参加伦敦中国艺术国际展览会出品图说

第 一 册　铜 器

ILLUSTRATED CATALOGUE OF CHINESE GOVERNMENT EXHIBITS FOR THE INTERNATIONAL EXHIBITION OF CHINESE ART IN LONDON

VOLUME I.　BRONZE

伦敦中国艺术国际展览会筹备委员会编辑

中央编译出版社
CCTP Central Compilation & Translation Press

图书在版编目（CIP）数据

参加伦敦中国艺术国际展览会出品图说 / 伦敦中国艺术国际展览会筹备委员会主编 . -- 北京：中央编译出版社，2022.9

ISBN 978-7-5117-4241-4

Ⅰ . ①参… Ⅱ . ①伦… Ⅲ . ①历史文物 – 中国 – 图集
Ⅳ . ① K870.2

中国版本图书馆 CIP 数据核字（2022）第 153392 号

参加伦敦中国艺术国际展览会出品图说

责任编辑　郑永杰
特约编辑　刘诗婷　杨　凌
责任印制　刘　慧
出版发行　中央编译出版社
地　　址　北京市海淀区北四环西路 69 号（100080）
电　　话　（010）55627391（总编室）　（010）55627312（编辑室）
（010）55627320（发行部）　（010）55627377（新技术部）
经　　销　全国新华书店
印　　刷　山东韵杰文化科技有限公司
开　　本　889 毫米 ×1194 毫米　1/16
字　　数　321 千字
印　　张　50.25
版　　次　2022 年 9 月第 1 版
印　　次　2022 年 9 月第 1 次印刷
定　　价　980.00 元（全四册）

新浪微博：@ 中央编译出版社　　**微　　信：**中央编译出版社（ID：cctphome）
淘宝店铺：中央编译出版社直销店（http://shop108367160.taobao.com）
（010）55627331

本社常年法律顾问：北京市吴栾赵阎律师事务所律师　闫军　梁勤
凡有印装质量问题，本社负责调换，电话：（010）55626985

參加倫敦中國藝術國際展覽會出品圖說

第 一 册　銅 器

ILLUSTRATED CATALOGUE OF CHINESE GOVERNMENT EXHIBITS FOR THE INTERNATIONAL EXHIBITION OF CHINESE ART IN LONDON

VOLUME I.　BRONZE

倫敦中國藝術國際展覽會籌備委員會編輯
商務印書館印行

序

中華民國二十三年十月國民政府行政院既決定選送本國藝術品於英倫。供國際展覽。目的在使西方人士得見中國藝術之偉美。乃組織籌備委員會掌其事。籌備委員會同人以本會任務莫重於出品之徵選。因選聘藝術專家若干人別組專門委員會司徵選之責。專門委員會自是年十一月成立。徵集研討。歷時數月。中間復與英國專家交換意見。而甄選乃定。用特編輯此册。附有照片。以備參稽。資考證。此本目錄所由成也。據目錄載出品類別爲銅器、瓷器、書畫、玉器、剔紅、景泰藍、織繡、摺扇、古書等。中國藝術之發展。自上古以迄近世。略具梗概。出品機關爲故宮博物院、古物陳列所、中央研究院、北平圖書館、河南博物館、安徽省立圖書館。而選自故宮博物院、古物陳列所者爲最多。此其大概也。

中華民國二十四年四月倫敦中國藝術國際展覽會籌備委員會

總　目

第一册 .... 銅器

第二册 .... 瓷器

第三册 .... 書畫

第四册 .... 其他

（織繡、玉器、景泰藍、剔紅、摺扇、珍本古書、傢具文具、考古選例、附私人玉器）

TABLE OF CONTENTS

Volume I. . . . . Bronze

Volume II. . . . . Porcelain (3 parts)

Volume III. . . . . Painting and Calligraphy

Volume IV. . . . . Miscellaneous

第　一　册

銅　器

Volume I.

BRONZE

參加倫敦中國藝術國際展覽會
銅器照片總目說明

			頁數
一	中國青銅器之起原		五
二	銅器之種類		五
三	銅器之時代		五
四	銅器之地域		七
五	中國銅器在藝術上之價值		七
六	中國銅器在史料上之價值		九
七	本次出品概要		
	(一) 烹飪器及食器類	三十八件	十三
	(二) 容器、溫器及飲器類	四十二件	四十一
	(三) 尋常用器類	九件	七十三
	(四) 樂器類	七件	八十一
	(甲) 新鄭銅器羣	八件	九十一
	(乙) 壽縣銅器羣	四件	九十七

總共壹百零捌件

TABLE OF CONTENTS

		PAGE
I.	Beginning of the Chinese Bronze	6
II.	Types of the Chinese Bronze	6
III.	Dating	6
IV.	Provenance	8
V.	Artistic Value of the Chinese Bronze	8
VI.	The Historical Value of Chinese Bronzes in Chinese Culture	10
VII.	The Bronzes for the present Exhibition	14

参加倫敦中國藝術國際展覽會
銅器照片目錄

一　中國青銅器之起原

中國青銅器之發明。最遲當在商初（西紀前一五〇〇年左右）。或尚遠在其前。以我人就現存之商代銅器觀之。其製作之技巧。已極進步矣。

冶金術之起原。與製陶極有影響。故古代銅器之形制。大部與陶器相同。如鬲、甗、豆等在古陶器內極多發見。然銅器之較遲者。或出於他種器物之摹倣。如簠卽仿諸竹製之筐是也。

二　銅器之種類

銅器之種類。自使用上分別之。大致可分爲下列之五類。

（一）烹飪器及食器　如鬲、甗、鼎、敦、簠、簋、豆等。

（二）容器、温器及飲器　如罍、壺、卣、盉、角、爵、斝、觚、觶、尊等。

（三）尋常用器　如盤、鑑、匜等。

（四）樂器　如鐘、鎛、鉦、鐃、鈴、鐸等。

（五）兵器　如戍、戈、矛、劍等。

註　以上一二三各類。舊時總稱爲禮器。與樂器相偶。實未確當。蓋此三類器及樂器。最初皆爲日用所需。其後遂兼爲祭祀及殉葬之用。卽兵器亦如此。故無論何類銅器。皆含有用器、禮器、明器三種用途。不能以禮器一名包括之也。

三　銅器之時代

中國銅器之有銘文者。常可藉以證明一確定之時代。就目前所知者。大體可分爲六期。

（一）商器　（約西紀前一七六六至一一二二年）

（二）西周器　（約西紀前一一二二至七六九年）

（三）春秋器　（約西紀前七二二至四八一年）

CHINESE BRONZE

I. Beginning of the Chinese Bronze

The use of bronze articles in China began, at the latest, in the beginning of the Shang Dynasty (circa 1500 B.C.). It is more than probable that their first appearance may be dated at a much earlier period, as we find that in the extant specimens of the Shang Dynasty, both the craftsmanship and the decorative designs evidence an advanced state of development.

As the potter's art exercised a good deal of influence on metal works in the early days, so we find that ancient bronze vessels were often modelled after earthenwares. For example, such forms as li (鬲), yen (甗), and tou (豆) are found in great numbers in ancient pottery, although they are best known in bronze. At a later date bronzes were modelled after objects of other make, as in the case of fu (簠) which derived its form from that of bamboo make.

II. Types of the Chinese Bronze

Bronze vessels classified according to their various uses may roughly be divided into five categories:

1. Cooking utensils and food vessels, such as li (鬲), yen (甗), ting (鼎), tui (敦), kuei (簋), fu (簠), tou (豆), etc.
2. Containers, heating and drinking vessels, such as lei (罍), hu (壺), yu (卣), ho (盉), chio (角), chueh (爵), chia (斝), ku (觚), chih (觶), tsun (尊), etc.
3. Vessels for ordinary use, such as p'an (盤), chien (鑑), yi (匜), etc.
4. Musical instruments, such as chung (鐘), po (鎛), cheng (鉦), nao (鐃), ling (鈴), to (鐸), etc.
5. Weapons, such as yueh (戉), ko (戈), mao (矛), chien (劍), etc.

Note: The practice formerly to include all bronzes in Classes (1), (2), and (3), under the term "Ceremonial Bronzes," in contradistinction with musical bronze instruments, is rather misleading. Originally, all bronzes in Classes (1), (2), and (3), together with musical bronze instruments, were articles of daily use. It was only later on that they were used for sacrificial and funeral purposes; and this is also true of military bronze weapons. Indeed, it may be said that all bronzes, no matter of what kind, have been used for daily, sacrificial and funeral purposes. The use of the term "Ceremonial Bronzes" is therefore inadequate for classificatory purposes.

III. Dating

Chinese bronze articles that have inscriptions can usually be given definite dates on the evidence of such writing. From our present knowledge, these articles may roughly be assigned to six periods as follows:

1. The Shang Dynasty (circa 1766–1122 B.C.)
2. The West Chou period (circa 1122–769 B.C.)
3. The Ch'un Ch'iu period, or that covered by the "Spring and Autumn Annals" (circa 722–481 B.C.)

（四）戰國器 （約西紀前四八一至二二一年）

（五）漢器 （約西紀前二〇六至西紀二二〇年）

（六）漢以後器

商、西周、春秋三時期。爲銅器時代中最主要者。其間變化較少。然樂器在商時尚未甚發達。鐘鎛一類。當起於西周時。食器之盨。亦西周末年始發見。故單就銅器之進化。有時亦可判別其時代也。

春秋末年及戰國時。銅器之形式、花紋、文字各方面。均有劇烈之變化。其主要原因。則以春秋以前。製銅器者。盡屬於王所居之都會。而春秋以後。各國均有製器。地方特性之發展。遂有各種歧異也。近時有稱此爲『秦式』者誤矣。

漢代銅器歸於素樸簡質。合於實用。漢以後則爲衰落時期。無特殊之風格矣。

四　銅器之地域

除時代不同外。苟銅器之製作地點不同。則其所表現之風格迴異。此種情況。春秋以前。尚未顯著。春秋時齊、秦、晉、楚等國之文化。在銅器中灼然可辨。如烹飪器中之敦。卽盡爲齊器。卽其顯證。戰國時器變化之繁夥。亦正以銅器產地之推廣耳。

五　中國銅器在藝術上之價值

由藝術眼光以研究中國銅器可分爲四點:

（一）色劑　由製造銅器之原料不同。則其所發之色澤及斑銹。亦因之不同。考工記言『金有六齊』。其別如下:

六分其金而錫居一。謂之鐘鼎之齊。

五分其金而錫居一。謂之斧斤之齊。

四分其金而錫居一。謂之戈戟之齊。

三分其金而錫居一。謂之大刃之齊。

4. The period of the "Warring States" (circa 481–221 B.C.)
5. The Han Dynasty (circa 206 B.C.–220 A.D.)
6. Post-Han period

The periods covered by the Shang and the West Chou Dynasty and the "Spring and Autumn Annals" are by far the most important of the Bronze Age in China. Bronze works of these periods maintain a more or less uniform tradition. But there are certain typological changes; musical instruments, for instance, were not much developed during the Shang Dynasty, but those of the chung and po type (both clapperless bells) began to appear in the West Chou period. The hsu (盨) type of food vessels did not appear until the end of that period. Therefore, the dating of bronze may sometimes be determined by their typology.

During the latter part of the period of the "Spring and Autumn Annals" and during the time of the "Warring States," the form, decoration, and style of writing of bronzes all underwent violent changes. The principal reason for such changes was that prior to the period of the "Spring and Autumn Annals," workers in bronze all congregated in the metropolis where the Emperor resided; but after that time, they were dispersed throughout the feudal principalities. Thus local variation of every sort was brought about; and each followed a different line of development. The result is that bronze articles of this period are richer in form and show more local colour. To call bronzes of this period "Ch'in bronzes" as some do, is clearly a mistake.

Bronze wares of the Han Dynasty are usually simple and devoid of rich ornament. They are mostly for practical use. The period after the Han Dynasty is one of decline, and is devoid of any particular characteristics.

IV. Provenance

Besides the difference in time, articles manufactured in different localities, assume features mutually distinct. Such a condition was not apparent before the period of the "Spring and Autumn Annals," but during that period, the states of Ch'i (齊), Ch'in (秦), Chin (晉), and Chu (楚), each had its individual production. The fact that the tui (敦) among cooking utensils were almost all Ch'i wares may be cited as a typical example of local production. The various changes stamped on the bronze works of the period of the "Warring States," were essentially due to the extension of centres of local manufacture.

V. Artistic Value of the Chinese Bronze

Chinese bronzes studied in their technical aspect may be grouped under the following four points:

1. Patination and Composition.—The difference in the constituents of the bronze, usually results in a variety of patina or mottles of rust. "K'ao Kung Chi" (考工記) states that there are six proportions for the making of this alloy which are as follows:

Five parts of copper, and one part of tin. This is known as the alloy for making chung (a kind of clapperless bells) and ting (caldrons).

Four parts of copper, and one part of tin. This is known as the alloy for making fu-chin (axes).

Three parts of copper, and one part of tin. This is known as the alloy for making ko and chi (military weapons).

Two parts of copper, and one part of tin. This is known as the alloy for making great swords.

五分其金而錫居二。謂之削殺矢之齊。

金錫半。謂之鑒燧之齊。

考工記爲戰國時書。古人製器不盡如記中所述之劃一。近來收藏家認爲色澤之不同。乃由於原料成分之不一。然尤爲重要者。蓋爲火候之優劣。同一原料。所得結果亦有不同也。

(二) 形式　銅器繼石、陶、竹、木等器而發達。所摹仿之範圍甚廣。因而其形式甚繁。且每一類器。必有其主要之形式。而其餘則時有變化。如圓形之器每變爲方形。圈足之器每於足下加以方几。圓柱形之足變成鳥獸形或人形。蓋頂及鋬飾以鳥獸形。器身上飾以牙狀之稜等。故雖同類之器。形式多不相同。

(三) 花紋　銅器雖間有素樸而無花紋者。然花紋實爲銅器藝術之重要部分。

商周銅器之花紋中。以回紋爲最重要。此種花紋。在中國古雕刻品內最爲普遍。且古代回字正作㔁形以象其狀。舊時稱爲雷紋者。雷卽回也。回紋亦有時用以塡補別種主要花紋之隙處。

鳥紋、獸紋、龍紋 (卽所謂蟠夔紋)、饕餮紋、蟬紋等。均此時代所習見之主要花紋也。

戰國時器。類多蟠螭、蟠虺等紋。且好嵌石類。與商代之刻骨同。其錯金銀爲花紋者。尤爲美觀。

除圖案化之花紋外。在銅器中亦有作鳥獸之圖形者。春秋以後。頗爲習見。

(四) 書法　銅器之銘文中。不乏優美之書法。且可窺見中國書法之源。其較古者。甚近於圖畫。有時以文字組合類似圖畫。有時以文字錯雜於花紋之內。幾不能辨。戰國時則作鳥蟲書。以鳥或蟲形配合於文字。使類於花紋。

六　中國銅器在史料上之價值

中國銅器。不僅在藝術及考古學方面。佔重要之位置。其有關於歷

Three parts of copper, and two parts of tin. This is known as the alloy for making knives and arrow-heads.

One half of copper, and the other half of tin. This is known as the alloy for making mirrors. "K'ao Kung Chi" (考工記) is a book probably written in the time of the "Warring States;" bronzes of an earlier period were not always made in strict conformity with the formulæ prescribed in that work. Differences of colour in bronzes result from slight differences in their make-up. But what is particularly important is the proper or improper mode of firing, for the same proportion in the materials used may have different results.

2. Shapes and Forms.—Since bronze objects were often modelled after those made of stone, pottery, bamboo, wood, etc., they have, therefore, assumed in the very beginning innumerable shapes or forms. In addition, every kind of object had a combination of features, of which some kept on changing in the course of time, while others remained more or less true to their prototype. For instance a round-shaped ware may become rectangular; cylindrical legs may assume the form of a bird, an animal or a human being; the same is true with the knob of a cover or the handle or even the complete article itself. Such changes are often gradual. In some cases, it is almost possible to trace back the different stages of such changes, and group them into typological series.

3. Ornamental Patterns.—Bronze works are sometimes found plain and devoid of any ornament, but it is the decorative patterns that have attracted the greatest amount of attention from collectors.

Of the decorative patterns found on the bronze works of the Shang and Chou periods, the "hui-pattern" (回紋, i.e. rectangular spirals) is the most important. This pattern is probably the most common of all the ancient Chinese decorative features. It is a modified form of the Chinese character 㔿, signifying "revolving." Formerly it was called "thunder-pattern" because the ancient character for thunder was 回. On bronze vessels, the "hui-pattern" was frequently used to fill up the intervening spaces of other patterns. Patterns of birds, animals, dragons (the so-called "p'an-kuei-wen"), ogremasks, and cicadas are the principal ones prevailing in these periods.

Bronze works assigned to the period of the "Warring States" are, in a large number, adorned with the patterns of p'an-chih (蟠螭, coiled lizard) and p'an-hui (蟠虺, coiled serpent). Occasionally we meet with vessels inlaid with turquois in the same way as the incised bones of the Shang Dynasty; frequently gold and silver were used for inlaying purposes. Besides this, very often after the period of the "Spring and Autumn Annals," we come across figures of birds and animals in bronzes.

4. Styles of Writing.—The inscriptions on bronze vessels are written in different styles of writing, and many of them show fine calligraphy. As time went on, changes were made in the style of writing. Some characters in the inscriptions of an earlier date are written in pictorial writing; sometimes the characters are so disposed as to form pictures; and sometimes they are so closely mixed up with the patterns that it is difficult to discern them. A kind of script known as the script of birds and insects was in vogue, during the period of the "Warring States;" it is formed by blending the characters with the figures of birds and insects. By means of the inscriptions on bronzes then, we are able to trace Chinese writing to its origin.

VI. The Historical Value of Chinese Bronzes in Chinese Culture

Chinese bronzes are not only important from the artistic and archæological point of view, but are also highly esteemed by scholars because of their great bearing on Chinese history and

史文化。尤爲學者所珍視。如盂鼎銘與周初之酒誥相似。散盤銘可藉以考見周厲王時夨散二國之分田。虢季子白盤銘可考見周宣王之伐玁狁。且其文與詩經相同。而宗周鐘爲厲王所自作。獻侯鼎記『成王』之名於其生時。皆中國文化上之瓌寶也。

七　本次出品概要

本次出品。以籌備時間太短。私家藏品散在各處。未能徵集。故僅就國立主要文化機關所藏。遴選精品。儘可能範圍內組成系統。

依上述銅器之種類。除兵器外。別爲四類。又新鄭及壽縣所發見之兩銅器羣。爲表現其由地域得來之特殊風格計。故各附於後。

(一)　烹飪器及食器類。
(二)　容器、溫器及飲器類。
(三)　尋常用器類。
(四)　樂器類。
(甲)　新鄭銅器羣。
(乙)　壽縣銅器羣。

culture. Many instances may be cited to illustrate this: The inscription on the yü-ting (盂鼎) resembles the "Wine Precept" (酒誥, a chapter in the "Canon of History") of the early part of the Chou Dynasty. The inscription on the San-p'an can be made use of to investigate the division of farm-land in the kingdoms of Tseh and San during the time of Emperor Li, of the Chou Dynasty. The inscription on the Kuo-chi-tze-pai p'an (虢季子白盤) throws light on the conquest of the Hsien-yuin barbarians by Emperor Hsuan of the Chou Dynasty; moreover, the language of this inscription is similar to that of the "Book of Poetry." The Chung Chou chung was cast by Emperor Li himself. The ting of the Marquis of Hsien was inscribed with the title of Ch'eng-Wang during his lifetime: this makes clear that Ch'eng-Wang is not a posthumous title. All these examples show the value of bronzes in the study of Chinese culture.

VII. The Bronzes for the Present Exhibition

The bronzes for the present exhibition were selected mainly from the Palace Museum and the National Museum, supplemented with a few from other collections. The bronzes from the above museums may be classified into four groups (1, 2, 3, and 4). Those from Hsin-cheng and Shou-hsien are put together into two groups (*a* and *b*), not because of any classificatory reason, but because of their having been discovered in those two places.

1. Cooking utensils and food vessels.
2. Containers, heating and drinking vessels.
3. Vessels for ordinary use.
4. Musical instruments.

a. Bronzes from Hsin-cheng (新鄭).
b. Bronzes from Shou-hsien (壽縣).

（一）烹飪器及食器類說明

本類可分爲二小類。卽烹飪器與食器。兩者爲相近。故合之。

烹飪器之主要者爲鬲、鼎及敦。由鬲所蛻化者爲甗。鬲、甗及鼎均遠自商世。已極盛行。敦在古時。殆以瓦製者爲多。春秋以後。始大行於齊國。

食器之重要者。爲簠、簋及豆。豆源流最古。然傳世銅豆。未見甚古者。簋自商世已有簠則起於西周末年或春秋時。簋後變爲盨。亦在西周末年發見。

前人不識敦。誤以爲鼎或鬵。又誤簋爲敦。盨爲簋。今並訂正。

1. Cooking Utensils and Food Vessels

This category is sub-divided into two classes: Cooking utensils and food vessels. They are put under the same category because they are closely associated in their uses.

The principal cooking vessels are the li, ting, and tui; the yen was developed from the li. The li, yen, and ting prevailed early in the Shang Dynasty. The tui, chiefly made of pottery in ancient times, gained prevalence in Ch'i State after the period of the "Spring and Autumn Annals."

The principal food vessels are the fu, kuei, and tou. The tou had its origin in remote antiquity, but it was cast in bronze only at a later period. The kuei (簋) made its appearance early in the Shang Dynasty, while the fu first appeared in the latter part of the West Chou or in the "Spring and Autumn Annals" period. The kuei developed into hsu (盨) at the end of West Chou.

Formerly scholars mistook the tui for the ting, or the hsün (甗); the kuei for the tui, or the hsu (盨) for the kuei. These mistakes should be corrected.

甲. 鬲屬
A. THE LI GROUP

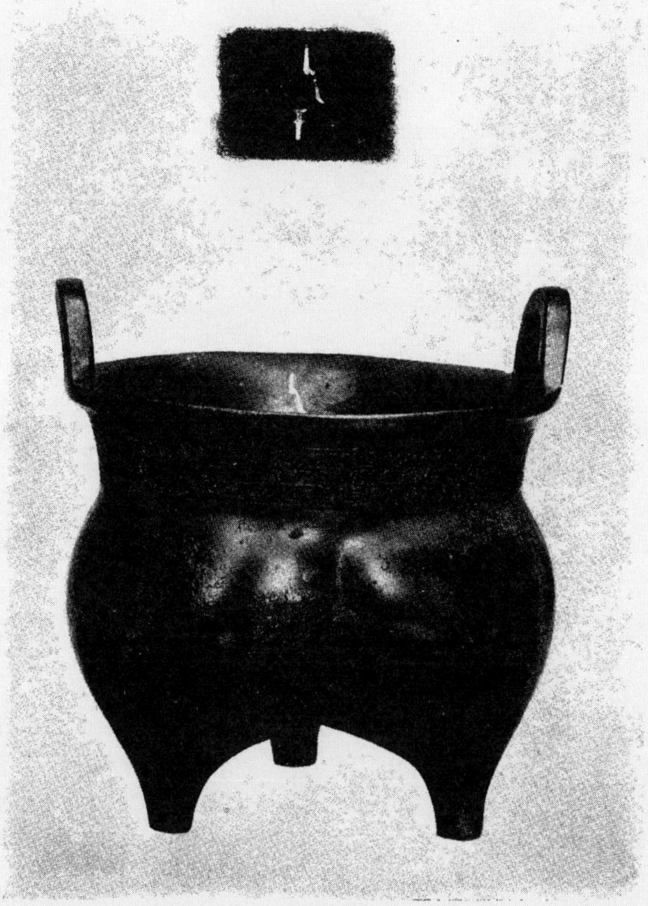

一 父辛鬲

故宮博物院藏(以下簡稱院)

商器。

有銘。有微傷。通耳高拾伍·貳公分。口徑拾叁·玖公分。最大腹圍肆拾貳·柒公分。重市秤貳拾伍兩捌錢。

1. Li to Worship Father Hsin

With inscription. Shang Dynasty. National Palace Museum (indicated hereafter with the initials N. P. M.).

二　鳥紋方鬲(院)

商或周初器。

舊稱蟠夔方鬲。口徑拾伍·玖公分。通耳高貳拾叁·玖公分。重市秤壹百壹拾伍兩正。

2. Square Li with Bird-pattern

Formerly called p'an k'uei square li. Shang or beginning of Chou Dynasty. N. P. M.

乙. 甗屬

B. THE YEN GROUP

三 父乙甗(院)

商器。錯金銀。

有銘。通耳高肆拾肆·伍公分。口徑貳拾柒·捌公分。重市秤拾玖斤捌兩正。

3. Yen to Worship Father I

With inscription. Inlaid with gold and silver. Shang Dynasty. N. P. M.

四 蟠螭紋方甗(院)

周器。

舊稱蟠夔方甗。有傷。口徑貳拾伍·柒公分。横貳拾玖·陸公分。通耳高叁拾柒·玖公分。重市秤叁百壹拾叁兩正。

4. Square Yen with P'an-chih-pattern

Formerly called p'an k'uei square yen. Chou Dynasty. N. P. M.

丙. 鼎屬

C. THE TING GROUP

五 婦鼎(院)

商器。

有銘。口徑拾玖·玖公分。通耳高貳拾肆·伍公分。最大腹圍陸拾肆·伍公分。重市秤壹百肆拾兩正。

5. Fu Ting

With inscription. Shang Dynasty. N. P. M.

六 饕餮鼎(院)

器甚大。足上飾以饕餮形。周初器。

舊稱蟠虺鼎。口徑最寬伍拾·柒公分。通耳高柒拾肆·捌公分。最大腹圍壹百陸拾貳公分。重市秤捌拾壹斤正。

6. Ting with Ogre-mask-pattern

Formerly called p'an hui ting. Unusually large. With ogre-mask-patterns at tops of legs. Early Chou. N. P. M.

七 父己鼎(院)

款足似鬲狀。商或周初器。

有銘。口徑拾玖·伍公分。通耳高貳拾肆·柒公分。最大腹圍陸拾壹·叁公分。重市秤玖拾陸兩正。

7. Ting to Worship Father Chi

With inscription. Legs shaped like the li. Shang or beginning of Chou Dynasty. N. P. M.

八　父辛方鼎(院)

商或周初器。

有銘。通耳高貳拾壹·貳公分。口縱拾肆·玖公分。橫拾柒·叁公分。底縱拾壹·肆公分。橫拾伍·捌公分。重市秤玖拾兩正。

8. Square Ting to Worship Father Hsin

With inscription. Shang or beginning of Chou Dynasty. N. P. M.

九 子京鼎

古物陳列所藏(以下簡稱所)
商器。

有銘。通耳高一邊貳拾叁公分。通耳高一邊貳拾貳·玖公分。口徑橫貳拾·壹公分。口徑縱拾玖·柒公分。腹圍陸拾貳·叁公分。重市秤玖拾捌兩捌錢。

9. Tze-chin Ting

With inscription. Shang Dynasty. National Museum (indicated hereafter with the initials N. M.)

一〇 文方鼎(所)

商或周初器。

有銘。通耳高貳拾柒·伍公分。口徑橫拾玖·柒公分。口徑縱拾陸·壹公分。深拾壹·伍公分。重市秤壹百壹拾陸兩捌錢。

10. Square Ting of Wen

With inscription. Shang or beginning of Chou Dynasty. N. M.

一一 獻侯鼎(所)

周成王時器(約西紀前一〇六〇至一〇三〇年)。

有銘。通耳高一邊貳拾叁·捌公分。通耳高一邊貳拾肆公分強。外口徑拾捌公分。腹圍伍拾陸·伍公分。重市秤玖拾伍兩捌錢。

11. Ting of the Marquis of Hsien (or Hsien-hou Ting)

With inscription. Vessel of the time of Ch'eng-Wang (about 1060–1030 B.C.) of Chou Dynasty. N. M.

一二 鄒父方鼎(院)

鼎腹作鳥紋。有八稜。作牙形。西周初年器。

舊稱錫貝鼎。有銘。口縱拾伍·柒公分。橫拾玖·伍公分。通耳高貳拾伍·陸公分。縱拾貳·貳公分。橫拾陸·壹公分。重市秤壹百零肆兩正。

12. 鄒-fu Square Ting

With inscription. Bird-pattern and eight indented flanges on the body. Beginning of West Chou. N. P. M.

一三 康鼎(院)

西周器。

有銘。口徑貳拾叁公分。通耳高貳拾貳·壹公分。最大腹圍陸拾柒·玖公分。重市秤壹百零叁兩正。

13. K'ang Ting

With inscription. West Chou. N. P. M.

一四 大鼎(院)

附耳。西周器。

有銘。口徑叁拾捌·壹公分。通耳高叁拾壹·柒公分。最大腹圍玖拾壹·貳公分。重市秤貳拾斤正。

14. Ta Ting

With inscription. "Ears" (loop-handles) projecting upward from the body. West Chou. N. P. M.

一五 芮公鼎(院)

芮國在今陝西朝邑。芮公器亦甚多。西周末或春秋時器。

有銘。口徑叁拾肆·伍公分。通耳高叁拾肆·柒公分。最大腹圍壹百零玖·叁公分。重市秤貳拾柒斤捌兩正。

15. Ting of the Duke of Jui (or Jui-kung Ting)

The Jui State is now Chao-i, Shensi Province. Bronze of the Duke of Jui are plentiful. End of West Chou or period of "Spring and Autumn Annals." N. P. M.

一六 鬣季鼎(所)

足尖而短。春秋時器。

有銘。通耳高一邊叁拾肆公分強。通耳高一邊叁拾貳·柒公分。口徑橫叁拾玖·叁公分。口徑縱肆拾公分。深拾柒·陸公分。腹圍壹百壹拾肆·貳公分。重市秤貳拾柒斤。

16. Lieh-chi Ting

With inscription. Legs short and conical. Period of "Spring and Autumn Annals." N. M.

一七 叔單鼎(所)

春秋時黃國器(今河南潢川)。

有銘。通耳高貳拾捌·捌公分。口徑貳拾捌公分。腹圍捌拾貳·肆公分。重市秤拾捌斤拾伍兩貳錢。

17. Shu-shan Ting

With inscription. Vessel of the Huang State. period of "Spring and Autumn Annals." Huang is now located at Huang-chuan, Honan Province. N. M.

一八 邿伯鼎(所)

附耳。春秋時邿國器(今山東濟寧)。

有銘。通耳高一邊叁拾·貳公分。通耳高一邊貳拾玖·玖公分。口徑橫叁拾伍·伍公分。口徑縱叁拾陸·壹公分。腹圍壹百零肆公分。重市秤拾捌斤柒兩捌錢。

18. Ting of the Earl of Shih

With inscription. "Ears" projecting upward from the body. Vessel of the Shih State. period of the "Spring and Autumn Annals." The Shih State is now located at Chi-ning, Shantung Province. N. M.

一九 蟠虺鼎(所)

附耳。蓋有三環。可仰置。戰國時器。

通耳高貳拾陸·貳公分。口徑貳拾·柒公分。深拾肆·貳公分。腹圍陸拾玖公分。連蓋重市秤壹百零伍兩捌錢。

19. Ting with Coiled-serpent-pattern (P'an-hui-pattern)

"Ears" projecting upward from the body. Three rings on the cover, which can be reversed to serve as a dish. Period of the "Warring States." N. M.

二〇 龍紋鼎(院)

附耳。蓋有鏤空之圓頂。可仰置。戰國時器。

舊稱蟠夔鼎。通蓋高拾玖·伍公分。口徑拾陸·叁公分。最大腹圍伍拾陸·叁公分。共重市秤柒拾伍兩正。

20. Ting with Dragon-pattern

Formerly called p'an k'uei ting. "Ears" projecting upward from the body. An open-work carved knob on the cover, which can be reversed. Period of the "Warring States." N. P. M.

(29)

二一 鳳耳鼎(院)

以鳥首代兩耳。平蓋。蓋有紐。可握。有四鳥首。可仰置。形製極奇。戰國時器。

有花紋。口徑拾叁·伍公分。通蓋高拾捌·伍公分。最大腹圍肆拾捌·捌公分。連蓋共重市秤柒拾捌兩正。

21. Ting with Phœnix-shaped "Ears"

Loop-handles in the form of the heads of bird. Flat cover with a loop-handle in the centre and four heads of bird on the margin to act as supporters when reversed. Unique in form and make. Period of the "Warring States." N. P. M.

丁. 敦屬

D. THE TUI GROUP

二二 陳侯午敦(所)

齊桓公時器(西紀前三八四至三七八年)。

有銘。通耳高上叁拾肆公分。通耳高下叁拾叁·陸公分。以敦字體分上下。口徑貳拾伍·陸公分。底徑横貳拾柒·壹公分。底徑縱貳拾伍·伍公分。底方圍壹百零伍公分。重市秤叁拾柒斤叁兩捌錢。

22. Tui of Wu, Marquis of Chen

With inscription. Vessel possessed by Huan-kung (384–378 B. C.) of the Ch'i State. N. M.

二三 雲紋敦(所)

三足爲環形所展成。戰國時器。

高拾壹·貳公分。口徑拾柒·伍公分。深捌·肆公分。腹圍伍拾壹·捌公分。重市秤肆拾貳兩叁錢。

23. Tui with Cloud-scrolls

Three legs formed of extended rings. Period of the "Warring States." N. M.

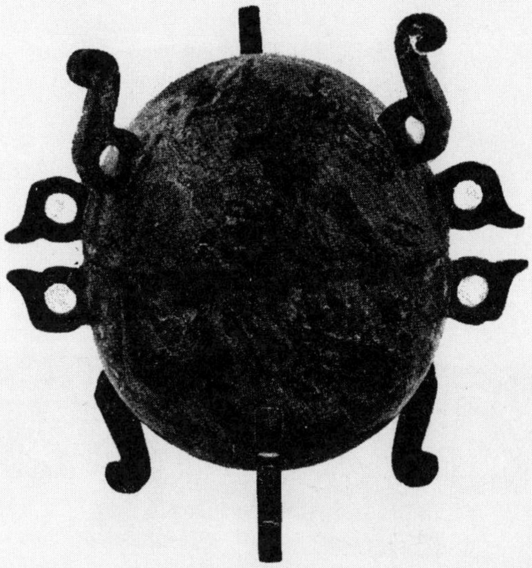

二四 素敦(院)

三足並蓋上三環。均爲環形所展長。戰國時器。

舊稱素鼎。口徑拾·捌公分。通蓋最高拾陸·叁公分。最大腹圍叁拾捌·叁公分。重市秤肆拾伍兩正。

24. Tui

The three legs and the three rings on the reversible cover are formed of extended rings. Period of the "Warring States." N. P. M.

戊. 簠屬
E. THE FU GROUP

二五 召叔山父簠(院)

春秋時鄭國器(今河南新鄭)。
有銘。口縱貳拾叁·肆公分。橫貳拾捌·叁公分。高柒·柒公分。底縱拾叁·肆公分。橫拾柒·貳公分。重市秤玖拾伍兩正。

25. Chao-shu-shan-fu Fu

With inscription. Vessel of the Cheng State (now Hsin-cheng, Honan), period of "Spring and Autumn Annals." N. P. M.

二六 陳曼簠(院)

春秋時齊國器。

舊稱齊陳曼簠。有銘。口縱拾玖·叁公分。橫叁拾壹·壹公分。高拾·捌公分。底縱柒·壹公分。重市秤壹百兩正。

26. Chen-man Fu

With inscription. Vessel of the Ch'i State, period of "Spring and Autumn Annals." N. P. M.

己. 簋屬

(舊稱敦)

F. THE KUEI GROUP

(formerly called the Tui Group)

二七 饕餮紋簋(所)

無耳。周身花紋。極精美。商器。

高拾貳·柒公分。口徑拾捌·壹公分。底徑拾肆·肆公分。深拾·叁公分。重市秤伍拾肆兩。

27. Kuei with Ogre-mask-pattern

Without "ears." Exquisite designs all over the body. Shang Dynasty. N. M.

二八 父丁簋(所)

腹作直紋。商器。

有銘。高拾陸·肆公分。口徑橫貳拾壹·捌公分。口徑縱貳拾貳·貳公分。底徑橫拾陸·玖公分。底徑縱拾柒·伍公分。深拾貳·玖公分。腹圍陸拾伍公分。重市秤壹百壹拾伍兩捌錢。

28. Kuei to Worship Father Ting

With inscription. Straight lines on body. Shang Dynasty. N. M.

二九 父乙簋(院)

斂口。商器。

有銘。高拾貳·伍公分。口徑拾伍·壹公分。足徑拾伍·伍公分。腹圍陸拾叁·捌公分。重市秤陸拾伍兩正。

29. Kuei to Worship Father I

With inscription. Narrow-mouthed. Shang Dynasty. N. P. M.

三〇 父癸簋(院)

商器。

有銘。口徑拾捌·叁公分。高拾叁·捌公分。足徑拾肆·陸公分。腹圍伍拾·叁公分。重市秤伍拾壹兩正。

30. Kuei to Worship Father Kuei

With inscription. Shang-Dynasty. N. P. M.

三一 「亞」方簋(院)

亞古代爵稱。口下作龍紋。腹作饕餮紋。腹下作鳥紋。並間以小冋紋。兩耳作怪鳥形。器四周有八稜。商器。

口縱拾壹·玖公分。橫拾柒公分。最高貳拾·陸公分。底縱拾貳·叁公分。橫拾肆·貳公分。重市秤壹百伍拾伍兩正。

31. "Ya" Square Kuei

With inscription. Dragon-pattern below the lip; ogre-mask-pattern on the body; and bird-pattern below the body. Two loop-handles assume the form of monstrous birds, with eight flanges round the body. These flanges are patterns of great antiquity. Shang Dynasty. N. P. M.

三二 詢辛簋(所)

素腹。西周初年器。

有銘。高拾·伍公分。口徑拾伍·壹公分。底徑拾壹·柒公分。深玖公分。腹圍肆拾陸·玖公分。重市秤肆拾叁兩貳錢。

32. Hsun-hsin Kuei

With inscription. Body plain. Beginning of West Chou. N. M.

三三 「作寶尊彝」簋(所)

腹作鳥紋。兩耳作鳥形。西周初年器。

有銘。通耳高一邊拾伍·壹公分。通耳高一邊拾伍·捌公分。口徑橫貳拾肆公分。口徑縱貳拾捌公分。底徑橫拾柒·壹公分。底徑縱拾柒·陸公分。深拾壹·捌公分。腹圍陸拾肆公分。重市秤玖拾伍兩捌錢。

33. "Tso-Pao-Tsun-I" Kuei

Tso, Pao, Tsun, and I (作, 寶, 尊, 彝) are the characters inscribed on the vessel. Bird-pattern on the body. Two "ears," bird-shaped. Beginning of West Chou. N. M.

三四 虢簋(所)

口甚侈。兩耳作獸形。花紋有金銀錯。春秋時器。

有銘。通耳高一邊拾陸·肆公分。通耳高一邊拾陸·陸公分。口徑貳拾肆·伍公分。底徑拾玖·伍公分。深拾壹·捌公分。腹圍柒拾壹公分。重市秤壹百陸拾壹兩。

34. Hsiung Kuei

With inscription. Wide-mouthed. Two "ears," animal-shaped. Pattern inserted with gold and silver. Period of "Spring and Autumn Annals." N. M.

三五 陳侯午簋(所)

兩耳作龍形。底連方几。齊桓公時器(西紀前三八四至三七八年)。

有銘。最高點計拾壹公分。口徑拾捌·玖公分。深玖·叁公分。腹圍伍拾捌·肆公分。重市秤肆拾捌兩壹錢。

35. Kuei of Wu, Marquis of Chen

With inscription. Two "ears," dragon-shaped. Square pedestal added to round base. Vessel of Huan-kung (384–378 B. C.) of Ch'i State. N. M.

庚. 盨屬

(舊稱簋)

G. THE HSU GROUP

(formerly called the Kuei Group)

三六 𨟻季獻盨(院)

春秋時器。

有銘。口縱拾捌·壹公分。橫貳拾伍·貳公分。通蓋高拾柒·捌公分。底縱拾叁·捌公分。橫貳拾壹·叁公分。共重市秤壹百叁拾兩正。

36. Hsu of Lo-chi-hsien

With inscription. Period of "Spring and Autumn Annals." N. P. M.

三七 華季盨(所)

此器是盨。而銘中稱爲簋。可證盨由簋蛻化而成。

有銘。高拾玖公分。口徑橫貳拾壹·叁公分。口徑縱拾伍·伍公分。底徑橫貳拾壹·貳公分。底徑縱拾伍·壹公分。深捌·肆公分。腹圍陸拾玖公分。重市秤玖拾兩捌錢。

37. Hsu of Hwa-chi

With inscription. This vessel is in reality a hsu, but it is called a kuei in the inscription. This gives evidence of the fact that the hsu was developed from the kuei. N. M.

辛. 豆屬
H. THE TOU GROUP

三八 星虬豆(所)

兩耳作環形。腹中有三鳥圖。戰國時器。

內鑲花紋。高拾柒公分。口徑拾捌·貳公分。深玖·壹公分。底徑拾壹·柒公分。腹圍伍拾玖·陸公分。重市秤肆拾貳兩。

38. "Hsing-ch'iu" Tou

Decorated with stars and dragons. "Two ears," ring-shaped. Figure of three birds inside the vessel. Period of the "Warring States." N. M.

（二）容器、溫器及飲器類說明

容器、溫器及飲器。在使用上頗有聯繫。蓋皆與酒有關係也。

罍、壺、卣等。用以容酒漿者。謂之容器。其源出於陶器。罍之小者稱瓿。春秋戰國時間有稱罐及鑘者。壺、漢時稱爲鍾。方壺稱爲鈁。春秋時又有所謂鉼者。實亦壺也。

卣皆有提梁。然古卣本無提梁。昔人所稱爲方彝者。實亦卣也。

盉、角、爵、斝等。均有長足可供溫酒之用。然角、爵、斝又兼爲飲器。角無柱。而爵、斝有柱。角蓋較古之型式也。

觚、觶皆飲器。尊似觚而較大。其用途未甚明瞭。

2. Containers, Heating and Drinking Vessels

Vessels of this category in most cases are used for serving wine and are in themselves more or less related to one another in use.

Of the containers there are the lei, hu, and yu. All of them are used to hold beverages. They were developed from pottery. The lei of a small size is called a pu (瓿). It was sometimes called a tan (罎) or a min (鑑) during the periods of "Spring and Autumn Annals" and the "Warring States." The hu (壺) and the square hu were called chung (鍾) and fang (鈁) respectively during the Han Dynasty. What was called p'ing (鉼) during the period of the "Spring and Autumn Annals" is in reality a hu. The yu (卣) has a swing-handle, but the yu of remote antiquity, however, had no swing-handle. What was formerly called a square yi (彝) is also in reality a yu (卣).

The ho (盉), chio (角), chueh (爵), and chia (斝) are supported by long legs in order to warm wine over the fire. But the chio, chueh, and chia are also used as drinking vessels. The chueh and chia have knobbed projections on the rim while the chio has none. The style of the chio is probably more archaic than those of the other two.

The ku (觚) and chih (觶) are drinking vessels. The tsun (尊) resembles the ku but is larger. The use of the tsun is not yet ascertained.

甲. 罍屬

A. THE LEI GROUP

三九 饕餮紋罍(院)

頸腹之間。飾三獸首。商或周初器。

舊稱缺蓋古銅提耳大爐。口徑念叁·柒公分。高念叁·貳公分。底徑拾玖·玖公分。最大腹圍壹百零陸公分。重市秤壹百柒拾玖兩正。

39. Lei with T'ao-t'ieh-pattern (Ogre-mask-pattern)

Decorated with three animal heads between the neck and the body. Shang or beginning of Chou. N. P. M.

四〇 饕餮紋方罍(院)

蓋有四鳥形。腹側飾兩獸首。商或周初器。

舊稱古銅彝。通蓋高念陸·肆公分。口縱拾陸·柒公分。橫拾柒·貳公分。底縱拾伍·柒公分。橫拾陸·壹公分。最大腹圍捌拾貳公分。重市秤壹百念叁兩正。

40. Square Lei with T'ao-t'ieh-pattern

With a bird-head on each of the four corners of the cover. Tow sides of body decorated with animal-heads. Shang or beginning of Chou. N. P. M.

四一 乳丁罍(院)

頸腹間飾獸首。間以鳥形及牙稜。腹有乳。間以回紋。極精美。商或周初器。

口徑叁拾壹·叁公分。高叁拾柒公分。底徑貳拾玖公分。重市秤貳拾柒斤陸兩正。

41. Lei with "Nipples" (Bosses)

Decorated with animal-heads between the neck and the body, and bird figures at the intervals between the heads. Indented flanges and "nipples" on the body and small hui-pattern in the intervening spaces. Shang or beginning of Chou. N. P. M.

乙. 瓿屬

B. THE PU GROUP

四二 獸耳囘紋瓿(所)

商或周器。

舊稱雲雷瓿。高拾玖·伍公分。口徑拾陸·伍公分。底徑拾捌公分。深拾柒·肆公分。腹圍玖拾叁·陸公分。重市秤壹百叁拾肆兩捌錢。

42. Pu with Animal-shaped "Ears" and Hui-pattern

Formerly called yun-lei pu. Shang or Chou Dynasty. N. M.

四三 饕餮紋瓿(所)

商或周器。

高拾柒·陸公分。口徑拾伍·壹公分。深拾伍·肆公分。底徑拾陸·伍公分。上腰圍柒拾壹·柒公分。重市秤玖拾伍兩捌錢。

43. Pu with T'ao-t'ieh-pattern

Shang or Chou Dynasty. N. M.

丙. 鑪屬

C. THE MIN GROUP

四四 寧鑪(所)

戰國時器。

有銘。高拾陸·捌公分。深拾伍·肆公分。口徑橫拾·貳公分。口徑縱拾·伍公分。底徑橫拾壹·陸公分。底徑縱拾壹·捌公分。腹圍陸拾柒公分。重市秤捌拾捌兩捌錢。

44. Min of Ning

With inscription. Period of the "Warring States." N. M.

丁. 壺及鍾屬

D. THE HU AND THE CHUNG GROUP

四五 曾伯陭壺(院)

蓋頂如花瓣。兩耳作獸首形。附環。通體作盤雲紋。西周或春秋時曾國器。

有銘。蓋口及頂均有銘。蓋有傷。通蓋高肆拾壹·貳公分。口徑拾肆·壹公分。底徑貳拾壹·捌公分。最大腹圍柒拾陸·玖公分。重市秤拾捌斤拾貳兩正。

45. Tseng-po-ch'i Hu

With inscription. The knob on the cover divided into petals. Two "ears," animal-head-shaped and with rings. Cloud-scrolls all over the body. Vessel of the Cheng State, West Chou or period of "Spring and Autumn Annals." N.P.M.

四六 芮公壺(院)

西周末或春秋時芮國器。
有銘。底足均傷。通蓋高叁拾柒公分。口縱玖·捌公分。横拾貳·柒公分。底縱拾叁公分。横拾陸·壹公分。最大腹圍陸拾玖·壹公分。重市秤拾捌斤捌兩正。

46. Hu of the Duke of Jui

With inscription. Vessel of the Jui State. Latter part of West Chou or period of "Spring and Autumn Annals." N. P. M.

四七 殷句壺(所)

西周末或春秋時器。

有銘。通蓋高一邊伍拾柒·叁公分。通蓋高一邊伍拾捌·壹公分。口徑橫拾玖·捌公分。口徑縱拾肆·陸公分。底徑橫貳拾捌·貳公分。底徑縱貳拾·叁公分。深肆拾壹·捌公分。腹圍玖拾玖·叁公分。蓋頂橫拾玖·陸公分。蓋頂縱拾伍公分。連蓋共重市秤肆拾叁斤叁兩捌錢。

47. Ying-kou Hu

With inscription on cover. Latter part of West Chou or period of "Spring and Autumn Annals." N. M.

四八 □侯壺(所)

西周或春秋時器。

有銘。高肆拾柒·柒公分。口徑橫拾玖·壹公分。口徑縱拾捌·捌公分。底徑橫貳拾捌·伍公分。底徑縱貳拾捌公分。深肆拾貳·叁公分。腹圍壹百零肆·伍公分。重市秤肆拾陸斤叁兩捌錢。

48. Hu of the Marquis of (?)

With inscription. West Chou or period of "Spring and Autumn Annals." N. M.

四九 伯庶父壺(院)

耳附兩環。西周或春秋時器。

有銘。蓋有傷。通蓋高叁拾叁·叁公分。口徑拾·壹公分。底徑拾伍·捌公分。最大腹圍伍拾柒·貳公分。重市秤壹百貳拾柒兩正。

49. Po-shu-fu Hu

With inscription. Rings appended to the "ears." West Chou or period of "Spring and Autumn Annals." N. P. M.

五〇 周𡖊壺(院)

耳附兩環。西周或春秋時器。
有銘。口縱拾伍·貳公分。橫貳拾公分。高肆拾捌·肆公分。底縱貳拾壹·肆公分。橫貳拾陸·肆公分。重市秤貳拾伍斤陸兩正。

50. Chou-𡖊 Hu

With inscription. Rings appended to the "ears." West Chou or period of "Spring and Autumn Annals." N. P. M.

五一 行獵圖壺(所)

以行獵圖與花紋相間。戰國時器。

高叁拾柒·貳公分。口徑拾壹·玖公分。底徑拾伍公分。腹圍柒拾玖·伍公分。重市秤玖拾兩捌錢。

51. Hu with Hunting Pictures

Hunting-pictures intermingled with patterns inlaid with metals. Period of the "Warring States." N. M.

五二 四獸圖壺(所)

腹有四獸圖。有提梁。戰國時器。

高叁拾·捌公分。口徑拾·肆公分。底徑橫拾貳公分。底徑縱拾壹·柒公分。深貳拾玖·伍公分。腹圍陸拾陸·肆公分。重市秤捌拾兩捌錢。

52. Hu with Picture of Four Animals

Picture of four animals on the body. With swing-handle. Period of the "Warring States." N. M.

五三 鳥獸圖壺(所)

腹有鳥獸圖。以金銀錯之。戰國時器。

兩耳有鼻。高叁拾叁·貳公分。口徑橫拾壹·壹公分。口徑縱拾·玖公分。深叁拾·陸公分。腹圍柒拾柒·柒公分。重市秤玖拾肆兩捌錢。

53. Hu with Picture of Birds and Animals

Picture of birds and animals on the body. Inlaid with gold and silver. Period of the "Warring States." N. M.

五四 龍鳳紋壺(所)

戰國時器。

舊稱夔鳳壺。高叁拾伍·叁公分。口徑橫拾貳·貳公分。口徑縱拾捌·捌公分。底徑橫拾陸公分。底徑縱拾叁·壹公分。深叁拾·貳公分。重市秤壹百陸拾壹兩捌錢。

54. Hu with Phœnix-dragon-pattern

Formerly called k'uei feng hu. Period of the "Warring States." N. M.

五五 瓠形壺(院)

戰國時器。

底邊似繩狀。口徑陸公分。通蓋頂高叁拾叁·伍公分。底徑捌·伍公分。最大腹圍肆拾貳·玖公分。重市秤肆拾捌兩正。

55. Gourd-shaped Hu

Period of the "Warring States." N. P. M.

(54)

五六 厤㚖扁壺(所)

戰國時器。

有銘。高貳拾伍·陸公分。口徑玖·肆公分。深貳拾叁·壹公分。底邊橫拾叁·貳公分。底邊縱柒·伍公分。腰厚柒·伍公分。腰橫貳拾伍·壹公分。重市秤捌拾捌兩捌錢。

56. 厤㚖 Flat Hu

With inscription. Period of the "Warring States." N. M.

五七 馭虎圖扁壺(所)

一旁爲獸圖。一旁爲有人馭虎之圖。有鏈狀之提梁。漢器。

鎖鍊提梁。高拾玖·陸公分。口徑橫陸公分。口徑縱伍·捌公分。底徑橫拾貳·陸公分。底徑縱肆·玖公分。深拾柒·伍公分。連鍊重市秤肆拾叁兩叁錢正。

57. Flat Hu with Picture of Tiger-driving

With picture of animal on one side of the body and picture of a man driving a tiger on the other. Swing-handle chain-shaped. Han Dynasty. N. M.

五八 南皮侯家鍾(所)

漢器。

有銘。高肆拾伍·玖公分。口徑拾玖·壹公分。底徑橫貳拾壹·陸公分。底徑縱貳拾壹·肆公分。深肆拾·捌公分。腹圍壹百壹拾貳公分。重市秤貳拾壹斤柒兩捌錢正。

58. Chung of the Marquis of Nan-p'i

With inscription. Han Dynasty. N. M.

戊. 鈁 屬

E. THE FANG GROUP

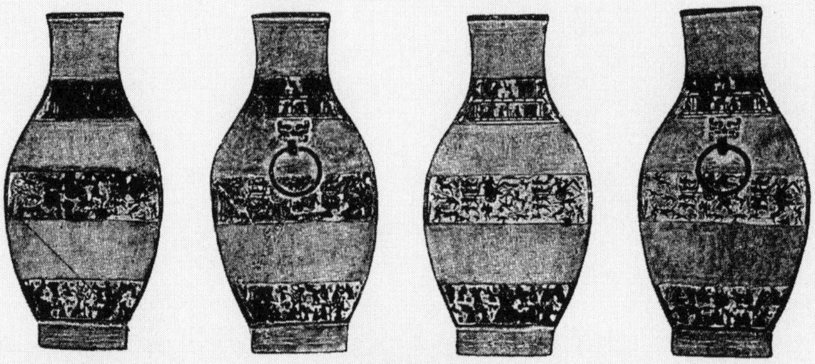

五九 畫像鈁(院)

頸、腹、足並有圖紋。似漢畫像。戰國時器。

舊名古銅雙耳方壺。口縱橫均拾壹·陸公分。高肆拾伍·叁公分。底縱橫均拾叁·肆公分。最大腹圍玖拾叁公分。重市秤壹百玖拾柒兩正。

59. Fang with Pictures

Pictures like bas-relief of the Han Dynasty on the neck, body, and base. Period of the "Warring States." N. P. M.

己. 鉼屬

F. THE P'ING GROUP

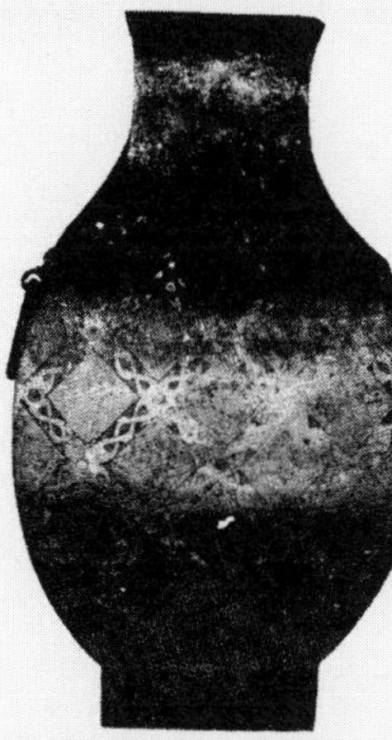

六〇 綯紋鈁(所)

腹以綯紋作斜方格。格中作雲紋。嵌綠松石。戰國時器。

高肆拾陸·叁公分。口徑橫拾貳·貳公分。口徑縱拾貳公分。底徑橫拾肆·伍公分。底徑縱拾肆·叁公分。深肆拾壹·肆公分。腹圍玖拾捌·捌公分。重市秤拾玖斤肆兩捌錢正。

60. Fang with Rope-pattern (T'ao-pattern)

The rhombs on the body are formed of rope-pattern (t'ao-pattern) and are filled up with cloud-scrolls and inlaid with turquois. Period of the "Warring States." N. M.

六一 盂城鉼(院)

春秋時器。

有銘。舊名古銅雙環扁瓶。口殘傷。口縱玖公分。橫拾壹·貳公分。高貳拾陸·伍公分。底縱捌·叁公分。橫拾貳·肆公分。最大腹圍伍拾伍·伍公分。重市秤陸拾捌兩正。

61. P'ing of Meng-cheng

With inscription. Period of "Spring and Autumn Annals." N. P. M.

庚. 卣屬

G. THE YU GROUP

六二 猆卣(院)

通身作龍紋。間以小回紋。有四棱。精美絕倫。商器。有銘。舊名用禾卣。口縱陸·玖公分。橫柒·貳公分。通蓋頂高貳拾叁·伍公分。底徑柒·玖公分。重市秤伍拾伍兩正。

62. Yu of 猆

With inscription. Dragon-pattern all over the body and hui-pattern in the intervening spaces. With four flanges. Unmatched in exquisiteness. Shang Dynasty. N. P. M.

六三 父庚卣(院)

有喙。商器。

有銘。舊稱父庚盉。口徑捌·肆公分。通蓋頂高貳拾肆·壹公分。底徑玖·柒公分。最大腹圍肆拾·柒公分。重市秤伍拾叁兩正。

63. Yu to Worship Father Keng

Formerly called ho, to worship Father Keng. With inscription and spout. Shang Dynasty. N. P. M.

六四 周乎卣(院)

西周器。
有銘。通高貳拾貳·捌公分。口縱玖·捌公分。橫拾叁·肆公分。底縱拾貳·貳公分。橫拾伍·柒公分。最大腹圍伍拾貳·伍公分。共重市秤玖拾陸兩正。

64. Chou-hu Yu

With inscription. West Chou. N. P. M.

辛. 盉屬
H. THE HO GROUP

六五 父丁盉(院)

商器。

有銘。通蓋高貳拾捌·柒公分、口徑拾壹·柒公分。最大腹圍伍拾肆·叁公分、重市秤壹百零叁兩正。

65. Ho to Worship Father Ting

With inscription. Shang Dynasty. N. P. M.

六六 足形盉(院)

四足。蓋頂作獸形。商或周初器。

有銘。舊名古銅壺。通蓋高貳拾柒·叁公分。口徑拾肆·壹公分。最大腹圍陸拾肆公分。共重市秤壹百肆拾柒兩正。

66. Ho Inscribed with a Character Resembling a Man's Foot

With inscription and four legs. Animal-shaped knob on cover. Shang or beginning of Chou Dynasty. N. P. M.

六七 龍紋方盉院

失蓋。商或周初器。

舊稱蟠夔方盉。木蓋帶玉頂。口縱拾壹·貳公分。橫拾肆·壹公分。通蓋頂高貳拾肆·貳公分。連木蓋帶玉頂共重市秤捌拾伍兩正。

67. Square Ho with Dragon-pattern

Formerly called p'an k'uei square ho. Cover lost. Shang or beginning of Chou Dynasty. N. P. M.

六八 獸盉(院)

喙作獸形。無鋬。有提梁。足短。戰國或漢器。

舊名古銅盉。帶銅蓋。口徑陸·伍公分。通梁高拾柒公分。最大腹圍肆拾公分。連蓋重市秤叁拾叁兩正。

68. Ho with an Animal-head-shaped Spout

Without a handle. A lizard-shaped swing-handle. Legs short. Period of the "Warring States" or Han Dynasty. N. P. M.

子. 爵屬 A. THE CHUEH GROUP

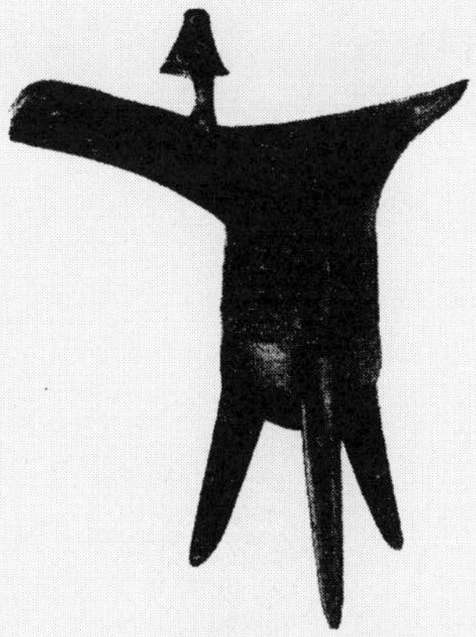

六九 一柱爵(所)

爵均兩柱。此以兩柱合爲一柱。商或周初器。

通柱高拾玖公分、口徑橫連流拾肆·伍公分。口徑縱柒公分。腹圍拾伍·肆公分。重市秤拾叁兩正。

69. Chueh with One Projection

Generally the chueh has two separate projections on the rim, but this one has them joined into one. Shang or beginning of Chou Dynasty. N. M.

丑. 斝屬 B. THE CHIA GROUP

七〇 非子異斝(院)

商器。

有銘。原稱古銅大爵。又稱子孫斝。口徑貳拾·壹公分。最高叁拾叁·玖公分。重市秤壹百捌拾貳兩正。

70. Chia of 非-tze-i

With inscription. Shang Dynasty. N. P. M.

七一 龍紋斝(所)

商或周初器。

舊名夔紋斝。連柱高叁拾肆·玖公分。口徑拾壹·玖公分。深拾柒·伍公分。腹圍肆拾伍·捌公分。重市秤壹百叁拾玖兩正。

71. Chia with Dragon-pattern

Formerly called k'uei wen chia. Shang or beginning of Chou Dynasty. N. M.

寅. 觚屬

C. THE KU GROUP

七二 鈴觚(院)

商或周初器。

舊稱古銅觚。又稱雲紋觚。有花紋。口徑拾貳·柒公分。高貳拾叁·柒公分。底徑柒·柒公分。重市秤貳拾壹兩捌錢。

72. Ku with a Bell

Formerly called ku. with cloud-scroll-pattern. Shang or the beginning of Chou Dynasty. N. P. M.

七三 回紋觚 所

商或周初器。

高貳拾肆·肆公分強。口徑拾肆·壹公分。深拾陸公分。重市秤貳拾伍兩叁錢。

73. Ku with Hui-pattern

Shang or beginning of Chou Dynasty. N. M.

卯. 尊屬

D. THE TSUN GROUP

七四 父辛尊(院)

商器。

有銘。舊名古銅掞盂。帶銅胆。口徑貳拾·叁公分。高貳拾伍·玖公分。底徑拾叁·捌公分。最大腹圍肆拾·捌公分。重市秤柒拾肆兩正。

74. Tsun to Worship Father Hsin

With inscription. Shang Dynasty. N. P. M.

七五 諸姛方尊(院)

有八稜腹上飾象首鹿首各四。饕餮紋與龍紋相間。隙處均飾以小回紋。商器。

有銘。口徑縱橫均叁拾叁·貳公分。高肆拾伍·柒公分。底徑貳拾貳·伍公分。重市秤肆拾貳斤捌兩正。底殘缺。

75. Chu-szu Square Tsun

With inscription. Eight flanges. Upper part of body decorated with four elephant heads and four deer heads. T'ao-t'ieh-pattern intermingled with dragon-pattern, and little hui-pattern filling up the intervening spaces. Shang Dynasty. N. P. M.

七六 邢季㚟尊(院)

腹作鳳紋。西周時邢國之器(今河北邢台)。
有銘。舊名古銅尊。口徑拾柒·貳公分。高拾柒·伍公分。足徑拾貳·玖公分。最大腹圍肆拾伍·伍公分。重市秤陸拾貳兩正。

76. Hsing-chi-㚟 Tsun

With inscription. Phœnix-pattern on body. Vessel of the Hsing State. Period of West Chou. Hsing State is located at Hsing-tai, Hopei Province. N. P. M.

七七 季尊(院)

周初器。

有銘。舊名周季受尊。口徑拾捌·柒公分。高貳拾·捌公分。底徑拾叁·伍公分。最大腹圍叁拾玖·伍公分。重市秤陸拾伍兩正。

77. Chi Tsun

With inscription. The beginning of Chou Dynasty. N. P. M.

七八 服尊(院)

有稜。有兩耳。作龍形。通體作鳥獸及龍紋。西周器。

有銘。舊名古銅尊。口徑拾玖·伍公分。高貳拾貳·捌公分。底縱拾·捌公分。橫拾壹·貳公分。最大腹圍肆拾陸·捌公分。重市秤壹百壹拾伍兩。

78. Fu Tsun

With inscription and flanges. Two dragon-shaped "ears." Bird, animal, and dragon-patterns all over the body. Period of West Chou. N. P. M.

七九 獸尊(院)

作獸形。鳥喙。以首爲蓋。頸部下爲器。形製絕奇。春秋或戰國時器。

舊名古銅天鷄薰爐。尾斷足斷。最高拾捌·玖公分。通長貳拾壹公分。最寬玖·伍公分。重市秤伍拾柒兩正。

79. Animal-shaped Tsun

The whole vessel is animal-shaped with a bird's beak. The head serves as a cover. Unique in form and make. Period of "Spring and Autumn Annals" or of the "Warring States." N. P. M.

八〇 犧尊(院)

錯金銀及綠松石。

舊名古銅犧尊。有花紋。有傷。最高貳拾捌·陸公分。最長肆拾·伍公分。最寬拾陸·伍公分。重市秤壹百陸拾伍兩正。

80. Tsun in the Shape of Cow-like Animal

Inlaid with gold, silver, and turquois. N. P. M.

（三）尋常用器類說明

尋常用器。在商周時。最主要者。爲盤、鑑及匜。皆盥洗所用器也。然盤亦用以盛食物。鑑可以鑑容。而匜之有足者。可以爲温器。

盂亦鑑類也。通常稱之爲洗。大抵皆漢器也。

奩、鐙等皆漢以後器。

3. Vessels for Ordinary Use

During the Shang and the Chou Dynasty, the principal vessels for ordinary use are the p'an (盤), chien (鑑), and yi (匜). They were in most cases used as washbasins.

The p'an might also be used to hold food; chien might serve as a mirror; and yi with legs might serve as a heating vessel.

The yü is a kind of chien, and is commonly called hsi (洗). Such vessels, for the most part, belong to the Han Dynasty.

Lien (奩, toilet-case), and teng (鐙, lamp-stand) belong to periods subsequent to Han.

甲. 盤屬

A. THE P'AN GROUP

八一 魚盤(所)

有流。有鋬。三足。盤内以十三魚字組成花紋。西周器。

最高點計拾壹·肆公分。口徑叁拾捌公分。連流徑肆拾·柒公分。深柒·柒公分。底口圍玖拾·柒公分。重市秤壹百陸拾叁兩捌錢正。

81. P'an, Decorated with Fish-like Figure

With open spout, handle. and three legs. Pattern formed of thirteen fish-like figures inside the vessel. West Chou. N. M.

乙. 鑑及盂屬

B. THE CHIEN AND THE YÜ GROUP

八二 蟠虺紋鑑(院)

戰國時器。

舊稱古銅鼓。有花紋。口徑貳拾捌公分。高拾壹公分。底徑拾壹·陸公分。最大腹圍捌拾·柒公分。重市秤陸拾捌兩正。

82. Chien with Coiled-serpent-pattern

Period of the "Warring States." N. P. M.

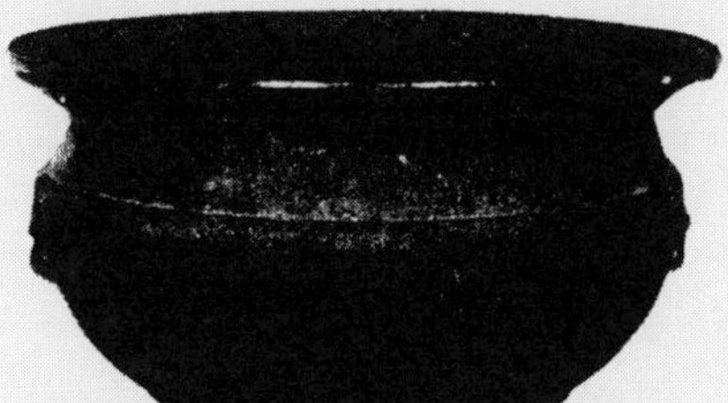

八三 「富貴昌宜侯王」盂(所)

漢器。

有銘。高拾柒·肆公分。口徑叁拾伍·壹公分。底徑貳拾壹·陸公分。深拾柒·壹公分。腹圍玖拾玖·伍公分。重市秤壹百壹拾柒兩捌錢正。

83. Fu-kuei-ch'ang-i-hou-wang Yü

With inscription. Han Dynasty. N. M.

丙. 匜 屬

C. THE YI GROUP

八四 陳伯元匜(院)

春秋時陳國器。

有銘。舊名古銅彝。最長貳拾柒公分。最寬拾伍·陸公分。最高拾柒·叁公分。重市秤陸拾兩正。

84. Yi of Yuan, Earl of Chen

With inscription. Vessel of the Chen State, period of "Spring and Autumn Annals." N. P. M.

八五 魚鳧圖匜(院)

匜內有魚鳧圖紋。春秋或戰國時器。
舊名漢魚鳧匜。最長貳拾陸·玖公分。最寬拾伍·肆公分。最高拾陸·貳公分。重市秤叁拾貳兩正。

85. Yi with Figures of Fish and Duck

Figure of fish and duck inside the vessel. Period of "Spring and Autumn Annals" or of the "Warring States." N. P. M.

八六 單環匜(院)

足爲圓輪形。匜身附一環。春秋或戰國時器。
通長貳拾捌·陸公分。最寬拾陸·貳公分。最高拾壹·捌公分。重市秤叁拾貳兩正。

86. Yi with a Single Ring

Legs wheel-shaped. A ring attached to the body. Period of "Spring and Autumn Annals" or of the "Warring States." N. P. M.

(77)

八七　王子匜(院)

銘字近鳥蟲書。器作獸形。以口爲流。無足。戰國時器。

有銘。舊稱王鑷匜。最大口徑拾捌·陸公分。最高拾叁·貳公分。最寬貳拾貳公分。重市秤肆拾壹兩陸錢。

87. Wang-tze Yi

With inscription. Script of the inscription similar to the "birds and insects" type. Vessel shaped like an animal. Mouth of the animal serves as spout. Without legs. Period of the "Warring States." N. P. M.

丁. 奩屬
D. THE LIEN GROUP

八八 錯金奩(所)

漢或漢後器。

高拾·肆公分。口徑捌·柒公分。底徑捌·捌公分。深捌·柒公分。腹圍貳拾柒·玖公分。重市秤拾叁兩正。

88. Lien, Inlaid with Gold

Han Dynasty or later. N. M.

戊. 鐙屬

E. THE TENG GROUP

八九 聖得鐙(院)

漢器。

柄有「聖得鐙」三字。盤徑貳拾叁·玖公分。鐙徑拾貳公分。通柄高捌公分。重市秤伍拾兩正。

89. Shen-te Teng

With inscription. Han Dynasty. N. P. M.

（四）樂器類說明

銅製樂器。可別爲三小類。

（一）執而擊者。鐃鉦是也。鐃多商或周初器。鉦多春秋器。蓋由鐃變成者。

（二）懸而擊者。鐘鎛是也。鐘之有銘詞者。最早爲西周末年。鎛則多春秋時器。鐘鎛之有甬者側懸。有紐者皆直懸。

（三）中有舌者。鈴鐸是也。此類之有銘詞者極少。亦西周以後之器。

4. Musical Instruments

Musical instruments made of bronze may be sub-divided into three classes:

(1) Those to be held in the hand when beaten. To this class belong the nao (鐃) and the cheng (鉦). Instruments of the type of the nao, for the most part, belong to the Shang Dynasty or the beginning of the Chou Dynasty. Those of the type of the cheng, for the most part, belong to the period of "Spring and Autumn Annals," for they were developed from the nao.

(2) Those to be hung up when beaten. To this class belong the chung (鐘) and the po (鎛). A chung with inscription dates at the earliest from the end of the West Chou period. Instruments of the type of the po, for the most part, belong to the period of "Spring and Autumn Annals." The chung and po that have on the top a stout stem (or handle), from which springs a loop on the side corresponding to the front of the body are hung oblique, while those that have on the top a loop are hung verticle.

(3) Those with clappers. To this class belong the ling (鈴) and the to (鐸). Very few of them have inscriptions. They also belong to periods subsequent to West Chou.

甲. 鐘屬

A. THE CHUNG GROUP

九〇 芮公鐘(院)

西周末或春秋時芮國器。

有銘。舊名古銅鐘。高叁拾伍·伍公分。口縱拾肆·捌公分。横拾玖·壹公分。口圍伍拾壹·壹公分。重市秤拾陸斤捌兩正。附玉璧一件。有傷。直徑拾壹·壹公分。孔徑肆·柒公分。厚零·捌公分。重市秤陸兩貳錢。

90. Chung of the Duke of Jui

With inscription. Vessel of Jui State, West Chou Dynasty or the period of "Spring and Autumn Annals." N. P. M.

九一 工𢻫王鐘(院)

清乾隆二十六年(西紀一七六一年)臨江(今江西清江縣)民耕地得十一鐘。獻之。今存此一器。可寶也。工𢻫卽吳國。春秋時吳國器。

有銘。帶銅環。有傷。高肆拾壹·伍公分。口縱拾陸·肆公分。橫貳拾貳·肆公分。口圍陸拾·叁公分。連環重市秤貳拾柒斤正。

91. Chung of the Prince of Kung-ngu

With inscription. Vessel of the Wu State in the period of "Spring and Autumn Annals." Kung-ngu was an archaic name of the Wu State. The people of Ling-kiang (now Ching-kiang hsien) in Kiangsi Province discovered eleven chung while cultivating their farms in the twenty-sixth year of Emperor Chien-lung of the Ch'ing Dynasty (1761). They were all presented to the Emperor. Only one survives at present.

九二 子穌編鐘(院)

春秋時器。

有銘。舊稱周從鐘。帶玉紐及木架。架上刻有[周從鐘]三字。架有散脫。鐘最長拾貳·叁公分。最寬玖·捌公分。最高貳拾貳·貳公分。連玉紐橫架共重市秤柒拾貳兩正。

92. Pien-chung of Tze-su

Formerly called tso ch'ung chung. With inscription. Period of "Spring and Autumn Annals." Pien-chung are small bells arrranged according to their different sounds to form a musical set. N. P. M.

乙. 鏄屬

B. THE PO GROUP

九三 盤雲紋鏄(院)

以交龍爲紐。乳作盤雲紋。春秋或戰國時器。

舊稱蟠虺鏄。通梁高伍拾柒·壹公分。頂縱貳拾叁·肆公分。橫貳拾玖·柒公分。底口縱貳拾玖·柒公分。橫叁拾陸·玖公分。最大腹圍壹百零陸·肆公分。重市秤柒拾壹斤捌兩正。

93. Po with Cloud-scroll-pattern

Formerly called p'an hui po. Two intertwining dragons serving as a loop. Cloud-scroll-pattern on "nipples" (bosses). Period of "Spring and Autumn Annals" or of the "Warring States." N. P. M.

九四 蟠虺紋鎛(院)

以交龍爲紐。乳作螺紋。春秋或戰國時器。

璧直徑拾肆·叁公分。孔徑陸·玖公分。連環共重拾肆兩正。帶玉璧銅環。底口傷。通梁高肆拾·貳公分。頂縱拾玖·肆公分。橫貳拾叁·壹公分。底口縱貳拾叁·柒公分。橫貳拾捌·陸公分。最大腹圍捌拾貳·貳公分。重市秤拾柒斤正。

94. Po with Coiled-serpent-pattern

Two intertwining dragons serving as a loop. Spiral lines on "nipples." Period of "Spring and Autumn Annals" or of the "Warring States." N. P. M.

九五 交螭紋鎛(院)

鈕兩端作獸首形。乳作螺紋。春秋或戰國時器。

通梁高伍拾叁·玖公分。頂縱貳拾柒·陸公分。橫叁拾叁·貳公分。底口縱叁拾貳·柒公分。橫叁拾玖·伍公分。最大腹圍壹百拾·肆公分。重市秤捌拾伍斤捌兩正。

95. Po with Intertwining-lizard-pattern

Two ends of the loop in the form of animal head. Spiral lines on "nipples" (bosses). Period of "Spring and Autumn Annals" or of the "Warring States." N. P. M.

丙. 鉦屬

C. THE CHENG GROUP

九六 素鉦(院)

帶木座。玉頂及木座皆乾隆時裝置。

通頂高叁拾貳·陸公分。口闊叁拾·伍公分。重市秤叁拾柒兩正。

96. Cheng without Decoration

Jade top and wooden stand made in the time of Ch'ien-lung. N. P. M.

（甲） 新鄭銅器羣說明

新鄭銅器羣。於中華民國十二年（西紀一九二三年）發見於河南新鄭縣城內，一坑中出成形之器七八十件。破碎者不計其數。現俱存河南博物館內。新鄭在春秋爲鄭地。此等銅器。大概爲東周時造。今選取八件。以見一斑。

a. The Hsin-cheng Bronzes

These bronzes were discovered in the city of Hsin-cheng, Honan Province, in 1923. About seventy to eighty complete pieces and innumerable fragments were found in one pit. Most of the finds are now kept in the Museum of Honan Province. Hsin-cheng belonged to the State of Cheng in the period of "Spring and Autumn Annals." These bronzes were probably cast in the period of East Chou. Eight vessels have been selected as specimens of this group.

九七 龍文鬲

高肆寸貳分。深貳寸伍分。口徑伍寸肆分。腹圍壹尺陸寸伍分。重肆拾兩。容捌合壹勺。

97. Li with Dragon-patterns

With beautiful green mottles of rust. Museum of Honan (indicated hereafter with the initials M. H.)

九八 牢鼎 (卽牛鼎)

器形較大。前後鼻上着牛首形。

高壹尺肆寸柒分。深壹尺零柒分。口徑壹尺捌寸叁分。腹圍伍尺捌寸叁分。耳高伍寸捌分。闊肆寸。足高陸寸伍分。重玖百肆拾肆兩。容肆斗捌升伍合。

98. Lao Ting, or Ting Decorated with Bull-heads

Of comparatively large size. Decorated with bull-heads at the fore and back of the body. M. H.

九九 蟠虺紋鼎(原名鼒)

器蓋全。

通蓋高壹尺伍寸捌分。深壹尺貳寸柒分。口徑壹尺貳寸柒分。腹圍肆尺伍寸貳分。耳高叁寸伍分。闊貳寸柒分。足高肆寸捌分。重陸百壹拾捌兩。容貳斗捌升柒合。

99. Ting with Coiled-serpent-pattern

Originally called tze. Complete with cover and body. M. H.

一〇〇 蟠螭紋簋(原名敦)

通蓋高捌寸陸分。深叁寸伍分。口徑柒寸伍分。腹圍貳尺柒寸壹分。足高貳寸玖分。重壹百捌拾肆兩。容肆升貳合叁勺。

100. Kuei with Coiled-lizard-pattern

Originally called tui. Complete with cover and body, both of which decorated with horizontal ridges. M. H.

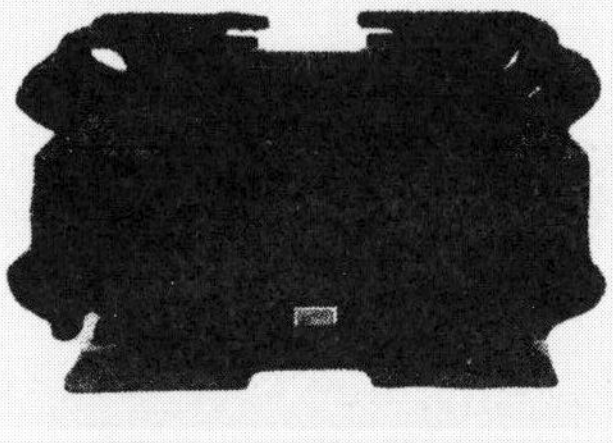

一〇一 蟠虺紋簠

器蓋全。花紋精細。

通蓋高陸寸壹分。深貳寸。口徑長玖寸叁分。闊陸寸陸分。腹圍叁尺貳寸。重壹百肆拾陸兩。容壹升玖合叁勺。

101. Fu with Coiled-serpent-pattern

Complete with cover and body. Pattern delicate. M. H.

一〇二 蟠螭紋壺(原名圜壺)

頸上作山紋。其下作螭紋。間以横紋。

高壹尺壹寸貳分。深玖寸陸分。口徑肆寸玖分。腹圍貳尺伍寸肆分。重壹百玖拾兩。容伍升捌合。

102. Hu with Coiled-lizard-pattern

Originally called yuan hu. Hill-pattern on the neck and lizard-pattern below it; horizontal ridges at the interval between them. M. H.

一〇三 蟠螭紋編鐘(一)

高伍寸貳分。甬高叁寸肆分。上徑縱肆寸。橫貳寸玖分。下徑縱伍寸。橫叁寸柒分。腹圍壹尺貳寸伍分。重壹百叁拾陸兩正。

103. Pien-chung with Coiled-lizard-pattern (A)

M. H.

一〇四 蟠螭紋編鐘(二)

高肆寸柒分。甬高貳寸玖分。上徑縱叁寸肆分。橫貳寸肆分。下徑縱叁寸捌分。橫貳寸捌分。腹圍玖寸伍分。重柒拾捌兩正。

編鐘原有二組。共存二十一件。今選其大小各一。

104. Pien-chung with Coiled-lizard-pattern (B)

Pien-chung are small bells arranged according to their different sounds. There are two sets of pien-chung (consisting of 21 pieces) in the Museum of Honan Province. A large and a small one have been selected from each set as specimens.

（乙）壽縣銅器羣說明

壽縣古物。發現於中華民國二十二年（西紀一·九三三年）夏。器物多有散出。惟安徽圖書館。尚保存七百餘件。壽縣於秦以前爲壽春。楚地。楚考烈王二十二年遷都於壽春。至楚王負芻五年。前後凡二十年（自西紀前二四一·至二二二年）。皆都於此。銅器之作。當在其時。此羣銅器冶鑄之術不甚精。然可以確知爲戰國末年楚國之銅器。且其形式頗多特異者。今由安徽圖書館選取四件。

b. The Shou-hsien Bronzes

These bronzes were discovered in the summer of 1933. Many of them have been scattered away through private hands, but some seven hundred pieces of them are still kept in the Library of Anhwei Province. Before the Ch'in Dynasty, Shou-hsien was called Shou-ch'un and belonged to the State of Ch'u. Shou-ch'un was the capital of Ch'u for twenty years (241–222 B. C.), from the twenty-second year of Prince Kao-li to the fifth year of Prince Fu-ch'u of Ch'u. These bronzes were probably cast during this time, and show characteristics of the bronzes of Ch'u at the end of this particular period. Four pieces have been selected as specimens from the Anhwei Library.

一〇五 楚王酓肯鼎

此器當爲楚考烈王作(西紀前二四一至二三八年)。形製極大。附耳。有流。三足。作獸首形。

有銘。高合今度壹尺零伍分。足高玖寸貳分。口徑壹尺伍寸捌分。流長肆寸。容深肆寸柒分。重準今衡捌拾叁斤。

105. Ting of Prince Yin-ken of Ch'u

With inscription. This vessel was cast for Prince Kao-li of Ch'u (241–238 B.C.). Of unusually large bulk. "Ears" projecting upward from the sides of the body. With a spout. Three legs decorated with animal heads.

一〇六 爼(全形)

一〇六 爼(面)

一〇六 爼(底)

此器前所未見。當係置於鼎上以供割肉者。古『䵼』字象置彐於鼎上。有肉而以刀割之。彐即爼形。與此正同。中作十字形孔。蓋以泄汁者。

器高今度肆寸玖分。左右徑長玖寸捌分。前後徑長肆寸玖分。重準今衡柒斤捌兩正。

106. Tsu (爼)

Probably used for meat cutting on the ting. The archaic ideograph "䵼" depicts a "tsu" (彐) put on a ting; on the "tsu" is meat (月) with a knife (刀) over it. When viewed sidewise the "tsu" looks exactly like the "彐." It has cross-shaped crevices in the centre to let fluid leak through it.

一〇七 盤雲紋簠

此次所出簠甚多。形狀皆同。

有銘。通高今度叁寸伍分。左右徑長玖寸肆分。前後徑長陸寸伍分。容深貳寸肆分。重準今衡拾斤捌兩正。

107. Fu with Cloud-scroll-pattern

With inscription. Many fu were discovered at Shou-hsien. All of them are similar in form.

一〇八 環梁方盤(盤長方形)

此器有兩環狀之提梁。形製罕見。盤長方形、

高今度叁寸陸分。左右徑長壹尺捌寸壹分。前後徑長玖寸捌分。容深壹寸柒分。重準今衡拾陸斤捌兩正。

108. Square P'an with Two Chain-shaped Swing-handles

Unusual in form and make.

(72422A)

参加倫敦中國藝術國際展覽會
出品圖說
第一册　銅器
Illustrated Catalogue of Chinese Government Exhibits for the International Exhibition of Chinese Art in London
Volume I Bronze

編輯者　倫敦中國藝術國際展覽會籌備委員會

發行人　上海河南路　王雲五

印刷所　上海河南路　商務印書館

發行所　上海及各埠　商務印書館

定價國幣叁元　外埠酌加運費匯費

中華民國二十五年二月初版

四〇〇上

（本書校對者翁際雲）

参加伦敦中国艺术国际展览会出品图说

第 二 册　瓷 器

ILLUSTRATED CATALOGUE OF CHINESE GOVERNMENT EXHIBITS FOR THE INTERNATIONAL EXHIBITION OF CHINESE ART IN LONDON

VOLUME II. PORCELAIN

伦敦中国艺术国际展览会筹备委员会编辑

CCTP 中央编译出版社
Central Compilation & Translation Press

图书在版编目 (CIP) 数据

参加伦敦中国艺术国际展览会出品图说 / 伦敦中国艺术国际展览会筹备委员会主编 . -- 北京：中央编译出版社，2022.9

ISBN 978-7-5117-4241-4

Ⅰ . ①参… Ⅱ . ①伦… Ⅲ . ①历史文物 – 中国 – 图集
Ⅳ . ① K870.2

中国版本图书馆 CIP 数据核字 (2022) 第 153392 号

参加伦敦中国艺术国际展览会出品图说

责任编辑 郑永杰
特约编辑 刘诗婷　杨　凌
责任印制 刘　慧
出版发行 中央编译出版社
地　　址 北京市海淀区北四环西路 69 号（100080）
电　　话 （010）55627391（总编室）　（010）55627312（编辑室）
（010）55627320（发行部）　（010）55627377（新技术部）
经　　销 全国新华书店
印　　刷 山东韵杰文化科技有限公司
开　　本 889 毫米 ×1194 毫米　1/16
字　　数 321 千字
印　　张 50.25
版　　次 2022 年 9 月第 1 版
印　　次 2022 年 9 月第 1 次印刷
定　　价 980.00 元（全四册）

新浪微博：@ 中央编译出版社　　**微　　信：**中央编译出版社（ID：cctphome）
淘宝店铺：中央编译出版社直销店（http://shop108367160.taobao.com）
（010）55627331

參加倫敦中國藝術國際展覽會出品圖說

第 二 册 瓷 器

ILLUSTRATED CATALOGUE OF CHINESE GOVERNMENT EXHIBITS FOR THE INTERNATIONAL EXHIBITION OF CHINESE ART IN LONDON

VOLUME II. PORCELAIN

倫敦中國藝術國際展覽會籌備委員會編輯
商務印書館印行

第　二　册

瓷　器

Volume II.

PORCELAIN

参加倫敦中國藝術國際展覽會
瓷器照片總目

瓷器概說

	頁數
瓷器原始	九
歷代名窯	一一
瓷器胎骨	一五
瓷器油色	一七
瓷器紋片	二一
景德鎮窯	二三
琺瑯彩瓷	二九

	名稱	件數	
一	宋定窯	四件	三五
二	宋鈞窯	十二件	三六
三	宋汝窯	十件	四四
四	宋官窯	十七件	五二
五	宋龍泉窯	四件	六二
六	宋哥窯	十三件	六四
七	宋章龍泉窯(即弟窰)	一件	六九
八	宋建陽窯	三件	六九
九	南宋官窯	十六件	七〇
一〇	南宋吉州窯	十五件	七八
一一	金宿州窯	四件	八七
一二	金平定窯	一件	八九
一三	南宋餘姚窯	一件	九〇
一四	南宋餘杭窯	一件	九一

TABLE OF CONTENTS

		PAGE
The Origin of Porcelain		10
Famous Yao of the Successive Dynasties		12
The Body Materials of Porcelain		16
Glaze Colours on Porcelain Wares		18
Marks and Crackles on Porcelain		22
The Ching-tê Chên Yao		24
Porcelain with Cloisonné Enamel		30

PART I

I.	Sung Ting Ware	4	Pieces	35
II.	Sung Chün Ware	12	,,	36
III.	Sung Ju Ware	10	,,	44
IV.	Sung Kuan Ware	17	,,	52
V.	Sung Lung-ch'üan Ware	4	,,	62
VI.	Sung Ko Ware	13	,,	64
VII.	Sung Chang Lung-ch'üan Ware (i.e. Ti Yao)	1	Piece	69
VIII.	Sung Chien-yang Ware	3	Pieces	69
IX.	Southern Sung Kuan Ware	16	,,	70
X.	Southern Sung Chi-chou Ware	15	,,	78
XI.	Chin Su-chou Ware	4	,,	87
XII.	Chin P'ing-ting Ware	1	Piece	89
XIII.	Southern Sung Yü-yao Ware	1	,,	90
XIV.	Southern Sung Yü-hang Ware	1	,,	91

	名稱	件數	頁數
一五	南宋湘湖窰	二件	九一
一六	南宋郊壇下官窰	五件	九二
一七	南宋廣窰	三件	九五
一八	元彭窰	七件	九七
一九	元臨川窰	三件	九八
二〇	元樞府窰	一件	九九
二一	明處州窰	四件	一〇〇
二二	明德化窰	一件	一〇二
二三	明廣窰	四件	一〇二
二四	明永樂窰	十一件	一〇六
二五	明宣德窰	二十四件	一一二
二六	明成化窰	十八件	一二六
二七	明弘治窰	一件	一三三
二八	明嘉靖窰	六件	一三四
二九	明隆慶窰	二件	一三七
三〇	明萬曆窰	三件	一三九
三一	明景德鎮窰	二件	一四一
三二	明周窰	一件	一四三
三三	明壺公窰	一件	一四四
三四	清康熙窰(一色泑器)	三件	一四五
	清康熙窰(青花器)	一件	一四八
	清康熙窰(泑裏三色器)	一件	一四九
	清康熙窰(三彩器)	一件	一五〇
	清康熙窰(五彩器)	一件	一五一
	清康熙窰(琺瑯彩器)	七件	一五二
三五	清康熙郎窰	四件	一五五
三六	清雍正窰(一色泑器)	十六件	一五八

PAGE

XV.	Southern Sung Hsiang-hu Ware	2 Pieces	91
XVI.	Southern Sung Kuan Ware under the Suburban Altar	5 ,, ...	92
XVII.	Southern Sung Kuang-tung Ware	3 ,, ...	95
XVIII.	Yüan Pêng Ware	7 ,, ...	97
XIX.	Yüan Lin-ch'üan Ware	3 ,, ...	98
XX.	Yüan Shu-fu Ware	1 Piece	99

PART II

I.	Ming Ch'u-chou Ware	4 Pieces	100
II.	Ming Tê-hua Ware	1 Piece	102
III.	Ming Kuang-tung Ware	4 Pieces	102
IV.	Ming Yung Lo Ware	11 ,, ...	106
V.	Ming Hsüan Tê Ware	24 ,, ...	112
VI.	Ming Ch'êng Hua Ware	18 ,, ...	126
VII.	Ming Hung Chih Ware	1 Piece	133
VIII.	Ming Chia Ching Ware	6 Pieces	134
IX.	Ming Lung Ch'ing Ware	2 ,, ...	137
X.	Ming Wan Li Ware	3 ,, ...	139
XI.	Ming Ching-tê Chên Ware	2 ,, ...	141
XII.	Ming Chou Ware	1 Piece	143
XIII.	Ming Hu-kung Ware	1 ,, ...	144

PART III

I.	Ch'ing K'ang Hsi Ware:		
	In Monochrome	3 Pieces	145
	In Under-glaze Blue	1 Piece	148
	In Three Under-glaze Colours	1 ,, ...	149
	In Enamel of Three Colours	1 ,, ...	150
	In Enamel of Five Colours	1 ,, ...	151
	In Cloisonné Enamel	7 Pieces	152
II.	Ch'ing K'ang Hsi Lang Ware	4 ,, ...	155
III.	Ch'ing Yung Chêng Ware:		
	In Monochrome	16 ,, ...	158

	名稱	件數	頁數
	清雍正窯(青花器)	二件	一七〇
	清雍正窯(琺瑯彩器)	三十四件	一七二
三七	清乾隆窯(一色洳器)	十六件	一八七
	清乾隆窯(青花器)	五件	一九八
	清乾隆窯(青花鬬彩器)	二件	二〇二
	清乾隆窯(粉彩器)	十一件	二〇四
	清乾隆窯(琺瑯彩器)	三十二件	二一三
三八	清康熙製(銅胎琺瑯彩器)	七件	二三七
	清乾隆製(玻璃胎琺瑯彩器	八件	二四六

總共三百五十二件

			PAGE
	In Under-glaze Blue	2 Pieces	170
	In Cloisonné Enamel	34 ,,	172
IV.	Ch'ing Ch'ien Lung Ware:		
	In Monochrome	16 ,,	187
	In Under-glaze Blue	5 ,,	198
	In Under-glaze Blue and Enamel of Contrasting Colours	2 ,,	202
	In Powder Enamel	11 ,,	204
	In Cloisonné Enamel	32 ,,	213
V.	Ch'ing K'ang Hsi Manufacture:		
	In Cloisonné Enamel on a Copper-body	7 ,,	237
VI.	Ch'ing Ch'ien Lung Manufacture:		
	In Cloisonné Enamel on a Glass-body	8 ,,	242

Totalling . . . . 352 Pieces

參加倫敦中國藝術國際展覽會

瓷器照片總目

瓷器概說

倫敦中國藝術國際展覽會籌備委員會專門委員郭葆昌述

瓷器原始

中國古用陶器。厥後精進爲瓷。陶與瓷雖同由埏埴鍛鍊所成。而其原質迥異。陶質爲土。土之用隨在可資。故產陶之地極廣。瓷則必採石製泥爲之。其原質復有美有惡。故產瓷有一定區域。而品類亦有精粗之別。

瓷字說文（說文解字、漢許慎撰、成於和帝永元十二年、西元一〇〇年、）本無。見徐鉉（宋太宗朝、徐鉉等奉勅校定說文解字、雍熙三年(西元九八六年)進上、）新附四百一字中。蓋漢世尚無其物。未制其字也。此字始見晉呂忱字林。（呂忱武帝時人(西元第三世紀)、原書已佚、此字見文選笙賦傾縹瓷以酌酃句下唐李善注引、）自陳顧野王玉篇（成於梁大同九年、西元五四三年、）以下。字書並因之。用於文字則肇自晉潘岳（武帝惠帝時人(西元第三世紀)）笙賦。六朝（晉宋齊梁陳隋(西元二六六年至六一八年)）以降。詩文用者益多。呂潘皆晉初人。是瓷器晉初

A BRIEF DESCRIPTION OF PORCELAIN

BY

KUO PAO-CH'ANG

Technical Expert to the Committee of Preparation for the London International Exhibition of Chinese Works of Art

I. The Origin of Porcelain

Pottery wares were in use among ancient people in China, and were in subsequent ages developed into porcelain. Pottery and porcelain, though both are formed from moulded clay and are afterward subjected to a firing process, are composed of entirely different materials. Since the material for pottery is earth, which is available for use almost everywhere, districts suitable for its production are naturally vast and well distributed. Porcelain, on the other hand, must be fabricated from paste which has been derived from pulverised stones specially quarried, and may be distinguished by the difference in the quality of paste. Hence ceramic wares can be manufactured only within certain areas, and may be graded by their relative coarseness or fineness.

The character tz'ŭ (瓷), meaning porcelain, did not originally figure in the Shuo Wên (說文),[1] but is found among the four hundred and one characters subsequently supplemented by Hsü Hsüan (徐鉉).[2] The reason is that since the ware was not yet in existence during the Han Dynasty, no character was adopted for it. The character first made its appearance in the Tzŭ Lin (字林) or Collection of Words, compiled by Lü Shên (呂忱) of the Chin Dynasty.[3] The Yü Pien (玉篇) or Scriptionary, compiled by Ku Yeh-wang (顧野王)[4] and later dictionaries followed suit by incorporating the word. Tz'ŭ or porcelain having made its début in the Idyll about Sheng (笙賦), composed by P'an Yo (潘岳),[5] has often been employed in odes and other literature, written since the "Six Dynasties."[6] Since Lü Shên and P'an Yo were both living in the early part of the Chin Dynasty, it seems that porcelain should already

1 Shuo Wên Chieh Tzŭ (說文解字) or Description of Scripts and Explanation of Characters, compiled by Hsü Shên (許慎) of the Han Dynasty, and completed in the twelfth year of Emperor Ho (100 A.D.).

2 During the reign of Emperor T'ai Tsung of the Sung Dynasty Hsü Hsüan and others were ordered by an imperial decree to revise the Shuo Wên Chieh Tzŭ, revision being submitted in the third year of Yung Hsi (986 A.D.).

3 Lü Shên lived in the time of Emperor Wu (third century A.D.). The original work is no longer in existence. The word appears in a verse of an idyll known as fu (賦) about a musical instrument of the organ-type known as sheng (笙), the idyll being found in the literary selection called Wên Hsüan (文選). The passage runs thus: "To tip azure porcelain while imbibing the liquor of ling (lu)"; the beverage was made in Hêng-yang, Hunan. In the glossary of that verse Li Shan of the T'ang Dynasty quoted Lü's work.

4 The work was completed in the ninth year of the reign of Ta T'ung of the Liang Dynasty (543 A.D.).

5 P'an Yo lived during the reigns of Emperor Wu and Emperor Hui (third century A.D.).

6 The "Six Dynasties"—Chin, Sung, Ch'i, Liang, Ch'ên, and Sui—extended from 266 to 618 A.D.

已有旣不見於漢代。當在魏晉之世也。

甆字亦見西京雜記所載鄒陽漢景帝時人(紀元前第二世紀)酒賦。西京雜記舊傳出於葛洪。亦有謂梁吳均撰者。吳均梁人無論矣。葛洪晉咸和時人。西元第四世紀亦在潘岳之後。書中各賦。皆漢建安獻帝年號以後文體。出魏晉間人依託。非漢初人作。

歷代名窯

窯之見於載籍者。莫古於晉之東甌窯建於魏晉之際、在今浙江永嘉縣境、其地爲古東甌國、因地而名、故稱東甌窯、見唐陸羽茶經引晉杜毓荈賦、陸羽、唐肅宗上元(西元七六〇年)前人、次則有元魏之關中窯建於元魏(西元四七一至五五六年)、在今陝西咸陽縣、洛京。窯建於元魏、在今河南洛陽縣、再次爲陳之昌南。見後卽今日馳譽寰中之景德鎭窯也。自唐而降。窯日以多。不勝縷舉，就其名著當時及今日有傳器者言之。唐越窯窯建於唐、在今浙江紹興縣、其地唐屬越州、故稱越窯、爲最。邢窯建於唐、在今河北邢台縣、次之。如杜詩杜甫、唐詩人之最有名者、甫集有於韋處乞大邑甆詩、甚稱其美、所稱大邑甆者。窯建於唐、屬邛州、通稱邛窯、在今四川大邑縣、器必甚精。惜今未見。五代西元九〇七至九六〇年則越窯秘色器外。柴窯建於後周世宗朝(西元九五四至九五九年)、在今河南鄭縣、世宗本姓柴、故名柴窯、獨著。北宋名窯最多。定、窯建於宋初、在今河北定縣、鈞、窯建於宋初、在今河南禹縣、其地有鈞臺、因名鈞窯、至今尚存、東、窯建於宋初、在今河南陳留縣、以其在汴京之東、故名東窯、汝、窯建於宋徽宗大觀元年(西元一一〇七年)、在今河南臨汝縣、創立之人爲蕭服、官、窯建於宋大觀間(西元一一〇七至一一一〇年)、在今河南開封縣、龍泉、窯建於宋初、地名琉田市、在今浙江龍泉縣、哥弟宋有處州人章生一生二兄弟、在龍泉琉田市分窯製器、故以哥窯弟窯別之、諸窯。

have existed at that time; and since it did not appear in the Han Dynasty, it must first have been introduced in the period between Wei (魏) and Chin (晉).[1]

II. Famous Yao of the Successive Dynasties

Of all the yao, or porcelain kilns, that are mentioned in books, none is anterior to the Tung Ou kilns (東甌窯) of the Chin Dynasty.[2] Next in order come the Kuan-chung Yao (關中窯),[3] and the Lo-ching Yao (洛京窯),[4] of the Yüan Wei period. Next comes the Ch'ang-nan factory (昌南) of the Ch'en Dynasty (*vide infra*), which have now become the well known kilns at Ching-tê Chên.

From the T'ang Dynasty downward the number of kilns gradually increased to the extent that they were too numerous to be mentioned. Taking those that were famous at the time or those of which we have extant specimens, we may say that among the kilns of the T'ang Dynasty, the Yüeh Yao (越窯)[5] ranks first, and the Hsing Yao (邢窯),[6] second. What was known as the Ta-yi ware[7] which was mentioned in a poem of Tu Fu (杜甫)[8] may be taken to be an article of very fine quality, but it is to be regretted that no specimens can now be seen.

In the "Five Dynasties" (907–960 A.D.), besides the Yüeh-chou wares of the "secret colour," or pi-sê (祕色), the Ch'ai Yao[9] alone enjoyed a high reputation.

The Northern Sung Dynasty had the greatest number of noted porcelain manufactures to its credit. The Ting,[10] the Chün,[11] the Tung,[12] the Ju,[13] the Kuan,[14] the Lung-chüan,[15] and

1 The word tz'ŭ also occurs in the Idyll on Wine, composed by Tsou Yang (鄒陽) who was a contemporary of Emperor Ching of the Han Dynasty (second century B.C.). This idyll was reproduced in the Hsi Ching Cha Chi (西京雜記) or Miscellanea of the West Capital, and was formerly said to have been from the pen of Ko Hung (葛洪) or perhaps Wu Chün (吳均). Wu Chün, being a man of the Liang Dynasty, needs no discussion. Ko Hung lived at the time of Hsien Ho of the Chin Dynasty (fourth century A.D.), also later than P'an Yo. All the idylls contained in that book are of the style prevalent after the Chien An period—a reign title of Emperor Hsien of the Han Dynasty (196–220 A.D.), and must have been composed by men of the Wei and Chin, who imputed them to men of the early part of the Han Dynasty, men who could never have been the authors of such literature.

2 The yao or kilns were established at the time of Wei and Chin, and may have been located in the territory of modern Yung-chia District (永嘉縣), Chekiang Province. The locality being the ancient state of East Ou the kiln came under the name of Tung Ou Yao, following that of its site. The kiln is mentioned in the Idyll of Ch'uan (荈)—the late and old leaves of the tea plant—composed by Tu Yü (杜毓) of the Chin Dynasty which is quoted in the Ch'a Ching (茶經)—or Classic on Tea—compiled by Lu Yü (陸羽) of the T'ang Dynasty. Lu Yü preceded Shang Yüan of the reign of Emperor Su Tsung (760 A.D.).

3 The yao was established in the period of the Yüan Wei (471–556 A.D.) and is situated in the modern district of Hsien-yang, Shensi Province.

4 This yao was established in the Yüan Wei period and is situated in what is now the Lo-yang District, Honan Province.

5 The kiln is situated in the Shao-hsing District, Chekiang Province. The locality belonged to Yüeh-chou in the T'ang Dynasty; hence the name Yüeh Yao.

6 The kiln was established in the time of T'ang, and is located in what is now known as Hsing-t'ai Hsien, Hopei Province.

7 The kiln was established in the T'ang Dynasty and came under the jurisdiction of Ch'iung-chou (邛州). Its wares are commonly called Ch'iung Yao. Its site is in the modern Ta-yi Hsien (大邑縣), Szechuan Province.

8 Tu Fu is the best known among T'ang poets. In his Poetical Work is a poem under the heading, "Begging for a Ta-yi Bowl at Wei's Place"; he speaks highly of the bowl's beauty.

9 The kiln was established during the reign of Emperor Shih Tsung of the Posterior Chou Dynasty (954–959 A.D.) in what is now known as Chêng Hsien (鄭縣), Honan Province. Shih Tsung's family name being Ch'ai, it is therefore named Ch'ai Yao (柴窯).

10 The Ting Yao (定窯) was established early in the Sung Dynasty in modern Ting Hsien, Hopei.

11 The Chün Yao (鈞窯) was established early in the Sung Dynasty in modern Yü Hsien, Honan. There is in the locality the Chün Tai or "Terrace of Chün" after which the factory has been named. The kilns are still in operation.

12 The Tung Yao (東窯) was established in the early part of the Sung Dynasty in modern Ch'ên-liu Hsien in Honan. Being situated to the east of the national capital, it was named Tung Yao or East Kiln.

13 The Ju Yao (汝窯) was established in the first year of Ta Kuan of Emperor Hui Tsung in the Sung Dynasty (1107 A.D.) in modern Lin-ju Hsien in Honan. The founder of the factory was Hsiao Fu (蕭服).

14 The Kuan Yao (官窯) was established early in the Sung Dynasty during the Ta Kuan period (1107–1110 A.D.) at modern K'ai-fêng Hsien, Honan.

15 The Lung-ch'üan Yao (龍泉窯) was established early in the Sung Dynasty in a place called Liu-t'ien Shih (琉田市) in modern Lung-ch'üan Hsien, Chekiang.

南北互峙。後先輝映。於時昌南易名景德。越窯仍稱祕色。製器多佳。而磁州、窯建於宋初、在今河北磁縣、現仍燒造、麗水、窯建於宋、在今之浙江麗水縣、蕭縣、窯建於宋、在今江蘇蕭縣之白土鎮、建安、窯建於宋、在今福建建甌縣、宋世卽遷建陽縣、建陽各窯。亦有可取。其監窯專官之可考者。太平興國中西元九七七至九八四年則有監越州瓷窯務之殿前承旨趙仁濟。大觀元年則有監設汝州瓷窯務之將作少監蕭服。南渡後。修內司官窯修內司、北宋屬將作監、掌宮城太廟繕修之事、南渡後將作監入工部、其職務多由修內司代掌、故官窯亦屬之、窯爲邵成章提舉後苑時所設、在鳳凰山下、今杭縣地、製襲舊京。吉、窯建於南宋、地名永和市、在今江西吉安縣。宿、窯建於金、在今安徽宿縣、泗窯建於金、在今安徽泗縣、及平定窯。建於金、在今山西平定縣、器法古定。祕色遷於餘姚。南宋時越窯改設於此、在今浙江餘姚縣、餘杭、窯建於南宋、在今浙江餘杭縣、湘湖景德鎮東南二十里外有湘湖市、南宋時建窯製器、亦設窯製器。郊壇下別立之新官窯。南宋末年建、在今浙江杭縣、陽江縣廣窯南宋時建窯製器、卽今廣東陽江縣、明代改設於石灣、在今南海縣佛山鎮、現仍燒造、之沙鈞。皆有佳品。元代彭均寶於霍州在今山西霍縣燒造。倣法定器。當時有彭窯之稱。新立之窯。臨川窯建於元、在今江西臨川縣、較佳。各地舊窯或已不存。或雖存而原質已劣。製作不良。

the Ko Ti (哥弟), or the Elder and Younger Brothers' ware[1] —each set up rival standards in the north and south, or else reflected glory one after another. Meanwhile Ch'ang-nan, which has assumed the name of Ching-tê, and the Yüeh-chou factory, whose product was still known as pi-sê, also turned out a great quantity of wares of a superior grade. Some of the Tz'ŭ-chou,[2] the Li-shui,[3] the Hsiao-hsien,[4] the Chien-an,[5] and the Chien-yang porcelains have something to recommend them.

As to the special officials for the supervision of porcelain manufacture, there were in the time of T'ai P'ing Hsing Kuo (977–984 A.D.), Chao Jên-chi (趙仁濟), who was Tien-ch'ien Ch'eng-chih (殿前承旨), or Attendant Han-lin at the Imperial Court and Superintendent of Porcelain Manufacture at Yüeh-chou; and in the Ta Kuan period, Hsiao Fu, who was Chiang-tso Shao-chien (將作少監), or Vice-Minister of the Imperial Household and Superintendent of the Establishment of Porcelain Kilns at Ju-chou.

After the Imperial Court moved to the south, the Kuan Yao of the Hsiu-nai Ssŭ (修內司)[6] followed the practice obtaining then in the old capital. The Chi-chou,[7] the Su-chou,[8] the Ssŭ-chou,[9] and the P'ing-ting[10] were all wares modelled after the ancient Ting. The pi-sê porcelains were made in Yü-yao instead.[11] Factories were also established in Yü-hang[12] and Hsiang-hu[13] for the manufacture of ceramic objects. A new Kuan Yao was established beneath the Altar of Heaven.[14] There are also good specimens of the Sha Chün (沙鈞) or siliceous Chün ware, which were being produced by the Kuang-tung kilns established at Yang-chiang Hsien.[15]

Pêng Chün-pao (彭均寶) in the Yüan period, manufactured a type of wares in Ho-chou[16] in imitation of Ting-chou porcelain, which were then given the name of Pêng Yao (彭窯). Among the kilns newly established in the dynasty, the Lin-ch'üan Yao[17] seemed to be doing

1 Two brothers, Chang Sheng-i and Chang Sheng-erh, natives of Ch'u-chou (處州) each operated kilns at Liu-t'ien Shih, Lung-ch'üan, for the manufacture of porcelain. These factories were therefore called Ko Yao (the Elder Brother's Factory) and the Ti Yao (the Younger Brother's Factory).

2 The Tz'ŭ-chou Yao (磁州窯) was established early in the Sung Dynasty in modern Tz'ŭ Hsien, Hopei Province. It is still in operation.

3 The Li-shui Yao (麗水窯) was established in the Sung period in what is now known as Li-shui Hsien, Chekiang.

4 The Hsiao-hsien Yao (蕭縣窯) was established in the Sung period at a place called Pai-t'u Chên (白土鎮) in modern Hsiao Hsien, Kiangsu.

5 The Chien-an Yao (建安窯) was established in the Sung Dynasty in a locality which is now called Chien-ou Hsien (建甌縣), Fukien Province. During the same dynasty the kilns were transferred to Chien-yang Hsien (建陽縣), Fukien.

6 Hsiu-nai Ssŭ was a department of the Imperial Household and in charge of the construction and repair of palaces, walls, ancestral temples, and so on. After the Court removed to the south, the Imperial Household was amalgamated with the Board of Works and its functions were mostly discharged by the Hsiu-nai Ssŭ. The Kuan kilns, therefore, came under its control. The kilns were established by Shao Ch'eng-chang (邵成章), who was Ti-chü Hou-yüan (提舉後苑) or General Manager of the Imperial Court, at Fêng-huang Shan (鳳凰山), or Phoenix' Hill, in modern Hang Hsien (杭縣).

7 The Chi-chou Yao (吉州窯) was established in the Southern Sung period, at Yung-ho Shih (永和市) in modern Chi-an Hsien (吉安縣), Kiangsi.

8 The Su-chou Yao (宿州窯) was established during the Chin period in modern Su Hsien, Anhui.

9 The Ssŭ-chou Yao (泗州窯) was established during the Chin period in modern Ssŭ Hsien, Anhui.

10 The P'ing-ting Yao (平定窯) was established during the Chin Dynasty in modern P'ing-ting Hsien, Shansi.

11 The Yüeh Yao was transferred in the Southern Sung period to what is now known as Yü-yao Hsien (餘姚縣), Chekiang Province.

12 The Yü-hang Yao (餘杭窯) was established in the Southern Sung Dynasty in modern Yü-hang Hsien, Chekiang.

13 Twenty li (or about seven miles) to the south-east of Ching-tê Chên is the Hsiang-hu Shih (湘湖市) where factories were founded for the manufacture of porcelains in the Southern Sung Dynasty.

14 The factory was established toward the latter part of the Southern Sung Dynasty in modern Hang Hsien, Chekiang.

15 In the Southern Sung Dynasty kilns were established for the manufacture of porcelain wares in present-day Yang-chiang Hsien (陽江縣), Kuangtung Province. In the Ming Dynasty the kiln site was moved over to what is now known as Shih-wan (石灣) in Fo-shan Chên (佛山鎮), district of Nan-hai. Wares are still being made there.

16 In modern Ho Hsien (霍縣) in Shansi.

17 The Lin-Ch'üan Yao (臨川窯) was founded during the Yüan Dynasty in modern Lin-ch'üan Hsien, Kiangsi Province.

景德鎮窯至是亦稍不振。惟內府進御及樞府用器。咸取供於此。尚有佳者。明清兩代。鎮窯獨步當世。諸窯莫能接武矣。明別有德化窯突起於福建之泉州。在今德化縣、現在仍存、通稱建瓷其所製器。品質並佳。石灣廣窯。見前注宜興歐窯。建於明、在今江蘇宜興縣、器式亦好。

瓷器胎骨

瓷器胎骨。皆由採石製泥淘鍊範成。窯地不同。原質亦判。今就有傳器者論之。唐越窯胎質瑩白如玉。邢窯澄泥爲範。細白如粉。後周柴窯純白而細膩。北宋越窯。與唐代同。定窯承邢之後。原質相類。白器多範澄泥。而淘鍊之精不及。鈞窯胎質。有白、有灰、有紅、有黃。而白者最上。東窯白中透灰。間有灰色者。則較粗也。汝窯質淺黃。細而堅。官窯原質有白、灰、紅之分。蓋取自東鈞兩地。而淘鍊極精純。白者多用含有鐵質之黑泑護胎足。亦有純用鐵骨泥者。細審可辨。龍泉哥弟胎質皆白。微帶灰色。弟窯淘鍊最純。哥窯別有黃與黑泥二種。龍泉窯有用紫金水合白泥者。驟觀之頗似紅泥。其實非也。麗水窯原質灰白。蕭窯質白。粗而堅。建安窯以烏泥著。建陽窯灰白。精而暗。磁州窯質白。粗而燥。南宋修內司官窯胎質、有灰黑、灰黃及純用紅泥者。郊壇下新立官窯原質亦與

comparatively well. But among the old kilns some ceased to exist, while others though continuing to run, turned out wares either of inferior workmanship or poor material. Even the Ching-tê Chên factories suffered from stagnation at that time. As they continued to supply the ceramic wares needed by the Imperial Household and the Privy Council, some fine specimens were still manufactured. The kilns at Ching-tê Chên were at their zenith in both the Ming and the Ch'ing Dynasty, and encountered no rivalry from other porcelain factories.

The Tê-hua Yao[1] established at Ch'üan-chou Fu in Fukien suddenly came into prominence in the Ming period, producing wares that were elegant in form and fine in texture. The Kuang-tung Kilns at Shih-wan (*vide supra*) and the Ou Yao[2] at I-hsing also manufactured vessels of good quality.

III. The Body Materials of Porcelain

Inasmuch as the paste of porcelain ware is made from the moulding of clay that has been obtained through the levigating of pulverised stones specially mined, the material varies with the different factory sites. We will discuss only those wares which have extant specimens. The Yüeh ware of the T'ang Dynasty had a paste "pure white like jade," while the Hsing Yao was made from the welding of elutriated clay which was fine and white like powder. The Ch'ai ware of the Posterior Chou Dynasty had a pure white body which was finely grained and unctuous.

In the Northern Sung period the Yüeh ware was the same as in the time of the T'ang. The Ting ware, being successor to the Hsing, was composed of the same body material, but the elutriated clay of which most of its white objects were made was less refined. The Chün ware was a body of white, grey, red, or yellow, the white being of the highest quality. The body of the Tung ware is white with a tinge of grey, and sometimes entirely grey. The latter constituted the coarser kind. The paste of the Ju is of light yellow, fine and compact. The Kuan ware is distinguishable by a white, grey, or red paste, because the materials were taken from the sites of both the Tung and the Chün, but were exceedingly refined. In the case of a white paste, a dark ferruginous glaze was usually applied in order to protect the ware and its base, sometimes a ferruginous clay being used for the whole article. The difference can easily be detected by a close examination. Wares from the Lung-ch'üan and from the Ko Ti kilns, that is of the Chang brothers, were made of white body with a slight tinge of grey. The clay used in the Ti Yao, or Kiln of the Younger Brother, was highly refined, while that used in the Ko Yao or Kiln of the Elder Brother consisted, in addition, of a yellow and black variety. Of the Lung-ch'üan ware, the body was occasionally made by mixing white clay with a purple metallic solution. At first sight the material appears to be a reddish clay, but it is really not so. The Li-shui ware has a greyish white body. The Hsiao ware has a white body which is coarse but hard. The Chien-an ware is famous for its body of black clay. The Chien-yang ware is provided with a greyish white body which is coarse but opaque. The Tz'ŭ-chou ware is white but dry and coarse.

The Southern Sung Kuan ware of the Hsiu-nai Ssŭ has a paste of blackish grey, yellowish grey, or entirely red; while the new Kuan ware made in kilns established beneath the Altar of Heaven, though of the same material, was less refined. These wares were also sometimes

1 The kilns are located in modern Tê-hua Hsien, and are still working. The products are commonly called Chien tz'ŭ or Fukien porcelain.

2 The kilns were established in the Ming Dynasty in modern I-hsing Hsien (宜興縣), Kiangsu Province.

之相類。而淘鍊欠純。兼有範白泥者。餘姚秘色繼越而作。其原質之瑩白相類而較粗。餘杭質白而堅。湘湖白而膩。吉、宿、泗皆白質。吉最堅。宿次之。泗又次之。平定窯原質灰白而粗。元霍州之彭窯。原質白膩而微黃。臨川原質與之彷彿而微粗。處州窯繼龍泉之後。胎質亦類似。明德化窯質白而瑩。佳者不減越泥。至於景德鎮窯。在唐以假玉器稱。其瑩白可知。原質取材最廣。近則本邑之麻倉、高嶺諸山。遠則星子縣之大陂嶺及安徽之祁門。產量既豐。配合有法。以故製造獨精。綿遠弗替。重振瓷業。非此莫屬也。廣窯宋時在陽江所製器。原質爲确沙。其色黑。明代在石灣製者。原質爲紫沙。其色紫。明之宜興器。原質亦爲紫沙。此二者。與諸窯之採石範泥。大不同矣。以上所舉。乃就諸窯分別略言之。若同出一窯之器。則淘鍊多者。其質純而細。淘鍊少者。其質粗而鬆。此又視乎工匠之技藝。及器物之品格耳。

瓷器泑色

瓷器泑色。初皆純一。後來演進。乃有花瓷。純色之始。曰青曰白。青者如竹曰縹。唐越窯秘色亦曰峯翠。五代、宋仍之。後周柴窯曰雨過天青。宋東窯有碧青、淡碧青、油青。汝窯有天青、深者蔚藍卵青、粉青。官窯有天青、翠

made by moulding white clay. The pi-sê ware of Yü-yao, succeeding the Yüeh-chou ware, has a singularly pure white paste, which is, however, somewhat coarser in texture. The body of the Yü-hang ware is white but hard. The Hsiang-hu ware has also a white body which is fine and smooth. The wares of the Chi-chou, the Su-chou, and the Ssŭ-chou are all white; while in compactness the Chi-chou ranks first, the Su-chou second, and the Ssŭ-chou third. The body of the P'ing-ting ware is greyish white and coarse.

The Pêng Yao of Ho-chou in the Yüan period has an unctuous white body material with a slightly yellow tinge. The Lin-ch'üan product is of a similar material which is slightly coarser in texture. Being successor to the Lung-ch'üan Yao, the wares of Ch'u-chou were fabricated with similar materials. The Tê-hua wares of the Ming have a body white and lustrous, of which the finer are quite comparable to the Yüeh-chou ware.

As to wares of Ching-tê Chên which were already renowned as "false jade vessels" in the T'ang Dynasty, their body must presumably be white and translucent. The raw material was taken from a wide expanse of territory. The nearer was quarried from the Ma-ts'ang and Kao-ling Mountains within the same district. Farther away materials were also obtained from Ta-po Ling in Hsing-tzŭ Hsien and from Ch'i-mên in Anhui. Since the quantity of production was vast, and the ingredients properly proportioned, the porcelain manufactured in Ching-tê Chên has alone attained a high standard of excellence, and has been capable of lasting through the long ages of the past without suffering any decline. If the ceramic industry should be revived, it is at Ching-tê Chên, and there only, that we should centre our attention.

The Kuang-tung wares which were fabricated at Yang-chiang in Sung times were made of a sandy paste, black in colour, called Chio-sha (确沙). Those which were manufactured in Shih-wan in the Ming Dynasty were of another sandy paste, purple in colour, called Tzŭ-sha (紫沙). The Ou wares made at I-hsing during the Ming period were also of the purple siliceous substance. These two materials are vastly different from the paste derived from pulverised stone that was in use at the other kilns.

What has just been stated is but a summary of the differences existing between the products of the various kilns. As regards the wares which constituted the output of one and the same kiln, the material that has undergone levigation the greater number of times would be purer and finer; and conversely, material which has undergone less refinement would be coarser and looser in texture. Both of these, it may be observed, depend a good deal on the skill of the craftsman and the nature of the wares themselves.

IV. Glaze Colours on Porcelain Wares

The colours of the glaze on porcelain wares were at first applied only in monochrome. It was from later development that variegated decoration began to evolve. At the very outset the monochrome was either of white or blue-green. Blue-green monochrome was known in the Chin Dynasty as p'iao (縹) or azure (light bluish-white). The pi-sê or "secret colour" of the Yüeh-chou wares in the T'ang Dynasty was also called fêng-ts'ui (峯翠) or "the verdure of mountain peaks," the same name being retained in the "Five Dynasties" and the Sung. The Ch'ai ware of the Posterior Chou was of "the blue of the sky after rain." Wares from the Tung Yao of the Sung were coloured blue-green, light blue-green, and yu-ch'ing (油靑) or "oil blue-green." The Ju wares have the colour of "sky blue,"[1] egg green (i.e. the green of a duck's egg),

[1] The darker shade of this is called yü-lan (蔚藍) or deep sky blue.

青、粉青、月下白、大綠。龍泉窯有天青、粉青、翠青、葱翠青。麗水窯色微似龍泉。有油青、灰青。哥窯有翠青、粉青、淺青、極淺者其色近白、灰青。弟窯色與龍泉同。此諸窯器。泑色雖有濃淡淺深之不同。大抵皆青。哥窯別有米色一種。其變例也。鈞窯器備衆色。而其初旨爲天青。以其色重而藍。後人遂名之曰天藍。又以青料中含有銅質。煅鍊而變綠或紅、紫者。於是窯變之名生焉。後乃利用銅質而製紅紫器。此由變而演進也。南宋官窯。色與舊京同。無其腴潤。而較爲瑩澈。郊壇下新立官窯。色雖仍舊。究不相侔。餘杭窯泑色似官。但不甚瑩潤。且無紋片。湘湖窯淺粉青一種。甚爲精瑩。餘姚秘色。則大不如前矣。白泑如元魏之關中、洛京二窯。唐之昌南、邛、邢。諸器皆是。北宋定窯。承邢之後。器泑初爲瑩白。後來踵事增華。乃有青花、紅、紫以及黑色者。磁州窯最初亦爲白泑。後更有色泑、黑花、青花以及雜彩者。南宋之吉州。金之宿、泗、平定及元之彭窯。做定製器。泑皆主白。惟吉州窯則白器之外。兼製紫泑。更有米色碎器。亦變例也。明之德化窯亦專製白器。色極腴潤。以上諸窯。以泑色分。可別爲青白二系。雖各有演進。而其變遷之蹟。絕然不同。宋建安烏泥器。以烏金泑兔毫著。遷陽後兼有紫金色。宋鈞窯附近之神后山所製另一種器。胎

and light greenish-blue. The Kuan wares are coloured "sky blue," kingfisher green, light greenish-blue, moon white, and green. The Lung-ch'üan wares are sky blue, light greenish-blue, kingfisher green, and onion green. Wares from the Li-shui kilns are somewhat similar to the Lung-ch'üan product in colour, which is either oil blue-green or bluish grey. Ko wares have the tint of kingfisher green, light blue-greenish grey, light blue,[1] and bluish grey; while the Ti wares are the same as the Lung-ch'üan vessels in hue. Of all these wares the colour of the glaze seems to vary greatly in lighter or deeper shades, but all are principally blue-green. The Ko wares have besides mi-sê (米色) or colour of roasted rice, though that is exceptional.

Chün wares are of a great variety of colours, although the original idea was to give the glaze the tint of sky blue. As the colour is rich and blue, it is therefore named the "blue of the sky." Moreover, since the glaze is impregnated with a copper compound, it tended to turn into green, red, or purple in the process of firing. Thus the name of furnace transmutation has been given to the phenomenon. At a subsequent period potters, by taking advantage of the action of copper element, deliberately made wares of a red or purple hue. Thus a development was made from an accidental change.

The Kuan wares of the Southern Sung Dynasty were of the same colour as those manufactured in the old capital, but while wanting the unctuousness of the latter, surpassed them in translucency. Kuan wares of the new kiln beneath the suburban Altar, though supposedly of the same colour as the older variety, were not to be compared with their senior contemporary. The Yü-hang ware had a coloured glaze similar to that of the Kuan, but had neither the former's unctuousness nor its crackles. Of the Hsiang-hu wares those with a glaze of light greenish-blue are very fine and lustrous. The pi-sê wares of the Yü-yao kilns were not of as fine a quality as those made in Yüeh-chou before them.

White glaze may be found among the wares of the Kuan-chung and Lo-ching kilns of the Yüan Wei Dynasty, and in the Ch'ang-nan, the Ch'iung-chou, and the Hsing-chou wares of the T'ang Dynasty. The Ting kilns of Northern Sung, following in the footstep of those at Hsing-chou, produced at the beginning wares of a pure white glaze. It was due to subsequent elaboration that there were produced wares of an under-glaze blue and a red, a purple, and a black glaze. The Tz'ŭ-chou wares were at first of a white glaze, but were subsequently of coloured glaze, or decorated in black, in under-glaze blue, and in variegated enamels. The Chi-chou of the Southern Sung, the Su-chou, the Ssŭ-chou, the P'ing-ting wares of the Chin, and the Pêng wares of the Yüan Dynasty, taking Ting vessels as their prototype, were all chiefly of a white glaze. But in the Chi-chou kilns, in addition to white wares, some with a purple glaze were also fabricated. A few wares were also made in rice colour with fine crackles called mi-sê shui-ch'i (米色碎器) which were out of the ordinary. During the Ming period the Tê-hua kilns specialized in making white wares which were most unctuous. The products of all the kilns above mentioned may, according to the colour of their glaze, be roughly divided into two categories, white and blue-green. Though individual development might be discernable in each kiln, traces of such changes were quite independent and totally different.

The Chien-an wares of black clay made in the Sung Dynasty were famous for their golden black glaze with "rabbit-hair" marks. After the removal of the kilns to Chien-yang, the wares had in addition a golden brown glaze. In the neighbourhood of the Chün factories during the Sung period there were kilns at Shên-hou Shan (神后山) which produced wares with a

1 The lightest shade is almost white.

白泑黑。通稱河南爲金泑。磁州黑泑。亦有此法。是皆色泑之別格。然大都粗品。意取堅固。爲通常之用耳。景德鎮窯。自宋以降。製器無所不備。兼取諸窯之長。蓋由天產獨豐。能盡人工之巧也。

唐代陶器。有筆拓三色泑。乃古代塗碌法之演進也。後人誤稱唐三彩。案色與彩皆藝術專名。而其用不同。合色於泑內。或拓或澆於器之坯胎上。入匣滿窯燒成。謂之色泑。亦稱泑色。若燒成素器。於泑上加繪花文。塡以配製之顏色。再經鑪火完成。乃謂之彩。色合泑內。彩塡泑外。世人不察。往往混而爲一。附辨於此。

瓷器紋片

瓷器紋片。種種不同。其始出於天然。乃泑之病態也。而人爲者亦從之而生。有隱合泑內者。如魚子紋、汽泡、蟹爪紋、蚯蚓紋是。有起於泑表者。如蒐絲子紋、橘皮紋、椶眼、刹所切駕眼、冷紋、鍇紋是。魚子紋、汽泡由於火稍烈。橘皮紋由於火稍微。前者過後者不及也。蟹爪紋、蚯蚓紋惟厚泑之器乃有之。案顏料與泑汁。性本不同。配合工作或有未盡精到之處。經火煅鍊而紋生焉。管就鈞窯器細爲審察。其配製色泑。法用調和。不加研乳。顏料與泑汁未能十分鎔合。經火仍現離合狀態。致有紋大如蚯蚓走泥然。此爲鈞器所特具。而其他各窯如汝、官、龍泉等。其配製色泑之法。則調和之後。再加研乳。顏料泑汁。務令鎔合。雖其性仍在。經火後間或不免有紋。但細如蟹爪行迹矣。蒐絲子紋。亦爲鈞窯所獨有。因製紅紫器。於靑泑上加拓銅花汁。燒成後往往現密點如蒐絲子狀。若銅汁鎔合泑內。則無是紋。此鈞器製法不同之點也。椶眼形如椶房。由於

white body and a black glaze commonly called the golden black glaze of Honan. The Tz'ŭ-chou wares of a black glaze had the same method of manufacture. All these constitute variations in the colour of glaze. They were, however, vessels crudely potted with strength and solidity to be serviceable for everyday use.

The Ching-tê Chên porcelain factories, ever since the Sung Dynasty, have manufactured wares of every description and have modelled them after the best specimens of other kilns. Being specially favoured with an abundance of natural resources, potters have been enabled to exercise the best of their skill.[1]

V. Marks and Crackles on Porcelain

The marks and crackles on porcelain wares are of different kinds. At first they appeared naturally on account of some defects in the glaze. This natural happening, however, has given rise to an artificial technique of marking. There are markings shown faintly in the glaze, such as marks in the shape of fishroe, air bubbles, crabs' claws, and earthworm tracks. There are yet some that appear on the surface of the glaze, such as markings like cuscuta (or dodder), elevations like orange peel, or marks of palm eye, and pin holes. Still others are known as cold crackles and silk crackles. The fishroe and air bubble markings are due to excessive heating, while the orange peel undulations are caused by insufficient firing. The former is overdone, the latter underdone. Crabs' claw markings and earthworm tracks only appear on wares with a thick glaze.

It is to be observed that the pigments and glaze are quite different in nature, and that if the mixing should not be done just right, markings or lines will appear after the wares are fired. A close scrutiny of a Chün ware reveals the fact that the method of mixing the coloured glaze was by stirring without grinding the composition thoroughly in a mortar. The pigment and the glaze did not blend in a perfect manner, so that they would ultimately show signs of separating and rejoining after being baked. Hence the appearance of marks like earthworm tracks in soft soil. These are peculiar to Chün wares.

As to the other kilns such as the Ju, the Kuan, and the Lung-ch'üan, the colour-glaze preparation consisted of first mixing, and then grinding the ingredients in a mortar to blend together as much as possible the pigment and the glaze paste. Though each of the component parts may still bear its own characteristics, and show some markings after being fired, these marks would be fine like the claw tracks of a crawling crab.

The cuscuta-like markings are also peculiar to the Chün ware. The reason is that in making the red or purple ware, copper oxide would be mixed with the blue glaze. After firing the porcelain would occasionally bear small dots close together like cuscuta seeds (菟絲子). If, however, the copper oxide should melt in the glaze, there would not be such small markings --a point revealing the difference of technique in fabricating Chün wares.

1 In pottery wares of the T'ang Dynasty there was a three-coloured glaze (三色釉) applied with the brush, a method developed from the application of cinnabar to the unglazed portion of the ware. This glaze, by people of a subsequent period, was called "three-coloured enamel of T'ang" (唐三彩). It is to be noted that "coloured glaze" (色釉) and coloured enamel are both technical terms in the ceramic art, but are different in their practical application. By coloured glaze or glaze colour is meant the mixing of coloured pigment with the glaze, and then applying the mixture to the biscuit of a ware by a brush or by pouring it over, so that the article is put in seggar or firing box and baked in a big kiln. If a white glazed piece is baked and decorated on the glaze with coloured pigments previously prepared, and is fired again in a small furnace, the colours so applied are called ts'ai (彩) or coloured enamel. Coloured glaze, or sê (色) is mixed with the glaze itself, while coloured enamel, or ts'ai (彩) is filled in on the glaze. As the two are usually confused by the undiscriminating public, a brief explanation is called for here.

胎質粗鬆。補水欠勻。列眼猶如針剌。由於泑汁合色濃厚。性烈而發。冷紋短而密。出窯卽現。縴紋長而疏。歷久乃顯。皆冷熱相激使然也。各窯配製色泑。其法不盡相同。故器紋亦形態各異。後人乃專據此以識特徵。其實無論何窯之器。工作火候。若能恰得其宜。皆不致出何紋片也。配合泑汁。若用玻璃質成分稍多。燒成卽現冰裂之狀。是曰冰裂紋。始亦出於天然。而汝、官、哥窯。乃專利用此法。以爲表異。是由天然而入於人爲矣。碎器紋純乎人爲。則由冷紋、冰裂紋變化而出者。

景德鎭窯

景德鎭窯。建始於陳至德間。西元五八三至五八六年其時地名昌南。以其在昌江之南也。歷隋至唐武德中。西元六一九至六二六年浮梁鍾秀里人陶玉。在鎭製素瓷。載之入關。稱假玉器。且貢於朝。而昌南鎭瓷名天下。新平人霍仲初。當時亦在鎭製素器。奉詔進御。宋眞宗景德時。西元一〇〇四至一〇〇七年在鎭置監鎭官。設御窯。亦稱官窯。製器進御。並命於器底書建景德年號款字。是時製作益精。著行海內。於是天下咸稱景德瓷器。而昌南之名遂微。倣定窯製青花器。卽自是始。至徽宗世。西元一一〇一至一一二五年鎭之官窯。更有天青、月下白泑色。且因天青窯變而有帶硃紅、粉紅者。亦因其變化而利用銅質爲之。猶之鈞器也。器之品類至是乃益備。元代改宋監鎭官爲提領。泰

The marking like a palm-eye has the appearance of the ovary of a palm fruit, and is caused by the biscuit being coarse and loose-grained, and being unevenly touched up with water. Pin holes are like the prickings of a pin. They are caused by the glaze being very rich in pigment and subjected to intensive heating. Cold crackles are short but close together, appearing immediately after the wares emerge from the kiln. Liu-wên or silk crackles are long and wide apart, and will not appear until after a great length of time. Both these marks represent the result of a sudden change of temperature.

Just as the methods of mixing the coloured glaze in different kilns varies, so the crackle lines or markings on different wares assume different patterns and forms, which have been taken by men of subsequent periods to be the distinguishing features of any particular ware. As a matter of fact, wares from whatever factory would not show any marking should their potting and firing be properly conducted.

If a slightly greater proportion of the vitreous ingredient be used in the composition of a glaze, lines in the shape of cracked ice would appear after firing; they are called ice crackles. Originally they appeared as a natural phenomenon, but this fortuitous occurrence was turned to good account in the Ju, Kuan, and Ko wares, such marks being wilfully produced as a distinction. Such then is the conversion of a natural appearance into one which can be induced by human agency. The shui-ch'i wên (碎器紋) or fine crackles on some wares are put on entirely artificially, being evolved from the cold crackles and the ice crackles.

VI. The Ching-tê Chên Yao

The factories at Ching-tê Chên were first established during the Chih Tê period (583–586 A.D.) of the Ch'ên Dynasty when the locality was known as Ch'ang-nan, being on the south of the Ch'ang River. Then it careered through the Sui Dynasty up to Wu Tê period (619–626 A.D.) of the T'ang Dynasty. At the time T'ao Yü (陶玉), a native of Chung-hsiu Li (鍾秀里), in the district of Fou-liang (浮梁), made plain white porcelains in the Chên called "false jade vessels," and carried them inside Han-ku Kuan, Shensi. He also presented some to the Court. Since then the porcelain wares of Ch'ang-nan Chên have enjoyed a high reputation throughout the Empire. Meanwhile, Ho Chung-ch'u (霍仲初), a native of Hsin-p'ing, who also manufactured plain white wares in the Chên was commanded to minister to the needs of the Imperial Court.

It was in the time of Ching Tê of Emperor Chên Tsung (1004–1007 A.D.) of the Sung Dynasty that an official was appointed to oversee the affairs of the Chên. Imperial factories were established which were also under the name of Kuan Yao (official kilns), and porcelain wares were potted to supply the palaces. It was further ordered that the date mark of Ching Tê should be inscribed at the base of the ware. During that time the vessels were of better workmanship, and were greatly renowned throughout the country. From then on people called them Ching-tê porcelains, the name Ch'ang-nan thus sinking into oblivion. The manufacture of wares after the model of the Ting vessels in under-glaze blue originated at that date. Up to the time of Emperor Hui Tsung (1101–1125 A.D.) the Kuan wares of the Chên were also of sky blue and moon white glaze. Besides similar to the case of the Chün ware, through the transmutation of wares in sky blue, porcelains with a tinge of cinnabar in the glaze, or of pink, were obtained. This was also done by the utilization of colour changes caused by the action of copper oxide. Wares were getting nearer to perfection in variety and quality.

定後。（西元一三二四至一三二八年）又以本路總管監陶。內府進御之粉青器。及樞府所
用之月下白器。倣法宣和。（西元一一一九至一一二五年）亦稱纖美。明洪武朝（西元一三六九至一三九八年）
設署於鎮之珠山。命工部員外郎段廷珪董瓷務。建官窰以供上方。設
備益周。色器有青黑二種。以純素爲佳。永樂朝（西元一四〇三至一四二四年）半脫胎甜
白最著。花文錐拱之法始此。又有厚胎翠青及青花器。色樣俱佳。祭紅
亦創於是時。以鮮紅爲貴。宣德朝（西元一四二六至一四三五年）於永樂甜白、祭紅、鮮紅之
外。有寶石紅、霽青甚著。倣定瓷白、青花亦佳。彩瓷至是頗備。成化朝（西元
一四六五至一四八七年）彩器精進。畫手極高。其時監瓷務者。朱元佐也。青花、祭紅則
較永、宣爲遜。弘治朝（西元一四八八至一五〇五年）製器。接迹成窰。功相埒。正德朝（西元一五〇六
至一五二一年）官窰改稱御器廠。器以回青泑爲著。嘉靖朝（西元一五二二至一五六六年）以鮮紅
器燒造維艱。改製礬紅色。是爲礬紅之始。回青盛作。幽菁可愛。隆慶朝
（西元一五六七至一五七二年）五彩。可繼成窰。萬曆朝（西元一五七三至一六一九年）彩瓷。色澤濃豔。畫塡荒
率。頗具自然之致。此明代官窰之大略也。至於民窰較著者。成、弘間崔
國懋所造。倣法宣窰。世稱崔公窰。隆、萬間吳人周丹泉名時臣。來鎮倣
製定器。爲當時名手。兼作嬌黃亦佳。世稱周窰。萬曆間又有吳十九名

In the Yüan period the overseeing officer of the Chên (or town) was changed into a superintendent or T'i-ling (提領). After the reign of T'ai Ting (1324–1328 A.D.), the Intendant of the Circuit, or Lu (路) was made Superintendent of pottery. Vessels of light greenish-blue for the use of the Imperial Court, and moon white for the use of the Privy Council, or Shu Fu (樞府), were patterned after those of the Hsüan Ho period (1119–1125 A.D.), and were said to equal the originals in beauty.

During the reign of Hung Wu in the Ming Dynasty (1369–1398 A.D.) an office was established at Chu-shan (珠山) or Pearl Hill of the town, with Tuan T'ing-kuei (段廷珪), Junior Secretary of the Ministry of Works, appointed to take charge of porcelain manufacture. Official factories were constructed to supply wares for the use of the Imperial Court. This porcelain centre was getting to be better equipped.

Coloured wares were of two kinds –blue and black, plain ones being considered the best. In the reign of Yung Lo (1403–1424 A.D.) the semi-bodiless or pan t'o-t'ai (半脫胎) wares of pure white were the most celebrated. Decorations in relief or chui-kung (錐拱)—meaning "to raise with an awl"—were introduced in this period. There were also some of a thick body, in bluish green glaze or decorated in under-glaze blue; these were beautiful in shape and tone. Chi-hung (祭紅), or wares in sacrificial red, were first made at this time, of which the hsien-hung, or fresh red, was highly prized.

In the Hsüan Tê period (1426–1435 A.D.) there were in addition to the pure white, sacrificial red, and fresh red wares of the preceding reign, vessels in ruby red and in deep sky blue or chi-ch'ing (霽青), which were of great renown. Wares in imitation of the Ting vessels in pure white and decorated in under-glaze blue were also exquisite. Porcelains decorated in over-glaze enamel were of a greater variety.

The same enamelled porcelain wares greatly advanced in the reign of Ch'êng Hua (1465–1487 A.D.), when the articles reflected the highest skill in limning. At the time the Superintendent of the Imperial Factory was Chu Yüan-tso (朱元佐). Wares decorated in under-glaze blue, and glazed in sacrificial red were inferior to those of the Yung Lo and the Hsüan Tê period.

Vessels manufactured under Hung Chih (1488–1505 A.D.) conformed to those of the Ch'êng Hua reign, and were quite equal to them. In the time of Chêng Tê (1506–1521 A.D.) the name of Kuan Yao was changed to Yü-ch'i Ch'ang (御器廠) or the Factory of Imperial Wares, in which the glaze of Mohammedan blue was well known. During the reign of Chia Ching (1522–1566 A.D.) wares in fresh red were considered difficult to fabricate, so those in fan-hung sê (礬紅色), or the red colour reduced from copper sulphate, were made instead. This was the beginning of fan-hung wares. Porcelains in Mohammedan blue were abundantly produced, the luxuriant colour being attractive. The wu-ts'ai, or five-coloured enamels of the Lung Ch'ing period (1567–1572 A.D.) may rival those of Ch'êng Hua, while the enamelled porcelains of Wan Li (1573–1619 A.D.) were gorgeous in colouring; and, being limned and decorated at pleasure, presented scenes that were natural and unaffected. The above then constitutes a brief account of the Government factory in the Ming Dynasty.

As to private kilns, the most famous was operated by Ts'ui Kuo-mou in the period between Ch'êng Hua and Hung Chih. The wares manufactured there were modelled after those of Hsüan Tê. The kiln was known as Ts'ui-kung Yao (崔公窯), or Factory of Old Mr. Ts'ui. In the Lung Ch'ing and the Wan Li period, Chou Tan-ch'üan (周丹泉), really named Shih-ch'ên (時臣), a native of Kiangsi, came to the Chên (or town) to make imitations of the Ting ware, and

爲。燒造諸器。色料並佳。而流霞琖、卵幕杯尤著。以其別號壺隱道人。世稱壺公窯。有清一代。康、雍、乾三朝御窯製器。美備精良。超越前古。康熙間督瓷有名者。二十年西元一六八一年臧應選。以工部郎中駐廠督造。所製瓷品。多循宜、成法度。諸色兼備。製造益精。世稱臧窯。四十四年西元一七〇五年郎廷極。巡撫江西。專窯燒製。獨出心裁。器皆精美。亦供進御。世稱郎窯。雍正四年西元一七二六年年希堯以內務府總管奉命督理淮安板閘關。兼景德鎮御窯廠總理。物力富裕。工事精良。世稱年窯。六年西元一七二八年唐英以內務府員外郎奉命駐廠協理瓷務。其時總理仍年希堯也。乾隆元年西元一七三六年英襲希堯任。自是總理瓷務。前後二十餘年。歷時最久。其人博學多識。復能與工匠同其食息。萃精會神。研究探討。卒乃融會貫通。別抒意匠。倣古肇今。並多妙悟。官窯器之發達。以英時爲最盛。三朝名瓷。康熙以鮮紅最著。而天青、翠青、碧青、嬌黃、粉黃及吹紅、吹紫、吹青、吹綠尤美。青花五彩。纖軼宜、成。實有過之無不及。琺瑯彩器。花文彩色悉倣銅胎琺瑯器爲之、故名琺瑯彩、俗訛稱古月軒器、說見後、即於是時肇其端。此臧窯也。郎窯則以寶石紅、寶石藍、寶石

was regarded as an artisan of considerable fame at the time. He also turned out wares of lemon colour which were considered creditable. His factory was then known as Chou Yao. During the reign of Wan Li there was a Wu Nineteenth (吳十九) whose personal name was Wei(爲), and who made all kinds of porcelain wares which were excellent in colour and material. His liu-hsia chan (流霞琖) or cup of a floating red cloud, and luan-mu pei (卵幕杯) or eggshell cup were particularly well known. His pseudonym being Hu-yin Tao-jên (壺隱道人) or Taoist Hermit of a Tea Pot, people called his wares Hu-kung Yao.

Of the Ch'ing Dynasty, the reigns of K'ang Hsi, Yung Chêng, and Ch'ien Lung produced wares in the Imperial Kilns which excelled in every respect, and surpassed all those fabricated previously. In K'ang Hsi's reign the Superintendents of the Porcelain Factories who achieved fame included the following:

Tsang Ying-hsüan (臧應選), as Senior Secretary to the Ministry of Works, was appointed in the twentieth year of K'ang Hsi (1681 A.D.) to reside in the Imperial Factory and to superintend the work. The wares manufactured under him followed the pattern of the Hsüan Tê and the Ch'êng Hua period. They were of every description, and of exquisite finish, bearing the name of Tsang Yao.

Lang T'ing-chi (郎廷極) in the forty-forth year of K'ang Hsi (1705 A.D.) was appointed Governor of Kiangsi, and operated his own factory for the manufacture of porcelain. Exercising his own ingenuity, he made wares that were highly finished and beautiful. His wares were also presented to the Imperial Court. They were called Lang Yao.

Nien Hsi-yao (年希堯) in the fourth year of Yung Chêng (1726 A.D.) was Minister of the Imperial Household, and was appointed Superintendent of Customs at Huai-an, to serve concurrently as Director-General of the Imperial Porcelain Factory at Ching-tê Chên. At the time he had an abundance of fine materials at his disposal, and many skilful and experienced workmen to do his bidding. His wares were known as Nien Yao.

T'ang Ying (唐英), who was Junior Secretary of the Imperial Household in the sixth year of the same Emperor (1728 A.D.) was appointed to reside at the factory to assist in supervising the work. At the time, Nien Hsi-yao was still Director-General. In the first year of Ch'ien Lung (1736 A.D.), T'ang Ying succeeded Nien Hsi-yao as Director-General. Thereafter he acted in that capacity for over twenty years, the longest term that it has ever been the lot of one man to serve. He was profound in his learning as well as mellow in his experience. He was able to eat and rest with his workmen, and he conducted his investigation with great concentration of mind. In the end he thoroughly mastered the intricacies of his subject, and applying his ingenuity, he set to work to imitate old types and introduce new forms with extraordinary understanding. The development of the imperial kilns attained its zenith during T'ang's term of office.

Of the celebrated wares manufactured in the reigns of these three emperors, the fresh red vessels of K'ang Hsi Yao were the most eminent, while those in sky blue, kingfisher green, bluish green, lemon, light yellow, *soufflé* red, *soufflé* purple, *soufflé* blue, and *soufflé* green were specially beautiful. Wares of this period decorated in under-glaze blue and in variegated enamel which followed the patterns of the Hsüan Tê and the Ch'êng Hua period, compared favourably with them. Porcelains decorated in cloisonné enamel[1] were an innovation of this date. All these wares of K'ang Hsi emanated from Tsang Yao.

[1] The cloisonné enamelled porcelain wares are imitations of cloisonné bronze wares both in design and colouring. Hence they are named cloisonné enamel. They are popularly though erroneously called Ku-yüeh Hsüan. For explanation, *vide infra*.

綠特著。倣古亦佳。雍、乾兩朝官窯。經唐英督造。倣法歷代名瓷。如宋之白定、東、鈞、汝、官、龍泉、哥、弟、湘湖。明之永、宣、成、弘無所不倣。亦無所不工。而彩繪一門。繼往開來。益臻精到。粉彩則獨開生面。無異寫生。琺瑯彩則取藍勝藍。尤爲絕詣。窯器至此。集大成矣。清代民窯製器。各沿其當時官窯之風氣。亦多精品。惟康熙時之嬌黃三彩、嫩綠三彩、烏金泐五彩三彩。師法明製。而精美過之。此則官窯所希也。

琺瑯彩瓷

清代瓷器中有一種至精極美。馳譽寰宇之品。而其名沿訛襲謬。積重難返者。即世所稱古月軒器是也。考此類彩瓷。肇端於康熙二十年後臧應選督造之時。器之彩色、繪畫、款式。悉照康熙御製銅胎琺瑯彩器作法。顏料亦用西來之品。故定名爲琺瑯彩。又名瓷胎琺瑯。宮中檔冊。則書瓷胎畫琺瑯。乾隆八年西元一七四三年後。改書瓷胎洋彩。雍正六年以後。乾隆十八年西元一七五三年以前。唐英督造時。此類彩器。益加精進。沿用其法而加以運化。變板滯爲生動。更參以我國赭墨等色。補所不足。彩色襯托。益覺鮮明。英卒後遂成絕響矣。器底款字。康熙器爲宋體康熙御製四字。用洋紅或藍料書之。字皆凸起。亦有楷書青花款字者。雍正器有

The Lang wares were particularly renowned for their glaze of ruby red, sapphire blue, and emerald green. Vessels in imitation of ancient objects were also praiseworthy. The official factory under the supervision of T'ang Ying during the reigns of Emperors Yung Chêng and Ch'ien Lung, manufactured wares after the reputed vessels of the various dynasties. Such objects as the white Ting, the Tung, the Chün, the Ju, the Kuan, the Lung-ch'üan, the Ko, the Ti, and the Hsiang-hu wares of the Sung Dynasty, and also those manufactured in the periods of Yung Lo, Hsüan Tê, Ch'êng Hua, and Hung Chih of the Ming Dynasty, were all followed without exception, all being finely executed. Coloured decoration which was done by taking patterns of the past and introducing new methods for the present was approaching nearer and nearer to perfection. Fên-ts'ai (粉彩), or decoration in enamel mixed with powder, was a novelty at the time and was instinct with life. Cloisonné enamelled wares, which excelled their prototype, were superior to anything in that field. In fact, Ch'ing Kuan wares as a whole were a galaxy of masterpieces, enfolding the finest porcelains of every class and every age.

Wares made in the private factories of the Ch'ing Dynasty, all following the rule of thumb prevailing at the time in the official factory, had a good number of choice pieces among them. During the time of K'ang Hsi wares in three colours on a lemon or light green ground, or those in five or three colours on a ground of mirror black glaze, were manufactured after the Ming practice, but were finer and more beautiful than the Ming specimens. Such wares are not common among ceramic vessels from the Imperial Factory.

VII. Porcelain with Cloisonné Enamel

Of all the porcelain of the Ch'ing Dynasty, one kind is famous throughout the world as the finest and most beautiful, yet it is known by a misnomer which is continued by a misconception and is most difficult to correct. This is what is vulgarly known as Ku-yüeh Hsüan.

This type of enamelled porcelain, it is found, originated with the régime of Tsang Ying-hsüan, who was Superintendent of the Imperial Factory after the twentieth year of K'ang Hsi. The style of painting on the porcelain, which was in coloured enamel, was entirely adapted from the technique of manufacturing cloisonné ware on a bronze body for the use of the Emperor. The colouring materials in use were also imported from the west. Thus the name of fa-lang ts'ai (珐瑯彩)—"cloisonné enamel" or tz'ŭ-t'ai fa-lang (瓷胎珐瑯)—"porcelain-bodied cloisonné" was given to these vessels. In the records on file in the Imperial Palace these porcelains are recorded as tz'ŭ-t'ai hua fa-lang (瓷胎畫珐瑯) or "porcelain-body painted in cloisonné enamel." Subsequently in the eighth year of Ch'ien Lung (1743 A.D.) the name was altered in favour of tz'ŭ-t'ai yang-ts'ai (瓷胎洋彩) or "porcelain-bodied foreign enamel."

During the period between the sixth year of Yung Chêng and the eighteenth year of Ch'ien Lung (1753 A.D.) when T'ang Ying was Superintendent of the Imperial Works, this kind of enamelled ware reached its highest stage of development. T'ang improved upon the method in use, and put a vivacity into what had been dull and stereotyped. He also employed such popular Chinese colours as brown and black to make up the deficiency in variety of pigment, thus adding freshness and brilliancy to the composition. This art perished with the death of T'ang Ying.

The date marks inscribed at the base in the case of K'ang Hsi wares, consisted of four characters in the Sung style of writing, thus Kang Hsi yü-chih (康熙御製), or "made for the Emperor in the time of Kang Hsi." The characters are written in foreign red or blue enamel, and are somewhat raised. There are also marks written in under-glaze blue in the formal square

宋體雍正年製四字藍料款凸起者。有楷書雍正御製及大清雍正年製青花款者。乾隆器則皆用藍料凸起宋體書乾隆年製四字。此種彩畫。不獨施於瓷器。後來玻璃器亦用之。乾隆御用器物中。有玻璃質小品鼻烟壺之屬。當日造辦處(專爲皇帝造辦御用器物、屬於內務府、)奉命所製。純用琺瑯彩瓷彩畫方法。蓋從瓷器推而廣之者。底款皆楷書乾隆年製四字。極工整。用藍料寫者凸起。用油紅寫者與器底平。故宮有一玻璃質小餅。彩畫題句悉與琺瑯彩瓷溫壺相同。而精工有所不及。底刻宋體乾隆年製四字。亦希品也。琺瑯彩瓷器。故宮所藏品類極夥。(民國十九年(西元一九三〇年)經審查考定、陳列於承乾宮)玻璃器則鼻烟壺居多。器底款字皆不出上述範圍。無署古月軒款者。至於古月名軒。遍訪現存宮苑。如故宮、三海、頤和園以及熱河避暑山莊。未之見也。又稽諸載籍之有關已燬宮苑如暢春園、圓明園等者。又未之見也。更遍檢有清歷朝御製詩文集。亦未之見也。高宗集內於所有各處宮殿。題詠殆遍。乃僅有眉月軒、待月軒。而獨無古月。可見宮苑之內。無此軒名。否則高宗不應獨遺之也。然古月軒款字。乾隆時乃實有之。惟是玻璃器而非瓷器。且爲私家款而非進御物耳。此類之

style called k'ai-shu (楷書). The Yung Chêng wares bear the date mark Yung Chêng nien chih (雍正年製), or "made in the year of Yung Chêng." These also are written of blue enamel in the Sung style of characters which are slightly raised. There are also other marks such as Yung Chêng yü-chih (雍正御製) or "made for the Emperor in the time of Yung Chêng"; and Ta Ch'ing Yung Chêng nien chih (大清雍正年製) or "made in the year of Yung Chêng in the Great Ch'ing Dynasty." These are written in the style known as K'ai-shu, in under-glaze blue. As to Ch'ien Lung wares, there is the mark of four characters Ch'ien Lung nien chih (乾隆年製), or "made in the year of Ch'ien Lung"; this is written in blue enamel and the Sung style in slight relief.

This kind of decoration in enamel was not only applied to porcelain, but was later employed on glass wares also. Among the vessels used by the Emperor Ch'ien Lung there are to be found small articles such as snuff-bottles which were made under an imperial decree by the Tsao-pan Ch'u (造辦處).[1] Upon these articles was applied the method of painting upon porcelain with enamel, that is cloisonné enamelled porcelain. The technique which was employed upon porcelain was thus extended to glass ware. The date marks at the base were invariably the four characters, Ch'ien Lung nien chih (乾隆年製) written in the k'ai-shu style, exceedingly formal and trim. Those written in blue enamel are raised and those in "oil red" flush with the base. In the Palace Museum there is a small glass bottle on which the coloured decoration and the accompanying epigraph are exactly the same as those on a hot water vase of cloisonné enamelled porcelain, though somewhat inferior to the latter in execution. At the base are engraved the four characters Ch'ien Lung nien chih (乾隆年製) in Sung style of writing. It is a rare piece.

Porcelain in cloisonné enamel is represented by many examples in the Imperial Collection at the Palace.[2] Glass wares of the same kind are mostly represented by snuff-bottles. The date marks at the base all conform to the same type as described in the previous paragraph. There are none of these with the mark of Ku-yüeh Hsüan (古月軒).

With regard to the Hsüan (or pavilion) that is named Ku-yüeh, visits have been made to all the palaces which are still in existence, such as those in the Forbidden City, known as Ku Kung, those in the parks enclosing the three lakes known as San Hai, those in the Summer Palace called I-ho Yüan, and those at Jehol, but the search has been in vain. Researches have also been made into books and records that deal with palaces that were destroyed by fire, such as Ch'ang-ch'un Yüan, and Yüan-ming Yüan, but the effort again has been fruitless. Collections of poems and other great literary works by the various emperors have been thoroughly examined, with no more encouragement. In the Collection of the Emperor Kao Tsung (Ch'ien Lung) practically every building in all the palaces in and out of Peking has formed a subject for his poetical effusion. Among these so treated there are Mei-yüeh Hsüan (眉月軒) and Tai-yüeh Hsüan (待月軒) but no Ku-yüeh Hsüan! It is obvious then that there is no pavilion of that name within the Palace Precinct, or Imperial Parks, for otherwise Emperor Kao Tsung would not have singled it out for neglect.

Nevertheless there was actually the mark of Ku-yüeh Hsüan in the time of Ch'ien Lung, but it was inscribed on glass and not on porcelain wares. Moreover, it was the mark of a private individual, and was not affixed on vessels for the imperial palaces. Objects of this

1 The Ch'u was a department of the Imperial Household and was charged with the duty of making and furnishing vessels for the use of the Emperor.

2 In the nineteenth year of the Chinese Republic (1930 A.D.) they were identified after due examination, and placed on exhibition in the Ch'êng-ch'ien Kung (承乾宮).

器。亦一種玻璃質小品鼻烟壺。原質、彩畫與乾隆款字者無少異。器底泥金楷書古月軒三字。亦出當日造辦處所製。蓋當時親貴或內務府權要用器。不書乾隆年製者。以非皇家所御也。款書古月軒者。所以自玩也。能使令造辦處爲之製器。非親貴或內務府權要。孰具此權力哉。古月軒器與琺瑯彩瓷器。雖彩畫相埒。而胎質款字則如風馬牛之不相及。然琺瑯彩瓷器乃轉以古月軒爲名者。蓋亦有故。緣琺瑯彩瓷器。皆出特辦之物。專供御用。昔歲外間莫獲見之。而古月軒款字之玻璃質器。既爲私家製品。不免流轉市廛。無以名之。則因其款字呼以古月軒器而已。及咸豐十年（西元一八六〇年）之後。內廷琺瑯彩瓷器。亦有流出。見者因其彩畫與古月軒款之玻璃質器相類也。則推古月軒之名以名之。而古月軒之名以立。從此以訛傳訛。琺瑯彩本名轉爲所掩矣。

中華民國二十四年二月六日寫訖　　武林王維周錫五甫記

kind consist of small glass snuff-bottles, being the same in substance and decoration as those with date marks of Ch'ien Lung. At the base of the object are three characters, Ku-yüeh Hsüan (古月軒), written in the k'ai-shu style and composed of ni-chin (泥金) or gold ground fine like ink. They were also made by the Tsao-pan Ch'u at the time, apparently for a member of the imperial family or an official of high authority in the Imperial Household, to be used for himself. The reason why the date mark of Chien Lung nien chih was not inscribed was because they were not meant for the use of the Emperor, and the reason why the mark of Ku-yüeh Hsüan was affixed was because they were intended for the owner to fondle. If any-one who could order the Tsao-pan Ch'u to make vessels for himself be not an imperial prince or a high official in the Imperial Household, who else, it may be questioned, could it have been with such authority?

These Ku-yüeh Hsüan wares, as compared with cloisonné enamelled porcelain, though having coloured decoration of an equal quality, have a body material and a base mark entirely different. Still porcelain in cloisonné enamel goes under the name of Ku-yüeh Hsüan. There is a reason for it. As porcelains in cloisonné enamel were "specially made" for the exclusive use of the Imperial Court, none could have been seen outside the forbidden enclosure. The glass wares with the mark of Ku-yüeh Hsüan, on the other hand, being articles made for a private individual, could not indefinitely escape from circulation in the market. For want of an appropriate name they were therefore called by their base mark, Ku-yüeh Hsüan. After the tenth year of Hsien Fêng (1850 A.D.) cloisonné enamelled porcelain also leaked out from the palaces to the market. Those who got a sight of it, observing the similarity of its coloured decoration to that of the glass wares of the base mark of Ku-yüeh Hsüan, extended the latter's name to the articles newly come from the palace. Thus the term has become inde-lible, and the misnomer has echoed and re-echoed until the real name of "cloisonné enamel" has been drowned in this persistent babel!

參加倫敦中國藝術國際展覽會

瓷器照片目錄

CHINESE PORCELAIN

(瓷器尺寸係根據故宮博物院點收清册加入)

宋金元瓷

宋定窯

PART I

I. SUNG TING WARE

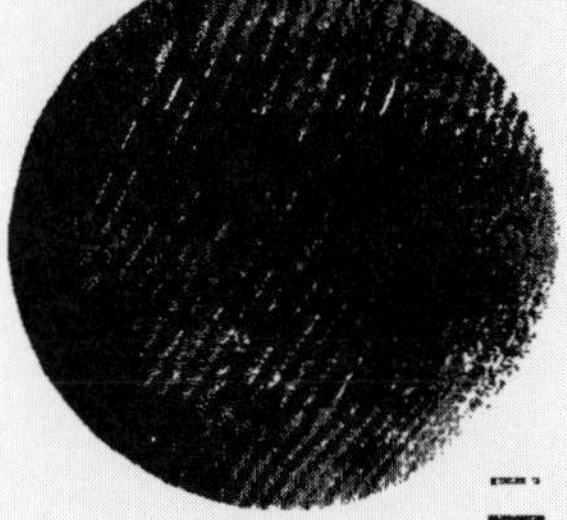

一

宋定窯瑩白劃文柳斗栝一件(原藏者故宮博物院、以下簡稱院)

原名白瓷銅口小罐鑲有鍍金銅口銅口既下底有傷。口徑伍·捌公分高柒·柒公分底徑肆·伍公分最大腹圍貳拾叁公分

Porcelain No. 1.

Ting Ware of the Sung Dynasty. Cup of pure white (ying-pai) in the shape of a plaited willow basket, with the design of willow twigs incised in the paste. Set with a gilded brass rim.

二

宋定窯瑩白劃花丹鳳朝陽盤口鵝頸瓶一件(院)

原名定瓷天盤口瓶帶木座底有鏘瓶有暗花。口徑肆貳公分高拾肆·捌公分底徑肆·肆公分最大腹圍貳拾捌公分

Porcelain No. 2.

Ting Ware of the Sung Dynasty. P'ing (vase) of pure white with dish-shaped mouth and goose-neck, with decoration of a phœnix facing the sun, incised in the paste. With a wooden stand.

三

宋定窰瑩白劃文柳編魚簍瓶一件(院)

原名白瓷銅口罇鑲有銅口口徑拾叁公分高拾柒·捌公分最大腹圍肆拾肆公分

Porcelain No. 3.

Ting Ware of the Sung Dynasty. Yü-lou p'ing (vase shaped like a plaited willow fish-basket), pure white, with design incised in the paste. With copper rim.

四

宋定窰瑩白劃花靈芝印泥合(早年出品)一件(院)

原名定瓷暗花印色盒有舉附木座口徑玖·捌公分通蓋高伍·貳公分底徑伍玖公分。

Porcelain No. 4.

Ting Ware of the Sung Dynasty. Seal vermilion box of ying-pai (pure white), decorated with ling chih fungi incised in the paste. This is an early product of the kiln. With a wooden stand.

宋鈞窰

II. SUNG CHÜN WARE

五

宋鈞窰粉青蓮花式大盌一件(院)

原名凍青釉瓷盌口有傷最大口徑貳拾公分。高拾壹·玖公分底徑柒·壹公分.

Porcelain No. 5.

Chün Ware of the Sung Dynasty. Large bowl of fên-ch'ing (light greenish-blue), shaped like a lotus flower.

六

宋鈞窯粉青窯變粉紅盌一件(院)

原名元瓷帶紅深沿盌口徑拾伍公分高捌玖公分底徑叁·捌公分

Porcelain No. 6.

Chün Ware of the Sung Dynasty. Bowl of fên-ch'ing (light greenish-blue), with furnace transmutation of pink. This shape is also called "palace bowl."

七

宋鈞窯月白尊一件(院)

原名出戟瓷觚底原刻有八字口徑拾陸·陸公分高貳拾貳公分底徑拾貳·伍公分

Porcelain No. 7.

Chün Ware of the Sung Dynasty. Tsun (vase) of yüeh-pai (moon white). On the base is the numeral "pa" (8) originally incised in the paste.

八

宋鈞窯丁香紫尊一件（院）

原名哥瓷花觚底有後刻，六字。底有傷，口徑拾玖·貳公分，高貳拾肆柒公分底徑拾肆·肆公分

Porcelain No. 8.

Chün Ware of the Sung Dynasty. Tsun (vase) of lilac purple. On the base is the numeral "liu" (6) subsequently engraved.

九

宋鈞窯月白窯變紫斑三足爐一件（院）

原名鈞窯三足爐帶木座及玉頂木蓋玉頂脫下。口有微傷口徑拾伍·玖公分高玖公分腹圍伍拾叁·壹公分

Porcelain No. 9.

Chün Ware of the Sung Dynasty. Three-footed incense burner of yüeh-pai (moon white) with furnace transmutation of purple mottles.

一〇

宋鈞窰天藍鼓式洗一件(陸)

原名均窰大洗底原刻有一字三足口徑貳拾伍伍公分高玖·玖公分底徑拾捌·叁公分

Porcelain No. 10.

Chün Ware of the Sung Dynasty. Washer of t'ien-lan (sky blue) in the shape of a drum, with the numeral "一" (1) originally incised in the paste of the base. With chip on one foot.

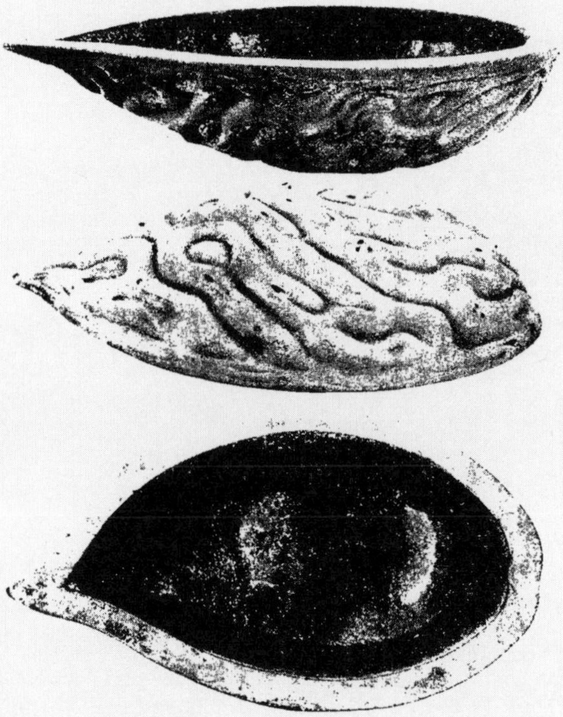

一一

宋鈞窰天藍窰變深紫蟠桃核筆洗一件(陸)

原名仿官與均窰寰蚌式洗口縱捌·叁公分橫拾貳·伍公分。高叁·捌公分

Porcelain No. 11.

Chün Ware of the Sung Dynasty. Brush-washer of t'ien-lan (sky blue) with furnace transmutation of deep purple, fashioned in the shape of the stone of a p'an-t'ao ("peach of life").

一二

宋鈞窯天藍渣斗式大花盆一件（院）

原名均釉瓷花盆底原刻有「二」字口有傷有璺口徑貳拾肆·肆公分高貳拾肆·叁公分底徑拾肆·貳公分最大腹圍柒拾玖·伍公分

Porcelain No. 12.

Chün Ware of the Sung Dynasty. Large flower-pot of t'ien-lan (sky blue), in the shape of a cha-tou (receptacle for discarded food). On the base is the numeral "erh" (2) originally incised in the paste.

一三

宋鈞窯月白窯變米色渣斗式大花盆一件（院）

原名宋瓷花盆底有傷口徑貳拾伍·壹公分高貳拾肆·肆公分底徑拾伍·壹公分最大腹圍柒拾柒·壹公分

Porcelain No. 13.

Chün Ware of the Sung Dynasty. Large flower-pot of yüeh-pai (moon white) with furnace transmutation of mi-sê (colour of roasted rice) in the shape of a cha-tou (receptacle for discarded food). With small chip on base.

一四

宋鈞窯玫瑰紫渣斗式花盆一件(院)

原名宋均窯渣斗式瓷花盆。底原刻有五字有璺口裡貳拾壹·貳公分高拾玖·伍公分底裡拾貳公分最大腹圍陸拾陸·伍公分

Porcelain No. 14.

Chün Ware of the Sung Dynasty. Flower-pot of rose purple glaze, fashioned in the shape of a cha-tou. On the base is the numeral "wu" (5) originally incised in the paste. With palace mark.

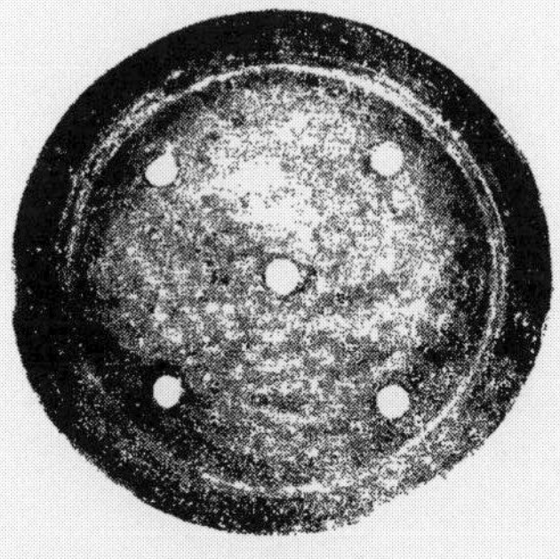

一五

宋鈞窯玫瑰紫大花盆一件（院）

原名宋均窯器鈴式花盆。底原刻有「二」字。底有傷。口縱貳拾柒·玖公分，橫貳拾捌·柒公分。高貳拾貳·伍公分。底徑拾伍·壹公分。

Porcelain No. 15.

Chün Ware of the Sung Dynasty. Large flower-pot of rose purple. On the base is the numeral "erh" (2) originally incised in the paste. With chip on base.

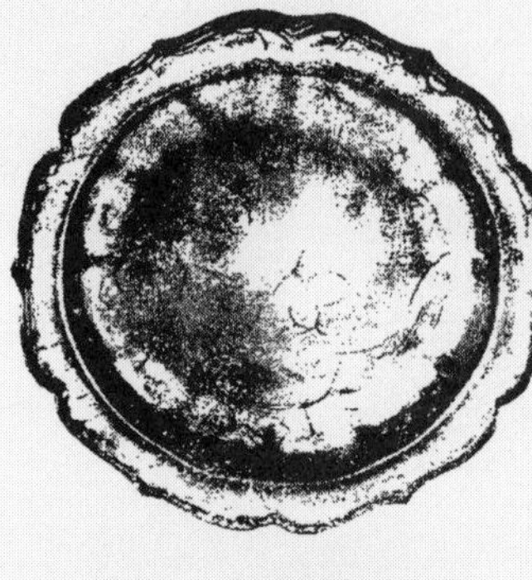

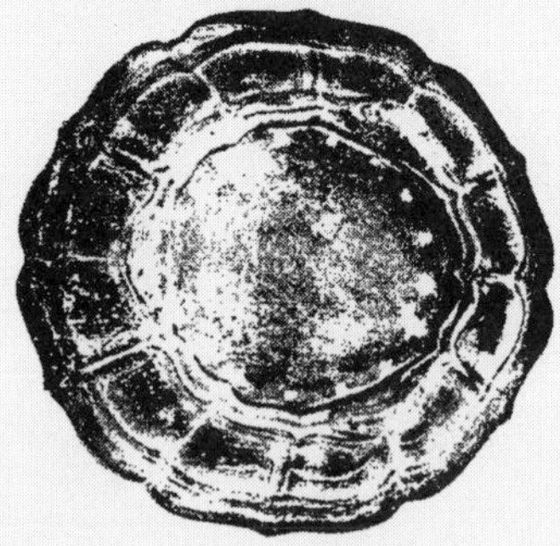

一六

宋鈞窯天青窯變深紫蓮花式盆托一件(院)

原名宋紫均蓮花瓣式奩底原刻有三字最大口徑貳拾貳·伍公分高肆·叁公分最大底徑拾叁·玖公分

Porcelain No. 16.

Chün Ware of the Sung Dynasty. Flower-pot stand of t'ien-ch'ing (sky blue) with furnace transmutation of deep purple, in the shape of a lotus flower. On the base is the numeral "san" (3) originally incised in the paste.

宋汝窯

III. SUNG JU WARE

一七

宋汝窯粉青盤一件(院)

原名乾隆御題哥窯瓷盤。底刻乾隆御題詩，因傷鑲有銅足。口徑貳拾壹·肆公分。高肆·捌公分。底徑拾伍·伍公分。

Porcelain No. 17.

Ju Ware of the Sung Dynasty. Plate in fên-ch'ing (light greenish-blue). On the base is inscribed an ode of Ch'ien Lung. With base rim mounted with a copper band, on account of damage there.

一八

宋汝窰粉青盤一件(院)

原名哥窰盤底刻「甲」字並乾隆御題詩·口足有傷·口徑拾伍·柒公分·高叁·柒公分·足徑拾·玖公分

Porcelain No. 18.

Ju Ware of the Sung Dynasty. Plate in fên-ch'ing (light greenish-blue). On the base are inscribed the character "chia" and an ode of Ch'ien Lung. Chip off the base rim.

一九

宋汝窯卵青碟一件(院)

原名祕窯碟。底刻「丙」字並乾隆御題詩。鑲有銅口。口徑拾叁公分。高叁·肆公分、底徑捌·捌公分.

Porcelain No. 19.

Ju Ware of the Sung Dynasty. Dish, in luan-ch'ing (the blue-green of a duck's egg). On the base are inscribed the character "ping" and an ode of Emperor Ch'ien Lung. With a copper rim.

二〇

宋汝窯粉青紙搥奉華瓶一件（院）

原名仿均窯長頸瓶，底刻有乾隆御題詩及「奉華」貳字，附木座，座上刻有乾隆御題詩，底刻「甲」字，帶銅口。口徑肆·伍公分，高貳拾貳·陸公分，底徑捌·伍公分，最大腹圍叁拾玖·伍公分。

Porcelain No. 20.

Ju Ware of the Sung Dynasty. Fêng-hua p'ing (vase) of fên-ch'ing (light greenish-blue), in the shape of a paper-beater. On the base are engraved the two characters "fêng-hua" and an ode composed by Ch'ien Lung. With a wooden stand, on the upper part of which is inscribed the same ode and on the under part the character "chia".

二一

宋汝窯粉青奉華尊一件(院)

原名乾隆御玩奉華出戟尊。底刻「奉華」二字。口徑最大拾叁·叁公分。高拾陸·伍公分,腹圍叁拾柒公分。底徑玖·肆公分。

Porcelain No. 21.

Ju Ware of the Sung Dynasty. Fêng-hua tsun (vase) in fên-ch'ing (light greenish-blue). On the base are inscribed the two characters "Fêng-hua."

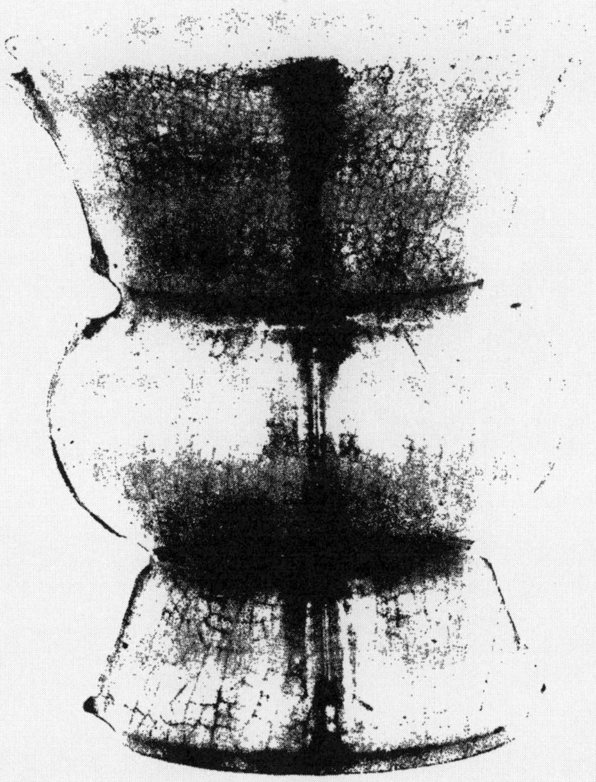

二二

宋汝窯天青窯變米色三犧尊一件(院)

原名六足獸頭盂。口徑拾貳·伍公分。高貳拾·肆公分。底徑最長玖·玖公分。最大腹圍叁拾捌公分。

Porcelain No. 22.

Ju Ware of the Sung Dynasty. Tsun (vase) of t'ien-ch'ing (sky blue) with furnace transmutation of mi-sê (rice colour) and fashioned in the shape of three sacrificial bulls.

二三

宋汝窯卵青橢圓洗一件(院)

原名哥瓷洗。帶木座。底有微傷。口縱玖·柒公分。橫拾肆·貳公分。高貳·捌公分。底徑肆·叁公分。

Porcelain No. 23.

Ju Ware of the Sung Dynasty. Elliptic washer of luan-ch'ing (the blue-green of a duck's egg). With a wooden stand.

二四

宋汝窯天青圓洗一件(院)

原名天青開片瓷盤,底刻「甲」字,並乾隆御題詩,附木座,上刻「安儀周家珍藏」,並乾隆御題詩,底刻「甲」字,口徑拾肆·捌公分,高叁·玖公分,底徑拾·玖公分。

Porcelain No. 24.

Ju Ware of the Sung Dynasty. Circular washer of t'ien-ch'ing (sky blue). On its base are engraved the character "chia," and an ode of Ch'ien Lung. With a wooden stand, on the base of which are engraved the character "chia," and on the upper part of which, the characters "An I-chou chia chên-ts'ang" (or in the precious collection of the family of An I-chou) and an ode composed by Emperor Ch'ien Lung.

二五

宋汝窯粉青無紋橢圓水仙盆一件（院）

原名冬青瓷洗底刻有乾隆御題詩。誤爲官窯附雕文木座匣
抽屜內藏乾隆御筆書畫合璧一冊計捌開。口縱拾陸・肆公分，
橫貳拾叁公分高陸・玖公分底縱拾貳・玖公分橫拾玖・貳公分。
此系精之品、舊題猫食盆清雍正間曾經內府發往景德鎮。命
照此釉色製器見唐英陶成記事碑記

Porcelain No. 25.

Ju Ware of the Sung Dynasty. Elliptical narcissus-pot of fên-ch'ing (light greenish-blue) without crackles. This exquisite piece was originally labelled wo-chih pêng—a feeding basin for a small dog. At the time of Yung Chêng, it was once sent down to Ching-tê Chên through the Imperial Household with the decree to make wares of its glaze-colour. See the "Tablet Giving an Account of the Completion of Porcelain Wares," composed by T'ang Ying. On the base is inscribed an ode composed by Ch'ien Lung, who mistook the piece to be a Kuan ware. With a chest-shaped finely carved wooden stand, in the drawer of which is an album of writing and painting from the brush of Emperor Ch'ien Lung.

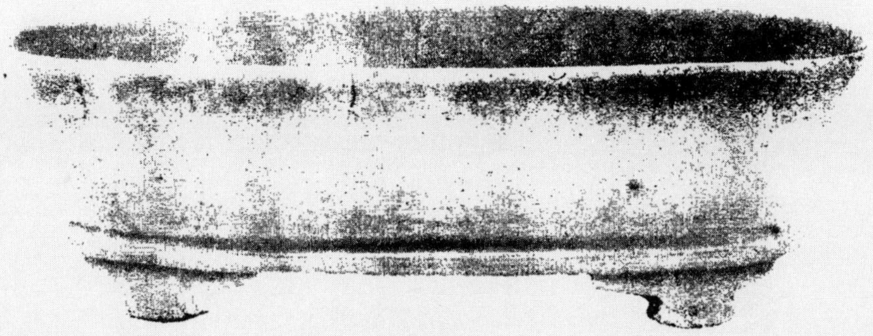

二六

宋汝窰粉青橢圓水仙盆一件(院)

原名豆青水仙瓷花盆沖口二道傷一塊、口縱拾伍·捌公分橫貳拾叁·壹公分高陸·玖公分底縱拾貳·玖公分橫拾玖·肆公分

Porcelain No. 26.

Ju Ware of the Sung Dynasty. Elliptical narcissus-pot, in fên-ch'ing (light greenish-blue). Two cracks on rim, and also a chip.

宋官窰

IV. SUNG KUAN WARE

二七

宋官窰翠青琮式瓶一件(院)

原名豆青四方開片瓷瓶帶木座口徑柒·伍公分高貳拾伍·陸公分底徑柒公分

Porcelain No. 27.

Kuan Ware of the Sung Dynasty. P'ing (vase) of ts'ui-ch'ing (blue-green) in the shape of a tsung (or yellow jade for the worship of earth). With a wooden stand.

二八

宋官窯粉青絃文八稜盤口瓶一件(院)

原名哥窯瓶.底刻乾隆御題詩。附木座.刻詩同上。瓶口有傷.口徑捌·壹公分.高貳拾貳公分.底縱橫均捌·壹公分.最大腹圍肆拾叁·柒公分.

Porcelain No. 28.

Kuan Ware of the Sung Dynasty. Pa-lêng p'ing (octagonal vase), in fên-ch'ing (light greenish-blue) with dish-shaped mouth and "bowstring" fillets. On the base is inscribed an ode of Ch'ien Lung. With a wooden stand, inscribed with the same ode. Damage to the mouth originally there.

二九

宋官窯粉青膽瓶一件(院)

原名冬青開片錐把瓶.帶木座.底有傷.口徑貳·叁公分.高拾叁·玖公分.底徑肆·柒公分.最大腹圍貳拾貳·壹公分

Porcelain No. 29.

Kuan Ware of the Sung Dynasty. Tan-p'ing (vase in the shape of a gall-bladder) of fên-ch'ing (light greenish-blue). With a wooden stand.

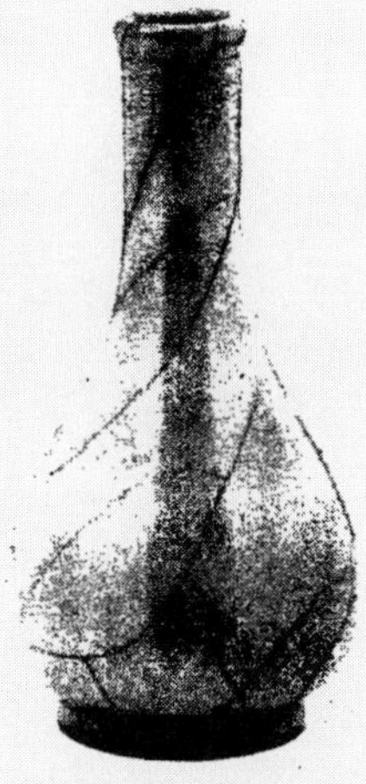

三〇

宋官窰粉青花觚一件(院)

原名哥窰花觚帶木座口徑拾伍·貳公分高拾柒·貳公分底徑伍·伍公分

Porcelain No. 30.

Kuan Ware of the Sung Dynasty. Ku (flower receptacle in the shape of a bronze goblet) of fên-ch'ing (light greenish-blue). With a wooden stand.

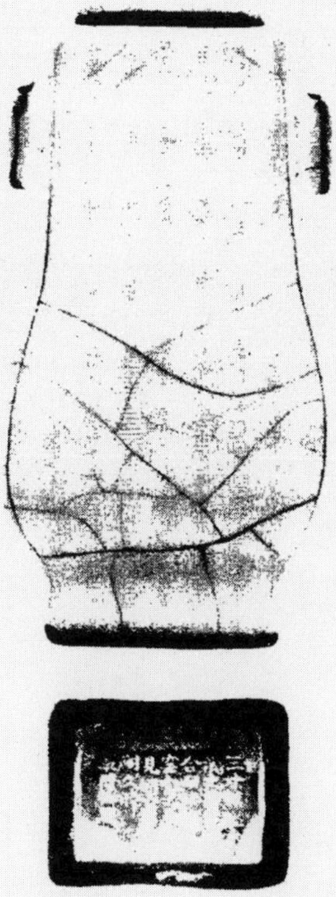

三一

宋官窰粉青貫耳穿帶小方壺一件(院)

原名開片小瓷瓶底刻乾隆御題詩帶景泰藍膽及木座均有乾隆御題詩瓶口縱貳·叁公分橫叁·貳公分高捌·肆公分底縱貳·伍公分橫叁·壹公分最大腹圍拾伍·叁公分膽頂縱貳公分橫叁公分底縱壹·叁公分橫貳·貳公分高陸公分

Porcelain No. 31.

Kuan Ware of the Sung Dynasty. Fang-hu (small quadrangular vase) of fêng-ch'ing (light greenish-blue), with "piercing handles" and tape holes. On the base of the ware is inscribed an ode composed by Emperor Ch'ien Lung. With a wooden stand on the upper part of which is inscribed the same ode.

三二

宋官窯粉青三登方壺一件(院)

原名哥窯三節瓶·底刻乾隆御題詩·帶木座座面刻乾隆御題座傷口徑縱叁·玖公分橫陸·壹公分高拾貳·貳公分底縱柒·貳公分橫拾·壹公分最大腹闊肆拾壹·玖公分

Porcelain No. 32.

Kuan Ware of the Sung Dynasty. Fang-hu (quadrangular vase) of fên-ch'ing (light greenish-blue), in the form of three tiers. On the base is inscribed an ode of Ch'ien Lung.

三三

宋官窯淺粉青弓耳扁壺一件(院)

原名哥窯雙耳小扁瓶口有微傷。口徑貳公分高拾壹·柒公分底縱叁·壹公分橫肆·貳公分.

Porcelain No. 33.

Kuan Ware of the Sung Dynasty. Pien-hu (flattened pot), in ch'ien fên-ch'ing (lighter shade of light blue-greenish grey), with handles shaped like a bow.

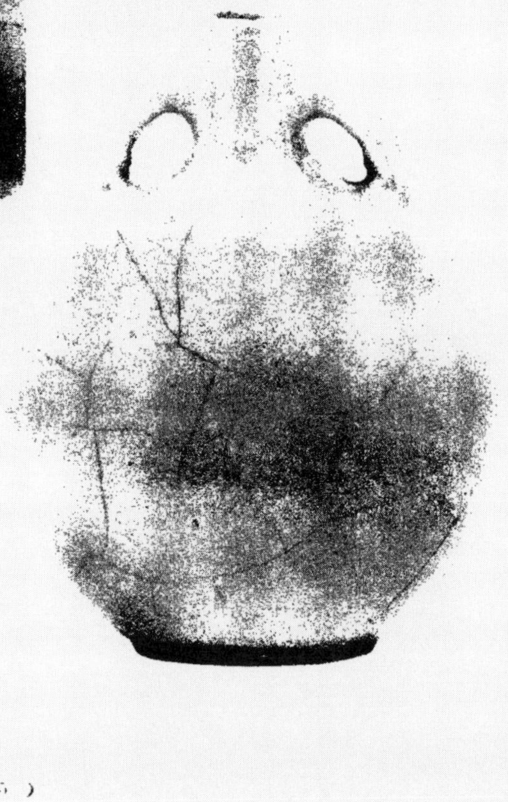

三四

宋官窯淺粉青方爐一件(院)

原名官窯瓷方爐底刻乾隆御題詩足有傷口縱橫均拾肆·捌公分·高拾·捌公分底縱橫均拾叁·玖公分。

Porcelain No. 34.

Kuan Ware of the Sung Dynasty. Fang-lu (square incense burner) in ch'ien fên-ch'ing (lighter shade of light blue-greenish grey). On the base is inscribed an ode of Ch'ien Lung. Chips off the legs.

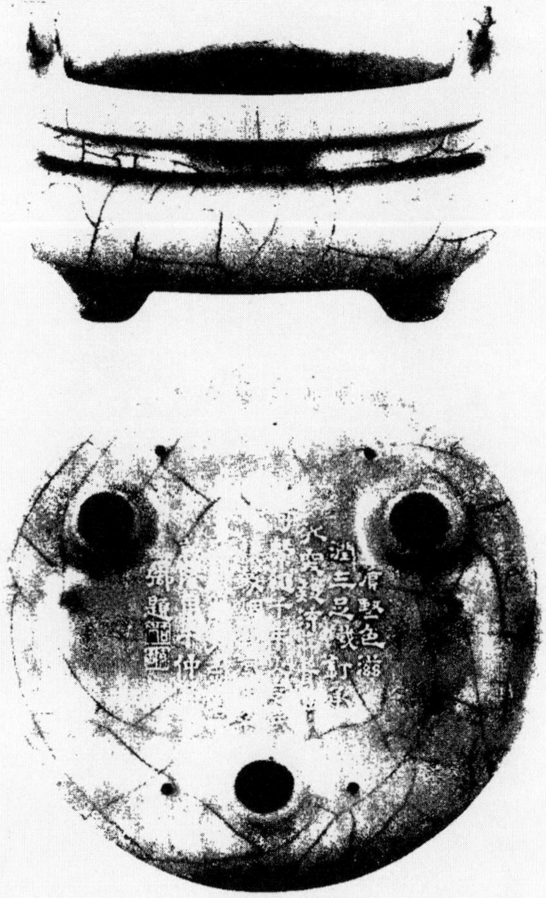

三五

宋官窯月白雙耳三足爐一件(院)

原名質堅色哀香爐底刻有乾隆御題詩帶木蓋蓋嵌玉頂口徑玖·玖公分通木蓋玉頂高捌·貳公分最大腹圍叁拾肆·柒公分

Porcelain No. 35.

Kuan Ware of the Sung Dynasty. Incense burner of yüeh-pai (moon white) with two handles and three feet. On the base is inscribed an ode composed by Emperor Ch'ien Lung.

三六

宋官窰天藍三足圓爐一件(院)

原名鈞窰三足爐帶木座及玉頂木蓋玉頂院下口徑拾·叁公分高玖·壹公分底最寬捌·玖公分最大腹圍叁拾肆·肆公分

Porcelain No. 36.

Kuan Ware of the Sung Dynasty. Circular incense burner of t'ien-lan (sky blue) with three feet. With a carved wooden cover fitted with a jade top and a wooden stand on the upper and lower parts of which are inscribed the two characters "Ch'ien Lung."

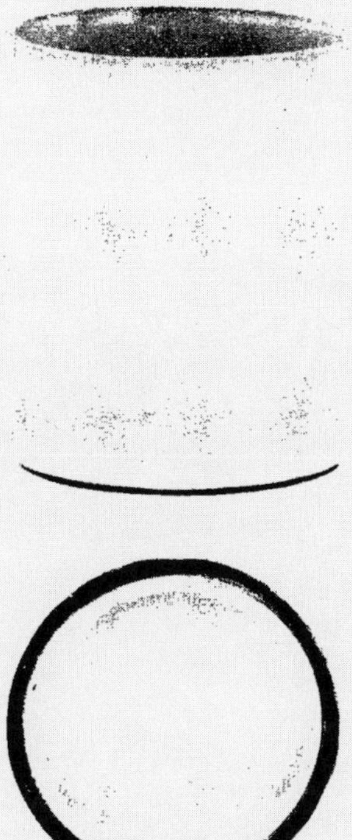

三七

宋官窰粉青筆筒一件(院)

原名哥瓷筆筒底刻乾隆御題詩·帶木座座面有乾隆御題詩。座底有「乾隆御玩」四字。口徑柒·柒公分。高玖·捌公分底徑柒·叁公分.

Porcelain No. 37.

Kuan Ware of the Sung Dynasty. Brush barrel of fên-ch'ing (light greenish-blue). On the base is inscribed an ode composed by Ch'ien Lung. With a wooden stand, on the upper part of which is inscribed the same ode, and on the lower part the four characters "Ch'ien Lung yü-wan" (for the imperial fondling of Ch'ien Lung).

(58)

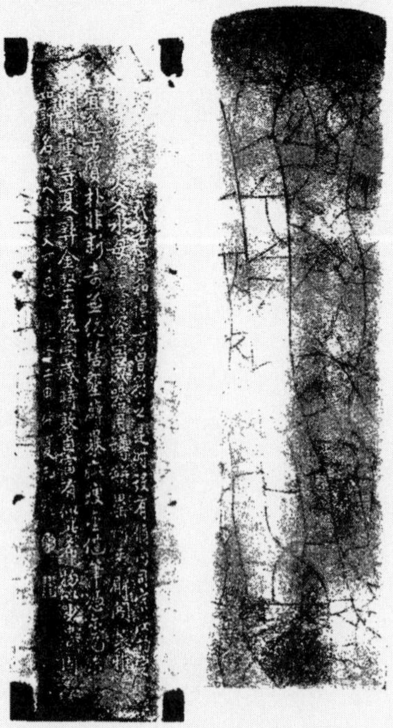

三八

宋官窰天青臂擱一件(院)

原名冬青瓷筆架,背面刻乾隆御題詩帶木座座下刻乾隆御題詩,上刻「乾隆御玩」四字最寬伍·玖公分最長貳拾貳·伍公分最高貳公分

Porcelain No. 38.

Kuan Ware of the Sung Dynasty. Arm-rest of t'ien-ch'ing (sky blue)—the reverse part being inscribed an imperial ode by Ch'ien Lung. With a wooden stand on the upper part of which is inscribed the four characters "Ch'ien Lung yü-wan" (for the imperial fondling of Ch'ien Lung), and on the lower part the same ode as on the arm-rest.

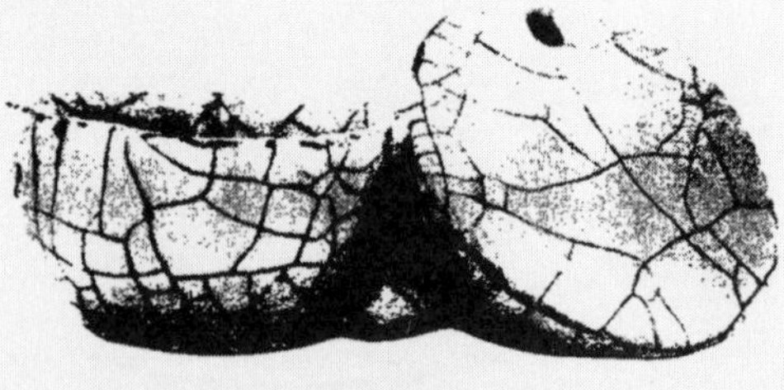

三九

宋官窰月白雙蓮房水注一件(院)

原名哥窰並蒂蓮蓬水盛帶木座最大口徑柒·玖公分最高陸·貳公分通長拾叁·柒公分

Porcelain No. 39.

Kuan Ware of the Sung Dynasty. Water-dropper of yüeh-pai (moon white) in the form of two lotus pods. With a wooden stand.

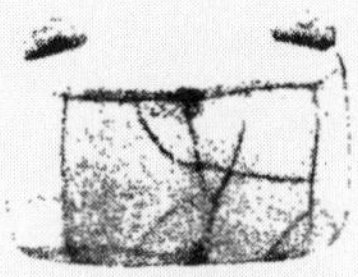

四〇

宋官窰月白小水注(上有珊瑚雙蝠蓋二個)一件(院)

原名哥瓷水盛帶木座最高叁·貳公分最大腹圍拾伍公分

Porcelain No. 40.

Kuan Ware of the Sung Dynasty. Small water-dropper of yüeh-pai (moon white), with two coral stoppers in the shape of bats (being a rebus for fu—blessing). With a wooden stand.

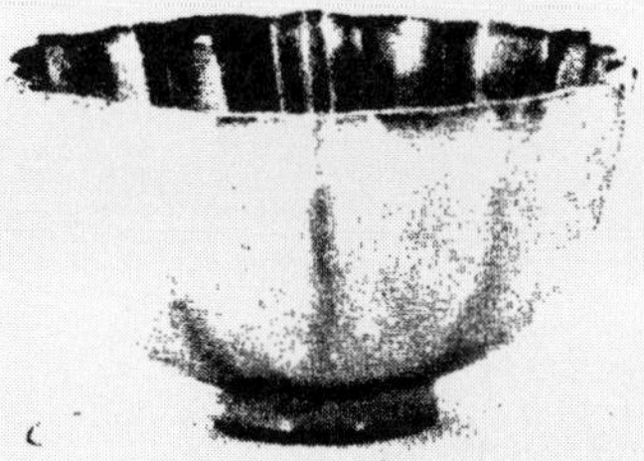

四一

宋官窯天青菱花式小盌一件(院)

原名凍青瓷盌帶木座有傷口徑捌·柒公分高伍·肆公分底徑叁·貳公分

Porcelain No. 41.

Kuan Ware of the Sung Dynasty. Small bowl of t'ien-ch'ing (sky blue) fashioned like a water-caltrop blossom. With a wooden stand.

四二

宋官窯粉青花插一件(院)

原名宋官窯一統花囊底刻乾隆御題詩帶木座銅囊均有乾隆御題座傷口傷口徑柒·伍公分高拾伍·陸公分底徑肆·肆公分

Porcelain No. 42.

Kuan Ware of the Sung Dynasty. Hua-ch'a (flower receptacle) of fên-ch'ing (light greenish-blue). On the base is inscribed an ode composed by Ch'ien Lung. With a wooden stand.

四三

宋官窯天青橢圓水仙盆一件(院)

原名官窯花盆底刻有乾隆御題詩附雕文木座匣抽屜內藏乾隆御臨王羲之五帖一冊。有墨口縱拾陸·柒公分橫貳拾叁叁公分高陸·捌公分底縱玖·柒公分橫拾陸·玖公分

Porcelain No. 43.

Kuan Ware of the Sung Dynasty. Elliptical narcissus-pot of t'ien-ch'ing (sky blue). On the base is inscribed an ode of Ch'ien Lung. With a carved wooden stand fashioned like a chest in the drawer of which is an album consisting of a copy of Wang Hsi-chih's writing, named "Wu T'ieh," made by the Emperor.

宋龍泉窯

V. SUNG LUNG-CH'ÜAN WARE

四四

宋龍泉窯粉青蓮瓣大盌一件(院)

原名凍青釉瓷盌口有微傷口徑貳拾貳·貳公分高拾·玖公分底徑陸·伍公分

Porcelain No. 44.

Lung-ch'üan Ware of the Sung Dynasty. Large bowl of fên-ch'ing (light greenish-blue), shaped like lotus petals.

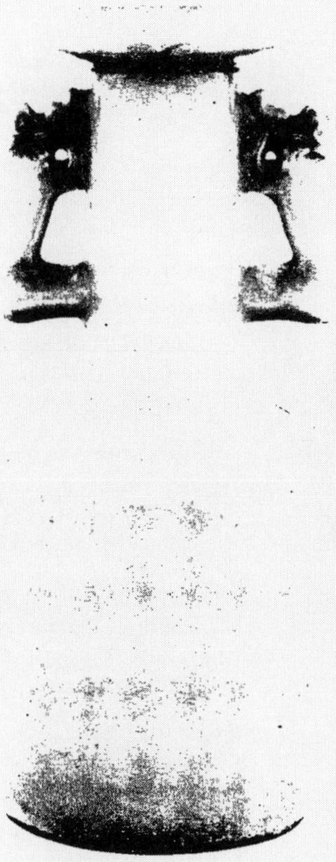

四五

宋龍泉窯粉青盤口鳳耳瓶一件(院)

原名豆青雙耳瓷瓶口徑最大玖·肆公分高貳拾伍·伍公分最大腹圍叁拾陸·捌公分底徑玖·陸公分

Porcelain No. 45.

Lung-ch'üan Ware of the Sung Dynasty. P'ing (vase) of fên-ch'ing (light greenish-blue), with dish-shaped mouth and phœnix-shaped handles.

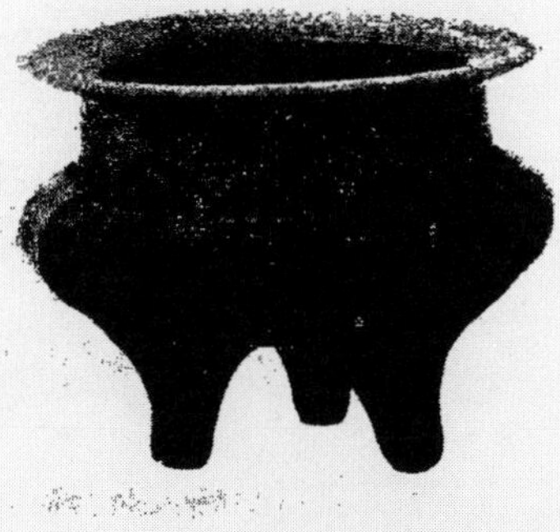

四六

宋龍泉窯粉青鬲式爐一件(院)

原名冬青三足鼎玉木蓋嵌蓋鈕玉頂頂脫下口徑拾伍·伍公分高拾貳·捌公分最大腹圍伍拾壹·柒公分。

Porcelain No. 46.

Lung-ch'üan Ware of the Sung Dynasty. Incense burner of fên-ch'ing (light greenish-blue), in the shape of a li (hollow-legged ting or tripod for ordinary use).

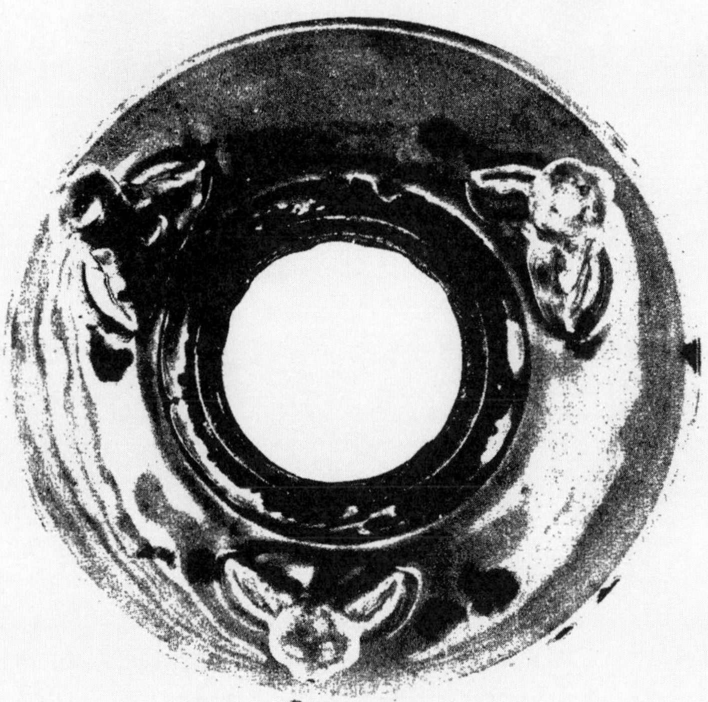

四七

宋龍泉窯葱翠青窯變匣鉢油斑點三足花囊一件(院)

原名龍泉釉三足盆藍花甕。口徑拾陸·捌公分。高拾陸·伍公分。孔徑玖·伍公分

按匣鉢油斑點。由於匣鉢經火煅鍊。溶汁濺於器上。始而出於天然。繼而人為。此種名稱乃得諸極有經驗之陶工。諸書無此記載。特注於此。

Porcelain No. 47.

Lung-ch'üan Ware of the Sung Dynasty. Hua-nang (flower receptacle) with three feet, in ts'ung ts'ui-ch'ing (onion blue-green), furnace transmutation of mottles from molten parts of the seggar (hsia-po yu pan-tien).

N. B. These mottles are caused by molten parts of the seggar splashing on the ware. Originally they were natural but were subsequently applied artificially. The name has been obtained from most experienced potters; no mention was ever made of it in books.

宋哥窯

VI. SUNG KO WARE

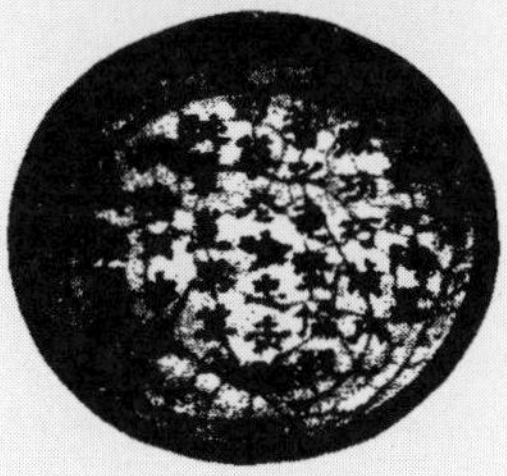

四八

宋哥窯粉青葵瓣口盤一件（院）

原名哥窯盤底刻乾隆御題詩口徑拾捌·玖公分高伍·貳公分底徑柒·貳公分

Porcelain No. 48.

Ko Ware of the Sung Dynasty. Plate of fên-ch'ing (light blue-greenish grey), with its upper rim shaped like althaea petals. On the base is inscribed an ode composed by Ch'ien Lung.

四九

宋哥窯灰青葵瓣口盤一件（院）

原名哥窯盤底刻乾隆御題詩口徑拾玖·肆公分高肆·肆公分底徑陸公分

Porcelain No. 49.

Ko Ware of the Sung Dynasty. Plate of hui-ch'ing (bluish grey) with its upper rim fashioned like althaea petals. On the base is inscribed an ode composed by Ch'ien Lung.

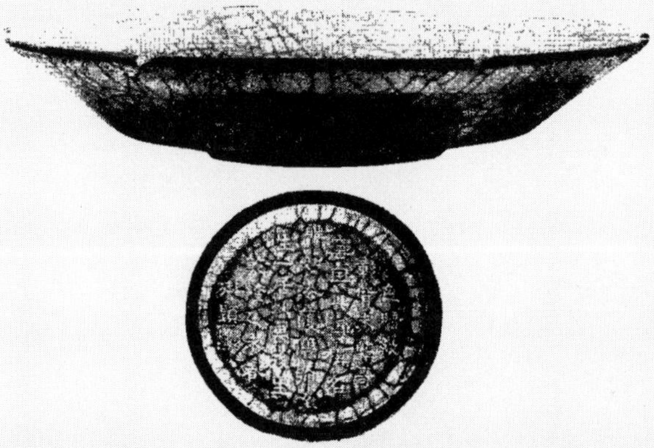

五〇

宋哥窰粉青葵瓣口盤一件(院)

原名哥窰盤。底刻乾隆御題詩。口徑拾柒·陸公分。高叁·肆公分。底徑陸·叁公分

Porcelain No. 50.

Ko Ware of the Sung Dynasty. Plate of fên-ch'ing (light blue-greenish grey), with its upper rim shaped like althaea petals. On the base is inscribed an ode composed by Emperor Ch'ien Lung.

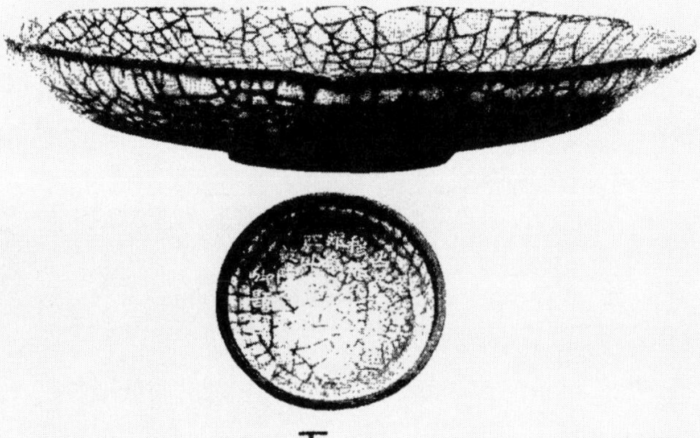

五一

宋哥窰灰青葵瓣口盤一件(院)

原名仿哥窰瓷盤。底刻乾隆御題詩。口徑拾捌·陸公分。高叁·伍公分底徑陸公分

Porcelain No. 51.

Ko Ware of the Sung Dynasty. Plate of hui-ch'ing (bluish grey) with its upper rim shaped like althaea petals. On the base is inscribed an ode of Ch'ien Lung.

五二

宋哥窰粉青雙耳盌一件(院)

原名哥窰雙耳洗鑲有銅口耳有傷、口徑拾捌·玖公分高柒·柒公分底徑陸·捌公分

Porcelain No. 52.

Ko Ware of the Sung Dynasty. Bowl of fên-ch'ing (light blue-greenish grey), with two handles. The upper rim is copper mounted.

五三

宋哥窰淺青葵瓣口盌一件(院)

原名哥窰瓜稜盌底刻乾隆御題詩口有微傷口徑拾玖·陸公分高柒·柒公分底徑陸·壹公分

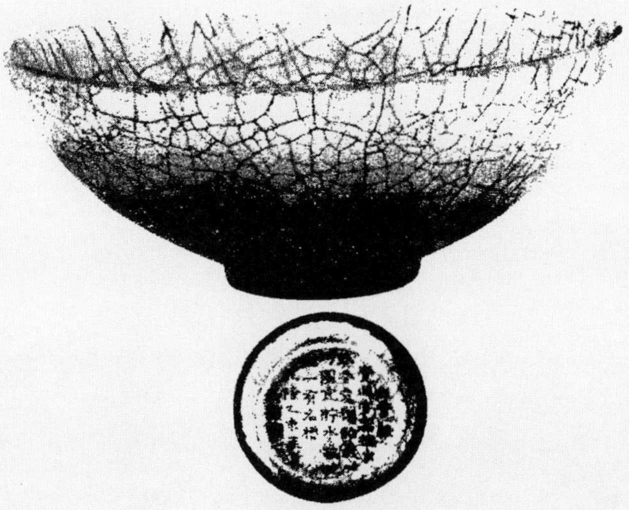

Porcelain No. 53.

Ko Ware of the Sung Dynasty. Bowl of ch'ien-ch'ing (light blue) with its rim shaped like althaea petals. On the base is inscribed an ode of Ch'ien Lung.

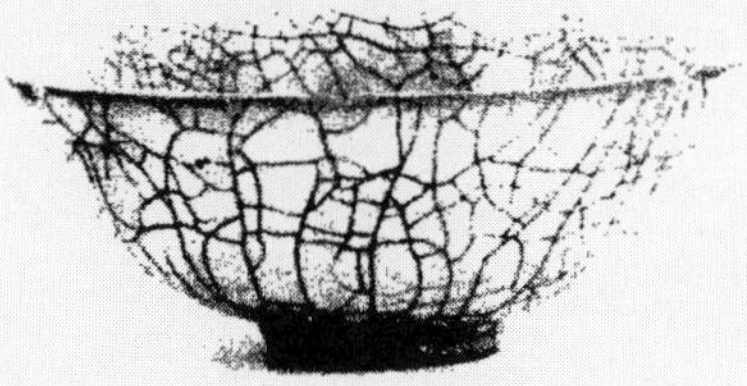

五四

宋哥窰灰青葵瓣口小盌一件(院)

原名哥窰盌口徑拾壹·捌公分高肆·玖公分底徑叁·陸公分

Porcelain No. 54.

Ko Ware of the Sung Dynasty. Small bowl of hui-ch'ing (bluish grey) with rim fashioned like althaea petals.

五五

宋哥窯米色高足盌一件(院)

原名無款哥窯靶盌口有傷口徑拾貳·柒公分高拾·貳公分,足徑肆公分

Porcelain No. 55.

Ko Ware of the Sung Dynasty. High-footed bowl of mi-sê (rice colour).

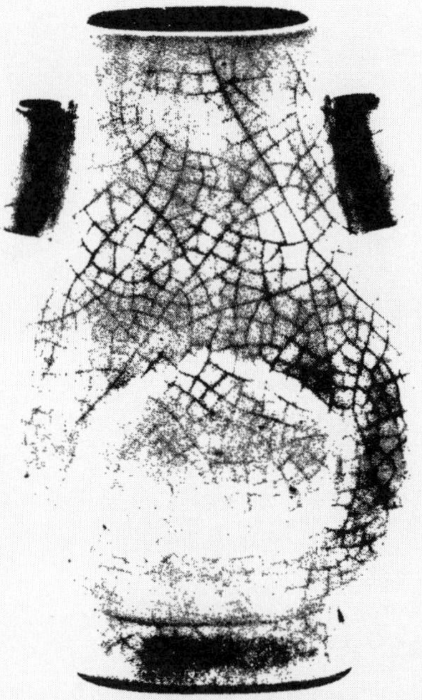

五六

宋哥窯粉青貫耳穿帶杏葉壺一件(院)

原名乾隆瓷提瓶底刻乾隆御題詩帶木座座面刻乾隆御題詩口縱伍·玖公分橫陸·玖公分高貳拾·叁公分底縱陸·陸公分橫捌伍公分最大腹圍叁拾柒公分.

Porcelain No. 56.

Ko Ware of the Sung Dynasty. Hu (vase) of fên-ch'ing (light blue-greenish grey), with "piercing handles" and tape holes, and bearing designs of apricot leaves. On the base is inscribed an ode from the pen of Ch'ien Lung. With a wooden stand on the upper part of which is inscribed the same ode.

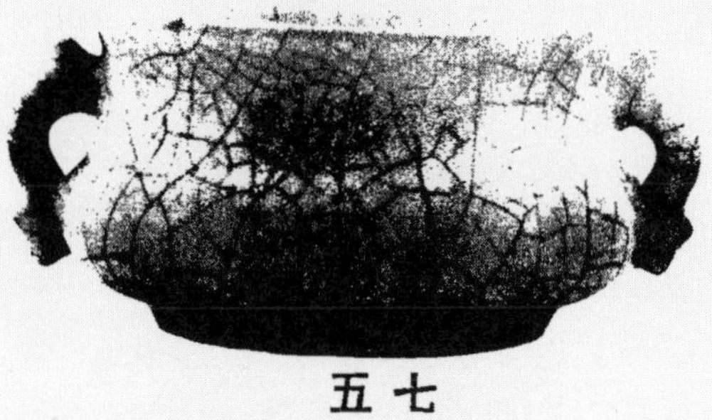

五七

宋哥窯粉青魚耳彝爐一件(院)

原名哥瓷雙耳爐帶玉頂木蓋玉頂已下口徑拾壹·貳公分高柒公分底徑捌·壹公分腹圍叁拾陸公分,

Porcelain No. 57.

Ko Ware of the Sung Dynasty. Incense burner of fên-ch'ing (light blue-greenish grey), in the form of an i (sacrificial vessel) with fish-shaped handles.

五八

宋哥窰粉靑窰變米色沖耳乳足爐一件(院)

原名哥窰嘤耳三足爐帶玉頂木蓋足有傷口徑拾貳·玖公分通耳高玖·陸公分最大腹圍肆拾伍·柒公分

Porcelain No. 58.

Ko Ware of the Sung Dynasty. Incense burner of fên-ch'ing (light blue-greenish grey), with furnace transmutation of mi-sê (rice colour), having loop handles (ch'ung-erh) and mammillated feet.

五九

宋哥窰米色三足圓爐一件(院)

原名哥窰三足鼷玉木蓋爐帶玉頂木蓋玉頂殘下口徑拾叁·貳公分高捌·肆公分底徑拾貳·貳公分腹圍肆拾叁·肆公分

Porcelain No. 59.

Ko Ware of the Sung Dynasty. Incense burner of mi-sê (rice colour) with round shape and three feet.

六〇

宋哥窰淺靑窰變米色筆掭一件(院)

原名鈞窰瓷片底刻乾隆御題詩帶木座座底刻乾隆御題詩最寬捌·柒公分最長拾貳·叁公分。最高壹·陸公分

Porcelain No. 60.

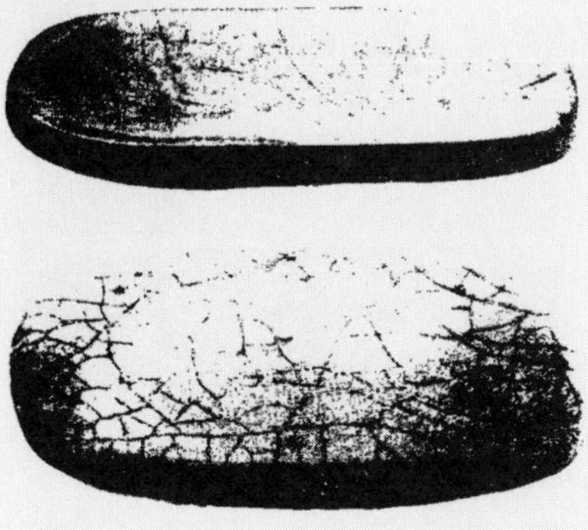

Ko Ware of the Sung Dynasty. Pi-t'ien (a slab to rub the writing brush upon) of ch'ien-ch'ing (light blue) with furnace transmutation of mi-sê (rice colour). On the base is inscribed an ode of Ch'ien Lung. With a wooden stand on the under part of which is inscribed the same ode.

宋章龍泉窰

VII. SUNG CHANG LUNG-CH'ÜAN WARE (TI YAO)

六一

宋章龍泉窰葱翠青象耳壺一件(院)

原名豆青直口瓶頸有壁口徑貳·柒公分高貳拾捌·肆公分最大腹圍肆拾肆·叁公分底徑柒·玖公分

Porcelain No. 61.

Chang Lung-ch'üan Ware of the Sung Dynasty. Hu (vase) of ts'ung ts'ui-ch'ing (onion blue-green) with handles shaped like elephant.

宋建陽窰

VIII. SUNG CHIEN-YANG WARE

六二

宋建陽窰烏金油盌一件(院)

原名無款紫窰銅鑲口淺盌鑲有銅口有壁口徑拾肆公分高伍·貳公分底徑叁·柒公分

Porcelain No. 62.

Chien-yang Ware of the Sung Dynasty. Bowl of golden black (mirror black) glaze. With a brass band on the rim.

六三

宋建陽窰烏金泐鷓鴣斑大盌一件(院)

原名銅鑲口黑色宋瓷撇口盌鑲有銅口口徑貳拾公分高伍·柒公分底徑肆·肆公分

Porcelain No. 63.

Chien-yang Ware of the Sung Dynasty. Large bowl of golden black glaze with mottles like partridge feathers. With a brass band on the rim.

六四

宋建陽窰烏金泐葉文盌一件(院)

原名銅鑲口黑色宋瓷撇口盌鑲有銅口帶木座座傷口徑拾伍·叁公分高伍·壹公分底徑叁·陸公分

Porcelain No. 64.

Chien-yang Ware of the Sung Dynasty. Bowl of golden black glaze with the design of a leaf. With a brass band on the rim.

南宋官窰

IX. SOUTHERN SUNG KUAN WARE

六五

南宋官窰粉青大盤一件(院)

原名官窰圓洗口底均傷有傷補口徑貳拾陸·玖公分高陸·貳公分底徑拾伍·捌公分

Porcelain No. 65.

Kuan Ware of the Southern Sung Dynasty. Large plate of fên-ch'ing (light greenish-blue). Chip on mouth rim.

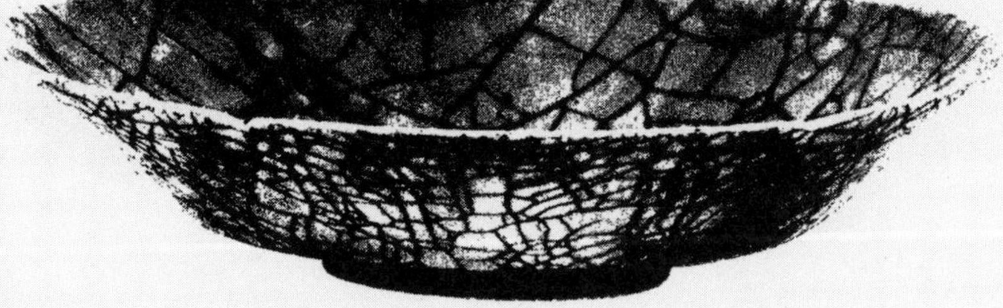

六六

南宋官窯粉青葵花式盤一件（院）

原名仿哥窯瓷盤口有微傷口徑貳拾叁·伍公分高伍·貳公分底徑柒·柒公分、

Porcelain No. 66.

Kuan Ware of the Southern Sung Dynasty. Plate of fên-ch'ing (light greenish-blue) shaped like an althaea flower.

六七

南宋官窯粉青葵花式盤一件（院）

原名仿官窯葵花式碟口徑拾捌·玖公分
高肆·玖公分底徑伍·玖公分

Porcelain No. 67.

Kuan Ware of the Southern Sung Dynasty. Plate fashioned in the shape of an althaea in fên-ch'ing (light greenish-blue).

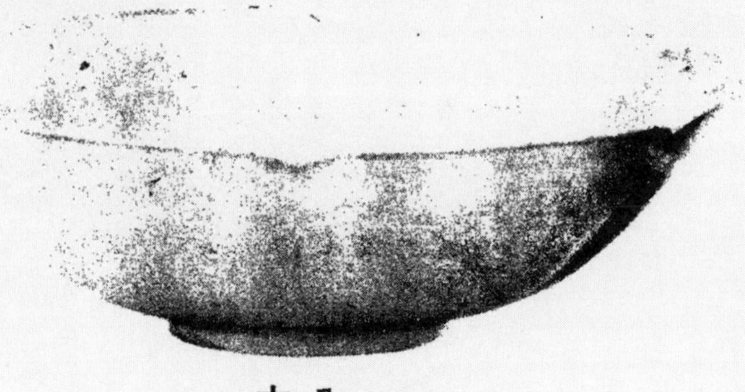

六八

南宋官窯粉青葵花式盌一件（院）

原名哥窯葵瓣洗口有傷口徑拾柒·玖公分高伍·捌公分底徑伍·柒公分

Porcelain No. 68.

Kuan Ware of the Southern Sung Dynasty. Bowl of fên-ch'ing (light greenish-blue) fashioned like an althaea.

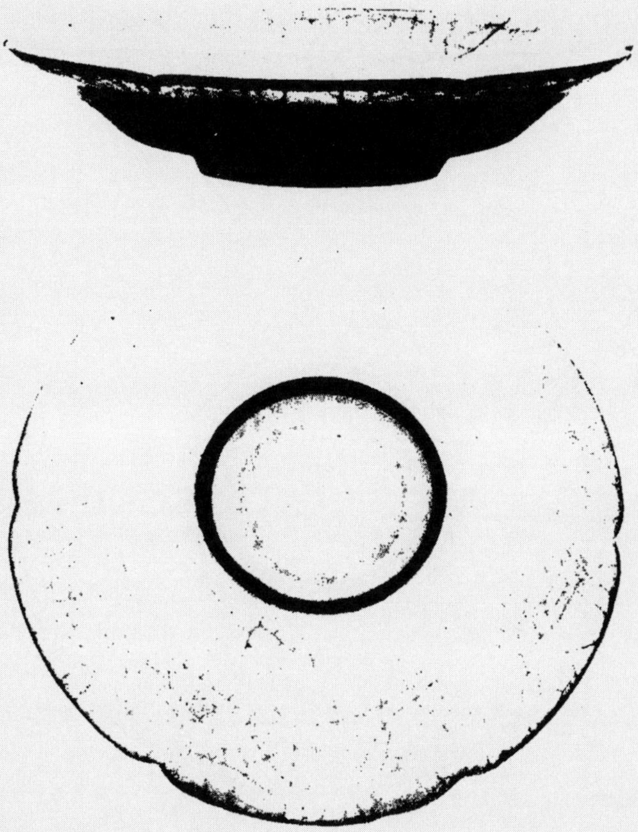

六九

南宋官窰月白葵瓣口碟一件(院)

原名哥窰盤底刻乾隆御題詩口徑拾肆·伍公分高叁·叁公分
底徑伍·陸公分

Porcelain No. 69.

Kuan Ware of the Southern Sung Dynasty. Dish of yüeh-pai (moon white) with rim fashioned like althaea petals. On the base is inscribed an ode composed by Ch'ien Lung.

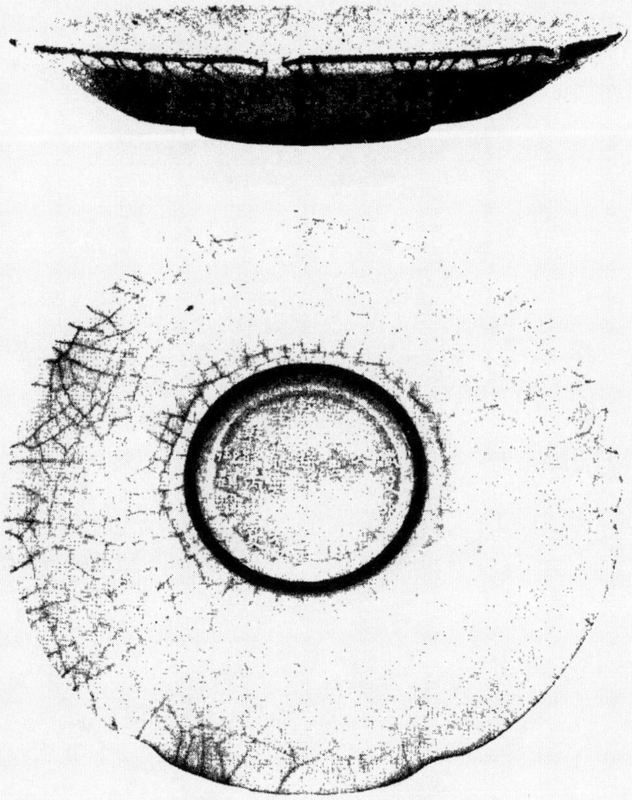

七〇

南宋官窰月白葵瓣口碟一件(院)

原名官窰盤底刻乾隆御題詩口徑拾肆·伍公分高貳·伍公分底徑伍·伍公分

Porcelain No. 70.

Kuan Ware of the Southern Sung Dynasty. Dish of yüeh-pai (moon white) with rim shaped like althaea petals. On the base is inscribed an ode composed by Ch'ien Lung.

七一

南宋官窯粉青紙槌小瓶一件(院)

原名紫窯小瓶底刻乾隆御題詩帶木座座刻乾隆御題詩口傷口徑叁·玖公分高拾貳·壹公分底徑肆·玖公分最大腹圍貳拾·柒公分

Porcelain No. 71.

Kuan Ware of the Southern Sung Dynasty. Small p'ing (vase) of fên-ch'ing (light greenish-blue) in the form of a paper beater. On the base is inscribed an ode of Ch'ien Lung. With a wooden stand inscribed with the same ode.

七二

南宋官窯月白凹稜膽瓶一件(院)

原名官窯小瓶底刻乾隆御題詩帶木座座上刻乾隆御題詩口徑叁公分高拾陸公分底徑伍·伍公分

Porcelain No. 72.

Kuan Ware of the Southern Sung Dynasty. Tan-p'ing (vase) of yüeh-pai (moon white) with indented edges. On the base is inscribed Ch'ien Lung's ode.

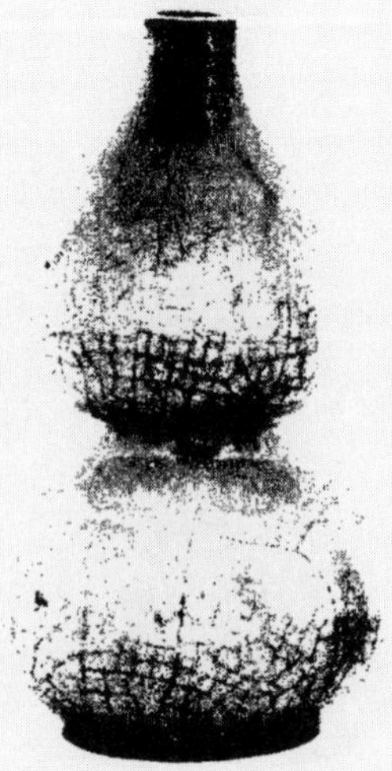

七三

南宋官窯月白葫蘆瓶一件(院)

原名開片葫蘆瓷瓶口徑叁公分高貳拾叁·玖公分底徑捌·伍公分最大腹圍肆拾伍·貳公分

Porcelain No. 73.

Kuan Ware of the Southern Sung Dynasty. P'ing (vase) of yüeh-pai (moon white) in the shape of a double-gourd.

七四

南宋官窯粉青貫耳八方壺一件(院)

原名官窯雙耳方瓶底刻乾隆御題詩帶木座上刻乾隆御題詩口縱肆公分橫伍·壹公分高拾肆·壹公分底徑肆·壹公分橫伍·貳公分最大腹圍貳拾伍·玖公分

Porcelain No. 74.

Kuan Ware of the Southern Sung Dynasty. Pa-fang hu (octagonal vase) with "piercing handles" glazed in fên-ch'ing (light greenish-blue). On the base of it is inscribed an ode of Ch'ien Lung.

七五

南宋官窰月白雙絃壺一件(院)

原名宋窰直口瓶底刻乾隆御題詩。帶木座座面刻乾隆御題詩。下刻「甲」字口有微傷口徑伍·肆公分高拾壹·捌公分底徑伍·玖公分最大腹圍貳拾捌·肆公分

Porcelain No. 75.

Kuan Ware of the Southern Sung Dynasty. Hu (vase) of yüeh-pai (moon white) with two "bowstring fillets." On the base is inscribed Ch'ien Lung's ode. With a wooden stand on the upper part of which is inscribed the same ode and on the under the character "chia".

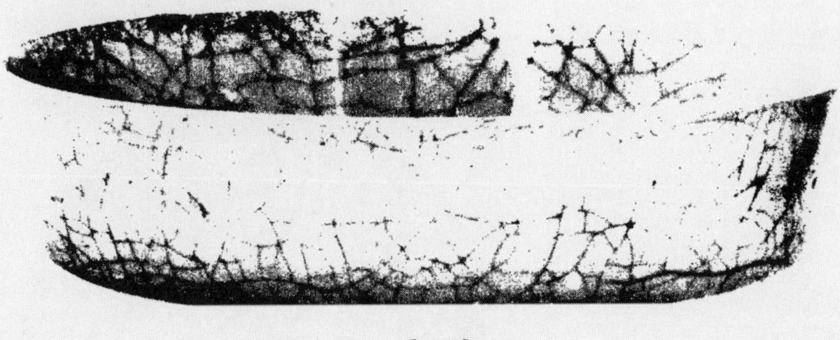

七六

南宋官窰翠青大圓洗一件(院)

原名哥窰槽羅洗口有傷口徑貳拾陸·伍公分高陸·捌公分底徑貳拾叁·肆公分

Porcelain No. 76.

Kuan Ware of the Southern Sung Dynasty. Large round washer of ts'ui-ch'ing or blue-green. Two chips on lip.

七七

南宋官窯粉青彫龍大圓洗一件(院)

原名無款豆青瓷洗口徑貳拾肆·柒公分高柒·捌公分底徑拾伍·伍公分

Porcelain No. 77.

Kuan Ware of the Southern Sung Dynasty. Large round washer of fên-ch'ing (light greenish-blue) with decoration of carved dragons in relief.

七八

南宋官窯粉青蔗段圓洗一件(院)

原名哥窯竹式圓洗口徑拾捌·貳公分高伍·捌公分底徑拾伍·柒公分

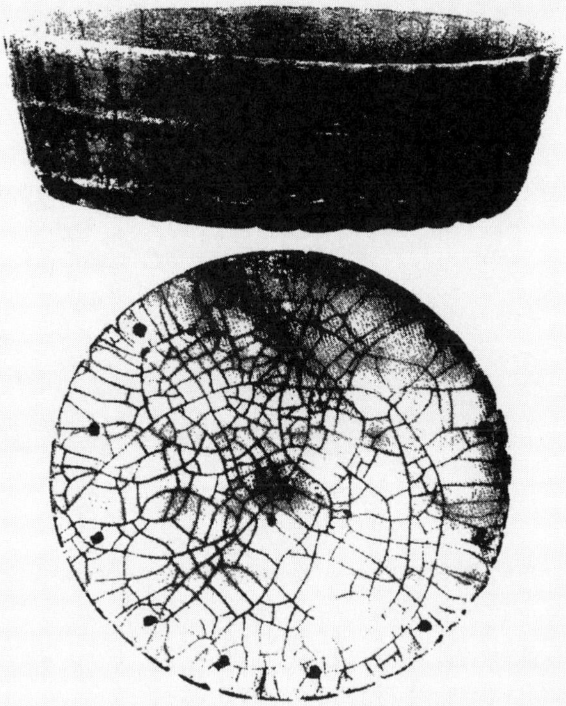

Porcelain No. 78.

Kuan Ware of the Southern Sung Dynasty. Round washer of fên-ch'ing (light greenish-blue) shaped like bundle of sugarcane.

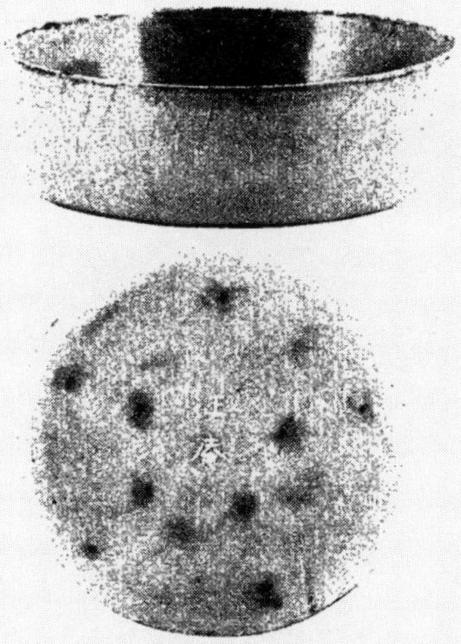

七九

南宋官窯粉青圓洗一件(院)

原名官窯樣雞洗底鐫正庵二楷字口有傷口徑拾伍·肆公分高伍·陸公分底徑拾叁·肆公分

Porcelain No. 79.

Kuan Ware of the Southern Sung Dynasty. Round washer of fên-ch'ing (light greenish-blue). On the base are inscribed the two characters "Chêng-an."

八〇

南宋官窯粉青菱花式洗一件(院)

原名仿官窯葵花式碟帶木座。口有傷補口徑拾貳·陸公分。高叁·陸公分。底徑玖·貳公分。

Porcelain No. 80.

Kuan Ware of the Southern Sung Dynasty. Washer of fên-ch'ing (light greenish-blue) shaped like a blossom of the water-caltrop. With a wooden stand.

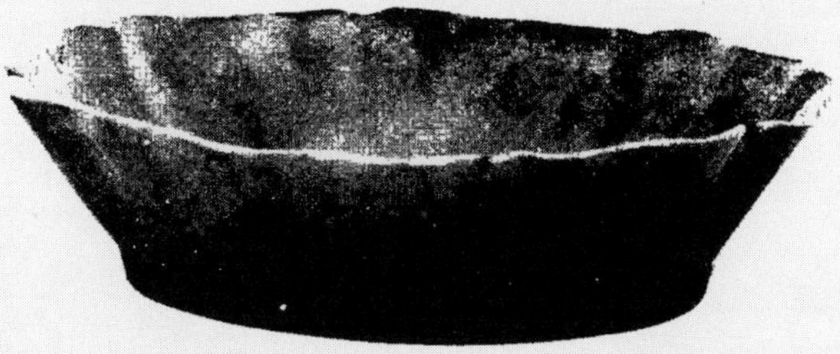

南宋吉州窯
X. SOUTHERN SUNG CHI-CHOU WARE

八一

南宋吉州窯牙白印花孩兒臥榴盌一件(院)

原名定窯銅口裏拱花鐃盌口徑拾玖·肆公分。高伍·叁公分。底徑叁·柒公分。

Porcelain No. 81.

Chi-chou Ware of the Southern Sung Dynasty. Bowl of ya-pai (ivory white), with the moulded decoration of children resting on pomegranates.

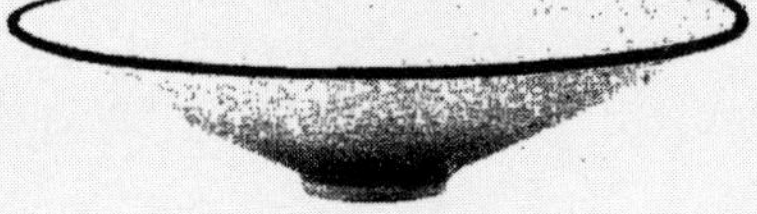

八二

南宋吉州窯牙白印花番蓮盌一件(院)

原名定窯裏拱花鐃盌。鑲有銅口。口徑拾柒·貳公分。高肆·貳公分底徑叁·肆公分。

Porcelain No. 82.

Chi-chou Ware of the Southern Sung Dynasty. Bowl of ya-pai (ivory white), with the decoration of Indian lotus moulded in the paste. With copper rim.

八三

南宋吉州窯牙白印花博古荷華盌一件(院)

原名定窯銅口裏拱花鐃盌。鑲有銅口。最大口徑貳拾·柒公分。高陸·捌公分底徑伍·陸公分。

Porcelain No. 83.

Chi-chou Ware of the Southern Sung Dynasty. Bowl of ya-pai (ivory white), with the decoration of antiques and lotus flowers moulded in the paste. With a brass band on the rim.

(79)

八四

南宋吉州窯米色碎器蓮瓣大盌一件(院)

原名甌瓷蓮花果洗鑲有銅口最大口徑貳拾陸·壹公分高拾叁公分底徑拾壹·伍公分

Porcelain No. 84.

Chi-chou Ware of the Southern Sung Dynasty. Large bowl of fine crackled rice colour (mi-sê shui-ch'i) shaped like lotus petals. With a brass rim.

八五

南宋吉州窯牙白繡花雲鶴琖一件(院)

原名定窯暗鳳茶鍾口徑拾·捌公分高伍公分底徑肆·柒公分

Porcelain No. 85.

Chi-chou Ware of the Southern Sung Dynasty. Chan (cup) of ya-pai (ivory white) with the raised decoration of clouds and cranes finely carved (hsiu) in the paste.

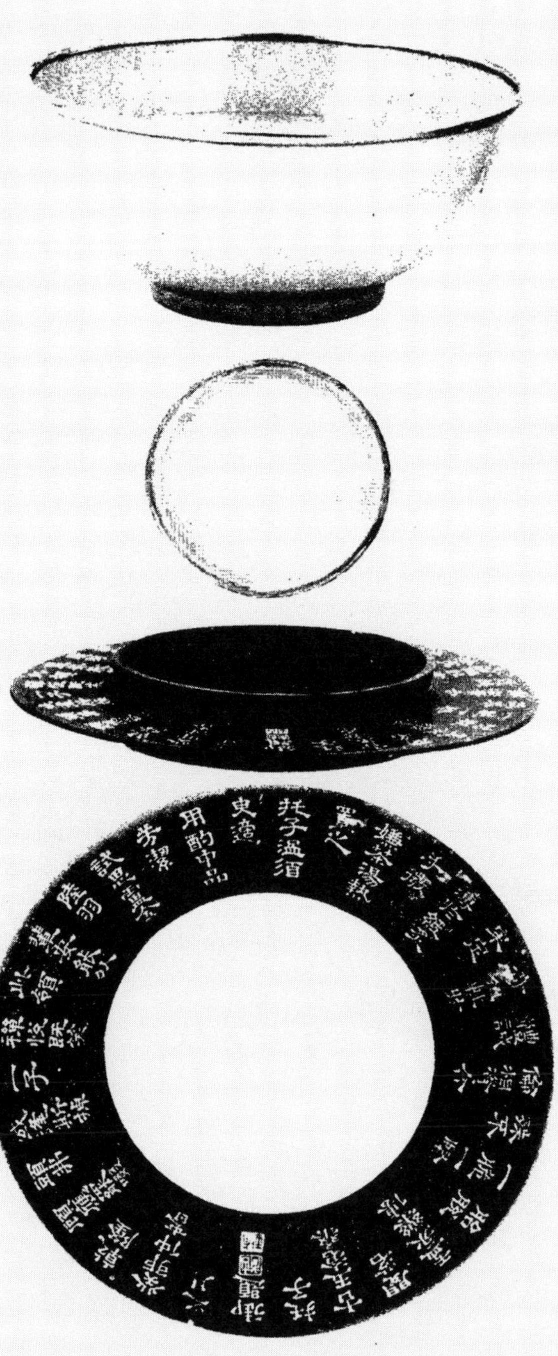

八六

南宋吉州窯牙白印花菊華琖一件（院）

原名定窯銅口拱花裏盤。底刻乾隆御題詩。附古玉托子。上刻詩同此器。高宗誤爲永樂茗盂。口徑拾·陸公分。高肆·玖公分。底徑肆·捌公分。

Porcelain No. 86.

Chi-chou Ware of the Southern Sung Dynasty. Chan (cup) of ya-pai (ivory white), with moulded decoration of chrysanthemums. On the base is inscribed an ode of Ch'ien Lung. With a stand of old jade inscribed with the same ode.

N.B. This piece was considered by the Emperor to be a ming-yü (tea-cup) of Yung Lo ware.

八七

南宋吉州窯牙白盤口瓶一件(院)

原名定窯直口瓶。底刻乾隆御題詩。帶木座。座面刻乾隆御題詩。口徑柒·壹公分。高拾伍·玖公分。底徑肆·壹公分。最大腹圍叁拾伍·玖公分。

Porcelain No. 87.

Chi-chou Ware of the Southern Sung Dynasty. P'ing (vase) of ya-pai (ivory white), with a dish-shaped mouth. On the base is inscribed an ode composed by Ch'ien Lung. With a wooden stand on the upper part of which is inscribed the same ode.

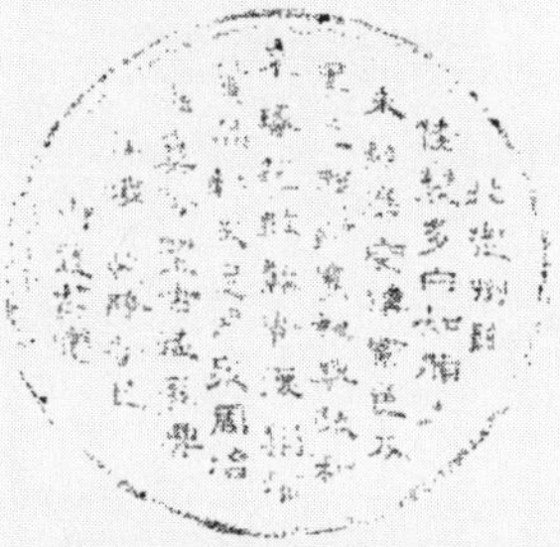

八八

南宋吉州窯牙白撇口小瓶一件(院)

原名定瓷小瓶。底刻乾隆御題詩。帶木座。座面刻乾隆御題詩。口徑叁·柒公分。高捌·肆公分。底徑叁·伍公分。最大腹圍拾捌·捌公分。

Porcelain No. 88.

Chi-chou Ware of the Southern Sung Dynasty. Hsiao-p'ing (small vase) of ya-pai (ivory white), with a spreading mouth. On the base is inscribed an ode of Ch'ien Lung. With a wooden stand on the upper part of which is carved an ode composed by Ch'ien Lung.

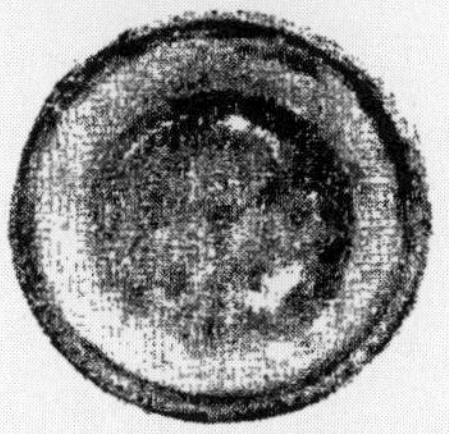

八九

南宋吉州窰牙白劃花雲龍天球瓶一件（院）

原名定窰槌瓶鑲有銅口。口徑柒·叁公分高叁拾伍·壹公分底徑拾壹公分。最大腹圍柒拾貳·伍公分

Porcelain No. 89.

Chi-chou Ware of the Southern Sung Dynasty. P'ing (vase) of ya-pai (ivory white) in the shape of a t'ien-ch'iu pear, decorated with clouds and dragons incised in the paste. With the upper rim mounted with brass.

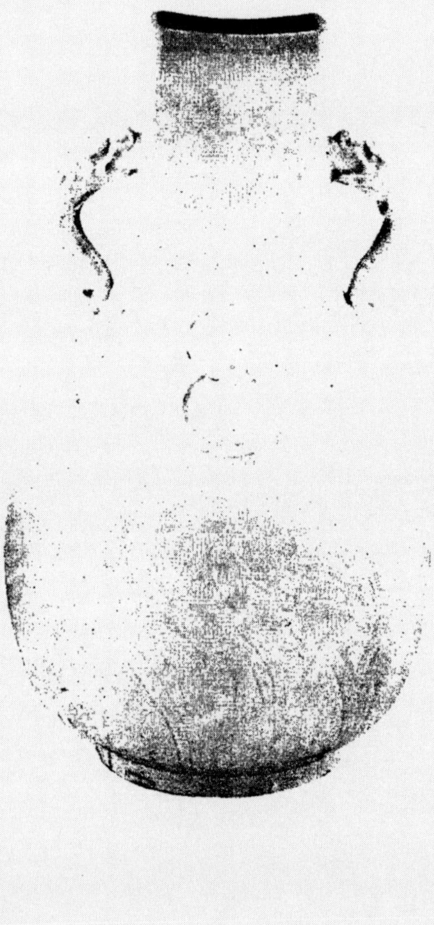

九〇

南宋吉州窰牙白劃花蓮華龍耳獸環壺一件（院）

原名填白瓷雙耳銅口尊有傷帶銅膽無銅口附銀質插花護口一個口縱肆·肆公分橫捌·肆公分高叁拾捌·陸公分最大腹圍陸拾柒·叁公分。底徑拾貳·叁公分

Porcelain No. 90.

Chi-chou Ware of the Southern Sung Dynasty. Hu (vase) of ya-pai (ivory white), with dragon-shaped handles attached animal masks with rings and the decoration of lotus blossoms incised in the paste. With silver mouthpiece for the insertion of flowers.

九一

南宋吉州窰牙白絃文敦一件(院)

原名定瓷雙耳爐.底有仲和珍玩四楷字及王鎔圖章.帶木蓋.蓋上嵌玉頂.蓋破.足有微傷.口徑拾叁·伍公分.通木蓋玉頂高拾陸·貳公分.最大腹圍伍拾公分.底徑玖·捌公分

Porcelain No. 91.

Chi-chou Ware of the Southern Sung Dynasty. Tui (a vessel for cereals), of ivory white, with "bowstring" fillets. On the base are written in ink the characters "Chung Ho ching-wan" or for the precious fondling of Chung Ho below which is affixed the seal of "Wang Yung."

九二

南宋吉州窑牙白包袱式把壶一件（陈）

原名填白袱形小瓷壶·带木座盖有伤口纵肆·贰公分横肆·玖公分通盖高柒·玖公分最长拾伍·肆公分

Porcelain No. 92.

Chi-chou Ware of the Southern Sung Dynasty. Pa-hu (pot with handle) of ya-pai (ivory white), fashioned like a cloth bundle. With a wooden stand.

九三

南宋吉州窯灰白印花天祿流雲方洗一件（陸）

原名瓷方洗。底刻乾隆御題詩。口縱拾肆·貳公分橫拾肆·捌公分。高肆·玖公分底縱橫均柒·陸公分

Porcelain No. 93.

Chi-chou Ware of the Southern Sung Dynasty. Square washer of hui-pai (greyish white), with the decoration of moving clouds and four beasts called t'ien-lu moulded in the paste. On the base is inscribed an ode of Ch'ien Lung.

九四

南宋吉州窯灰白印花天祿流雲方洗一件(院)

原名定瓷暗花方洗底刻乾隆御題詩口有微傷口縱拾肆·壹公分橫拾肆·陸公分高肆·玖公分底縱柒·柒公分橫柒·玖公分

Porcelain No. 94.

Chi-chou Ware of the Southern Sung Dynasty. Square washer of hui-pai (greyish white) with moulded decoration of moving clouds and four beasts called t'ien-lu. On the base is inscribed an ode composed by Ch'ien Lung.

九五

南宋吉州窯灰白印花菊花方洗一件(院)

原名宋瓷方洗帶木座口縱橫均拾壹·壹公分。高貳·伍公分底縱橫均陸·伍公分

Porcelain No. 95.

Chi-chou Ware of the Southern Sung Dynasty. Square washer of hui-pai (greyish white), with moulded decoration of chrysanthemum. With a wooden stand.

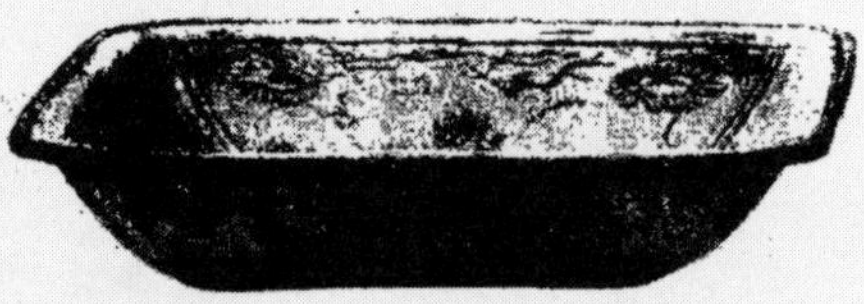

金宿州窯

XI. CHIN SU-CHOU WARE

九六

金宿州窯牙白琖一件(院)

原名定窯盞口徑拾壹·陸公分高柒·陸公分底徑肆陸公分

Porcelain No. 96.

Su-chou Ware of the Chin period. Cup (chan) of ya-pai (ivory white).

九七

金宿州窯瑩白印花回文蒲搥瓶一件(院)

原名墳白棒捶式瓶口徑伍·伍公分高貳拾叁·捌公分最大腹圍叁拾柒公分底徑陸·壹公分

Porcelain No. 97.

Su-chou Ware of the Chin period. P'ing (vase) of ying-pai (pure white) shaped like a bulrush head (p'u-ts'ui) with the hui-wen (or fine linear squared-spiral ornament) incised in the paste.

九八

金宿州窯瑩白象耳尊一件(院)

原名白定瓷象耳花瓶底有微傷口徑拾·捌公分高叁拾伍·玖公分底徑拾·玖公分最大腹圍伍拾貳·陸公分

Porcelain No. 98.

Su-chou Ware of the Chin period. Tsun (vase) of ying-pai (pure white) with elephant-shaped handles.

九九

金宿州窯瑩白葵花式渣斗一件(院)

原名定窯鑲銅口瓷斗帶木座底有紋傷口徑拾貳·肆公分高玖公分底徑陸公分最大腹圍叁拾叁·柒公分.

Porcelain No. 99.

Su-chou Ware of the Chin period. Ch'a-tou (receptacle for discarded food) of ying-pai (pure white) shaped like an althaea.

金平定窯

XII. CHIN P'ING-TING WARE

一〇〇

金平定窯灰白繡花雲龍大盤一件(院)

原名定窯銅口暗花洗鑲有銅口最大口徑叁拾玖·貳公分高柒·肆公分底拾捌·陸公分

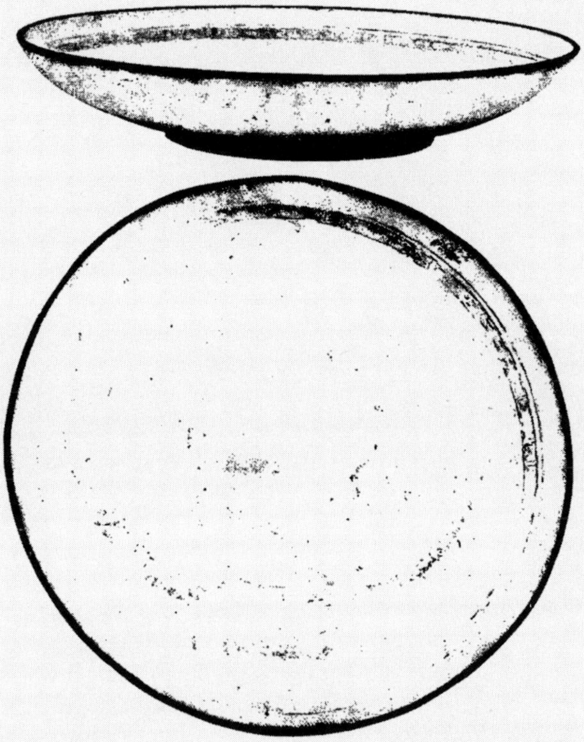

Porcelain No. 100.

P'ing-ting Ware of the Chin period. Large plate of ju-pai (creamy white), with the raised decoration of clouds and dragons finely carved (hsiu or embroidered) in the paste. With a brass band set on the rim.

南宋餘姚窰

XIII. SOUTHERN SUNG YÜ-YAO WARE

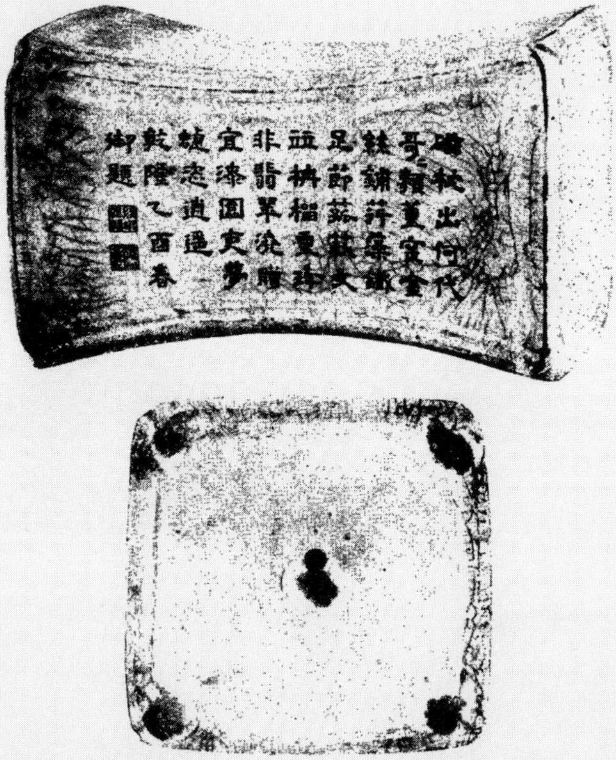

—〇—

南宋餘姚窰祕色枕一件(院)

原名哥窰瓷枕枕面刻乾隆御題詩,帶木座座面刻有乾隆御題詩.最長拾柒·伍公分最寬拾·捌公分.

Porcelain No. 101.

Yü-yao Ware of the Southern Sung Dynasty. Pillow of pi-sê (secret colour). On the upper side of it is inscribed an ode composed by Emperor Ch'ien Lung. With a wooden stand on the upper part of which is inscribed the same ode.

南宋餘杭窰

XIV. SOUTHERN SUNG YÜ-HANG WARE

一〇二

南宋餘杭窰油青三羊尊一件(院)

原名淡青銅口瓷搽盂鑲有銅口底有傷口徑拾叁·壹公分高拾伍·陸公分底徑捌·柒公分最大腹圍叁拾柒·伍公分

Porcelain No. 102.

Yü-hang Ware of the Southern Sung Dynasty. Tsun (vase) of oil blue-green, attached on the shoulder with three rams' heads. With a brass mounted rim.

南宋湘湖窰

XV. SOUTHERN SUNG HSIANG-HU WARE

一〇三

南宋湘湖窰淺粉青劃花芙蓉葵花式盌一件(院)

原名粉定窰小瓷盌鑲有銅口口徑貳拾公分高伍·玖公分底徑陸公分

Porcelain No. 103.

Hsiang-hu Ware of the Southern Sung Dynasty. Bowl of ch'ien fên-ch'ing (light greenish-blue) fashioned like an althaea blossom, with the design of hibiscus (fu-yung) incised in the paste. With a brass rim.

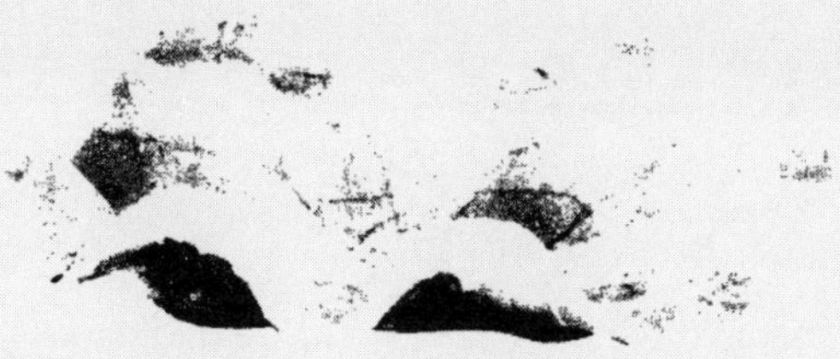

一〇四

南宋湘湖窯淺粉青荷葉小筆洗一件(院)

原名帶雕座蚌殼式瓷水盂附木座座傷橫拾·捌公分·縱捌·伍公分高叁·伍公分

Porcelain No. 104.

Hsiang-hu Ware of the Southern Sung Dynasty. Small brush washer, in ch'ien fên-ch'ing (lighter shade of light greenish-blue) in the shape of a lotus leaf. With a wooden stand.

南宋郊壇下官窯

XVI. SOUTHERN SUNG KUAN WARE UNDER THE SUBURBAN ALTAR

一〇五

南宋郊壇下官窯粉青穿帶瓶一件(院)

原名開片瓷瓶底刻乾隆御題詩帶木座座底刻乾隆御題詩口徑肆·肆公分高拾貳·肆公分底徑伍·貳公分最大腹圍貳拾伍·陸公分

Porcelain No. 105.

Kuan Ware under the Suburban Altar of the Southern Sung Dynasty. P'ing (vase) of fên-ch'ing (light greenish-blue) with two tape holes. On the base is inscribed an ode composed by Ch'ien Lung. With a wooden stand on the under part of which is inscribed the same ode.

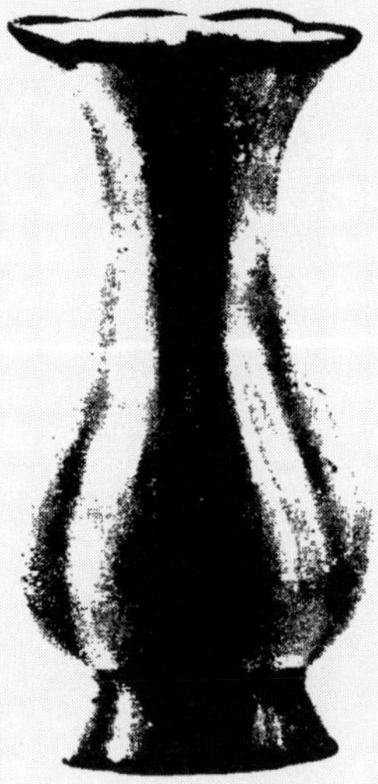

一〇六

南宋郊壇下官窯粉青海棠式小瓶一件(院)

原名汝窯海棠式小口尊帶木座口縱叁·壹公分橫伍·伍公分高拾壹·肆公分底縱叁·武公分橫肆·肆公分

Porcelain No. 106.

Kuan Ware under the Suburban Altar of the Southern Sung Dynasty. Hsiao-p'ing (small vase) of fên-ch'ing (light greenish-blue) in the shape of a pyrus blossom. With a wooden stand.

一〇七

南宋郊壇下官窯油灰三孔扁方壺一件(院)

原名哥窯雙管瓷瓶底刻乾隆御題詩帶木座座面刻乾隆御題詩口縱橫均肆公分高拾柒·陸公分底縱肆·壹公分橫陸·捌公分最大腹圍叁拾叁·武公分

Porcelain No. 107.

Kuan Ware under the Suburban Altar of the Southern Sung Dynasty. Pien fang-hu (flattened oblong pot) of yu-hui (oil grey) with three spouts. On the base is inscribed an ode composed by Ch'ien Lung. With a wooden stand, on the upper part of which is carved the same ode.

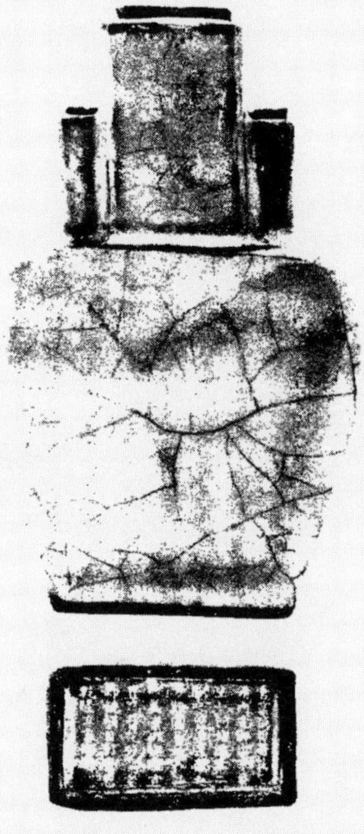

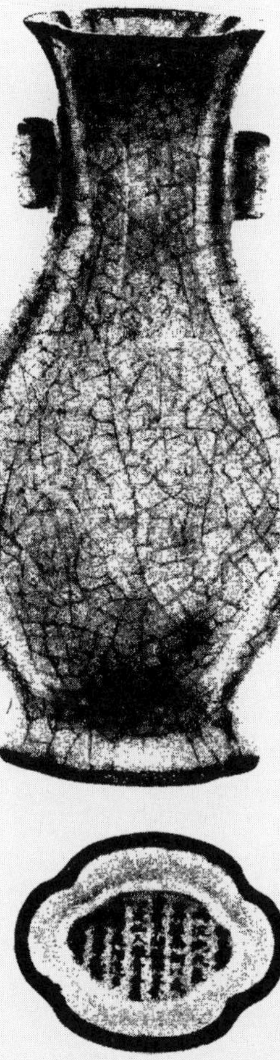

一〇八

南宋郊壇下官窯月白海棠式貫耳壺一件(睒)

原名祕色窯雙耳尊底刻乾隆御題詩帶木座座上嵌銀質乾隆御題詩口縱肆·伍公分橫伍·叁公分高拾陸·柒公分底縱肆·柒公分橫伍·捌公分

Porcelain No. 108.

Kuan Ware under the Suburban Altar of the Southern Sung Dynasty. Hu (vase) of yüeh-pai (moon white) shaped like the begonia blossom (ch'iu hai-tang) and with "piercing handles." On the base is inscribed an ode from the brush of Emperor Ch'ien Lung. With a wooden stand inlaid with silver characters being the same imperial ode.

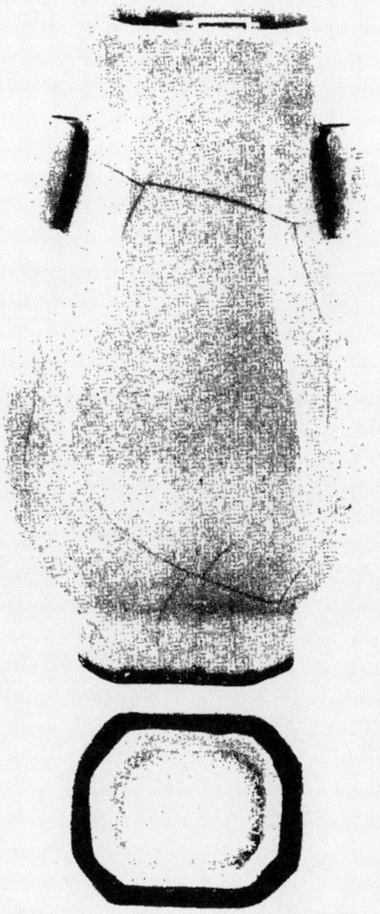

一〇九

南宋郊壇下官窯月白貫耳八方壺一件(睒)

原名雙耳瓷瓶底刻乾隆御題詩帶木座座上刻乾隆御題詩有璺口縱叁·柒公分橫伍·肆公分高拾伍·壹公分底縱肆·壹公分橫肆·玖公分最大腹圍貳拾肆·玖公分。

Porcelain No. 109.

Kuan Ware under the Suburban Altar of the Southern Sung Dynasty. Pa-fang hu (octagonal vase) of yüeh-pai (moon white) with "piercing handles." On the base is inscribed an ode of Ch'ien Lung. With a wooden stand on the upper part of which is engraved the same ode.

南 宋 廣 窯

XVII. SOUTHERN SUNG KUANG-TUNG WARE

一一〇

南宋廣窯天藍號筒式小瓶 一件 (院)

原名汝釉瓷瓶帶木座有傷口徑弍·弍公分。高拾肆·叁公分底徑叁·叁公分最大腹圍拾壹·肆公分

Porcelain No. 110.

Kuang-tung Ware of the Southern Sung Dynasty. Small p'ing (vase) of t'ien-lan (sky blue) in the shape of a hao-t'ung (Chinese bugle). Slight damage on shoulder. With a wooden stand.

一一一

南宋廣窯葱綠小尊 一件 (院)

原名冬青釉小瓷瓶帶木座底有微傷口徑肆·弍公分。高柒·叁公分底徑叁公分最大腹圍弍拾壹·捌公分

Porcelain No. 111.

Kuang-tung Ware of the Southern Sung Dynasty. Hsiao-tsun (small vase) of ts'ung-lü (onion green). With a wooden stand.

(95)

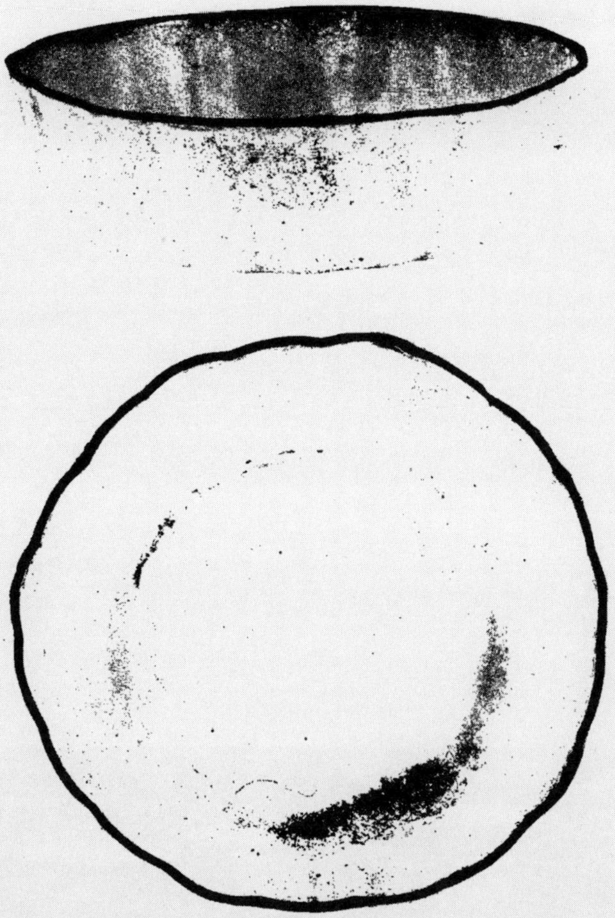

一一二

南宋廣窯月白劃花牡丹圓洗　一作（院）

原名定窯鑲銅口帶銅蓋菊瓣洗無銅蓋底有墨口徑叁拾叁·壹公分最高拾公分

Porcelain No. 112.

Kuang-tung Ware of the Southern Sung Dynasty. Round washer of yüeh-pai (moon white). With the decoration of peonies incised in the paste. With a brass rim.

元 彭 窯

XVIII. YÜAN PÊNG WARE

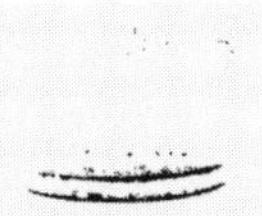

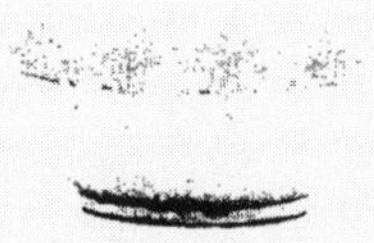

一一三

元彭窯牙白杯一件(院)

原名定窯暗花茶鍾口徑玖·壹公分高叁·捌公分底徑叁·伍公分

Porcelain No. 113.

Pêng Ware of the Yüan Dynasty. Cup of ya-pai (ivory white).

一一四

元彭窯牙白劃花雙螭杯一件(院)

原名定窯暗花茶鍾有劃花口徑玖·壹公分高叁·捌公分底徑叁·伍公分

Porcelain No. 114.

Pêng Ware of the Yüan Dynasty. Cup of ivory white with decoration of two ch'ih (or hornless dragons) incised in the paste.

一一五

元彭窯牙白劃花饕餮套杯一套五件(院)

原名象窯饕餮套壹套之一口徑玖公分高肆·貳公分底徑叁·捌公分之二口有微傷口徑捌·肆公分高伍公分底徑叁·伍公分之三有裂痕口徑捌公分高肆·叁公分底徑叁·肆公分之四底有三口徑柒·叁公分高叁·伍公分底徑叁·肆公分之五口徑陸·玖公分高貳·玖公分底徑叁·叁公分

Porcelain No. 115.

Pêng Ware of the Yüan Dynasty. T'ao-pei (or set of cups one fitting into another) of ivory white, with the decoration of t'ao-tieh (avaricious and gluttonous monsters) incised in the paste. Set of five pieces.

元臨川窯

XIX. YÜAN LIN-CH'ÜAN WARE

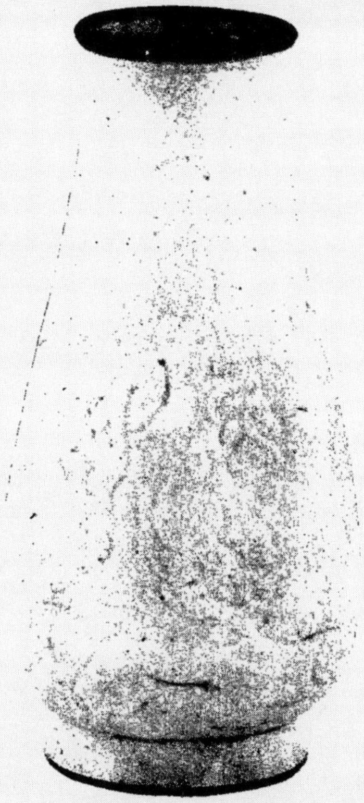

一一六

元臨川窯牙白劃花蟠螭靈芝小瓶一件(院)

原名定瓷暗花小瓶鑲有銅口帶木座座底刻乾隆御題詩注意乾隆認爲定窯口徑叁·貳公分·高拾壹·貳公分底徑叁·柒公分最大腹圍拾柒·壹公分

Porcelain No. 116.

Lin-ch'üan Ware of the Yüan Dynasty. Small p'ing (vase) of ya-pai (ivory white) decorated with coiled hornless dragons and ling-chih fungi incised in the paste. The rim is set with a brass band. With a wooden stand on the base of which is inscribed an ode composed by Ch'ien Lung. Note that Emperor Ch'ien Lung considered this to be a tan-p'ing of Ting Yao.

一一七

元臨川窯牙白劃花牡丹撇口小瓶一件(院)

原名白瓷小瓶。口徑叁·叁公分。高拾貳·伍公分。底徑叁·玖公分。最大腹圍拾玖公分。

Porcelain No. 117.

Lin-ch'üan Ware of the Yüan Dynasty. Small p'ing (vase) of ivory white, with flaring mouth and decoration of peonies incised in the paste.

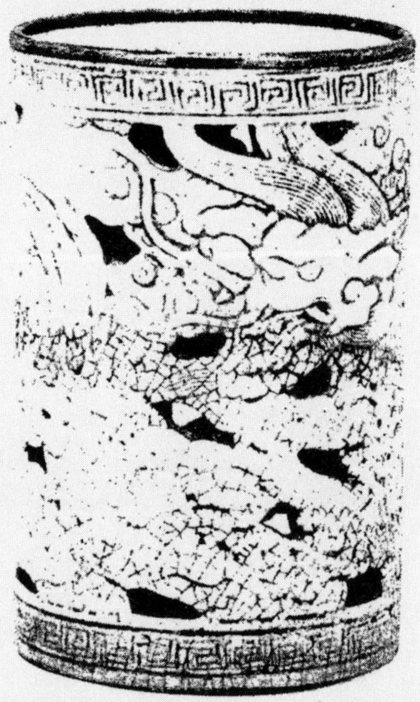

一一八

元臨川窯牙白鏤空龍鳳筆筒一件(院)

原名銅口白瓷筆筒。銅鍍金鑲口。有璺。口徑柒·柒公分。高拾貳·貳公分底徑柒·貳公分。

Porcelain No. 118.

Lin-ch'üan Ware of the Yüan Dynasty. Brush barrel of ya-pai (ivory white) decorated with dragon and phœnix carved in openwork. The rim is set with a gilded brass band.

元樞府窯

XX. YÜAN SHU-FU WARE

一一九

元樞府窯月白
印花纏枝番蓮
洗一件(院)

原名雨過天青暗
花瓷洗盤內口沿
有樞府二字暗款、
口徑拾貳公分高
肆·伍公分底徑叁·
捌公分。

Porcelain No. 119.

Shu-fu Ware of the Yüan Dynasty. Washer of yüeh-pai (moon white) with the moulded decoration of entwining sprays of Indian lotus.

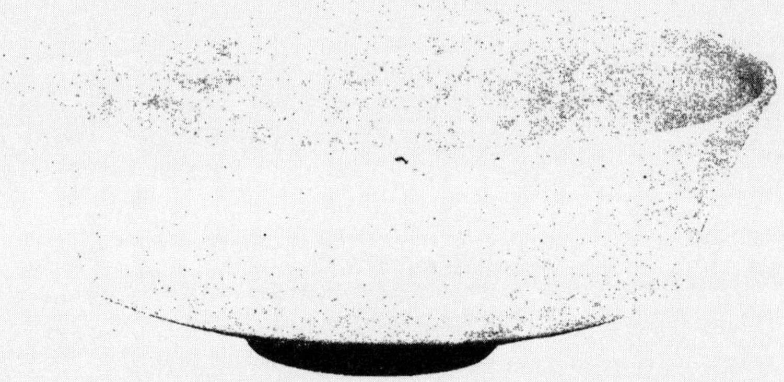

明瓷　明處州窯

PART II

I. MING CH'U-CHOU WARE

一二〇

明處州窯葱翠青錐拱蓮花大盌一件(院)

原名龍泉暗花大瓷盤有璺口徑叁拾叁公分高拾肆公分底徑拾叁·柒公分

Porcelain No. 120.

Ch'u-chou Ware of the Ming Dynasty. Large bowl of onion green with the decoration of lotus flowers "raised with an awl" (chui-kung).

一二一

明處州窯葱翠青壺(通稱玉壺春)一件(院)

原名冬青瓷膽瓶有微傷口徑捌·玖公分高叁拾·伍公分底徑拾·捌公分最大腹圍陸拾公分

Porcelain No. 121.

Ch'u-chou Ware of the Ming Dynasty. Hu (vase, commonly called yü-hu ch'un) in onion green.

一二二

明處州窯葱翠青蓋罐一件(院)

原名豆青瓷罐罐口有盤口徑拾壹公分通蓋高貳拾捌·叁公分底徑拾叁·捌公分最大腹圍陸拾叁·捌公分

Porcelain No. 122.

Ch'u-chou Ware of the Ming Dynasty. Covered jar (kai-kuan) in onion green.

一二三

明處州窯葱翠青錐拱雙魚洗一件(院)

原名龍泉釉大瓷盤口徑叁拾肆·捌公分高玖公分

Porcelain No. 123.

Ch'u-chou Ware of the Ming Dynasty. Washer in onion green with the decoration of two fish, "raised with an awl" (chui kung).

明德化窰

II. MING TÊ-HUA WARE

一二四

明德化窰瑩白雙貛紐方印一件（院）

原名瓷印角有微傷高伍·叁公分縱橫均伍·肆公分

Porcelain No. 124.

Tê-hua Yao of the Ming Dynasty. Square seal of ying-pai (pure white) with knob in the shape of a pair of badgers (huan).

明廣窰

III. MING KUANG-TUNG WARE

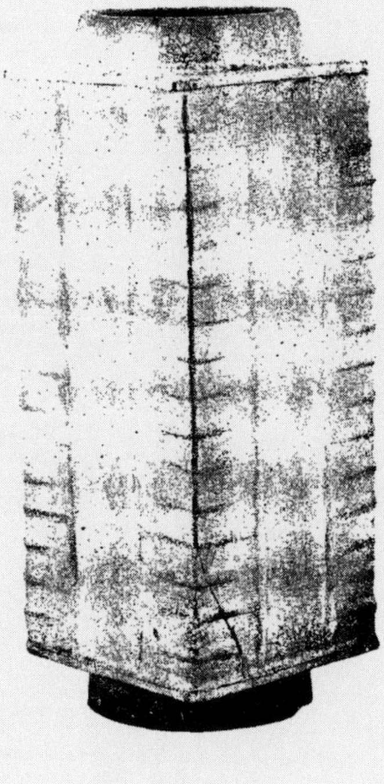

一二五

明廣窰月白琮式瓶一件（院）

原名白地青花瓶有傷口徑拾公分高叁拾叁·壹公分縱橫均拾貳·伍公分底徑拾·伍公分

Porcelain No. 125.

Kuang-tung Ware of the Ming Dynasty. P'ing (vase) in the shape of a tsung in yüeh-pai (moon white).

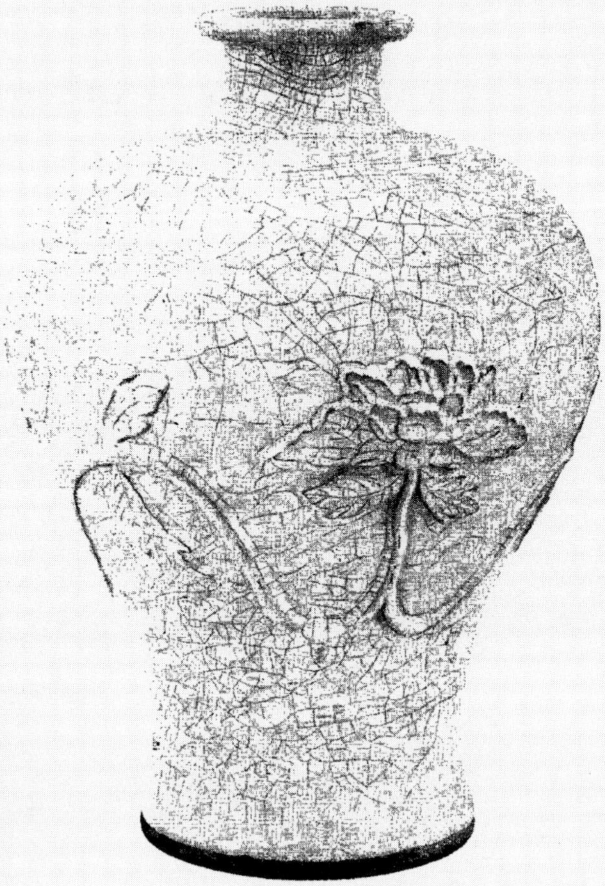

一二六

明廣窯月白彫鑲纏枝牡丹梅瓶一件（院）

原名白開片暗花瓶。足有微傷。口徑捌·陸公分。高叁拾肆·貳公分最大腹圍柒拾伍·陸公分底徑拾肆公分。

Porcelain No. 126.

Kuang-tung Ware of the Ming Dynasty. Mei-p'ing (vase) glazed in yüeh-pai (moon white) with the carved decoration of twining sprays of peonies attached thereto.

(103)

一二七

明廣窯天藍窯變鱔魚青方壺一件（院）

原名明廣窯方瓶口每邊捌·貳公分高貳拾陸·柒公分底每邊壹·叁公分最大腹闊陸拾壹公分

Porcelain No. 127.

Kuang-tung Ware of the Ming Dynasty. Square hu (vase) in t'ien-lan (sky blue) with furnace transmutation of eel blue. Engraved on the base are two characters "yu-chien."

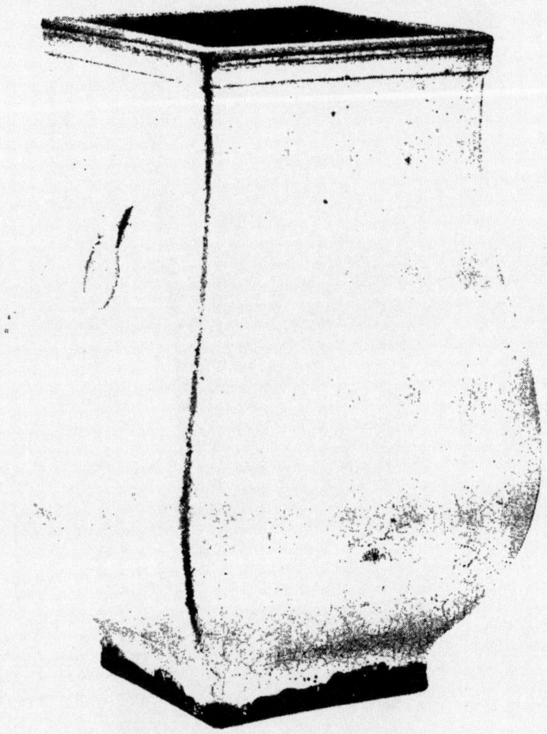

一二八

明廣窯月白影鑲獸環鈁一件(院)

原名仿宋瓷雙耳方尊.有傷.口縱橫均拾貳·伍公分高貳拾陸·叁公分最大腹圍陸拾叁公分底縱橫均玖·伍公分

Porcelain No. 128.

Kuang-tung Ware of the Ming Dynasty. Fang (vase, originally a quadrangular bronze vessel for measurement) in yüeh-pai (moon white) with animal-masks and rings carved and attached (tiao-hsiang).

明永樂窯

IV. MING YUNG LO WARE

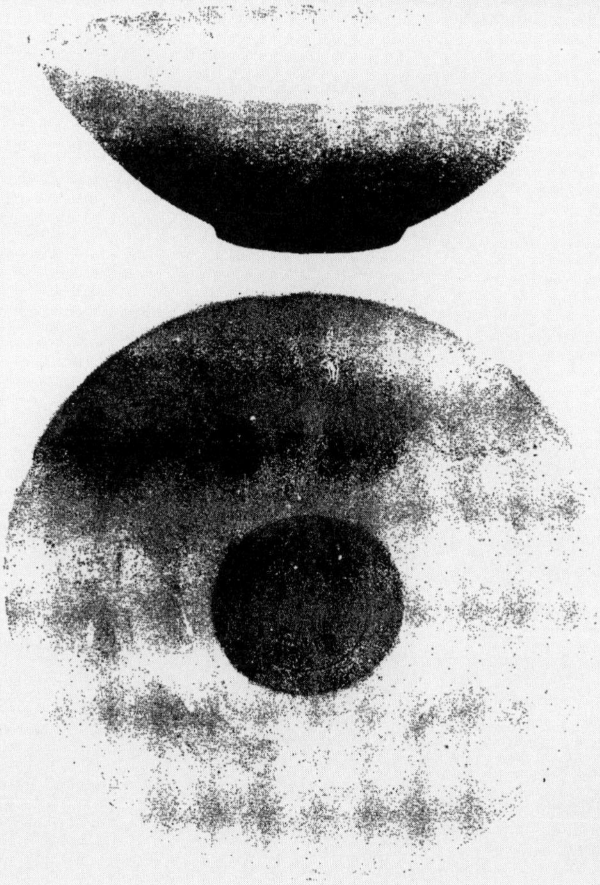

一二九

明永樂窯甜白半脫胎錐拱五龍葵瓣口盌一件(院)

原名永樂款塡白脫胎暗龍葵瓣瓷鏇盌盌裏有「永樂年製」四篆字暗款口徑貳拾·壹公分高陸·伍公分底徑陸·伍公分

Porcelain No. 129.

Yung Lo Ware of the Ming Dynasty. Pan t'o-t'ai (semi-bodiless) bowl of t'ien-pai (beautiful white), decorated with raised design of five dragons (chui-kung), and with rim shaped like an althaea flower. The finest specimen.

一三〇

明永樂窯甜白半脫胎錐拱雙龍小盌一件(院)

原名永樂款脫胎暗龍瓷茶鍾。鍾內有「永樂年製」四篆字暗款口徑玖·玖公分。高肆·捌公分底徑叁·玖公分強。

Porcelain No. 130.

Yung Lo Ware of the Ming Dynasty. Semi-bodiless bowl of t'ien-pai (beautiful white) with the decoration of a pair of dragons raised by chui-kung.

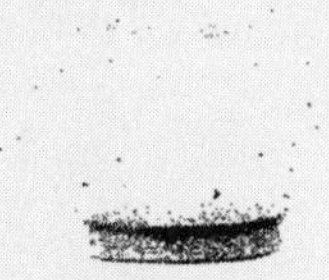

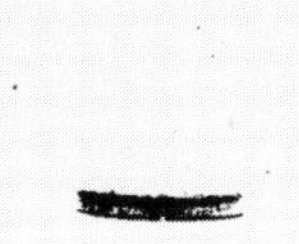

一三一

明永樂窯甜白半脫胎錐拱番蓮八寶撇口小盌一件（院）

原名永樂款脫胎暗花鐃式瓷茶鍾。鍾內有「永樂年製」四篆字暗款。口徑玖·柒公分高叁·柒公分底徑叁·伍公分

Porcelain No. 131.

Yung Lo Ware of the Ming Dynasty. Semi-bodiless everted-mouthed small bowl of t'ien-pai (beautiful white) with decoration of Indian lotus supporting eight Buddhist emblems.

一三二

明永樂窯甜白半脫胎錐拱雙龍高足盌一件（院）

原名永樂款塡白脫胎暗龍瓷靶盌口徑拾·玖公分。高玖·陸公分足徑叁·陸公分

Porcelain No. 132.

Yung Lo Ware of the Ming Dynasty. High-footed bowl of t'ien-pai (beautiful white) with the decoration of a pair of dragons raised by chui-kung.

一三三

明永樂窯甜白劃花番蓮八寶高足盌一件（院）

原名塡白暗花磬鈴靶盌盌內有「永樂年製」四篆字暗款口徑拾壹·柒公分高拾叁公分足徑伍·貳公分

Porcelain No. 133.

Yung Lo Ware of the Ming Dynasty. High-footed bowl of t'ien-pai (beautiful white) with incised designs of Indian lotus supporting eight Buddhist emblems.

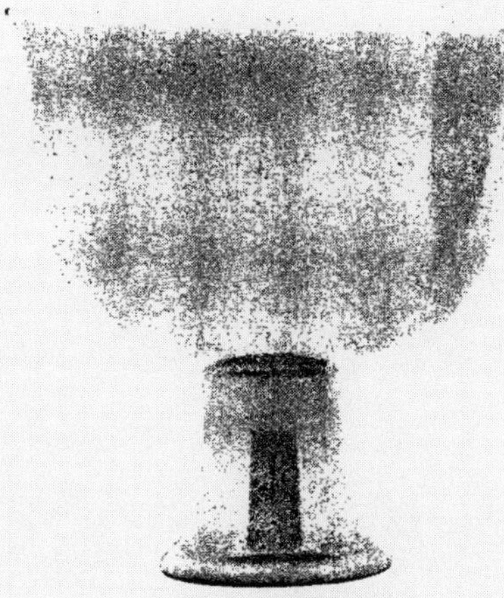

一三四

明永樂窯甜白劃花番蓮八寶高足盌一件(院)
原名填白暗花䓤鈴靶盌口徑拾壹·柒公分高拾叁公分足徑伍·貳公分

Porcelain No. 134.

Yung Lo Ware of the Ming Dynasty. High-footed bowl of t'ien-pai (beautiful white) with incised designs of Indian lotus supporting eight Buddhist emblems.

一三五

明永樂窯甜白錐拱葵花琖一件(院)
原名無款填白脫胎葵花式瓷茶鍾口徑玖·陸公分高肆·叁公分底徑叁·肆公分。

Porcelain No. 135.

Yung Lo Ware of the Ming Dynasty. Chan (cup) of t'ien-pai (beautiful white) in the shape of an althæa flower, worked by chui-kung (raised with an awl).

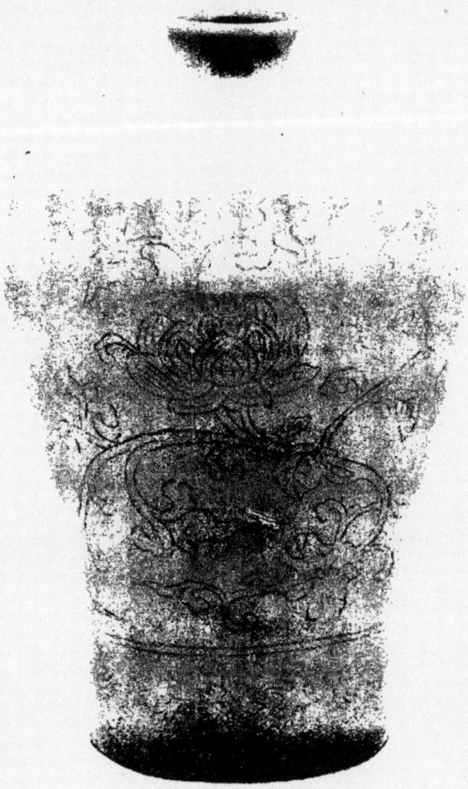

一三六

明永樂窯甜白剔花纏枝蓮梅瓶一件（院）

原名填白暗花瓶口徑肆·叁公分，高貳拾伍貳公分，底徑拾公分最大腹圍肆拾捌·陸公分。

Porcelain No. 136.

Yung Lo Ware of the Ming Dynasty. Mei-p'ing (vase for the prunus) of t'ien-pai (beautiful white) with the incised designs of twining sprays of lotus blossoms.

一三七

明永樂窯甜白三繫把壺一件(院)

原名白瓷茶壺。帶木座。口徑肆公分。通把高拾壹·壹公分。底徑拾貳·玖公分。通嘴把長拾玖·肆公分。

Porcelain No. 137.

Yung Lo Ware of the Ming Dynasty. Handled pot with three loops for suspension, glazed in t'ien-pai (beautiful white). With a wooden stand.

一三八

明永樂窯祭紅錐拱雙龍戲珠高足盌一件(院)

原名霽紅高足盌。盌裏有「永樂年製」四篆字暗款口徑拾陸·肆公分。高拾·肆公分。底徑肆·壹公分注意祭紅創於是時。

Porcelain No. 138.

Yung Lo Ware of the Ming Dynasty. High-footed bowl of chi-hung (sacrificial red) with the raised (chui-kung) decoration of a pair of dragons sporting with a pearl. Note that wares of sacrificial red were first made at this time.

一三九

明永樂窯翠青三繫蓋罐一件(院)

原名冬青三喜蓋罐。口徑捌·柒公分。通蓋高玖·伍公分最大腹圍肆拾玖·伍公分。底徑拾貳·叁公分。

Porcelain No. 139.

Yung Lo Ware of the Ming Dynasty. Covered jar (kai-kuan) in kingfisher green with three fastening loops.

(111)

明宣德窰

V. MING HSÜAN TÊ WARE

一四〇

明宣德窰寶石紅小盌一件(院)

原名宣紅瓷盌底有大明宣德年製六字暗款口徑拾·壹公分高伍·伍公分底徑肆·貳公分

Porcelain No. 140.

Hsüan Tê Ware of the Ming Dynasty. Small bowl of ruby red.

一四一

明宣德窰寶石紅小盌一件(院)

原名宣紅瓷盌口徑拾·貳公分高伍·肆公分。底徑肆·貳公分

Porcelain No. 141.

Hsüan Tê Ware of the Ming Dynasty. Small bowl of ruby red.

一四二

明宣德窯寶石紅撇口盌一件(院)

原名宣霽瓷盌。底刻乾隆御題詩。口徑貳拾·肆公分。高柒·肆公分底徑捌·玖公分。

Porcelain No. 142.

Hsüan Tê Ware of the Ming Dynasty. Bowl with flaring mouth in pao-shih hung (ruby red). On the base is inscribed an ode composed by Emperor Ch'ien Lung.

一四三

明宣德窯寶石紅菊瓣盌一件(院)

原名霽紅帶輪瓷盌帶木座鑲銅口有微傷口徑拾捌·捌公分。高捌·陸公分。底徑捌·柒公分。

Porcelain No. 143.

Hsüan Tê Ware of the Ming Dynasty. Bowl of pao-shih hung (ruby red) fashioned in the shape of chrysanthemum petals. With a copper rim and a wooden stand.

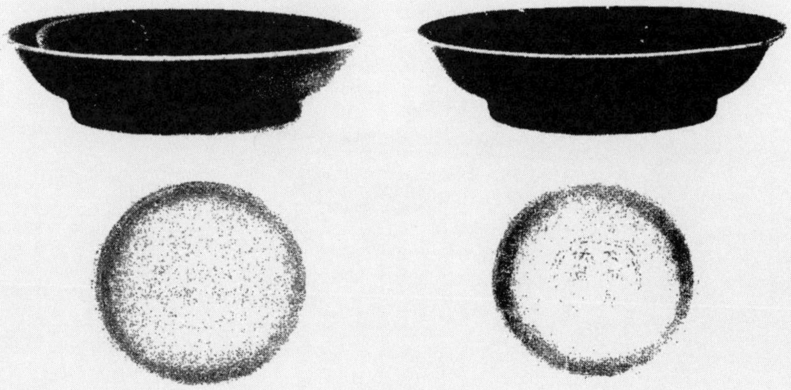

一四四

明宣德窯寶石紅碟二件(院)

原名宣德款霽紅瓷盤。底均有「大明宣德年製」六楷字暗款。口徑均拾伍公分高叁·捌公分。底徑玖·壹公分。

Porcelain No. 144.

Hsüan Tê Ware of the Ming Dynasty. Dishes of pao-shih hung (ruby red). Two pieces.

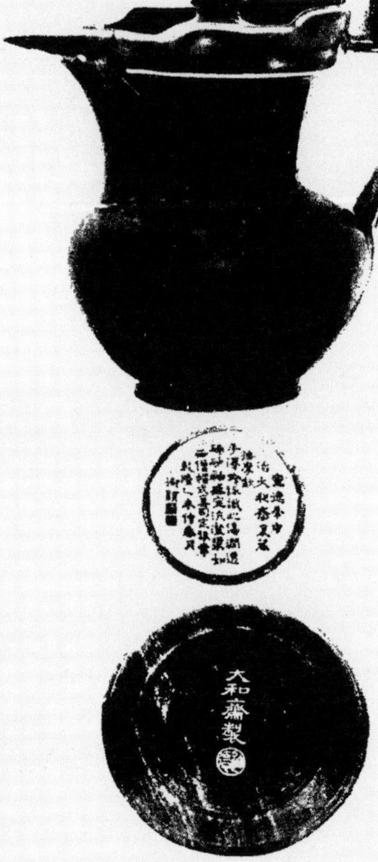

一四五

明宣德窯寶石紅僧帽壺一件(院)

原名宣德硃砂釉單耳壺底刻乾隆御題詩帶蓋蓋帶套套有玉扣帶木座座上刻「太和齋藏」下刻「雍邸清玩」並乾隆御題詩口縱拾壹·壹公分通嘴把橫貳拾·貳公分通蓋頂高拾玖·貳公分、底徑柒·肆公分、最大腹圍肆拾叁·伍公分。

Porcelain No. 145.

Hsüan Tê Ware of the Ming Dynasty. Hu (pitcher) in ruby red, with mouth shaped in the form of a priest's hat. On the base is inscribed an ode composed by Ch'ien Lung. With a wooden stand on the upper part of which is inscribed "Tai Ho Chai tsang" (in the collection of Tai Ho Chai) and on the under part "Yung Ti ch'ing-wan" (for the Yung Principality to take delight in)—Tai Ho Chai being the study of Prince Yung before he became enthroned as Emperor Yung Chêng—and the same ode of Ch'ien Lung.

一四六

明宣德窯寶石紅三足圓爐一件(院)

原名郎窯嵌玉木蓋爐帶玉頂木蓋玉頂腔下有傷口徑拾壹·伍公分高陸·捌公分底徑陸·柒公分。

Porcelain No. 146.

Hsüan Tê Ware of the Ming Dynasty. Round tripedal incense burner in pao-shih hung (ruby red). With repaired lip.

一四七

明宣德窯寶石紅印泥盒一件(院)

原名霽紅瓷盒帶木座座有傷口徑玖·陸公分通蓋高伍·柒公分底徑伍·伍公分。

Porcelain No. 147.

Hsüan Tê Ware of the Ming Dynasty. Seal vermilion box of pao-shih hung (ruby red). With a wooden stand.

一四八

明宣德窯寶石紅爆竹式花插一件(院)

原名霽紅一統瓷花插口徑壹·伍公分高拾肆·肆公分底徑肆·肆公分

Porcelain No. 148.

Hsüan Tê Ware of the Ming Dynasty. Flower receptacle (hua-ch'a) shaped like a fire-cracker made of bamboo, in pao-shih hung (ruby red).

(116)

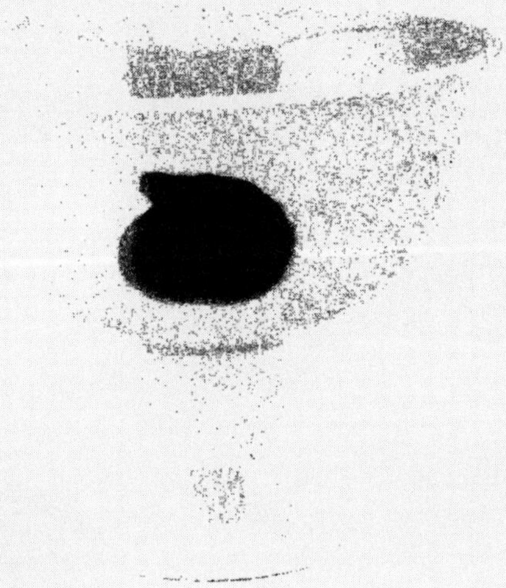

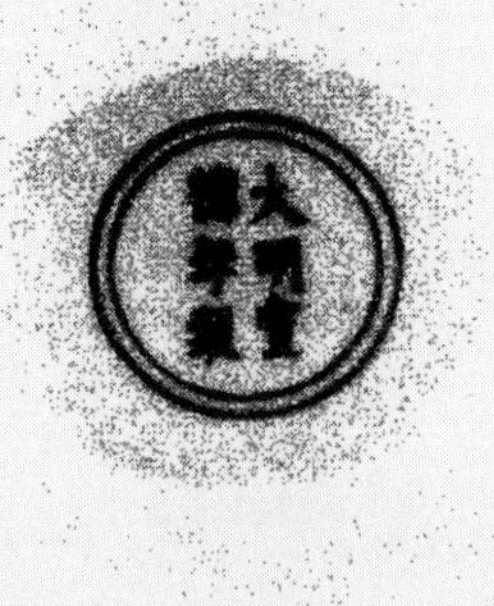

一四九

明宣德窯㴭裏鮮紅三果高足盌一件(院)

原名瓊白甆寳燒三菓靶盌盌內有「大明宣德年製」六字楷款，
口徑拾壹·陸公分高拾·貳公分底徑肆·伍公分

Porcelain No. 149.

Hsüan Tê Ware of the Ming Dynasty. High-footed bowl, decorated with three fruits in under-glaze fresh red (hsien-hung).

一五〇

明宣德窰青花泑裏紅趕珠龍合盌一件(院)

原名宣窰紅龍合盌盌內及蓋內均有「大明宣德年製」六字楷款盌口及蓋邊均有傷口徑拾柒·伍公分通蓋高拾伍公分底徑捌·玖公分

Porcelain No. 150.

Hsüan Tê Ware of the Ming Dynasty. Covered bowl decorated with pearl-chasing dragons in under-glaze blue and fresh red.

一五一

明宣德窯祭紅錐拱蓮瓣滷壺一件(院)

原名宣德紅藍瓷壺底有「大明宣德年製」六字楷款帶嵌牙木座口徑貳·捌公分通蓋頂高拾·陸公分底徑柒·壹公分

Porcelain No. 151.

Hsüan Tê Ware of the Ming Dynasty. Sauce-pot of chi-hung (or sacrificial red), decorated with lotus petals, raised by an awl (or chui-kung).

一五二

明宣德窯霽青錐拱蓮瓣滷壺一件(院)

原名宣德紅藍瓷壺底有「大明宣德年製」六字楷款帶嵌牙木座口徑貳·捌公分通蓋頂高拾·陸公分底徑柒·壹公分

Porcelain No. 152.

Hsüan Tê Ware of the Ming Dynasty. Sauce-pot of chi-ch'ing (or the blue of the sky after rain), decorated with lotus petals, raised with an awl (or chui-kung).

一五三

明宣德窯洳裏鮮紅纏枝石榴瓶一件(院)

原名白地紫花瓷花瓶口有微傷口徑肆·壹公分。高叁拾叁·壹公分底徑拾·叁公分最大腹圍伍拾伍·捌公分

Porcelain No. 153.

Hsüan Tê Ware of the Ming Dynasty. P'ing (vase) decorated with twining sprays of pomegranate blossoms in under-glaze fresh red.

一五四

明宣德窯洳裏鮮白澤(神獸)貫耳壺一件(院)

原名宣窯紅獸雙管瓶底款油紅楷書大明宣德年製六字楷款帶木座口有傷口縱伍·柒公分橫柒·捌公分高拾伍·壹公分底縱陸·玖公分橫玖·貳公分最大腹圍叁拾·肆公分

Porcelain No. 154.

Hsüan Tê Ware of the Ming Dynasty. Hu (vase) with "piercing handles" (kuan-erh), decorated with two pai-tze (legendary beasts) in under-glaze fresh red. With a wooden stand. Note that the date mark is in oil red of the characters "Ta Ming Hsüan Tê nien chih" or made in the year of Hsüan Tê of the Great Ming.

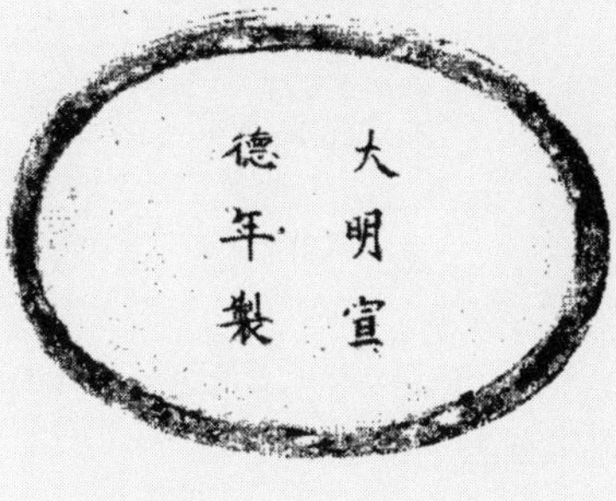

(120)

一五五

明宣德窰青花纏枝牡丹大盌一件（院）

原名白地青花大瓷盌底有「大明宣德年製」六字楷款口徑貳拾柒公分高拾叁·陸公分底徑拾叁·陸公分

Porcelain No. 155.

Hsüan Tê Ware of the Ming Dynasty. Large bowl decorated with twining sprays of peonies in under-giaze blue. With a wooden stand.

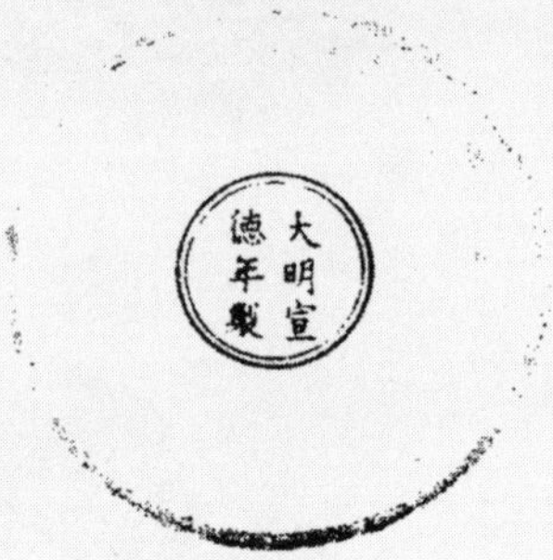

一五六

明宣德窰青花纏枝牡丹甒一件（院）

原名白地藍花瓷罇通蓋高叁拾陸·柒公分口徑伍公分底徑拾貳公分最大腹圍陸拾肆·叁公分注意酒器

Porcelain No. 156.

Hsüan Tê Ware of the Ming Dynasty. Wu (wine vessel with cover) with decoration of interlacing sprays of peonies in under-glaze blue.

一五七

明宣德窰青花纏枝花卉執壺一件(院)

原名白地青花無蓋瓷執壺帶瓷蓋口徑柒·叁公分通蓋高叁拾陸·肆公分底徑拾壹·肆公分最大腹圍伍拾柒公分

Porcelain No. 157.

Hsüan Tê Ware of the Ming Dynasty. Chih-hu (beverage vessel with handle for ritual use) decorated with twining sprays of flowers in under-glaze blue.

一五八

明宣德窰青花纏枝番蓮絃文三足爐一件(院)

原名宣德年製白地青花瓷玉頂木蓋爐口沿有「大明宣德年製」六字楷款帶木座口徑拾肆·捌公分，通木蓋玉頂高拾捌公分底徑拾肆·貳公分。

Porcelain No. 158.

Hsüan Tê Ware of the Ming Dynasty. Tripedal incense burner decorated with "bowstring" fillets and twining sprays of Indian lotus in under-glaze blue.

一五九

明宣德窯青花纏枝番蓮鏤空花薰一件（院）

原名白地藍花高足帶蓋瓷爐爐蓋均有𨻶通蓋高肆拾公分。口徑拾柒·叁公分底徑拾叁·伍公分.

Porcelain No. 159.

Hsüan Tê Ware of the Ming Dynasty. Hua-hsün (flower perfumer) with openwork decoration of twining sprays of Indian lotus in under-glaze blue.

（123）

一六〇

明宣德窯青花纏枝蓮鉢式缸一件(院)
原名青花白地鉢式瓷缸口徑貳拾叁·壹公分高拾叁·貳公分。
底徑玖·捌公分

Porcelain No. 160.

Hsüan Tê Ware of the Ming Dynasty. Jar (kang) in the shape of a patra decorated with twining sprays of lotus in under-glaze blue.

一六一

明宣德窯青花纏枝花卉圓洗一件(院)
原名白地青花瓷洗口徑貳拾陸·陸公分。高拾貳·貳公分底徑
拾玖公分

Porcelain No. 161.

Hsüan Tê Ware of the Ming Dynasty. Round washer decorated with twining sprays of flowers in under-glaze blue.

一六二

明宣德窯沕裏鮮紅三友(竹石芭蕉)壺(通稱玉壺春)一件(院)

原名宣德款鮮紅玉壺春瓶，底有「大明宣德年製」六字楷款，口徑玖·叁公分，長叁拾壹·捌公分，底徑拾貳·柒公分，最大腹圍陸拾叁·肆公分

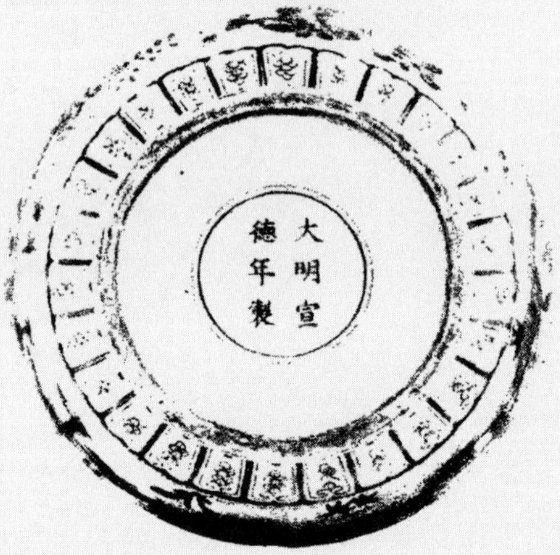

Porcelain No. 162.

Hsüan Tê Ware of the Ming Dynasty. Hu (vase, commonly called yü-hu ch'un) with decoration of three friends (i.e. bamboo, rocks and bananas) in under-glaze fresh red.

明成化窯

VI. MING CH'ÊNG HUA WARE

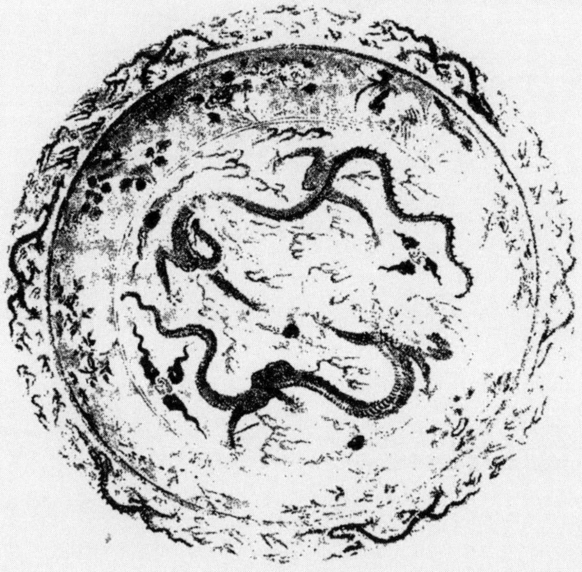

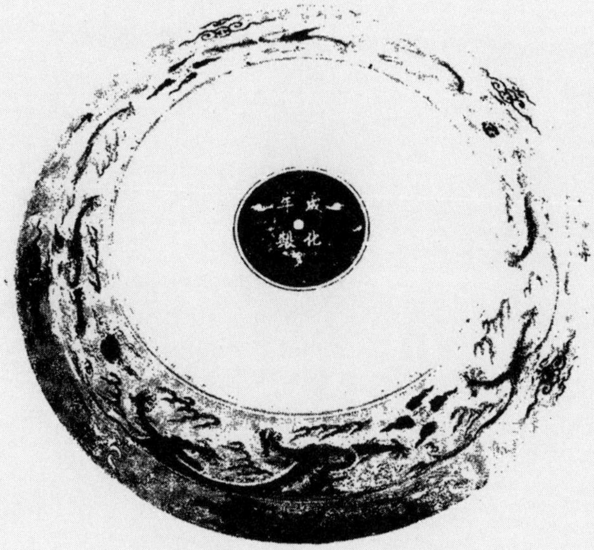

一六三

明成化窯紫地五彩

雲龍大盤一件(院)

原名紫地綫龍三彩大

瓷盤底有成化年製四

字楷款口徑肆拾柒公

分高柒肆公分底徑貳

拾伍捌公分

Porcelain No. 163.

Ch'êng Hua Ware of the Ming Dynasty. Large plate decorated with yün-lung (clouds and dragons) in variegated enamels over a purple ground.

(126)

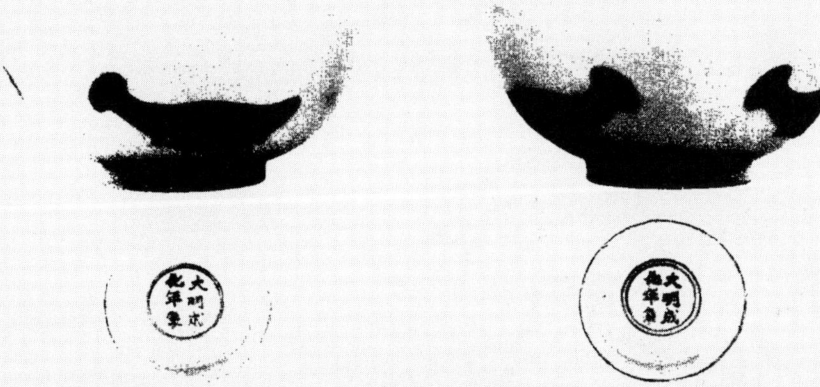

一六四

明成化窯詩裏鮮紅三魚大盌二件(院)

原名白地紅魚大完盌底均有大明成化年製六字楷款口徑均貳拾·柒公分高玖·貳公分底徑捌公分

Porcelain No. 164.

Ch'êng Hua Ware of the Ming Dynasty. Pair of large bowls decorated with three fish in under-glaze fresh red.

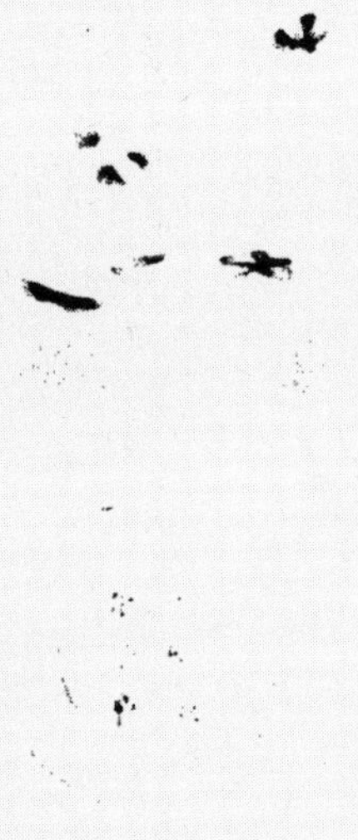

一六五

明成化窯半脫胎青花鬬彩梅蝶葵瓣口盌一件(院)

原名成化款填白脫胎五彩花蝶葵瓣完鏇盌底有大明成化年製六字楷款口徑拾伍·玖公分高伍·伍公分底徑肆·柒公分

Porcelain No. 165.

Ch'êng Hua Ware of the Ming Dynasty. Semi-bodiless (pan t'o-t'ai) bowl, with rim shaped like althaea petals, and decoration of the prunus and butterflies in under-glaze blue and enamels in contrasting colours.

一六六

明成化窰半脫胎青花鬬彩梅蝶葵瓣口盌一件(院)

原名成化款填白脫胎五彩花蝶葵瓣瓷鏇盌、口徑拾伍·叁公分高伍·貳公分底徑肆·陸公分

Porcelain No. 166.

Ch'êng Hua Ware of the Ming Dynasty. Semi-bodiless (pan t'o-t'ai) bowl, with rim shaped like althaea petals, and decoration of the prunus and butterflies in under-glaze blue and enamels in contrasting colours.

一六七

明成化窰青花鬬彩鴛鴦臥蓮盌一件(院)

原名成化款帶木座彩花瓷盌底有大明成化年製六字楷款口徑拾陸·叁公分高柒·壹公分底徑拾·伍公分

Porcelain No. 167.

Ch'êng Hua Ware of the Ming Dynasty. Bowl with decoration in under-glaze blue and enamels of contrasting colours of mandarin ducks resting amidst lotus flowers— yüan-yang wo-lien.

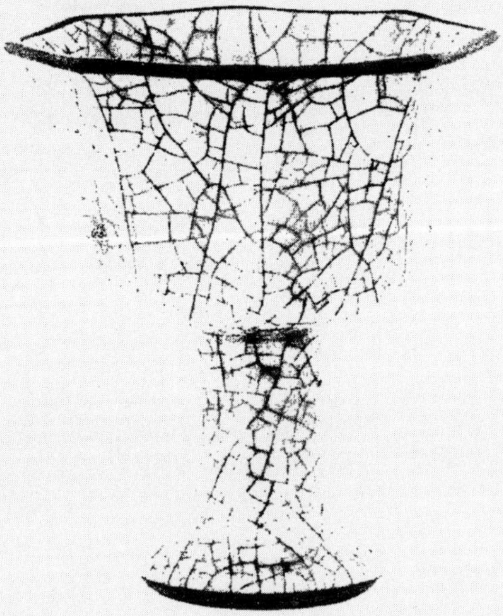

一六八

明成化窯仿哥淺青八方高足桮一件(院)

原名哥瓷淨水碗。底有「大明成化年製」六字楷款口有傷。口徑柒·捌公分高玖·肆公分底徑叁·柒公分

Porcelain No. 168.

Ch'êng Hua Ware of the Ming Dynasty. Octagonal high-stemmed cup, of ch'ien-ch'ing (light blue) modelled after a Ko ware.

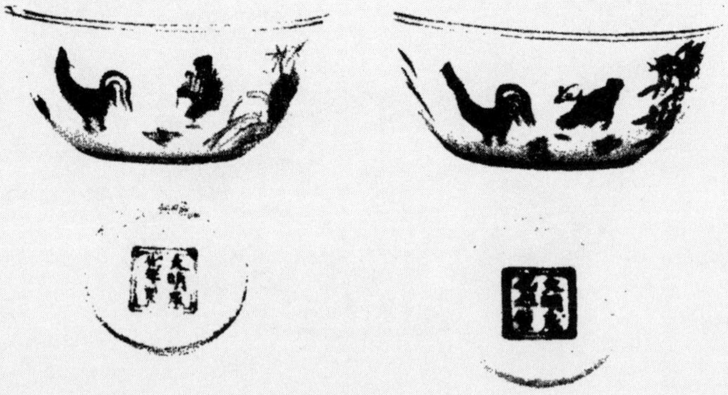

一六九

明成化窯青花鬬彩雞桮二件(院)

原名成化瓷雞缸底有「大明成化年製」六字楷款帶木架架上有乾隆御題口徑均捌·貳公分高叁·捌公分足徑壹爲叁·肆公分壹爲叁·陸公分

Porcelain No. 169.

Ch'êng Hua Ware of the Ming Dynasty. Pair of cups decorated with chickens in underglaze blue and enamels of contrasting colours. Two pieces. With a wooden tea-poy, on the top of which are inlaid with silver characters, being a song composed by Emperor Ch'ien Lung.

一七〇

明成化窯青花鬭彩雞桮二件(院)

原名成化瓷雞缸·底有「大明成化年製」六字楷款帶木座壹件口徑均柒·陸公分高叁·伍公分足徑叁·壹公分·

Porcelain No. 170.

Ch'êng Hua Ware of the Ming Dynasty. Pair of cups decorated with chickens in under-glaze blue and enamels of contrasting colours. Two pieces. With a stand in the form of a wooden tray.

一七一

明成化窯青花鬭彩雞缸桮二件(院)

原名五彩雞缸酒圓底均有「大明成化年製」六字楷款壹件口徑陸·叁公分高肆·捌公分底徑貳·玖公分壹件口徑陸·肆公分高肆·柒公分底徑貳·玖公分

Porcelain No. 171.

Ch'êng Hua Ware of the Ming Dynasty. Pairs of cups in the shape of jars with decoration of chickens in under-glaze blue and enamels of contrasting colours. Two pieces.

一七二

明成化窯油紅雙龍桮二件(院)

原名成化款白地紅龍瓷酒盃底均有大明成化年製六字楷款帶木座座底刻乾隆御玩四字口徑均陸公分高肆公分底徑貳伍公分

Porcelain No. 172.

Ch'êng Hua Ware of the Ming Dynasty. Pair of cups decorated with double dragons in yu-hung (oil red). Two pieces.

一七三

明成化窯青花油紅番蓮桮二件(院)

原名明成化款白地鈎蓮瓷盅底均有大明成化年製六字楷款帶木座口徑均捌·叁公分高肆·叁公分底徑叁·壹公分

Porcelain No. 173.

Ch'êng Hua Ware of the Ming Dynasty. Pair of cups decorated with Indian lotus in under-glaze blue and yu-hung (oil red). Two pieces.

一七四

明成化窯仿定青花雲龍小瓶一件(陸)
原名成化款白地青龍尊底有成化年製四字楷款口徑叁·叁公分高拾柒·肆公分最大腹圍貳拾叁公分底徑伍·肆公分

Porcelain No. 174.

Ch'êng Hua Ware of the Ming Dynasty. Small p'ing (vase) decorated with clouds and dragons in under-glaze blue, after the fashion of a Ting ware.

(132)

明弘治窯

VII. MING HUNG CHIH WARE

一七五

明弘治窯嬌黃地錐花綠彩趕珠龍高足盌一件（院）

原名黃地綠龍高足瓷盤盤內有弘治年製四字篆款.口有微傷口徑拾伍·陸公分.高拾·肆公分.足徑肆·叁公分

Porcelain No. 175.

Hung Chih Ware of the Ming Dynasty. High-footed bowl with the decoration of pearl-chasing dragons worked with an awl (chui) in green enamel over a lemon ground.

明嘉靖窯

VIII. MING CHIA CHING WARE

一七六

明嘉靖窯回青小盌一件(院)

原名霽青酒圓銅口口徑拾壹·捌公分高伍公分底徑貳·捌公分

Porcelain No. 176.

Chia Ching Ware of the Ming Dynasty. Small bowl in Mohammedan blue.

一七七

明嘉靖窯回青小盌一件(院)

原名霽青酒圓銅口口徑拾壹·捌公分高伍公分底徑貳·捌公分

Porcelain No. 177.

Chia Ching Ware of the Ming Dynasty. Small bowl in Mohammedan blue.

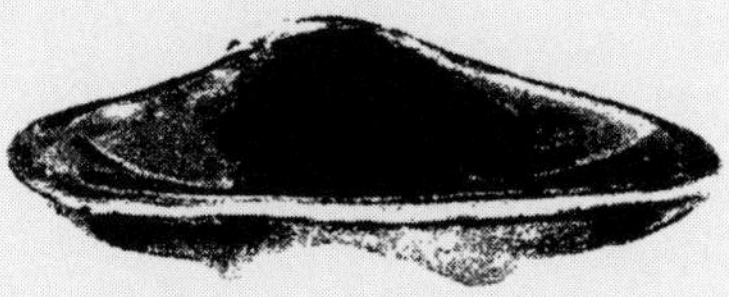

一七八

明嘉靖窯回青蚌式小筆洗一件(院)

原名帶雕座蚌殼式瓷水盂座傷橫拾·捌公分縱捌·伍公分高叁·伍公分

Porcelain No. 178.

Chia Ching Ware of the Ming Dynasty. Small brush-washer in the shape of a clam-shell (pêng) in Mohammedan blue. With a wooden stand.

一七九

明嘉靖窯青花鬬彩纏枝蓮方葫蘆小瓶一件(院)

原名嘉靖彩花小瓷瓶。底有「大明嘉靖年製」六字楷款帶木座。口縱橫均零玖公分高捌·捌公分底徑縱橫均貳叁公分

Porcelain No. 179.

Chia Ching Ware of the Ming Dynasty. Small p'ing (vase) fashioned in the form of a square double-gourd and decorated with twining sprays of lotus blossoms in under-glaze blue and enamels of contrasting colours. With a wooden stand.

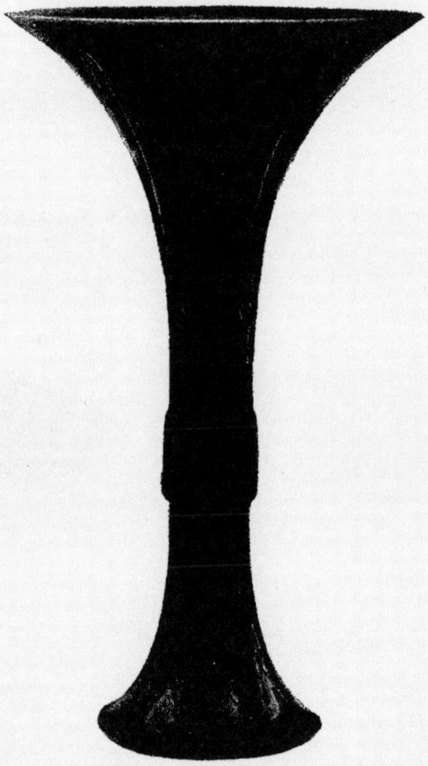

一八〇

明嘉靖窯孔雀綠錐拱蕉葉方夔雷文觚一件(院)

原名綠釉暗花觚。口徑拾陸·玖公分。高叁拾·壹公分底徑捌·柒公分

Porcelain No. 180.

Chia Ching Ware of the Ming Dynasty. Ku (vase) in peacock green decorated with banana leaves, square one-footed dragons and thunder scrolls carved in relief (chui-kung). Note that this is the finest specimen.

一八一

明嘉靖窯青花雲龍繩耳三足爐一件(院)

原名大明青龍爐、口沿有「大明嘉靖年製」六字楷款帶玉頂木蓋壹耳有傷口徑拾·伍公分通耳高拾·壹公分最大腹圍肆拾壹·伍公分

Porcelain No. 181.

Chia Ching Ware of the Ming Dynasty. Tripedal incense burner with rope-shaped handles, decorated with clouds and dragons in under-glaze blue.

(136)

明隆慶窯

IX. MING LUNG CH'ING WARE

一八二

明隆慶窯青花雲龍提梁壺一件(院)

原名白地青花提梁瓷壺，底有大明隆慶年造六字楷款，原傷，口徑拾壹·壹公分，通梁高叁拾壹·捌公分，底徑拾伍·壹公分。

Porcelain No. 182.

Lung Ch'ing Ware of the Ming Dynasty. Hu (pot) with over-top handle (t'i-liang) decorated with clouds and dragons in under-glaze blue.

一八三

明隆慶窯青花雲龍銀錠式盒 一件(院)

原名白地藍龍銀錠式瓷盒底有大明隆慶年造六字楷款蓋底均有裂痕最長貳拾貳·壹公分最寬叁拾·捌公分通蓋高捌·貳公分

Porcelain No. 183.

Lung Ch'ing Ware of the Ming Dynasty. Ho (box) in the shape of a silver ingot, with decoration of yün-lung (clouds and dragons) in under-glaze blue. Cracks on lower portion.

明 萬 厤 窯

X. MING WAN LI WARE

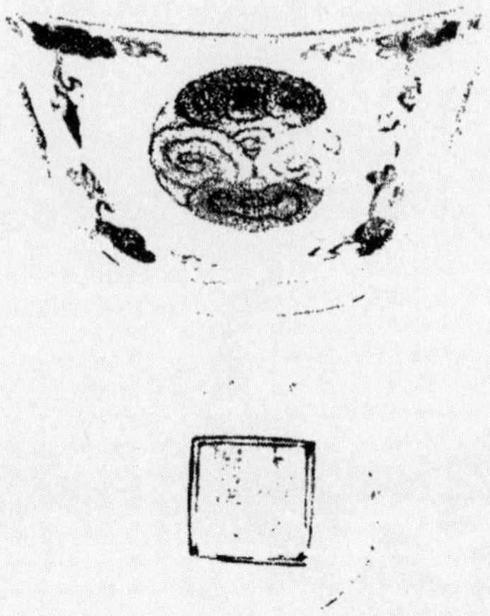

一八四

明萬厤窯青花鬬彩凌雲桮一件（院）

原名萬窯青轉枝蓮白裏瓷酒圓底有「大明萬厤年製」六字楷款口徑柒·伍公分。高肆·柒公分。底徑叁·伍公分。

Porcelain No. 184.

Wan Li Ware of the Ming Dynasty. Cup decorated with soaring clouds in under-glaze blue and enamels of contrasting colours.

一八五

明萬厤窯青花鬬彩凌雲桮一件（院）

原名萬窯青轉枝蓮白裏瓷酒圓底有「大明萬厤年製」六字楷款口徑柒·伍公分高肆·柒公分底徑叁·伍公分。

Porcelain No. 185.

Wan Li Ware of the Ming Dynasty. Cup decorated with soaring clouds in under-glaze blue and enamels of contrasting colours.

一八六

明萬曆窯青花人物六稜提梁壺一件(院)

原名大明青人大角瓷壺底有大明萬曆年製六字楷款蓋頂有傷口縱柒公分橫陸·壹公分通把高貳拾貳·伍公分底縱捌·伍公分橫柒玖公分

Porcelain No. 186.

Wan Li Ware of the Ming Dynasty. Liu-lêng hu (hexagonal pot) with over-top handle (t'i-liang) and under-glaze blue decoration of human figures.

明景德鎮窯

XI. MING CHING-TÊ CHÊN WARE

一八七

明景德鎮窯仿定瑩白錐拱天雞尊一件(院)

原名白瓷鳳拾艦口徑柒·叁公分高貳拾肆·壹公分

Porcelain No. 187.

Ching-tê Chên Ware of the Ming Dynasty. Tsun (vase) of ying-pai (pure white) in the shape of a t'ien-chi (pheasant) by chui-kung, modelled after a Ting piece.

一八八

明景德鎮窯彫塡綠彩趕珠龍壺(通稱玉壺春)
·件(院)

原名白地綠龍瓷膽瓶底有𥂕口徑捌·伍公分高叁拾叁·叁公分底徑拾·柒公分最大腹圍陸拾公分。

Porcelain No. 188.

Ching-tê Chên Ware of the Ming Dynasty. Hu (vase of the shape commonly called yü-hu ch'un) decorated with pearl-pursuing dragons carved and filled in with green enamel.

明周窯

XII. MING CHOU WARE

一八九

明周窯嬌黃錐拱饕餮鼎一件(陸)

原名黃瓷爐通耳高拾陸·貳公分口徑拾叁·伍公分足高陸·柒公分

Porcelain No. 189.

Chou Ware of the Ming Dynasty. Ting (tripod) of lemon colour, with the raised (chui-kung) decoration of t'ao-t'ieh (avaricious and gluttonous ogres).

明壺公窯

XIII. MING HU-KUNG WARE

一九〇

明壺公窯嬌黃凸彫九龍方盂一件(院)

原名黃瓷方花囊。帶銅鑲木座。口有鈞爾陶分文爾寶龍函潤珠燿東璧萬曆年吳爲製貳拾字。口縱橫均伍·柒公分。高叁·捌公分。底徑縱橫均肆·柒公分。

Porcelain No. 190.

Hu-kung Ware of the Ming Dynasty. Fang-yu (square water-pot) of lemon colour decorated with nine dragons carved in relief. With a wooden stand.

清瓷

清康熙窯

PART III

I. CH'ING K'ANG HSI WARE

一九一

清康熙窯甜白半脫胎錐拱番蓮八寶葵瓣口盌一件（碗）

原名康熙脫胎葵瓣鏡盌盌裏有「大清康熙年製」六篆字暗款。口原有微傷口徑貳拾公分高陸·貳公分底徑陸公分。

Porcelain No. 191.

K'ang Hsi Ware of the Ch'ing Dynasty. Semi-bodiless (pan t'o-t'ai) bowl of beautiful white (t'ien-pai) with rim shaped like althaa petals, and raised decoration (chui-kung) of Indian lotus supporting eight Buddhist emblems. Note that there is a slight damage to the rim.

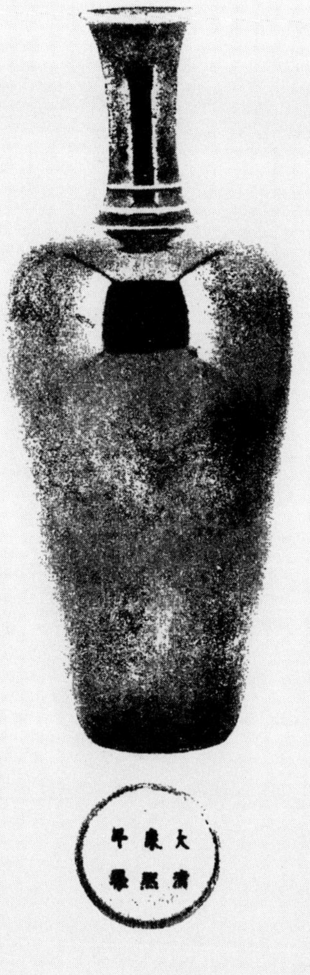

一九二

清康熙窰鮮紅萊菔尊(通稱豇豆紅)一件(院)
原名霽紅瓷小長瓶附木座底有「大清康熙年製」六字楷款口徑叁·貳公分高貳拾·貳公分底徑叁·玖公分最大腹圍貳拾伍·貳公分

Porcelain No. 192.

K'ang Hsi Ware of the Ch'ing Dynasty. Tsun (vase) in the shape of a turnip in hsien-hung (fresh red, commonly called chiang-tou hung or the red of the fresh small kidney-bean). With a wooden stand.

(146)

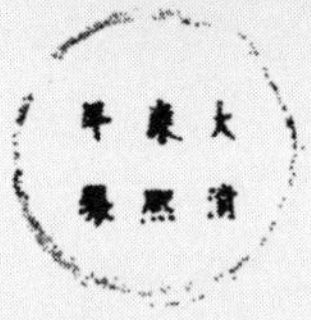

一九三

清康熙窯鮮紅萊菔尊(通稱豇豆紅)一件(院)

原名霽紅小長瓷瓶附木座底有「大清康熙年製」六字楷款。口有唇口徑叁·壹公分。高貳拾·貳公分底徑叁·捌公分最大腹圍貳拾伍·捌公分

Porcelain No. 193.

K'ang Hsi Ware of the Ch'ing Dynasty. Tsun (vase) shaped like a turnip in hsien-hung (fresh red, commonly called chiang-tou hung or bean red). With a wooden stand.

一九四

清康熙窰青花魚龍變化大圓洗一件（院）

原名康熙款白地青魚龍面盆底有「大清康熙年製」六字楷款，
口徑連邊叁拾玖公分高柒·叁公分底徑貳拾捌·貳公分

Porcelain No. 194.

K'ang Hsi Ware of the Ch'ing Dynasty. Large round washer decorated with "fish turning into dragon" in under-glaze blue.

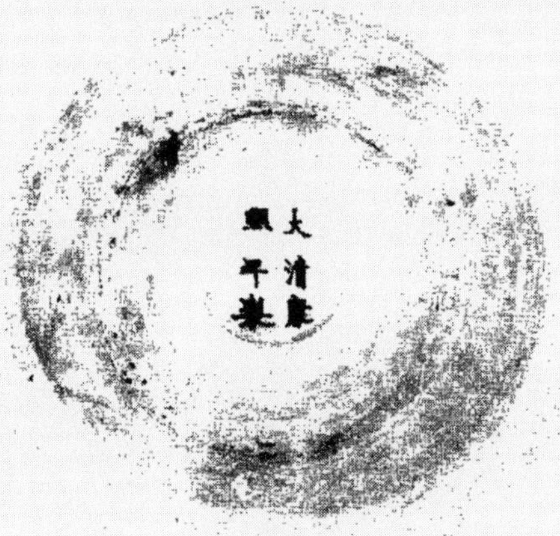

一九五

清康熙窯泑裏三色山水筆筒一件(瓷)

原名康熙款白地藍花茄紫筆筒。底有「大清康熙年製」六字楷款。口徑拾柒捌公分。高拾肆公分。底徑拾柒·玖公分。腹圍伍拾陸·陸公分

Porcelain No. 195.

K'ang Hsi Ware of the Ch'ing Dynasty. Brush barrel decorated with landscape in three under-glaze colours.

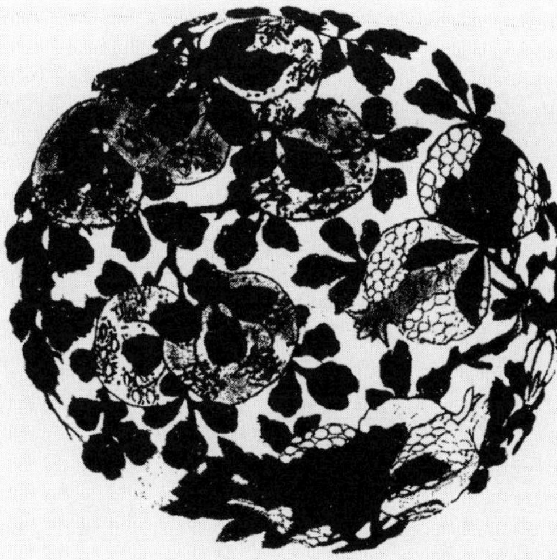

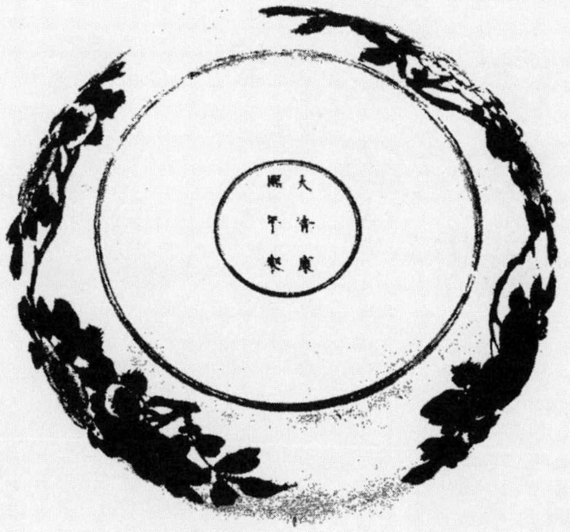

一九六

清康熙窯三彩福壽三多盤一件(院)

原名康熙款白地彩花瓷盤底有大清康熙年製六字楷款口徑貳拾肆·陸公分高肆·柒公分底徑拾陸·叁公分

Porcelain No. 196.

K'ang Hsi Ware of the Ch'ing Dynasty. Plate decorated in enamel of three colours with fu-shou san-to—a rebus with apple standing for to-fu or many blessings, peach for to-shou or longevity, and pomegranates for to-nan-tzŭ or many sons.

一九七

清康熙窯五彩鏤空方夔三節官薰一件(院)

原名瓷香薰實係連蓋三層底層口徑貳拾叁·貳公分中層口徑拾柒公分通蓋頂高貳拾肆·捌公分底徑拾玖·叁公分底層腹圍陸拾貳·伍公分

Porcelain No. 197.

K'ang Hsi Ware of the Ch'ing Dynasty. Palace perfumer in three sections, decorated in variegated enamel with openwork of square kuei (one-footed dragons).

(151)

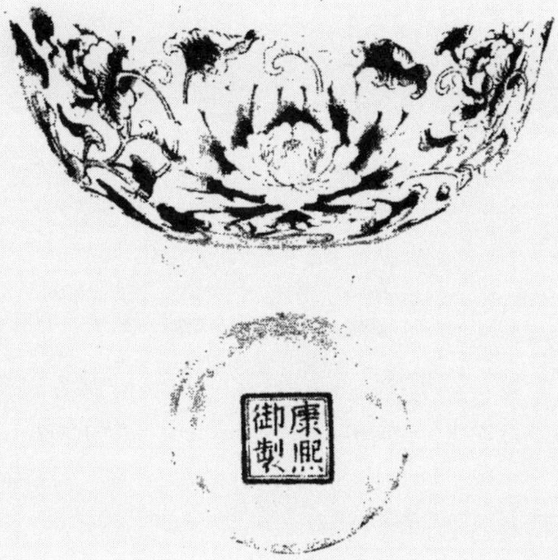

一九八

清康熙窯琺瑯彩黃地纏枝牡丹盌一件（院）

原名瓷胎畫琺瑯五彩西番花黃地大盌底款藍料凸起康熙御製四字楷款口徑拾伍公分高柒·柒公分底徑陸·壹公分

Porcelain No. 198.

K'ang Hsi Ware of the Ch'ing Dynasty. Bowl decorated with twining sprays of peonies in cloisonné enamel over a yellow ground. One piece. The date mark on the base is "Kang Hsi yü-chih" in raised characters of blue enamel.

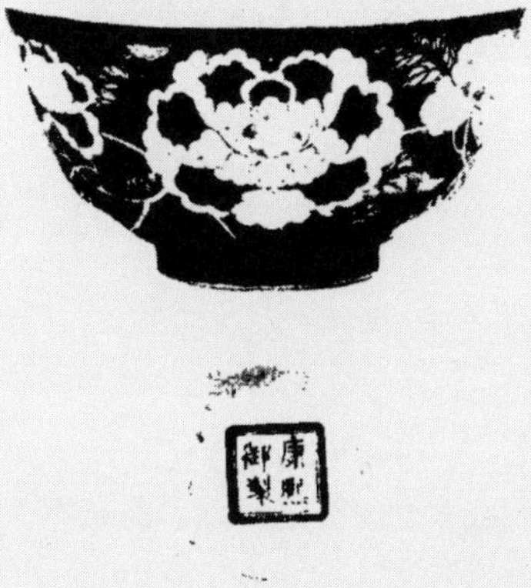

一九九

清康熙窯琺瑯彩洋紅地纏枝牡丹小盌一件（院）

原名瓷胎畫琺瑯五色西番花紅地茶盌底款藍料凸起康熙御製四字楷款口徑拾壹公分高伍·柒公分底徑肆·陸公分。

Porcelain No. 199.

K'ang Hsi Ware of the Ch'ing Dynasty. Small bowl decorated with interlacing sprays of peonies in cloisonné enamel over a foreign red ground. The date mark on the base is "K'ang Hsi yü-chih" in raised characters of blue enamel.

二〇〇

清康熙窯琺瑯彩洋紅地纏枝秋葵月季小盌一件（院）

原名瓷胎畫琺瑯五色西番花紅地茶盌底款藍料凸起康熙御製四字楷款口徑拾壹公分高伍·柒公分底徑肆·陸公分

Porcelain No. 200.

K'ang Hsi Ware of the Ch'ing Dynasty. Small bowl with decoration of twining sprays of ch'iu-kuei (hibiscus manihot) and roses in cloisonné enamel over a foreign red ground. The date mark on the base is "K'ang Hsi yü-chih" in raised characters of blue enamel.

二〇一

清康熙窯琺瑯彩藍地四季花卉盌·件(院)

原名瓷胎畫琺瑯四季花藍地碗口盌底款藍料凸起康熙御製四字楷款口徑拾貳·肆公分高陸·肆公分底徑肆·捌公分

Porcelain No. 201.

K'ang Hsi Ware of the Ch'ing Dynasty. Bowl decorated with flowers of the four seasons in cloisonné enamel over a blue ground. The date mark on the base is "Kang Hsi yü-chih" in raised characters of blue enamel.

二〇二

清康熙窯琺瑯彩粉紅地纏枝牡丹盌·件(院)

原名瓷胎畫琺瑯宮盌底款藍料凸起康熙御製四字楷款口徑拾伍·壹公分高陸·捌公分底徑伍·叁公分

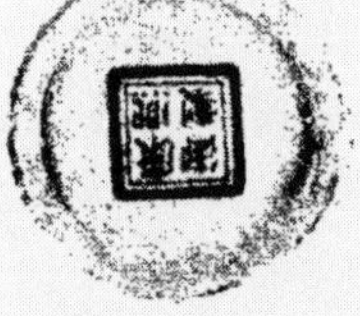

Porcelain No. 202.

K'ang Hsi Ware of the Ch'ing Dynasty. Bowl decorated with twining sprays of peonies in cloisonné enamel over a pink ground. The date mark on the base is "Kang Hsi yü-chih" in raised characters of blue enamel.

二〇三

清康熙窯琺瑯彩貢粉地折枝花卉撇口盌一件(院)
原名瓷胎畫琺瑯黃菊花白地茶盌底款洋紅凸起「康熙御製」四字楷款口徑拾壹·陸公分。高肆·叁公分底徑伍·玖公分

Porcelain No. 203.

K'ang Hsi Ware of the Ch'ing Dynasty. Bowl with spreading mouth, decorated with sprays of flowers in cloisonné enamel over a ground of white powder (kung-fên). The date mark on the base is "K'ang Hsi yü-chih," in raised characters of foreign red.

二〇四

清康熙窯琺瑯彩粉紅地開光綠地四季花盌一件(院)

原名瓷胎畫琺瑯花卉盌底款洋紅凸起康熙御製四字楷款口徑拾肆·玖公分高柒·貳公分底徑伍·柒公分

Porcelain No. 204.

K'ang Hsi Ware of the Ch'ing Dynasty. Bowl decorated with flowers of the four seasons in cloisonné enamel over a green ground enclosed in panels over a pink ground. The date mark on the base is "K'ang Hsi yü-chih" in raised characters of foreign red.

清康熙郎窯

II. CH'ING K'ANG HSI LANG WARE

二〇五

清康熙郎窯寶石紅觀音瓶(通稱觀音尊)一件(院)

原名霽紅瓷花瓶鑲有銅口底有磨口徑肆·肆公分高貳拾·玖公分底徑柒·貳公分最大腹圍叁拾叁·貳公分

Porcelain No. 205.

K'ang Hsi Lang Ware of the Ch'ing Dynasty. Kuan-ying p'ing (commonly called Kuan-ying tsun or the shape of the water bottle used by Avalokitesvala) in pao-shih hung or ruby red. With the rim bound with a copper band.

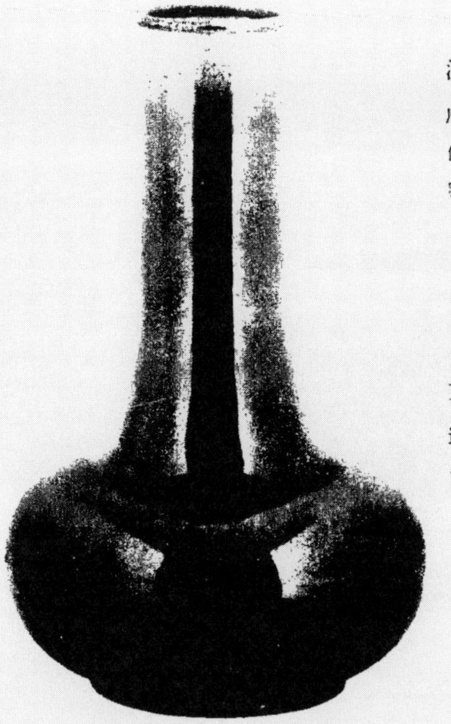

二〇六

清康熙郎窯寶石紅荸薺尊一件（陸）

原名銅鑲口郎窯瓶。銅鍍金鑲口底有傷口徑捌·伍公分。高叁拾捌·肆公分底徑拾肆·柒公分最大腹圍柒拾伍·貳公分

Porcelain No. 206.

K'ang Hsi Lang Ware of the Ch'ing Dynasty. Pi-ch'i tsun (vase shaped like a water-chestnut) in pao-shih hung (ruby red). With a gilded brass rim

二〇七

清康熙郎窯寶石紅觶一件（陸）

原名霽紅瓷瓶帶木座座傷口徑陸·叁公分高貳拾貳·伍公分底徑陸·壹公分最大腹圍叁拾柒·肆公分

Porcelain No. 207.

K'ang Hsi Lang Ware of the Ch'ing Dynasty. Chih (wine vessel in the form of a pear-shaped vase, with slightly spreading lip and hollow foot) of pao-shih hung (ruby red).

(156)

二〇八

清康熙郎窰寶石紅三足圓爐一件(院)

原名霽紅三足瓷花盆有墨口徑拾叁·壹公分高拾壹·叁公分。
底徑拾貳·陸公分腹圍肆拾貳·貳公分

Porcelain No. 208.

K'ang Hsi Lang Ware of the Ch'ing Dynasty. Round tripedal incense burner in pao-shih hung (ruby red).

清 雍 正 窯

III. CH'ING YUNG CHÊNG WARE

二〇九

清雍正窯鈞紅窯變深紫絃紋壺一件（院）

原名霽藍具鈞瓷扁壺底有雍正年製四字篆款底有傷口徑陸·捌公分高貳拾肆·肆公分底徑拾壹·捌公分最大腹圍柒拾肆·貳公分

Porcelain No. 209.

Yung Chêng Ware of the Ch'ing Dynasty. Hsien-wên hu (water-bottle with "bow-string" fillets) glazed in Chün-hung (or the red of Chün ware) with furnace transmutation of deep purple.

(158)

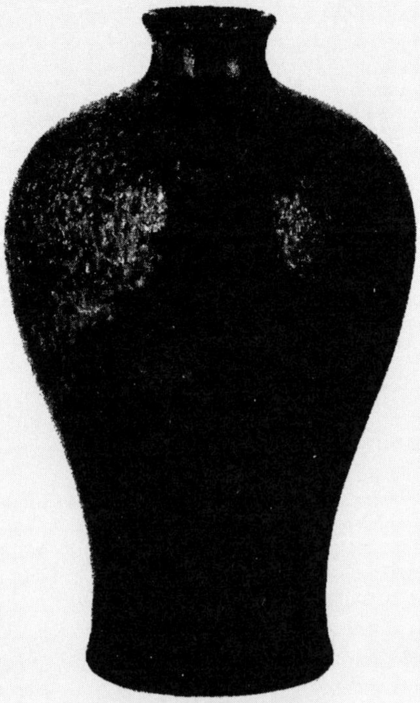

二一〇

清雍正窯爐鈞泑梅瓶一件(院)

原名均釉瓷梅瓶。底有「雍正年製」四字篆款。口徑肆·叁公分。高貳拾壹·玖公分。底徑捌公分。最大腹圍肆拾貳·伍公分。

Porcelain No. 210.

Yung Chêng Ware of the Ch'ing Dynasty. Mei-p'ing (vase) of Lu Chün-yu or the Chün glaze separately baked in a small furnace.

二一一

清雍正窯爐鈞泑三孔小花插一件(院)

原名仿均釉小花插。底有「雍正年製」四字篆款。項直徑伍·叁公分。高柒公分。底徑伍·陸公分。最大腹圍貳拾伍·叁公分。

Porcelain No. 211.

Yung Chêng Ware of the Ch'ing Dynasty. Miniature hua-ch'a (flower receptacle) with three spouts in Chün glaze separately baked in a small furnace (Lu Chün-yu).

二一二

清雍正窯粉青雙連瓶一件（院）

原名豆綠和合瓶口有「大清雍正年製」六字楷款口徑壹·柒公分。高拾貳·陸公分。底徑肆公分。

Porcelain No. 212.

Yung Chêng Ware of the Ch'ing Dynasty. Shuang-lien p'ing (double vase) of fên-ch'ing (light greenish-blue).

二一三

清雍正窯粉青銅骨無紋汝泑溫壺一件（院）

原名雨過天晴瓷小胆瓶底有「大清雍正年製」六字篆款。口徑叁·捌公分。高貳拾肆·壹公分。底徑拾壹·貳公分。最大腹圍伍拾壹·玖公分。

注意銅骨無紋汝泑。唐英命名。乃仿是時內府發宋汝窯無紋水仙盆泑色。

Porcelain No. 213.

Yung Chêng Ware of the Ch'ing Dynasty. Wên-hu (hot-water bottle used as a vase) in the "copper-bodied crackleless glaze of a Ju ware" of fên-ch'ing (light greenish-blue) (t'ung-ku wu-wên Ju-yu).

Note that "copper-bodied crackleless glaze of Ju ware" is a name given by T'ang Ying, being patterned after the glaze colour of a Sung Ju ware narcissus-pot without crackles, sent down by the Imperial Household at the time.

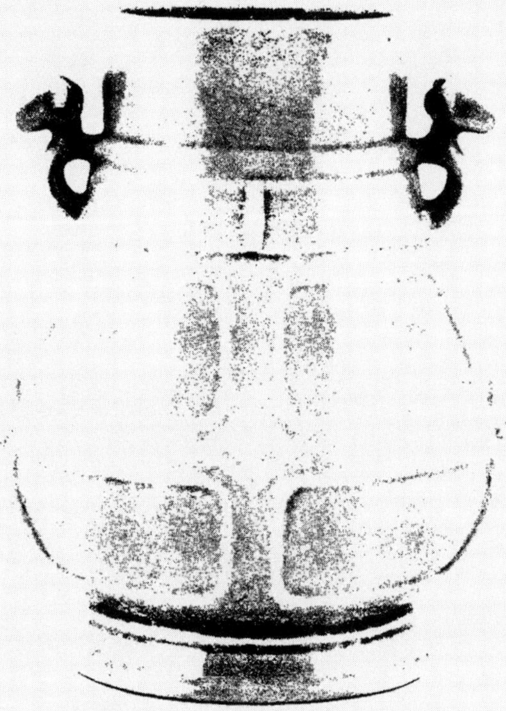

二一四

清雍正窯仿汝天青蚪耳壺一件（院）

原名雍窯雙耳月白瓷瓶，底有「大清雍正年製」六字篆款。口縱玖·柒公分，橫拾貳·貳公分，底縱拾壹·伍公分，橫拾肆·玖公分，最大腹圍伍拾肆·叁公分。

Porcelain No. 214.

Yung Chéng Ware of the Ch'ing Dynasty. Hu (vase) of t'ien-ch'ing (sky blue) modelled after a Ju porcelain, with two handles in the shape of the head of a ch'iu dragon.

二一五

清雍正窯淺天青鐵骨大觀泑繩紋尊一件(院)

原名雍正款乳釉瓷腰帶花尊。底有「大清雍正年製」六字篆款。口徑玖·伍公分。高拾捌·玖公分底徑拾叁·貳公分最大腹圍肆拾玖·叁公分。

注意鐵骨大觀。唐英命名。乃仿是時內府發宋器色澤。

Porcelain No. 215.

Yung Chêng Ware of the Ch'ing Dynasty. Shêng-wên tsun (vase) in "iron-bodied Ta Kuan glaze" (t'ieh-ku Ta Kuan yu) of ch'ien t'ien-ch'ing (light sky blue) with decoration of "twine" fillets.

Note that the "iron-bodied glaze of the Ta Kuan ware" was a name given by T'ang Ying, being patterned after the glaze colour of a Sung Kuan ware sent down by the Imperial Household at the time.

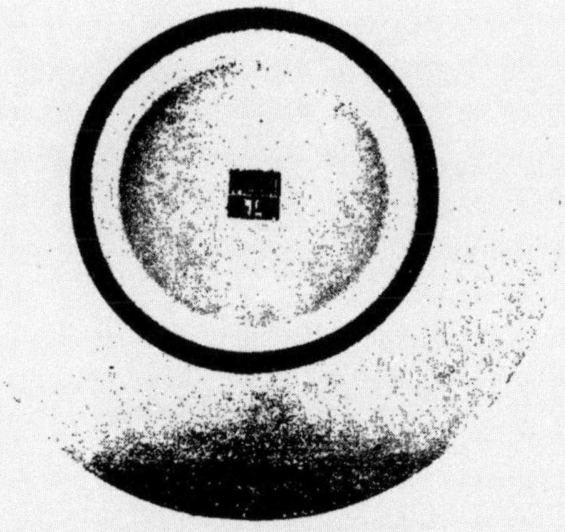

二一六

清雍正窯月白鐵骨大觀泑三羊尊一件(院)

原名雍正款三耳淺豆青瓷瓶。底有「大清雍正年製」六字篆款。有璺。口徑拾貳·叁公分。高叁拾貳·玖公分。底徑拾叁·捌公分。最大腹圍柒拾玖公分。

注意鐵骨大觀。唐英命名。乃仿是時內府發宋器色澤。

Porcelain No. 216.

Yung Chêng Ware of the Ch'ing Dynasty. San-yang tsun (vase) of the yüeh-pai (moon white) "iron-bodied Ta Kuan glaze" (t'ieh-ku Ta Kuan yu) decorated with masks of three rams.

Note that the "iron-bodied glaze of the Ta Kuan ware" was a name given by T'ang Ying, being patterned after the glaze colour of a Sung Kuan ware sent down by the Imperial Household at the time.

二一七

清雍正窯淺天藍小缸一件(院)

原名瓷缸。底有「雍正年製」四字篆款。口徑拾叁公分。高拾壹公分。底徑陸·陸公分。

Porcelain No. 217.

Yung Chêng Ware of the Ch'ing Dynasty. Small jar (kang) in light sky blue (t'ien-lan).

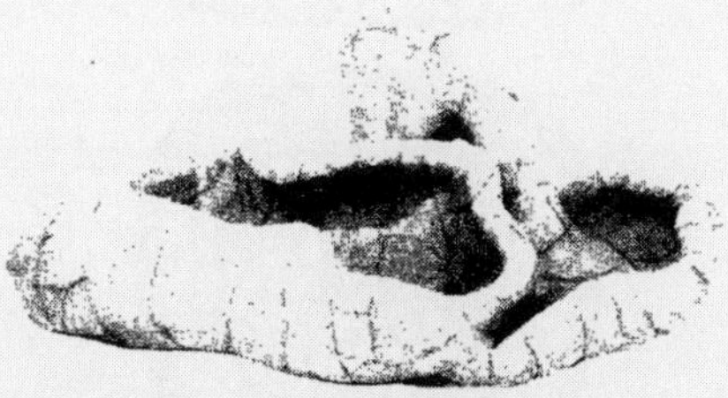

二一八

清雍正窯仿官粉青靈芝一件(院)

原名荷葉式瓷洗。最高肆·叁公分。最寬捌·壹公分。最長拾壹·陸公分。

Porcelain No. 218.

Yung Chêng Ware of the Ch'ing Dynasty. Ling-chih fungi of fên-ch'ing (light greenish-blue), modelled after the glaze colour of a Sung Kuan ware.

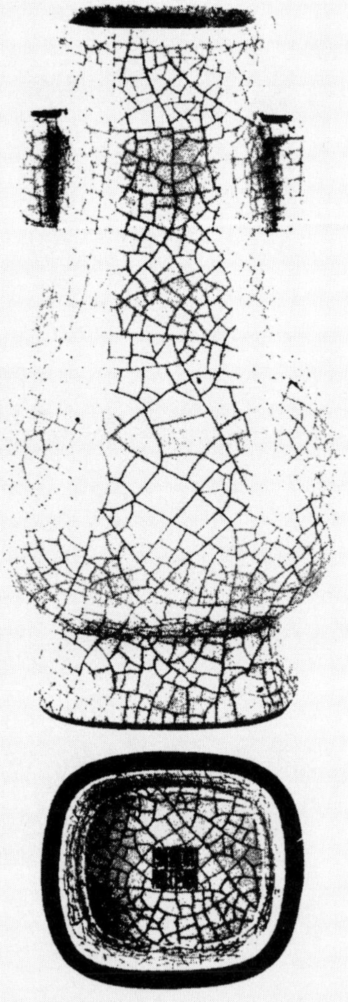

二一九

清雍正窰仿哥淺青貫耳壺一件（院）

原名雍正款豆青開片雙耳尊。底有「大清雍正年製」六字篆款。口有微傷。口縱橫均捌·捌公分。高貳拾柒·玖公分。底縱玖·伍公分。橫拾·肆公分。最大腹圍肆拾伍·伍公分。

Porcelain No. 219.

Yung Chêng Ware of the Ch'ing Dynasty. Kuan-erh hu (vase with "piercing handles") modelled after a Ko porcelain in the lightest greenish-blue (ch'ien-ch'ing).

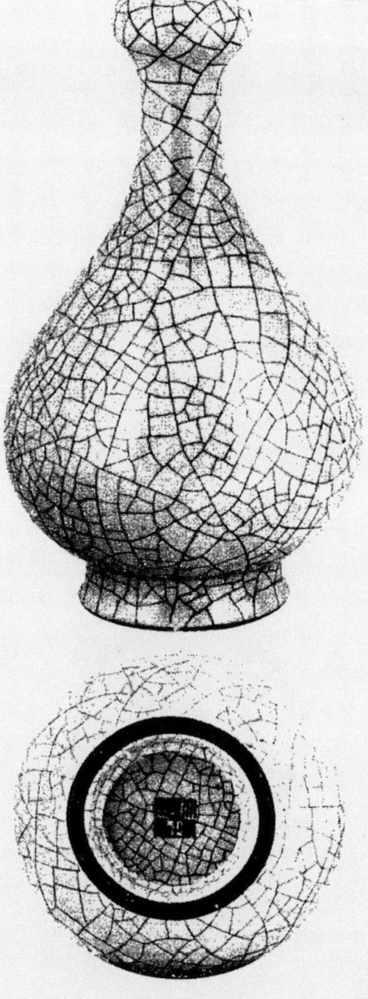

二二〇

清雍正窯仿哥淺青溫壺一件(院)

原名雍正款冰紋瓷瓶。底有「大清雍正年製」六字篆款。口徑叁·肆公分。高貳拾柒·柒公分。底徑捌·陸公分。最大腹圍肆拾捌·玖公分。

Porcelain No. 220.

Yung Chêng Ware of the Ch'ing Dynasty. Wên-hu (hot-water bottle used as a vase) modelled after a Ko porcelain in the lightest greenish-blue (ch'ien-ch'ing).

(166)

二二一

清雍正窯仿南宋官窯泑粉青獸環壺一件(院)

原名仿乳釉直口花囊底有「大清雍正年製」六字篆款口徑柒·陸公分,高貳拾·貳公分,底徑捌·伍公分最大腹圍伍拾伍·貳公分。

Porcelain No. 221.

Yung Chêng Ware of the Ch'ing Dynasty. Shou-huan hu (vase with handles in the shape of animal-mask and ring) in fên-ch'ing (light greenish-blue) glaze patterned after a Kuan porcelain of Southern Sung.

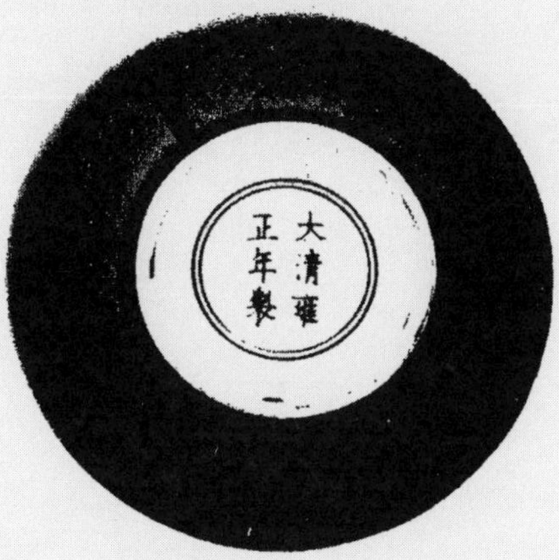

二二二

清雍正窯祭紅膽瓶一件

(院)

原名霽紅瓷小膽瓶底有大清雍正年製六字楷款口徑叁公分高貳拾公分底徑伍·伍公分最大腹圍叁拾肆公分

Porcelain No. 222.

Yung Chêng Ware of the Ch'ing Dynasty. Tan-p'ing (vase) in chi-hung (sacrificial red)

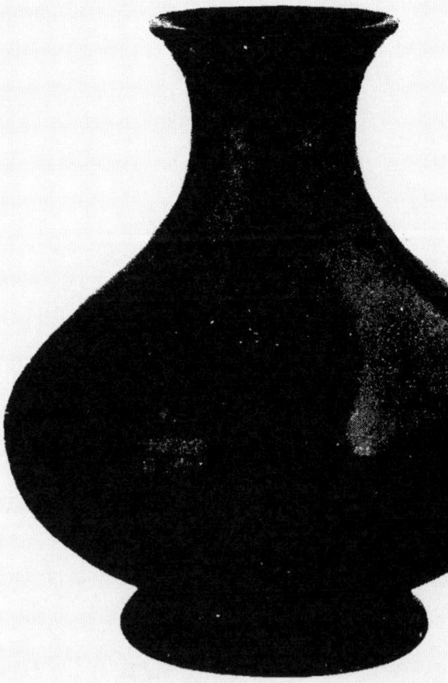

二二三

清雍正窯鱔魚青撇口絃文壺一件（院）

原名鱔魚青瓷瓶底有「大清雍正年製」六字篆款口徑柒·捌公分，高貳拾·貳公分底徑玖·伍公分最大腹圍伍拾肆公分

Porcelain No. 223.

Yung Chêng Ware of the Ch'ing Dynasty. Hsien-wên hu (vase with "bow-string" fillets) of eel green, with spreading mouth.

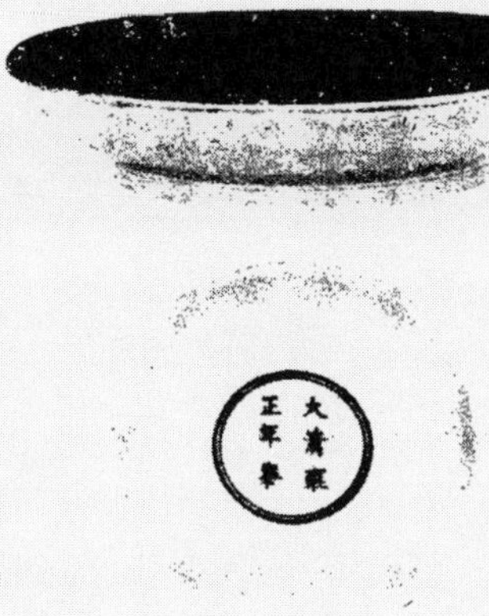

二二四

清雍正窯吹綠錐花纏枝蓮八寶碟一件(院)

原名翡翠釉瓷碟。底有「大清雍正年製」六字楷款。口徑拾肆·陸公分。高叁·叁公分。底徑玖·肆公分

Porcelain No. 224.

Yung Chêng Ware of the Ch'ing Dynasty. Dish with incised decoration (chui-hua) of twining sprays of lotus supporting eight Buddhist emblems in soufflé green.

二二五

清雍正窯青花番蓮貫耳六方壺一件(院)

原名雍正款青花白地雙耳六楞瓶。底有「大清雍正年製」六字篆款。口縱捌·陸公分。橫拾壹·壹公分。高貳拾捌·柒公分。底縱捌·捌公分。橫拾貳·壹公分。最大腹圍肆拾玖·柒公分

Porcelain No. 225.

Yung Chêng Ware of the Ch'ing Dynasty. Kuan-erh liu-fang hu (hexagonal vase with "piercing handles") decorated with Indian lotus in under-glaze blue.

二二六

清雍正窯青花錐拱菊瓣花澆一件（院）

原名雍正款白地藍花帶把壺底有「大清雍正年製」六字篆款。口縱陸·壹公分橫柒·玖公分。最高叁拾壹·貳公分底徑拾壹·貳公分最大腹圍伍拾柒·玖公分

Porcelain No. 226.

Yung Chêng Ware of the Ch'ing Dynasty. Hua-chiao (watering pot) with raised decoration (chui-kung) of chrysanthemum petals in under-glaze blue.

(172)

二二七

清雍正窯琺瑯彩梅竹先春盤二件(院)

原名瓷胎畫琺瑯黃地梅竹六寸盤。底款青花「大清雍正年製」六字楷款。之一。口徑拾柒·伍公分。高叁·捌公分。底徑拾·玖公分。之二。口徑拾柒·肆公分。高肆·玖公分。底徑拾·玖公分。

Porcelain No. 227.

Yung Chêng Ware of the Ch'ing Dynasty. Pair of plates decorated in cloisonné enamel with mei-chu hsien-ch'un or the prunus and the bamboo ushering in the spring. On the base is the date mark of "Ta Ch'ing Yung Chêng nien chih' in under-glaze blue. Two pieces.

(173)

(171)

二二八

清雍正窯琺瑯彩歲寒三友(柏天竹臘梅)盤二件(院)

原名瓷胎珐瑯黃地花卉六寸盤。底款青花「大清雍正年製」六字楷款。口徑均拾柒·伍公分。高叁·捌公分。底徑拾·捌公分。

Porcelain No. 228.

Yung Chêng Ware of the Ch'ing Dynasty. Pair of plates decorated in cloisonné enamel with shui-han san-yu—or the three friends in the cold weather, meaning three kinds of trees, the nandina, the yellow prunus and the cypress. On the base is the date mark "Ta Ch'ing Yung Chêng nien chih" in under-glaze blue. Two pieces.

二二九

清雍正窯琺瑯彩洋紅地梅竹先春盌二件(院)

原名瓷胎畫琺瑯白梅花紅地瓷宮盌底款藍料凸起「雍正年製」四字楷款。口徑均拾伍·壹公分。高柒·貳公分。底徑陸·壹公分。

Porcelain No. 229.

Yung Chêng Ware of the Ch'ing Dynasty. Pair of bowls decorated with the prunus and bamboo ushering in the spring. (mei-chu hsien ch'un) in cloisonné enamel on a foreign red ground. Two pieces. The base mark is "Yung Chêng nien chih," in raised characters of blue enamel.

二三〇

清雍正窯琺瑯彩茶梅拾貳喜盌二件(院)

原名瓷胎畫琺瑯白地時時報喜瓷宮盌。底款藍料凸起「雍正年製」四字楷款。口徑均拾陸·壹公分。高柒·伍公分。底徑陸·玖公分。

Porcelain No. 230.

Yung Chêng Ware of the Ch'ing Dynasty. Pair of bowls decorated in cloisonné enamel with camillia, prunus and twelve magpies (ch'a-mei shih-erh-hsi). Two pieces. The base mark is "Yung Chêng nien chih" in raised characters of blue enamel.

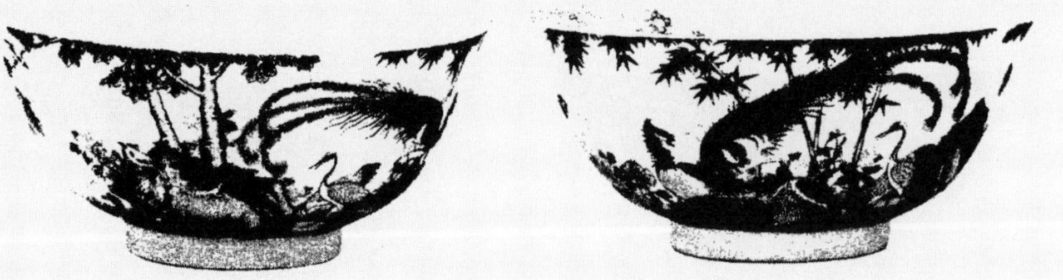

二三一

清雍正窯琺瑯彩伍倫圖盌二件(院)

原名瓷胎畫琺瑯伍倫圖白地大瓷盌之一原有沖口底款藍料凸起雍正年製四字楷款口徑均陸·壹公分高柒·陸公分底徑陸·柒公分

Porcelain No. 231.

Yung Chêng Ware of the Ch'ing Dynasty. Pair of bowls decorated in cloisonné enamel with wu lun t'u (picture of five kinds of birds and flowers a rebus for the five human relationships). Two pieces. One with a small crack originally there. The base mark is "Yung Chêng nien chih" in raised characters of blue enamel.

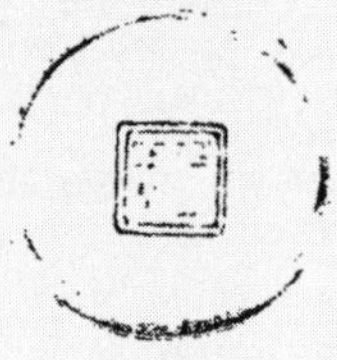

二三二

清雍正窯琺瑯彩粉黃地牡丹小盌一件(院)

原名瓷胎畫琺瑯茶鍾底款藍料雙方圈洋紅凸起雍正年製四字楷款口徑拾壹·肆公分。高伍·柒公分。底徑肆·壹公分

Porcelain No. 232.

Yung Chêng Ware of the Ch'ing Dynasty. Small bowl decorated in cloisonné enamel with peonies on a fên-huang (powder yellow) ground. On the base is the date mark "Yung Chêng nien chih" – made in the year of Yung Chêng – in raised characters of yang-hung or foreign red enamel enclosed in double rings of blue enamel.

(177)

二三三

清雍正窯琺瑯彩赭墨牡丹盌二件（院）

原名瓷胎畫琺瑯墨牡丹白地宮盌、底款藍料凸起「雍正年製」四字楷款。口徑均拾肆·玖公分、高柒·貳公分、底徑陸·壹公分。

Porcelain No. 233.

Yung Chêng Ware of the Ch'ing Dynasty. Pair of bowls decorated with peonies in cloisonné enamel. Mixed with Chinese brown and ink. Two pieces. The date mark on the base is "Yung Chêng nien chih" in raised characters of blue enamel.

二三四

清雍正窯琺瑯彩粉黃地芝蘭壽石圖小盌一件（院）

原名瓷胎畫琺瑯黃地芝仙祝壽茶盅、底款藍料凸起「雍正年製」四字楷款口徑拾壹·玖公分、高陸·壹公分、底徑肆·肆公分。

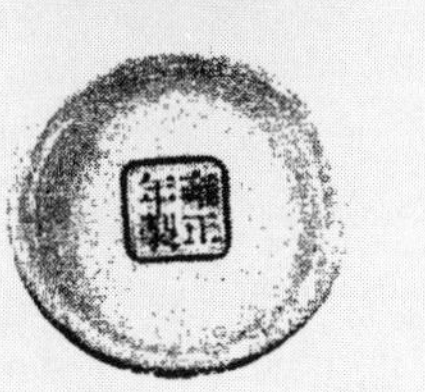

Porcelain No. 234.

Yung Chêng Ware of the Ch'ing Dynasty. Small bowl decorated in cloisonné enamel with sacred fungi, orchid and rocks (chih-lan shou-shih), over a fên-huang (light yellow) ground. The date mark on the base is "Yung Chêng nien chih" in raised characters of blue enamel.

二三五

清雍正窯琺瑯彩玉堂富貴小盌二件（院）

原名瓷胎畫琺瑯玉堂富貴白地茶鍾底款藍料凸起雍正年製四字楷款口徑均拾貳公分高伍·肆公分底徑肆·壹公分

Porcelain No. 235.

Yung Chêng Ware of the Ch'ing Dynasty. Pair of small bowls decorated with the magnolia, the pyrus spectabilis, and the peony (yü-t'ang fu-kuei) in cloisonné enamel. Two pieces. The date mark on the base is "Yung Chêng nien chih" in raised characters of blue enamel.

二三六

清雍正窯琺瑯彩萬壽圖小盌二件（院）

原名瓷胎畫琺瑯萬地長春白地茶盌底款藍料凸起雍正年製四字楷款口徑均拾壹·叁公分高伍·捌公分底徑肆·壹公分。

Porcelain No. 236.

Yung Chêng Ware of the Ch'ing Dynasty. Pair of small bowls decorated in cloisonné enamel with wan shou t'u or marigold and rockery. Two pieces. The date mark on the base is "Yung Chêng nien chih" in raised characters of blue enamel.

二三七

清雍正窯琺瑯彩竹雀圖器二件(院)

原名瓷胎畫琺瑯諸子百家白地大盌底款藍料凸起「雍正年製」四字楷款口徑拾陸公分高柒·柒公分底徑陸·柒公分.

Porcelain No. 237.

Yung Chêng Ware of the Ch'ing Dynasty. Pair of bowls decorated with sparrows and bamboos (chu-ch'iao t'u) in cloisonné enamel. Two pieces. The date mark on the base is "Yung Chêng nien chih" in raised characters of blue enamel.

二三八

清雍正窯琺瑯彩菊花器二件(院)

原名瓷胎畫琺瑯五色菊花白地瓷宮盌底款藍料凸起雍正年製」四字楷款口徑均拾伍·壹公分高柒·貳公分底徑陸·貳公分

Porcelain No. 238.

Yung Chêng Ware of the Ch'ing Dynasty. Pair of bowls decorated with chrysanthemums in cloisonné enamel. Two pieces. The date mark on the base is "Yung Chêng nien chih" in raised characters of blue enamel.

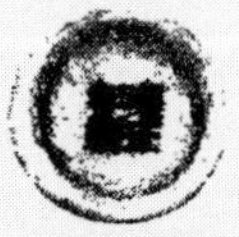

二三九

清雍正窯琺瑯彩竹雀圖酒鍾二件（院）

原名瓷胎畫琺瑯絲竹猗猗白地鍾底款藍料凸起「雍正年製」四字楷款口徑均肆·叁公分高叁·叁公分底徑貳·叁公分

Porcelain No. 239.

Yung Chêng Ware of the Ch'ing Dynasty. Pair of small wine cups decorated with bamboos and sparrows (chu-ch'iao t'u) in cloisonné enamel. Two pieces. The date mark on the base is "Yung Chêng nien chih" in raised characters of blue enamel.

二四〇

清雍正窯琺瑯彩鸜鵒秋光酒鍾二件（院）

原名瓷胎畫琺瑯秋樹八哥白地鍾底款藍料凸起「雍正年製」四字楷款口徑均肆·壹公分高叁公分底徑貳·壹公分

Porcelain No. 240.

Yung Chêng Ware of the Ch'ing Dynasty. Pair of small wine cups decorated with ch'ü-yü (the mainah) and red (maple) leaves (chü-yü ch'iu-kuang) in cloisonné enamel. Two pieces. The date mark on the base is "Yung Chêng nien chih" in raised characters of blue enamel.

(182)

二四一

清雍正窯琺瑯彩菊花碟二件(院)

原名瓷胎畫琺瑯黃菊花白地三寸碟。底款藍料凸起「雍正年製」四字楷款。內壹件口徑拾·捌公分高貳·玖公分。底徑陸·柒公分。又壹件口徑拾·柒公分高貳·玖公分。底徑陸·柒公分。

Porcelain No. 241.

Yung Chêng Ware of the Ch'ing Dynasty. Pair of small dishes with the decoration of chrysanthemums in cloisonné enamel. Two pieces. The date mark on the base is "Yung Chêng nien chih" in raised characters of blue enamel.

二四二

清雍正窯琺瑯彩梅竹先春酒柸二件(院)

原名瓷胎畫琺瑯節節長春白地鍾底款青花「雍正年製」四字楷款口徑均柒·壹公分高叁·伍公分底徑貳·陸公分。

Porcelain No. 242.

Yung Chêng Ware of the Ch'ing Dynasty. Pair of wine cups with decoration in cloisonné enamel of mei-chu hsien-ch'un or the prunus and the bamboo heralding the approaching spring. On the base is the date mark of "Yung Chêng nien chih" in under-glaze blue.

二四三

清雍正窯琺瑯彩洋紅地開花折枝花卉酒柸二件(院)

原名瓷胎畫琺瑯四季花紅地盅底款青花「雍正年製」四字楷款內壹件有微傷口徑均陸·肆公分高肆·叁公分底徑貳·肆公分

Porcelain No. 243.

Yung Chêng Ware of the Ch'ing Dynasty. Pair of wine cups, decorated in panels on yang-hung (foreign red) grounds with sprays of flowers in cloisonné enamel. On the base is the date mark "Yung Chêng yü-chih" of under-glaze blue. Two pieces.

(184)

二四四

清雍正窰琺瑯彩赭墨纏枝蓮開光喜報雙安把壺一件（院）

原名瓷胎畫琺瑯節節雙喜白地茶壺底款藍料凸起「雍正年製」四字楷款口徑陸·壹公分通蓋項拾壹·壹公分底徑陸·陸公分

Porcelain No. 244.

Yung Chêng Ware of the Ch'ing Dynasty. Handled pot decorated in cloisonné enamel with hsi-pao shuang-an (being a rebus for magpies and bamboos and two quails) in panels over grounds of twining sprays of lotus in dark brown and black ink. One piece. The date mark on the base is "Yung Chêng nien chih" in raised characters of blue enamel.

(185)

二四五

清雍正窯琺瑯彩百花地開光藍料山水把壺一件(院)

原名瓷胎畫琺瑯青山水白地茶壺。底款藍料凸起「雍正年製」四字楷款。口徑捌·壹公分。通蓋高捌·玖公分。底徑柒·陸公分

Porcelain No. 245.

Yung Chêng Ware of the Ch'ing Dynasty. Handled pot decorated with landscape painting in blue material, enclosed in panels over brocaded grounds in cloisonné enamel. The date mark on the base is "Yung Chêng nien chih" in raised characters of blue enamel.

清乾隆窯

IV. CH·ING CH·IEN LUNG WARE

二四六

清乾隆窯仿定塋白錐拱雲蝠絃文壺一件(院)
原名瓷胎甜白錐拱雲蝠絃紋壺,口徑陸·壹公分,高叁拾·伍公分,底徑拾公分,最大腹圍伍拾伍公分。

Porcelain No. 246.

Ch'ien Lung Ware of the Ch'ing Dynasty. Hsien-wên hu (vase with "bowstring" fillets) of ying-pai (pure white) modelled after a Ting porcelain, with raised decoration (chui-kung) of clouds and bats.

二四七

清乾隆窯仿定瑩白錐花饕餮百壽扁方壺一件(院)

原名白瓷瓶,底有「大清乾隆年製」六篆字暗款,口縱貳·柒公分,橫叁·柒公分。高貳拾·叁公分,底縱叁公分,橫肆·肆公分。

Porcelain No. 247.

Ch'ien Lung Ware of the Ch'ing Dynasty. Pien-fang hu (square flattened vase) of ying-pai (pure white) modelled after a Ting porcelain with incised decoration (chui-hua) of t'ao-t'ieh (or avaricious and gluttonous monsters) and hundred shou (longevity) characters in different forms of writing. One piece.

(188)

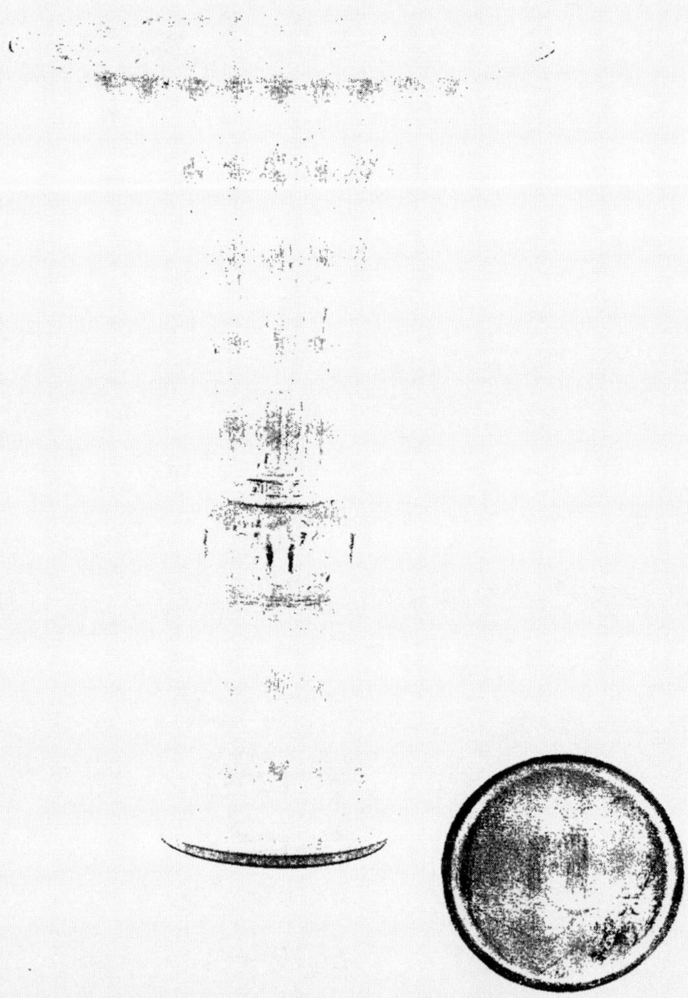

二四八

清乾隆窯仿定瑩白蕉葉雷文觚一件（院）

原名白瓷花觚。底有「大清乾隆年製」六字暗款。有壂。口徑拾伍·柒公分。高貳拾肆·捌公分。底徑陸·玖公分。腹圍拾肆·壹公分。

Porcelain No. 248.

Ch'ien Lung Ware of the Ch'ing Dynasty. Ku (goblet) of ying-pai (pure white) modelled after a Ting porcelain with decoration of banana leaves and lei-wên (linear squared spiral ornament).

二四九

清乾隆窯爐鈞汋雙耳燈籠尊一件（院）

原名仿均釉瓶。底有「大清乾隆年製」六字篆款。口徑柒·捌公分。高貳拾叁·叁公分。底徑分。腹圍肆拾貳公分。底徑捌·叁公分。

Porcelain No. 249.

Ch'ien Lung Ware of the Ch'ing Dynasty. Tsun (vase) in the shape of a Chinese lantern, with two handles, glazed in the Chün glaze separately baked in a small furnace (Lu Chün-yu).

二五〇

清乾隆窯天青銅骨無紋汋錐拱蓮瓣瓶一件（院）

原名乾隆款天藍瓷瓶。底有「大清雍正年製」六字篆款。口徑肆·貳公分。高拾柒·玖公分。底徑陸·肆公分。最大腹圍叁拾玖公分。

Porcelain No. 250.

Ch'ien Lung Ware of the Ch'ing Dynasty. Vase of t'ien-ch'ing (sky blue) crackleless copper-bodied Ju glaze (t'ung-ku wu-wên Ju yu) fashioned in the shape resembling lotus petals "raised with an awl" (chui-kung).

(190)

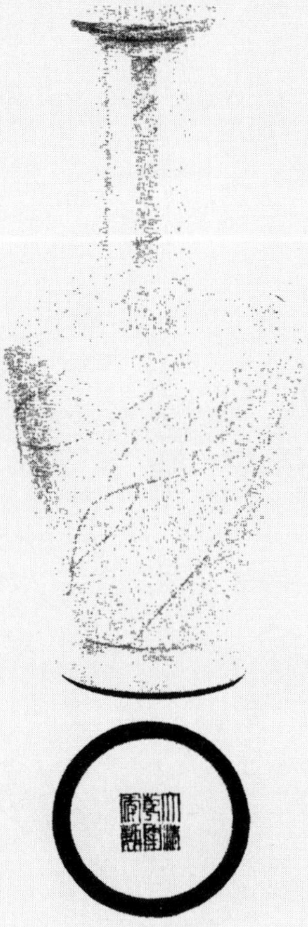

二五一

清乾隆窯月白鐵骨大觀汋盤口瓶一件(院)

原名冬青開片小瓷瓶。底有「大清乾隆年製」六字篆款。口徑肆·柒公分，高貳拾·陸公分，底徑伍·伍公分，最大腹圍叁拾壹公分。

Porcelain No. 251.

Ch'ien Lung Ware of the Ch'ing Dynasty. P'ing (vase) with a dish-shaped mouth in the "Ta Kuan iron-bodied glaze" (t'ieh-ku Ta Kuan yu') of yüeh-pai (moon white).

二五二

清乾隆窯粉青花觚一件(院)

原名乾隆款冬青小瓷觚。底有「大清乾隆年製」六字篆款。口徑拾叁·捌公分，高貳拾壹·柒公分，底徑伍·陸公分。

Porcelain No. 252.

Ch'ien Lung Ware of the Ch'ing Dynasty. Hua-ku (goblet used as a flower receptacle) in fên-ch'ing (light greenish-blue).

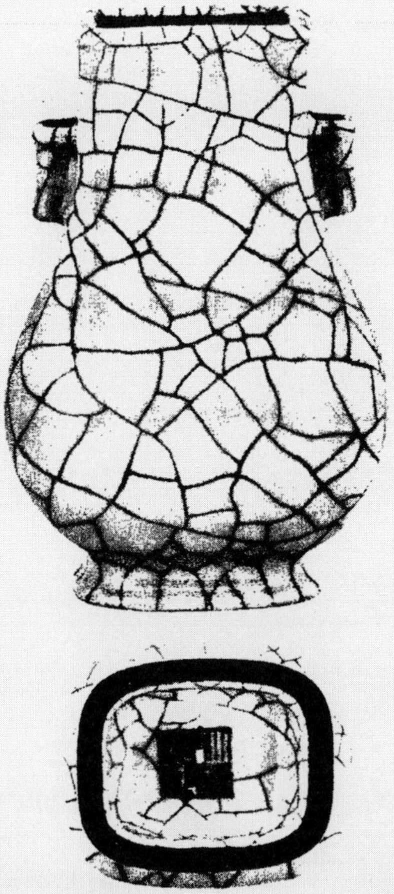

二五三

清乾隆窯仿哥淺青貫耳小方壺一件(院)

原名汝釉瓷雙管瓶底有大清乾隆年製六字篆款.口縱叁·柒公分橫肆·捌公分高拾壹·陸公分最大腹圍貳拾肆·陸公分底縱肆·肆公分橫伍·壹公分.

Porcelain No. 253.

Ch'ien Lung Ware of the Ch'ing Dynasty. Miniature kuan-erh fang-hu (quadrangular vase with "piercing handles") glazed in ch'ien-ch'ing (light blue-greenish grey) after the model of a Ko ware.

二五四

清乾隆窯仿哥粉青穿帶壺一件（院）

原名乳釉哥瓷穿帶瓶口徑拾壹·贰公分高叁拾叁·伍公分最大腹圍柒拾贰·柒公分底徑拾叁·捌公分

Porcelain No. 254.

Ch'ien Lung Ware of the Ch'ing Dynasty. Ch'üan-tai hu (vase with tape holes) in fên-ch'ing (light greenish-blue) glaze, patterned after a Ko porcelain.

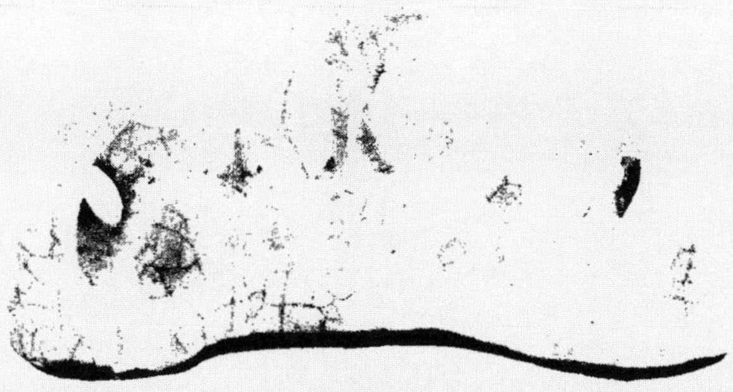

二五五

清乾隆窯仿哥淺青冰裂鱔血紋硯山一件（院）

原名瓷筆架最高玖·伍公分最長拾陸·柒公分

Porcelain No. 255.

Ch'ien Lung Ware of the Ch'ing Dynasty. Yen-shan (brush-rest in the shape of hills), in ch'ien-ch'ing (light blue-greenish grey) with ice-crackles of eel-blood, modelled after a Ko ware.

二五六

清乾隆窯仿湘湖泑淺粉青錐拱纏枝番蓮瓶一件（院）

原名乾隆款冬青暗花瓷瓶底有「大清乾隆年製」六字篆款口徑柒·陸公分高貳拾柒·捌公分底徑陸·陸公分最大腹圍肆拾·玖公分

Porcelain No. 256.

Ch'ien Lung Ware of the Ch'ing Dynasty. P'ing (vase) in ch'ien fên-ch'ing (the lighter shade of a light greenish-blue) modelled after the glaze of a Hsiang-hu ware and decorated with interlacing sprays of Indian lotus carved in relief (chui-kung).

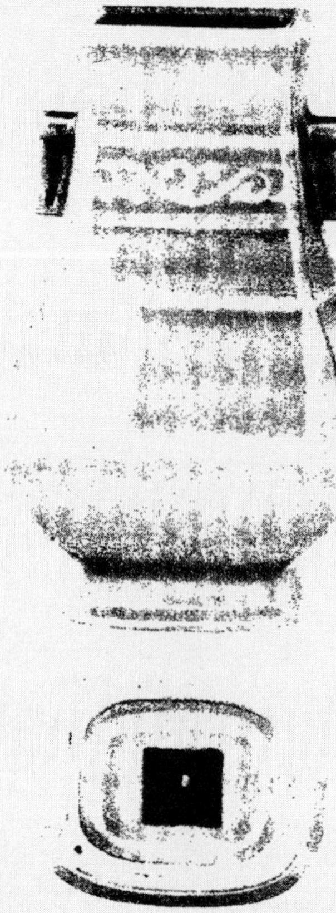

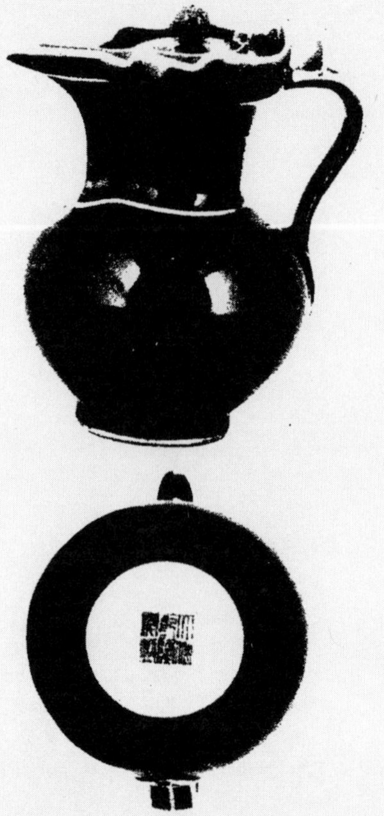

二五七

清乾隆窯仿湘湖泑淺粉青貫耳小方壺一件（院）

原名哥窯瓷貫耳管瓶底有大清乾隆年製六字篆款口縱叁·捌公分横伍公分高拾叁公分最大腹闊贰拾陸公分底縱肆·伍公分横伍·贰公分

Porcelain No. 257.

Ch'ien Lung Ware of the Ch'ing Dynasty. Miniature kuan-erh fang-hu (quadrangular vase with "piercing handles") in ch'ien fên-ch'ing (a lighter shade of light greenish-blue) modelled after the glaze colour of a Hsiang-hu ware.

二五八

清乾隆窯寶石紅僧帽壺一件（院）

原名乾隆年製祭紅僧帽壺底有大清乾隆年製六字篆款帶木座口最長柒·柒公分通蓋頂高拾壹·捌公分、底徑肆公分

Porcelain No. 258.

Ch'ien Lung Ware of the Ch'ing Dynasty. Sêng-mao hu (pitcher with the rim in the shape of a monk's hat) in pao-shih hung (ruby red). With a wooden stand.

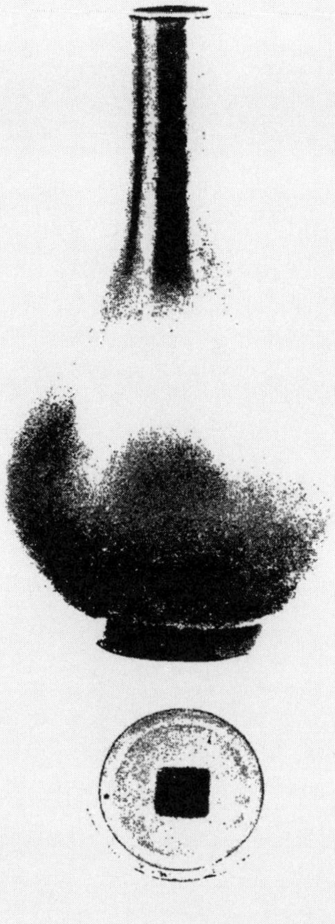

二五九

清乾隆窯鱔魚黄膽瓶一件(院)

原名乾隆款鱔魚青錐把瓷瓶底有大清乾隆年製六篆字暗款口徑叁·捌公分高貳拾柒·捌公分底徑柒·陸公分最大腹圍肆拾柒·柒公分

Porcelain No. 259.

Ch'ien Lung Ware of the Ch'ing Dynasty. Tan-p'ing (vase in the shape of a gall-bladder) of eel yellow (shan-yü huang).

二六〇

清乾隆窯鱔魚青膽瓶一件(院)

原名魚青錘式小瓷瓶底有大清乾隆年製六字篆款口徑叁·捌公分高貳拾柒伍公分底徑柒·叁公分最大腹圍肆拾陸·肆公分

Porcelain No. 260.

Ch'ien Lung Ware of the Ch'ing Dynasty. Tan-p'ing (vase in the shape of a gall-bladder) of eel green (shan-yü ch'ing).

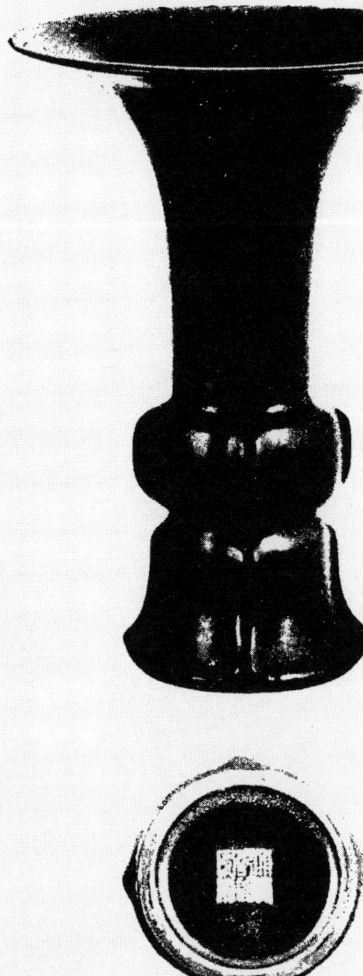

二六一

清乾隆窯茶葉末花觚一件(院)

原名廠官釉瓷花觚底有大清乾隆年製六字篆款口徑拾肆·伍公分高貳拾·柒公分底徑陸·柒公分最大腹圍貳拾·捌公分

Porcelain No. 261.

Ch'ien Lung Ware of the Ch'ing Dynasty. Hua-ku (goblet used as vase) in the colour of tea-dust.

二六二

清乾隆窯青花雲蝠海棠式貫耳瓶一件(院)

原名白地藍花壹吋出福海瓶底有大清乾隆年製六字篆款口縱肆·壹公分橫捌·陸公分高叁拾陸·壹公分底縱肆公分橫玖公分最大腹圍肆拾伍·伍公分

Porcelain No. 262.

Ch'ien Lung Ware of the Ch'ing Dynasty. Kuan-erh p'ing (vase with "piercing handles") shaped like a begonia flower and decorated in underglaze blue with clouds and bats.

二六三

清乾隆窯青花纏枝海石榴貫耳瓶一件(陸)

原名乾隆款青花白地雙耳小瓶底有大清乾隆年製六字篆款口徑伍·貳公分高拾玖·肆公分底徑陸·肆公分最大腹圍叁拾叁·壹公分

Porcelain No. 263.

Ch'ien Lung Ware of the Ch'ing Dynasty. Kuan-erh p'ing (vase with "piercing handles") decorated in under-glaze blue with twining sprays of hai shih-liu (foreign pomegranate).

二六四

清乾隆窰青花纏枝牽牛獸耳折方瓶一件(院)

原名乾隆款雙耳青花插底有大清乾隆年製六字篆款口徑陸·貳公分高拾陸公分底徑玖·壹公分

Porcelain No. 264.

Ch'ien Lung Ware of the Ch'ing Dynasty. Chê-fang p'ing (cubic vase faceted at the angles), with animal-mask handles, decorated with twining sprays of pharbitis hederacea in under-glaze blue.

二六五

清乾隆窯青花三友(竹石芭蕉)壺(通稱玉壺春)一件(院)

原名乾隆款白地青竹芭蕉花瓷膽瓶底有「大清乾隆年製」六字篆款有座口徑捌·伍公分高貳拾玖·壹公分底徑拾壹·叁公分最大腹圍伍拾陸·捌公分

Porcelain No. 265.

Ch'ien Lung Ware of the Ch'ing Dynasty. Hu (vase, commonly called yü hu ch'un) with decoration of three friends (i.e. bamboo, rocks and bananas) in under-glaze blue.

二六六

清乾隆窯青花番蓮高足桮一·件(院)

原名乾隆款白地藍花高足盌。底沿有「大清乾隆年製」六字篆款口有傷。口徑柒·伍公分。高捌·柒公分。足徑伍·肆公分

Porcelain No. 266.

Ch'ien Lung Ware of the Ch'ing Dynasty. High-stemmed cup with decoration of Indian lotus in under-glaze blue.

二六七

清乾隆窯青花鬭彩番蓮梅瓶一·件(院)

原名乾隆款白地彩花小口瓷瓶底有「大清乾隆年製」六字篆款口徑陸·捌公分高叁拾叁·貳公分底徑拾叁·肆公分最大腹圍柒拾壹·柒公分

Porcelain No. 267.

Ch'ien Lung Ware of the Ch'ing Dynasty. Mei-p'ing (vase) decorated with Indian lotus in under-glaze blue and enamel in contrasting colours.

二六八

清乾隆窯青花鬬彩九子蓋罐一件(院)

原名白地瓷彩罐底有大清乾隆年製六字篆款通蓋高貳拾玖·陸公分。口徑拾公分底徑拾壹公分最大腹圍肆拾肆·玖公分

Porcelain No. 268.

Ch'ien Lung Ware of the Ch'ing Dynasty. Kai-kuan (jar with cover) with decoration of "nine children at play" in under-glaze blue and enamel of contrasting colours.

二六九

清乾隆窯御題粉彩菊花梅瓶特辦精品二件(院)

原名乾隆款洋彩白地菊花瓷梅瓶·底均有大清乾隆年製六字篆款·口徑均肆公分高貳拾壹·肆公分底徑陸·柒公分最大腹圍叁拾壹·捌公分

Porcelain No. 269.

Ch'ien Lung Ware of the Ch'ing Dynasty. Mei-p'ing (vases) decorated with chrysanthemum in fên-ts'ai (enamel mixed with powder) and an imperial epigraph. Specially made by imperial decree—an exquisite specimen. Two pieces.

(204)

二七〇

清乾隆窯直粉三彩錦上添花轉心雙活環鏤空雲龍花薰冠架一件(院)

原名玲瓏旋轉瓷帽架底有「大清乾隆年製」六字篆款帶蓋。口徑肆·玖公分通蓋高叁拾·玖公分底徑拾柒·壹公分最大腹圍肆拾伍·玖公分。

Porcelain No. 270.

Ch'ien Lung Ware of the Ch'ing Dynasty. Hua-hsün kuan-chia (flower perfumer—hat stand), decorated in fên-ts'ai of three colours with flowers over brocaded ground, two movable rings revolving round the centre and with openwork of clouds and dragons.

二七一

清乾隆窯霽青描金番蓮鏤空轉心粉彩落花游魚四繫瓶一件(院)

原名瓷胎洋彩青地金花魚游春水瓷瓶底有大清乾隆年製六字篆款口徑伍·壹公分高貳拾叁·肆公分底徑捌·叁公分最大腹圍肆拾貳·捌公分

Porcelain No. 271.

Ch'ien Lung Ware of the Ch'ing Dynasty. Ssu-hsi p'ing (vase with four fastening loops), with openwork body decorated with Indian lotus painted in gold over a ground of chi-ch'ing (or the blue of the sky after rain) and a revolving centre decorated with swimming fish and falling flowers in fên-ts'ai (or enamel mixed with powder).

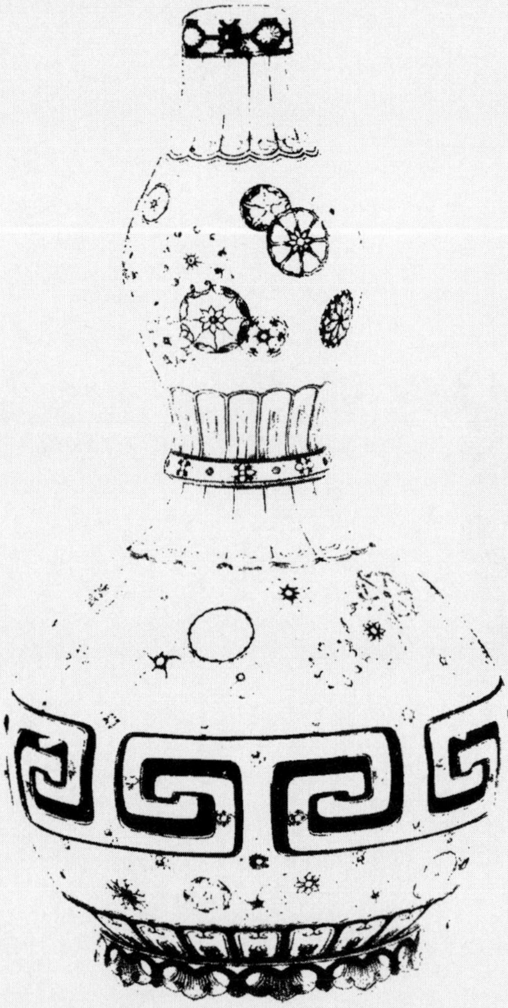

二七二

清乾隆窯粉彩黃地錦上添花粉青鏤空雷文葫蘆轉心瓶一件（陵）

原名乾隆款葫蘆旋轉瓷瓶底有「大清乾隆年製」六字篆款有盤口徑叁·叁公分高貳拾玖·捌公分底徑拾·貳公分最大腹圍伍拾·貳公分

Porcelain No. 272.

Ch'ien Lung Ware of the Ch'ing Dynasty. Hu-lu chuan-hsin p'ing (revolving vase in shape of double-gourd) decorated with flowers in fên-ts'ai (enamel mixed with powder) over a yellow brocaded ground and the body with openwork of linear squared spiral ornament (lei-wên) in fên-ch'ing (light greenish-blue).

二七三

清乾隆窯粉青地粉彩鏤空垂雲八卦轉心瓶一件(院)

原名瓷胎洋彩八卦如意旋轉瓷瓶底有大清乾隆年製六字篆款口徑柒·玖公分高貳拾貳·捌公分底徑玖·叁公分腹圍叁拾陸·陸公分

Porcelain No. 273.

Ch'ien Lung Ware of the Ch'ing Dynasty. Chuan-hsin p'ing (revolving vase) with decoration in fên-ts'ai over a fên-ch'ing (light greenish-blue) ground of openwork of pendent clouds and the "eight trigrams" (pa-kua).

二七四

清乾隆窯貢粉三彩錦上添花鏤空雲蝠轉心瓶一件(陸)

原名乾隆洋彩如意旋轉瓷瓶底有「大清乾隆年製」六字篆款。口徑柒公分高貳拾柒公分底徑拾玖·叁公分最大腹圍叁拾柒·玖公分

Porcelain No. 274.

Ch'ien Lung Ware of the Ch'ing Dynasty. Chuan-hsin p'ing (revolving vase) decorated in fên-ts'ai of three colours, with flowers over a brocaded ground and the body with openwork of clouds and bats.

(209)

二七五

清乾隆窯粉彩紫地錦上添花粉青鏤空蟠螭套瓶一件(院)

原名乾隆款洋彩玲瓏瓷膽瓶底有「大清乾隆年製」六字篆款口徑玖·肆公分高叁拾捌·伍公分底徑拾叁·柒公分最大腹圍柒拾貳·柒公分

Porcelain No. 275.

Ch'ien Lung Ware of the Ch'ing Dynasty. T'ao-p'ing (enveloping vase) decorated with flowers in fên-ts'ai (enamel mixed with powder) over a purple brocaded ground, the body of openwork with coiled ch'ih (hornless dragons) in fên-ch'ing (light greenish-blue).

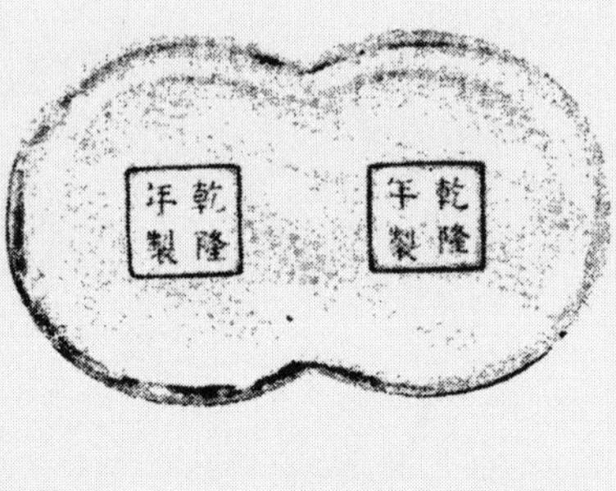

二七六

清乾隆窰粉彩久安圖雙連蓋罐一件（院）

原名畫琺瑯合歡蓋罐。底有「乾隆年製」四字楷款。口縱最大伍·柒公分，橫玖公分。高拾柒·陸公分。底縱最大陸·壹公分，橫玖·伍公分

Porcelain No. 276.

Ch'ien Lung Ware of the Ch'ing Dynasty. Shuang-lien kai-kuan (joint-jar with cover) decorated in fên-ts'ai (enamel mixed with powder) with chiu-an t'u or chrysanthemums and quails.

二七七

清乾隆窯粉彩紫地錦上添花春燈嬰戲如意雙耳瓶一件(院)

原名彩花人物雙耳瓷瓶底有大清乾隆年製六字篆款口徑拾貳公分高肆拾壹伍公分底徑拾壹柒公分最大腹圍陸拾陸伍公分

Porcelain No. 277.

Ch'ien Lung Ware of the Ch'ing Dynasty. P'ing (vase) with handles shaped like ju-i, decorated with flowers in fên-ts'ai over a purple brocaded ground, and on the white space of the body, with children sporting with lanterns in spring—ch'un-têng ying-hsi.

二七八

清乾隆窯粉彩雞缸桮一件(院)

原名瓷胎鷄缸盃底有大清乾隆仿古六字篆款桮上有乾隆御題口徑柒捌公分高柒公分底徑叁玖公分

Porcelain No. 278.

Ch'ien Lung Ware of the Ch'ing Dynasty. Chi-kang pei (chicken cup) in fên-ts'ai (enamel mixed with powder). The base mark is "Ta Ch'ing Ch'ien Lung fang-ku" or reproduction of an antique ware of the year of Ch'ien Lung of the Great Ch'ing Dynasty, in underglaze blue.

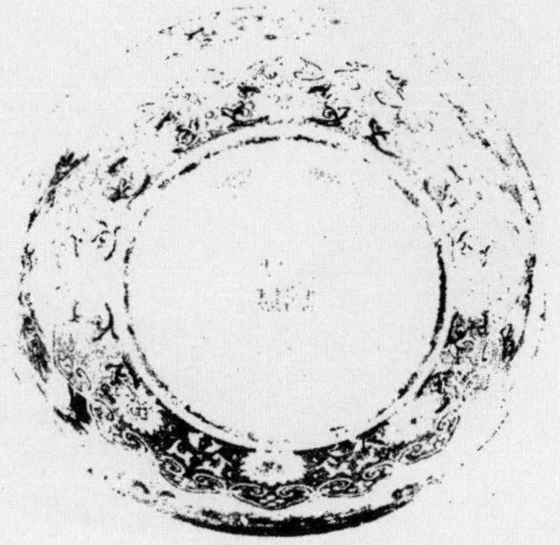

212

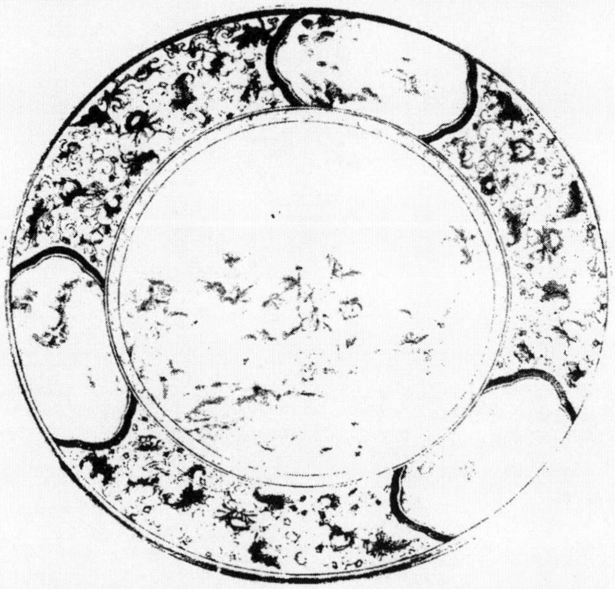

二七九

清乾隆窯琺瑯彩海棠春燕碟一件(院)

原名瓷胎洋彩花鳥四寸碟。底款藍料凸起「乾隆年製」四字楷款。口徑拾叁伍公分。高壹·玖公分。底徑陸·捌公分

Porcelain No. 279.

Ch'ien Lung Ware of the Ch'ing Dynasty. Dish decorated in cloisonné enamel with hai-t'ang ch'un-yen—cydonia flowers and spring swallows. The date mark of the base consists of "Ch'ien Lung nien chih." in raised characters of blue material.

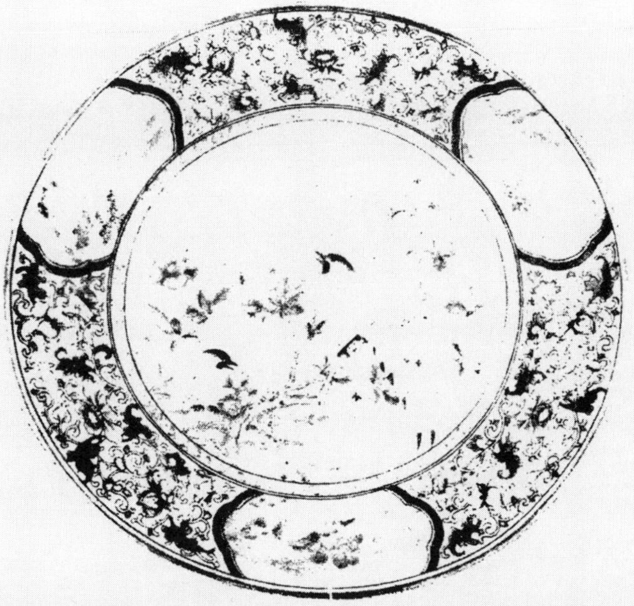

二八〇

清乾隆窯琺瑯彩海棠壽帶碟一件（陸）

原名瓷胎洋彩花鳥四寸碟底款藍料凸起「乾隆年製」四字楷款口徑拾叁·伍公分高壹·玖公分底徑陸·捌公分

Porcelain No. 280.

Ch'ien Lung Ware of the Ch'ing Dynasty. Dish decorated in cloisonné enamel with hai-t'ang shou-tai --cydonia flowers and shou-tai birds. The date mark on the base is "Ch'ien Lung nien chih" in raised characters of blue material.

(215)

二八一

清乾隆窯珐瑯彩山水樓閣盤二件(陸)

原名瓷胎珐瑯紅地白裏山水六寸盤底款藍料凸起“乾隆年製”四字楷款内壹件口徑拾柒·肆公分高肆·叁公分底徑拾·玖公分又壹件口徑拾柒·叁公分高肆·叁公分底徑拾壹公分之二原有沖口

Porcelain No. 281.

Ch'ien Lung Ware of the Ch'ing Dynasty. Pair of plates with the decoration of belvederes and landscape in cloisonné, enamel. Two pieces. One with a small crack originally there. With the base mark of "Ch'ien Lung nien chih" in raised characters of blue material.

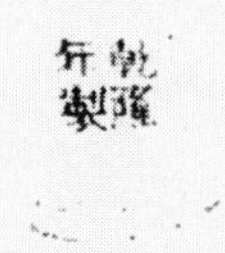

二八二

清乾隆窯琺瑯彩紅錦地折枝花卉魚藻盌二件(院)

原名瓷胎畫琺瑯錦上添花茶盌底款藍料凸起「乾隆年製」四字楷款、口徑均拾壹·叁公分高伍·玖公分底徑肆公分

Porcelain No. 282.

Ch'ien Lung Ware of the Ch'ing Dynasty. Pair of small bowls decorated in cloisonné enamel inside with fish and water plants and outside with sprays of flowers over red brocaded ground. With the base mark of "Ch'ien Lung nien chih" in raised characters of blue material.

(217)

二八三

清乾隆窯琺瑯彩藍錦地折枝花卉小盌二件(院)

原名瓷胎畫琺瑯錦上添花藍地茶盌底款藍料凸起「乾隆年製」四字楷款口徑均拾壹·玖公分高陸·壹公分底徑肆·伍公分。

Porcelain No. 283.

Ch'ien Lung Ware of the Ch'ing Dynasty. Pair of small bowls with decoration in cloisonné enamel of sprays of flowers on blue brocaded ground. Two pieces. The date mark on the base is "Ch'ien Lung nien chih" in raised characters of blue material.

二八四

清乾隆窯琺瑯彩洋紅折枝月季酒鍾二件(院)

原名瓷胎畫琺瑯洋紅酒鍾底款藍料凸起「乾隆年製」四字楷款口徑均肆·壹公分高叁公分底徑貳·壹公分

Porcelain No. 284.

Ch'ien Lung Ware of the Ch'ing Dynasty. Pair of small wine cups in foreign red, decorated in cloisonné enamel, inside, with sprays of roses. The date mark on the base is "Ch'ien Lung nien chih" in raised characters of blue material.

（ 219 ）

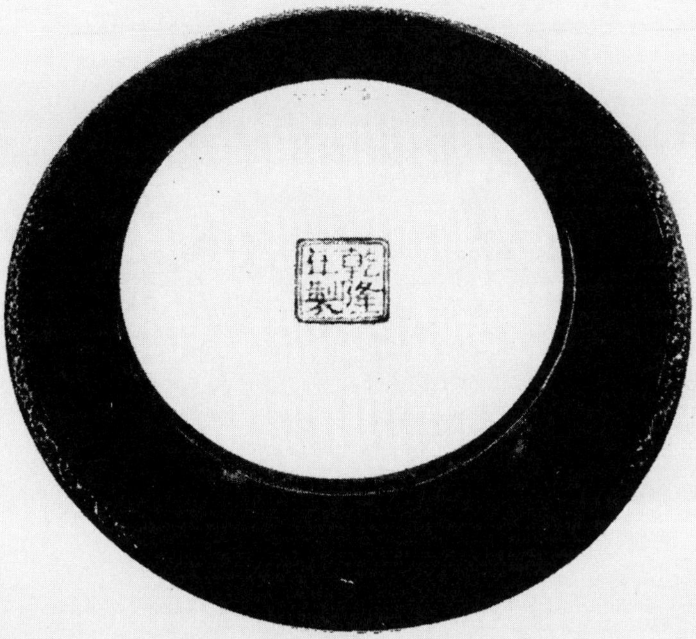

二八五

清乾隆窯琺瑯彩堆藍立粉開光春閨課子碟二件（院）

原名藍地暗花美瓷盤，底款藍料凸起「乾隆年製」四字楷款，口徑均拾叁·貳公分。高貳·柒公分，底徑捌公分。

Porcelain No. 285.

Ch'ien Lung Ware of the Ch'ing Dynasty. Pair of dishes with panels painted over a ground of floral designs of piled blue and heaped powder, with the picture in cloisonné enamel, of ch'un-kuei ko-tzŭ or mother teaching her child in her chamber in spring. Two pieces. The date mark on the base is "Ch'ien Lung nien chih" in raised characters of blue material.

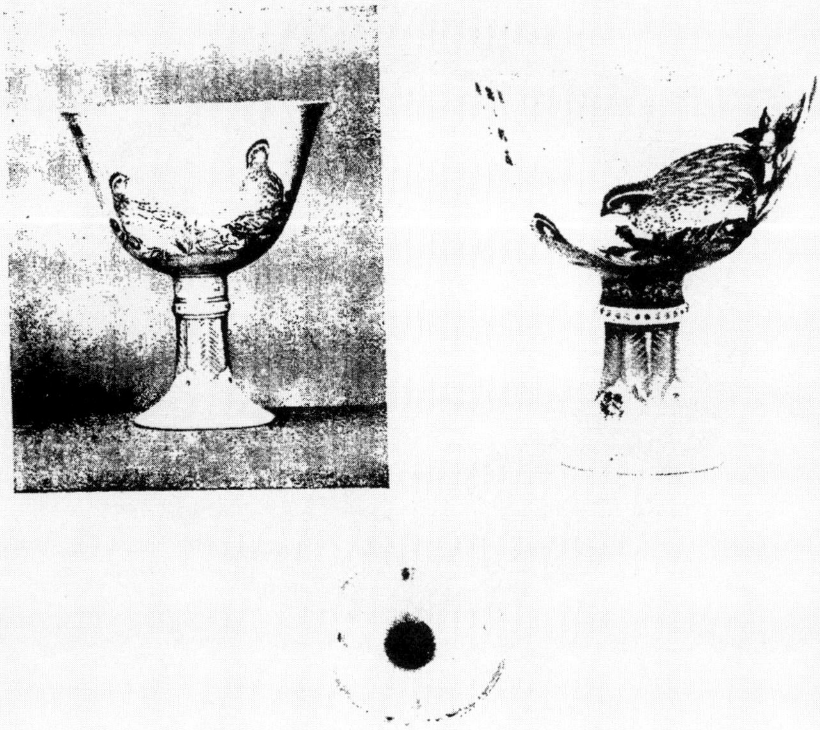

二八六

清乾隆窯琺瑯彩月季雙安圖高足杯（至精之品）二件（院）

原名瓷胎畫琺瑯花鳥靶鍾底款藍料凸起「乾隆年製」四字楷款内壹件口有微傷口徑柒·叁公分高捌·玖公分底徑叁·捌公分又壹件口徑柒·壹公分高捌·陸公分底徑叁·伍公分

Porcelain No. 286.

Ch'ien Lung Ware of the Ch'ing Dynasty. Pair of high stemmed wine cups decorated in cloisonné enamel with roses and shuang-an t'u—picture of two quails (an), signifying double peace (an). Two pieces. These are exquisite specimens. The date mark on the base is "Ch'ien Lung nien chih" in raised characters of blue material.

二八七

清乾隆窯琺瑯彩鸜鵒梅花膽瓶一件(院)

原名瓷胎畫琺瑯禽鳥梅花瓶底款藍料凸起「乾隆年製」四字楷款口徑叁·陸公分高貳拾·肆公分底徑肆·陸公分最大腹圍叁拾貳·伍公分

Porcelain No. 287.

Ch'ien Lung Ware of the Ch'ing Dynasty. Tan-p'ing (gall-shaped vase) with decoration in cloisonné enamel of ch'ü-yü (black thrushes) and the prunus. The date mark on the base is "Ch'ien Lung nien chih" in raised characters of blue material.

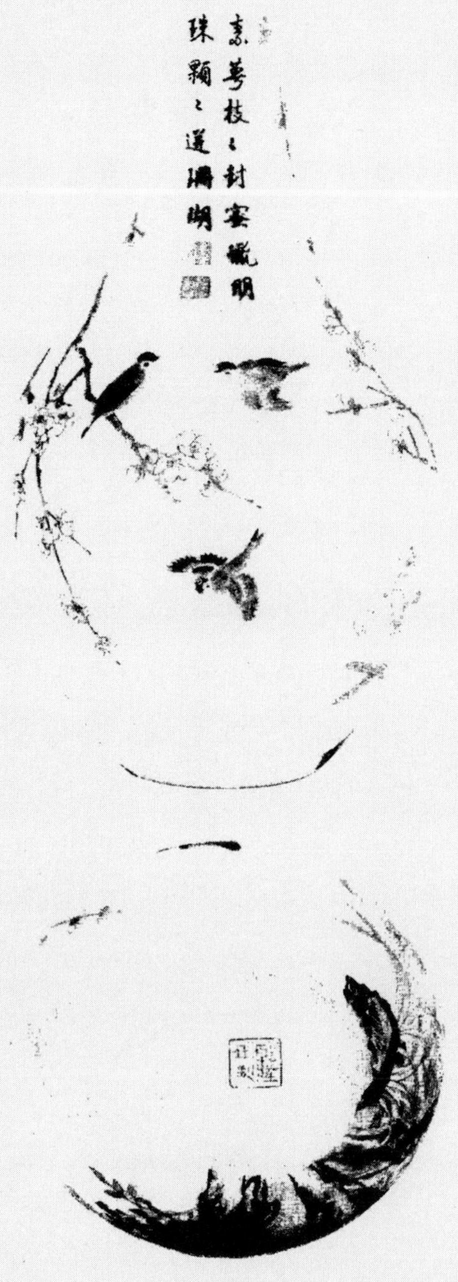

二八八

清乾隆窯珐瑯彩天仙梅壽膽瓶一件(院)

原名瓷胎畫珐瑯禽鳥梅花瓶。底款藍料凸起「乾隆年製」四字楷款。口徑叁·伍公分，高貳拾·叁公分，底徑肆·肆公分，最大腹圍叁拾壹·捌公分。

Porcelain No. 288.

Ch'ien Lung Ware of the Ch'ing Dynasty. Tan-p'ing (gall-shaped vase) with decoration in cloisonné enamel of t'ien-hsien mei-shou, i.e. the nandina domestica, narcissus, prunus and shou-tai bird—being a rebus for "long life of a heavenly immortal." The date mark on the base is "Ch'ien Lung nien chih" in raised characters of blue material.

221

二八九

清乾隆窯琺瑯彩藍地錦上添花開光折枝花卉瓶二件（院）

原名乾隆洋彩紙搥瓶底款藍料凸起「乾隆年製四字楷款口徑均肆·貳公分高拾捌·柒公分底徑柒·叁公分最大腹圍叁拾陸·捌公分

Porcelain No. 289.

Ch'ien Lung Ware of the Ch'ing Dynasty. Pair of p'ing (vases) with the decoration of sprays of flowers painted in panels over a blue brocaded ground—all in cloisonné enamel. The date mark on the base is "Ch'ien Lung nien chih" in raised characters of blue material.

(226)

二九〇

清乾隆窯琺瑯彩藍地錦上添花開光折枝番蓮菊花膽瓶二件(院)

原名瓷胎洋彩錦上添花玉環膽瓶底款綠地藍料凸起「乾隆年製」四字篆款口徑均叁·貳公分高貳拾叁·捌公分底徑陸·壹公分最大腹圍肆拾·貳公分

Porcelain No. 290.

Ch'ien Lung Ware of the Ch'ing Dynasty. Pair of tan-p'ing (gall-shaped vases) with decoration in cloisonné enamel of sprays of Indian lotus and chrysanthemums painted in panels over blue brocaded grounds. Two pieces. The date mark on the base is "Ch'ien Lung nien chih" in raised characters of blue material on a green ground.

二九一

清乾隆窯琺瑯彩洋紅鈎蓮地開光十八羅漢瓶二件（院）

原名瓷胎洋彩人物膽瓶。底款藍料凸起「乾隆年製」四字楷款。均口徑叁·肆公分。高貳拾叁·貳公分。底徑伍·捌公分最大腹圍肆拾·捌公分

Porcelain No. 291.

Ch'ien Lung Ware of the Ch'ing Dynasty. Pair of p'ing (vases) with decoration in cloisonné enamel in panels of "eighteen Ahrats" painted on grounds of hooked lotus (kou-lien) in foreign red. Two pieces. The date mark on the base is "Ch'ien Lung nien chih" in raised characters of blue material.

二九二

清乾隆窯琺瑯彩蝗螂秋色小梅瓶二件（院）

原名瓷地畫琺瑯三秋花白地三喜瓶。底款藍料凸起「乾隆御製」四字楷款。口徑貳·貳公分。高玖·貳公分底徑貳公分最大腹圍拾陸·伍公分

Porcelain No. 292.

Ch'ien Lung Ware of the Ch'ing Dynasty. Pair of miniature mei-p'ing (vases) decorated in cloisonné enamel with tang-lang ch'iu-sê—or mantis and autumn flowers. Two pieces. The date mark on the base is "Ch'ien Lung yü-chih" in raised characters of blue material.

（ 229 ）

二九三

清乾隆窯琺瑯彩梅鶴膽瓶一件(院)

原名瓷胎畫琺瑯仙山樓閣膽瓶底款藍料凸起「乾隆年製」四字篆款口徑叁·伍公分高貳拾·柒公分底徑肆·貳公分最大腹圍叁拾叁公分

Porcelain No. 293.

Ch'ien Lung Ware of the Ch'ing Dynasty. Tan-p'ing (gall-shaped vase) with decoration in cloisonné enamel of the prunus and the crane. The date mark on the base is "Ch'ien Lung nien chih" in raised characters of blue material.

(231)

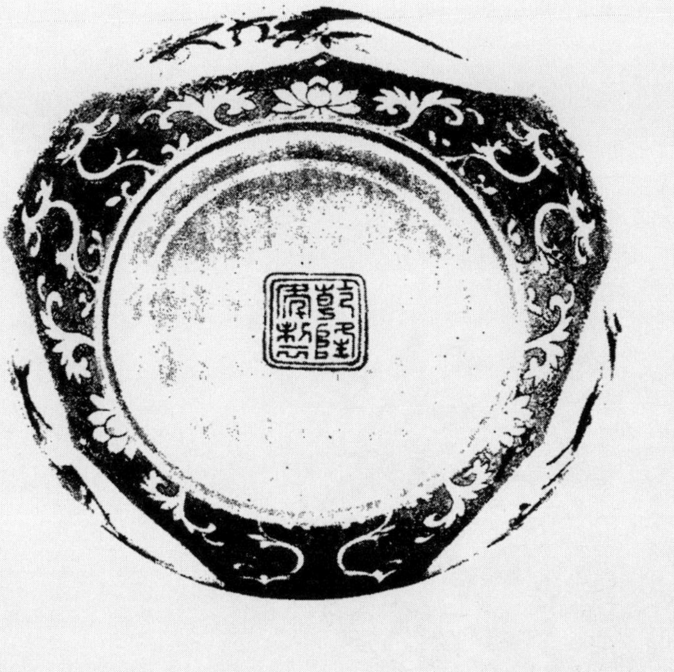

二九四

清乾隆窯琺瑯彩洋紅地錦上添花開光靈仙圖瓶二件（院）

原名瓷胎洋彩三多紙搥瓶底款藍料凸起「乾隆年製」四字篆款。之一。口徑肆·壹公分。高拾玖·叁公分。底徑柒·肆公分。最大腹圍叁拾陸·肆公分之二口徑肆·壹公分。高拾玖·壹公分。底徑柒·肆公分。最大腹圍叁拾陸·捌公分

Porcelain No. 294.

Ch'ien Lung Ware of the Ch'ing Dynasty. Pair of p'ing (vases) decorated with panels over brocaded grounds of foreign red, painted with ling-hsien t'u (or the ling-chih fungus and the narcissus) in cloisonné enamel. Two pieces. The date mark on the base is "Ch'ien Lung nien chih" in raised characters of blue material.

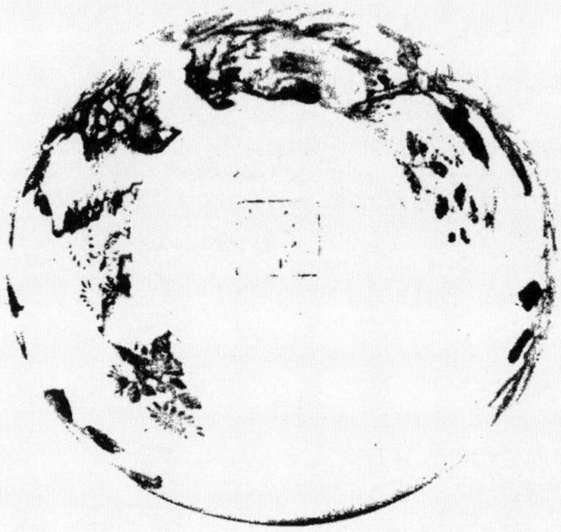

二九五

清乾隆窯琺瑯彩牡丹壺

(通稱玉壺春)一件(院)

原名乾隆款白地花卉玉壺春瓶。底款藍料凸起「乾隆年製」四字楷款。口徑肆公分,高陸·叁公分,底徑肆·玖公分,最大腹圍叁拾貳·貳公分。

Porcelain No. 295.

Ch'ien Lung Ware of the Ch'ing Dynasty. Hu (vase, commonly called yü-hu ch'un) with decoration of peonies in cloisonné enamel. The date mark on the base is "Ch'ien Lung nien chih" in raised characters of blue material.

二九六

清乾隆窯琺瑯彩山茶碧桃壺(通稱玉壺春)一件(院)

原名乾隆款白地花卉玉壺春瓶。底款藍料凸起「乾隆年製」四字楷款。口徑肆·壹公分。高陸·貳公分。底徑伍·貳公分。最大腹圍叁拾貳·伍公分。

Porcelain No. 296.

Ch'ien Lung Ware of the Ch'ing Dynasty. Hu (vase, commonly called yü-hu ch'un) with decoration of wild camillia and peach blossoms (the white double kind) in cloisonné enamel. The date mark on the base is "Ch'ien Lung nien chih" in raised characters of blue material.

二九七

清乾隆窯琺瑯彩桃柳爭春溫壺一件（院）

原名瓷胎畫琺瑯白地桃葉蒜頭瓶。底款藍料凸起「乾隆年製」四字楷款。口徑貳·叁公分。高拾柒·伍公分。底徑肆·柒公分。最大腹圍叁拾·伍公分。

Porcelain No. 297.

Ch'ien Lung Ware of the Ch'ing Dynasty. Wên-hu (hot-water bottle used as a vase) decorated in cloisonné enamel with t'ao-liu tsêng-ch'un or the peach and the willow rivalling in spring. The date mark on the base is "Ch'ien Lung nien chih" in raised characters of blue material.

二九八

清乾隆窯琺瑯彩杏柳春燕溫壺一件(院)

原名瓷胎畫琺瑯白地桃葉尊頭瓶底款藍料凸起「乾隆年製」四字楷款口徑貳·叁公分高拾柒·伍公分底徑肆·柒公分最大腹圍叁拾·伍公分

Porcelain No. 298.

Ch'ien Lung Ware of the Ch'ing Dynasty. Wên-hu (hot-water bottle used as a vase) decorated in cloisonné enamel with hsing-liu ch'un-yen or the apricot, the willow and spring swallows. The date mark on the base is "Ch'ien Lung nien chih" in raised characters of blue material.

二九九

清乾隆窯琺瑯彩開光三羊圖長方盒一件（院）

原名瓷胎畫琺瑯三羊開泰長方盒，底款藍料凸起「乾隆年製」四字楷款，通蓋高叁·玖公分，口縱伍·貳公分，橫陸·捌公分，底縱肆·肆公分，橫陸公分

Porcelain No. 299.

Ch'ien Lung Ware of the Ch'ing Dynasty. Oblong box decorated in cloisonné enamel with san-yang t'u, or the picture of three rams (a rebus meaning the revivifying power of spring). The date mark on the base is "Ch'ien Lung nien chih" in raised characters of blue material.

清康熙製

V. CH'ING K'ANG HSI MANUFACTURE

三〇〇

清康熙銅胎琺瑯彩紫地纏枝百合小盌一件（院）

原名銅胎畫琺瑯蓋盌，底款藍料康熙御製四字楷款，口徑拾貳·叁公分，通蓋頂高玖·貳公分，底徑陸·叁公分

Porcelain No. 300.

Ch'ing K'ang Hsi small bowl of cloisonné enamel on a copper-body, with decoration of twining sprays of lily over a purple ground. The base mark is "K'ang Hsi yü-chih" of blue enamel.

三〇一

清康熙銅胎琺瑯彩荷花蓋盌一件(院)

原名銅胎畫琺瑯蓮花蓋盌，底款洋紅凸起「康熙御製」四字楷款，口徑拾·柒公分，通蓋頂高玖·壹公分，底徑肆·捌公分。

Porcelain No. 301.

Ch'ing K'ang Hsi covered bowl (kai-wan) of copper-body with decoration of lotus flowers in cloisonné enamel. The date mark on the base is "K'ang Hsi yü-chih" in raised characters of foreign red.

三〇二

清康熙銅胎琺瑯彩黃地折枝牡丹瓶一件(院)

原名銅胎琺瑯五彩牡丹黃地觀音瓶。底款藍料「康熙御製」四字楷款，口徑玖公分，高叁拾肆·肆公分，底徑拾·叁公分，最大腹圍伍拾肆公分

Porcelain No. 302.

Ch'ing K'ang Hsi copper-bodied p'ing (vase) with sprays of peonies in cloisonné enamel over a yellow ground. The base mark is "K'ang Hsi yü-chih" in blue enamel.

三〇三

清康熙銅胎琺瑯彩歲朝圖小瓶 ·件(院)

原名銅胎畫琺瑯白地花卉瓶底款洋紅凸起「康熙御製」四字楷款口徑貳·叁公分高拾公分底徑叁·肆公分最大腹圍拾陸·玖公分

Porcelain No. 303.

Ch'ing K'ang Hsi miniature p'ing (vase) with decoration of shui-ch'ao t'u or the levee on a New Year's Day, i.e. of the narcissus, the nandina domestica, the prunus, the camillia and the ling-chih fungus, in cloisonné enamel on a copper body. The base mark is "K'ang Hsi yü-chih" in raised characters of foreign red. But it looks black on account of insufficient firing.

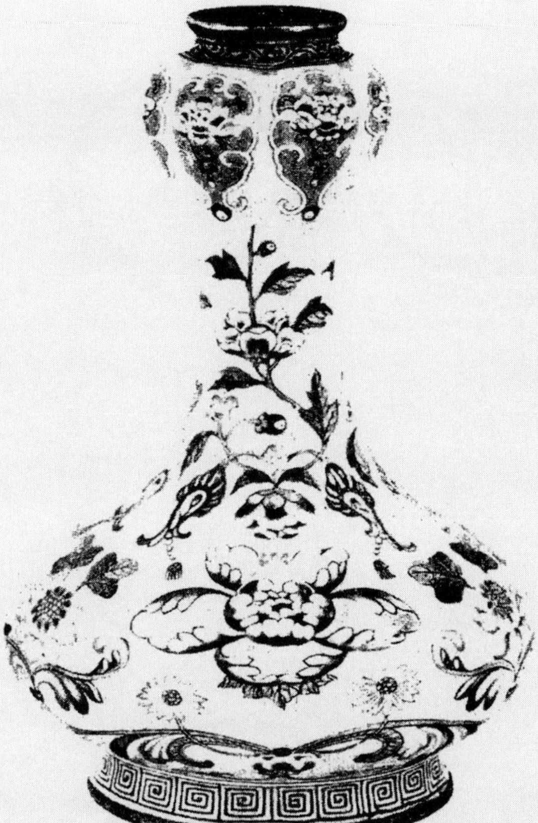

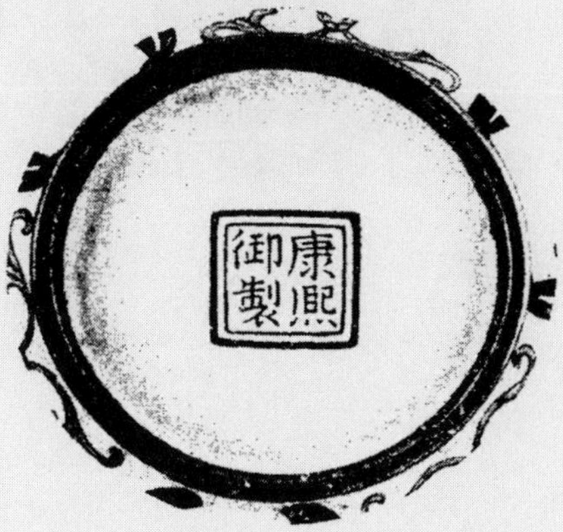

三〇四

清康熙銅胎琺瑯彩黃地纏枝花卉溫壺一件（院）

原名銅胎琺瑯黃地花卉瓶，底款藍料凸起康熙御製四字楷款，帶木座，口徑貳·伍公分，高拾叁·肆公分，底徑伍·玖公分，最大腹圍貳拾陸·捌公分。

Porcelain No. 304.

Ch'ing K'ang Hsi copper-bodied wên-hu (hot-water bottle used as vase) with decoration of interlacing sprays of flowers in cloisonné enamel over a yellow ground. The date mark on the base is "K'ang Hsi yü-chih" in raised characters of blue material. With a wooden stand.

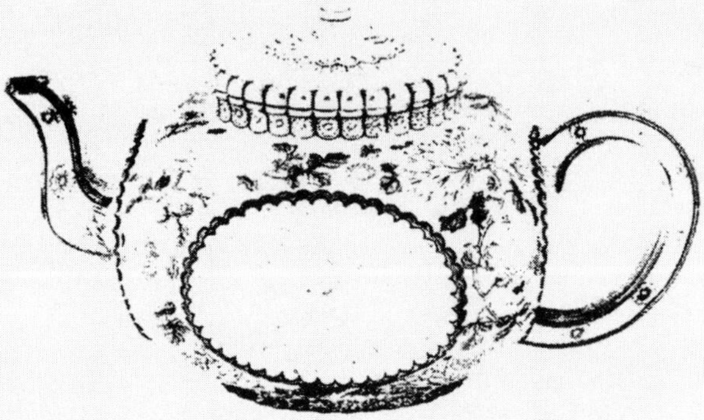

三 〇 五

清康熙銅胎珐瑯彩黃地開光菊花把壺 一件(院)

原名銅胎珐瑯四方滿鏤底款藍料康熙御製四字楷款口徑陸·壹公分通蓋頂高玖·壹公分通長拾陸公分底徑陸公分.

Porcelain No. 305.

Ch'ing K'ang Hsi pa-hu (pot with handle) of a copper body with decoration of chrysanthemums in cloisonné enamel enclosed in medallions over a yellow ground. With the date mark of "K'ang Hsi yü-chih" in blue enamel on the base.

三 〇 六

清康熙銅胎珐瑯彩黃地纏枝牡丹唾盂 一件(院)

原名銅胎珐瑯五彩西番花玉壺春瓶底款藍料凸起康熙御製四字楷款帶木座口徑伍·陸公分高柒·伍公分底徑陸·柒公分最大腹圍貳拾柒·肆公分

Porcelain No. 306.

Ch'ing K'ang Hsi cuspidore of copper decorated with twining sprays of peonies in cloisonné enamel over a yellow ground. The date mark on the base is "K'ang Hsi yü-chih" in raised characters of blue enamel. With a wooden stand.

清乾隆製

VI. CH'ING CH'IEN LUNG MANUFACTURE

(In cloisonné enamel on a glass-body.)

三〇八

清乾隆玻璃胎琺瑯
彩蘆汀採魚圖扁方
鼻烟壺一件(院)

原名古月軒料鼻烟壺底
款藍料乾隆年製四字楷
款口有傷帶布坌口縦連
邊壹·貳公分高陸·肆公分
底縦壹·叁公分横壹·捌公
分

Porcelain No. 308.

Ch'ing Ch'ien Lung glass snuff-bottle of a flattened quadrangular shape, decorated with lu-chiang ts'ai-yü t'u (or fisher-women picking their fish on a rushy bank), in cloisonné enamel. The base mark consists of "Ch'ien Lung nien chih," four raised characters of blue material.

三〇七

清乾隆玻璃胎琺瑯彩秋郊課子小瓶一件(院)

原名乾隆款玻璃畫琺瑯人物詩意瓶底款刻宋體「乾隆年製」
四字底有璺腹有微傷口徑貳·壹公分高拾·伍公分底徑貳·柒
公分最大腹圍拾陸·伍公分

Porcelain No. 307.

Ch'ing Ch'ien Lung glass-bodied small p'ing (vase) decorated in cloisonné enamel with ch'iu-chiao ko-tzŭ, mother teaching her child in the suburb in autumn amidst flowers, plants, and rocks on a slope. On the base is carved the mark of "Ch'ien Lung nien chih," four characters, in the Sung style of writing.

(72422B)

参加倫敦中國藝術國際展覽會出品圖說

第二册　瓷器

Illustrated Catalogue of Chinese Government Exhibits for the International Exhibition of Chinese Art in London

Volume II Porcelain

編輯者　倫敦中國藝術國際展覽會籌備委員會

發行人　王雲五　上海河南路

印刷所　商務印書館　上海河南路

發行所　商務印書館　上海及各埠

定價國幣伍元　外埠酌加運費匯費

中華民國二十五年四月初版 七月再版

四七九六上

(本書校對者翁際雲)

参加伦敦中国艺术国际展览会出品图说

第 三 册　书 画

ILLUSTRATED CATALOGUE OF CHINESE GOVERNMENT EXHIBITS FOR THE INTERNATIONAL EXHIBITION OF CHINESE ART IN LONDON

VOLUME III. PAINTING AND CALLIGRAPHY

伦敦中国艺术国际展览会筹备委员会编辑

中央编译出版社
CCTP Central Compilation & Translation Press

图书在版编目（CIP）数据

参加伦敦中国艺术国际展览会出品图说 / 伦敦中国艺术国际展览会筹备委员会主编．-- 北京：中央编译出版社，2022.9

ISBN 978-7-5117-4241-4

Ⅰ．①参… Ⅱ．①伦… Ⅲ．①历史文物－中国－图集
Ⅳ．① K870.2

中国版本图书馆 CIP 数据核字（2022）第 153392 号

参加伦敦中国艺术国际展览会出品图说

责任编辑 郑永杰
特约编辑 刘诗婷 杨 凌
责任印制 刘 慧
出版发行 中央编译出版社
地　　址 北京市海淀区北四环西路 69 号（100080）
电　　话 （010）55627391（总编室）　（010）55627312（编辑室）
（010）55627320（发行部）　（010）55627377（新技术部）
经　　销 全国新华书店
印　　刷 山东韵杰文化科技有限公司
开　　本 889 毫米 ×1194 毫米 1/16
字　　数 321 千字
印　　张 50.25
版　　次 2022 年 9 月第 1 版
印　　次 2022 年 9 月第 1 次印刷
定　　价 980.00 元（全四册）

新浪微博：@ 中央编译出版社　　**微　　信：**中央编译出版社（ID：cctphome）
淘宝店铺：中央编译出版社直销店（http://shop108367160.taobao.com）
（010）55627331

參加倫敦中國藝術國際展覽會出品圖說

第三册　書畫

ILLUSTRATED CATALOGUE OF CHINESE GOVERNMENT EXHIBITS FOR THE INTERNATIONAL EXHIBITION OF CHINESE ART IN LONDON

VOLUME III.　PAINTING AND CALLIGRAPHY

倫敦中國藝術國際展覽會籌備委員會編輯
商務印書館印行

Volume III.

PAINTING

AND

CALLIGRAPHY

第　三　册

書　畫

參加倫敦中國藝術國際展覽會

書畫照片總目

書畫說明	頁數
第一章 總綱	五
第二章 書學之演進及其名家	五
第三章 畫學之演進及其名家	七
第四章 中國畫之特點及其繪畫之法	一一
第五章 此次出品概要	一三

	名稱	件數	
一	唐代畫	三件	一七
二	五代畫	三件	二〇
三	宋代書畫	五十六件	三四
四	元代書畫	四十一件	一二八
五	明代書畫	四十三件	一八六
六	清代書畫	二十九件	二二五

總共壹百柒拾伍件

TABLE OF CONTENTS

PAGE

INTRODUCTORY NOTE

Capt. I. General Principles 6

Capt. II. The Evolution of Chinese Calligraphy and Its Eminent Exponents. . . 6

Capt. III. The Evolution of Chinese Painting and Its Famous Painters 8

Capt. IV. The Special Features and Technique of Chinese Painting 12

Capt. V. The Principal Exhibits 14

T'ang Dynasty 17

Five Dynasties 20

Sung Dynasty 34

Yuan Dynasty 128

Ming Dynasty 186

Ch'ing Dynasty 225

參加倫敦中國藝術國際展覽會

書畫照片總目

書畫說明

第一章 總綱

中國書畫之學。有極悠久之歷史存在。其特色尤在書學與繪畫之學互相貫通。故足於世界藝術上占一重要位置。蓋各國祇有畫學而無書學。日本雖有書學。乃以中國之書學爲書學者也。中國之書與畫。皆以表現內心之感想爲前提。其間書與畫息息相通。互無止境。凡人格之高尚。學識之深邃。皆本精神之所寄。內蘊而外發。與僅止描寫物像實體者不同。而技巧復足以副之。古代遺物之尚存者（指絹本紙本）。如六朝之鍾繇、王羲之、顧愷之等。年代較遠。頗難斷定其眞僞。唐宋以降。則所存猶繁。足資研索。今就歷代書與畫之源流派別。擇要縷舉以介於海內外究心中國書畫之學者如下。

第二章 書學之演進及其名家

書學爲中國藝術之一種。其發展約分五時期。商周至秦。由含圖畫性之文字。演進爲籀文小篆。此爲第一時期。此期之字。存者爲銅器及石刻等。尙多可考。

秦末創八分。漢復創隸書、章草、草書。魏鍾繇、晉王羲之以如今體之行、楷、草書著名。眞迹猶存於世。遂爲今體書之集大成者。歷代書家。皆莫能出其範圍。以迄於六朝之末。其間惟北朝略成別派（如鄭羲等）。雄奇峻整。自具特長。此爲第二時期。

PAINTING AND CALLIGRAPHY

INTRODUCTORY NOTE

Chapter I—General Principles

Chinese calligraphy and Chinese painting both have a history of great antiquity. They are moreover distinguished by the existence between them of a peculiar close affinity. The art of painting is known in many countries, but the art of calligraphy is known only in China, and what is known of the art of calligraphy in Japan is also that of China. Characterized as they are by this very special relationship in their parallel existence, Chinese calligraphy and painting would seem to deserve a position of first importance in the realm of art.

Primarily both Chinese calligraphy and painting serve as media of the revelation of the spirit of man and have always exercised great influence upon each other. Nobility of character and profundity of learning find expression in Chinese paintings and writings, which, with an adequate technique of their own, are essentially different from the simple reproductions of concrete substances.

Of the old writings and paintings that are extant (that is, those done on silk and paper), there are examples of Chung Yu, Wang Hsi-chi, Ku Kai-chi of the Six Dynasties. But owing to their great antiquity, it is difficult to ascertain their genuineness. Those of the T'ang and Sung Dynasties are more numerous and are worth careful study. It is now proposed to describe briefly and in their main aspects the origins and types of the various writings and paintings in their historical order for the benefit of those who are interested in the art of Chinese calligraphy and painting.

Chapter II—The Evolution of Chinese Calligraphy and Its Eminent Exponents

Calligraphy as one kind of Chinese art may be said to have passed through approximately five stages. From the dynasties of Shang and Chou to the Chin Dynasty, Chinese calligraphy evolved from picture-writing to chou-wen (籀文), and siao-chuan (小篆). This may be regarded as the first period of which many specimens may be found on various bronze-ware and stone inscriptions.

Pa-fen (八分), a composite and transitional type of writing, first appeared at the end of the Chin Dynasty, while during the Han Dynasty such styles as li-shu (隸書), chang-tsao (章草), and tsao-shu (草書) were evolved. During Wei, there was Chung Yu and during Tsing there was Wang Hsi-chi, both of whom were famous for their writing in what is known to-day as the formal and running styles and of whose handwriting true representative specimens are still in existence to-day. It might be said that in their writings the art of Chinese calligraphy as known in its present styles reached its height. In fact, no subsequent artist up to the end of the Six Dynasties ever went beyond these two eminent calligraphists. The only slight deviation occurred during Pei Chao (North Dynasty) when such man as Chen Hsi developed a style possessing singular vigour and a sheer ruggedness all its own. This is the second period in the history of Chinese calligraphy.

至隋代而南北匯合。遂開唐代之先聲。唐之太宗皇帝、歐陽詢、虞世南、褚遂良、薛稷、陸柬之、孫虔禮、張旭、顏眞卿、懷素、柳公權、李邕、徐浩。各具專長。自立門戶。文人中如李白、林藻、杜牧。皆以書傳至五代楊凝式集成各家。堪稱後勁。此爲書學第三時期。

兩宋代興。斯道益昌。蔡襄、蘇軾、黃庭堅、米芾、繼武楊氏。開宋四家書學專派。其後徽宗皇帝獨倡瘦金書體。高宗皇帝居德壽宮二十年。潛心二王書法。於是文人中如蔡京、周邦彥、范成大、張孝祥、姜夔、陸游、吳琚、吳說、朱熹、岳珂等。亦皆以善書著名。迨金入主中國。而文化上實受中國之同化。故金之任詢、王廷筠。元之趙孟頫。連翩而起。趙孟頫兼工書畫。可稱爲此期之集大成者。此外元之鮮于樞、康里巙巙、虞集、張雨、揭傒斯、俞和等。亦皆各有其獨具之特色。是爲第四時期。

明衍元之餘緒。書家若宋克、宋濂、李東陽、祝允明、文徵明、王寵等。皆具專長。至董其昌復集大成。亦書畫兼精。清初各家。強半爲所籠罩。其間王鐸、汪士鋐、姜宸英、金農、王澍、劉墉、翁方綱、伊秉綬等。較爲傑出。嘉慶以後。人厭臺閣體之無生氣。一轉而學碑刻。風尚爲之一變。書道亦復稍振。如鄧石如、包世臣、張裕釗輩。卽其代表。此爲第五時期。

第三章 畫學之演進及其名家

畫學繁賾。茲分山水、人物、寫生三系說明之。

(一) 專畫山水。蓋源於六朝。而盛於唐。就便利說明計。可分南北二宗。南宗以柔取韻。在實處得虛神。重於用筆。北宗以剛取勢。借虛處見實

The Sui Dynasty witnessed a commingling of the styles of writing as they were known in the north and the south, and this led up to the flourishing period as represented by the T'ang Dynasty. The Emperors Tai Tsung, Ou-Yang Hsun, Yu Shih-nan, Chu Sui-liang, Hsueh Chih, Lu Chien-chi, Sun Chien-li, Chang Hsu, Yen Cheng-ching, Hwai Su, Liu Kung-chuan, Li Yung, and Hsu Hao are all calligraphists with individual styles. Among the poets, Li Po, Lin Tsao and Tu Mu are also known for their distinguished penmanship. During Wu Tai (Five Dynasties) a worthy successor was found in Yang Ning-shih, who seemed to represent the best of his predecessors. This is the third period.

During the Sung Dynasty the art of Chinese calligraphy saw further and greater development. Succeeding Wu-yang Shih, Tsai Hsiang, Su Shih, Wang Ting-chien and Mi Fei developed four distinctive styles of the Sung Dynasty. Later the Emperor Hui Tsung invented what is known as shou-chin-shu (瘦金書), while the Emperor Kao Tsung spent twenty years in the Teh Shou Palace learning the art of the two Wangs (Wang Hsi-chi and Wang Hui-chi). In the meantime, such scholars as Tsai Ching, Chou Pang-yen, Fan Cheng-ta, Chang Hsiao-shiang, Chiang Kwei, Lu Yu, Wu Chu, Wu Yueh, Chu Shih, Yao Ke and others all won fame as calligraphists. The conquest of China by the Manchus (Liao-Chin) and Mongols was, as is known, largely political and Chinese civilization was in each case adopted by the invaders. Thus it was that Yin Hsun and Wang Ting-tsun of Chin and Chao Meng-fu of Yuan rose one after another as distinguished artists. Chao Meng-fu who was as eminent a painter as he was a calligraphist may be regarded as the supreme representative of this fourth period during which lived also such famous men as Shien Yu-shu, Kang Li-kwei, Yu Chih, Chang Yu, Chieh Hsi-ssu, Yu Ho and others who were each distinguished in his own particular style.

The Ming Dynasty carried on the heritage of the Yuan Dynasty and had such famous artists as Sun Ke, Sun Lien, Li Tung-yang, Chu Jung-ming, Wen Chung-ming, and Wang Chung who were all known for their special talent. The most distinguished calligraphist of the period, however, was Tung Chih-chang, who was equally proficient as a painter. Indeed, he attained such artistic heights that most of the later calligraphers of the early Ch'ing Dynasty were overshadowed by him. There were, nevertheless, such comparatively outstanding men as Wang To, Wang Shih-hung, Chiang Chen-ying, Ching Nung, Wang Shu, Liu Jung, Weng Fang-kang and Yi Ping-shou who were all representatives of the Ch'ing Dynasty. After the reign of Chia Ching, there was a general distaste for the rigidity and dullness of the tai-ko style (臺閣體), into which Chinese calligraphy had largely fallen at the time. A new interest in the study of old stone inscriptions was aroused and the art of calligraphy took a sudden turn, acquiring in the process a new vitality. Representatives of this phase were such men as Teng Shih-ju, Pao Shih-chen and Chang Yu-chao. This is the fifth period.

Chapter III—The Evolution of Chinese Painting and the Famous Painters

The art of painting is very complicated. It may be described in three divisions—landscape, figures and sketch.

(1) The origin of painting of landscapes is attributed to the Six Dynasties, but it flourished in the T'ang Dynasty. For convenience's sake, it may be divided into two schools, northern and southern. The southern school secures harmony of tone by means of soft touches and gains illusive charm in its drawing of realities. This school lays stress upon the handling of

力重於用墨。南宗以王維爲祖。唐之楊昇、盧鴻。五代之荆浩、關仝、董源、巨然。宋之李成、范寬、惠崇、燕文貴、許道寧、郭熙、趙大年、米芾、江參、米友仁。元之趙孟頫、錢選、高克恭、黃公望、曹知白、吳鎮、王蒙、倪瓚、盛懋、朱德潤、唐棣、陳汝言、徐賁。明之王紱、劉珏、沈周、文徵明、董其昌。清之王時敏、王鑑、王翬、王原祁、吳歷、惲壽平、石溪、石濤、八大山人、高宗皇帝、湯貽汾、戴熙。相承法乳。千餘年來。未有間斷。

北宗山水。每兼工人物樓臺之屬。縝密生辣者。兼而有之。唐之李思訓、李昭道。號爲大小李將軍者。卽其代表。北宗中之縝密者。宋之王詵、趙宗漢、趙伯駒、趙伯驌、劉松年、閻次平。元之王振鵬。明之仇英、吳彬爲一系。生辣者。宋之李唐、朱銳、馬遠、夏圭。元之劉貫道。明之戴進、周臣、唐寅、藍瑛爲一系。清初畫派。尙沿明末作風。如王鐸、戴明說、傅山、法若眞等。皆近北宗。此二宗有時互相混合。並非劃若鴻溝。在觀覽者善爲辨別耳。

(二) 人物畫殆始於漢。六朝因之。而稍參以外來之影響。現傳之作。自唐代起。爲較可靠。唐之閻立本、吳道子、大小尉遲、周昉。五代之周文矩、邱文播。宋之石恪、晁无咎、李伯時、蘇漢臣、馬和之、張擇端、賈師古、梁楷、李嵩、龔開。元之趙孟頫、趙雍、趙彥徵祖孫、顏輝、任仁發。明之吳偉、郭詡、杜堇、唐寅、仇英、丁雲鵬、崔子忠。清之陳洪綬、張飄、華嵒、改琦。或寫事實。或攝神韻。工草兼施。各擅勝槩。

(三) 寫生則唐之韓幹、戴嵩、韓滉、邊鸞。五代之刁光胤、徐熙、黃筌、滕昌祐。宋則黃筌之子居寀、徐熙之孫崇嗣。各具家法。趙昌、崔白、艾宣、吳元瑜、林椿、吳炳、李迪、馬麟、魯宗貴。遼之蕭瀜。元之錢選、王淵。明之宣宗皇

the brush. The northern school makes powerful rhythm predominant in its compositions, showing real strength by means of empty spaces. This school emphasizes the application of colours. The founder of the southern school was Wang Wei. Yang Shen and Lu Hung of the T'ang Dynasty, Ching Hao, Kwan Tung, Tung Yuan, and Chu Jan of the Five Dynasties, Li Cheng, Fan K'uan, Hwei Chung, Yen Wen-kuei, Hsu Tao-ning, Kuo Hsi, Chao Ta-nien, Mi Fei, Chiang Shen and Mi Yu-jen of the Sung Dynasty, Chao Meng-fu, Chien Hsuan, Kao K'e-kung, Huang Kung-wang, Tsao Chih-po, Wu Chen, Wang Mang, Ni Ts'an, Sheng Mou, Chu T'e-chen, T'ang Ti, Chen Yu-yen, and Hsu Pun of the Yuan Dynasty, Wang Fu, Liu Yu, Shen Chou, Wen Cheng-ming and Tung Chi-chang of the Ming Dynasty, and Wang Shih-ming, Wang Chien, Wang Hui, Wang Yuan-chi, Wu Li, Yun Shou-ping, Shih Hsi, Shih Tao, Pa-ta Shan-jen, Emperor Kao Tsung, T'ang Yi-fen and Tai Hsi of the Ch'ing Dynasty: —all these painters carried on the tradition of this school for more than a thousand years without interruption.

The painting of landscapes by the northern school often included drawings of human and animal figures and of buildings and towers. Their execution was of two kinds, elaborate and rough, and the representative artists were Li Sze-hsun, and Li Chao-tao, alias the "Big" and "Little" Generals Li, of the T'ang Dynasty. Well-known for elaborate execution were Wang Hsien, Chao Tsung-han, Chao Po-chu, Chao Po-hsiao, Liu Sung-nien and Yen Tz'e-ping of the Sung Dynasty, Wang Chen-peng of the Yuan Dynasty, and Chou Ying and Wu Pin of the Ming Dynasty:—all these artists formed one school. For the rough and rugged style, may be mentioned Li T'ang, Chu Jui, Ma Yuan and Hsia Kuei of the Sung Dynasty, Liu Kwan-tao of the Yuan Dynasty, Tai Chin, Chou Chen, T'ang Yin and Lan Ying of the Ming Dynasty;—these artists also formed one school. The different schools of painting in the beginning of the Ch'ing Dynasty followed the tradition of the artists of the latter part of the Ming Dynasty. For example, Wang To, Tai Ming-yueh, Fu Shan and Fa Jo-chen all showed approaches to the northern school. Sometimes the southern and northern schools showed intermixture in their technique and exhibited no clear line of demarcation. It is for connoisseurs to distinguish them.

(2) The painting of human and animal figures had its origin in the Han Dynasty, and it was followed up through the Six Dynasties, but touched a little by extraneous influences. The extant works of this category date back to the T'ang Dynasty and they are comparatively authentic. Yen Li-pen, Wu Tao-tse, the junior and the senior Yu Chih, and Chou Fang of the T'ang Dynasty, Chou Wen-chu and Chiu Wen-po of the Five Dynasties, Shih Ke, Chao Wu-chiu, Li Pai-shih, Su Han-chen, Ma Ho-chih, Chang Tse-tuan, Chia Hsi-ku, Liang Kai, Li Sung and Kung Kai of the Sung Dynasty, Chao Meng-fu, Chao Jung, Chao Yen, Cheng Chu-sun, Yen Hui and Jin Jin-fa of the Yuan Dynasty, Wu Wei, Kuo Hsu, Tu Chin, T'ang Yin, Chou Ying, Ting Yun-peng and Ts'ui Tse-chung of the Ming Dynasty, these painters either depicted real scenery and living figures or ethereal charm and airy grace by means of either elaborate drawing or rough sketch, and each of them was eminent in his particular category of painting.

(3) Famous for painting real scenery and life-like figures were the following artists: Han Kan, Tai Sung, Han Huang and Pien Luan of the T'ang Dynasty, T'iao Kwan-yin, Hsu Hsi, Hwang Chuan, Teng Chang-yu of the Five Dynasties, Chu Tsai, on of Hwang Chuan, and Chung Ssu, grandson of Hsu Hsi: each had his own technique. Chao Chang, Ts'ui Po, Ai Hsuan, Wu Yuan-yu, Lin Chun, Wu Ping, Li Ti, Ma Lin, and Lu Tsung-kuei, Hsiao Jung of

帝、林良、呂紀、陸治、陳道復、王穀祥、徐渭、周之冕、陳栝、清之惲壽平、王武、金農、蔣廷錫、鄒一桂。皆具專長。此派之畫在工麗之中。仍具氣韻。調色敷彩備極精能。其中亦有寫意一派。善用減筆。著墨不多。而神氣具足。且不流於蠢獷。較之一般院畫徒以摹仿爲能。超出多多矣。

第四章 中國畫之特點及其繪畫之法

以上三系不過就各人所專精者而言。往往一人而擅三長。茲亦毋庸詳述。惟中國之畫。幾純於全可以表現作者之人格、性情、興趣。此一點爲研究中國畫者所必須明瞭及承認者。其所以如此之故。(一)因藝術與人生幾於打成一片。(二)因畫法完全與書法相通。(三)因所用之工具及使用之法。均甚微妙。故得形成此項結果。中國畫具純用毛筆。復有粗細剛柔之別。每落筆後。卽不再改。故山水之皴染。與堆砌塗飾不同。而力量及趣味卽寓其中。又陰陽向背及諸比例。雖不十分嚴格。而大體不致差違。亦因有氣勢爲之籠罩映帶也。又用墨及用各顏色除特別注意其研磨調溶之法外。其用時。復因著筆之先後。用力之輕重。水與各色暨色與色間配合之成分。以及筆與紙(或絹)及顏色三方面相接觸時。錯綜融會而產生之光彩及情味。因而構成種種之功能。故製紙、絹、顏料、筆及畫時。對紙、絹、顏料之加工。(如紙先水浬。絹先上礬及調色須用某種質地之水等。)亦須特殊之技術。卽如筆之種類。卽有三四十種之多。他可知也。至用紙絹之外。有繪之建築物及器皿上

the Liao Dynasty, Chien Hsuan and Wang Yuan of the Yuan Dynasty, Emperor Hsuan Tsung, Lin Liang, Lu Chih, Chen Tao-fu, Wang Ku-Hsiang, Hsu Wei, Chou Tse-mien and Chen Chieh of the Ming Dynasty, Yun Shou-ping, Wang Wu, Chin Nung, Chiang Ting-hsi and Tsou I-kuei of the Ch'ing Dynasty;—each of these painters had his own special qualities. The paintings of this school are characterized by exquisite beauty, as well as powerful rhythm and show excellent skill in the mixing and laying on of colours. In this school there was also a group of painters, who specialized in producing pictures just by a few touches, chiefly in outline. Though they made sparing use of colours, they could produce pictures full of life and vitality, without at the same time being coarse and vulgar. Thus their works are far superior to the pictures of the "patronized" type, which were mainly imitative.

Chapter IV—The Special Features and Technique of Chinese Painting

The three general divisions of Chinese painting as described in the previous chapter were discussed merely from the standpoint of the highest individual attainments of the representative artists. However, as it often happened, one person might be equally skilled in several or all of the three divisions. But in the study of Chinese painting one must first of all realize and appreciate the important fact that it is almost entirely a medium for the expression of the character, the temperament and the taste of the painter. This is so because (1) Chinese art is an integral part of life, because (2) the technique of Chinese painting and that of calligraphy are bound up with each other, and because (3) the implements and the manner in which they are employed are both highly elaborate and refined.

The principal instrument used in Chinese painting is, of course, the brush. But the brushes are highly differentiated according to the degree of fineness and suppleness. Every stroke of the brush is irrevocable and is not retouched. Therefore the effects thus obtained in landscape painting are quite different from those achieved by the piling of colours and the process of endless retouching, while the force and appeal thus produced will be found in the intangible whole of the picture.

The laws of perspective, of light and shade and of proportion, though not rigidly observed, are respected in the main through rhythm as well as the atmosphere which generally envelops and illuminates the entire picture.

Particular attention is also paid to the employment of ink and colours. Besides the preliminary care usually exercised in the preparation and mixing of the pigments, the order in which they are applied, the force or pressure with which they are brushed on, the proportion between the water and colour used as well as that between their various combinations, and finally the quality of the brush, the silk or paper and of the colours themselves are all supremely important in the moment of contact in order that the desired brilliance and appeal of a picture might be achieved. Therefore, in the manufacture of paper, silk, pigments and the brush, special skill is always required. Even at the moment of painting, the various materials to be used must be suitably prepared. For instance, the dampening of the paper ground, or the treatment of silk with alum, or even the selection of the right kind of water for the mixing of colours. In the matter of the brush alone, as many as forty kinds are used, not to mention the various other things required in the pursuit of this art.

者有用指用舌用刷而不用筆者。此外尚有火畫、鐵畫、紙織畫、貼絨畫等。應列入美術工藝內。尚有一節應聲明者。中國畫固自有其真面目與精神。然歷來所受外來之影響。亦復不少。如佛教之傳播。使節之交通物產工藝品之輸入。皆曾令繪畫之作風。發生甚大之衝動。但大半皆能咀嚼融化。而形成一本國色彩之作品。此世界畫派中之東方畫派。所以必推中國爲巨擘也。

第五章 此次出品概要

此次書畫出品。限於故宮博物院及古物陳列所所藏。於上列各派各家雖不能完全備具。然各派重要作家之作品。已盡量選出。觀者亦可得中國書畫家之大凡及其特色。其他各品。或祇存孤本。未便令其遠行或品質稍次。無須舉以濫列。或年久紙絹脆裂。不能懸掛。或長卷大幅舒展維艱。再三斟酌之餘。得如斯册所錄。

綜 計

唐五代	作品(畫)	六 件
宋	作品(書畫)	五十六件
元	作品(書畫)	四十一件
明	作品(書畫)	四十三件
清	作品(書畫)	二十九件

總共一百七十五件。雖漏略難免。而統系堪稽。此則希望觀衆引爲滿意者也。又中國書畫裝裱之法。爲各國所無。因其技術之精能。可令書畫之優點。完全表露。如有缺損。幷能加以補救。其間著名之技術家如湯傑、吳文玉之輩。至與書畫作者齊名。其裝裱之式。如卷如册。便於存儲展覽。亦爲各國所無。此亦足供觀衆參考者。合爲附及。兹爲易於參考起見。將中西歷摘要列後。

Besides paper and silk, painting is also done on buildings and various kinds of utensils. Similarly, the finger or even the tongue is sometimes used instead of the brush. In addition to these varieties, pictures are also made by the process of charring, and others out of wrought iron, paper and velvet, which may be classified as industrial art.

There is finally another point that should be made clear in connection with Chinese painting. Though it has a style and spirit all its own, Chinese painting has in its contact with foreign influences, shown considerable reaction. The effects of Buddhism, of communication with the outside world through envoys and of the importation of foreign industrial artcraft and materials can be seen in the upheavals in the style of Chinese painting. However, most of the foreign elements have been digested and assimilated, and made an integral part of the original art of the nation. It would not, therefore, be too much to claim for Chinese painting the position of leadership in Oriental art.

Chapter V—The Principal Exhibits

Selected as they are from the collections of the National Palace Museum and National Museum, the exhibits displayed in London are by no means comprehensive but they may be considered as fairly representative of the various important schools of Chinese calligraphy and painting. It is believed that an inspection of these exhibits will be sufficient to give an idea of the general nature as well as the special characteristics of the art of Chinese calligraphy and painting. Such other examples as are not found in the Exhibition are either solitary originals which should rather be saved from the risks of transportation over long distances or works of a somewhat secondary quality which need not be indiscriminately shown. There are still others which, due to the extreme delicacy of their condition resulting from their very antiquity, can no longer withstand rough hanging, or which, due to their extraordinary dimensions, cannot be properly displayed. It is, therefore, after considerable deliberation that the following list was compiled:

T'ang and the Five Dynasties	6 exhibits.
Sung	56 exhibits.
Yuan	41 exhibits.
Ming	43 exhibits.
Ch'ing	29 exhibits.

There are altogether 175 exhibits representing the art of Chinese calligraphy and painting. It is hoped that in spite of the omissions their presentation in the chronological order will prove satisfying.

Finally, a word may be added in regard to the type of mounting which is also peculiar to Chinese calligraphy and painting. In fact, it is a distinct art, the parallel of which cannot be found in any other country. This art consists in completely bringing out and enhancing the beauty of the subject in the process of mounting, and also, in the case of damage to the original ground, in skillful mending. There are a number of such skilled men as T'ang Chieh and Wu Wen-yu who actually enjoyed as great fame as the artists. There are, moreover, several styles of mounting. Some are in scrolls and others are in book form, while all of them are aimed at convenience in handling as well as in keeping.

For the convenience of reference, the various Chinese dynastic periods are appended below together with the Western chronology:

漢 · · · · · · · · 由公元前二〇六至公元二二〇

三國 · · · · · · · 由公元二二〇至公元二六五

晉至隋 · · · · · · 由公元二六五至公元六一八

唐 · · · · · · · · 由公元六一八至公元九〇七

五代 · · · · · · · 由公元九〇七至公元九六〇

宋 · · · · · · · · 由公元九六〇至公元一二七九

元 · · · · · · · · 由公元一二七九至公元一三六八

明 · · · · · · · · 由公元一三六八至公元一六四四

清 · · · · · · · · 由公元一六四四至公元一九一二

Han	206 B.C.–220 A.D.
San Kuo (Three Kingdoms)	220–265 A.D.
Tsing & Sui	265–618 A.D.
T'ang	618–907 A.D.
Wu Tai (Five Dynasties)	907–960 A.D.
Sung	960–1279 A.D.
Yuan	1279–1368 A.D.
Ming	1368–1644 A.D.
Ch'ing	1644–1912 A.D.

唐

T'ANG DYNASTY (618 – 907 A. D.)

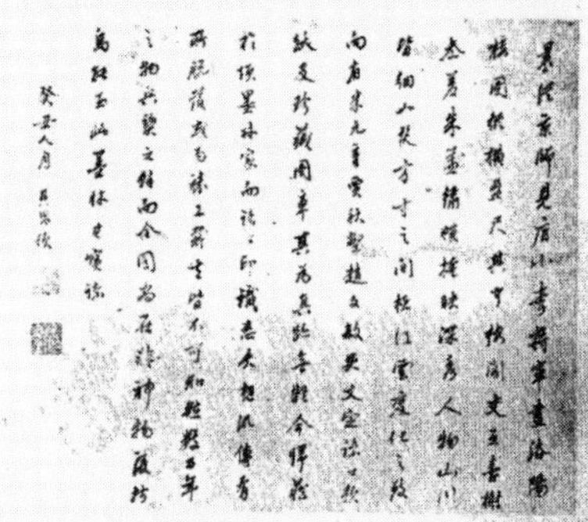

一　唐李昭道洛陽樓圖（傳）

絹地寶笈重編著錄右上角有「李昭道」三字題款。有傷補。縱叁拾柒·叁公分。橫叁拾玖·伍公分。詩堂上有「董其昌」題識。紙地有摺痕。縱叁拾貳·玖公分橫叁拾捌·伍公分。又有乾隆御書「自足千古」四字紙地。縱貳拾公分。橫叁拾捌·伍公分。下邊緣有「于敏中」題識。帶綾裱。

李昭道(約西歷716年時人)。思訓子。太原府倉曹直集賢院。官至太子中書舍人。世稱思訓爲大李將軍。昭道爲小李將軍。

「附註」以下人名後括弧內生卒年。俱僅註數目字。例如(約西歷716年時人)。省作(約716)。餘倣此。

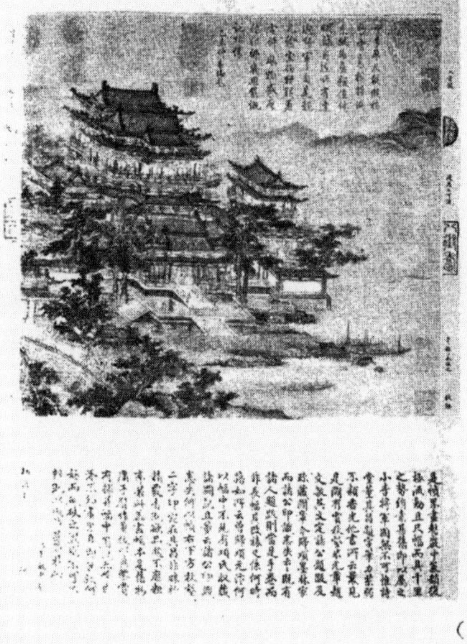

1. Li Chao-tao "Loyang Lou T'u"

Loyang Mansion (attributed).

Li Chao-tao (circa 716).—Son of Sze-hsun (思訓). At T'aiyuan Fu (太原府) he was an official with the rank of Ts'ang Ts'ao Chih Chi Hsien Yuan (倉曹直集賢院). Afterwards, he became "T'ai Tse Chung Shu She Jen (太子中書舍人). After generations call Sze-hsun General Li, senior, and Chao-tao General Li, junior.

二 唐李昭道 春山行旅圖(傳)

絹地。寶笈三編著錄。縱玖拾伍·伍公分。橫伍拾伍·肆公分。

2. Li Chao-tao "Ch'un Shan Hsing Lu T'u"

Travelling in the Mountains in Spring (attributed).

(18)

三 唐人

雪景山水(傳)

絹地·寶笈重編著錄無款·上端有乾隆辛亥新正月御題題識有傷補及摺痕縱壹百叁拾陸·叁公分。橫陸拾捌·陸公分。

3. "Hsueh Ching Shan Shui"

By an un-identifiable T'ang painter

A Snow Scene(attributed).

五　代

FIVE DYNASTIES (907–960 A. D.)

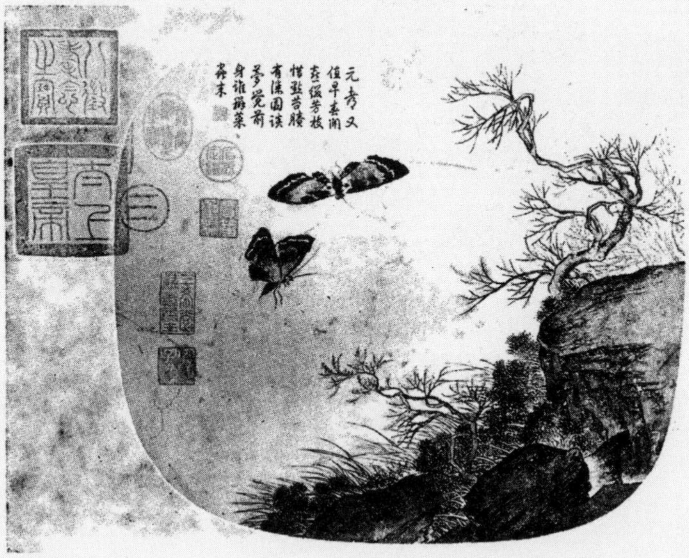

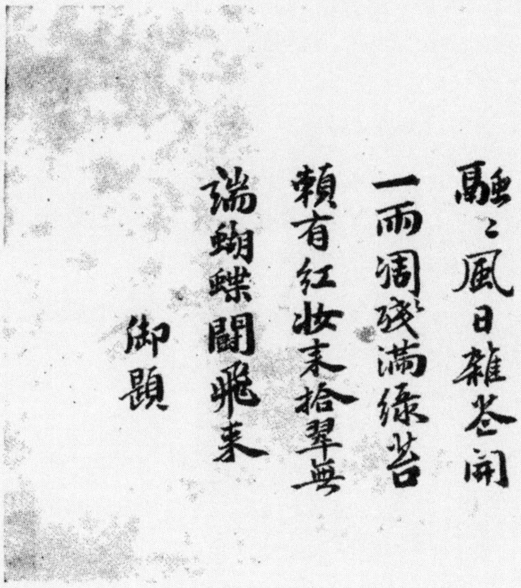

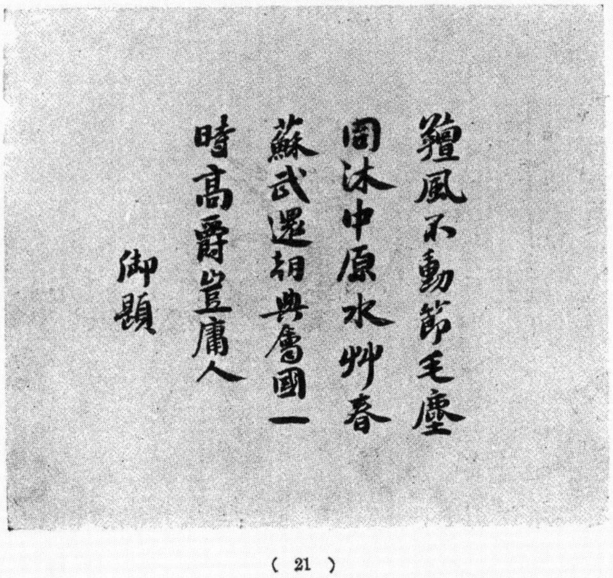

(21)

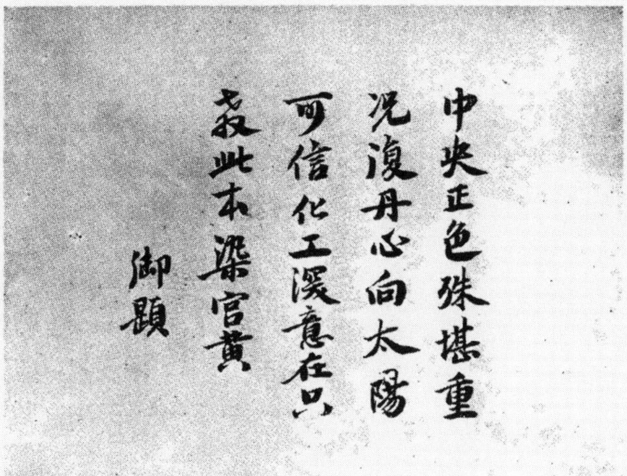
中央正色殊堪重
況復丹心向太陽
可信化工溪意在只
裒此本染宮黄
御題

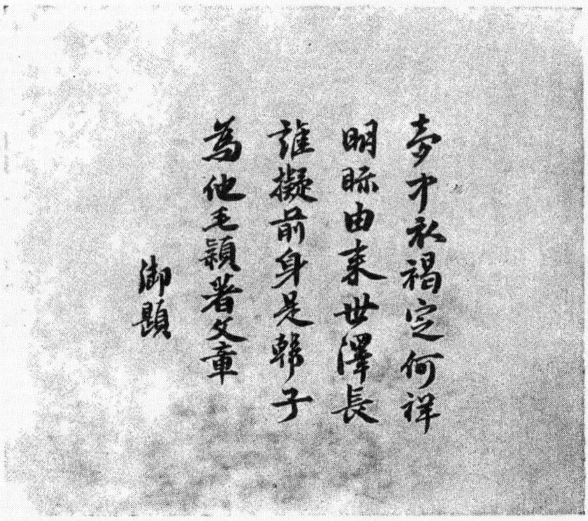
麥才秋禍定何祥
明際由來世澤長
誰擬前身是韓子
為他毛穎著文章
御題

賦得閒情思獨工
想携卮酒對芳叢
鉛華不為春爭艷留
得先生醉頰紅
御題

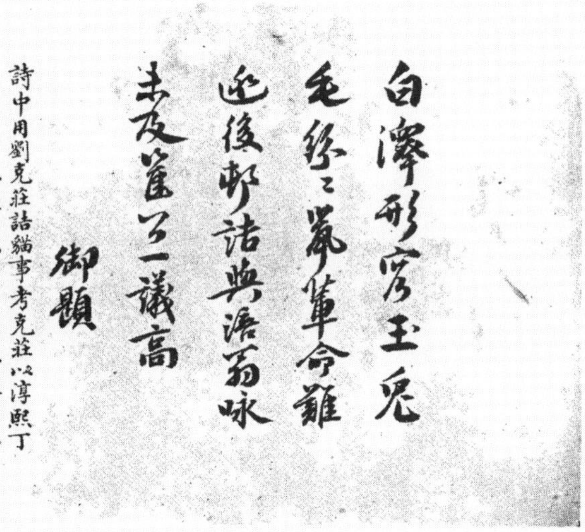

白澤形容玉兔
毛絲々氣革命雖
迹後郵詰與潛蜀咏
未及崔公一議高

御題

詩中用劉克莊語貓事考克莊以淳熙丁
未生上距乾道之元二十二年此題贋也
既用其韻並正之御識

臣汪由敦奉
敕敬書

（25）

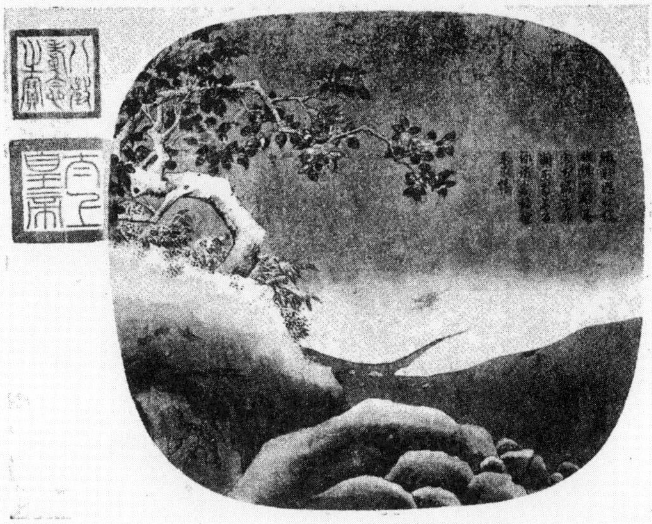

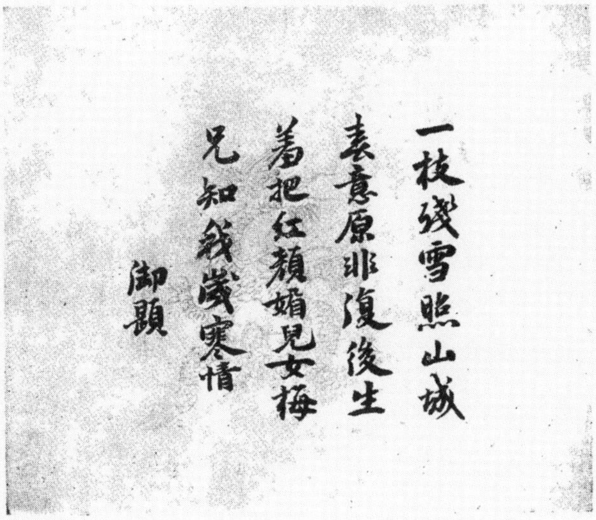

一枝殘雪照山城
素意原非復後生
羞把紅顏媚兒女梅
兄知我歲寒情
御題

（ 26 ）

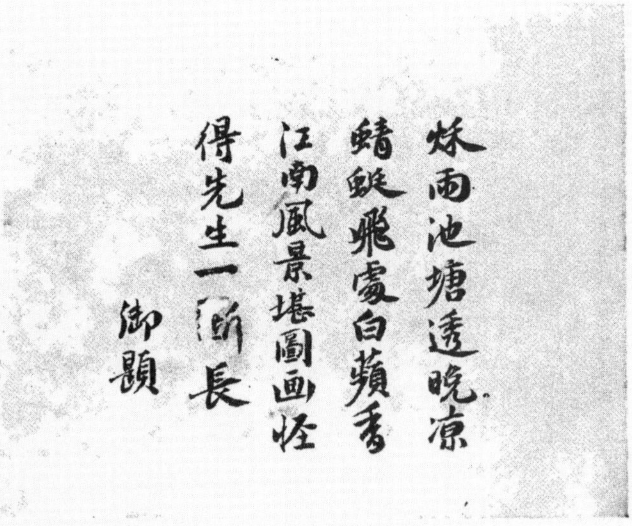

(27)

黄絹翠帔玉為姿
何處春風一見之
未到湘江清絶地試
看山谷老人詩
御題

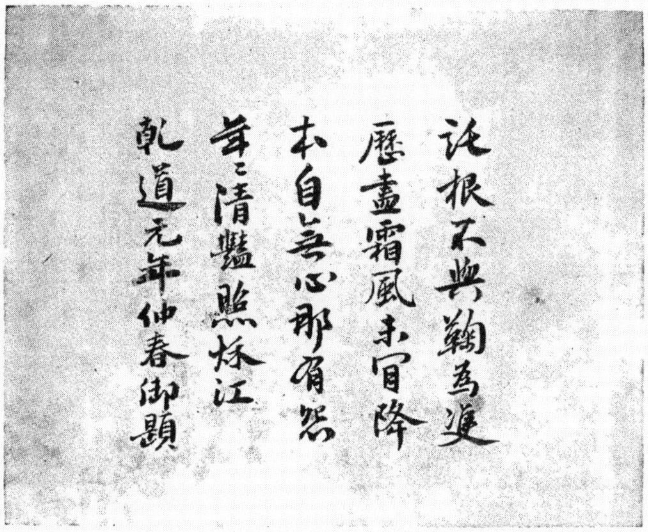

託根不與菊為叢
歷盡霜風未肯降
本自無心那有怨
年年清豔照秋江
乾道元年仲春御題

唐刁光胤長安人自昭宗天復初入蜀
善畫湖石花竹貓兔鳥雀之類慎交
游所與皆一時佳士黃筌孔嵩咸師事
之議者謂孔類升堂黃得入室年踰八
十益不廢所學今傳於世者絕少此十幅
乃宋宣和御府後有孝宗御題真為鴻
寶二十年前購於遼安劉魯一侍郎家每
幅有飛白暗款在樹石間真定梁公聞之
特札借觀款未曾有己巳攜歸拓上明年庚
午重加裝潢藏信天巢又十年今請養閒
居長夏無事取而細觀慮後來者々不知
愛護為詳跋於後或曰自靖康之變宣
和內府諸物盡已散失孝宗安得而題之

蓋自高宗內禪以後孝宗極意搜覓
天下之珍奇以充奉養宣和舊藏有
仍歸者又何致疑乎至其畫格之超妙
書法之渾厚真鑒賞者自能別之
大清康熙三十八年己卯七月四日伏暑中涼
風颯至建蘭已放一花用宋硯與自製書
畫墨記於簡靜齋年五十有五
江邨 竹窗 高士奇

（ 30 ）

四 五代刁光胤 花卉寫生册

絹地。石渠寶笈重編著錄。拾開。跋壹開。第壹開畫縱叁拾貳·陸公分。橫叁拾陸·叁公分。對題縱貳拾陸·捌公分。橫叁拾壹·貳公分。第貳開畫縱叁拾肆公分。橫叁拾陸·肆公分。對題縱貳拾柒·叁公分。橫叁拾壹·貳公分。第叁開畫縱叁拾貳·捌公分。橫貳拾陸·伍公分。對題縱貳拾柒·柒公分。橫叁拾壹·叁公分。第肆開畫縱叁拾貳·伍公分。橫叁拾伍·貳公分。對題縱貳拾柒·捌公分。橫叁拾壹·貳公分。第伍開畫縱叁拾肆·肆公分。橫叁拾柒·肆公分。對題縱貳拾捌公分。橫叁拾壹·叁公分。第陸開畫縱叁拾肆公分。橫叁拾陸·肆公分。對題縱貳拾伍·捌公分。橫叁拾壹·叁公分。第柒開畫縱叁拾肆公分。橫叁拾陸公分。對題縱貳拾柒·肆公分。橫叁拾壹·伍公分。第捌開畫縱叁拾貳·伍公分。橫叁拾陸·肆公分。對題縱貳拾肆·陸公分。橫叁拾壹·肆公分。第玖開畫縱叁拾肆·壹公分。橫叁拾陸·伍公分。對題縱貳拾捌·伍公分。橫叁拾壹·肆公分。第拾開畫縱叁拾叁·伍公分弱。橫叁拾陸·肆公分。對題縱貳拾肆·捌公分。橫叁拾壹·貳公分。跋紙縱肆拾肆·伍公分。橫肆拾肆公分。

刁光胤(約 901)。長安人。天復中避地入蜀。

4. T'iao Kwan-yin "Hua Hui Hsieh Sheng Ch'e"

Album of Flowers.

T'iao Kwan-yin (circa 901).—Native of Ch'angan (長安). In the time of Tien Fu (天復), he moved to Hsueh (蜀).

五 五代人

秋林羣鹿圖（傳）

絹地。石渠寶笈初編養心殿著錄。有傷補。縱壹百壹拾捌·壹公分。橫陸拾叁·柒公分。

5. "Ch'iu Lin Chun Lu T'u"

By an un-identifiable painter of the Five Dynasties

A Herd of Deer in an Autumn Grove (attributed).

六 五代人 雪漁圖（傳）

絹地。石渠寶笈御書房著錄。無款。有傷補及裂痕。縱陸拾貳·貳公分。橫叁拾貳·玖公分。

6. "Hsueh Yu T'u"

By an un-identifiable painter of the Five Dynasties

Fishing on a Snowy Day (attributed).

宋

SUNG DYNASTY (960 – 1279 A. D.)

七 宋董源 龍宿郊民圖

絹地。石渠寶笈重編著錄。上邊緣有「董其昌」及「王鴻緒」「清高宗」等題識。紙地。剝落。縱壹百伍拾陸·叁公分。橫壹百陸拾·壹公分。

董源（約 903）。字叔達。又字北苑。江南鍾陵人。事南唐爲後苑副使。

7. Tung Yuan "Lungshu Chiao Min T'u"

Natives of Lungshu Suburb.

Tung Yuan (circa 930).—Tung Yuan, with the pseudonyms of Shu-ta (叔達), and Peh-yuan (北苑), was a native of Chungning (鍾陵) in Kiangnan. He served in the Southern T'ang Dynasty as the Hou Yuan Fu Shih (後苑副使), or vice minister of the Imperial Household.

八 宋巨然

寒林晚岫圖

紙地。寶笈重編著錄。無款。上端有「黃宣」等題識。縱壹百肆拾公分。橫伍拾伍·捌公分。

巨然（約 930）。江寧人。隨僞李至京師。居開元寺。

8. Chu Jan "Han Lin Wan Hsiu T'u"

Winter Grove and Peaks in the Evening Light.

Chu Jan (circa 930).—Chu Jan, a monk, was a native of Kiangning (江寧), now Nanking. He followed Li Yu (the last emperor of the Southern T'ang Dynasty) to the capital, where he resided in the K'ai Yuan Monastery (開元寺).

九 宋范寬 臨流獨坐圖

絹地。寶笈重編著錄。無款。上端有「何樾」等題識。有傷補。縱壹百伍拾陸·貳公分。橫壹百零陸·陸公分。

范寬(約 977)。名中正。字仲立。華源人。性緩。世謂之范寬。

9. Fan K'uan "Lin Liu Tu Tso T'u"

Sitting Alone Overlooking a Stream.

Fan K'uan (circa 977).—Fan K'uan, named Chung-cheng (中正), with the pseudonym of Chung-li (仲立), was a native of Huayuan (華源). Being slow in temperament, he was called Fan K'uan (meaning slowness).

一〇 宋燕文貴 三仙授簡圖(傳)

絹地。無款。縱肆拾陸·肆公分。橫肆拾壹·肆公分。

燕文貴(967–1044)。吳興人。隸軍中。入圖畫院。

10. Yen Wen-kuei "San Hsien Shou Kan T'u"

Presentation of Tablets Among Three Arhats (attributed).

Yen Wen-kuei (967–1044).--Yen Wen-kuei was a native of Wuhsing (吳興). He was first of the soldiery but joined the Academy of Painting.

一一 宋趙昌 歲朝圖

絹地。寶笈重編著錄。下端有「臣昌」題款。詩堂有乾隆御筆。縱壹百零肆公分。橫伍拾壹·貳公分。

趙昌(約1010)。字昌之。廣漢人。

11. Chao Ch'ang "Sui Ch'ao T'u"

New Year's Day.

Chao Ch'ang (circa 1010).—Chao Ch'ang, with the pseudonym of Ch'ang-chih (昌之), was a native of Kwanghan (**廣漢**).

一二 宋趙昌

牡丹

絹地。寶笈三編著錄。下端有「趙昌」題款。有傷補。縱壹百肆拾叁·陸公分。橫伍拾玖·玖公分。

12. Chao Ch'ang "Mu Tan"

Peonies.

一三 宋崔白蘆汀宿雁圖

絹地。無款。縱壹百零陸·伍公分。橫伍拾壹·貳公分。

崔白(約1070)。字子西。濠梁人。仁宗時畫院藝學。

13. Ts'ui Po "Lu Ting Hsu Yen T'u"

Wild Goose Resting in a Rushy Beach.

Ts'ui Po (circa 1070).—Ts'ui Po, with the pseudonym of Tse-hsi (子西), was a native of Haoliang (濠梁). In the reign of Jen Tsung he was I-hsueh (藝學) or expositor of art in the Academy of Painting.

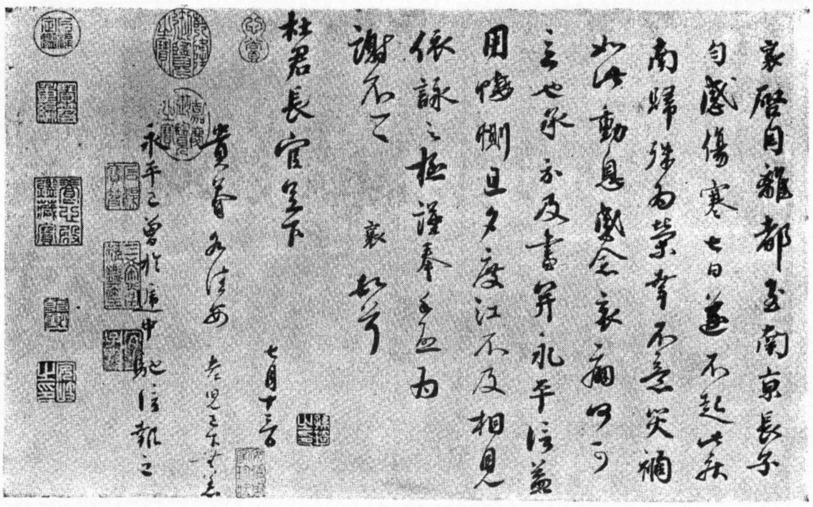

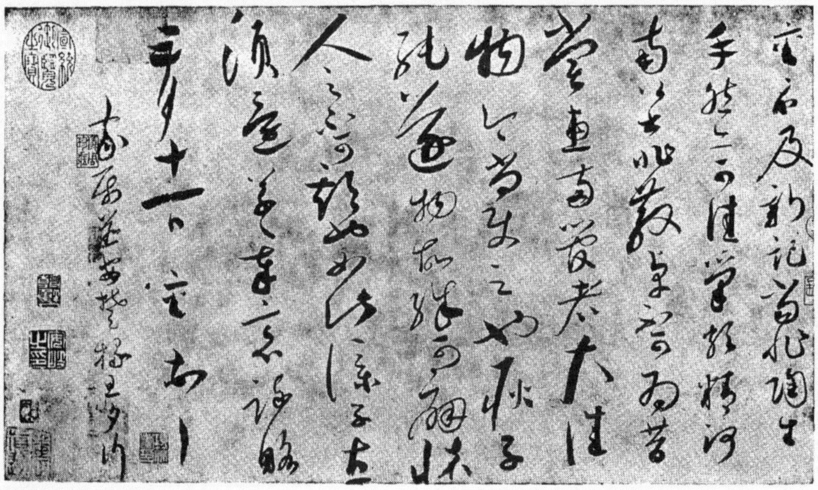

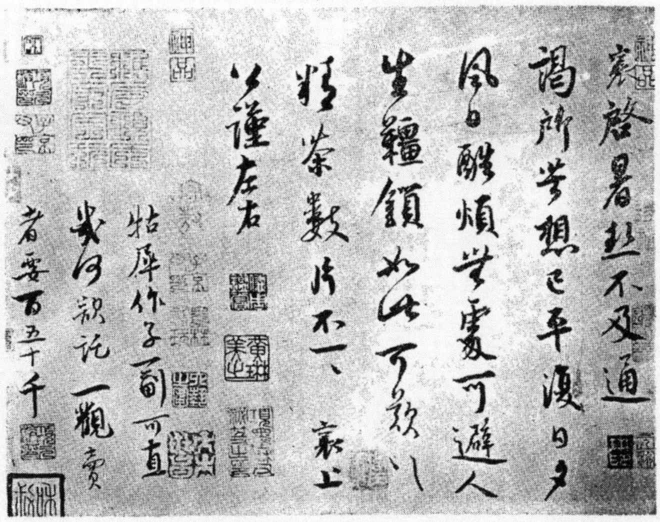

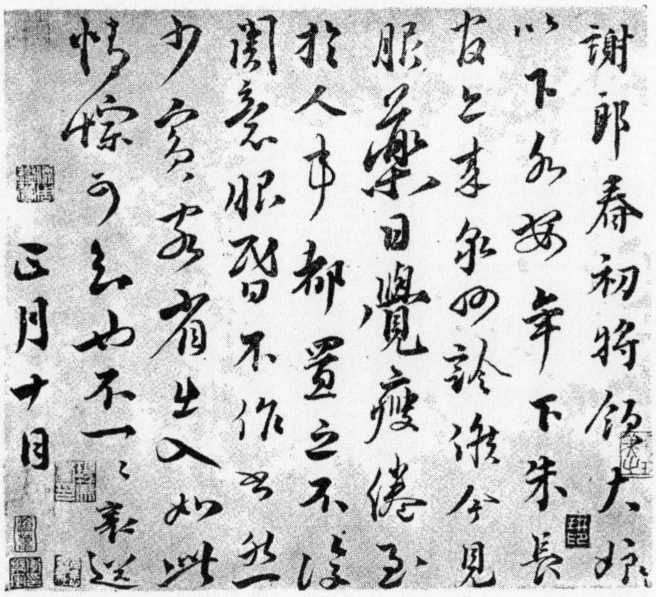

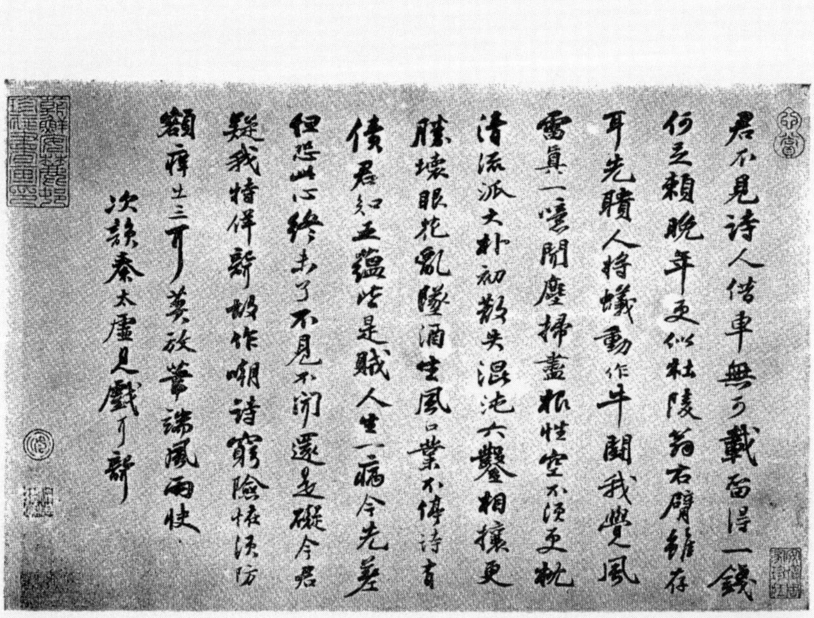
君不見詩人借車無可載留得一錢
何足賴晚年更似杜陵翁右臂雖存
耳先聵人將蟻動作牛鬭我覺風
雷真一噫聞塵掃盡根性空不須更枕
清流派大朴初散失混沌六鑿相攘更
勝壞眼花亂墜酒生風口業不停詩有
債君知五蘊皆是賊人生一病今先差
但恐此心終未了不見不聞還是礙今君
疑我特佯聾故作嘲詩窮險怪須防
額癢出三耳莫放筆端風雨快
次韻秦太虛見戲耳聾

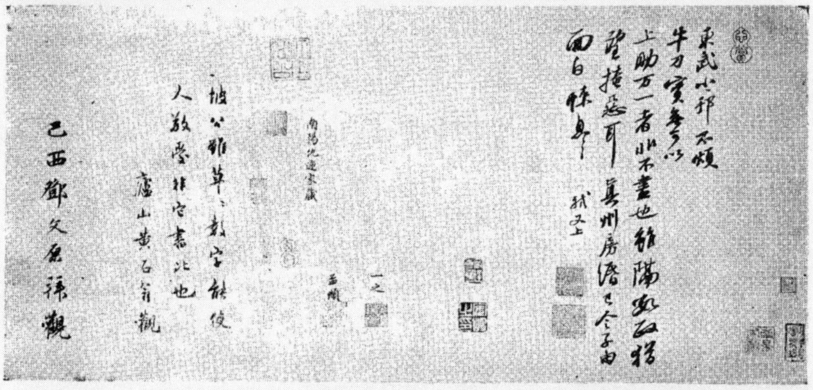

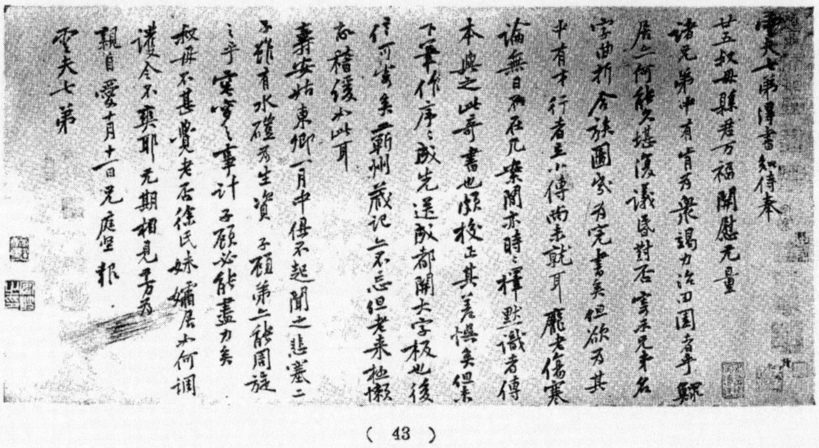

(43)

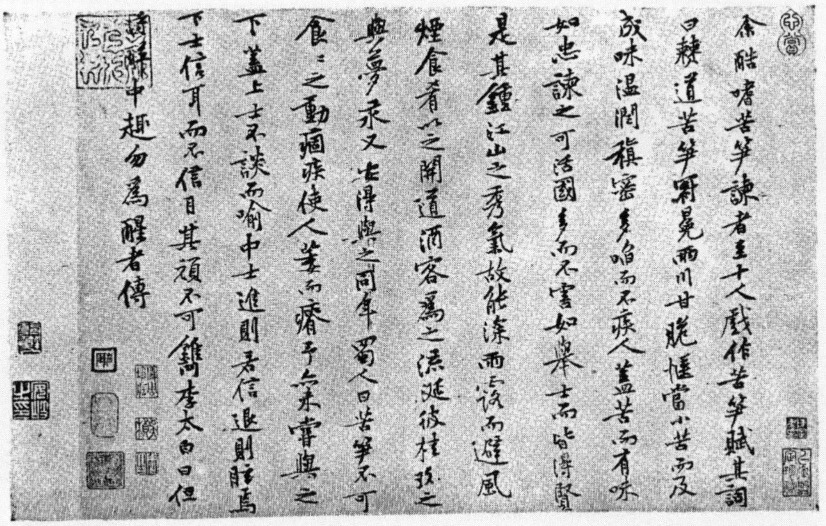

余酷嗜苦笋諫者至十人戲作苦笋賦其詞
曰僰道苦笋冠冕兩川甘脆愜當小苦而及
成味溫潤縝密多啗而不疾人蓋苦而有味
如忠諫之可活國多而不害如舉士而皆得賢
是其鍾江山之秀氣故能深雨露而避風
煙食肴以之開道酒客為之流涎彼桂玫之
與夢汞又安得與之同年蜀人曰苦笋不可
食食之動痼疾使人萎而瘠予亦未嘗與之
下蓋上士不談而喻中士進則若信退則眩焉
下士信耳而不信目其頑不可鐫李太白曰但
得醉中趣勿為醒者傳

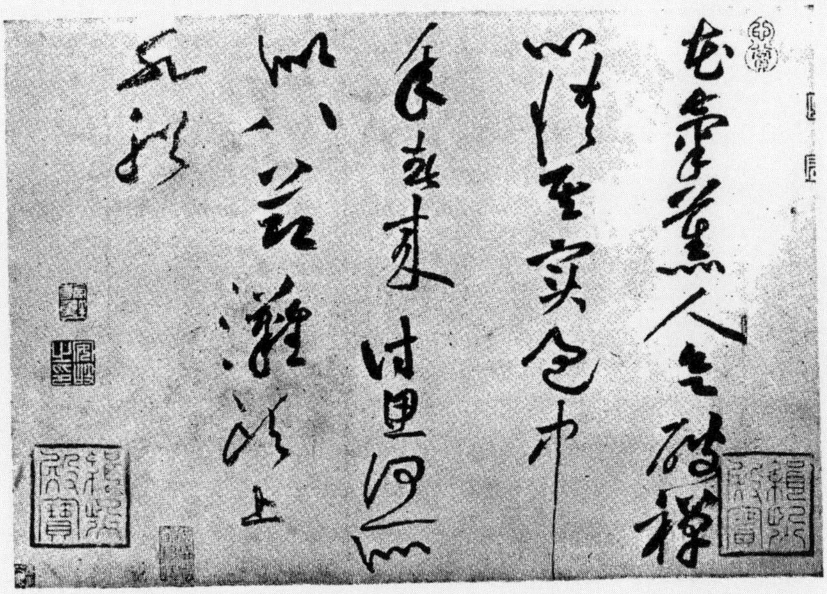

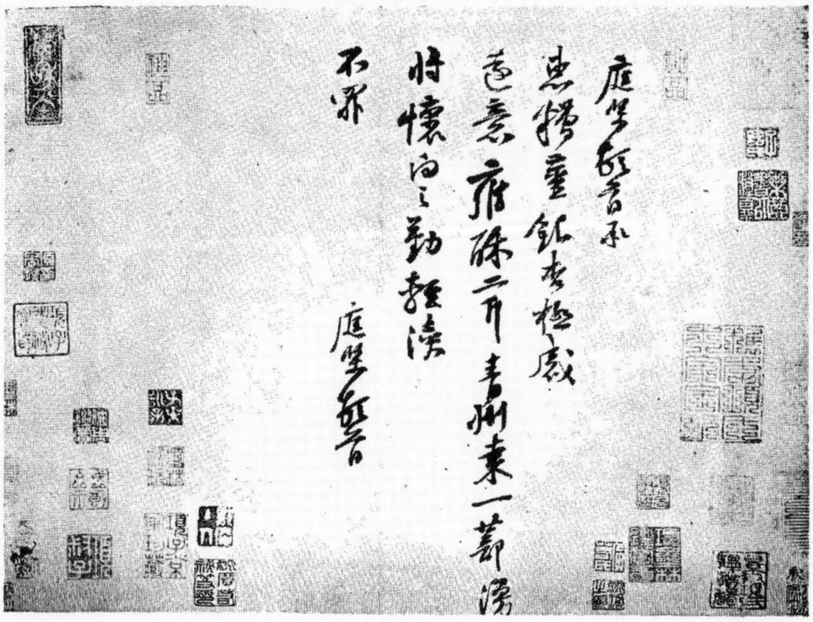

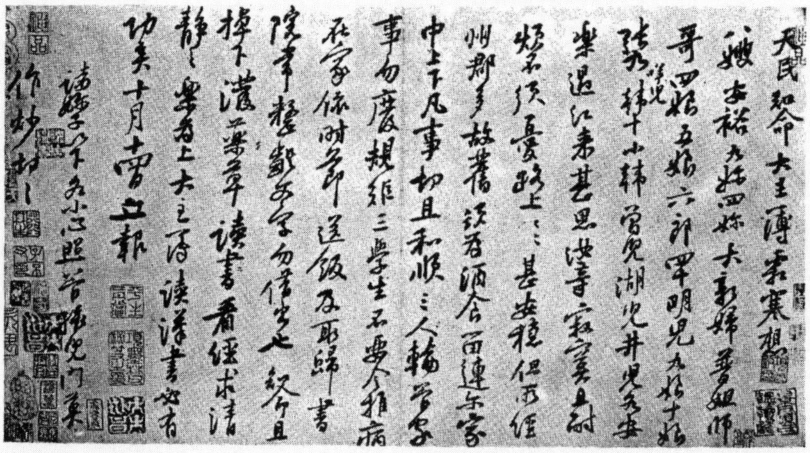

(45)

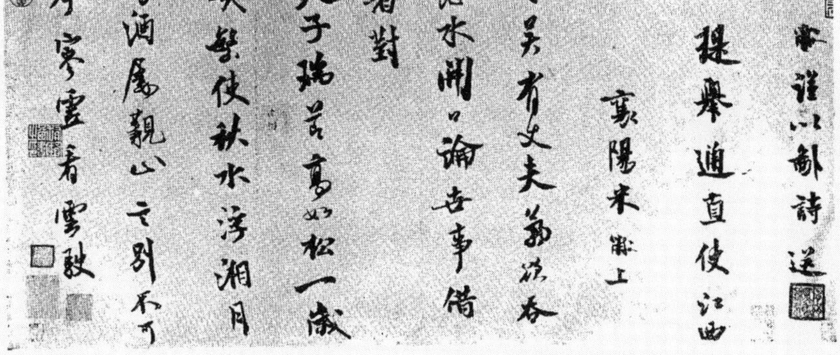

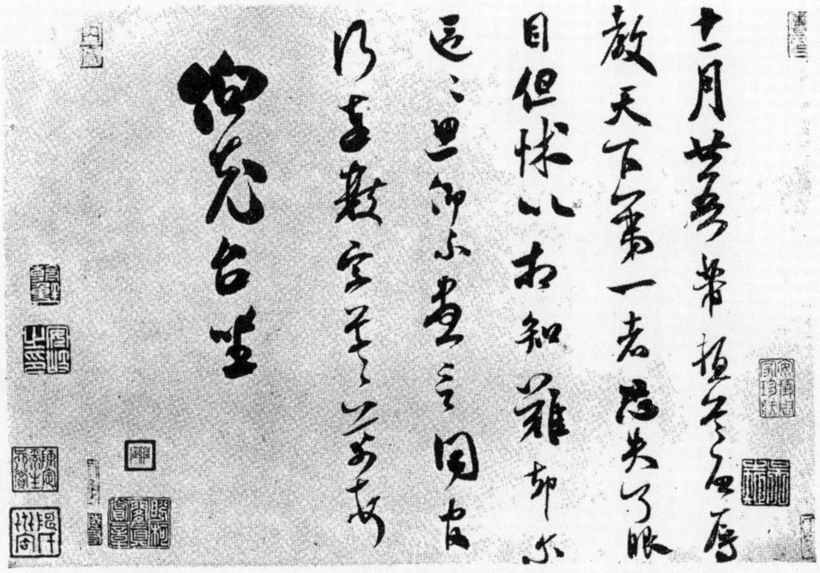

（ 46 ）

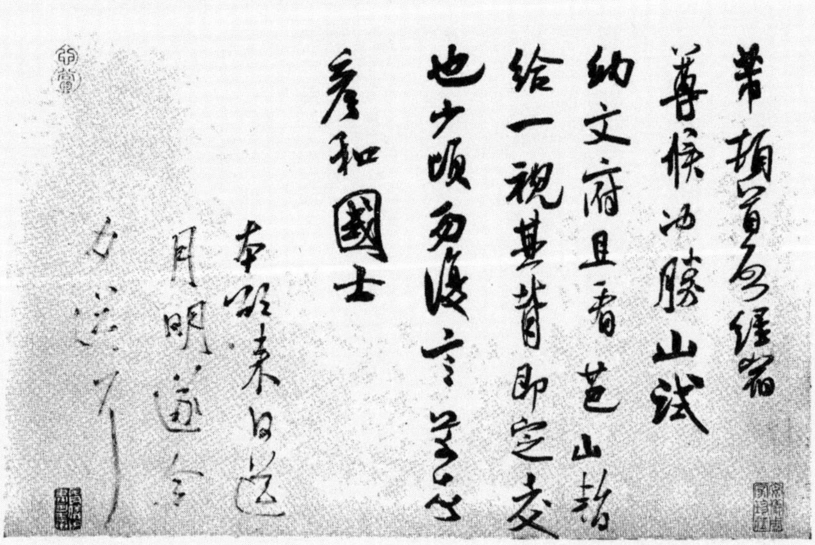

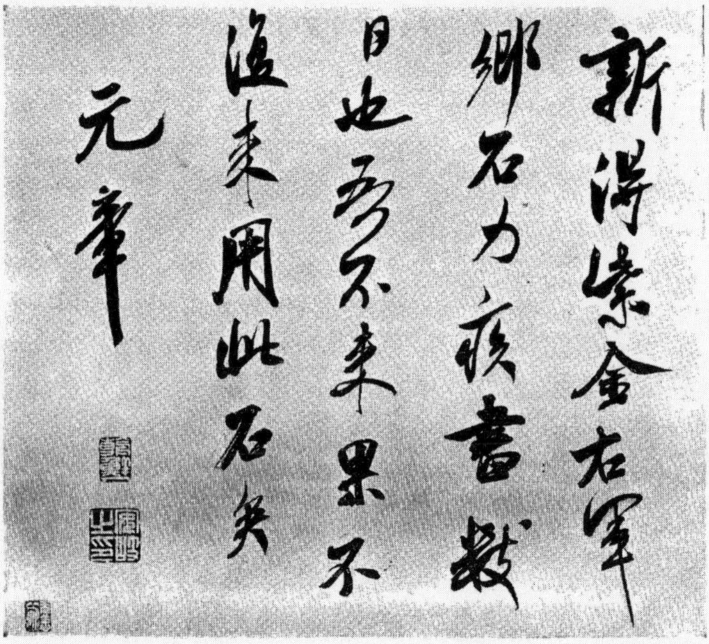

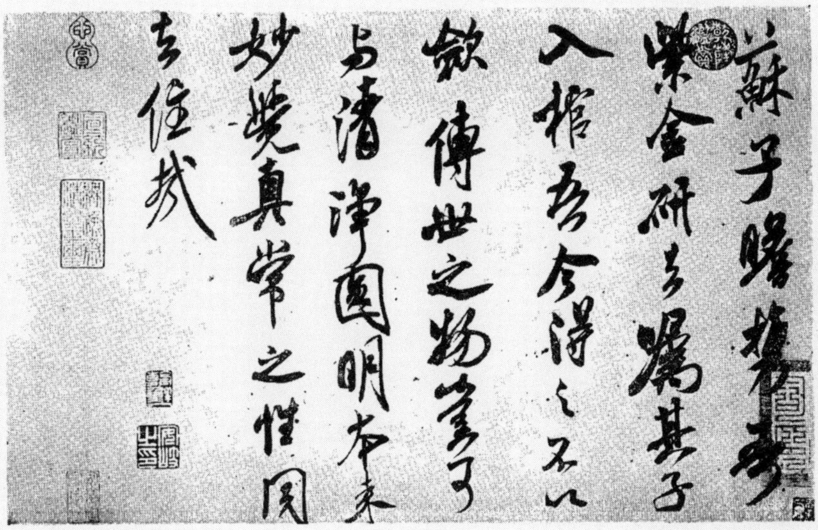

一四 宋四家 墨寶

拾伍開。(第拾肆開空白半開。)又空白叁開。均紙地。寶笈重編著錄。第壹開「宋蔡忠惠公杜君帖」。宋蔡君謨(1012–1067)。名襄。仙遊人。擅書法。紙地剝落。縱貳拾玖·貳公分。橫叁拾玖公分。第貳開「宋蔡君謨陶生帖」。紙地剝落。縱貳拾玖·玖公分。橫伍拾·玖公分。第叁開「宋蔡君謨暑熱春初二帖」。紙地剝落。暑熱帖縱貳拾叁·壹公分。橫貳拾玖·叁公分。春初帖縱貳拾陸·柒公分。橫貳拾玖·壹公分。第肆開「宋蘇文忠公秦太虛詩帖」。宋蘇子瞻(1036–1101)。名軾。號東坡。眉州眉山人。擅書法。世稱蘇體。并長文學。紙地剝落。縱叁拾·玖公分。橫肆拾伍·叁公分。第伍開「宋蘇子瞻東武帖」。縱貳拾捌·捌公分。橫肆拾肆·叁公分。第陸開「宋黃魯直雲夫帖」。宋黃庭堅(1045–1105)。字魯直。號涪翁。又號山谷道人。分寧人。舉進士。徽宗初。知太平州。縱叁拾貳·壹公分。橫陸拾壹·貳公分。第柒開「宋黃山谷苦筍帖」。縱叁拾壹·壹公分。橫肆拾貳·貳公分。第捌開「宋黃山谷花氣詩一帖」。縱叁拾壹公分。橫叁拾叁·伍公分。第玖開「宋黃文節公庭堅書」。縱貳拾捌·玖公分。橫叁拾柒·陸公分。第拾開「宋黃文節公庭堅書」。縱貳拾伍·伍公分。橫肆拾伍·玖公分。第拾壹開「宋米海岳三吳帖」。宋米芾(1051–1107)。字元章。別號海岳外史、襄陽漫士、溪堂、鹿門居士、淮陽外史。世居太原。後徙襄陽。定居潤州。是以一作吳人。官書畫學博士。縱叁拾·陸公分。橫陸拾叁公分。第拾貳開「宋米海岳伯老帖」。縱貳拾柒·玖公分。橫叁拾伍·陸公分。第拾叁開「宋米元章彥和帖」。縱叁拾·貳公分。橫肆拾貳·陸公分。第拾肆開「宋米海岳紫金帖」。縱貳拾捌·肆公分。橫叁拾·陸公分。第拾伍開「宋米海岳紫金研帖」。縱貳拾捌·叁公分。橫叁拾玖·柒公分。

14. Sung Sze Chia "Mo Pao"

Calligraphy of Four Calligraphists of the Sung Dynasty.

一五 宋郭熙 關山春雪圖

絹地。寶笈三編著錄。下端有「熙寧壬子二月奉王旨畫關山春雪之圖臣熙進」題款。有傷補及霉傷。縱壹百柒拾玖·壹公分。橫伍拾壹·貳公分。

郭熙 (約 1085)。河陽温縣人。爲御畫院藝學。

15. Kuo Hsi "Kuan Shan Ch'un Hsueh T'u"

Spring Snow on a Mountain Pass.

Kuo Hsi (circa 1085).—Kuo Hsi was a native of Wenhsien, Hoyang (河陽温縣). He was I-hsueh (藝學) or expositor of art in the Academy of Painting.

一六 宋郭熙
設色山水(傳)

絹地。寶笈三編著錄。右邊有「河陽郭熙」題款。有摺紋、縱壹百捌拾捌·陸公分。横玖拾伍·貳公分。帶錦褾。

16. Kuo Hsi "Shan Shui"

Landscape (attributed).

一七 宋郭熙 山莊高逸圖(傳)

絹地。下端有「河陽郭熙寫」題款。縱壹百捌拾玖·壹公分。
橫壹百零捌·玖公分。

17. Kuo Hsi "Shan Chuang Kao I T'u"

Eminent Recluse in a Mountain Abode (attributed).

(51)

一八 宋米芾 "春山瑞松圖"

紙地。石渠寶笈初編御書房著錄。左下角有「米芾」二字。紙地剝落。縱叁拾伍·壹公分。橫肆拾肆·壹公分。詩堂有題字。縱貳拾柒·伍公分。橫叁拾捌·捌公分。

米芾 (1051-1107)。字元章。別號海岳外史、襄陽漫士、溪堂、鹿門居士、淮陽外史。世居太原。後徙襄陽。定居潤州。是以一作吳人。官書畫學博士。

18. Mi Fei "Ch'un Shan Jui Sung T'u"

Pine Trees and Mountains in Spring.

Mi Fei (1051–1107).—Mi Fei, with the pseudonyms of Yuan-chang (元章), Hai-yo Wai-shih (海岳外史), Hsiang-yang Man-shih (襄陽漫士), Ch'i-t'ang (溪堂), Lu-men Chu-shih (鹿門居士), and Huai-yang Wai-shih (淮陽外史), lived for generations in T'aiyuan. He subsequently moved to Hsiangyang and settled down in Junchou (潤州). It was therefore once alleged that he was a native of Wu (吳). He served as Doctor of Painting.

一九 宋徽宗 紅蓼白鵝圖

絹地。石渠寶笈養心殿著錄。無款。有傷補。縱壹百叁拾叁·壹公分。橫捌拾陸·肆公分。

徽宗 (1083–1135)。諱佶。神宗第十一子。在位二十五年。

19. Emperor Hui Tsung "Hung Liao Po E T'u"

White Goose and Red Polygonums.

Emperor Hui Tsung (1083–1135).—Emperor Hui Tsung of the Sung Dynasty was named Chi (佶). He was the eleventh son of Shen Tsung. He reigned twenty-five years.

徽宗皇帝御製池塘秋晚
圖向曾大父
樞密在政府時侍
紫宸宴酒酣樂作
上乃聲其慶會之意出斯圖
以賜曾大父暨大父侍郎先君
知郡傳至易從迨今四世百有
餘年矣拜觀寶圖筆精墨妙
超卓今古豈凡子所能作哉
謹當珍藏以示子孫垂之不
朽堅忠孝大節仰答
聖眷隆渥也

淳熙丁酉春南陽鄒易從拜書

（55）

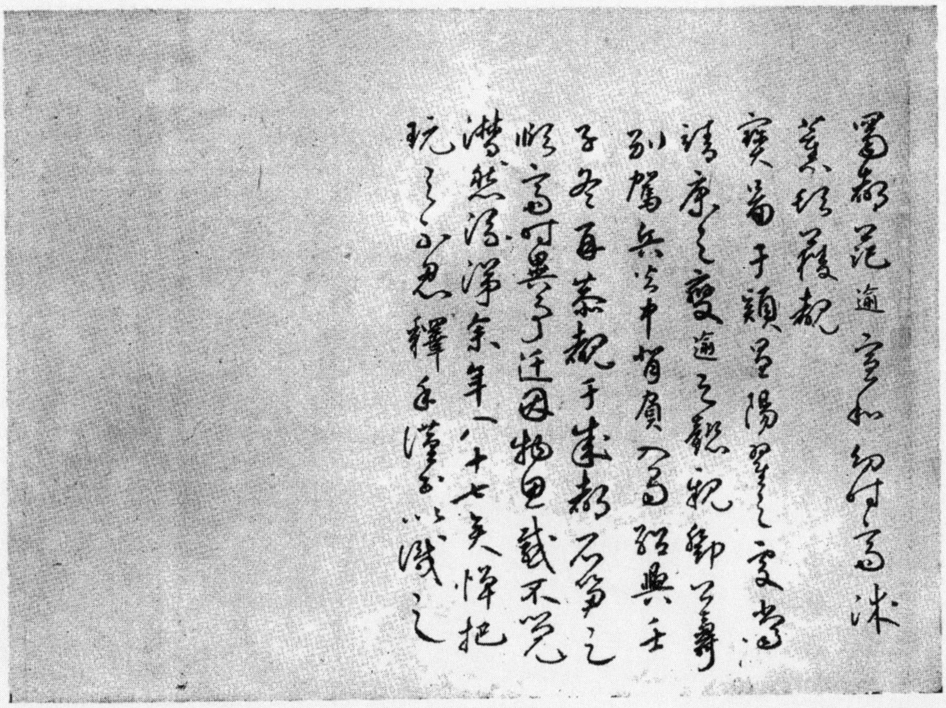

(56)

(58)

（ 59 ）

（ 61 ）

二〇 宋徽宗 池塘秋晚圖卷

紙地。石渠寶笈御書房著錄。最後有御押及御書圖章。縱叁拾叁·壹公分。橫貳百叁拾叁·柒公分。拖尾有「南陽鄧易從」題識。縱叁拾叁·壹公分。橫捌拾玖·伍公分。帶錦袱木盒各壹件。

20. Emperor Hui Tsung "Ch'ih T'ang Ch'iu Wan T'u Ch'uen"

An Autumn Evening by a Lake (a scroll).

怪石

殊狀難名各蔽虧高低萃
羌聞巍巍直疑伏獸身將
動常恐是蛟發〻起〻現
幾層蒼檜藹凝嵐四接老
松園各封三品非無美歛
羽曾今壯奮衣

牡丹一本同榦二花其紅深
淺不同名品寔兩種也一曰
疊羅紅一曰勝雲紅艷麗尊
榮皆冠一時之妙造化密移
如此褒賞之餘因成口占
異品殊葩共翠柯嫩紅拂拂
醉金荷春羅幾疊敷丹陛雲
縷重縈浴絳河玉鑑和鳴鸞
對舞寶枝連理錦成窠東
君造化勝前歲吟繞清香故
琢磨

（63）

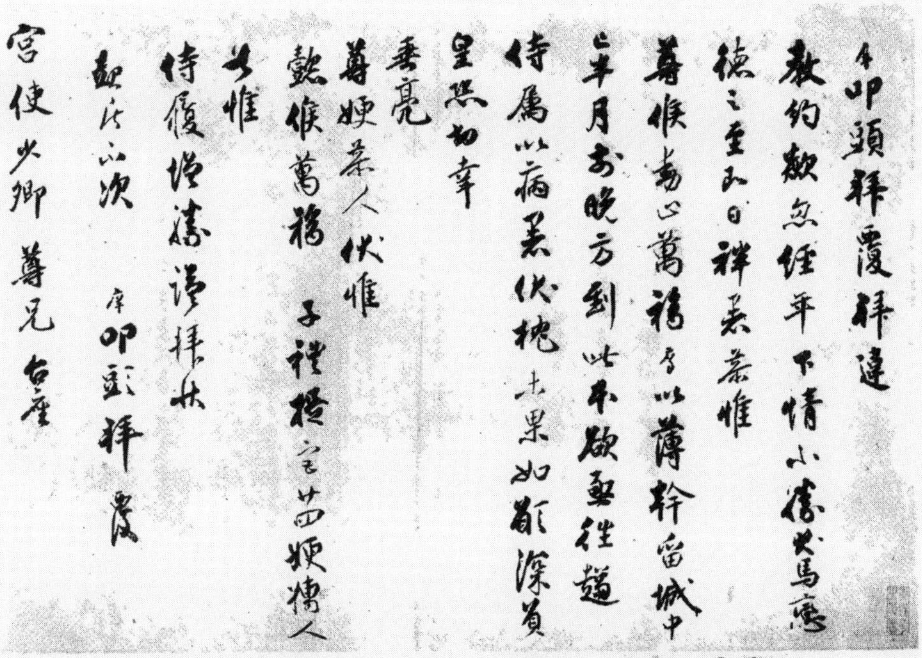

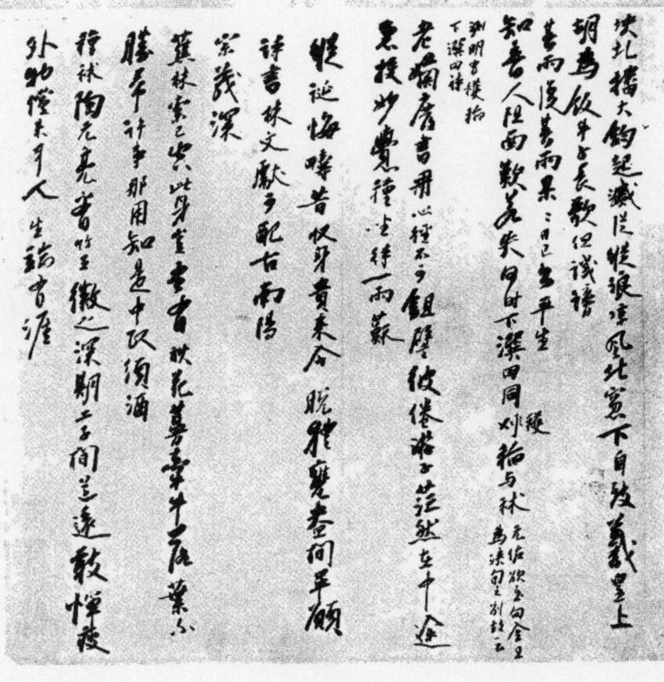

(64)

家洛目頓首再拜別久不勝馳
仰厚
示伏審
辦嚴之暇
台候曼福感慰克家衰疾多冝昇遠蒙
恩入輿機政懇辭不獲日深憂懼
不識何以見教也
新除未足為
公賀
望實兼隆冝居
近密
武林徒湯
公重豈淹郵之地耶
所諭以克家兩日肺喘謁歸来日与
丞相議之
贍集未間千万
眠食加護不宣克家洛目頓首再拜
泰發知府待制台坐

觀啓出京忽草不獲
再奉違俟忽累月爲勝馳
仰近中厚示
手教伏承
履此新涼
起居殊勝爲慰、轍到此幸無恙
學中全無職事歸以日甚但恐違
素親舊無与往還耳未卜
會面惟
順候自重不勝區區謹奉手啓布
謝不宣轍再
子瞻秘丞仁丈執事
七月廿四日

(65)

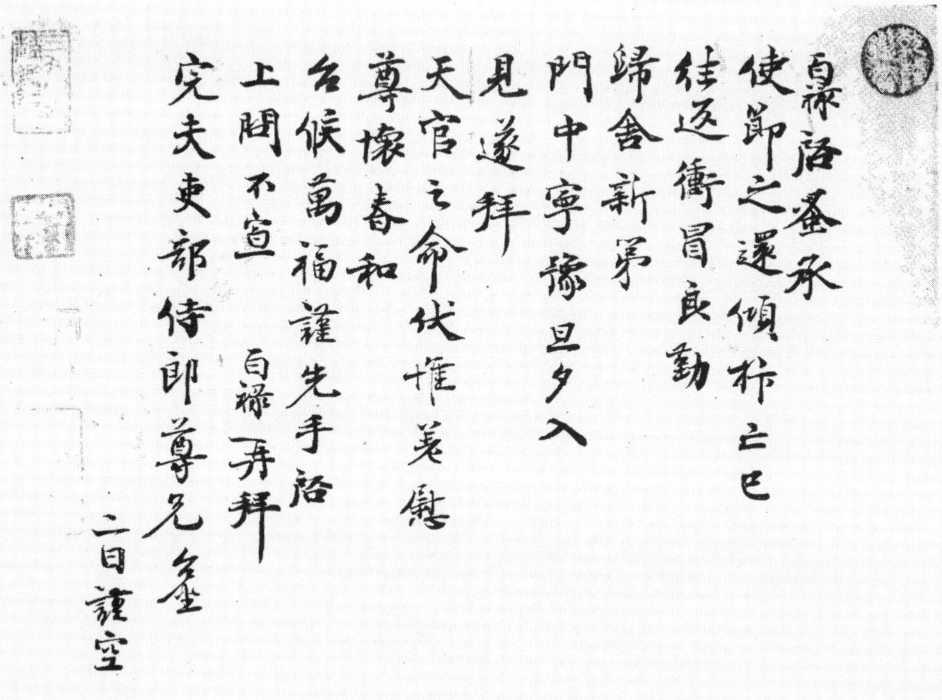
百祿啓蚤承
使節之還傾杼之已
往返衝冒良勤
歸舍新第
門中寧豫旦夕入
見遂拜
天官之命伏惟慶慰
尊懷春和
台候萬福謹先手啓
上問不宣 百祿再拜
究夫吏部侍郎尊兄台坐
二日謹空

二一 宋代墨寶

柒開。紙地。寶笈重編著錄。第壹開宣和御筆怪石詩帖。字有浸傷。縱叁拾伍·貳公分。橫肆拾貳·叁公分。第貳開宣和御筆牡丹詩帖。縱叁拾肆·玖公分。橫伍拾貳·貳公分。第叁開□庠尺牘。縱叁拾壹·捌公分。橫肆拾柒·壹公分。第肆開無款五言詩帖。雙幅。上幅縱叁拾肆·伍公分。橫拾肆·柒公分。下幅縱叁拾肆·伍公分。橫拾捌·貳公分。第伍開□克家書尺牘。有傷補。縱叁拾伍·捌公分。橫肆拾伍·貳公分。第陸開蘇轍書尺牘。有傷補。縱貳拾伍·捌公分。橫叁拾貳公分。第七開□百祿書尺牘。有傷補。縱貳拾陸·陸公分。橫叁拾柒公分。空白四開。

21. Sung Tai "Mo Pao"

An Album of Calligraphy by Hui Tsung and Others.

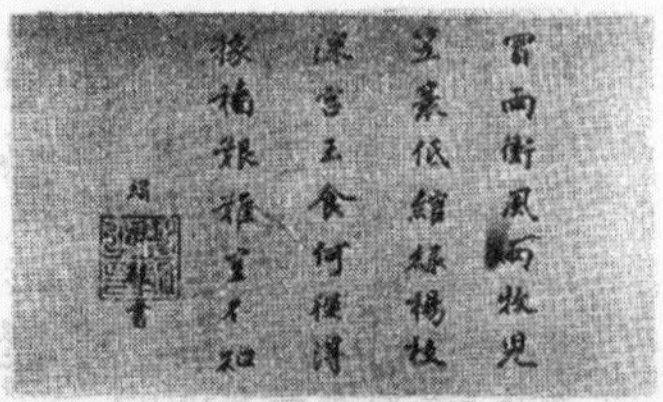

二二 宋李迪
風雨歸牧圖(傳)

絹地。石渠寶笈三編著錄。下端有「甲午歲李迪筆」題款。詩堂有「緝熙殿書」題跋。縱壹百貳拾·陸公分。橫壹百零叁公分。

李迪(1089-1161)。河陽人。宣和時蒞職畫院。授成忠郎。紹興間復職畫院副使。歷事孝光朝。

22. Li Ti "Feng Yu Kuei Mu T'u"

Herdsmen Returning Home in a Rain Storm (attributed).

Li Ti (1089-1161).—Li Ti was a native of Ho-yang (河陽). During the reign of Hsuan Ho he served in the Academy of Painting. He was subsequently appointed Ch'eng Chung Lang (成忠郎). In the Shao Hsing (紹興) period, he was reappointed to the Academy as vice-director, serving through the reigns of Emperors Hsiao Tsung and Kuang Tsung.

(68)

二三 宋李唐 乳牛圖

絹地。無款。右邊緣有「李晞古乳牛圖蕉林重裝」。縱肆拾陸·陸公分。橫陸拾貳·陸公分。

李唐(1049–1130)。字晞古。河陽三城人。徽宗朝補入畫院。建炎間。授成忠郎。畫院待詔。賜金帶。

23. Li T'ang "Ju Niu T'u"

Milch Cow.

Li T'ang (1049–1130).—Li T'ang, with the pseudonym of Hsi-ku (晞古), was a native of Sanch'eng, in Hoyang (河陽三城). During the reign of Emperor Hui Tsung he was appointed to the Imperial Academy of Painting. Later on, in the Chien Yen period, he was conferred the official title of Ch'eng Chung Lang (成忠郎), and probationer or Tai Chao in the Academy. He was given a golden belt by the Emperor.

二四 宋趙伯駒 春山圖

紙地。寶笈重編著錄。無款。上端有「乾隆」題識。紙地剝落。縱捌拾玖·捌公分。橫叁拾貳·肆公分。

趙伯駒(1120–1182)。字千里。宋宗室。太祖七世孫。官至浙東兵馬鈐轄。

24. Chao Po-chu "Ch'un Shan T'u"

Mountain in Spring.

Chao Po-chu (1120–1182).—Chao Po-chu, with the pseudonym of Chien-li (千里), was of the imperial clan. He was a grandson of Emperor Tai Tsu (960–975 A.D.) of the seventh generation. He served as Che Tung Ping Ma Chien Hsia (浙東兵馬鈐轄), or commanding officer of the army in east Chekiang.

二五 宋趙伯駒 阿閣圖

絹地。寶笈重編著錄。無款。有傷補及摺痕。縱柒拾叁·肆公分。橫伍拾伍·捌公分。

25. Chao Po-chu "Ah Ke T'u"

Ah Ke Building.

(71)

二六 宋蘇漢臣
秋庭戲嬰圖

絹地。寶笈重編著錄。無款。有傷補。縱壹百玖拾柒·伍公分。橫壹百零捌·陸公分。

蘇漢臣(約1120)。開封人。宣和畫院待詔。隆興初。補承信郎。

25. Su Han-chen "Ch'iu T'ing Hsi Ying T'u"

Children at Play in a Courtyard in Autumn.

Su Han-chen (circa 1120).—Su Han-chen was a native of K'aifeng (開封), Honan. In Hsuan Ho's reign he was a Tai Chao or probationer in the Academy of Painting. In the early part of the Lung Hsing (隆興) period, he was made Ch'eng Hsin Lang (承信郎).

二七

宋蘇漢臣
貨郎圖

絹地。寶笈三編著錄。無款。有傷補及摺痕霧傷。縱壹百伍拾玖·肆公分。橫玖拾柒·叁公分。

27. Su Han-chen "Hou Lang T'u"

A Pedlar of Toys.

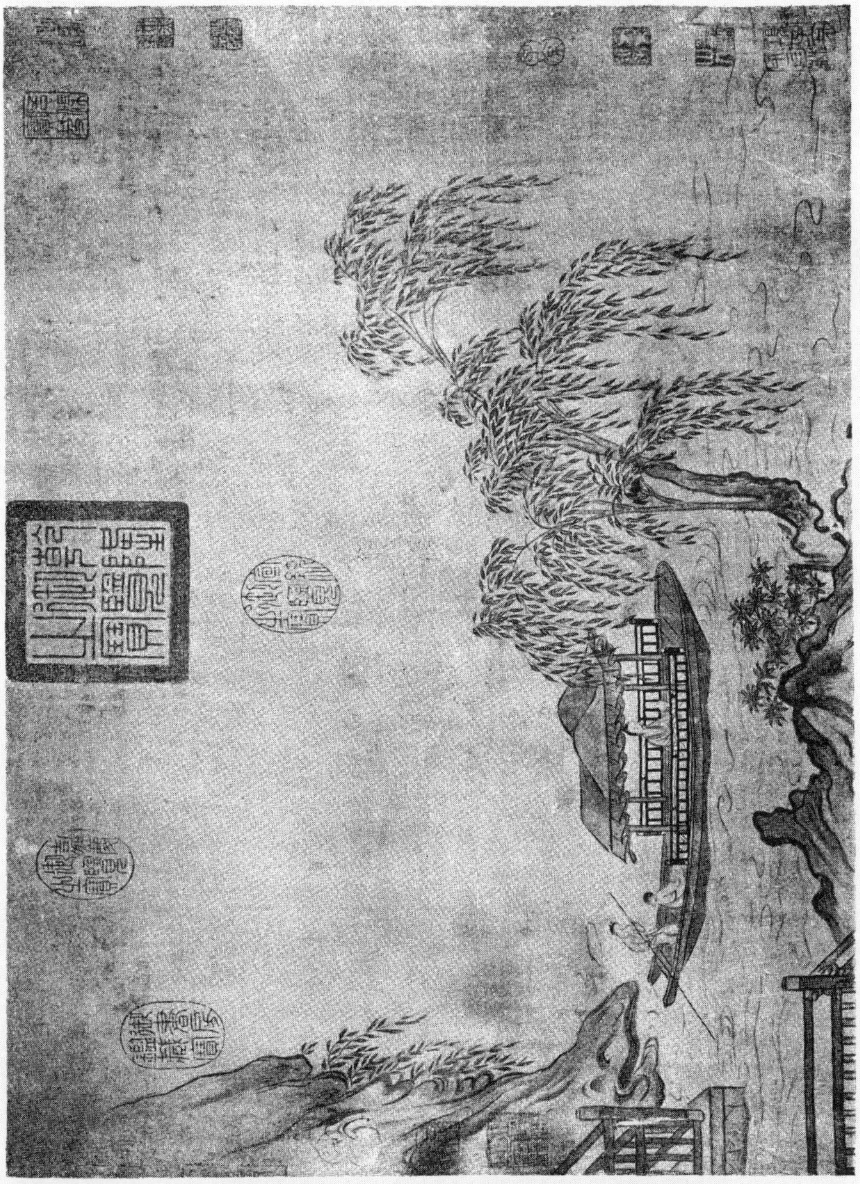

二八 宋馬和之 柳溪春舫圖

絹地。石渠寶笈初編御書房著錄。左下角有「和之」二字題款。有傷補。縱叁拾陸·玖公分。橫伍拾壹·伍公分。

馬和之(1130–1180)。錢塘人。紹興中登第。官至工部侍郎。高孝兩朝深重其筆。

28. Ma Ho-chih "Liu Ch'i Ch'un Fang T'u"

A Boat in a Willowy Stream in Spring.

Ma Ho-chih (1130–1180).—Ma Ho-chih was a native of Ch'ient'ang (錢塘). In the Shao Hsing (紹興) period, he passed the officer-examination, and later on, he became Kung Pu Shih Lang (工部侍郎). During the reigns of Emperor Kao and Emperor Hsiao, he was greatly admired for his brushwork.

(74)

二九

宋馬和之
閒忙圖(傳)

絹地。無款。有傷補。縱壹百貳拾肆·伍公分。橫陸拾柒·貳公分。

29. Ma Ho-chih "Hsien Mang T'u"

Working at Leisure (attributed).

三〇 宋劉松年 絲綸圖

紙地。寶笈三編著錄。無款。跋尾有「攝李汪砢玉源崑甫」題識。有傷補及摺痕。縱玖拾捌·陸公分。橫叁拾叁·貳公分。

劉松年(1073-1157)。錢塘人。淳熙畫院學生。紹熙年待詔。

30. Liu Sung-nien "Sze Lun T'u"

Women Weaving.

Liu Sung-nien (1073-1157).—Liu Sung-nien was a native of Ch'ient'ang (Chekiang). In the time of Shun Hsi (淳熙), he was made a student in the Academy of Painting, and later was appointed Tai Chao (待詔) or probationer there.

三一 宋劉松年 唐五學士圖

絹地。寶笈三編著錄。無款。有傷補。縱壹百柒拾伍·叁公分。橫壹百零陸·伍公分。

31. Liu Sung-nien "T'ang Wu Hsueh Shih T'u"

Five Scholars of the T'ang Dynasty.

三二 宋林椿 十全報喜圖

絹地。寶笈三編著錄。下端有「畫院待詔林椿畫」題款。均係半字。詩堂有「黃鉞書御題詩」。有傷補。縱壹百柒拾叁·壹公分。橫玖拾柒·肆公分。

林椿(約 1176)。錢塘人。淳熙間。官畫院待詔。賜金帶。

32. Lin Ch'un "Shih Ch'uan Pao Hsi T'u"

Magpies Singing.

Lin Ch'un (circa 1176).—Lin Ch'un was a native of Ch'ient'ang (Chekiang). In the time of Shun Hsi he served as a Tai Chao (待詔) or probationer in the Academy of Painting, and was conferred a golden belt by the Emperor.

(79)

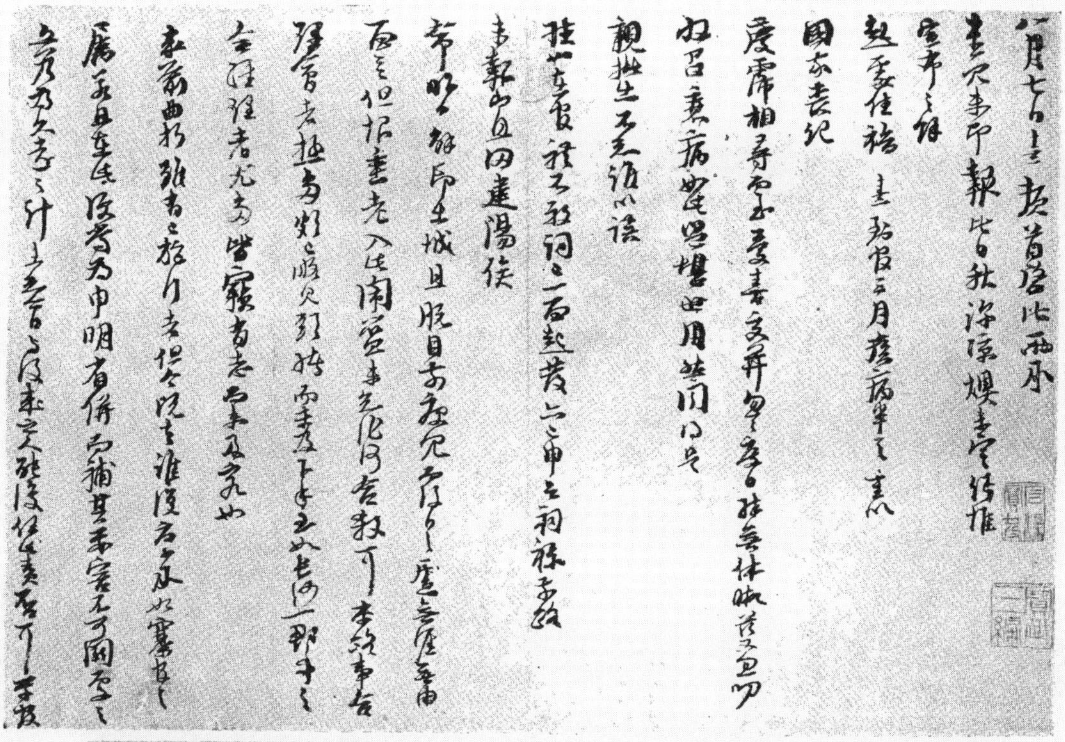

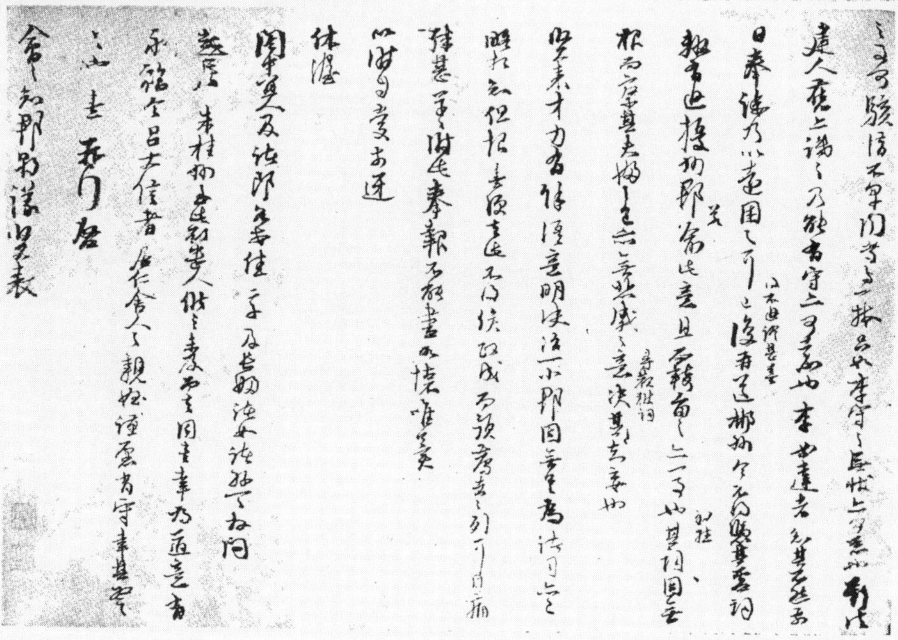

題晦庵翰墨卷後

右晦庵翰墨文卷乃有宋沈著卿出雜色倭
紙奉邀徵國朱文公走書晉彭澤令陶淵明歸去
來辭令闕郡幕賓宛陵陳君家世寶藏之舊物
迹迹相付抱持弗置至君又能裝池成卷是所以承遺
澤於前而垂蓋庇于後可遺啟紫桑翁元亮嘗
祖晉世宰輔自少家貧耕植自給餅無儲粟不求見
需爲能固守其窮袁呂叔父見用爲令當風波未靜
之時在官八十餘日見宋業漸隆不復肯仕劃然
賦辭自免去職可謂潔靖節之純也耶有謂元亮
恥事二姓在晉所作皆題年號入宋之詩惟書甲
子皆載於傳記之外雖有識如黃庭堅秦觀李燾

真德秀亦疑其謬而指之際獨蕭統撰本爲是所
以予朱子述通鑑綱目遂書曰晉徵士陶潛卒可謂
得其實矣曩昔晦庵然舜卿先請不他銘記書
而是特筆者當唱疾之作楚景慕淵明之清致遂
有乘興捉筆不覺終篇之讙而紀述不曰晦庵而曰
雲壑者時築室於建陽廬峯之巔號曰雲谷蓋在
然陽書堂之後因創草堂而扁曰晦庵亦曰雲壑老
人後得武夷五曲之地結廬其間曰武夷精舍晚卜築
於考亭作精舍曰竹林更名曰滄洲因號曰滄洲病叟
家後構著遇遯之同人更號遯翁而晦庵之號甚顯
於世故多晦庵云年譜序次如是其雲壑爲文公別
號明矣顧其筆勢遒勁天機逸發如枯藤朽木雲

(81)

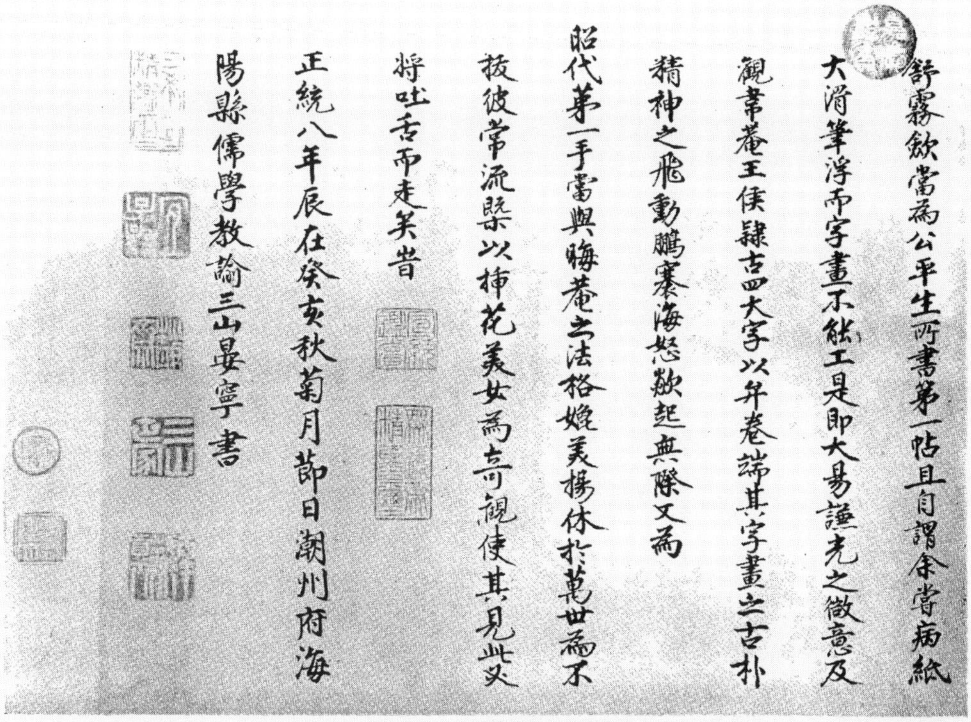
許霧歛當爲公平生所書第一帖且自謂余嘗病紙
大滑筆浮而字畫不能工是即大易謙光之微意及
觀韋菴王侯隸古四大字以弁卷端其字畫之古朴
精神之飛動鵬騫海怒欻起無際又爲
昭代第一手當與晦菴之法格媲美揚休於萬世爲不
拔彼常流槩以插花美女爲奇觀使其見此必
將吐舌而走矣旹
正統八年辰在癸亥秋菊月節日潮州府海
陽縣儒學教諭三山晏寧書

三三 宋朱熹 尺牘

陸開。(內有半開空白。)最後附空白頁貳開。紙地。石渠寶笈三編著錄。第一開有「宋徽國朱文公遺像」字樣。縱貳拾捌·肆公分。橫貳拾貳·肆公分。第二開紙地剝落。有「熹頓首啓」字樣。縱叁拾叁·叁公分。橫肆拾柒·柒公分。第三開紙地剝落。有「熹再拜啓」字樣。縱叁拾叁·叁公分。橫肆拾柒·壹公分。第四開有蟲蛀痕。有「題晦庵翰墨卷後」字樣。縱叁拾壹·伍公分橫肆拾壹·叁公分。第五開有蟲蛀痕。縱叁拾壹·肆公分。橫肆拾叁·壹公分。第六開有蟲蛀痕。有「三山晏寧」題識。縱叁拾壹·肆公分。橫叁拾陸·玖公分。

朱熹(1130–1200)。字元晦。改字仲晦。婺源人。紹興進士。累官轉運副使、煥章閣待制、祕閣修撰。

33. Chu Hsi "Ch'ih Tu"

Letters.

Chu Hsi (1130–1200).—Chu Hsi, with the pseudonym of Yuan-hui (元晦) which was changed into Chung-hui (仲晦), was a naive of Wuyuan (婺源) in Anhui. He graduated as Chin-shih in the time of Shao Hsing (紹興) and served as assistant commissioner of transportation, Huan-chang Ko Tai Chih (煥章閣待制), and compiler in Pi Ko (祕閣).

三四 宋閻次平

四樂圖

絹地。左邊下端有「閻次平」題款。有補痕。縱壹百玖拾貳·陸公分。橫玖拾柒·貳公分。

閻次平(約1164)。閻仲之子。隆興初。補將仕郎。畫院祇候。賜金帶。

34. Yen Tz'e-ping "Sze Lo T'u"

Four Toys (Fishing, Gathering Fuel, Tilling and Reading).

Yen Tz'e-ping (circa 1164).—Yen Tz'e-ping was a son of Yen Chung (閻仲). In the early part of Lung Hsing (隆興), he was appointed Chiang Shih Lang (將仕郎), and the Chih Hou (祇候) in the Academy of Painting. He was given a golden belt by the Emperor.

三五 宋李嵩
羅漢圖

絹地。祕殿珠林三編著錄。無款。有傷補。縱壹百零肆·壹公分。橫肆拾玖·伍公分。

李嵩(1166-1243)。錢塘人。光宗、寧宗、理宗三朝畫院待詔。

35. Li Sung "Lo Han T'u"

A Lohan.

Li Sung (1166-1243).—Li Sung was a native of Ch'ient'ang (Chekiang). In the reigns of Kuang Tsung, Ning Tsung, and Li Tsung (thirteenth century A.D.). He served as Hua Yuan Tai Chao (畫院待詔), or probationer in the Imperial Academy of Painting.

三六 宋馬遠 對月圖

絹地。寶笈三編著錄、無款、有折裂痕。縱壹百肆拾玖·捌公分·橫柒拾捌·貳公分。

馬遠(約1195)。字欽山。光宗寧宗朝。畫院待詔。

36. Ma Yuan "Tui Yueh T'u"

Looking at the Moon.

Ma Yuan (circa 1195).—Ma Yuan, with the pseudonym of Ch'ien-shan (欽山), was a Tai Chao (待詔) or probationer in the Academy of Painting, in the time of Kuang Tsung and Ning Tsung (1190–1224 A.D.).

(85)

三七 宋馬遠 秋江漁隱圖

紙地。寶笈重編著錄。無款。左中段有乾隆辛卯秋御題。有傷補及摺痕。縱叁拾陸·陸公分。橫貳拾捌·柒公分。

37. Ma Yuan "Ch'iu Chiang Yu Yin T'u"

The Peace and Quiet of Angling by a River in Autumn.

三八 宋夏珪

西湖柳艇圖

絹地。寶笈重編著錄。無款。上端有「天錫郭畀」題識。有折傷。縱壹百零柒·貳公分。横伍拾玖·叁公分。

夏珪(約 1208)。字禹玉。錢塘人。寧宗朝待詔。

38. Hsia Kuei "Hsi Hu Liu T'ing T'u"

Boating Under the Willows of the West Lake.

Hsia Kuei (circa 1208).—Hsia Kuei, with the pseudonym of Yu-yu (禹玉), was a native of Ch'ient'ang, (Chekiang) and was a Tai Chao (待詔) or probationer of the Academy of Painting in the reign of Emperor Ning Tsung (1195–1224 A.D.).

(88)

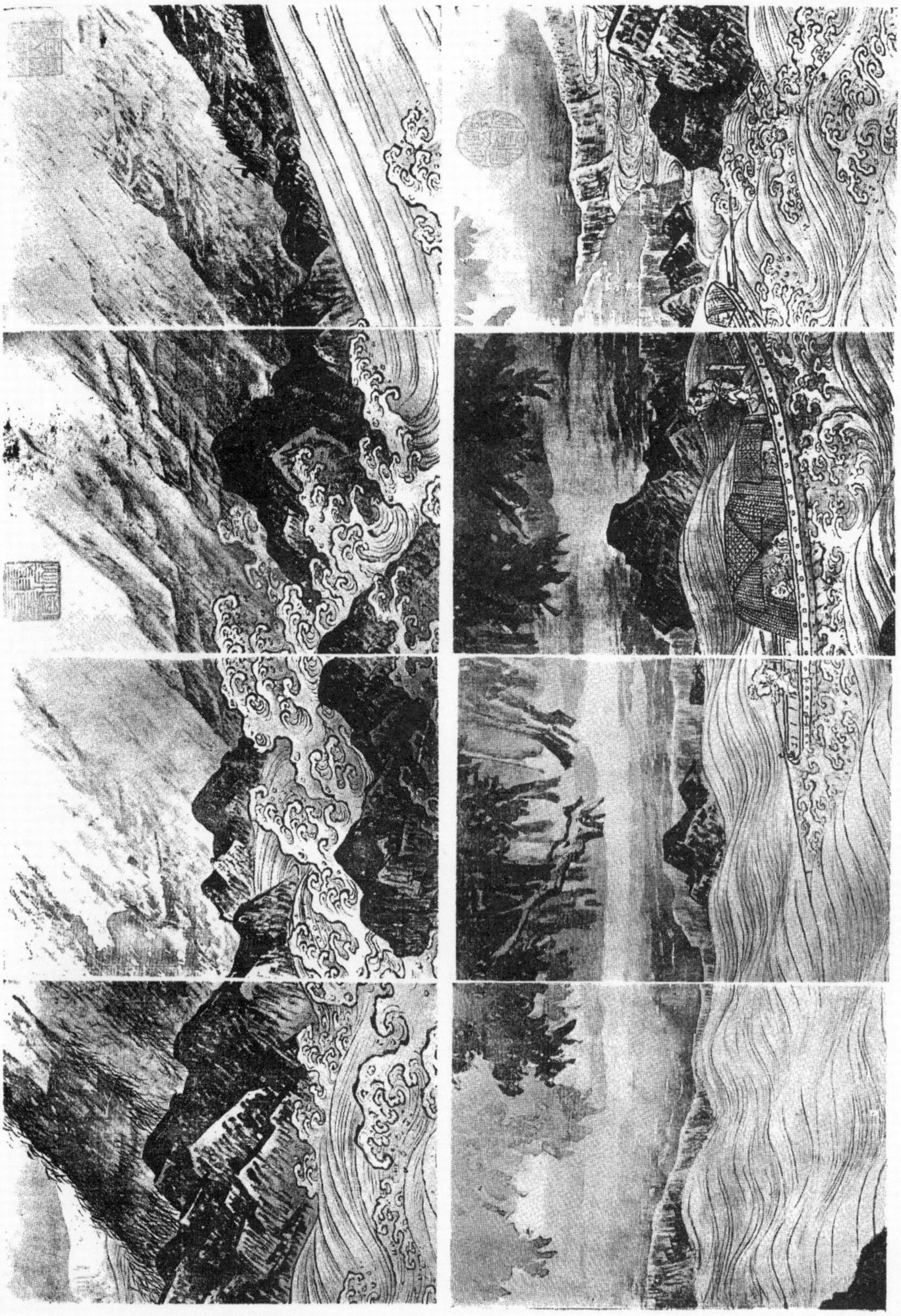

(89)

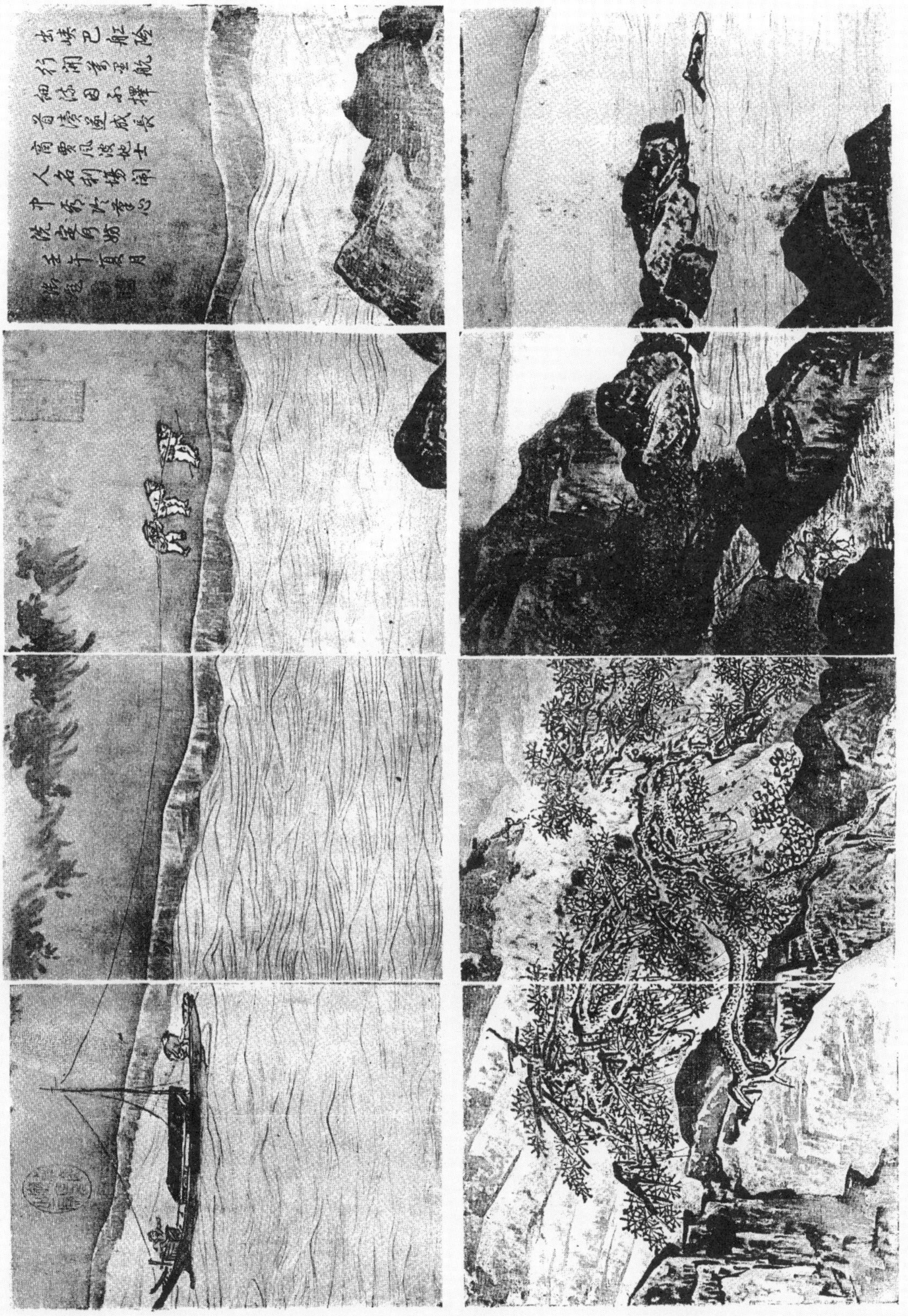

(90)

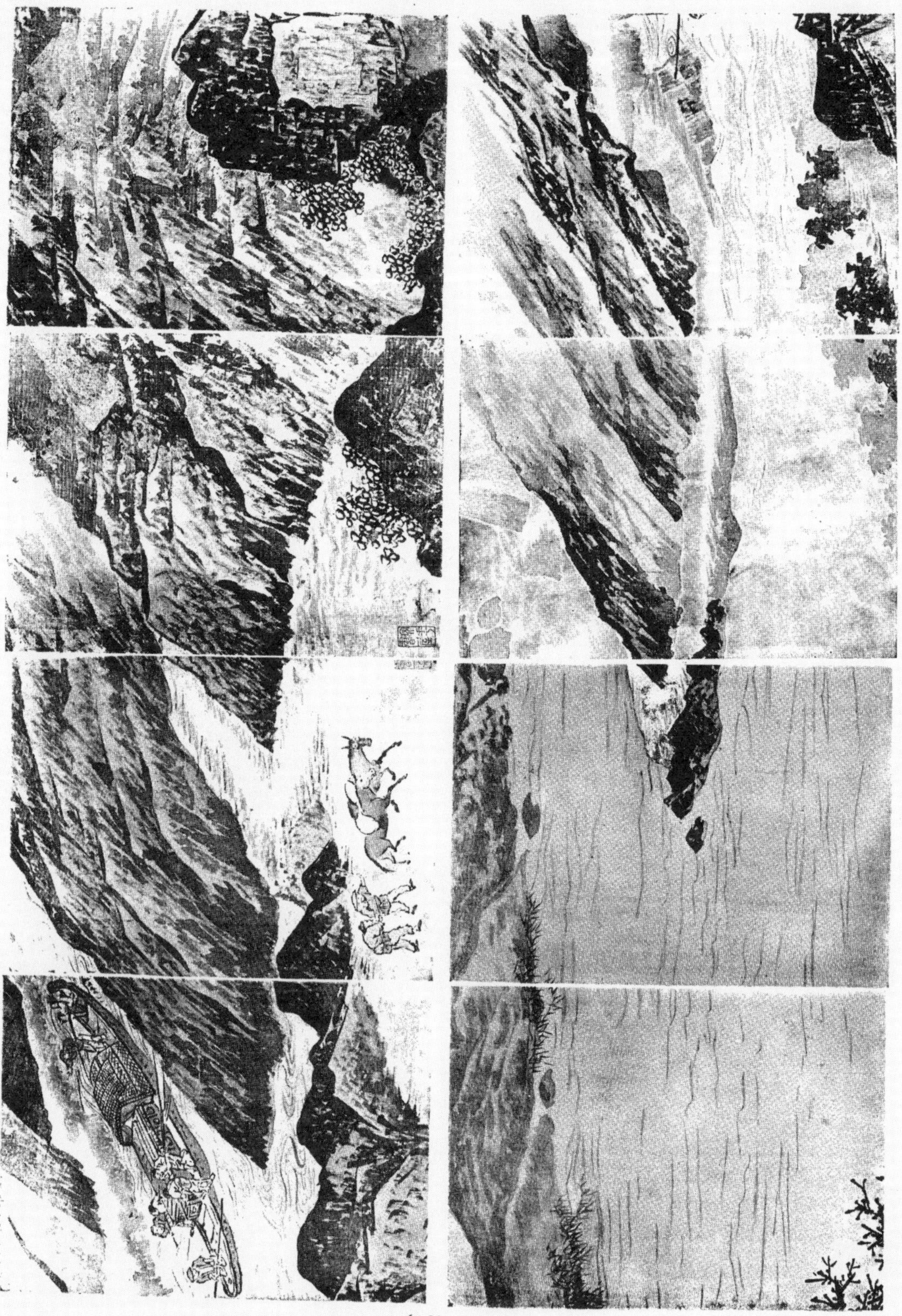

(91)

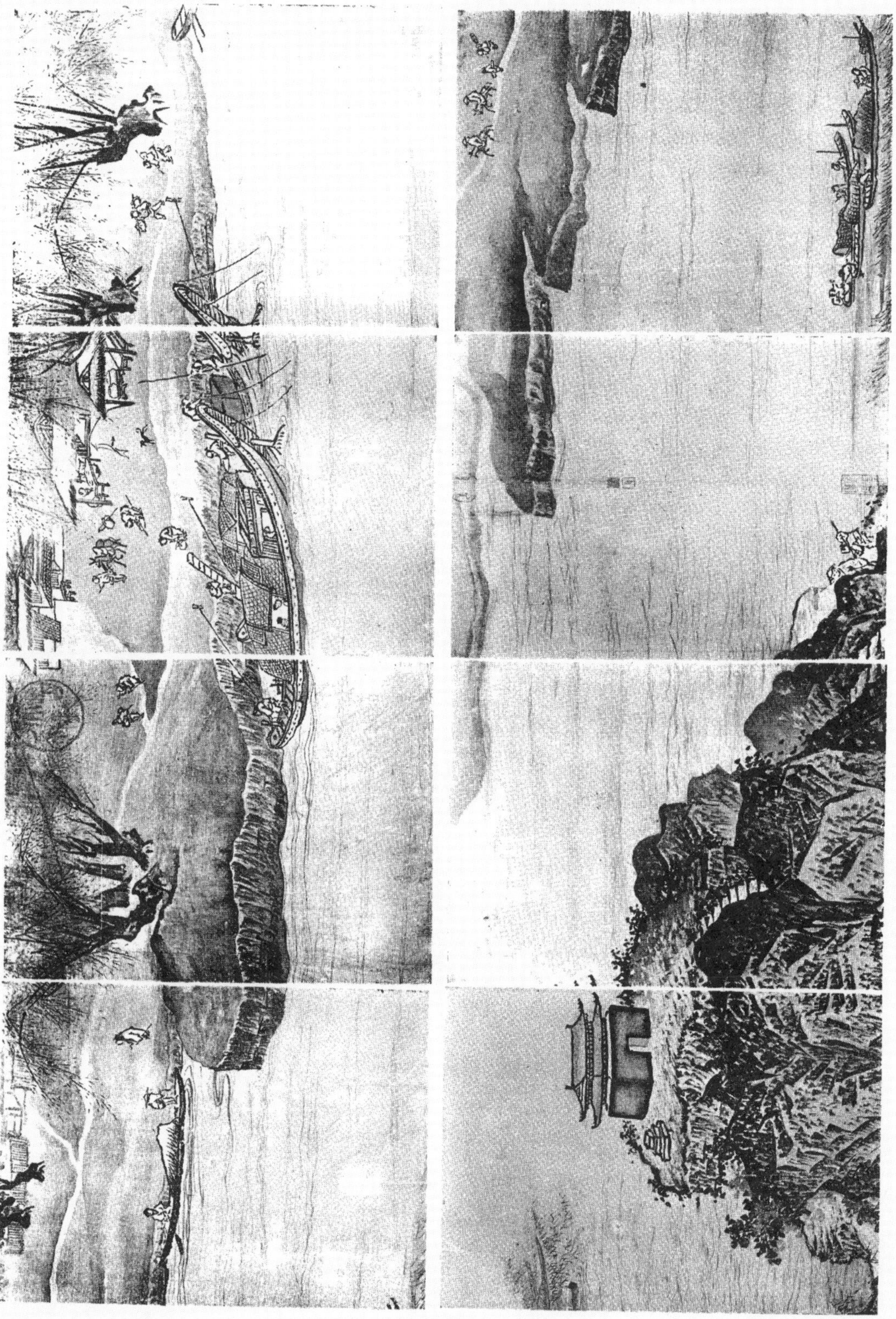

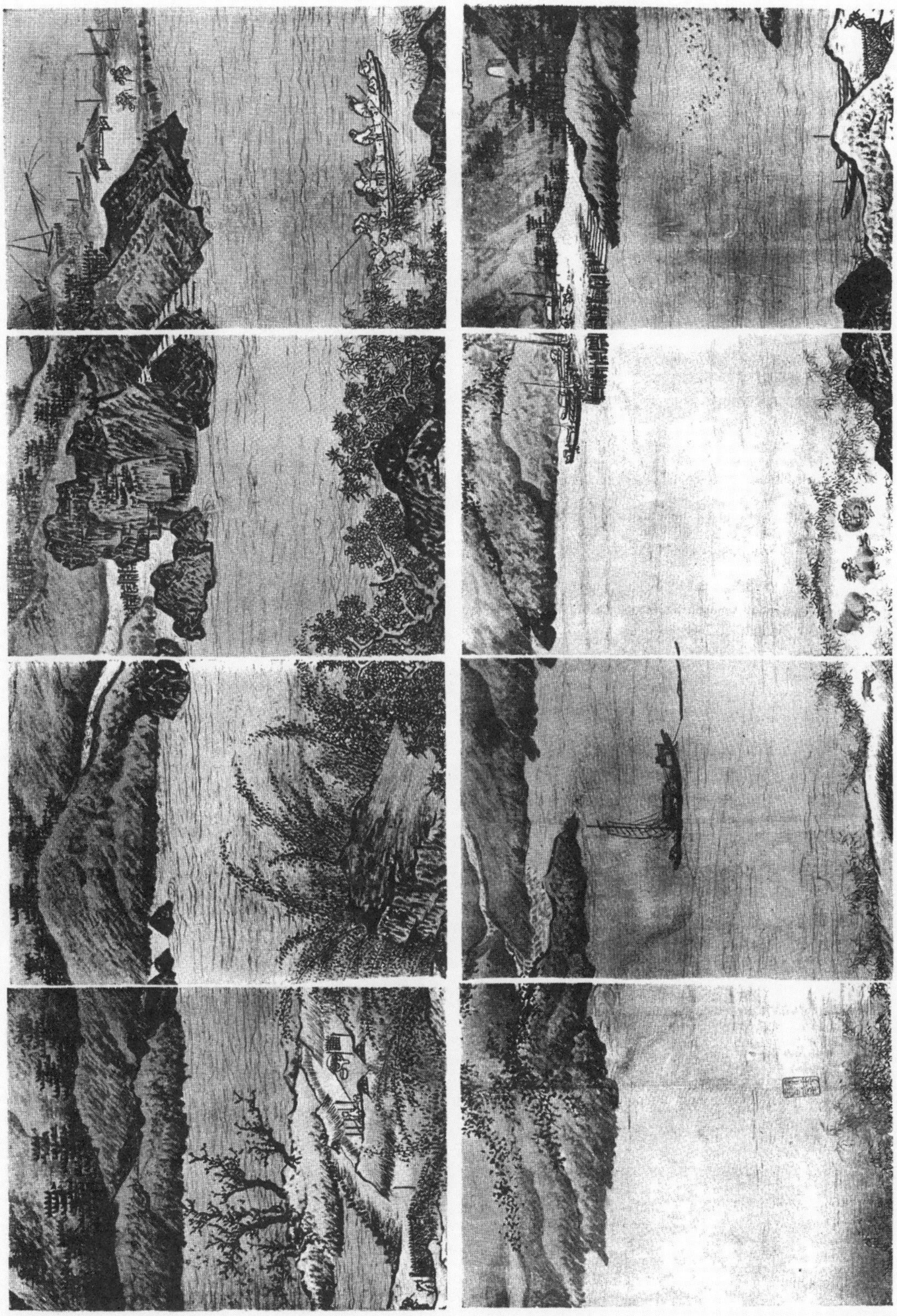

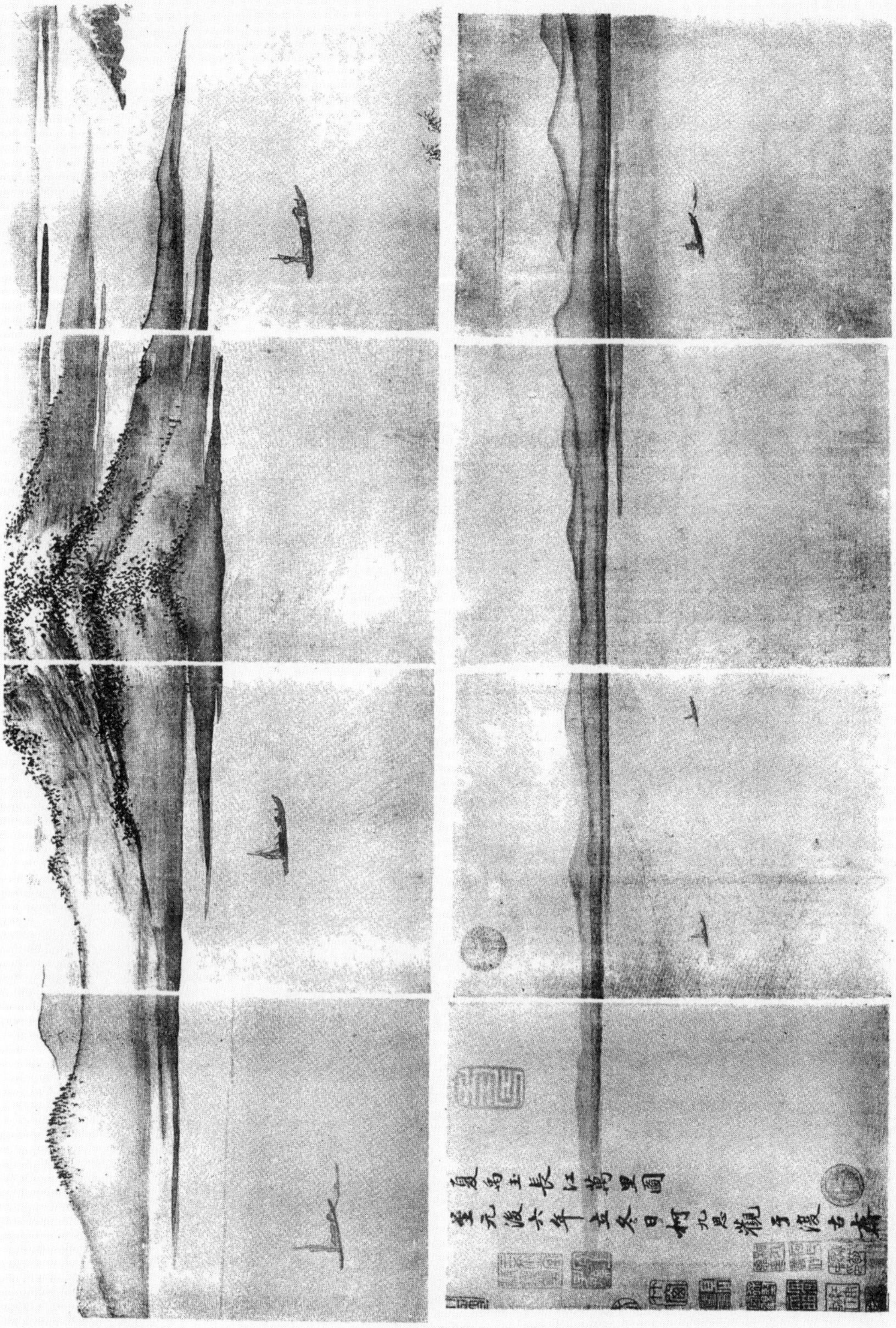

（ 95 ）

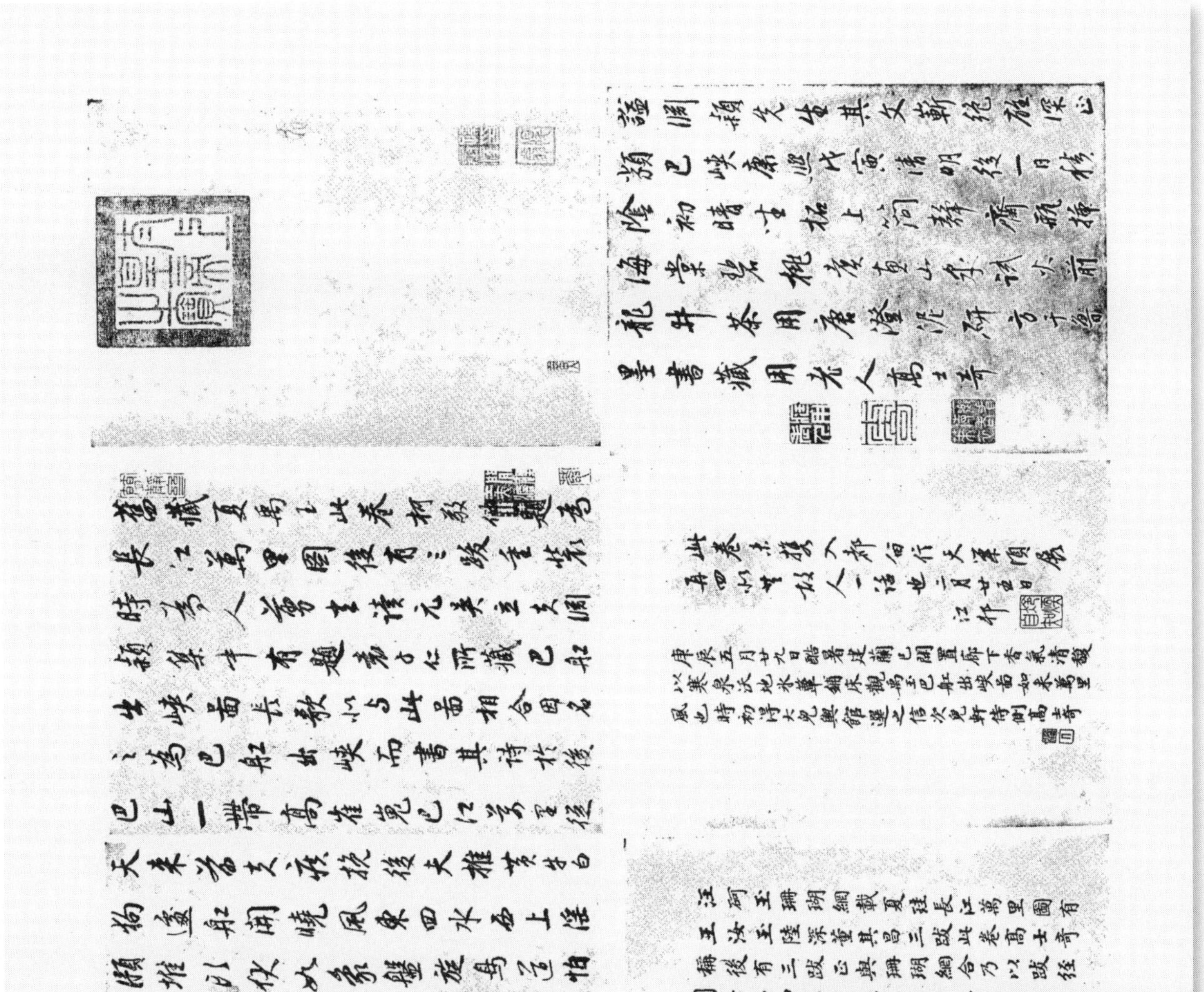

三九 宋夏珪 長江萬里圖卷

絹地。寶笈重編著錄。無款。最後有「柯九思觀於復古齋」題識。絹地。有黴傷及缺損。縱貳拾陸·玖公分。橫壹千壹百壹拾肆·叁公分。引首有「岷流壯觀」四字。縱貳拾陸·玖公分。橫柒拾伍·捌公分。拖尾有「高士奇」等跋語四段。縱貳拾陸·玖公分。橫壹百貳拾柒公分。帶木盒。

39. Hsia Kuei "Ch'ang Chiang Wan Li T'u Ch'uen"

Ten Thousand Miles of the Yangtze (a scroll).

四〇 宋馬麟

花鳥

絹地。下端有「臣馬麟」題款。縱壹百壹拾玖·捌公分。橫伍拾陸·肆公分。

馬麟(約 1302)。遠子。爲畫院祗候。能世家學。遠多以己畫作麟畫。

40. Ma Lin "Hua Niao"

Birds and Flowers.

Ma Lin (circa 1302).—Ma Lin was the son of Ma Yuan (馬遠). He served as Chih Hou (祗候) in the Academy of Painting.

四一 宋魯宗貴

春韶鳴喜圖

絹地。下端有「宗貴製」題款。有蟲蛀。縱壹百陸拾·肆公分。橫柒拾柒·玖公分。

魯宗貴(約 1229)。錢塘人。紹定時畫院待詔。

41. Lu Tsung-kuei "Ch'un Shao Ming Hsi T'u"

Birds Welcoming the Spring.

Lu Tsung-kuei (circa 1229).—Lu Tsung-kuei was a native of Ch'ient'ang (Chekiang). In the Shao Ting period he was Tai Chao (待詔) or probationer in the Academy of Painting.

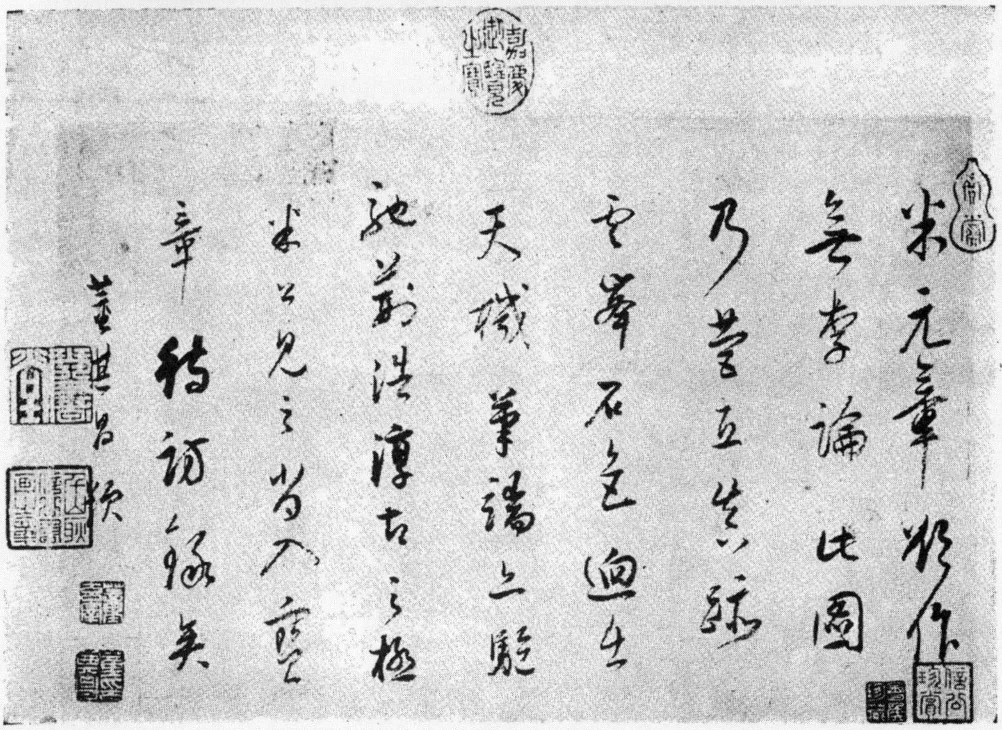

（ 100 ）

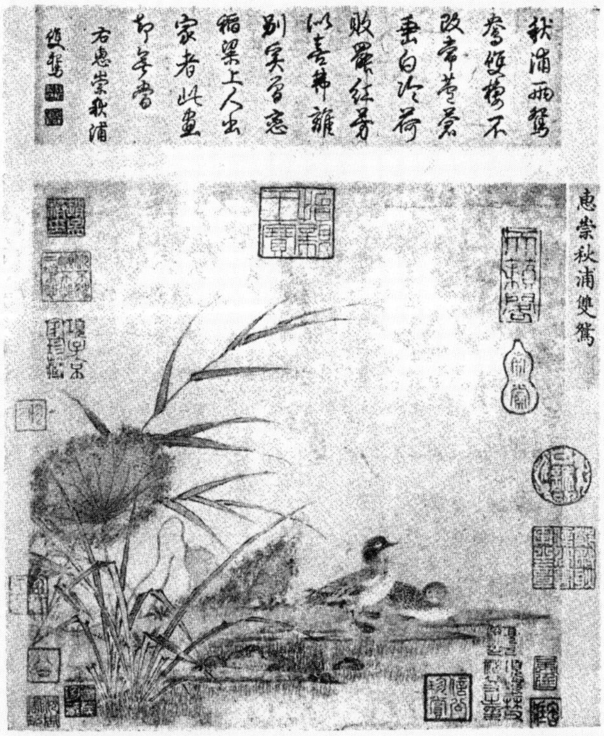

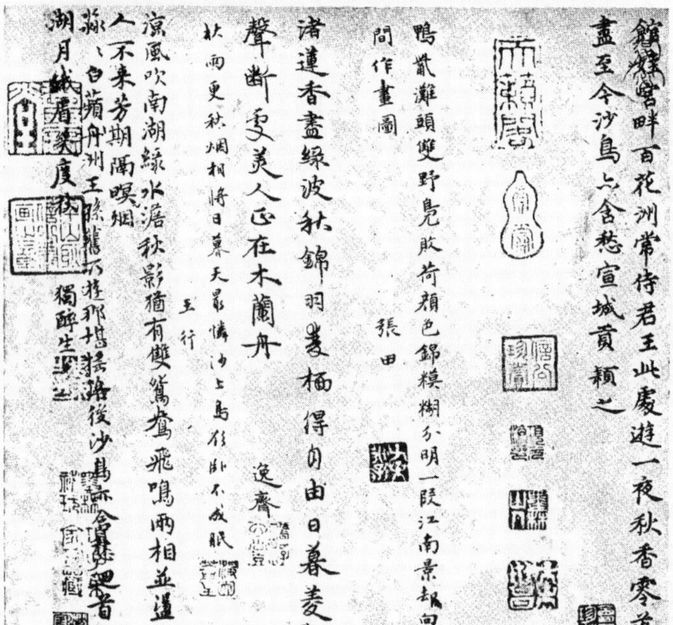

(101)

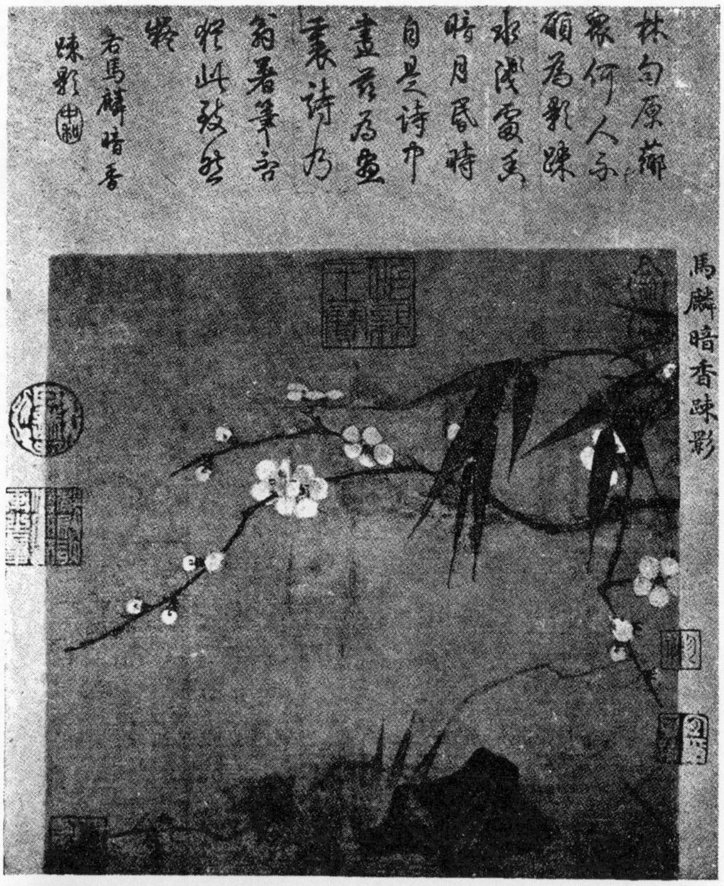
馬麟暗香疎影

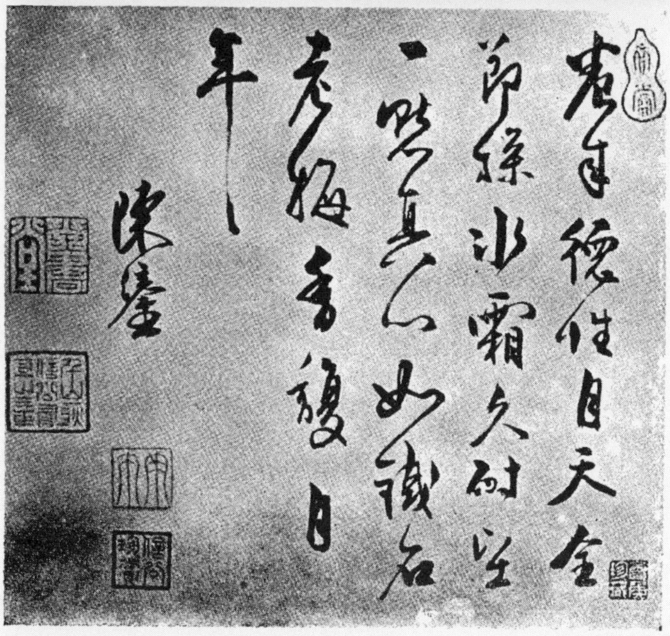

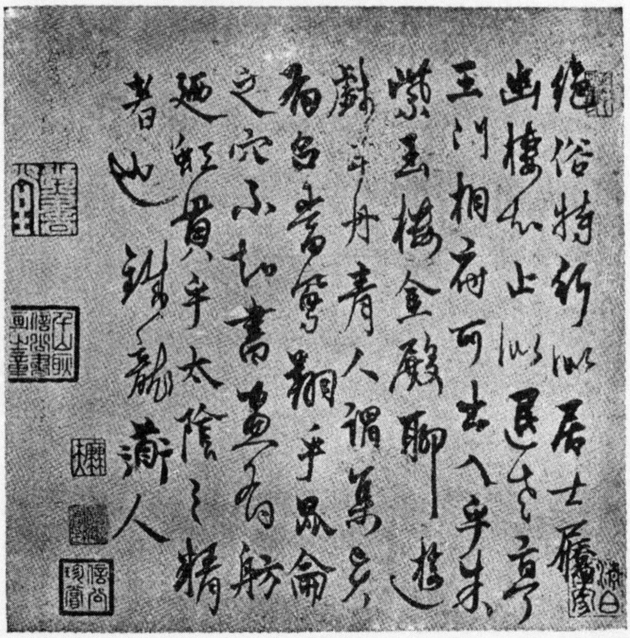

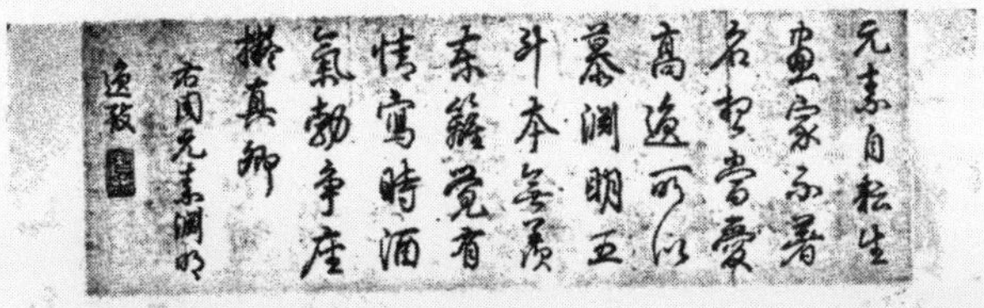
元素自松生
畫家不著
名譽當愛
高逸可以
慕淵明五
斗米不爲
束帶覺有
情寫時酒
氣勃爭座
擬真卿
右周元素淵明
逸致

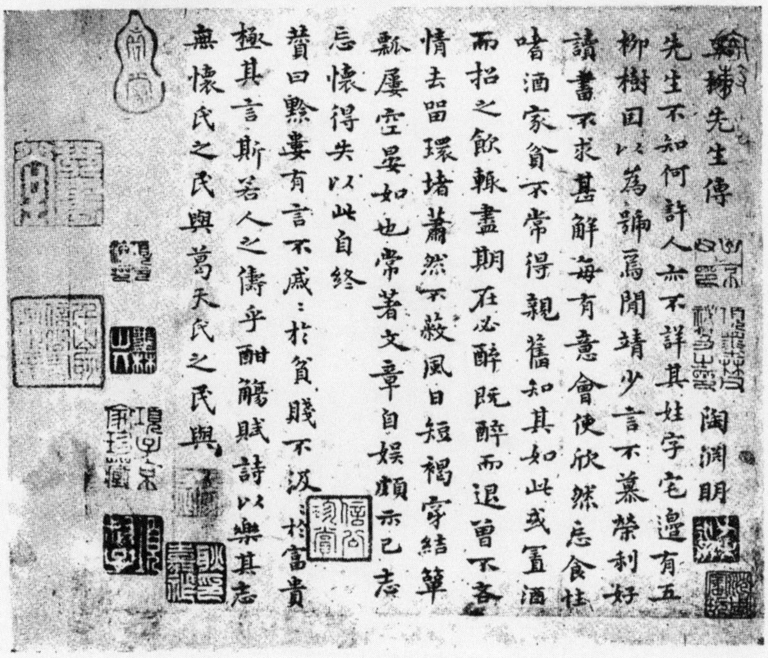
五柳先生傳　陶淵明
先生不知何許人亦不詳其姓字宅邊有五
柳樹因以為號焉閑靖少言不慕榮利好
讀書不求甚解每有意會便欣然忘食性
嗜酒家貧不常得親舊知其如此或置酒
而招之飲輒盡期在必醉既醉而退曾不吝
情去留環堵蕭然不蔽風日短褐穿結簞
瓢屢空晏如也常著文章自娛頗示己志
忘懷得失以此自終
贊曰黔婁有言不戚戚於貧賤不汲汲於富貴
極其言斯若人之儔乎酣觴賦詩以樂其志
無懷氏之民與葛天氏之民與

（ 104 ）

钱選野芳拳石
大德七年三月吴興錢選舜舉

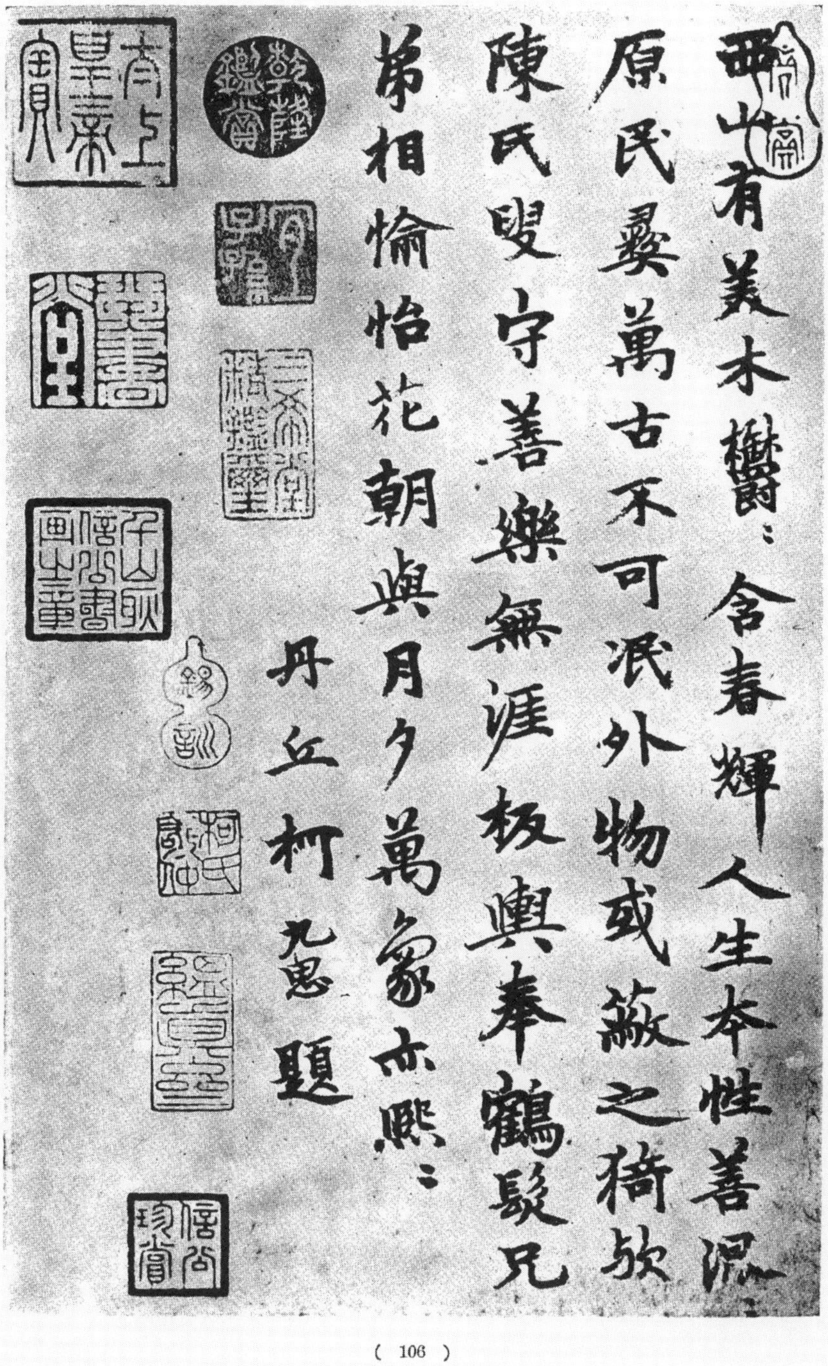
西山有美木欎欎含春輝人生本性善混
原民彝萬古不可泯外物或蔽之猗歟
陳氏叟守善樂無涯板輿奉鶴髮兄
弟相愉怡花朝與月夕萬象亦熙熙
丹丘柯九思題

（ 106 ）

四二 歷代畫幅集册

(陸開。寶笈重編著錄。)

李成　瑤峯琪樹圖

絹地。無款。有傷補。縱貳拾肆·壹公分。橫叁拾陸·壹公分。頂幅有「乾隆」題識。紙地。縱柒·捌公分。橫叁拾陸·貳公分。對幅有「董其昌」題識。紙地。縱貳拾肆·貳公分。橫叁拾陸·貳公分。

李成(916–975)。字咸熙。長安人。唐末徙家青州。名畫評云。營邱人。工山水。

惠崇　秋浦雙鴛圖

紙地。無款。縱貳拾柒·肆公分。橫貳拾陸·肆公分。頂幅有「乾隆」題識。紙地。縱柒·貳公分。橫貳拾陸·伍公分。對幅有「貢穎之」「張田」「逸齋」「王行」及「獨醉生」五人題識。紙地。縱貳拾柒·伍公分。橫貳拾陸·肆公分。

惠崇(約1024)。建陽人。工畫鵝、雁、鷺鷥。尤工小景。善爲寒汀遠渚。瀟灑虛曠之象。人所難也。

馬麟　暗香疏影圖

絹地。無款。有傷補。縱貳拾伍公分。橫貳拾肆·陸公分。頂幅有「乾隆」題識。紙地。縱柒·玖公分。橫貳拾伍·伍公分。對幅有「陳鎏」題識。紙地。縱貳拾肆·玖公分。橫貳拾肆·捌公分。

馬麟(小傳見前)。

林椿　花木珍禽圖

絹地。無款。有裂痕。縱貳拾伍·捌公分。橫貳拾陸·肆公分。頂幅有「乾隆」題識。紙地。縱捌·肆公分。橫貳拾柒公分。對幅有「鐵龍道人」題識。紙地。縱貳拾柒·柒公分。橫貳拾伍·捌公分。

林椿(小傳見前)。

周元素　淵明逸致圖

紙地。下端有「元素」題款。縱貳拾伍·肆公分。橫貳拾肆·玖公分。頂幅有「乾隆」題識。紙地。縱捌·陸公分。橫貳拾肆·捌公分。對幅書有「陶淵明五柳先生傳」。紙地。縱貳拾壹·玖公分。橫貳拾叁·捌公分。

周元素(約 1370)。名位。太倉人。

錢選　野芳拳石圖

紙地。有「大德七年三月吳興錢選舜舉」題款。縱叁拾捌公分。橫貳拾貳·伍公分。隔水有「乾隆」題識。紙地。縱拾壹·伍公分。橫拾叁·肆公分。對幅有「丹丘柯九思題」題識。紙地。縱叁拾·陸公分。橫拾柒·壹公分。

錢選(1239–1302)。字舜舉。號玉潭。霅川人。宗景定間。鄉貢進士。入元不仕。

42. "Li Tai Hua Fu Chi Ch'e"

An Album of Paintings of Successive Dynasties.

(107)

四三 宋人 溪山暮雪圖

絹地。寶笈重編著錄。無款。縱壹百零貳·壹公分。橫伍拾伍·玖公分。

43. “Ch‘i Shan Mu Hsueh T‘u”

By an un-identifiable Sung artist

A Snowy Evening.

(108)

四四 宋人 寒林樓觀圖

絹地。石渠寶笈初編御書房著錄。詩堂有「畫禪有李」四字。有傷補及摺痕。縱壹百伍拾·貳公分。橫捌拾玖·伍公分。

44. "Han Lin Lou Kuan T'u"

By an un-identifiable Sung artist

A Mansion in a Winter Grove.

(109)

四五 宋人

仿張僧繇沒骨山水

絹地。石渠寶笈三編著錄。有傷補。左下角有「僧繇」二字。縱貳百壹拾·玖公分。横捌拾·伍公分。

45. "Fang Chang Sheng-yu Shan Shui"

By an un-identifiable Sung artist

Landscape After the Style of Chang Sheng-yu.

(110)

四六 宋人 賞月空山圖

絹地。無款。有摺傷。縱柒拾壹·玖公分。橫玖拾叁·陸公分。

46. "Shang Yueh K'ung Shan T'u"

By an un-identifiable Sung artist

Drinking to the Moon on a Deserted Mountain Lake.

(111)

四七 宋人
觀梅圖

絹地。石渠寶笈養心殿著錄。無款。有折傷。縱壹百零玖·玖公分。橫伍拾叁·陸公分。

47. "Kuan Mei T'u"

By an un-identifiable Sung artist

Looking at Plum Blossoms.

(112)

四八 宋人 浣月圖

絹地。寳笈初編御書房著錄。無款。有傷補及摺痕。縱柒拾柒·伍公分。横伍拾伍公分。

48. "Wan Yueh T'u"

By an un-identifiable Sung artist

Cleansing of the Moon.

(113)

四九 宋人
卻坐圖

絹地。寶笈初編養心殿著錄。無款。有傷補及摺痕。縱壹百肆拾柒公分。橫柒拾柒·柒公分。

49. "Ch'ou Tso T'u"

By an un-identifiable Sung artist

Refusing a Seat.

(114)

五〇 宋人 采芝圖

絹地。祕殿珠林重編著錄。無款。有傷補。縱壹百零貳·陸公分。橫肆拾捌·肆公分。

50. "T'sai Ch'ih T'u"

By an un-identifiable Sung artist

A Girl Gathering Fungi.

五一 宋人 枇杷猿戲圖

絹地。石渠寶笈初編養心殿著錄。無款。有傷補及折痕蟲蛀霉傷。縱壹百玖拾伍·玖公分。横壹百零柒·玖公分。

51. "Pi Pa Yuan Hsi T'u"

By an un-identifiable Sung artist

Monkeys at Play on a Pi-pa Tree.

(116)

五二 宋人 安和圖

絹地。無款。縱壹百零伍·陸公分。橫伍拾貳·伍公分。

52. "An Ho T'u"

By an un-identifiable Sung artist

A Picture of Peace and Harmony: Quails.

(117)

五三 宋人 山羊圖

絹地。無款。有傷補摺痕剝落蟲蛀。縱柒拾陸·貳公分。橫伍拾·伍公分。

53. "Shan Yang T'u"

By an un-identifiable Sung artist

Goats.

(118)

五四 宋人 富貴花狸圖

絹地。石渠寶笈御書房著錄。無款、有傷補及裂痕。縱壹百肆拾壹·叁公分。橫壹百零柒·捌公分。

54. "Fu Kuei Hua Li T'u"

By an un-identifiable Sung artist

Peonies and a Cat.

五五　宋人　江帆山市圖卷

紙地。石渠寶笈重華宮著錄。無款。有摺傷。縱貳拾捌·陸公分。橫肆拾肆公分。

55. "Chiang Fan Shan Shih T'u Ch'uen"

By an un-identifiable Sung artist

Sailing Boat by a Market on the Mountain (a scroll).

五六 宋人 秋瓜圖

紙地。石渠寶笈初編養心殿著錄。紙地剝落。縱貳拾陸·捌公分。橫肆拾伍·伍公分。

56. "Ch'iu Kua T'u"

By an un-identifiable Sung artist

Autumn Melons.

五七 宋人 布畫山水

布地。石渠寶笈重編著錄。詩堂有「別裁超藝」四字。下邊緣有「和坤」等題字拾壹段。有傷補。縱壹百伍拾肆·玖公分。橫壹百叁拾陸·肆公分。

57. "Pu Hua Shan Shui"

By an un-identifiable Sung artist

Landscape on Cloth.

五八 宋人
華燈侍宴圖

絹地。石渠寶笈御書房著錄。無款。有傷補及摺痕。上詩堂有乾隆御題。下詩堂有「董誥」題識。縱壹百壹拾貳·壹公分。橫伍拾叁·柒公分。

58. "Hua Teng Shih Yen T'u"

By an un-identifiable Sung artist

Reception Under Lantern Light.

五九 宋人 畫杜甫麗人行圖

絹地寶笈重編著錄無款有傷補及裂痕縱肆拾公分橫肆拾壹·壹公分

59. "Hua Tu Fu Li Jen Hsing T'u"

By an un-identifiable Sung artist

Pictorial Representation of Tu Fu's Poem, Entitled "Li Jen Hsing."

六〇 宋人 上林瑞雪圖

絹地。寶笈重編著錄。無款。有傷補。縱肆拾貳·壹公分。橫肆拾貳·貳公分。

60. "Shan Lin Jui Hsueh T'u"

By an un-identifiable Sung artist

Snowing in Shan Lin Garden.

(125)

六一 宋太祖像(古物陳列所)

絹地。下左端有「寶蘊樓書畫錄」章壹方。縱壹百玖拾壹公分。横壹百陸拾玖公分。

61. "Sung T'ai Tsu Hsiang"

Portrait of Sung T'ai Tsu.

(126)

六二 宋太宗像(古物陳列所)

絹地。下左端有「寶蘊樓書畫錄」章壹方。縱柒拾肆公分。橫肆拾柒·壹公分。

62. "Sung T'ai Tsung Hsiang"

Portrait of Sung T'ai Tsung.

(127)

元

YUAN DYNASTY (1279–1368 A.D.)

六三 元錢選 秋瓜圖

紙地。石渠寶笈御書房著錄。上端有「吳興錢選」題款。有傷。縱陸拾叁公分。橫叁拾貳公分。

錢選（1239–1302）。字舜舉。號玉潭。霅川人。宋景定間鄉貢進士。入元不仕。

63. Ch'ien Hsuan "Ch'iu Kua T'u"

Autumn Melon.

Ch'ien Hsuan (1239–1302).—Ch'ien Hsuan, with the pseudonyms of Shun-chu (舜舉), and Yu-tan (玉潭), was a native of Chach'uan (霅川), in Chekiang. In the Ching Ting period of the Sung Dynasty, he graduated as Chin-shih, but did not serve under the Yuan.

六四 元錢選 桃枝松鼠圖卷

紙地。寶笈重編著錄。無款。左下角有「舜舉」朱文方印。紙地破損。縱貳拾陸·肆公分。橫肆拾肆叁公分。拖尾有「歐大任」題跋。縱貳拾陸·伍公分。橫貳拾玖·叁公分。

64. Ch'ien Hsuan "T'ao Chih Sung Shu T'u Ch'uen"

Squirrel on a Peach Branch (a scroll).

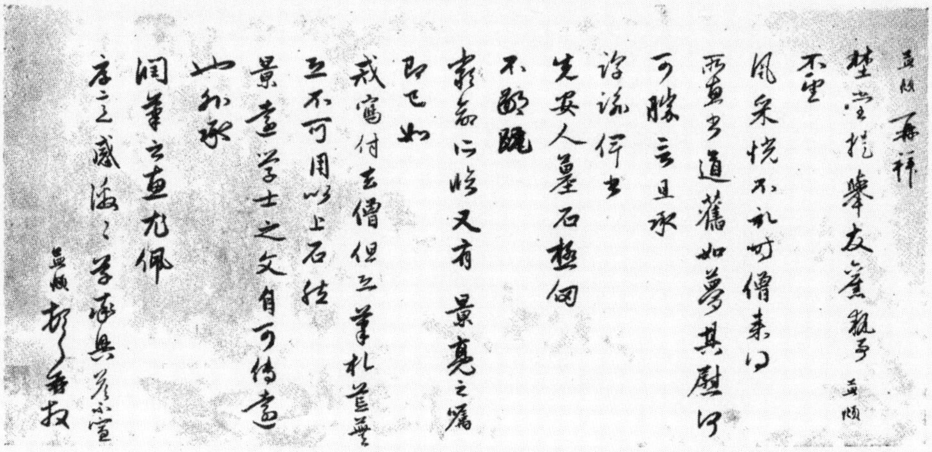

孟頫再拜
埜堂提舉友愛足下 孟頫
不審
風采悅不[illegible]時僧來得
兩書手道舊如夢其歷何
可勝言且承
諭說作者
先安人墓石極[illegible]
不敢[illegible]
[illegible]已臨又有 景亮之請
即也如
我當付去僧但此筆札甚[illegible]
本不可用以上石結
景嘉學士之文自可傳遠
也知承
聞筆之道尤佩
孟之感激之[illegible]承與[illegible]
孟頫頓首

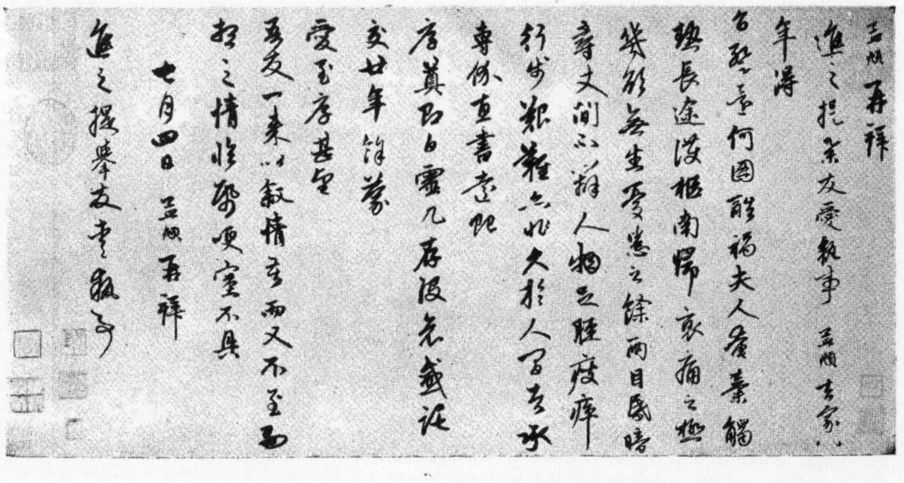

孟頫再拜
進之提舉友愛足下 孟頫[illegible]家
年得
[illegible]何圖能福夫人奄棄館
[illegible]長途[illegible]南歸哀痛之極
[illegible]無生憂患之餘兩目昏暗
尋丈間不辨人物足脛疲痒
行步艱難亦非久於人間者承
專价直書[illegible]
厚莫[illegible]靈几存沒[illegible]感[illegible]
交廿年餘矣
受足下甚至
[illegible]一來以叙情素而又不至再
相之情非紙墨可盡不具
七月四日 孟頫再拜
進之提舉友愛足下

(130)

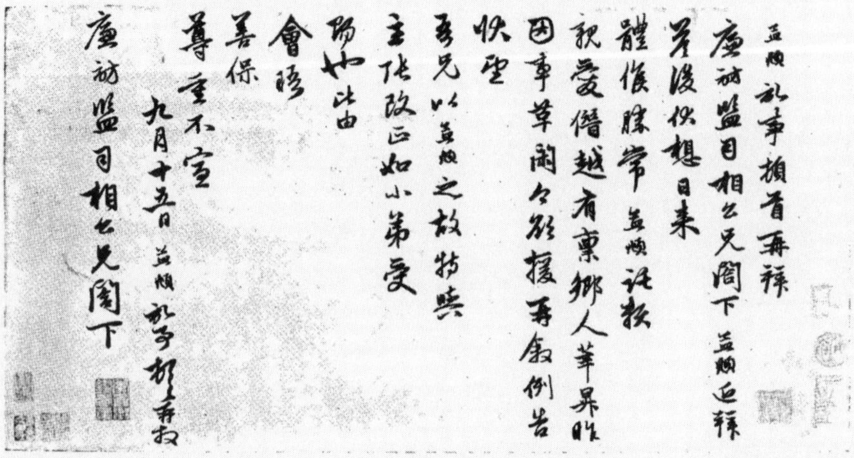

孟頫記事頓首再拜
廣胡監司相公兄閣下 孟頫近拜
書後伏想日來
體候勝常 孟頫竊叨
親愛僭越有東鄉人華昇昨
因事草閙々然援拜敘例告
恱望
吾兄以孟頫之故特與
主張改正如小弟受
賜也 此由
會聆
善保
尊重不宣
九月十五日 孟頫記事頓首再拜
廣胡監司相公兄閣下

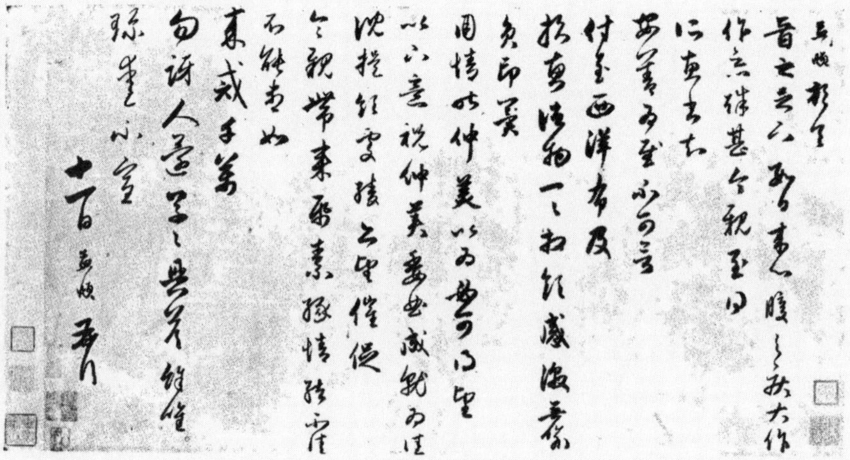

(131)

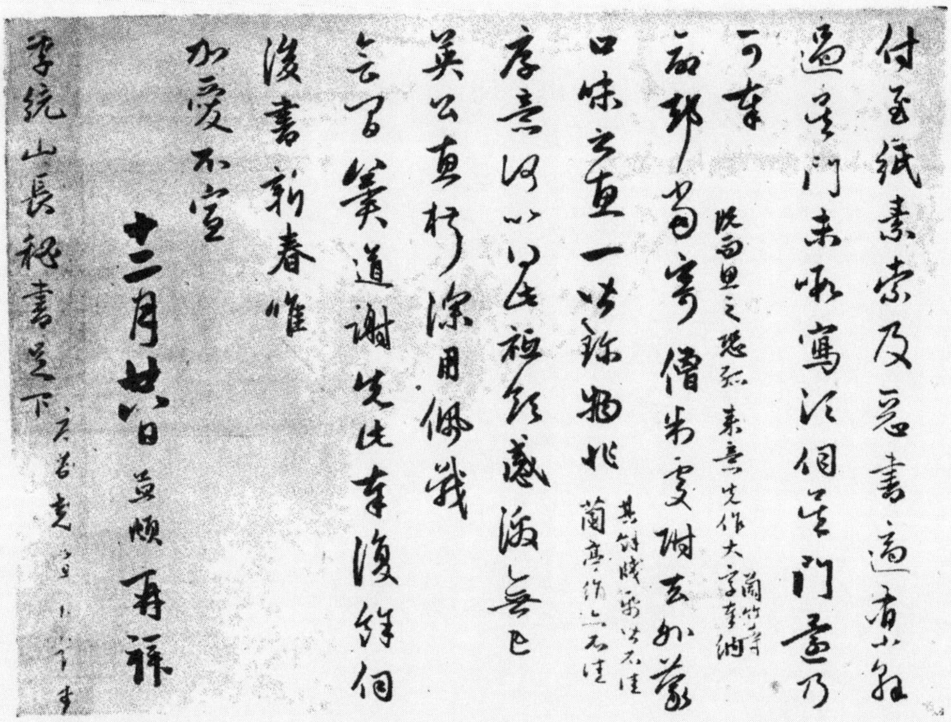
付至纸素索及恳书适逍有小补
适至门来取写治伺至门遣乃
可奉
而邦尚寄僧米爱树玄外蒙 此面里之悉知 东来先作大字 简竹宇李纳
口味之直一以锦物此 其余贱恙少不佳 简斋作亦不佳
存意何以屡被行感激无已
真公直行深用怅戕
会可筹道谢先此奉复余伺
后书新春惟
加爱不宣
十二月廿日 益顺 再拜
季统山長秘书足下

执尚奉礼
伯埔教授 友生之
益顺 执尚奉礼
德楣教授仁弟足下 益顺
李長玄後至今不以
前书中间亦尝具礼不審
得达否发去物扫已脱手
望示为
催促答前项余钞付下为
感乡间大水可畏虽水者
稻早未知可收否米又大贵
未知何以卒岁因便略
此专候
执音不宣
益顺 执尚奉礼
益顺 执封

(132)

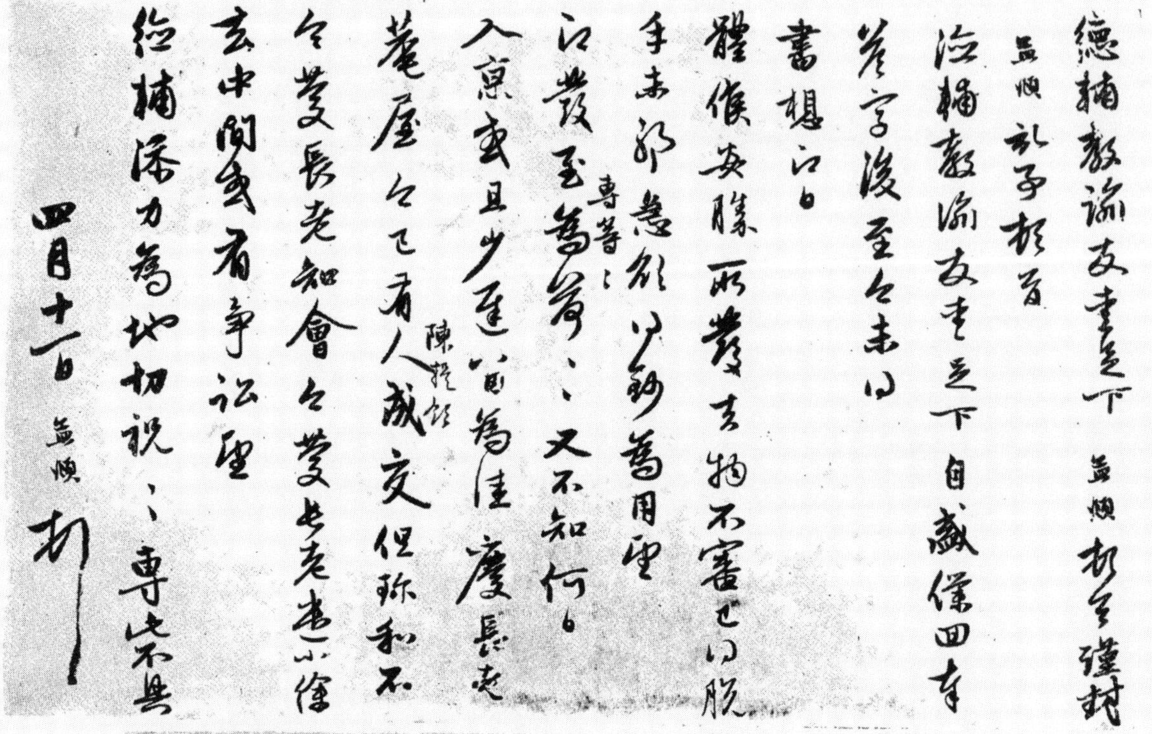

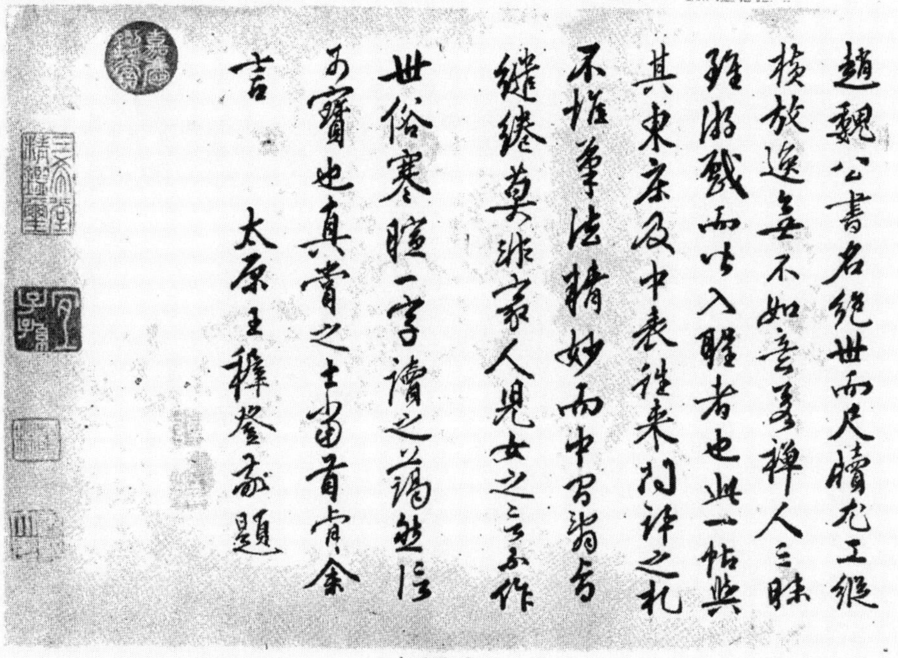

（ 133 ）

六五 元趙孟頫 七札册

捌開。每開壹幅。紙地。石渠寶笈三編著錄。第壹開有「孟頫再拜」字樣。縱叁拾·陸公分。橫陸拾貳·捌公分。第貳開有「孟頫再拜」字樣。縱貳拾捌·伍公分。橫伍拾叁·伍公分。第叁開有「孟頫禮事頓首再拜」字樣。縱貳拾伍公分。橫肆拾叁公分。第肆開有「孟頫再拜」字樣。縱貳拾陸·柒公分。橫肆拾柒·陸公分。第伍開有「孟頫再拜」字樣。縱貳拾玖·柒公分。橫肆拾·柒公分。第陸開有「孟頫頓首奉禮」字樣。縱貳拾伍·捌公分。橫肆拾壹公分。第柒開有「孟頫頓首」字樣。縱貳拾陸·捌公分。橫肆拾貳公分。第捌開王稺登跋有「太原王稺登敬題」字樣。

趙孟頫(1254–1322)。字子昂。號松雪道人。湖州人。官至翰林學士承旨。諡文敏。

65. Chao Meng-fu "Ch'i Cha Ch'e"

Album of Seven Letters.

Chao Meng-fu (1254–1322).—Chao Meng-fu, with the pseudonyms of Tse-ang (子昂) and Sung-hsueh Tao-jen (松雪道人), was a native of Huchou, (Chekiang). He served as Han-lin attendant on the imperial court and was cannonized Wen-ming (文敏).

(134)

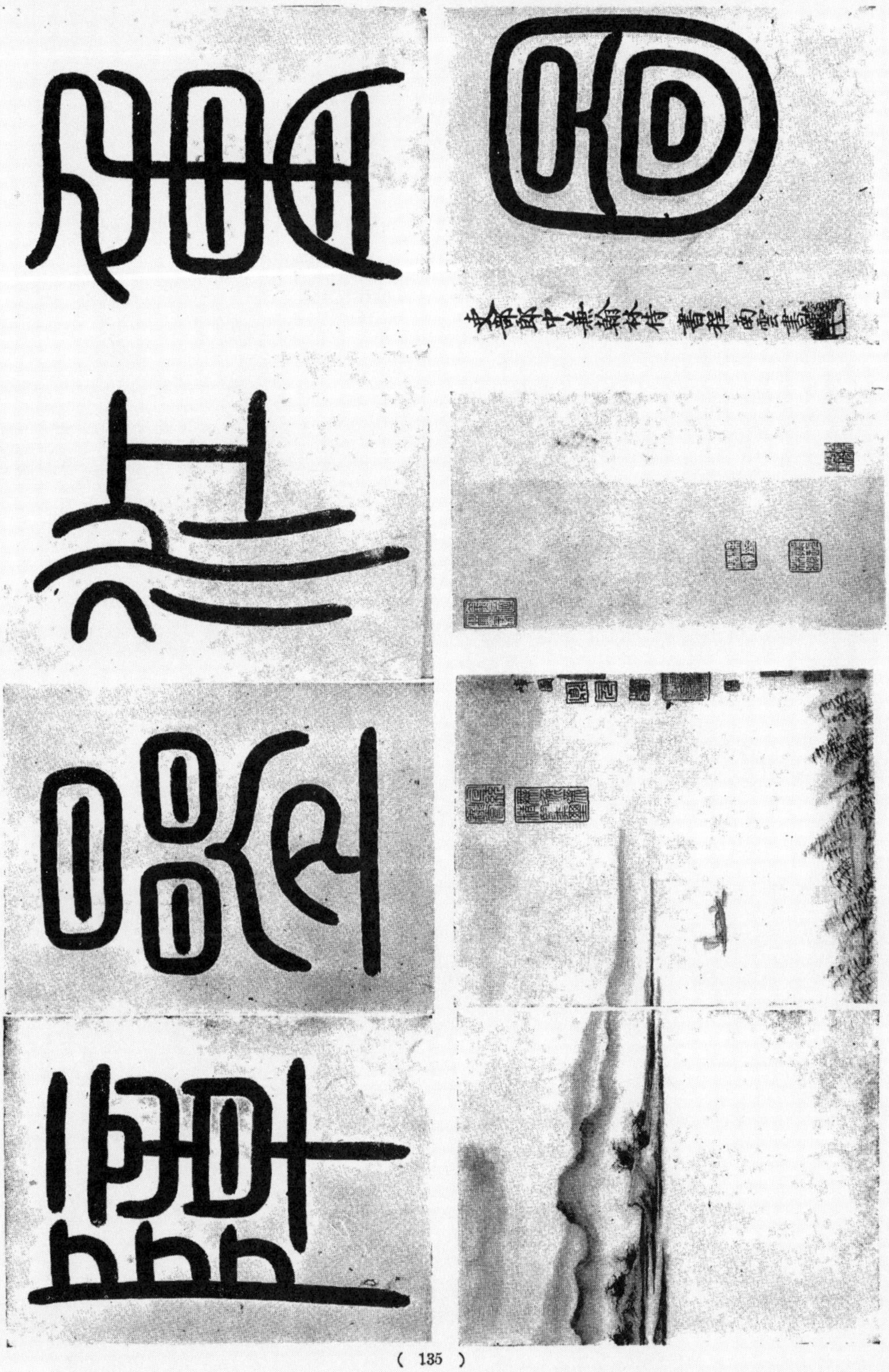

(135)

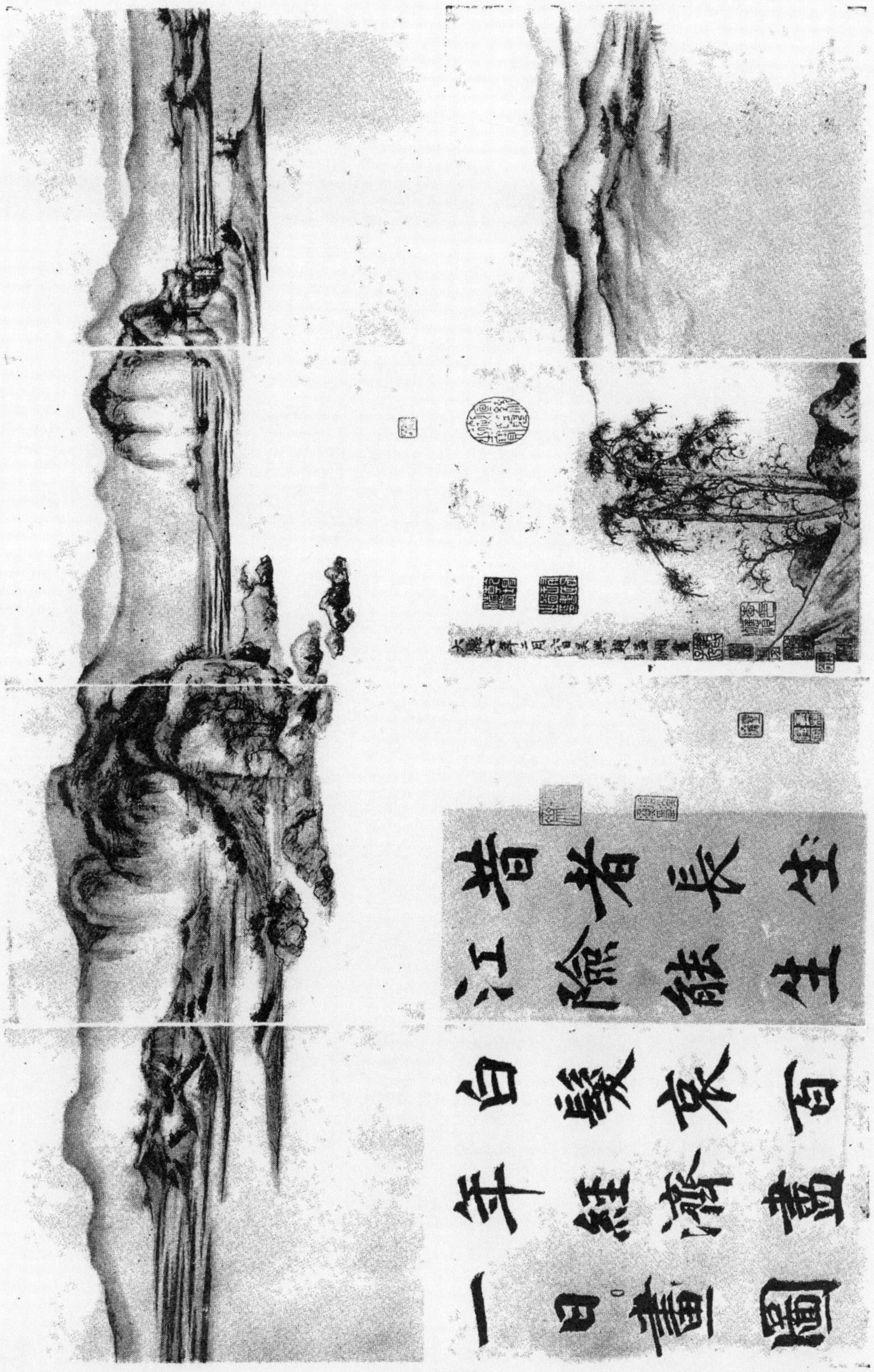

(136)

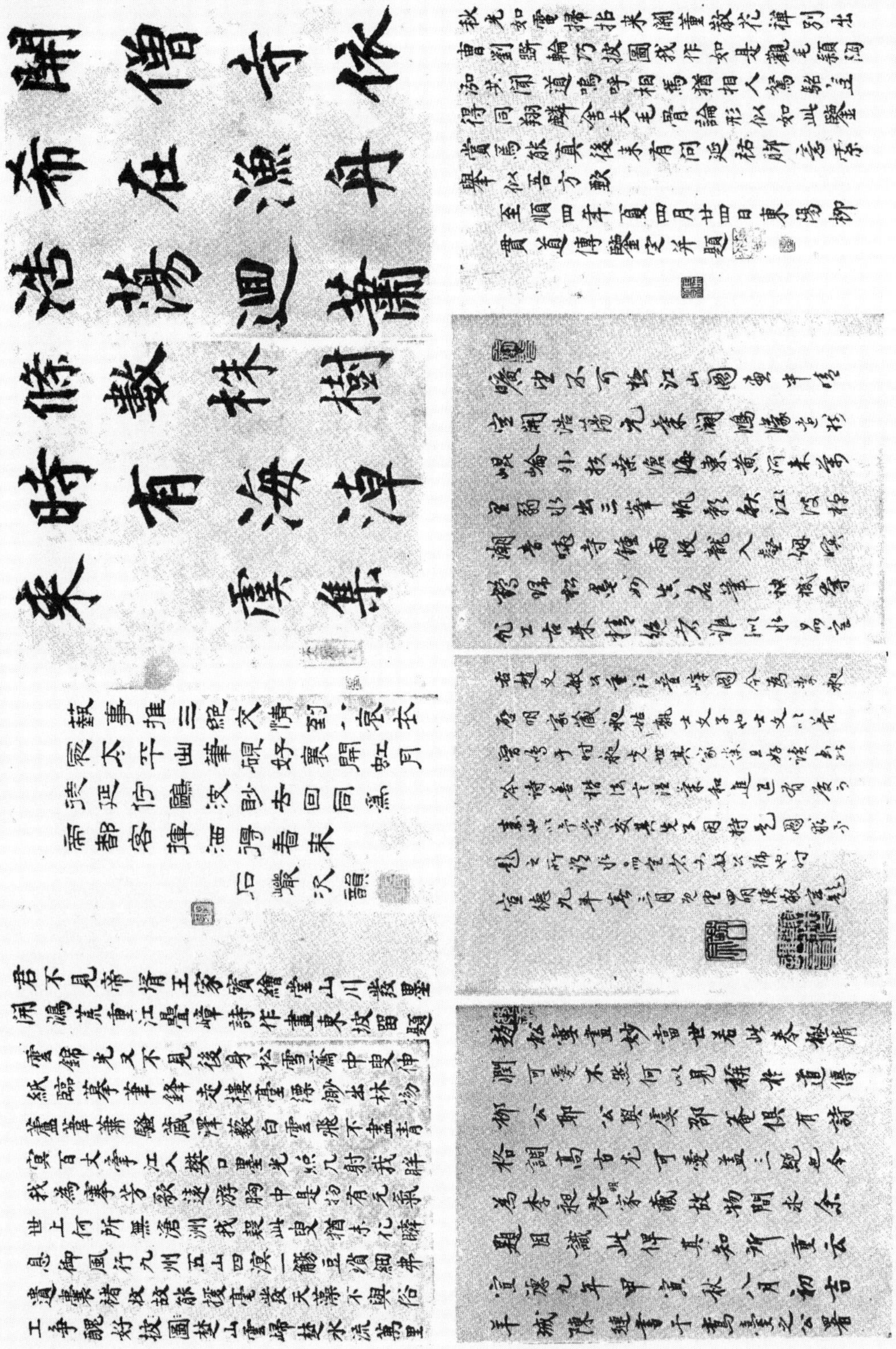

(137)

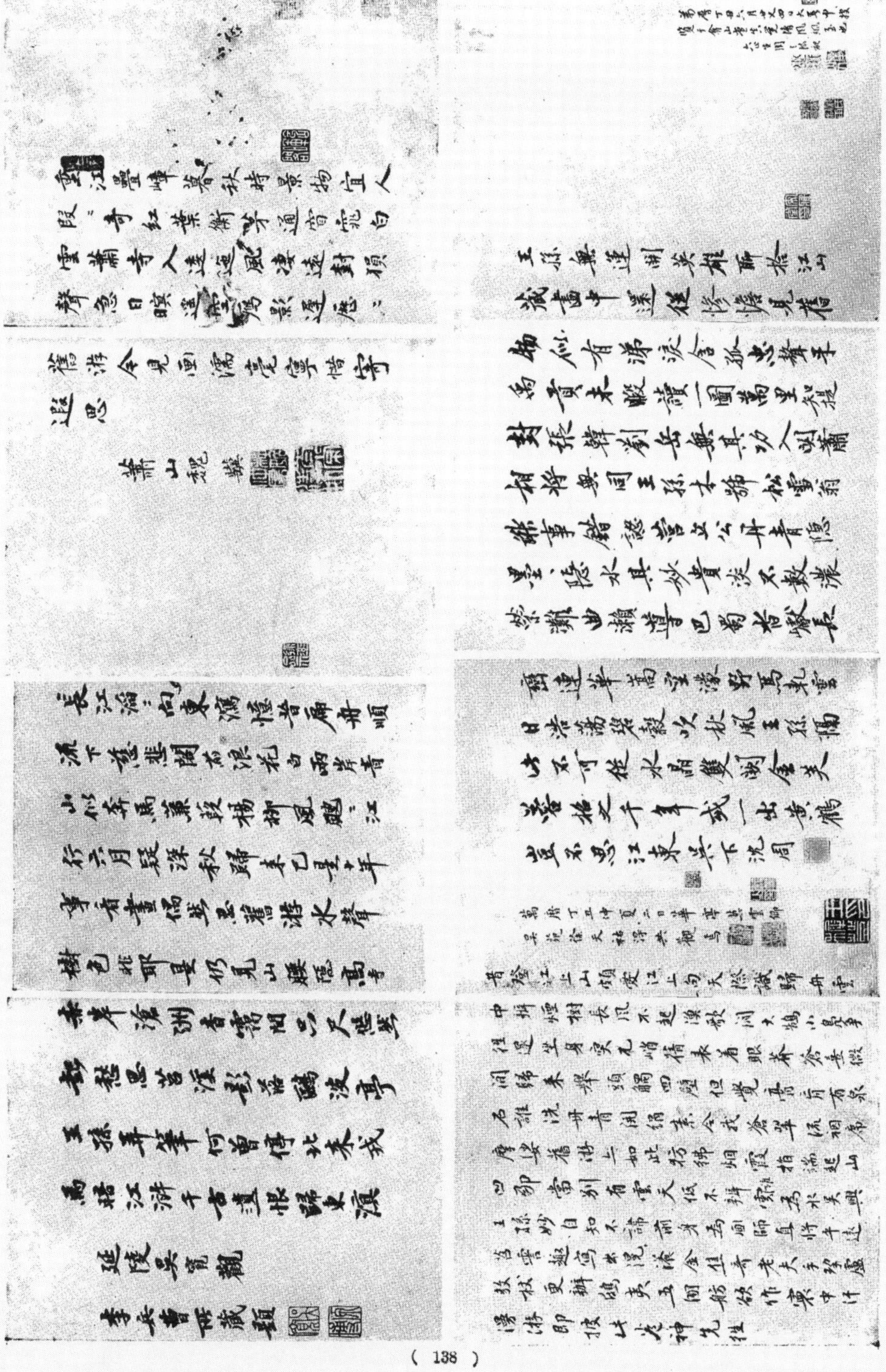

(138)

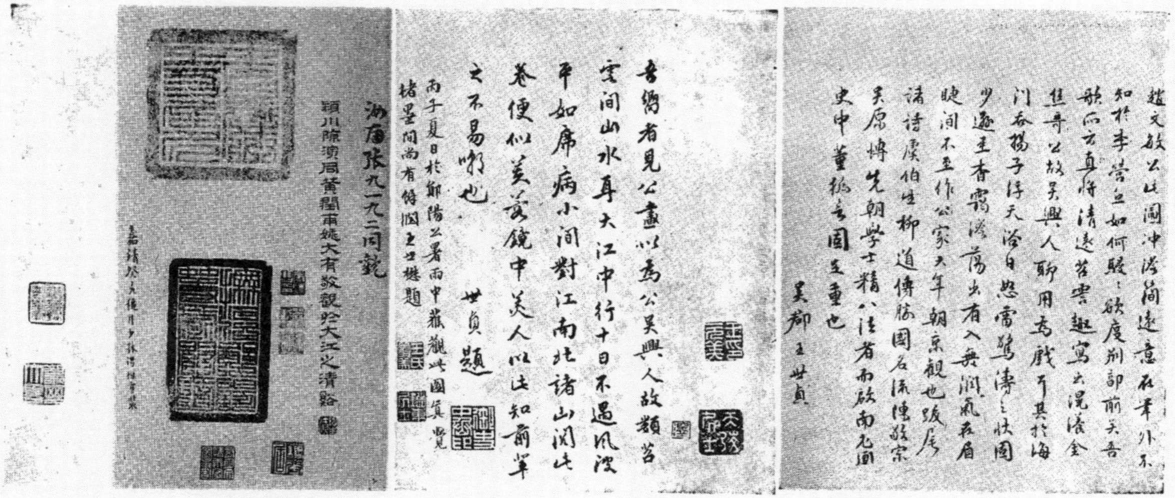

六六 元趙孟頫 重江疊嶂圖卷

紙地。左端有「大德七年二月六日吳興趙孟頫畫」題識。有傷補。縱貳拾捌·伍公分。橫壹百柒拾陸·伍公分。引首紙地。有程南雲篆書「重江疊嶂圖」五字。縱貳拾捌·伍公分。橫壹百貳拾叁·貳公分。拖尾有「虞集」等跋語拾伍段。末尾有「嘉靖癸酉秋月少林湯傑重裝」字樣。縱貳拾捌·伍公分。橫肆百柒拾肆·貳公分。

66. Chao Meng-fu "Chung Chiang Tieh Chang T'u Ch'uen"

Mountain Folds by a Many Tributaried River (a scroll).

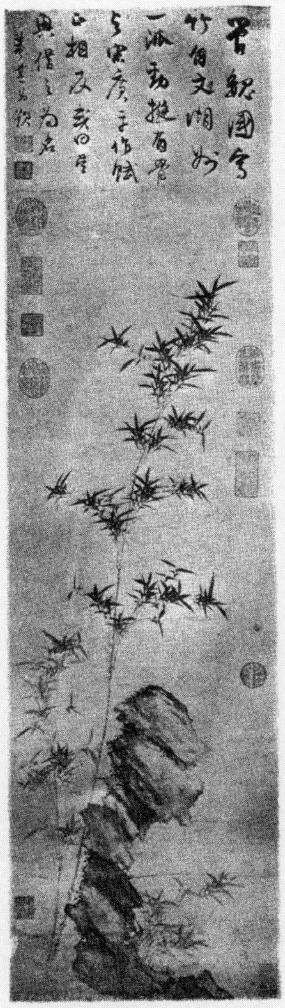

六七 元管道昇 竹石

紙地。石渠寶笈御書房著錄。無款。上詩堂有「董其昌」題識。縱捌拾柒·壹公分。橫貳拾捌·柒公分。

管道昇(1262–1319)。字仲姬。趙文敏室。封魏國夫人。翰墨詞章。不學而能。善畫墨竹。亦工山水佛像。

67. Kuan Tao-sheng "Chu Shih"

Bamboos and Stones.

Kuan Tao-sheng (1262–1319).—With the pseudonym of Chung-chi (仲姬). Wife of Chao Wen-ming. Given the title of Lady from Wei State. Excellent in calligraphy and poetry, with an inborn talent for the same. Good in black and white drawings of bamboos, and also in landscape and religious painting.

六八 元高克恭 雨山圖

紙地。寶笈重編著錄。上端有「克恭爲孟載畫雨山圖畫竟雨如澍快事也」題識。下邊緣有「蕉林收藏」章。有傷痕。縱壹百貳拾壹·捌公分。橫捌拾壹·柒公分。

高克恭（約1280）。字彥敬。號房山。大同人。官至刑部尚書。

68. Kao K'e-kung "Yu Shan T'u"

Mountain in Rain.

Kao K'e-kung (circa 1280).—Kao K'e-kung, with the pseudonyms of Yen-ching (彥敬) and Fang-shan (房山), was a native of Tatung (大同). He served as president of the Board of Punishments.

(141)

六九 元高克恭

林巒煙雨圖(傳)

紙地。石渠寶笈御書房著錄。上端有「元統癸酉夏六月克恭」題款。縱壹百貳拾叁·肆公分。橫陸拾壹·叁公分。

69. Kao K'e-kung "Lin Luan Yen Yu T'u"

Mist and Rain in a Grove (attributed).

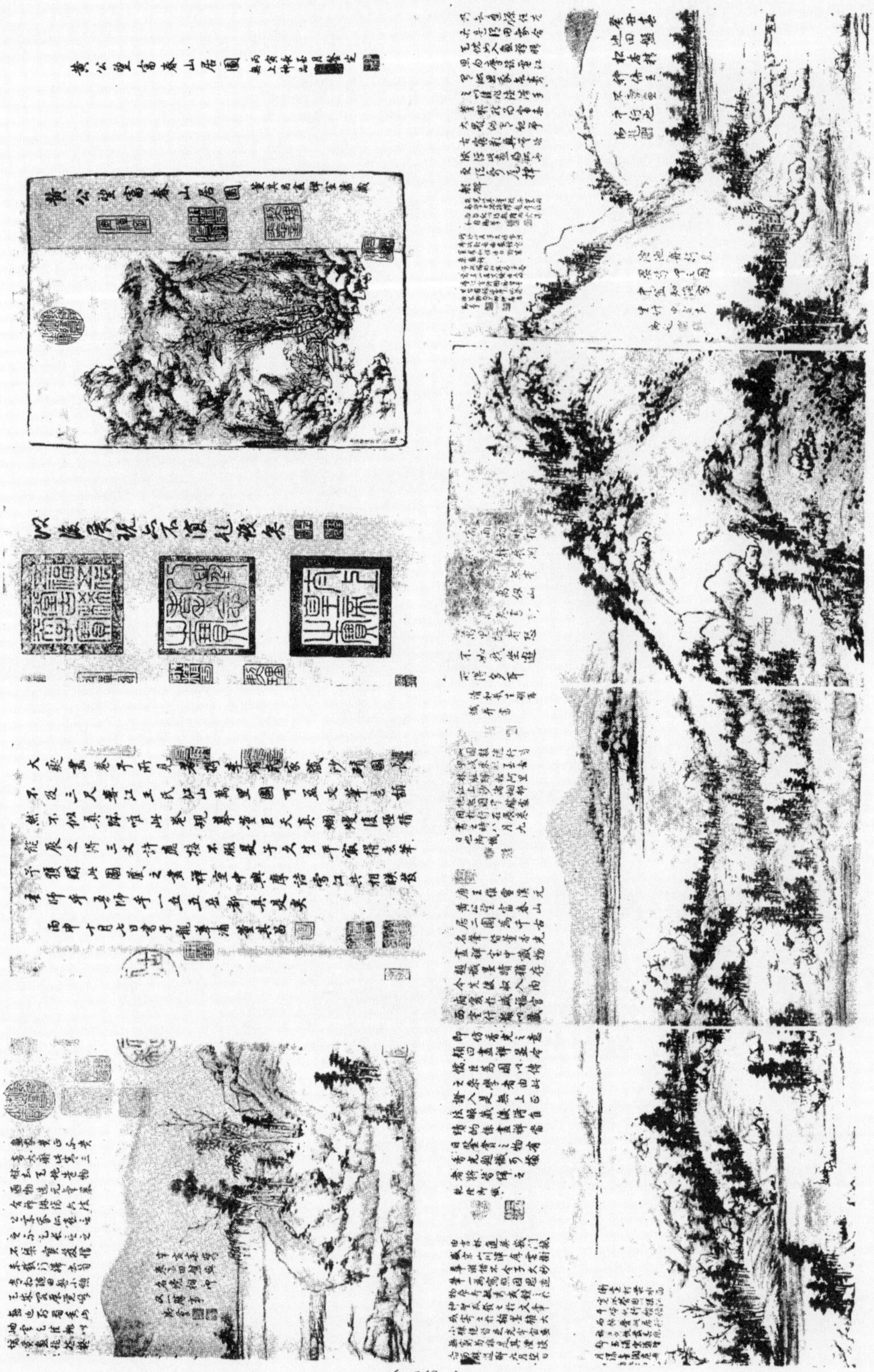

(143)

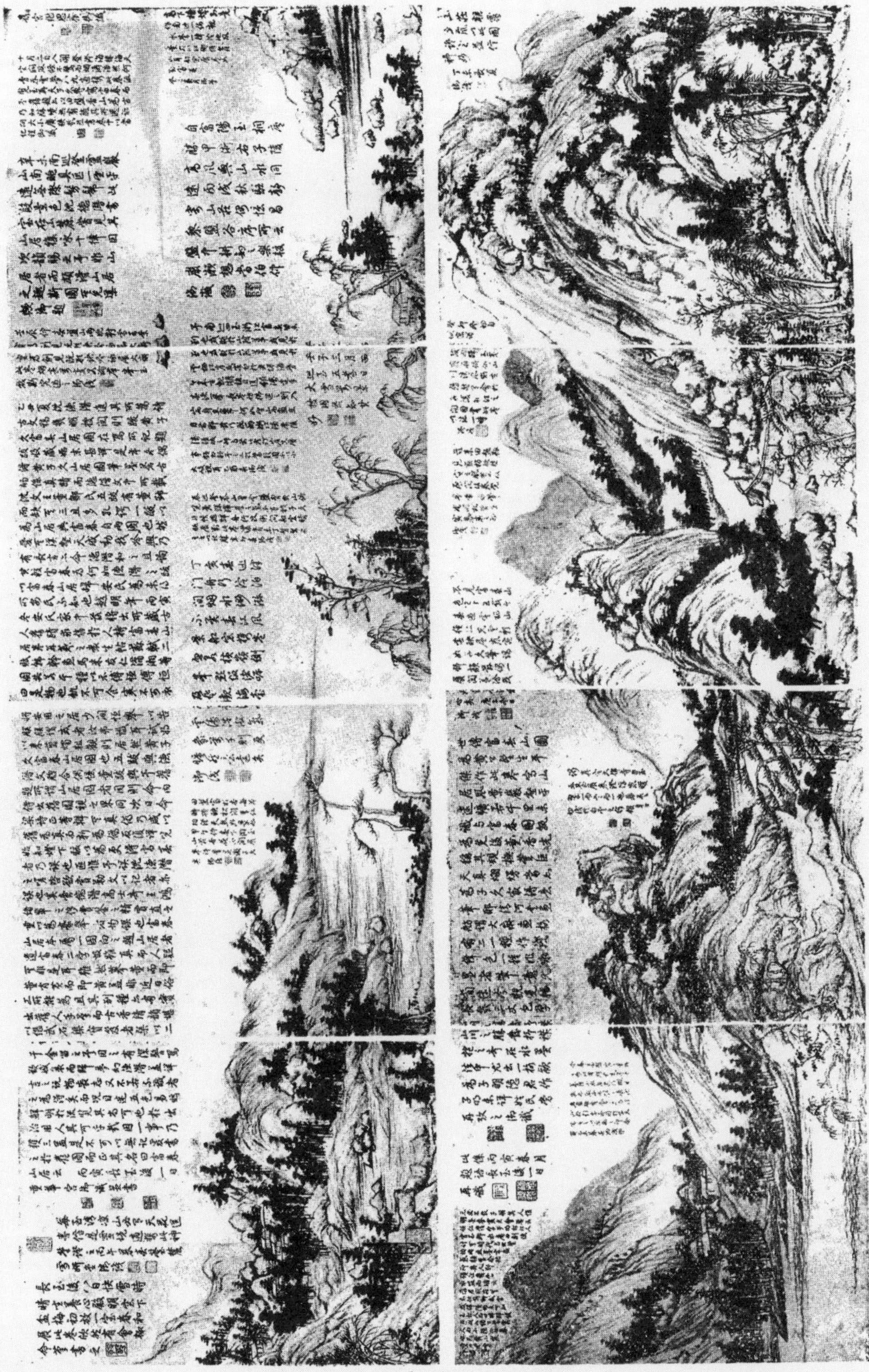

(144)

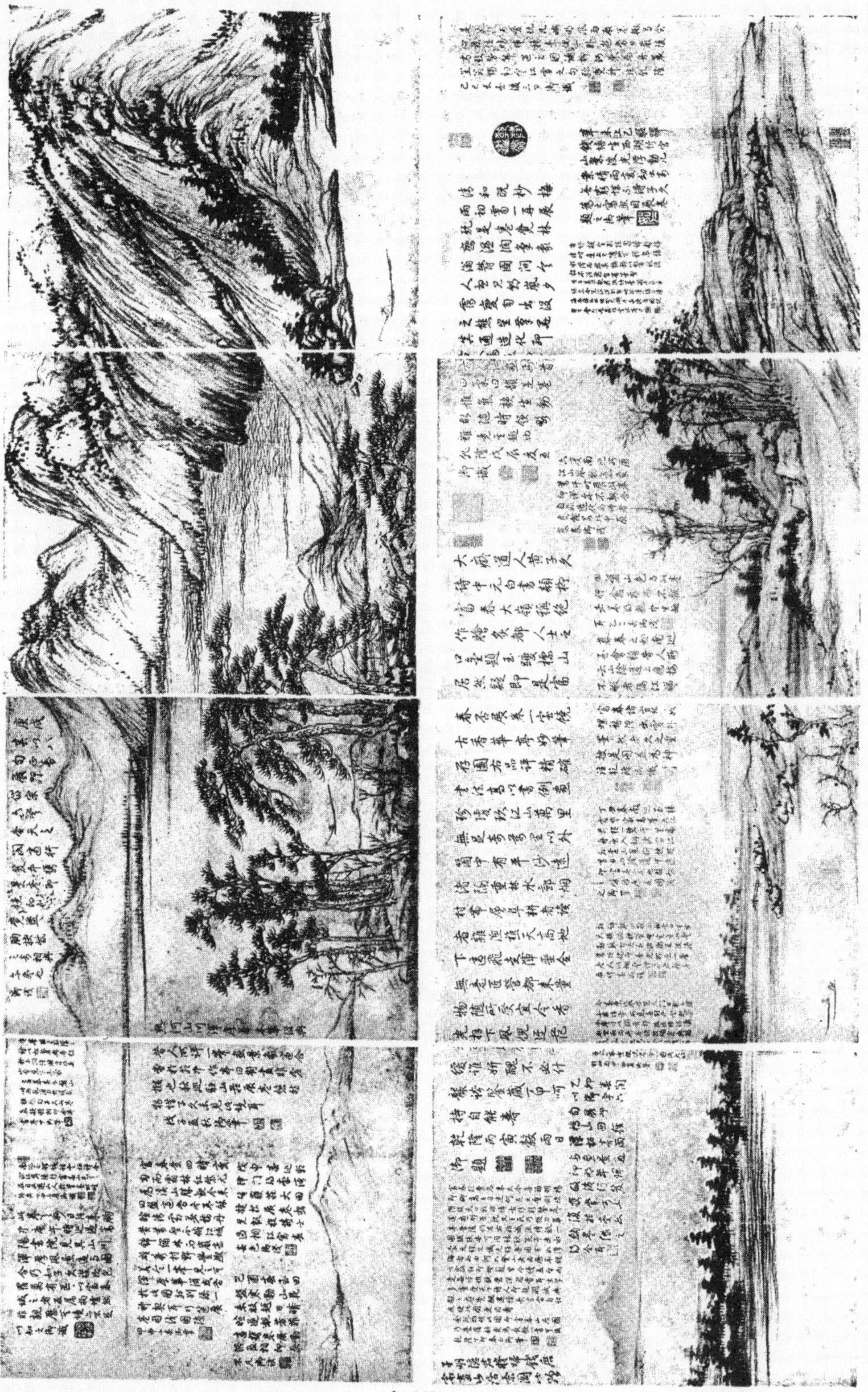

(145)

(146)

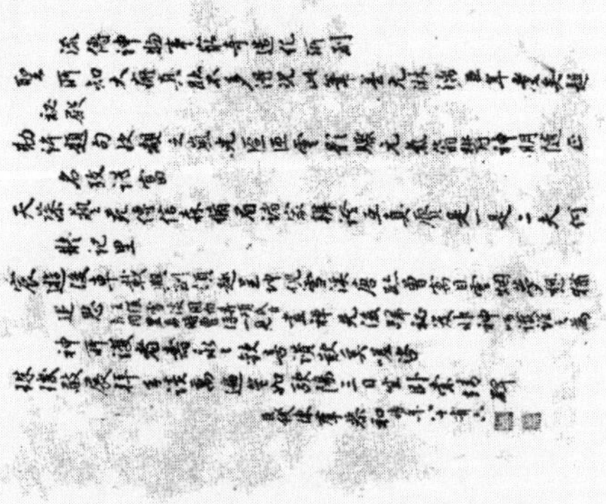

七〇 元黃公望 富春山居圖卷

紙地。有「大癡道人」題識。「黃氏子久」白文印壹方及「劉珏」「乾隆」題識。引首有「乾隆」「董其昌」題字。拖尾有「乾隆」「鄒之麟」「孔諤」「沈德潛」「錢陳羣」等題跋。有破裂。縱叁拾叁公分。橫伍百捌拾玖·肆公分。包首連隔水縱叁拾貳·柒公分。橫陸拾玖公分。拖尾連隔水縱叁拾貳·柒公分。橫壹百玖拾伍·伍公分。帶破錦套壹個。裏上有董邦達繪山水。縱叁拾叁·捌公分。橫拾柒·捌公分。

黃公望(1269–1354)。字子久。號一峯。又號大癡道人。平江常熟人。

70. Huang Kung-wang "Fu Ch'un Shan Chu T'u Ch'uen"

Dwelling on the Fu Ch'un Mountains (a scroll).

Huang Kung-wang (1269–1354).—Huang Kung-wang, with the pseudonyms of Tse-chiu (子久), I-feng (一峯), and Ta-ch'ih Tao-jen (大癡道人), was a native of Ch'angshu (常熟), Pingchiang (now Kiangsu).

七一 元曹知白

雙松圖

絹地。上端有「天歷二年人日雲西作此松樹障子遠寄石末伯善以寓相思」題識。有折紋。縱壹百叁拾貳·壹公分、橫伍拾柒·伍公分。

曹知白(1272–1355)。字又元。一字貞素。別號雲西。華亭人。至元中爲崑山教諭。

71. Tsao Chih-po "Shuang Sung T'u"

Two Pine Trees.

Tsao Chih-po (1272–1355).—Tsao Chih-po, with the pseudonyms of Yu-yuan (又元), Chen-su (貞素), and Yun-hsi (雲西), was a native of Huat'ing (華亭). In the reign of Chih Yuan (1277–1294 A.D.), he served as director of studies in K'unshan (Kiangsu).

(148)

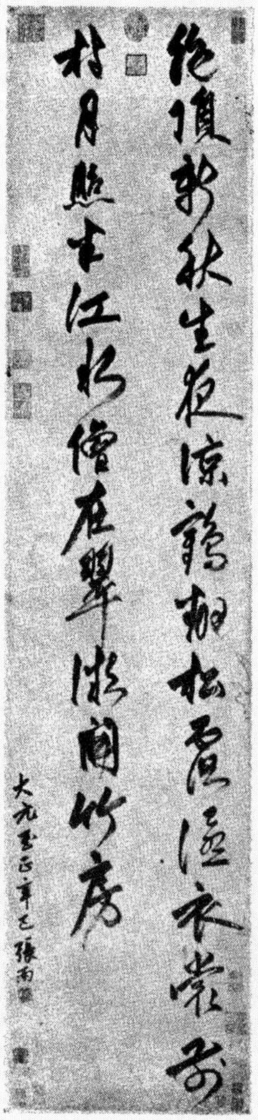

七二 元張雨 書七言詩

紙地。石渠寶笈三編著錄。有「大元至正辛巳張雨」題款。縱壹百伍拾叁公分。橫叁拾叁·陸公分。

張雨(1277–1348)。字伯雨。號句曲外史。又號貞居子。錢塘道士。

72. Chang Yu "Shu Ch'i Yen Shih"

Ode of Seven Characters, Written in a "Running Hand."

Chang Yu (1277–1348).—Chang Yu, with the pseudonyms of Po-yu (伯雨), Chu-ch'u Wai-shih (句曲外史), and Chen-chu Tse (貞居子), was a Taoist in Ch'ient'ang.

(149)

七三 元吳鎮

雙松圖

絹地石渠寶笈重華宮著錄上端有「吳鎮」題款有僞縱壹百捌拾·陸公分橫壹百壹拾·柒公分。

吳鎮(1280-1354)。字仲圭。號梅花道人。嘉興人。爲人抗簡孤潔。勢力不能奪。山水師巨然。墨竹效文同。俱臻妙品。

73. Wu Chen "Shuang Sung T'u"

Two Pine Trees.

Wu Chen (1280–1354).—With the pseudonym of Chung-kuei (仲圭). Called a "Plum-blossom" Taoist (梅花道人). Native of Chiahsing. A man distinguished for his simplicity, independence and honesty, not to be tempted even by power. In landscape painting, he followed Chu Jan, and in his black and white drawing of bamboos, he followed Wen T'ung. Everything from his hand is good.

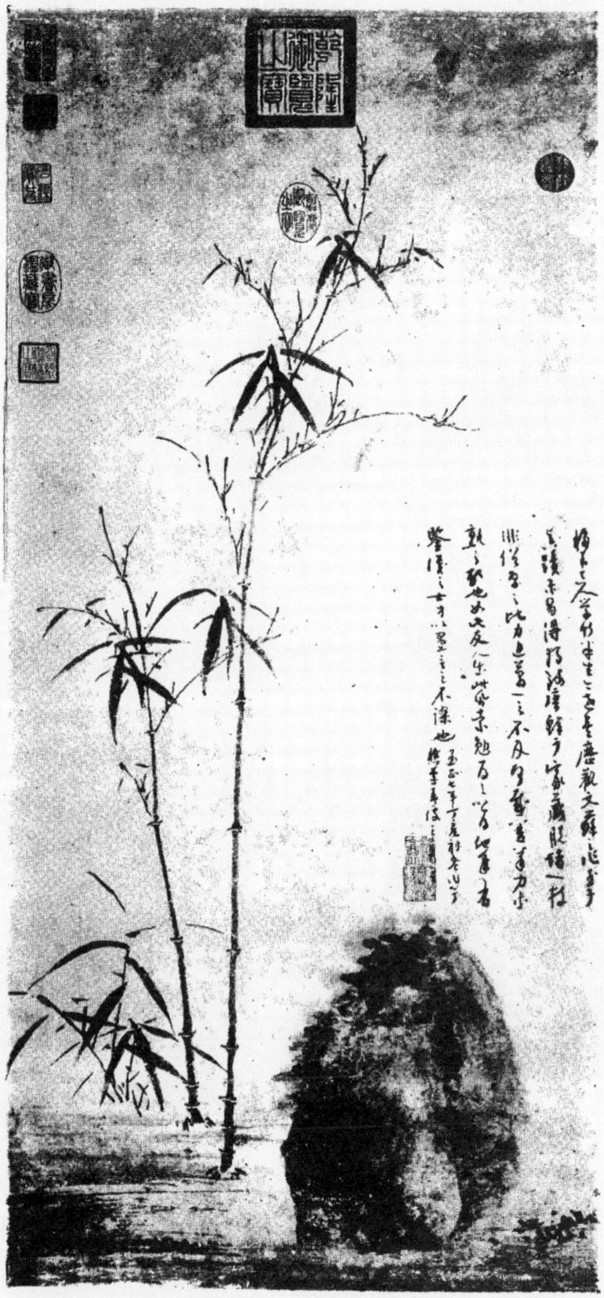

七四　元吳鎮

竹石

紙地寶笈初編御書房著錄。中端有「至正七年丁亥初冬作」題識。縱玖拾陸公分，橫肆拾貳·伍公分。

74. Wu Chen "Chu Shih"

Bamboos and Rocks.

七五 元吳鎮
洞庭漁隱圖

紙地。石渠寶笈御書房著錄。上下端均有「梅花道人戲墨」題識。有傷補。縱壹百肆拾陸·肆公分。橫伍拾捌·陸公分。

75. Wu Chen "Tung T'ing Yu Yin T'u"

A Hermit Fishing in Tung T'ing Lake.

七六 元盛懋 秋林高士圖

絹地。寶笈三編著錄。下端有「武唐盛懋」題款。有傷補及折痕。縱壹百叁拾伍·伍公分。橫伍拾捌·玖公分。

盛懋(約 1300)。字子昭。臨安人。

76. Sheng Mou "Ch'iu Lin Kao Shih T'u"

Eminent Scholar in an Autumnal Grove.

Sheng Mou (circa 1300).—Sheng Mou, with the pseudonym of Tse-ch'ao (子昭), was a native of Linan (臨安).

(153)

七七 元朱德潤
林下鳴琴圖

絹地。石渠寶笈御書房著錄。上端有「朱澤民作」題款。有傷。縱壹百貳拾貳公分。橫伍拾捌·壹公分。

朱德潤(1294-1365)。字澤民。睢陽人。官至鎮東行中書省儒學提舉。

77. Chu T'e-jen "Lin Hsia Ming Ch'in T'u"

Playing the Lute Under the Trees.

Chu T'e-jen (1294-1365).—Chu T'e-jen, with the pseudonym of Tse-min (澤民), was a native of Chuiyang (睢陽). He served as Chen Tung (鎮東) (Governor of the East), acting grand secretary and chancellor of the Imperial Academy of Learning.

七八 元柯九思 墨竹

紙地。石渠寶笈養心殿著錄。上端有「丹丘生寫贈」題款。有傷補。縱壹百·柒公分。橫肆拾玖·柒公分。

柯九思(1312-1365)。字敬仲。號丹丘生。台州人。文宗置奎章閣時。授學士院鑒書博士。

78. K'o Chiu-sze "Mo Chu"

Bamboos in Black and White.

K'o Chiu-sze (1312-1365).—K'o Chiu-sze, with the pseudonym of Chin-chung (敬仲). Called Tan-ch'iu Sheng (丹丘生). Native of T'aichou (台州). Emperor Wen Tsung made him Librarian of the Academy.

七九 元王淵 鷹逐畫眉圖

（古物陳列所）

絹地。上端中有「乾隆御覽之寶」壹方。詩堂有「陳從儒」題跋及印章貳方。畫上端有「趙俶」「杜元誠」「楊深」「許汝霖」「班帷志」諸人題詩並印章捌方。下右端有「若水」二字（字蹟模糊）及印章壹方。下左端有「寶蘊樓書畫錄」章壹方。縱壹百壹拾陸·陸公分。橫伍拾叁·貳公分。原簽題「五代黃荃鷹逐畫眉」。

元王淵（約1314）。字若水。號澹軒。錢塘人。幼習丹青。趙文敏多指教之。故所畫皆師古人。無一筆院體。山水師郭熙。花鳥師黃荃。人物師唐人。一一精妙。

79. Wang Yuan "Yin Chu Hua Mi T'u"

A Hawk Swooping on a Thrush.

Wang Yuan (circa 1314).—With his pseudonym of Jo-shui (若水). He is also called Tan-hsuen (澹軒). Native of Hangchow. When a child, he loved to paint. Chao Wen-ming taught him. His drawings are modelled after the styles of the old masters, following no one school in particular. His "landscapes" are after the style of Kuo Hsi (郭熙), his "birds and flowers" after the style of Huang Chuan (黃荃), and his "human figures" after the style of the T'ang artists, but in all, excellent.

(156)

八〇 元李士行

喬松竹石圖

絹地。下端有「薊丘李士行遵道作」題款。縱壹百捌拾壹·玖公分。橫壹百零陸·叁公分。

李士行(1282-1328)。字遵道。薊丘人。衎子。官黃巖知州。

80. Li Shih-hsing "Ch'iao Sung Chu Shih T'u"

Bamboos and Rocks Under a Tall Tree.

Li Shih-hsing (1282-1328).—Li Shih-hsing, with the pseudonym of Tsun-tao (遵道), was a native of Kueichiu (薊丘) and the son of Li K'an (李衎). He served as magistrate of the Department of Huangyen (黃巖).

八一 元王蒙

東山草堂圖

紙地寶笈重編著錄上端有「至正三年四月望日爲東山良友畫黃鶴山樵王蒙」題識縱壹百拾壹·肆公分橫陸拾·壹公分

王蒙（1308-1385）。字叔明。號黃鶴山樵。湖州人。元末爲理問。

81. Wang Mang "Tung Shan Ts'ao T'ang T'u"

Thatched Pavilion in Tung Shan.

Wang Mang (1308-1385).—Wang Mang, with the pseudonyms of Shu-ming (叔明) and Huang-hao Shan-ch'ao (黃鶴山樵), was a native of Hu-chou (湖州), Che-kiang. He served as law secretary (理問) of a provincial judge in the end of the Yuan.

八二 元王蒙 谷口春耕圖

紙地。石渠寶笈重華宮著錄。上端有「黃鶴山人王蒙」題款。縱壹百貳拾肆·玖公分。橫叁拾柒·叁公分。

82. Wang Mang "Ku K'ou Ch'un Keng T'u"

Ploughing in Spring, at the Entrance of a Gorge.

八三 元顧安 平安磐石圖

絹地。寶笈三編著錄。上端有「至正庚寅孟秋顧定之作」題款。有傷補。縱壹百捌拾陸·玖公分。橫壹百零叁·玖公分。

顧安(約 1330)。字定之。官泉州路判官。

83. Ku An "P'ing An P'an Shih T'u"

Bamboos and Rocks.

Ku An (circa 1330).—Ku An, with the pseudonym of Ting-chih (定之), served as sub-prefect of Ch'uanchou (泉州).

(159)

八四 元倪瓚
江岸望山圖

紙地。寶笈重編著錄。上端有「倪瓚」題識。縱壹百壹拾壹·叁公分。橫叁拾叁·貳公分。

倪瓚(1301–1374)。字元鎮。號雲林子。無錫人。隱居不仕。

84. Ni Ts'an "Chiang An Wang Shan T'u"

Descrying the Hills from a River Bank.

Ni Ts'an (1301–1374). — Ni Ts'an, with the pseudonyms of Yuan-chen (元鎮), and Yun-lin Tse (雲林子), was a native of Wusih. He lived in retirement without becoming an officer.

八五 元倪瓚
容膝齋圖

紙地。石渠寶笈養心殿著錄。上端有「壬子歲七月五日雲林生寫」題款及題識。有折痕。縱柒拾叁·叁公分。橫叁拾伍·陸公分。

85. Ni Ts'an "Jung Hsi Chai T'u"

The Jung Hsi Studio.

八六 元顧安倪瓚合作 古木竹石

紙地。寶笈初編御書房著錄。上端有「癸丑初月二十一日雪齋示此幅並爲添作一石又賦此詩以贈通玄隱士倪迂」題識。有傷補。縱玖拾叁肆公分。橫玖拾貳玖公分。

86. Ku An and Ni Ts'an "K'u Mu Chu Shih"

Bamboos and Rocks and an Old Tree.

(161)

八七 元張中 花鳥

紙地。寶笈三編著錄。下端有「張中」題款。有傷補。縱壹百貳拾貳·柒公分。橫｛肆拾叁·陸公分。

張中(約 1350)。又名守中。字于正。一作子政。松江人。山水師黃公望。亦能墨戲。

87. Chang Chung "Hua Niao"

Flowers and Birds.

Chang Chung (circa 1350).—His other Christian name is So-chung (守中); and his pseudonym Yu-chen (于正). Another pseudonym of his is Tse-chen (子政). Native of Sungchiang (松江). In landscape painting, he followed after Huang Kung-wang. Also good in calligraphy.

(162)

八八 元陸廣 五瑞圖

紙地。石渠寶笈三編著錄。下角有「陸廣」題款。有傷補。縱壹百貳拾陸公分。橫陸拾·伍公分。

陸廣(約 1333)。字季弘。號天游生。吳人。

88. Lu Kuang "Wu Jui T'u"

Five Felicitous Objects.

Lu Kuang (circa 1333).—Lu Kuang, with the pseudonyms of Chi-hung (季弘) and T'ien-yu Sheng (天游生), was a native of Wu (吳), now Kiangsu.

八九 元朱叔重 春塘柳色圖

紙地。寶笈重編著錄。上端有「叔重作」題款。縱肆拾壹·叁公分。橫肆拾伍·伍公分。

朱叔重(約1322)。吳人。

89. Chu Shu-ch'ung "Ch'un T'ang Liu She T'u"

Green Willows by a Lake in Spring.

Chu Shu-ch'ung (circa 1322).—Chu Shu-ch'ung was a native of Wu (吳), now Kiangsu.

九〇 元顏輝 袁安臥雪圖

絹地。寶笈重編著錄。無款。有傷補。縱壹百陸拾·柒公分。橫壹百零伍·柒公分。

顏輝(約1340)。字秋月。江山人。

90. Yen Hui "Yuan An Wo Hsueh T'u"

Yuan An Indifferent to the Cold and Snow.

Yen Hui (circa 1340).—Yen Hui, with the pseudonym of Ch'iu-yueh (秋月), was a native of Chiangshan (江山).

九一 元張舜咨 樹石

紙地。寶笈重編著錄。上端有「張師夔」題識。有傷補。縱壹百壹拾貳·伍公分。橫叁拾伍·貳公分。

張舜咨（生卒年不詳）。字師夔。號櫟里子。

91. Chang Shun-tze "Shu Shih"

Trees and Rocks.

Chang Shun-tze.—Chang Shun-tze had the pseudonyms of Shih-kuei (師夔) and Li-li Tse (櫟里子).

九二 元吳廷暉

龍舟奪標圖

絹地。無款。有傷補。縱壹百貳拾肆·壹公分。橫陸拾伍·陸公分。

吳廷暉（生卒年不詳）。吳興人。工青綠山水。花鳥亦精密。

92. Wu T'ing-hui
"Lung Chou Tou Piao T'u"

Dragon Boat Race.

Wu T'ing-hui.—Native of Wuhsing. Good in landscape painting and in drawing bird and flowers.

九三 元郭畀 畫高使君詩意

紙地。石渠寶笈御書房著錄。上端有「郭天錫」題款。有傷補。縱捌拾壹·伍公分。橫叁拾·陸公分。

郭畀(1301-1355)。字天錫。一字佑之。號北山。京口人。爲平江路吳江儒學教授。未上。浙江行省辟充椽吏。竹木窠石有米家風。書法出入趙孟頫。

93. Kuo Pi "Hua Kao Shih-ch'un Su Yi"

Illustration of Kao Shih-ch'un's Poem.

Kuo Pi (1301–1355).—He has two pseudonyms, one T'ien-hsi (天錫), and the other Yu-tze (佑之). He is also called Pei-shan (北山). Native of Chingk'ou (京口). His drawings of bamboos, trees and rocks are after the style of Mi Fei, while in calligraphy he follows Chao Meng-fu.

(168)

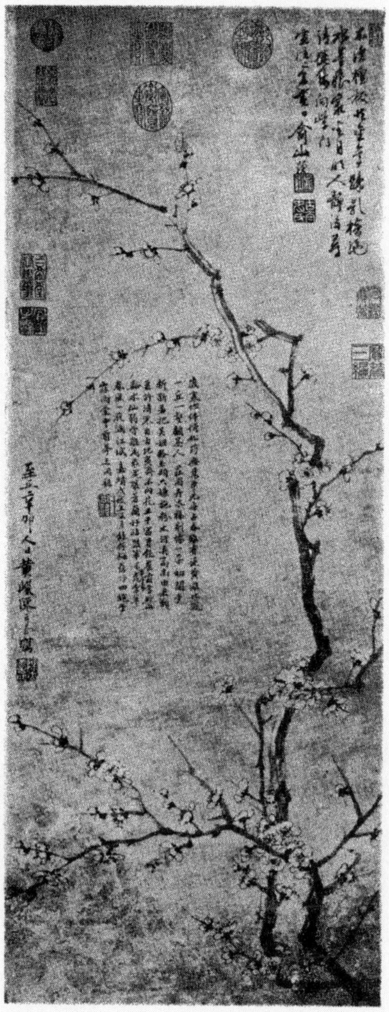

九四 元陳立善 墨梅

紙地。寶笈三編著錄。左中端有「至正辛卯人日黃巖陳立善寫」題款。有傷補。縱捌拾肆·玖公分。橫叁拾貳·壹公分。

陳立善(約1340)。黃巖人。至正中爲慶元路照磨。

94. Chen Li-shan "Mo Mei"

An Ink Study of the Plums.

Chen Li-shan (circa 1340).—Chen Li-shan was a native of Huangyen. In the time of Chih Cheng (1341–1368 A.D.), he served as Chao Mo (照磨) or commissary of the seal in the circuit of Ch'ing-yuan (慶元).

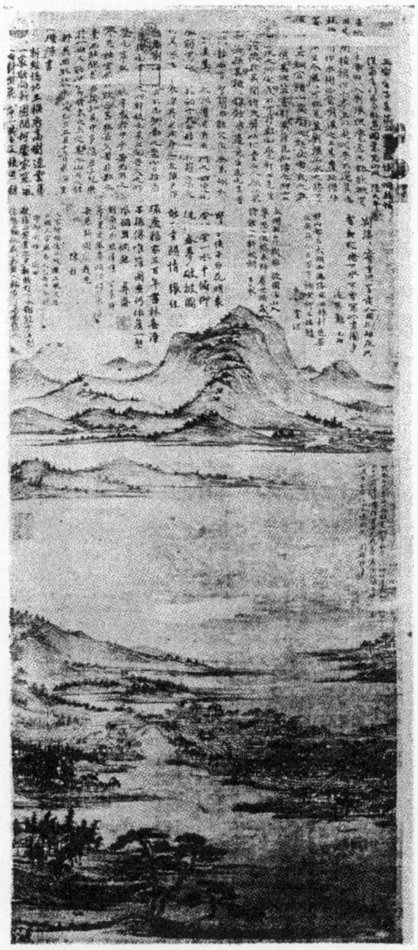

九五 元陳汝言 荆溪圖

絹地。寶笈重編著錄。無款。上有「倪瓚」「王蒙」等題識。有傷補。縱壹百貳拾玖·陸公分。橫伍拾肆·壹公分。

陳汝言(約 1360)。字惟允。號秋水。汝秩弟。與兄有大髯小髯之稱。工詩。倜儻有謀略。嘗參張士誠軍事。洪武初。以荐任濟南經歷坐事死。

95. Chen Ju-yen "Ching Ch'i T'u"

View of Ching Ch'i.

Chen Ju-yen (circa 1360).—His pseudonym is Wei-yung (惟允). Also called Ch'iu-shui (秋水). Younger brother of Ju-tieh (汝秩). The two brothers are called "Big Beard" and "Small Beard." Ju-yen is a poet and skillful in military strategy.

九六 元方從義 山陰雲雪圖

紙地。石渠寶笈初編御書房著錄。有「金門羽客方方壺」題識。詩堂有「建安蘇絅」題識。紙地剝落。連詩堂縱捌拾壹·肆公分。横貳拾伍·陸公分。

方從義(約 1336)。字無隅。號方壺。貴溪人。上清宮道士。山水瀟灑。有董巨二米遺韻。品之逸者也。

69. Fang Ch'ung-yi "San Yin Yun Hsueh T'u"

Clouds and Snow in San Yin.

Fang Ch'ung-yi (circa 1336).—With the pseudonym of Wu-yu (無隅). Called Fang-hu (方壺). Native of Kuei-ch'i (貴溪). Became a Ch'ing Kung Taoist. His landscape has an atmosphere of peace and calm. Influenced by Tung Yuan, Chu Jan and the two Mi's.

九七 元方從義

高高亭圖

紙地。石渠寶笈御書房著錄。左端有「方方壺」題款。有傷補。縱陸拾貳·叁公分。橫貳拾捌公分。

97. Fang Ch'ung-yi "Kao Kao T'ing T'u"

Kao Kao Pavilion.

九八 元人

江天樓閣圖

紙地。石渠寶笈御書房著錄。無款。有傷補。縱捌拾叁·捌公分。橫肆拾·肆公分。

98. "Chiang T'ien Lou Ke T'u"

By an un-identifiable artist of the Yuan Dynasty

Pavilion by a River.

(173)

九九 元人 射雁圖

絹地。石渠寶笈重華宮著錄。無款。有傷補。縱壹百叁拾壹·捌公分。橫玖拾叁·陸公分。

99. "She Yen T'u"

By an un-identifiable artist of the Yuan Dynasty

Shooting Wild Geese.

(174)

一〇〇 元人

嘉穀鳴禽圖

絹地。石渠寶笈御書房著錄。無款。有傷補。縱壹百柒拾捌公分。橫玖拾叁玖公分。

100. "Chia Ku Ming Ch'in T'u"

By an un-identifiable artist of the Yuan Dynasty

Singing Amidst Abundance.

一〇一 元人 翠竹翎毛圖

絹地。無款。有傷補。縱壹百捌拾伍·伍公分。橫壹百零玖·捌公分。

101. "Ts'ui Chu Ling Mao T'u"

By an un-identifiable artist of the Yuan Dynasty

Bamboos and Birds.

元太祖皇帝

即青吉思汗諱特穆津在位二十二年父曰伊蘇克伊是為烈祖皇帝起宋寧宗開禧二年丙寅金章宗泰和六年終宋理宗寶慶三年丁亥金哀宗正大四年

元太宗皇帝

諱諤格德依太祖第三子在位十三年起宋理宗紹定二年己丑終宋理宗淳祐元年辛丑金正大六年

（ 177 ）

元世祖皇帝

即色辰諱呼必賚睿宗第四子在位三十八年起宋理宗景定元年庚申終于元貞三年乙酉

元成宗皇帝

即諤勒哲依圖諱特穆爾世祖曾孫在位十一年起元貞三年乙酉終大德十一年丁未

（ 178 ）

元武宗皇帝

即庫魯克諱海桑成宗長子在位六年起大德十一年丁未終至大五年壬子即皇慶元年

元仁宗皇帝

諱阿裕爾巴里巴特喇成宗次子在位九年起至大五年壬子終延祐七年庚申即至治元年

元文宗皇帝

即濟雅圖諱托克特穆爾武宗子在位六年起至和元年戊辰終至順四年癸酉

元寧宗皇帝

諱伊埒哲伯明宗次子在位一月

（ 180 ）

一〇二 元帝像册（古物陳列所）

絹地。內帝像捌頁。附空白四頁。其像爲元太祖、元太宗、元世祖、元成宗、元武宗、元仁宗、元文宗、及元寧宗。附木匣黃綢袱各一件。

102. "Yuan Ti Hsiang Ch'e"

Portraits of Yuan Emperors (an album).

(182)

(183)

(184)

一〇三 元后像册（古物陳列所）

絹地。內捌頁。共后像十五像。附空白肆頁。其像爲世祖皇后、順宗皇后、武宗皇后、仁宗皇后、英宗皇后、明宗皇后、寧宗皇后等。附木匣黃綢袱各一件。

103. "Yuan Hou Hsiang Ch'e"

Portraits of Yuan Empresses (an album).

(185)

明

MING DYNASTY (1368–1644 A. D.)

一〇四 明朱芾 蘆洲聚雁圖

紙地。寶笈重編著錄。無款。上端有「蘆洲聚雁圖」字樣。縱壹百壹拾柒·伍公分。橫叁拾·玖公分。

朱芾(約 1390)。字孟辨。松江人。洪武初爲中書舍人。

104. Chu Fei "Lu Chou Chu Yen T'u"

Wild Geese Gathering on a Rushy Islet.

Chu Fei (circa 1390).—Chu Fei, with the pseudonym of Meng-pien (孟辨), was a native of Sungchiang in Kiangsu. He was Chung Shu She Jen (中書舍人) of the grand secretariat.

一〇五 明王紱 山亭文會圖

紙地。寶笈重編著錄。上端有「永樂甲申中秋日九龍山人王孟端畫」題款。縱壹百貳拾玖·肆公分。橫伍拾壹·肆公分。

王紱 (1362–1416)。字孟端。號友石。又號九龍山人。無錫人。永樂間拜中書舍人。

105. Wang Fu "Shan Ting Wen Hui T'u"

Gathering of Litterati in a Mountain Bower.

Wang Fu (1362–1416).—Wang Fu, with the pseudonyms of Meng-tuan (孟端), Yu-shih (友石), and Chiu-lung Shan-jen (九龍山人), was a native of Wusih in Kiangsu.

(186)

一〇六 明夏昶半窗晴翠圖

紙地。石渠寶笈御書房著錄。有「東吳夏昶仲昭作」題款。紙地剝落。縱壹百叁拾玖·叁公分。橫肆拾伍·叁公分。

夏昶(1388–1470)。初名昶。太宗改名昶。字仲昭。崑山人。永樂乙未進士。正統中官至太常卿。

106. Hsia Ch'ang "Pan Ch'ung Ch'ing Ts'ui T'u"

Glimpse of Bamboo Through a Window.

Hsia Ch'ang (1388–1470).—Hsia Ch'ang, with the pseudonym of Chung-ch'ao (仲昭), was a native of Kun-shan in Kiangsu. He graduated as Chin-shih in the thirteenth year of Yung Lo (1415 A.D.), and in the time of Cheng Tung (1436–1449 A.D.) served as director of the Court of Sacrificial Worship (太常卿).

一〇七 明夏昶三祝圖

紙地。石渠寶笈三編著錄。有「東吳夏昶」題款。紙地傷補。縱壹百壹拾貳·肆公分。橫貳拾陸·柒公分。

107. Hsia Ch'ang "San Chu T'u"

Three Bamboos.

(187)

一〇八
明戴進
風雨歸舟圖

絹地。右下端有「錢塘戴進寫」五字款識。有傷補及摺痕。縱壹百肆拾叁·壹公分。橫捌拾壹·玖公分。

明戴進(約1430)。字文進。號靜庵。又號玉泉山人。錢塘人。

108. Tai Chin "Feng Yu Kuei Chou T'u"

A Boat Homeward Bound in Rain and Wind.

Tai Chin (circa 1430). — Tai Chin, with the pseudonyms of Wen-chin (文進), Ching-an (靜庵), and Yu-chuan Shan-jen (玉泉山人), was a native of Ch'ient'ang in Chekiang.

(188)

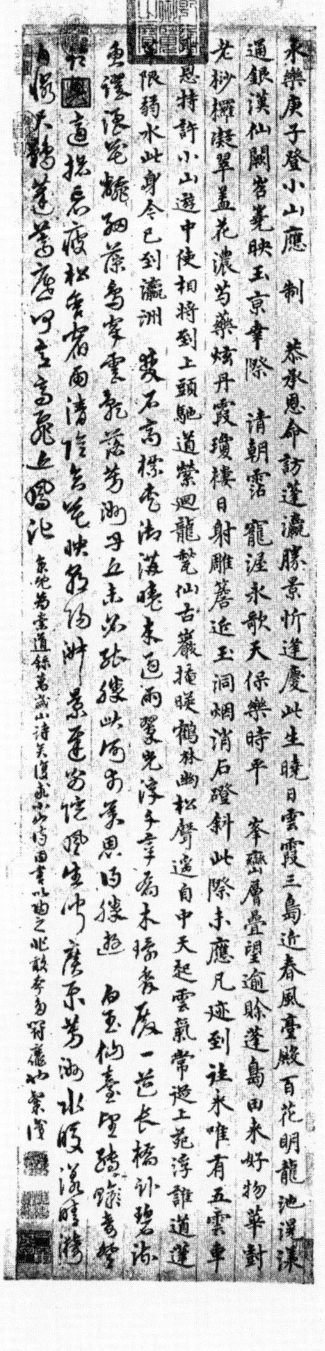

一〇九 明沈粲 書應制詩

紙地。石渠寶笈初編御書房著錄。有「粲識」題識。有霉傷及摺痕。縱壹百貳拾壹·肆公分。橫貳拾捌·捌公分。

沈粲(約 1428)。字民望。號簡庵。華亭人。官至大理少卿。

109. Shen Ts'an "Shu Ying Chih Shih"

Poem Composed Under Imperial Command.

Shen Ts'an (circa 1428).—Shen Ts'an, with the pseudonyms of Min-wang (民望) and Chien-an (簡庵) was a native of Huating in Kiangsu. He served as sub-director of the Grand Court of Revision.

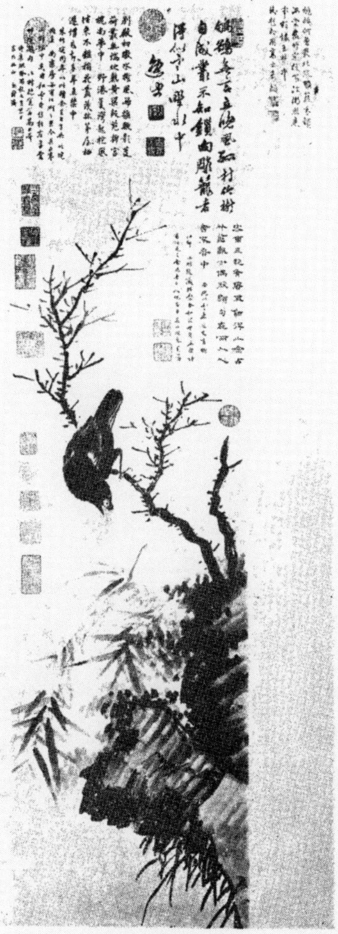

一一〇 明姚綬 寒林鸜鵒圖

紙地、石渠寶笈重編著錄、有「逸史」題識及「高士奇」「朱彝尊」題跋、紙地有剝落。縱壹百壹拾陸·柒公分、橫貳拾玖·陸公分。

姚綬(1423–1495)。字公綬。號穀庵子。又號雲東逸史。嘉善人。天順進士。成化初爲永甯郡守。人稱丹邱先生。

110. Yao Shou "Han Lin Chu Ku T'u"

Mynah on a Tree in Winter.

Yao Shou (1423–1495).—Yao Shou, with the pseudonyms of Kung-shou (公綬), Ku-an Tse (穀庵子), and Yun-tung Yi-shih (雲東逸史), was a native of Chiashan (嘉善) in Chekiang. He graduated as Chin-shih in the T'ien Shung period (1458–1464 A.D.). In the early part of Cheng Hua (1465–1487 A.D.) he served as prefect of Yungning (永甯郡守). He was commonly called Master Tan-hsui (丹邱先生).

一一一 明沈周
廬山高圖

紙地。石渠寶笈養心殿著錄。上端有「成化丁亥端陽日門生長洲沈周詩畫敬爲醒庵有道尊先生壽」題款。縱壹百玖拾叁·伍公分。横玖拾捌·貳公分。

沈周(1427–1509)。字啓南。號白石翁。世稱石田先生。長洲人。

111. Shen Chou "Lu Shan Kao T'u"

Lu Shan.

Shen Chou (1427–1509).—Shen Chou, with the pseudonyms of Ch'i-nan (啓南) and Pai-shih Weng (白石翁), also familiarly called Master Shih-t'ien (石田先生), was a native of Changchou in Kiangsu.

一一二 明吳偉

採芝圖

絹地。寶笈重編著錄。上端有「湖湘小僊作」題款。有折傷。縱伍拾捌·叁公分。横貳拾陸·陸公分。

吳偉(1459–1508)。字士英。一字魯夫。更字次翁。江夏人。弱冠謁成國。諸公呼爲小仙。遂以爲號。憲宗召授錦衣衛。鎮撫。待詔仁智殿。孝宗命畫稱旨。授錦衣百戶。賜印章曰畫狀元。

112. Wu Wei "Hsien Chih T'u"

Arhat with Fungus.

Wu Wei (1459–1508).—With the pseudonyms of Shih-ying (士英), Lu-fu (魯夫) and Tz'e-weng (次翁). Native of Chiang-hsia. As a youth, he went to Ch'eng State. Chu-kung calls him Hsio-hsien; hence his appellation of Hsio-hsien.

一一三

明吳偉

仙踪侶鶴圖

紙地。秘殿新編珠林重定著錄。右下端有「江夏吳偉」題款。有傷補。縱陸拾捌·捌公分。横叁拾玖公分。

113. Wu Wei "Hsien Ch'ung Lu E T'u"

Arhats Keeping Company with a Heron.

一一四 明陳憲章
萬玉圖

絹地。石渠寶笈養心殿著錄。右中端有「陳憲章」題識。有傷補。縱壹百壹拾貳·壹公分。横伍拾柒·柒公分。

陳憲章(生卒年不詳)。名錄。以字行。號如隱居士。會稽人。

114. Ch'en Hsien-chang "Wan Yu T'u"

Plum Blossoms.

Ch'en Hsien-chang.—Ch'en Lu (陳錄), with the pseudonym of Hsien-chang and Ju-yin Chu-shih (如隱居士), was a native of Kueichi (會稽), now Chekiang. He was generally known by his pseudonym, Hsien-chang.

一一五 明呂紀

杏花孔雀圖

絹地。寶笈三編著錄。右中端有「呂紀」題款。有傷補。縱貳百零叁·陸公分。橫壹百壹拾·伍公分。

呂紀(約 1477–1494 之時)。字廷振。鄞人。宏治間爲錦衣指揮使。

115. Lu Chi "Hsing Hua K'ung Ch'iao T'u"

Peacocks and Apricot Blossoms.

Lu Chi (circa 1477–1494).—Lu Chi, with the pseudonym of T'ing-cheng (廷振), was a native of Chin (鄞) in Chekiang. He served as captain of the imperial guards.

一一六 明呂紀
雪景翎毛圖

絹地。石渠寶笈養心殿著錄。下端有「呂紀」題款。有傷補。縱壹百柒拾貳公分。橫玖拾柒公分。

116. Lu Chi "Hsueh Ching Ling Mao T'u"

Birds in a Snow Scene.

(196)

一一七 明唐寅

山路松聲圖

絹地。寶笈三編著錄。上端有「治下唐寅畫呈李父母大人先生」題款。縱壹百玖拾肆·陸公分。橫壹百零貳·捌公分。

唐寅(1470-1523)。字子畏。一字伯虎。號六如。吳人。宏治戊午舉應天解元。

117. T'ang Yin "Shan Lu Sung Sheng T'u"

Murmuring of Pines on a Mountain Path.

T'ang Yin (1470-1523).—T'ang Yin, with the pseudonyms of Tse-wei (子畏), Pu-hu (伯虎), and Lu-ju (六如), was a native of Wu (now Kiangsu). He graduated as Chia-yuan or first in the interprovincial examination at Nanking in the tenth year of Hung Chih (1498 A.D.).

一一八 明唐寅 杏花

紙地。石渠寶笈御書房著錄。下端有「吳郡唐寅」題款。縱壹百拾肆·玖公分。橫叁拾貳·壹公分。

118. T'ang Yin "Hsing Hua"

Apricot Blossoms.

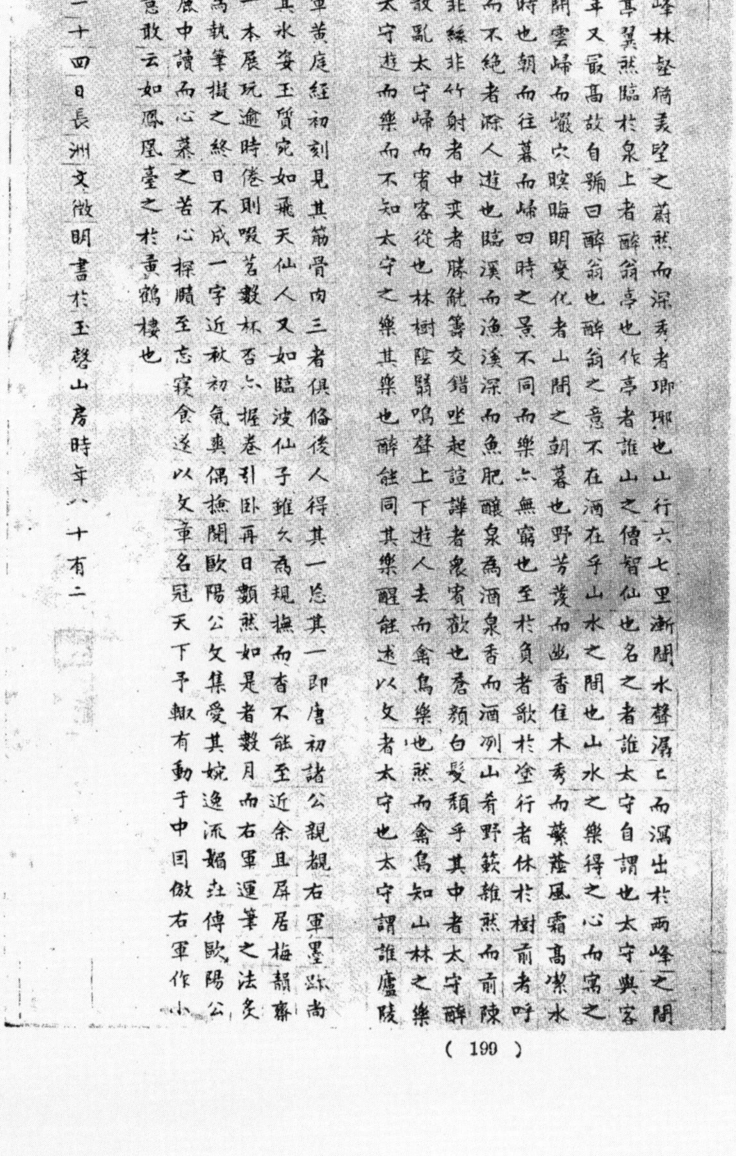

醉翁亭記

環滁皆山也其西南諸峰林壑尤美望之蔚然而深秀者瑯琊也山行六七里漸聞水聲潺潺而瀉出於兩峰之間者釀泉也峰回路轉有亭翼然臨於泉上者醉翁亭也作亭者誰山之僧智仙也名之者誰太守自謂也太守與客來飲於此飲少輒醉而年又最高故自號曰醉翁也醉翁之意不在酒在乎山水之間也山水之樂得之心而寓之酒也若夫日出而林霏開雲歸而巖穴暝晦明變化者山間之朝暮也野芳發而幽香佳木秀而繁陰風霜高潔水落而石出者山間之四時也朝而往暮而歸四時之景不同而樂亦無窮也至於負者歌於塗行者休於樹前者呼後者應傴僂提攜往來而不絕者滁人遊也臨溪而漁溪深而魚肥釀泉為酒泉香而酒洌山肴野蔌雜然而前陳者太守宴也宴酣之樂非絲非竹射者中弈者勝觥籌交錯坐起而諠譁者衆賓歡也蒼顏白髮頹乎其中者太守醉也已而夕陽在山人影散亂太守歸而賓客從也樹林陰翳鳴聲上下遊人去而禽鳥樂也然而禽鳥知山林之樂而不知人之樂人知從太守遊而樂而不知太守之樂其樂也醉能同其樂醒能述以文者太守也太守謂誰廬陵歐陽修也

余於梅韻堂展玩右軍黃庭經初刻見其筋骨肉三者俱備後人得其一忘其一即唐初諸公覩右軍墨跡尚不能得何況今日至其水姿玉質宛如飛天仙人又如臨波仙子雖久為規撫而杳不能至近余且屏居梅韻齋中案頭日置黃庭經一本展玩逾時倦則啜茗數杯否亦握卷引卧再日類然如是者數月而右軍運筆之法炙之愈出味之愈永然為執筆擬之終日不成一字近秋初氣爽偶檢閱歐陽公文集愛其婉逸流暢往傳歐陽公得呂黎遺稿于廢書簏中讀而心慕之苦心探賾至忘寢食遂以文章名冠天下予輒有動于中因倣右軍作小楷數百餘字聊以寄意敢云如鳳凰臺之於黃鶴樓也

皆

嘉靖三十年辛亥七月二十四日長洲文徵明書於玉磬山房時年八十有二

一一九

明文徵明
書醉翁亭記

紙地。有「文徵明」題款。縱伍拾叁·伍公分。橫貳拾捌·伍公分。

文徵明（1470-1559）。字徵仲。號衡山。長洲人。授翰林院待詔。

119. Wen Cheng-ming "Shu Tsui Weng T'ing Chi"

Transcription from an Essay, Entitled: Tsui Weng Pavilion.

Wen Cheng-ming (1470–1559).—Wen Cheng-ming, with the pseudonyms of Cheng-chung (徵仲) and Heng-shan (衡山), was a native of Ch'angchou (長洲) in Kiangsu. He served as Tai Chao (待詔), or probationer in the Hanlin Academy.

一二〇 明文徵明

江南春圖

紙地。寶笈重編著錄。上端有「嘉靖丁未春二月徵明畫并書。追和雲林先生詞二首」題識。縱壹百零陸·壹公分。橫叁拾·陸公分。

120. Wen Cheng-ming "Chiang Nan Ch'un T'u"

Spring in Kiang Nan.

(200)

一二一 明文徵明

影翠軒圖

紙地。上端有「徵明」題款縱陸拾柒·壹公分。横叁拾壹公分。

121. Wen Cheng-ming "Ying Ts'ui Hsuan T'u"

Ying Ts'ui Balcony.

一二二 明文徵明

洞庭西山圖

紙地。上端有「徵明」題識。縱壹百貳拾壹·壹公分。横貳拾捌·捌公分。

122. Wen Cheng-ming "Tung T'ing Hsi Shan T'u"

The Western Hills of Tung T'ing Lake.

一二三　明仇英　柳塘漁艇圖

紙地。寶笈三編著錄。下端有「仇英實父製」題款。縱壹百零貳·玖公分。橫肆拾柒·陸公分。

仇英(約 1530)。字實父。號十洲。太倉人。移居吳郡。

123. Ch'ou Ying "Liu T'ang Yu T'ing T'u"

Fishing Boat by the Willow Trees.

Ch'ou Ying (circa 1530).—Ch'ou Ying, with the pseudonyms of Shih-fu (實父) and Shih-chou (十洲), was a native of T'ai-ts'ang (太倉), but moved to live in Wuchun (吳郡), now Kiangsu.

(202)

一二四 明仇英 秋江待渡圖

絹地。寶笈重編著錄。無款。下端有「仇英之印」章及「仇氏實父」章。有摺紋。
縱壹百伍拾肆·肆公分。橫壹百叁拾叁·叁公分。

124. Ch'ou Ying "Ch'iu Chiang Tai Tu T'u"

Waiting to Cross a River in Autumn.

一二五 明仇英

梅石撫琴圖(傳)

絹地。寶笈重編著錄下端有「實父仇英製」題識。縱壹百零捌·叁公分橫叁拾壹·貳公分。

125. Ch'ou Ying "Mei Shih Fu Ch'in T'u"

Lute Playing Beside Plum Blossoms and Rocks (attributed).

一二六　明陸治　支硎山圖

紙地。上端有「包山陸治」題識。縱捌拾叁·陸公分。橫叁拾肆·捌公分。

陸治(1426–1576)。字叔平。號包山子。吳諸生。

126. Lu Chih "Chih Hsing Shan T'u"

Chih Hsing Mountain.

Lu Chih (1426–1576).—Lu Chih, with the pseudonyms of Shu-p'ing (叔平) and Pao-shan Tse (包山子), was a Licentiate in Kiangsu.

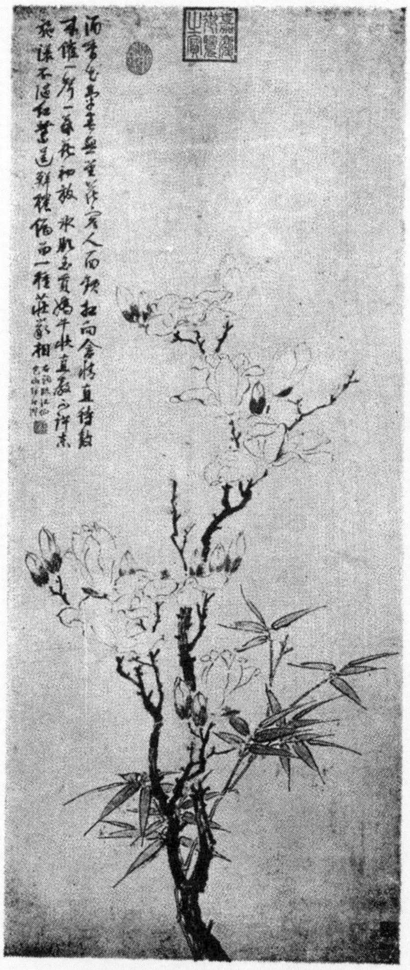

一二七　明陸治　玉蘭

紙地。上端有「陸治」題款。縱壹百貳拾肆·捌公分。橫伍拾壹·玖公分。

127. Lu Chih "Yu Lan"

Magnolia Flowers.

一二八 明文嘉 瀛洲仙侶圖

紙地。寶笈三編著錄。上端有「文嘉」題款。詩堂上有「文嘉」題識。縱柒拾·陸公分。橫貳拾伍·柒公分。

文嘉(1501–1583)。字休承。號文水。長洲人。徵明仲子。

128. Wen Chia "Yin Chou Hsien Lu T'u"

The Immortals in Fairyland.

Wen Chia (1501–1583).—Wen Chia, with the pseudonyms of Hsiu-ch'eng (休承) and Wen-shui (文水), was a native of Ch'angchou (長洲) and the second son of Cheng-min (徵明).

一二九 明錢穀

杏花喜鵲圖

紙地。寶笈三編著錄。上端有「錢穀」題款。縱壹百壹拾陸·伍公分。横叁拾肆·貳公分。

錢穀 (1508–1572)。字叔寶。吳人。

129. Ch'ien Ku "Hsing Hua Hsi Ch'iao T'u"

A Magpie on a Branch of Apricot Blossoms.

Ch'ien Ku (1508–1572).—Ch'ien Ku, with the pseudonym Shu-pao (叔寶), was a native of Wu (吳) (Kiangsu).

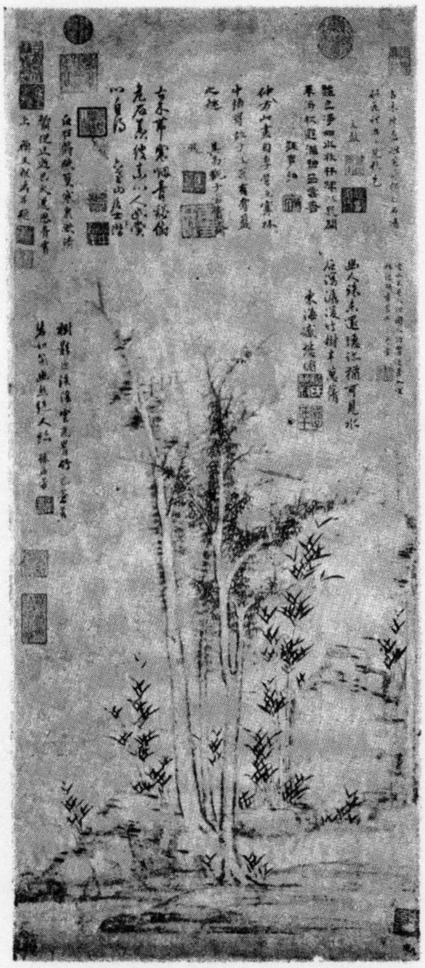

一三〇 明顧正誼
仿雲林樹石

紙地。上端有「顧正誼畫幷題」題款。縱玖拾貳·柒公分。橫叁拾捌·柒公分。

顧正誼(約 1580)。字仲方。自號亭林。華亭人。官中書舍人。

130. Ku Cheng-yi "Fang Yun Ling Shu Shih"

Trees and Rocks, After the Style of Ni T'san.

Ku Cheng-yi (circa 1580).—Ku Cheng-yi, with the pseudonyms, Chung-fang (仲 方) and T'ing-lin (亭林), was a native of Huating (華亭) in Kiangsu. He served as Chung Shu She Jen (中書舍人), in the grand secretariat.

一三一 明徐渭
榴實圖

紙地。寶笈重編著錄。上端有「文長」題款。有傷補。縱玖拾壹·捌公分。橫貳拾陸·陸公分。

徐渭 (1521–1593)。字文淸。更字文長。號天池。山陰諸生。總督胡宗憲招致幕府。知兵好奇計。擒徐海。誘王直。皆與其謀。

131. Hsu Wei "Liu Shih T'u"

Pomegranate.

Hsu Wei (1521–1593).—With the pseudonyms of Wen-ch'ing (文淸) and Wen-ch'ang (文長). Called T'ien-ch'ih (天池). Licentiate of Shanyin. Expert in military tactics.

(209)

一三二 明孫枝
梅花水仙圖

紙地。下端有「嘉靖己未冬月孫枝」題款。縱柒拾壹·伍公分.橫叁拾壹·伍公分。

孫枝(約1630)。字叔達。號華林居士。

132. Sun Chih "Mei Hua Shui Hsien T'u"

Narcissus and Plum Blossoms.

Sun Chih (circa 1630).—Sun Chih has the pseudonyms of Shu-ta (叔達) and Hua-lin Chu-shih (華林居士).

一三三 明項元汴 蘭竹

紙地。寶笈三編著錄。上端有「項元汴寫」題款。縱柒拾捌公分。橫叁拾肆·叁公分。

項元汴(1525–1590)。字子京。號墨林居士。檇李人。畫山水學黃公望倪瓚。尤醉心於倪。得其勝趣。每作縑素。自爲韻語題之。

133. Hsiang Yuan-pien "Lan Chu"

Bamboos and Orchids.

Hsiang Yuan-pien (1525–1590).—With the pseudonym of Tse-ching (子京). Called Mo-lin Chu-shih (墨林居士). Native of Tsunli (檇李). In landscape painting, he followed after Huang Kung-wang and Ni Ts'an, but especially after the latter from whom he derived his special characteristic of simplicity. His drawings are accompanied by his own writing.

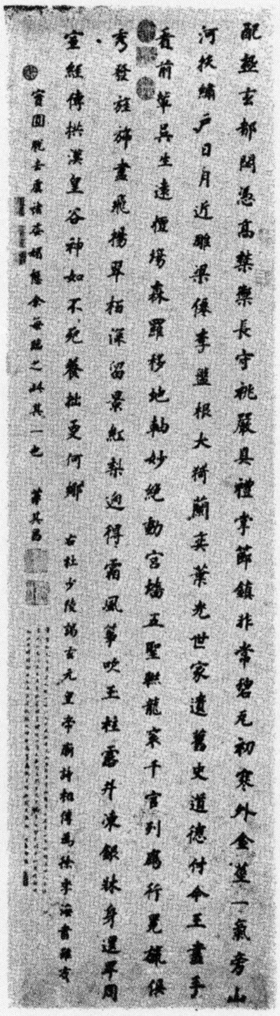

一三四 明董其昌書杜甫詩

紙地。寶笈三編著錄。下端有「董其昌」題款。縱壹百捌拾壹·肆公分。橫肆拾陸公分。

董其昌(1555–1636)。字元宰。號思白。華亭人。萬曆進士。累官至禮部尙書。

134. Tung Chi-chang "Shu Tu Fu Shih"

Transcription of One of Tu Fu's Poems.

Tung Chi-chang (1555–1636).—Tung Chi-chang, with the pseudonyms Yuan-tsai (元宰) and Sze-po (思白), was a native of Huating (華亭), now Sung-chiang, Kiangsu. He graduated as Chin-shih in the reign of Wan Li (1573–1619 A.D.) and served as president of the Board of Rites.

一三五 明董其昌 秋林書屋圖

紙地。石渠寶笈養心殿著錄。上端有「思翁」題識。縱伍拾肆·肆公分。橫伍拾捌·壹公分。

135. Tung Chi-chang "Ch'iu Lin Shu Wu T'u"

A Studio in the Forest in Autumn.

一三六 明董其昌 東岡草堂圖

紙地。寶笈重編著錄。上端有「其昌」題識。縱捌拾柒·肆公分。橫陸拾伍·叁公分。

136. Tung Chi-chang "Tung Kang Ts'ao T'ang T'u"

Thatched Pavilion in Tung Kang.

(214)

一三七 明董其昌 夏木垂陰圖

紙地。寶笈三編著錄。上端有「董玄宰」題識。有傷補縱叁百貳拾壹·柒公分。橫壹百零貳·叁公分。

137. Tung Chi-chang "Hsia Mu Sui Yin T'u"

Trees in Summer.

一三八 明王綦 溪橋紅樹圖

紙地。石渠寶笈重編著錄。上端有「丙寅春寫于長生館王綦」題識。紙地有剝落。縱捌拾捌·貳公分。橫伍拾柒·捌公分。

王綦(約 1368–1398 之時)。字履若。吳諸生。

138. Wang Chi "Ch'i Ch'iao Hung Shu T'u"

Trees by a Bridge.

Wang Chi (circa 1368–1398).—Wang Chi, with the pseudonym Lu-jao (履若), was a Licentiate of Wu (Kiangsu).

(215)

一三九 明宋旭
雲巒秋瀑圖(傳)

紙地。石渠寶笈養心殿著錄。上端有「宋旭」題款。縱壹百貳拾伍·陸公分。橫叁拾貳·捌公分。

宋旭(1523–1602)。字初暘。崇德人。家石門。游寓多居精舍。禪燈孤榻。世以髮僧高之。

139. Sung Hsu "Yuan Luan Ch'iu Pao T'u"

Waterfall and Clouds in Autumn (attributed).

Sung Hsu (1523–1602).—With the pseudonym of Ch'u-yang (初暘). Native of Ts'ungte (崇德). His home is in Shihmen (石門), but he lived everywhere, always in beautiful places. Very simple in habits. Hence after generations call him a "monk with hair."

一四〇 明關思

秋林聽泉圖

絹地。上端有「庚午仲春日虛白道人關思」題款。縱壹百伍拾公分。橫伍拾玖·捌公分。

關思(約 1580)。字何思。一名九思。字仲通。號虛白。烏程人。

140. Kuan Sze "Ch'iu Lin T'ing Chuan T'u"

Listening to a Bubbling Spring from a Grove.

Kuan Sze (circa 1580).—Kuan Sze, with another name Chiu-sze (九思), and the pseudonyms Chung-t'ung (仲通), Ho-sze (何思), and Hsu-po (虛白), was a native of Wuch'eng (烏程) in Chekiang.

一四
明李士達
坐聽松風圖

紙地。寶笈重編著錄。上端有「萬曆丙辰秋寫吳郡李士達」題款。縱壹百陸拾柒·貳公分。横玖拾玖·陸公分。

李士達(約1580)。號仰槐。吳縣人。

204. Li Shih-ta "Tso T'ing Sung Feng T'u"

Listening to the Wind Among the Pines.

Li Shih-ta (circa 1580).—Li Shih-ta, with the pseudonym of Yang-huai (仰槐), was a native of Wuhsien (吳縣) in Kiangsu.

一四二 明崔子忠
桐陰博古圖

紙地。石渠寶笈初編養心殿著錄。上端有「庚辰中秋長安崔子忠畫」題款。紙地剝落。縱壹百捌拾壹·叁公分。橫柒拾伍·伍公分。

崔子忠(約1644)。字道母。號北海。山東人。崇禎時順天諸生。明亡殉國。

142. Ts'ui Tse-chung "T'ung Yin Po Ku T'u"

Antiques Under the Shade of the Elecococa.

Ts'ui Tse-chung (circa 1644).—Ts'ui Tse-chung, with the pseudonyms of Tao-mu (道母) and Pei-hai (北海), was a native of Shantung. He was a Hsiu-t'sai or Licentiate in the time of Ts'ung Cheng (1628–1644 A.D.), and became a martyr for the state at the overthrow of the Ming Dynasty.

(219)

一四三 明張宏
琳宮晴雪圖

紙地。寶笈三編著錄。上端有「天啓丙寅十月張宏寫」題款。縱壹百叁拾陸公分。橫肆拾陸·叁公分。

張宏(約 1630–1650 之時)。字君度。號鶴澗。吳人。

143. Chang Hung "Lin Kung Ch'ing Hsueh T'u"

Sunshine After Snow in the Jade Palace.

Chang Hung (circa 1630–1650).—Chang Hung, with the pseudonym of Chun-tu (君度) and Hao-chien (鶴澗), was a native of Wu, now Kiangsu.

(220)

一四四 明藍瑛

秋老梧桐圖

紙地。石渠寶笈御書房著錄。上端有「蜨叟藍瑛」題款。縱壹百叁拾陸·陸公分。橫叁拾壹·壹公分。

藍瑛(約 1630)。字田叔。號蝶叟。錢塘人。

144. Lan Ying "Ch'iu Lao Wu T'ung T'u"

A Bird on An Old Elecococa Branch in Autumn.

Lan Ying (circa 1630).—Lan Ying, with the pseudonyms of T'ien-shu (田叔) and Tieh-sou (蝶叟), was a native of Ch'ient'ang in Chekiang.

(221)

一四五 明邢慈靜

觀音大士像(泥金畫)

紙地。祕殿珠林重編著錄。上有「慈靜」畫井贊。縱伍拾伍·貳公分。橫貳拾貳·叁公分。

邢慈靜(生卒年未詳)。臨清邢侗妹。叅議馬拯室。善墨花白描大士。宗管道昇。有髮繡大士。極工書。體頗類其兄。工詩。著非非草。

145. Hsing Ch'ih-ching "Ta Shih Hsiang"

Bodhisattva.

Hsing Ch'ih-ching.—Native of Lingch'ing (臨清). Sister of Hsing T'ung (邢侗). Wife of Ma Chen (馬拯). Good in black and white drawings of flowers, and in making delicate tracings of Bodhisattvas. Followed after Kuan Tao-sheng. Good in calligraphy and poetry. Composed a poem called "Fei Fei Ts'ao."

(222)

(223)

一四六 明郭甸 寒鵶宿雁圖

絹地。石渠寶笈養心殿著錄。上端有「古亳郭甸」題款。縱壹百陸拾玖·壹公分。橫玖拾柒·陸公分。

郭甸(生卒年不詳)。字海田。亳人。

144. Kuo Tien "Han Ya Hsu Yen T'u"

Winter Magpies and Swans Resting.

Kuo Tien.—Kuo Tien, with the pseudonym of Hai-tien (海田), was a native of Po (亳) in Honan.

清

CH'ING DYNASTY (1644 – 1912 A.D.)

一四七 清王時敏
仿黃公望山水

絹地。寶笈重編著錄。上端有「王時敏」題識。有微傷。縱壹百肆拾柒·玖公分。橫陸拾柒·伍公分。

王時敏（1592–1680）。字遜之。號煙客。太倉人。明末官至太常寺少卿。

147. Wang Shih-ming "Fang Huang Kung-wang Shan Shui"

Landscape After the Style of Huang Kung-wang.

Wang Shih-ming (1592–1680).—Wang Shih-ming, with the pseudonyms Hsun-chih (遜之) and Yen-k'o (煙客), was a native of T'aits'ang (太倉) in Kiangsu. He served as sub-director of the Court of Sacrificial Worship at the end of the Ming Dynasty.

(225)

一四八 清王鑑

煙浮遠岫圖

絹地。寶笈三編著錄。上端有「王鑑」款識。有摺痕及傷。縱壹百叁拾肆·玖公分。橫柒拾捌·捌公分。

王鑑(1598–1677)。字圓照。號湘碧。又號染香菴主。太倉人。官至廉州知府。

148. Wang Chien "Yen Fo Yuan Ti T'u"

Mist Floating over a Distant Ravine.

Wang Chien (1598–1677). —Wang Chien, with the pseudonyms Yuan-chao (圓照), Hsiang-pi (湘碧), and Jan-hsiang An-chu (染香菴主), was a native of T'ai-ts'ang (太倉) in Kiangsu. He served as prefect of Lienchou (廉州) in Kuang-tung.

一四九 清世祖
墨鍾馗

紙地。上右角「賜戶部尙書戴明說」八字。有斷折。縱壹百叁拾貳·陸公分橫陸拾肆·壹公分。

世祖(1638-1661)。名福臨。太宗第九子。在位十八年。年號順治。

149. Emperor Shih Tsu "Mo Chung K'uei"

An Ink Study of Chung K'uei.

Emperor Shih Tsu (1638-1661).—Emperor Shih Tsu, named Fu-lin (福臨) was the ninth son of T'ai Tsung (太宗). He reigned for eighteen years under the name of Shun Chih (順治).

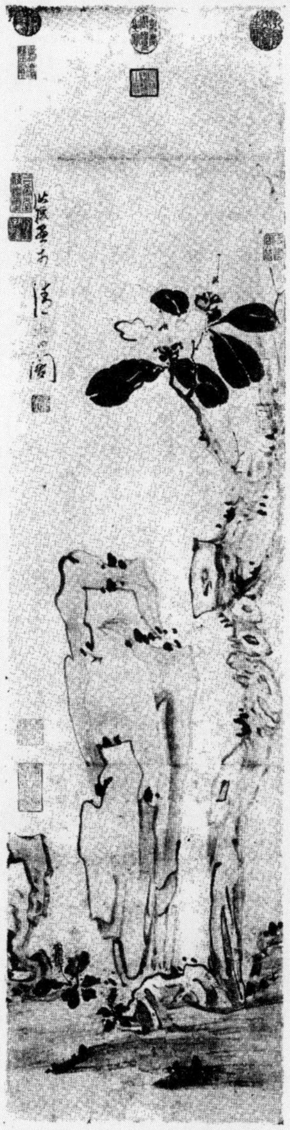

一五〇 清陳洪綬
卷石山茶

紙地。寶笈三編著錄。上端有「洪綬」題識。有傷補。縱壹百拾叁·陸公分。橫貳拾柒·玖公分。

陳洪綬 (1599–1652)。字章侯。號老蓮。諸暨人。以明經不仕。崇禎間召入爲供奉。甲申後自稱悔遲。

150. Chen Hung-shou "Chu Shih San Ch'e"

Rock and Camellias.

Chen Hung-shou (1599–1652).—Chen Hung-shou, with the pseudonym of Chang-hou (章侯). Called Lao-lien (老蓮). Native of Chuk'ai (諸暨). Good at landscape painting.

一五一 清吳歷 仿梅道人山水

紙地。寶笈三編著錄。上端有「吳歷」題識。有傷補。縱壹百玖拾玖·柒公分。橫壹百零陸·叁公分。

吳歷 (1632–1718)。字漁山。號墨井道人。常熟人。

151. Wu Li "Fang Mei Tao-jen Shan Shui"

Landscape After the Style of Mei Tao-jen.

Wu Li (1632–1718).—Wu Li, with the pseudonyms Yu-shan (漁山), and Mo-ching Tao-jen (墨井道人), was a native of Ch'angshu (常熟) in Kiangsu.

一五二 清王翬 仿趙孟頫 江村清夏圖

紙地。石渠寶笈重編著錄。有「琴川石谷」題識。紙地剝落。縱壹百壹拾捌公分。横陸拾壹公分。

王翬(1632-1720)。字石谷。號耕煙散人。又號清暉主人。常熟人。康熙中供奉內廷。

152. Wang Hui "Fang Chao Meng-fu Chiang Ts'un Ch'ing Hsia T'u"

Village by a River in Summer, After the Style of Chao Meng-fu.

Wang Hui (1632–1720).—Wang Hui, with the pseudonyms Shih-ku (石谷), Keng-yen San-jen (耕煙散人), and Ch'ing-hui Chu-jen (清暉主人), was a native of Ch'angshu (常熟) in Kiangsu. In the time of K'ang Hsi (1662–1722 A.D.), he was attendant painter to the Imperial Court.

(230)

一五三 淸王翬

一梧軒圖

紙地。寶笈重編著錄。上端有「石谷王翬」題識。縱壹百零肆·肆公分。橫伍拾肆·叁公分。

153. Wang Hui "I Wu Hsuan T'u"

I Wu Pavilion.

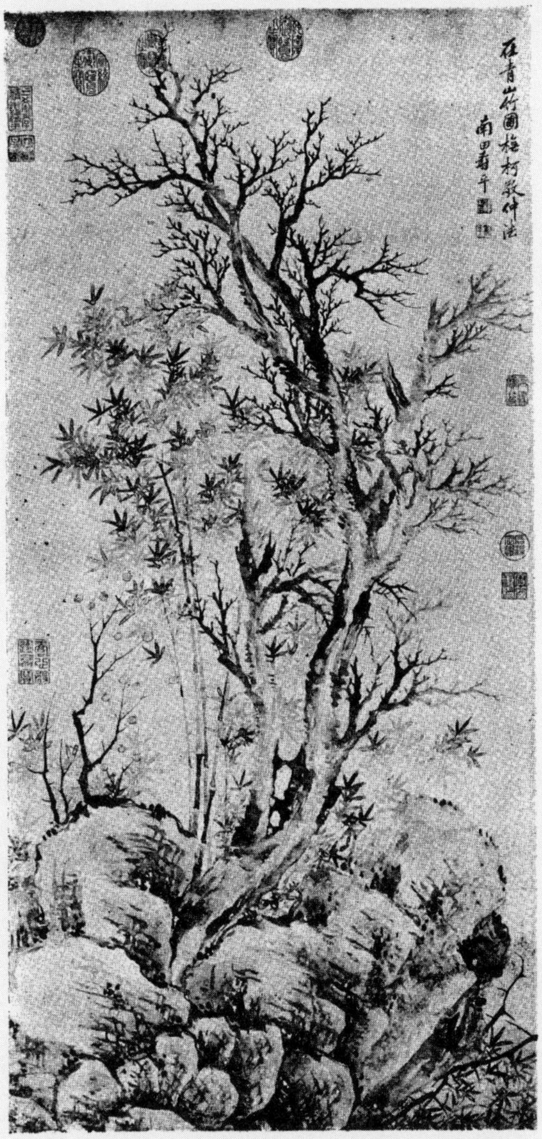

一五四 清惲壽平

喬柯修竹圖

紙地。寶笈重編著錄。上端有「南田壽平」題款。有傷補。縱壹百零壹·陸公分。橫肆拾柒·捌公分。

惲壽平(1633–1690)。名格。以字行。一字正叔。號南田。又號白雲外史。武進人。

154. Yun Shou-p'ing "Ch'iao Ko Hsiu Chu T'u"

Slim Bamboos Under a Tree.

Yun Shou-p'ing (1633–1690).—Yun Shou-p'ing was named Ko (格) but was famous by his pseudonym Shou-p'ing (壽平). His other pseudonyms were Cheng-shu (正 叔), Nan-tien (南田), and Po-yun Wai-shih (白雲外史). He was a native of Wuchin (武進) in Kiangsu.

一五五 清王武 溪亭對菊圖

紙地。上端有「丁未秋日王武識」題款。縱壹百陸拾柒·柒公分。横肆拾伍·肆公分。

王武(1632–1690)。字勤中。號忘庵。吳縣人。

155. Wang Wu "Ch'i T'ing Tui Chu T'u"

Looking at Chrysanthemums from a Pavilion by a Stream.

Wang Wu (1632–1690).—Wang Wu, with his pseudonyms Ch'in-chung (勤中) and Wang-an (忘庵), was a native of Wuhsien (吳縣) in Kiangsu.

一五六 清王武 花鳥

絹地。寶笈三編著錄。上端有「震澤王武」題款。有霉傷。

縱壹百陸拾陸·柒公分。橫伍拾捌·柒公分。

156. Wang Wu "Hua Niao"

Flowers and a Bird.

一五七 清王原祁
松壑流泉圖

紙地。寶笈三編著錄。上端有「麓臺祁」題款。縱伍拾柒·壹公分。橫叁拾柒·叁公分。

清王原祁(1643–1715)。字茂京。號麓臺。時敏孫。太倉人。康熙庚戌進士。官至戶部侍郎。

157. Wang Yuan-chi "Sung Ho Liu Ch'uan T'u"

Running Spring in a Pine-covered Ravine.

Wang Yuan-chi (1643–1715).—Wang Yuan-chi, with the pseudonyms Mao-ching (茂京) and Lu-t'ai (麓臺), was a native of T'ai-ts'ang (太倉) in Kiangsu. He graduated as Chin-shih in the reign of K'ang Hsi. He served as vice-president of the Board of Revenue.

(235)

一五八

清僧元濟王原祁合作蘭竹

紙地。石渠寶笈養心殿著錄。上端有「清湘石濤濟道人」及「麓臺補坡石」題款。縱壹百叁拾肆·貳公分。橫伍拾柒·柒公分。

僧元濟(生卒年不詳)。又名道濟。字石濤。號靑湘老人。一云清湘陳人。一云淸湘遺人。又號大滌子。又自號苦瓜和尚。又號瞎尊者。明楚藩後也。

158. The Monk Yuan-chi and Wang Yuan-chi "Lan Chu"

Orchids and Bamboos.

Yuan-chi—Yuan-chi, with the pseudonyms of Shih-t'ao (石濤), Ch'ing-hsiang Lao-jen (靑湘老人), Ta-ti Tse (大滌子), K'u-kua Ho-shang (苦瓜和尙), and Hsia-tsun Ch'e (瞎尊者), was a scion of the feudal state of Ch'u (楚) in the Ming Dynasty.

一五九 清赫奕

晴嵐晚翠圖

絹地。石渠寶笈養心殿著錄。下端有「臣赫奕恭畫」款識。縱玖拾玖·肆公分。橫伍拾壹·貳公分。

赫奕(約 1750)。號澹士。滿洲人。官大司空。

159. Ho Yi "Ch'ing Lan Wan Ts'ui T'u"

Verdure of Misty Peaks in the Evening Sky.

Ho Yi (circa 1750).—Ho Yi, with the pseudonym Tan-shih (澹士), was a Manchu. He served as president of the Board of Works.

一六〇 清蔣廷錫

四瑞慶登圖

絹地。寶笈重編著錄。下端有「雍正元年九月禮部右侍郎臣蔣廷錫恭畫」題款。縱壹百捌拾伍·伍公分。橫捌拾柒·壹公分。

蔣廷錫(1669–1732)。字揚孫。號西君。又號西谷。常熟人。康熙中入詞林。官至大學士。

160. Chiang T'ing-hsi "Sze Jui Ch'ing Teng T'u"

Four Happy Omens.

Chiang T'ing-hsi (1669–1732).—Chiang T'ing-hsi, with the pseudonyms Yang-sun (揚孫), Yu-chun (西君), and Hsi-ku (西谷), was a native of Ch'angshu (常熟). In the reign of K'ang Hsi, he entered into the Han-lin Academy, serving as grand secretary.

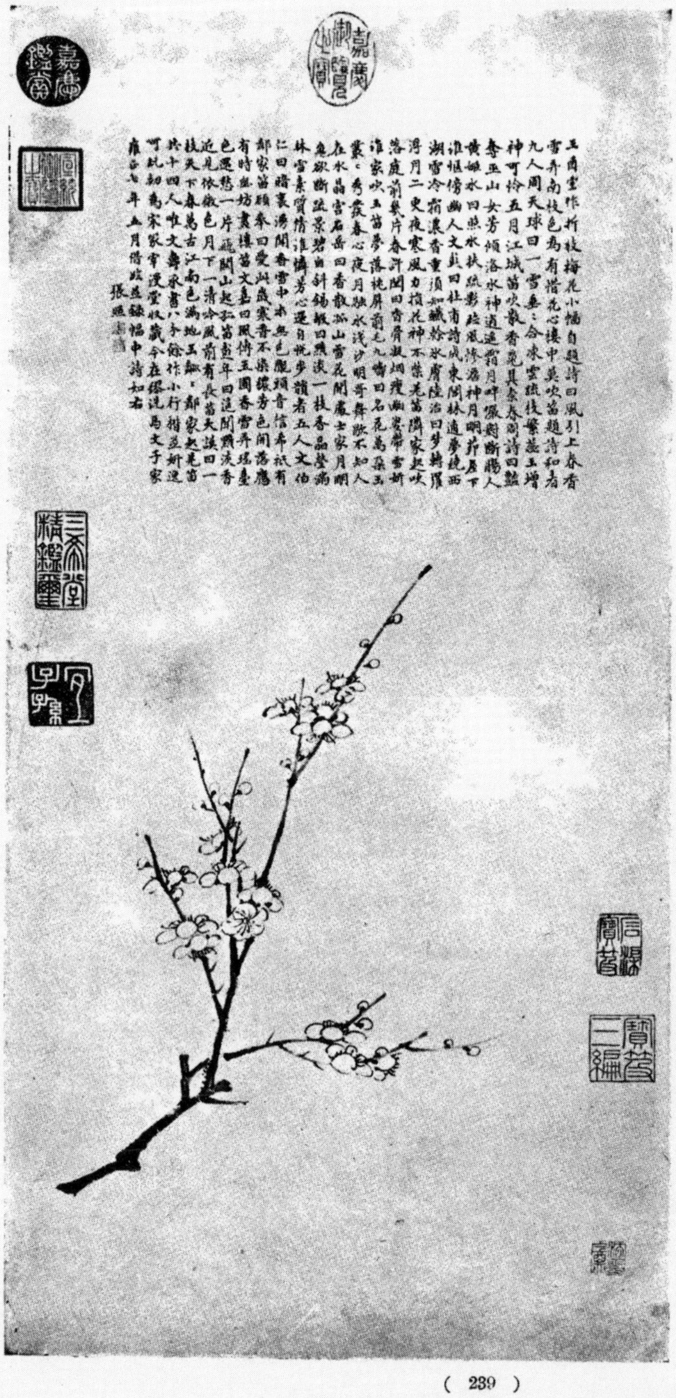

一六一 清張照

墨梅

紙地。寶笈三編著錄。上端有「張照」題款。縱陸拾壹·伍公分。横叁拾·貳公分。

張照(1691-1745)。字得天。華亭人。康熙乙丑進士。官至刑部尙書。

161. Chang Chao "Mo Mei"

An Ink Study of Plum Blossoms.

Chang Chao (1691-1745).—Chang Chao, with the pseudonym of Te-t'ien (得天), was a native of Huating, Kiangsu. He graduated as Chin-shih in the time of K'ang Hsi, and served as president of the Board of Punishments.

一六二 清高其佩
廬山瀑布圖

紙地。石渠寶笈重華宮著錄。下端有「高其佩」題款。有傷補。縦玖拾捌·伍公分。橫肆拾玖·玖公分。

清高其佩(1672–1734)。字韋之。號且園。又號南村。爲鐵嶺漢軍人。父天爵爲耿精忠所害。其佩官至刑部侍郎。善指畫。

162. Kao Chi-pei "Lu Shan Pao Pu T'u"

Waterfall in Lu Shan.

Kao Chi-pei (1672–1734).—With the pseudonym of Wei-chih (韋之). Has two appelations: Ch'ieh-yuan (且園) and Nan-ts'un (南村). Good in drawing with his fingers.

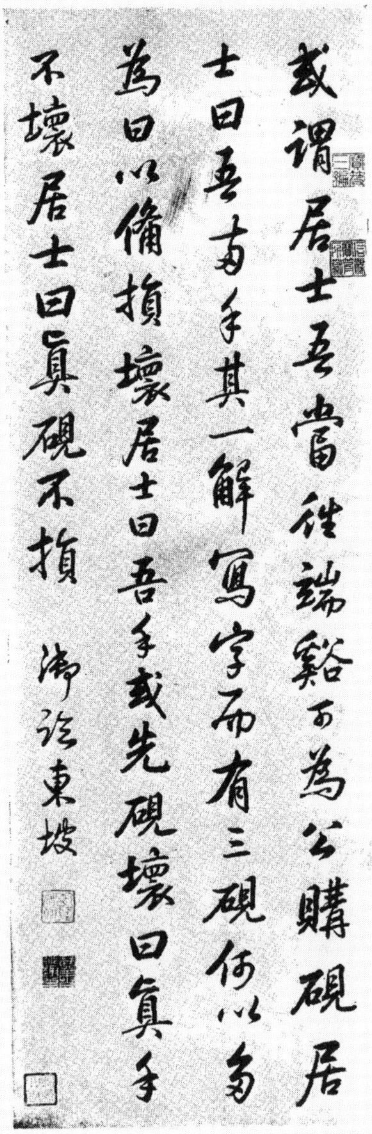

一六三 清高宗 臨蘇軾書

紙地。寶笈三編著錄。下端有「御臨東坡」題款。縱玖拾玖·玖公分。橫叁拾貳·貳公分。

高宗(1711–1799)。名弘曆。世宗子。在位六十年。年號乾隆。

163. Emperor Kao Tsung "Lin Su Shih Shu"

Calligraphy After the Style of Su Shih.

Emperor Kao Tsung (1711–1799).—Emperor Kao Tsung, named Hung-li (弘曆), was the son of Emperor Shih Tsung (世宗). He reigned sixty years, taking for his reign name Ch'ien Lung (乾隆).

一六四　清高宗　煙波釣艇圖

紙地。石渠寶笈三編著錄。右上角有「重華宮御製」題識。縱伍拾玖公分。橫叁拾柒公分。

164. Emperor Kao Tsung "Yen Po Tio T'ing T'u"

A Fishing Boat on a Misty Lake.

一六五 清張宗蒼
仿黄公望山水

紙地。寶笈三編著錄。下端有「臣張宗蒼恭摹黄公望筆」題款。有傷補。縱壹百貳拾肆·壹公分。横肆拾柒·伍公分。

張宗蒼(1686–1762)。字默存。一字墨岑。號篁村。吳縣人。乾隆時官戶部主事。

165. Chang Tsung-ts'ang "Fang Huang Kung-wang Shan Shui"

Landscape After the Style of Huang Kung-wang.

Chang Tsung-ts'ang (1686–1762).—Chang Tsung-ts'ang, with the pseudonyms Mo-ts'un (默存), Mo-ts'en (墨岑), and Huang-ts'un (篁村), was a native of Wu-hsien (Soochow). In Ch'ien Lung's reign he served as second class assistant secretary of the Board of Revenue.

一六六 清鄒一桂
墨梅

絹地。寶笈重編著錄。下端有「臣鄒一桂恭畫」題款。縱壹百捌拾陸·捌公分。橫玖拾叁·肆公分。

鄒一桂(1686–1774)。字原褒。號小山。無錫人。雍正丁未傳臚。官至禮部侍郎。

166. Tsou I-kuei "Mo Mei"

An Ink Study of Plum Blossoms.

Tsou I-kuei (1686–1774).—Tsou I-kuei, with the pseudonyms Yuan-pao (原褒) and Hsiao-shan (小山), was a native of Wusih in Kiangsu. He graduated as Quarters in the fifth year of Yung Cheng (1727 A.D.), and served as vice-president of the Board of Rites.

一六七 清鄒一桂 盎春生意圖

紙地。寶笈重編著錄。下端有「臣鄒一桂恭寫」題款。縱肆拾貳·叁公分。橫柒拾肆·伍公分。

167. Tsou I-kuei "Ang Ch'un Sheng I T'u"

Life in Spring

(246)

一六八 清錢維城 春花三種

紙地。寶笈三編著錄。下端有「臣錢維城恭畫」題款。縱壹百壹拾貳·玖公分。橫捌拾·貳公分。

錢維城（1720–1772）。字宗磐。號紉菴。又號稼軒。武進人。乾隆乙丑狀元。官至工部侍郎。

168. Ch'ien Wei-ch'eng "Ch'un Hua San Chung"

Three Kinds of Spring Flowers.

Ch'ien Wei-ch'eng (1720–1772).—Ch'ien Wei-ch'eng, with the pseudonyms of Tsung-p'an (宗磐), Jen-an (紉菴), and Chia-hsuan (稼軒), was a native of Wuchin, Kiangsu. He graduated as Optimus Han-lin graduate in the time of Ch'ien Lung (1736–1795 A.D.), and served as vice president of the Board of Works.

一六九 清永瑢
山水

紙地。寶笈三編著錄。下端有「子臣永瑢恭畫」題款。有傷補。縱壹百叁拾壹·壹公分。横陸拾肆公分。

永瑢(約 1790)。清高宗第六子。封質親王。

169. Yung Jung "Shan Shui"

Landscape.

Yung Jung (circa 1790).—Yung Jung was the sixth son of Emperor Kao Tsung. He was named Chih Ch'in Wang (質親王) or Prince Chih.

一七〇 清金廷標 移桃圖

紙地。寶笈三編著錄。下端有「臣金廷標恭繪」題款。縱壹百捌拾柒·壹公分。橫陸拾叁·肆公分。

金廷標(約 1750)。字士揆。烏程人。乾隆時供奉內廷。

170. Chin T'ing-piao "I T'ao T'u"

Transplanting Peaches.

Chin T'ing-piao (circa 1750).—Chin T'ing-piao, with the pseudonym of Shih-k'uei (士揆), was a native of Wuch'eng in Chekiang. In the time of Ch'ien Lung he became attendant painter to the Imperial Court.

(249)

一七一 清金廷標 罱泥圖

紙地。寶笈重編著錄。下端有「臣金廷標恭畫」題款。縱壹百肆拾貳·伍公分。橫捌拾玖·柒公分。

171. Chin T'ing-piao "Nan Ni T'u"

Dredging Mud.

一七二 清徐揚
雨景山水

紙地。下端有「臣徐揚恭寫」題款。縱柒拾玖公分。橫叁拾陸·柒公分。

徐揚(約 1750)。號雲亭。吳縣人。官內閣中書。

172. Hsu Yang "Yu Ching Shan Shui"

A Rainy Scene.

Hsu Yang (circa 1750).—Hsu Yang, with the pseudonym of Yun-ting (雲亭), was a native of Wuhsien, in Kiangsu. He served as secretary of the grand secretariat.

(252)

一七三 清丁觀鵬 摹宋人漁樂圖

紙地。寶笈重編著錄。下端有「乾隆十二年十月臣丁觀鵬」題款。縱叁拾·肆公分。横叁拾·玖公分。

丁觀鵬(約 1750)。乾隆時供奉內廷。

173. Ting Kuan-peng "Mo Sung Jen Yu Lo T'u"

Angler's Happiness, After the Style of a Sung Artist.

Ting Kuan-peng (circa 1750).—Ting Kuan-peng was a painter attendant to the Imperial Court in Ch'ien Lung's time.

(254)

附

一七四 清郎世寧 山水

絹地。右下角有「臣郎世寧恭畫」題款。有破損。縱壹百肆拾叁·陸公分。橫捌拾玖·貳公分。

郎世寧(生卒年不詳)。意大利人。工翎毛花卉。以海西法爲之。

174. Lang She-ning "Shan Shui"

Landscape.

Lang She-ning (Giuseppe Gastiglione).—An Italian. A good painter of animals and flowers in the western manner.

一七五

清郎世寧

瓶中富貴圖

絹地。寶笈三編著錄。左下角有「臣郎世寧恭畫」題款。有蟲蛀。縱壹百壹拾叁·陸公分。橫伍拾玖·陸公分。

175. Lang She-ning

(Giuseppe Gastiglione)

"Ping Chung Fu Kuei T'u"

Peonies in a Vase.

以上各件除註明故物陳列所外。均古宮博物院藏。

(72422C)

參加倫敦中國藝術國際展覽會出品圖說

第三冊　書畫

Illustrated Catalogue of Chinese Government Exhibits for the International Exhibition of Chinese Art in London

Volume III Painting and Calligraphy

編輯者　倫敦中國藝術國際展覽會籌備委員會

發行人　王雲五　上海河南路

印刷所　商務印書館　上海河南路

發行所　商務印書館　上海及各埠

（本書校對者翁際雲）

定價國幣伍元　外埠酌加運費匯費

中華民國二十五年四月初版

参加伦敦中国艺术国际展览会出品图说

第 四 册　其他类

ILLUSTRATED CATALOGUE OF CHINESE GOVERNMENT EXHIBITS FOR THE INTERNATIONAL EXHIBITION OF CHINESE ART IN LONDON

VOLUME IV.　MISCELLANEOUS

伦敦中国艺术国际展览会筹备委员会编辑

中央编译出版社
CCTP Central Compilation & Translation Press

图书在版编目 (CIP) 数据

参加伦敦中国艺术国际展览会出品图说 / 伦敦中国艺术国际展览会筹备委员会主编 . -- 北京 : 中央编译出版社 , 2022.9

ISBN 978-7-5117-4241-4

Ⅰ . ①参… Ⅱ . ①伦… Ⅲ . ①历史文物 – 中国 – 图集

Ⅳ . ① K870.2

中国版本图书馆 CIP 数据核字 (2022) 第 153392 号

参加伦敦中国艺术国际展览会出品图说

责任编辑 郑永杰
特约编辑 刘诗婷 杨 凌
责任印制 刘 慧
出版发行 中央编译出版社
地 址 北京市海淀区北四环西路 69 号 (100080)
电 话 (010) 55627391 (总编室) (010) 55627312 (编辑室)
(010) 55627320 (发行部) (010) 55627377 (新技术部)
经 销 全国新华书店
印 刷 山东韵杰文化科技有限公司
开 本 889 毫米 ×1194 毫米 1/16
字 数 321 千字
印 张 50.25
版 次 2022 年 9 月第 1 版
印 次 2022 年 9 月第 1 次印刷
定 价 980.00 元 (全四册)

新浪微博： @ 中央编译出版社 **微 信：** 中央编译出版社 (ID：cctphome)
淘宝店铺： 中央编译出版社直销店 (http://shop108367160.taobao.com)
(010) 55627331

本社常年法律顾问： 北京市吴栾赵阎律师事务所律师 闫军 梁勤
凡有印装质量问题，本社负责调换，电话： (010) 55626985

參加倫敦中國藝術國際展覽會出品圖說

第四冊　其他類

ILLUSTRATED CATALOGUE OF CHINESE GOVERNMENT EXHIBITS FOR THE INTERNATIONAL EXHIBITION OF CHINESE ART IN LONDON

VOLUME IV.　MISCELLANEOUS

倫敦中國藝術國際展覽會籌備委員會編輯
商務印書館印行

第　四　册

其　他　類

Volume IV

MISCELLANEOUS

參加倫敦中國藝術國際展覽會

其他類照片目錄

名稱	件數	頁數
(一) 織繡	二十九件	一
(二) 玉器 水晶、瑪瑙、青田石、雄精、犀角、銀器等附。(另附張乃驥(叔馴)先生參加倫敦中國藝術國際展覽會玉器六十五件簡目)	七十件	三十一
(三) 景泰藍	十六件	六十九
(四) 剔紅	五件	八十三
(五) 摺扇	二十柄	八十九
(六) 傢具文具	十九件	一百零三
(七) 考古選例	一百十三件	一百一十七
(八) 珍本古書	五十種	一百五十五

總共叄百捌拾柒件

TABLE OF CONTENTS

PAGE

1. Tapestry and Embroidery 1

2. Jade (Including Crystal, Agate, Ch'ing T'ieng Stone, Hsiung Ching Stone, Rhinoceros Horn, and Silver, and a Supplementary List of Jade Lent by Mr. Ch'ang Nai-chi) 31

3. Cloisonné 69

4. Red Lacquer 83

5. Fans 89

6. Furniture and Writing Accessories 103

7. Archæological Exhibits 117

8. Ancient Books 155

織　　　　繡

TAPESTRY AND EMBROIDERY

參加倫敦中國藝術國際展覽會
織繡照片目錄
TAPESTRY AND EMBROIDERY

宋
SUNG DYNASTY (960–1279 A. D.)

一

宋緙絲花鳥　一軸（故宮博物院藏以下簡稱院）
絹地。寶笈三編著錄。有傷。縱肆拾伍·陸公分。橫肆拾玖·壹公分。

1. Birds and Flowers.

二

宋緙絲喜報生孫圖　一軸（院）

絹地。上端有「無逸齋精鑑璽」之章。有傷。縱壹百壹拾叁·叁公分。橫陸拾捌·伍公分。

2. Birds Rejoicing at the Sprouting of Bamboo Shoots.

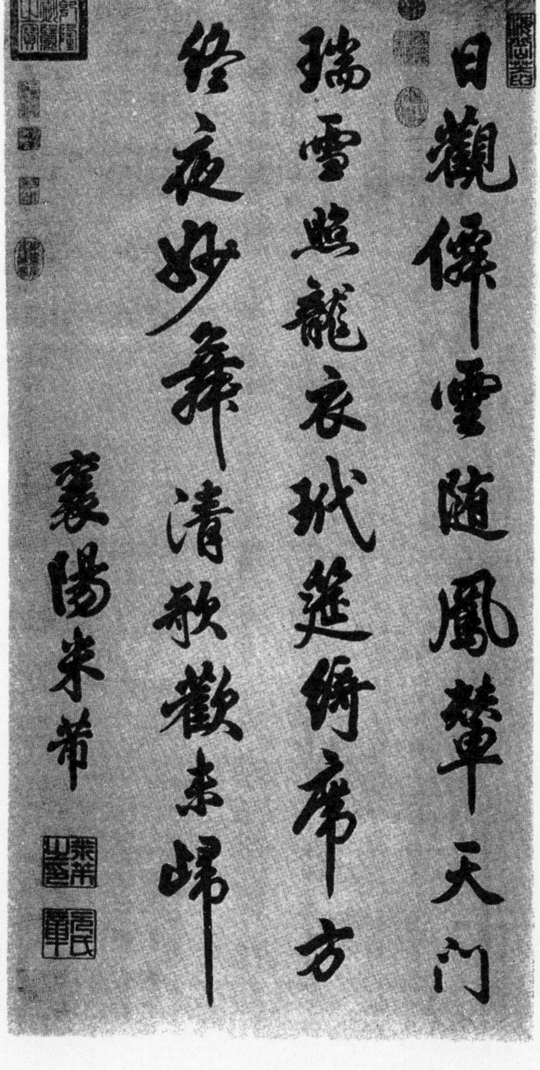

三

宋緙絲米芾書七言詩　一軸(院)

絹地。石渠寶笈御書房著錄。下端有「襄陽米芾」題款。縱壹百壹拾叁·壹公分。横伍拾伍·叁公分。

3. Mi Fei's Poem.

四

宋緙絲趙昌竹梅雙喜圖　一軸(院)

絹地。寶笈重編著錄。上端有「趙昌製」題款。有傷。縱玖拾玖·貳公分。橫肆拾貳公分。

4. Chao Ch'ang's Bamboos, Plum Blossoms, and Magpies.

(6)

五

宋緙絲羣仙祝壽圖　一·軸（院）

絹地。石渠寶笈御書房著錄。有傷。縱壹百肆拾叁·肆公分。横玖拾捌·柒公分。

5. Arhats Wishing Someone's Birthday.

六

宋緙絲山水　一軸（院）

絹地。寶笈重編著錄。縱玖拾·貳公分。橫叁拾伍·陸公分。

6. Landscape.

七

宋緙絲青牛老子圖　一軸（院）

絹地。上有「乾清宮鑒藏寶」等圖章。縱壹百零捌·叁公分。橫伍拾壹·柒公分。

7. Lao-tze on a Cow.

八

宋緙絲蓉塘戲鷺　一軸 (院)

絹地。寶笈三編著錄。有傷。縱壹百貳拾叁·玖公分。橫肆拾玖·叁公分。

8. Herons at Play.

九

宋緙絲和鳴鸞鳳圖　一軸（院）

絹地。寶笈三編著錄。有傷。縱壹百肆拾捌·柒公分。橫肆拾捌·柒公分。

9. Phœnixes Singing.

一〇

宋緙絲沈子蕃花鳥　一軸（院）

絹地。寶笈重編著錄。下端有「子蕃」題款。縱玖拾伍·玖公分。橫叁拾捌·肆公分。

10. Sheng Tze-p'an's Birds and Flowers.

一一

宋緙絲崔白天仙壽芝圖　一軸

(古物陳列所以下簡稱所)

絹地。上端中有「乾隆御覽之寶」壹方。下右端緙有「崔白製」三字及印章壹方。下左有「寶蘊樓書畫錄」章壹方。縱壹百零貳·陸公分。橫肆拾伍公分。

11. Rocks and Plants after Ts'ui Po.

一二

宋緙絲陳居中天仙拱壽圖

一軸（院）

絹地。寶笈重編著錄。上端有「陳居中製」題款。縱玖拾玖·叁公分。橫肆拾貳·貳公分。

12. Flowers and Birds, after Ch'en Chu-chung.

一三

宋緙絲蟠桃獻壽圖　一軸(院)

絹地。石渠寶笈養心殿著錄。詩堂有「御題」繡字。連詩堂縱壹百肆拾柒·柒公分。橫伍拾肆·叁公分。

13. Peaches.

一四

宋繡大士像　一軸（院）

綾地。祕殿新編著錄。縱捌拾柒公分。橫肆拾捌·陸公分。

14. Bodhisattva (Embroidery).

一五

宋繡白鷹　一軸（院）

絹地。寶笈重編著錄。有傷補。縱壹百零柒·柒公分。橫伍拾伍公分。

15. White Eagle (Embroidery).

元

YUAN DYNASTY (1279–1368 A. D.)

一六

元繡先春四喜　一·軸（院）

絹地。寶笈三編著錄。縱捌拾柒公分。橫肆拾捌·肆公分。

16. Birds in Spring (Embroidery).

明

MING DYNASTY (1368–1644 A. D.)

一七

明緙絲戲嬰圖　一軸（院）

絹地、寶笈重編著錄、有傷、縱陸拾叁·貳公分。橫捌拾捌·捌公分。

17. Children at Play.

一八

明織崔白花卉　一軸(院)

絹地。石渠寶笈養心殿著錄。下端有「崔白製」題款。有傷。縱壹百零貳·叁公分。横肆拾肆·捌公分。

18. In Imitation of Ts'ui Po's Flowers.

一九

明織竹杖化龍圖　　一軸（院）

絹地。石渠寶笈養心殿著錄。有傷。縱玖拾伍·叁公分。橫肆拾貳·柒公分。

19. Bamboo Stick Changing into a Dragon.

（ 20 ）

清

CH'ING DYNASTY (1644–1912 A. D.)

二〇

清綼絲村農韶慶圖　一軸（院）

絹地。寶笈重編著錄。縱捌拾捌·伍公分。橫陸拾陸·壹公分。

20. Springtime in the Country.

二一

清緙絲銅柱銘勳圖　　一軸（院）

絹地。寶笈三編著錄。有微傷。縱壹百叁拾叁·壹公分。橫陸拾肆·壹公分。

21. Memorial of Great Deeds.

二二

清緙絲李靖遇虬髯公圖 一軸（院）

絹地。寶笈重編著錄。縱壹百壹拾陸·伍公分。橫陸拾·伍公分。

22. Li Ch'ing Meeting Ch'iu Yen Kung.

二三

清緙絲周處擊蛟圖

一軸（院）

絹地。寶笈三編著錄。縱壹百肆拾壹公分。橫柒拾貳柒公分。

23. Chou Ch'u Fighting the Dragon.

二四

清緙絲御題周文矩大禹治水圖　一軸（院）

絹地。寶笈重編著錄。本幅連上下題字縱貳百叁拾叁·玖公分。橫捌拾陸·柒公分。

24. Emperor Yu Overcoming the Deluge.

二五

清緙絲白蘋紅蓼圖　一軸（院）

絹地。寶笈重編著錄。縱肆拾·壹公分。橫陸拾柒·捌公分。

25. Red Polygonums and White Pin Flowers.

二六

清緙絲武王受丹書圖 ·軸（院）

絹地，寶笈重編著錄。有蟲蛀。縱壹百壹拾·捌公分。横肆拾叁·陸公分。

26. Emperor Wu Receiving the Tan Book.

二七

清緙絲春溪浴鴨圖　　一軸(院)

絹地寶笈重編著錄縱壹百零陸·柒公分、橫肆拾陸·貳公分。

27. Ducks Bathing in a Stream in Spring.

二八

清緙絲荷花　一軸（院）

絹地。上端有「宣統御覽之寶」。縱壹百貳拾貳·陸公分。橫伍拾捌·柒公分。

28. Lotus Flowers.

二九

清緙絲場圃秋成圖　一軸（院）

絹地。寶笈重編著錄。縱捌拾捌·陸公分。橫陸拾伍·玖公分。

29. Garnering and Winnowing of the Autumn Harvest.

玉 器

水晶、瑪瑙、青田石、雄精、犀角、銀器等附

(另附張乃驥(叔馴)先生參加倫敦中國藝術國際展覽會玉器六十五件簡目)

JADE

(Including Crystal, Agate, Ch'ing T'ieng Stone, Hsiung Ching Stone, Rhinoceros Horn, and Silver, and a Supplementary list of Jade Lent by Mr. Ch'ang Nai-chi.)

參加倫敦中國藝術國際展覽會
玉器照片目錄
JADE

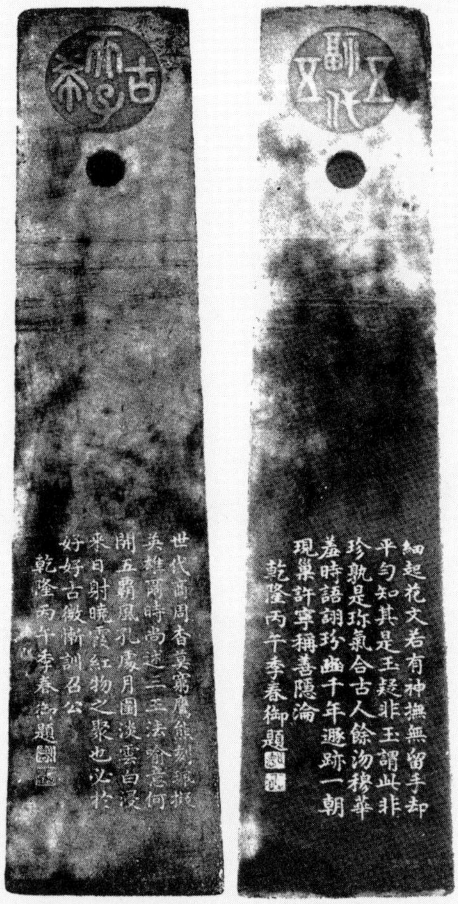

一

舊玉圭　一件(院)

原名「漢玉圭」.兩面上鐫「古希天子」及「五福五代」陽文兩寶.下鐫「乾隆御題」.最寬柒·壹公分.最長叁拾·陸公分.最厚壹·貳公分.重市秤拾玖兩肆錢.

1.　Kuei of Old Jade.

It has a wooden stand. Engraved on it on one side are the characters "Ku Hsi T'ien Tze," and on the other side are the characters "Wu Fu Wu Tai." Underneath is carved Ch'ien-lung's inscription.

二

舊玉圭　一件(院)

原名「漢玉圭」帶木匣.錦袱線繐.繐帶玉豆貳粒.匣蓋刻「庇豐式古」四字.圭最寬肆·捌公分。長拾貳·壹公分最厚零·玖公分.連繐及玉豆共重市秤肆兩陸錢.

2.　Kuei of Old Jade.

Wrapped in brocade. With a box, carved with dragons. The top of the box is carved with four characters "Pi Feng Shih Ku."

三

舊玉素璧　一件（院）

原名「舊玉插屏」。帶木座。璧上有「乾隆御題」。直徑拾叁•捌公分。孔徑伍•陸公分。厚零•伍公分。重市秤伍兩陸錢。

3. A Plain Piece of Old Jade.

It has a wooden stand. On it is engraved Ch'ien-lung's inscription.

四

舊玉琮　一件（院）

原名「漢玉槓頭」。帶木座。座破。高貳·捌公分。最寬伍·肆公分。孔徑肆·陸公分。重市秤叁兩肆錢。

4. An Octagonal-Shaped Piece of Old Jade with a Ring Hole in Its Center.

With a wooden stand.

五

舊玉璜　一件（院）

原名「漢玉璜」。帶木架。架傷。璜最寬叁·柒公分。最長拾貳·肆公分。厚零·肆公分。連架共重市秤捌兩正。

5. Huang of Old Jade.

With a wooden stand.

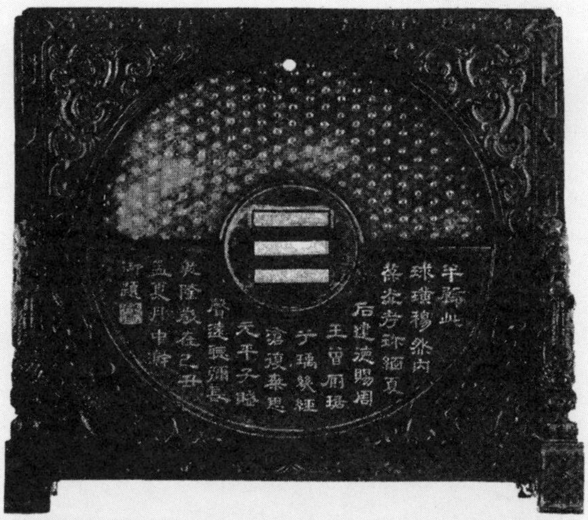

六

舊玉璜　一件（院）

原名「漢玉半璧」。璜邊刻有「乾隆御題」。帶木架；架嵌有銅字「乾隆御題」。璜最寬陸公分，最長拾柒·捌公分。最厚零·陸公分；重市秤肆兩捌錢。

6. Huang of Old Jade.

With Ch'ien-lung's inscription on its wooden stand.

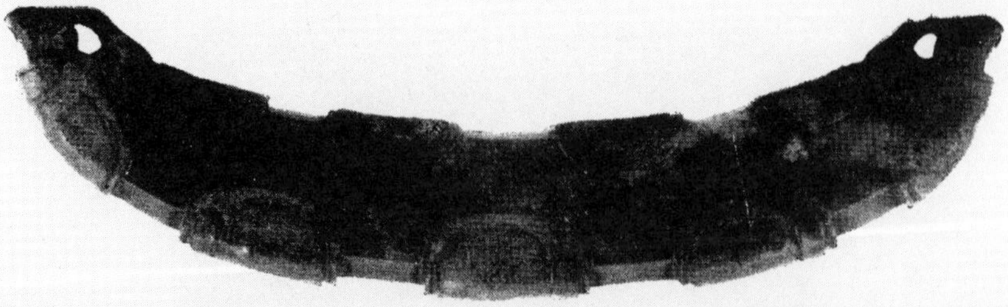

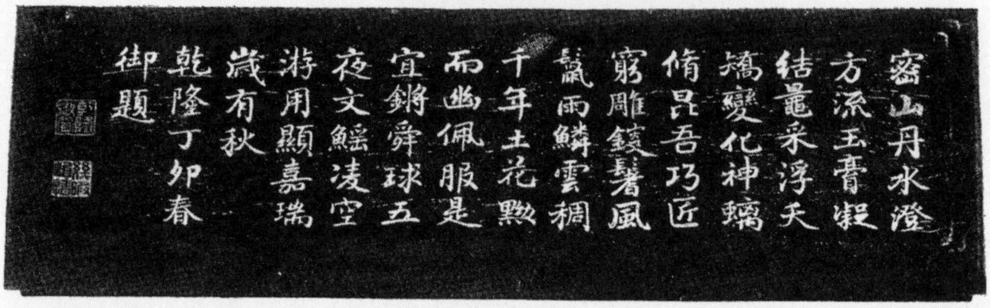

七

舊玉瓏 一件(院)

原名「舊玉璜」。帶木座。座上刻「乾隆御題」。最長貳拾·叁公分。最寬叁·柒公分最高壹·伍公分。重市秤捌兩肆錢。

7. Fine Open-Work Carving of Old Jade.

It has a wooden stand. On the stand is carved Ch'ien-lung's inscription.

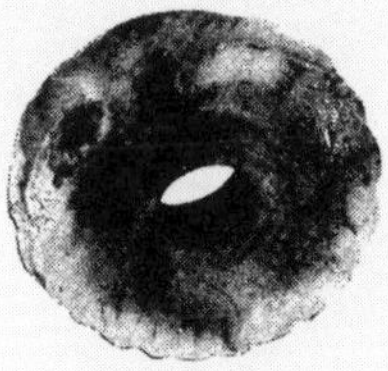

八

舊玉環 一件(院)

原名「漢玉環」。帶漆盒。直徑伍·貳公分。厚貳公分。重市秤貳兩捌錢。

8. Ring of Old Jade.

With a lacquer box.

九

舊玉璧

舊玉環

舊玉瑗(院)

以上三件。原名「漢玉壽環」。帶嵌玉三層小盒一件。盒底有「朴崖鑒賞」四字楷款。內附嘉慶御書小册頁三册。均四開。璧直徑肆·捌公分。孔徑壹·玖公分。厚零·貳公分。環直徑肆·陸公分。孔徑貳·肆公分。厚零·肆公分。瑗直徑肆·伍公分。孔徑叁·貳公分。厚零·捌公分。共重市秤壹兩貳錢。

9. Pi of Old Jade.
Ring of Old Jade.
A Large Ring of Old Jade.

The above three pieces are contained in a round box, carved with dragons, bearing the inscription "Pu Ya Chien San." On top of the box is inserted a jade ring. There are also in it three small albums written by Chia-ching.

一〇

舊玉璧　　一件(院)

原名「漢玉璧」。實係木盒上之嵌件。直徑陸·玖公分。孔徑貳·柒公分。連木盒共重市秤肆兩肆錢。

舊玉環　　一件(院)

原名「漢玉環」。直徑最長柒·柒公分。高叁·壹公分。重市秤叁兩捌錢。

舊玉魚　　一件(院)

原名「漢玉琀」。最長伍·伍公分。最高叁·壹公分。重市秤壹兩正。以上三件。合成圓盒形。

10. Pi of Old Jade.

Ring of Old Jade.

Fish of Old Jade.

The above three pieces when put together have the appearance of a round box.

一一

舊玉璪　　一件(院)

原名「漢玉素璧」。帶雕漆盒。盒傷。直徑伍·叁公分。最厚壹·叁公分。重市秤貳兩正。雕漆盒口徑陸·叁公分。通蓋高肆·貳公分。

11. Chi of Old Jade.

With a carved box in red lacquer.

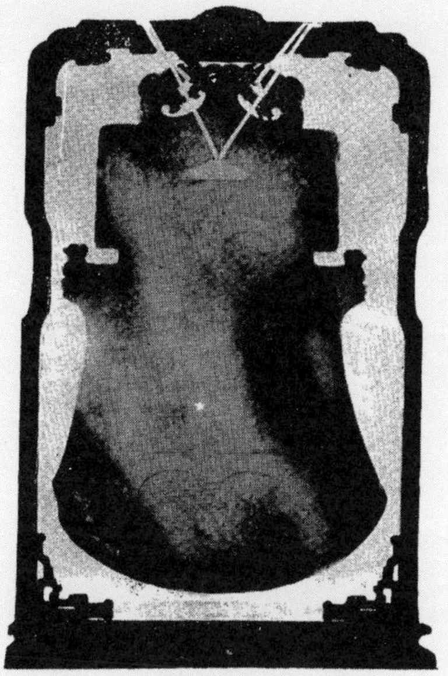

一二

舊玉戚　一件（院）

原名「舊玉磬」。帶木架。最寬拾肆公分。最長貳拾叁·貳公分。最厚零·捌公分。重市秤拾玖兩貳錢。

12. Ch'i of Old Jade.

With a wooden stand.

一三

舊玉辟邪　一件（院）

原名「漢玉飛馬」。上有「乾隆御題」。帶木座。座上刻「乾隆御玩」及「乾隆御題」。最高玖·伍公分。最寬拾叁公分。最厚叁·肆公分。重市秤拾壹兩陸錢。

13. Pi Hsieh of Old Jade.

It has a wooden stand, on which are carved "Ch'ien-lung's Plaything," and Chien-lung's inscription.

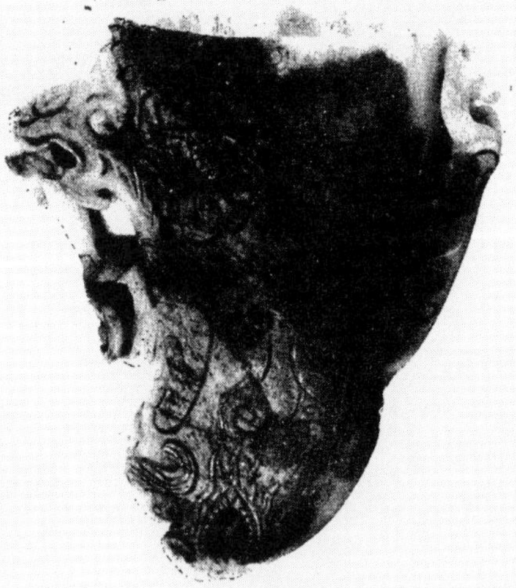

一四

舊玉蟠龍觥　　一件(院)

原名「舊玉觥」內口沿有「乾隆御題」。帶木座。座底刻「乾隆御題」有緒口縱伍·捌公分。横玖·叁公分。高拾肆·伍公分。重市秤拾陸兩正。

14. Dragon-Carved Wine Cup of Old Jade.

With a wooden stand bearing Ch'ien-lung's inscription.

一五

舊玉蟠龍觥　　一件(院)

原名「漢玉瓶」帶木座座上刻有「商山品帰兌式」六字。最高拾捌公分最寬拾·叁公分重市秤拾柒兩肆錢

15. Dragon-Carved Wine Cup of Old Jade.

With a wooden stand.

一六

舊玉杯　　一件(院)

原名「漢玉羽觴洗」。帶木座。底有「乾隆年製」篆款。口縱玖公分。横拾壹·壹公分。高叁·捌公分。重市秤捌兩貳錢。

16. Cup of Old Jade Stamped with the Inscription "Made in Ch'ien-lung's Reign."

With a wooden stand.

一七

舊玉雙桮　　二件（院）

原名「漢玉雙桮」。一件桮內刻有「題漢玉雙桮詩序」。一件桮內刻有「乾隆御題」。帶木座。一個座上刻有「題漢玉雙桮詩序」。口徑均肆公分。高柒·捌公分。底徑叁·貳公分。共重市秤肆兩捌錢。

17. A Pair of Cups of Old Jade.

With a wooden stand, bearing an Imperial inscription.

一八

舊玉雙螭桮　　一件（院）

原名「舊玉螭虎把桮」。帶雕龍紫檀匣及木座。盒壁刻乾隆御製「玉桮記」。口徑陸·伍公分。通耳高伍·肆公分。底徑叁·貳公分。重市秤肆兩正。

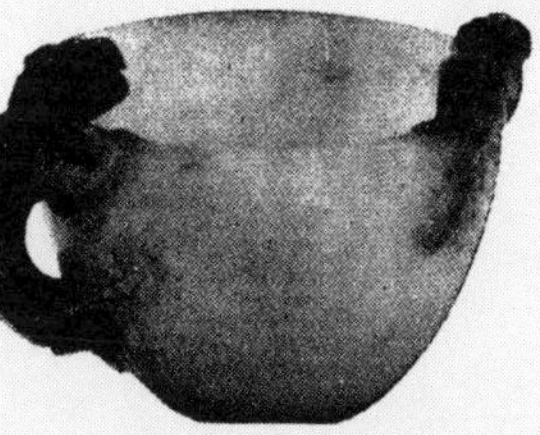

18. Cup of Old Jade, Carved with a Pair of Lizards.

With a wooden stand and teak box, carved with dragons. On the box is Ch'ien-lung's writing entitled "Yu Pei Chi."

一九

舊玉單把桮　　一件（院）

原名「漢玉帶把桮」。帶木座。口徑肆·柒公分。高拾貳·貳公分。底徑叁·壹公分。重市秤叁兩捌錢。

19. A Cup with One Handle, Made of Old Jade.

With a wooden stand.

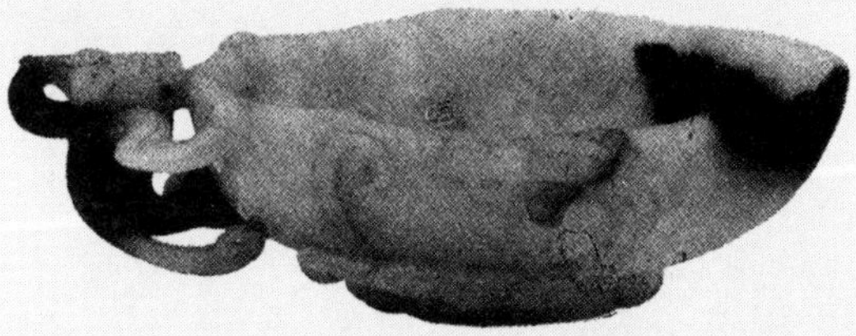

二〇

舊玉螭把海棠式洗　一件(院)

原名「白漢玉洗子」。口縱玖·貳公分。橫拾壹·玖公分。通耳長拾伍公分。高肆·貳公分。底縱肆·伍公分。橫伍·捌公分。重市秤柒兩正。

20. A Writing-Brush Washer of Old Jade, Shaped Like a Crab-Apple Blossom, with a Lizardlike Handle.

二一

舊玉刀　一件(所)

刀口長貳拾捌·伍公分。(刀頭至刀柄計)刀闊叁·捌公分。重市秤叁兩壹錢強。

21. Knife of Old Jade.

With a brocade box, edged with bamboo.

二二

舊玉鵝　一件(院)

原名「漢玉鵝」。帶木座。座底嵌有「乾隆御題」。最高肆·貳公分。最寬伍·柒公分。最厚壹·玖公分。重市秤貳兩正。

22. Goose of Old Jade.

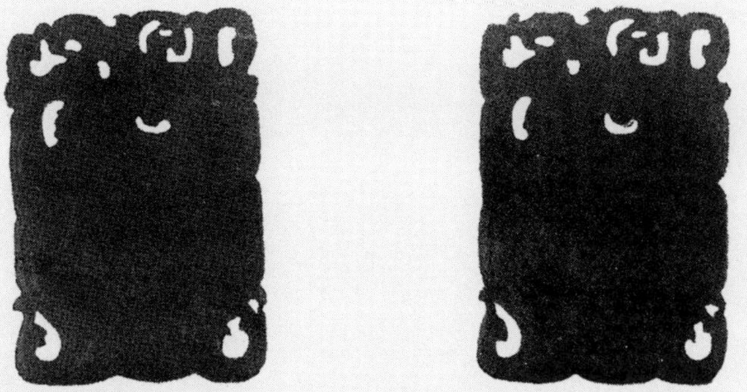

二三

白玉夔紋方珮　二件（院）

原名「羊脂玉珮」。邊上刻有「乾隆年製」四字篆款。帶木座。座有傷。均縱伍·壹公分。均橫柒·玖公分。均厚零·陸公分。均重市秤貳兩貳錢。

23. Square Pendants of White Jade with Serpent Design.

With wooden stands.

二四

白玉瑞獸尊　一件（院）

口沿有「大清乾隆倣古」六字隸款。帶木座。高貳拾貳·壹公分。口縱拾·貳公分。橫肆·壹公分。重市秤伍拾貳兩正。

24. Animal-Shaped Wine Cup of White Jade.

With a wooden stand.

(44)

二五

白玉兕觥一件(院)

原名「青白玉虎首匜」。底有「大清乾隆倣古」隸款。帶玉蓋。蓋有「乾隆御題」。有綹。通蓋最高柒·捌公分口縱最大陸·叁公分。橫拾伍公分。底縱伍公分。橫柒·伍公分。連蓋共重市秤貳拾叁兩陸錢。

25. A Wine Cup of White Jade Carved in the Shape of a Cowlike Animal.

Underneath are engraved in Ku Chuan characters "Ch'ien-lung of the Ch'ing Dynasty." On the cover of the wine cup is carved Ch'ien-lung's inscription.

二六

白玉觥　一件(院)

原名「漢玉觶」。帶木座。座破。最高拾貳·貳公分。口最長拾·貳公分。口最寬陸·貳公分。重市秤拾陸兩捌錢。

26. Wine Cup of White Jade.

With a wooden stand.

二七

白玉蟠夔小方壺　一件(院)

原名「青白玉蟠夔方壺」。底有「大清乾隆倣古」六字楷款。帶木座及玉蓋。口縱叁公分。橫叁·叁公分。通玉蓋頂高拾叁·貳公分。底縱貳·玖公分。橫叁·貳公分。最大腹圍貳拾·伍公分。重市秤拾兩肆錢。

27. Small Square Pot of White Jade with a Coiled Serpent Design.

With a jade cover and a wooden stand.

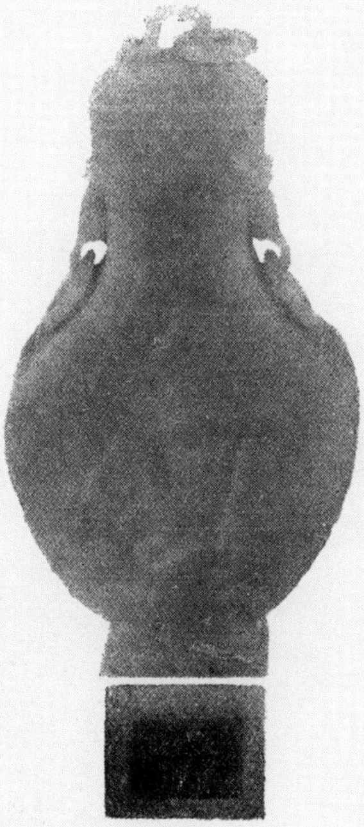

二八

白玉穀紋扁方瓶　一件（院）

原名「青白玉乳丁扁方瓶」。帶木座及玉蓋。通蓋高拾捌·玖公分。口縱叁·貳公分橫肆·貳公分。底縱貳·陸公分。橫叁·陸公分。重市秤拾兩捌錢。

28. Flat Square Vase of White Jade, with a Design of Some Grain-Producing Plant.

With a jade cover and a wooden stand.

二九

白玉桮　一件（院）

原名「白玉羽觴」。帶木座。口縱陸·肆公分。橫玖公分。高貳·伍公分。底縱肆公分。橫伍·捌公分。重市秤叁兩貳錢。

29. Cup of White Jade.

With a wooden stand.

三〇

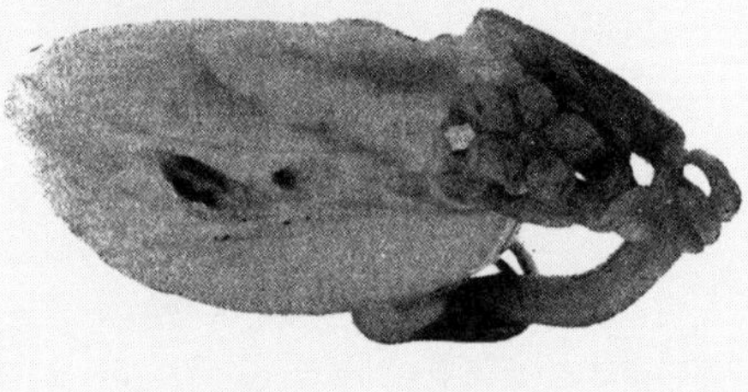

白玉鸚鵡蟠桃桮　一件（院）

原名「漢玉鸚鵡桃式桮」。帶木座。最寬捌·肆公分。最長拾貳·陸公分。最高伍·肆公分。重市秤伍兩正。

30. Cup of White Jade, with a Peach-and-Parrot Design.

With a wooden stand.

三一

白玉雕花盌　一件(院)

原名「痕都斯坦白玉洗」。口徑拾叁·陸公分。高叁·玖公分。底徑陸·伍公分。重市秤叁兩正。

31. A Bowl of White Jade, Carved with Flowers.

三二

白玉茶壺　一件(院)

底有「嘉慶御用」四字隸款。通玉蓋高拾·柒公分。口徑柒·伍公分。通嘴柄長拾陸·柒公分。底徑陸·捌公分。重市秤貳拾貳兩陸錢。

32. Teapot of White Jade.

Stamped with an inscription in Li-shu style "For Emperor Chia-ching's Use."

(48)

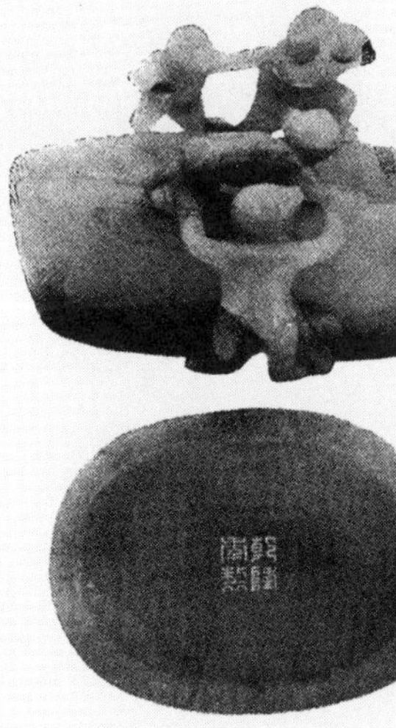

三三

白玉五子洗　一件 (院)

底有「乾隆年製」四字篆款。口橫拾壹·壹公分。最高柒·叁公分。重市秤拾貳兩捌錢。

33. A Writing-Brush Washer of White Jade, with Figures of Five Children.

With the inscription "Made in Ch'ien-lung's Reign."

三四

白玉玲瓏三友洗　一件 (院)

原名「青玉雕玲瓏洗」。帶木座。最高伍·陸公分。橫拾肆·伍公分。縱玖·陸公分。重市秤捌兩正。

34. A Writing-Brush Washer of White Jade, with Open-Work Carvings of Plum Blossoms, Bamboos and Pines.

With a wooden stand.

三五

白玉雕花雙耳三足爐　　一件（院）

無蓋。口徑拾貳·肆公分。通耳高玖·柒公分。最大腹圍肆拾貳·伍公分。重市秤貳拾貳兩捌錢。

35. Incense Burner of White Jade, Carved with Flowers.

Two ears and three legs.

三六

白玉四耳彝爐　　一件（院）

原名「白玉四足活環爐」。口徑拾·貳公分。通玉蓋頂高拾貳·捌公分。底徑捌·貳公分。最大腹圍叁拾玖·陸公分。連玉蓋共重市秤貳拾捌兩正。

36. Incense Burner of White Jade with Four Ears.

三七

黄玉穀紋方唾盂　　一件(院)

原名「黃玉乳丁痰盂」最高伍·肆公分縱捌·玖公分橫拾·玖公分重市秤拾玖兩陸錢。

37. A Square Yu of Yellow Jade, with a Design of Some Grain-Producing Plant.

三八

黄玉四螭橢圓洗　　一件(院)

原名「白玉螭虎洗」底有「乾隆年製」四字篆款帶木座最高柒·伍公分最長拾捌·伍公分。最寬拾叁·肆公分底縱捌·伍公分橫拾·肆公分重市秤貳拾肆兩肆錢

38. An Elliptical Writing-Brush Washer of Yellow Jade, with Four Lizards Carved on It.

With the inscription "Made in Ch'ien-lung's Reign."

(51)

三九

黃玉連環鈕印　一件係三方（所）

第一方通鈕高叁·玖公分強。橫叁·伍公分。縱貳·肆公分。底圍玖·陸公分。第二方通鈕高叁·陸公分。方徑貳·陸公分。方圍拾·貳公分。第三方通鈕高叁·伍公分。方徑貳·柒公分。方圍拾·貳公分。鍊環叁拾貳枚。三方共重市秤肆兩叁錢。

39. Three Seals, Connected Together by a Chain, of Yellow Jade.

With a brocade box.

四〇

碧玉雙耳活環菊瓣洗　一件（院）

原名「碧玉雙環菊瓣盤」。底有「乾隆年製」四字隸款。口徑貳拾伍·肆公分。通耳高捌·叁公分。底徑拾陸·肆公分。重市秤肆拾伍兩肆錢。

40. A Writing-Brush Washer of Pi Jade, with Two Ears, a Movable Ring, and Chrysanthemum Designs on It.

With the inscription "Made in Ch'ien-lung's Reign."

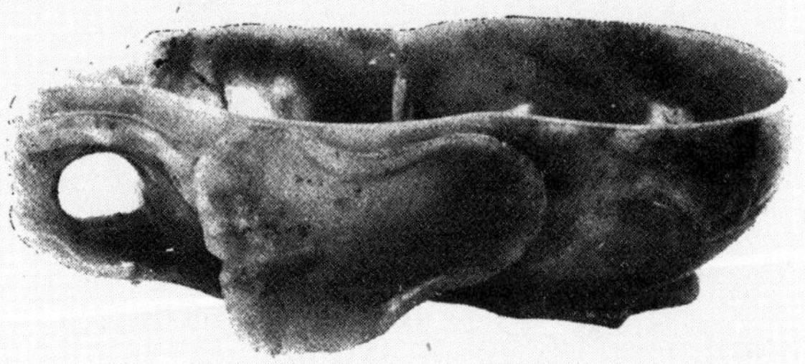

四一

碧玉纏枝葫蘆洗　　一件(院)

原名「青玉金枝葫蘆洗」。帶木座。高伍·叁公分。最長拾陸·肆公分。重市秤拾兩捌錢。

41. A Writing-Brush Washer of Pi Jade, with a Design of Intertwining Branches of the Gourd Plant on It.

四二

碧玉雕花龍耳爐　　一件(院)

原名「碧玉四足雕花雙耳盒」。帶玉蓋。通蓋高拾叁·壹公分。通耳長拾陸·伍公分。口縱陸·壹公分。橫拾·捌公分。底縱陸公分。橫拾·捌公分。重市秤叁拾玖兩貳錢。

42. Incense Burner of Pi Jade, with Flower Carvings and a Dragon-Shaped Ear.

It has a jade cover.

四三

碧玉石室藏書筆筒　一件(院)

原名「碧玉雕室石藏書筆筒」。口沿刻有「石室藏書」四隸字及「乾隆御題詩」。口徑拾肆·玖公分。高拾陸公分底徑拾肆·叁公分重市秤柒拾陸兩正。

43. A Shih Shih Ts'ang-Shu Writing-Brush Holder of Pi Jade Carved with a Picture of an Imperial Library.

With Ch'ien-lung's inscription on its mouth.

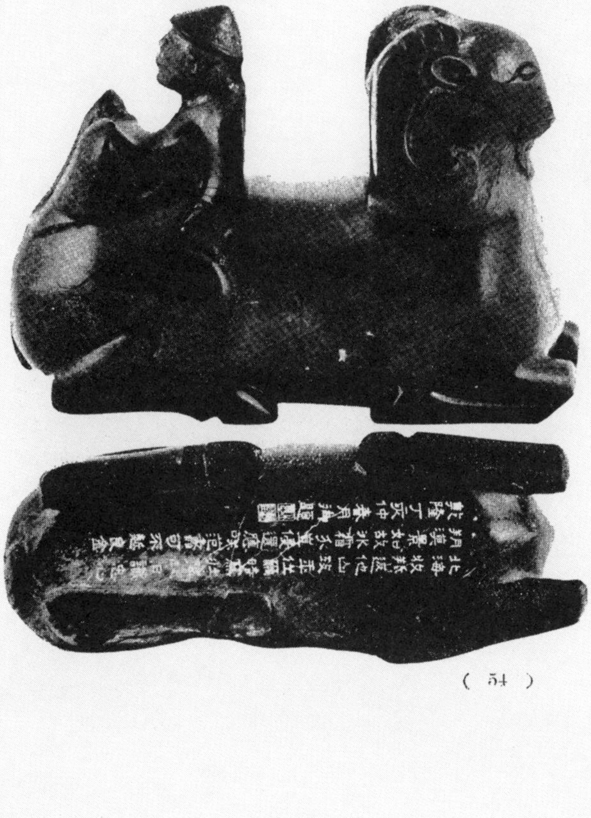

四四

墨玉北海牧羝　一件(院)

原名「墨玉牧羝」。底刻「乾隆御題」。帶木座。座底刻「乾隆御題」。有傷。最高拾壹·伍公分最長拾陸公分。重市秤伍拾叁兩正。

44. Piece of Jade in the Shape of a Lamb, with the Figure of a Shepherd Carved on It.

With Ch'ien-lung's inscription underneath. Its wooden stand has a poem cut into it, which has for its theme the carving on the jade.

(54)

四五

青玉降龍伏虎筆筒　一件（院）

原名「青玉筆筒」帶木座座上鐫有「乾隆御玩」四隸字。口徑玖·捌公分，高拾陸·貳公分，底徑玖·伍公分。腹圍叁拾壹公分，重市秤叁拾肆兩貳錢。

45. A Writing-Brush Washer of Ch'ing Jade, Carved with a Dragon and a Tiger.

四六

青玉雙魚吉慶香薰　一件（院）

原名「青玉雕花香盒」帶描金漆座及玉蓋蓋有傷。通蓋高肆·壹公分，横拾柒·壹公分，縱拾叁·叁公分。連蓋共重市秤拾貳兩正。

46. Incense Box of Ch'ing Jade, with Two Ears.

With a gilded lacquer stand.

四七

翠玉白玉韘　二件(院)

以上二件原名「玉搬指」帶嵌玉蓋銀盒。內一件係翠玉。高貳·陸公分。直徑叁·壹公分。又一件係白玉。高貳·捌公分。最寬叁·肆公分。共重市秤貳兩捌錢。

47. Two Thumb-Rings, One of White Jade and the Other of Ts'ui Jade.

With a silver box, which has jade inserted in it.

四八

翠玉蓋盌　一件(院)

帶玉蓋。口有傷。通玉蓋頂高捌·貳公分。口徑拾貳·壹公分。底徑肆·伍公分。共重市秤捌兩正。

48. Bowl with Cover Made of Ts'ui Jade.

四九

翠玉盌　二件(院)

原名「碧玉盌」以上二件。底均有「嘉慶年製」四字隸款。帶銀鍍金托蓋。托底均刻有「宣統二年泰興樓造京平足重叁兩叁錢」。蓋內均刻有「宣統二年泰興樓造京平足貳兩柒錢」。口徑均拾·玖公分。高伍·叁公分。底徑肆·陸公分。共重市秤拾兩正。

49. Bowl of Ts'ui Jade.

Made in Chia-ching's reign. With a gilded silver plate and cover.

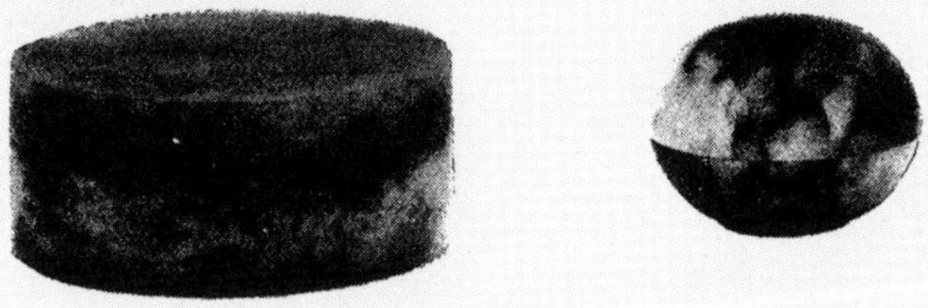

五〇

大小翠玉盒　二件(院)

以上二件。帶金雙桃形盒。一件底刻有「光緒十年三月日義和足金貳兩平重拾叁兩壹錢」。內一件通玉蓋高貳·伍公分。口徑底徑均伍·壹公分。一件通玉蓋高貳·陸公分。口徑叁·貳公分。底徑壹·伍公分。共重市秤肆兩正。金盒重市秤拾肆兩捌錢。

50. A Big and a Small Box of Ts'ui Jade.

They are put in a golden box which has the shape of two peaches.

五一

翠玉印泥盒　·件(院)

原名「翠玉印色盒」。帶木座。通玉蓋高貳·柒公分。口徑陸·柒公分。底徑肆公分。重市秤貳兩陸錢。

51. A Seal Vermilion Box of Ts'ui Jade.

With a wooden stand.

五二

翠玉松鶴插屏　一件（院）

原名「彫花插屏」。帶木座。座有傷。寬拾伍·肆公分。長貳拾壹·柒公分。厚壹公分。重市秤叁拾壹兩肆錢。

52. A Ts'ui Jade Screen with Carvings of Pine Trees and Herons.

With a wooden stand.

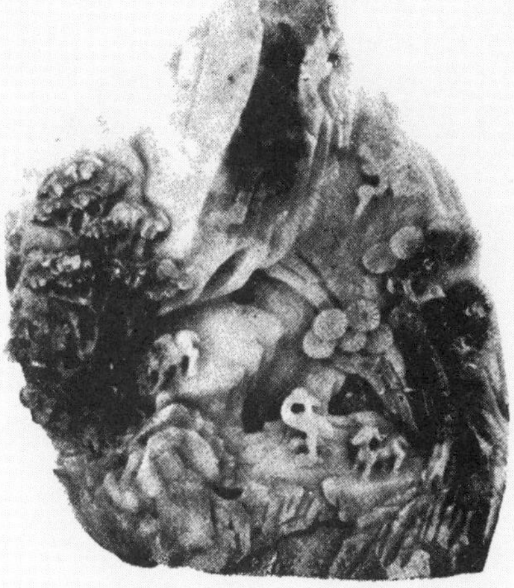

五三

翠玉松鶴山子　一件（院）

原名「雕刻翠石山子」。最高拾肆公分。最長拾壹·伍公分。最寬肆·伍公分。重市秤叁拾壹兩正。

53. A Ts'ui Jade Mountain with Pines and Herons.

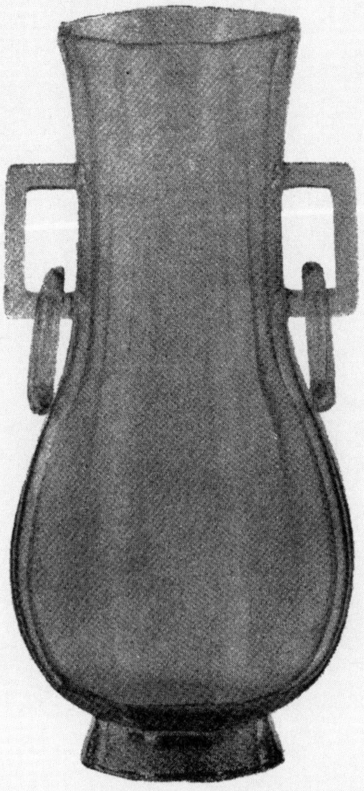

五四

水晶雙耳活環八方瓶　一件(院)

原名「水晶雙環瓶」。高貳拾壹·柒公分。口縱伍·捌公分。横陸·柒公分。底縱肆·伍公分。横伍·柒公分。重市秤貳拾兩貳錢。

54. An Octagonal-Shaped Crystal Vase, with Two Ears and a Movable Ring.

五五

紅瑪瑙巧作福壽花插　一件(院)

原名「紅瑪瑙筆洗」。有微傷。最高玖·捌公分。口縱最長伍·叁公分。横最長柒·壹公分。重市秤拾壹兩肆錢。

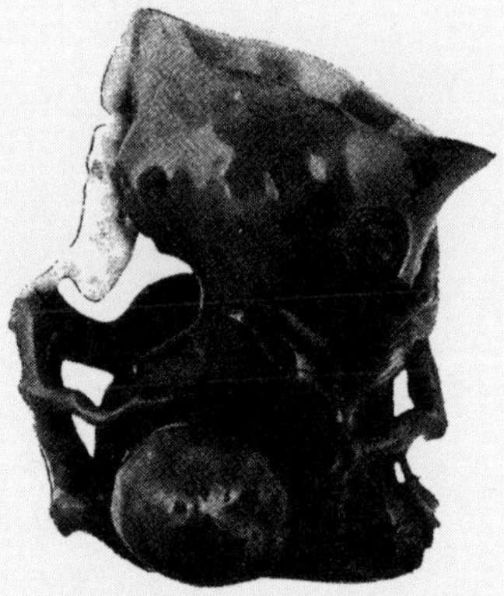

55. Red Agate Carved with Figures which Symbolize Long Life and Good Luck.

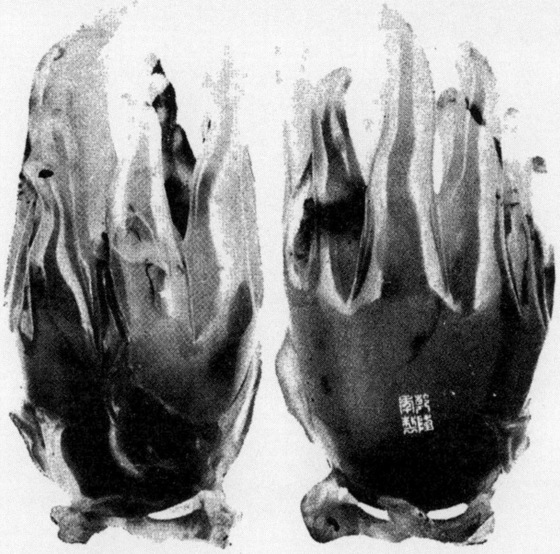

五六

瑪瑙佛手　一件(院)

原名「瑪瑙佛手花插」。帶木座。有「乾隆年製」四字篆款。最高拾肆·玖公分。最寬柒·壹公分。重市秤拾伍兩陸錢。

56. Agate Citron.

With inscription "Made in Ch'ien-lung's Reign" carved on its wooden stand.

五七

靑田石圖章　一件(院)

原名「凍石圖章」。帶嵌螺鈿木盒及錦袱木匣。通紐高拾伍·壹公分。縱橫均拾叁·叁公分。重市秤拾貳斤肆兩正。

57. A Seal of Ch'ing T'ieng Stone.

Originally called "Tung Shih," which may be the same as "Shou Shan Shih." The seal is wrapped up in brocade, and is put in a wooden box.

五八

雄精天中瑞景山子　一件(院)

上鐫「天中瑞景」四字。帶木座。最高貳拾叁·玖公分。最寬叁拾叁·柒公分。重市秤貳拾玖斤陸兩正。

58. T'ien Chung Jui Ching Mountain of Hsiung Ching Stone.

On it are engraved the four characters "T'ien Chung Jui Ching."

五九

雕龍犀角觥　一件(所)

底刻「子孫永寶」四字。連柄高拾貳·玖公分。口徑縱拾柒·貳公分。口徑橫拾壹公分。深捌·貳公分。重市秤拾陸兩肆錢。

59. A Wine Cup of Rhinoceros Horn, Carved with Dragons.

Underneath it are carved four characters "Tze Sun Yung Pao."

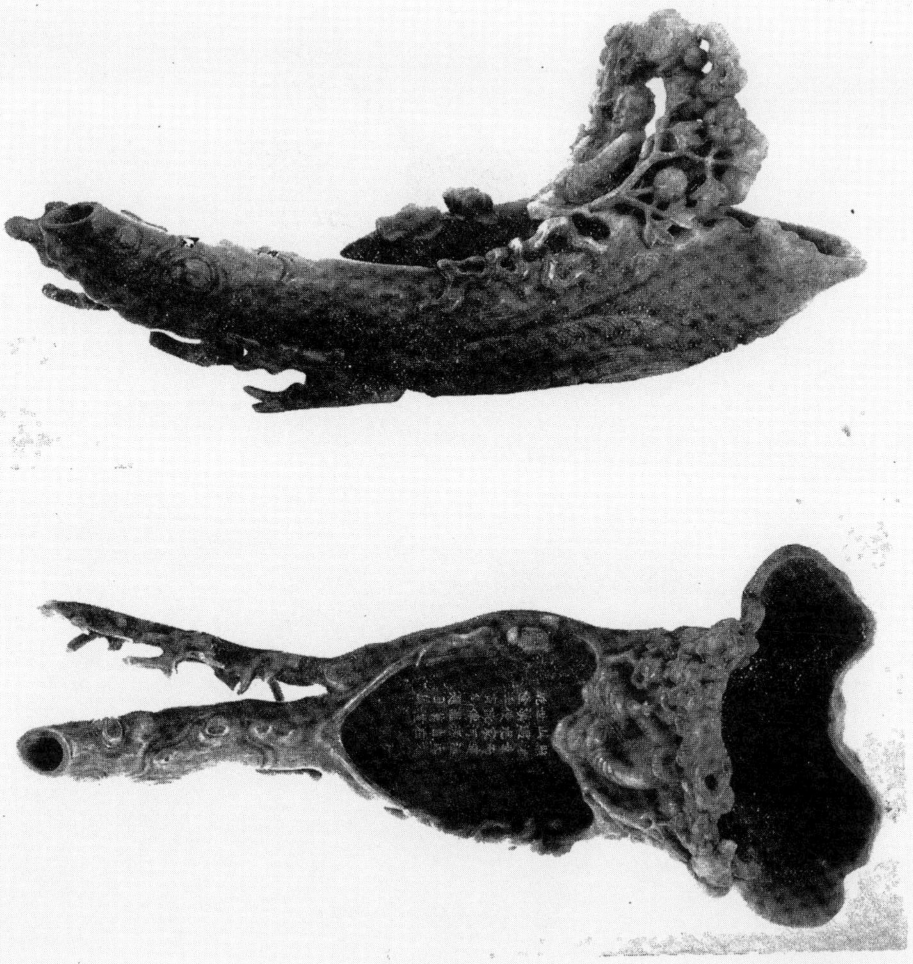

六〇

雕刻犀角桮　　·件(所)

鐫有「清高宗御製詩」高拾貳公分頭至尾長貳拾柒公分。腹深肆·玖公分。重市秤拾貳兩玖錢。

60. A Cup of Rhinoceros Horn with Carvings.

On it is engraved a poem composed by the Emperor Kao Chung of the Ch'ing Dynasty.

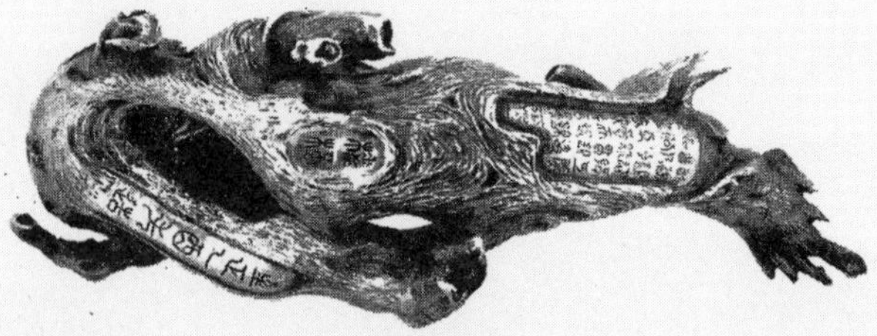

六一

元銀槎桮　一件(所)

鐫有「至正乙酉年造」六字。有銘。高拾伍·叁公分。長貳拾壹·壹公分。重市秤拾玖兩。

61. A Boat-Shaped Silver Cup of the Yuan Dynasty.

On it are engraved six characters "Chih Chen I Yu Nien Tsao."

另附張乃驥（叔馴）先生參加倫敦中國藝術國際展覽會玉器六十五件簡目

編號	名稱	件數	備考
(一)	玉箭頭	一	河南彰德府安陽出土
(二)	玉刀頭	一	仝上
(三)	出脊玉刀	一	仝上
(四)	出脊玉刀 有柄	一	仝上
(五)	出脊圓形玉柄	一	仝上
(六)	玉象頭	一	仝上
(七)	玉刀 有花紋	一	仝上
(八)	帶面具玉人	一	仝上
(九)	圓身玉獸頭	一	仝上
(一〇)	圓身玉虎	一	仝上
(一一)	玉蝗螂	一	仝上
(一二)	玉盤獸	一	仝上
(一三)	大玉蛹	一	仝上
(一四)	玉封泥印	一	仝上
(一五)	玉蟬	一	仝上
(一六)	玉四脚螭虎	一	仝上
(一七)	小玉熊 一面人面	一	仝上
(一八)	長耳玉兔	一	仝上
(一九)	陰文花薄片	一	仝上
(二〇)	圓身鳥	一	仝上
(二一)	長鈎魚	一	仝上
(二二)	出脊大玉魚	一	仝上
(二三)	出脊大玉魚	一	仝上
(二四)	有字陰紋花片	一	仝上
(二五)	玉魚形挖耳	一	河南省洛陽出土
(二六)	玉人形	一	仝上
(二七)	銀把玉刀	一	仝上
(二八)	玉鳥	一	仝上
(二九)	玉蛙蟆	一	仝上
(三〇)	玉牛頭	一	仝上

SUPPLEMENTARY LIST OF JADE

(LENT BY CH'ANG NAI-CHI, 張乃驥)

1. Jade Arrowhead.
2. Jade Knife Blade.
3. Jade Knife with Ridge.
4. Jade Knife with Ridge and Handle.
5. Round Jade Handle with Ridges.
6. Jade carved like an Elephant's Head.
7. Jade Knife with carvings.
8. Man with a Mask.
9. Round Piece of Jade carved like an Animal's Head.
10. Round Piece of Jade carved like a Tiger.
11. A Mantis-Shaped Piece of Jade.
12. Animal-Shaped Piece of Jade.
13. A Large Pupa-Shaped Piece of Jade.
14. A Jade Sea.
15. Cicada-Shaped Piece of Jade.
16. A Four-Legged Lizard of Jade.
17. A Small Piece of Jade, carved with a Bear on one side, and a Man's Face on the other.
18. Long-Eared Elephant of Jade.
19. A Chip of Jade with designs carved in it.
20. Round Piece of Jade carved like a Bird.
21. Long Fish-Shaped Hook.
22. A Large Fish of Jade.
23. A Large Fish of Jade.
24. A Chip of Jade with inscriptions and designs carved in it.
25. A Scooped-Out Ear of Jade, fishlike in shape.
26. Piece of Jade in the shape of a Man.
27. Jade Knife with Silver Handle.
28. Bird of Jade.
29. Frog of Jade.
30. A Cow's Head of Jade.

編號	名稱	件數	備考
(三一)	玉龜	一	河南省洛陽出土
(三二)	玉雁	二(一對)	仝上
(三三)	玉鳥 翼有小鳥二只	一	仝上
(三四)	玉龍璜	一	仝上
(三五)	蜜蠟花方塊	一	仝上
(三六)	蜜蠟鳳凰 均已斷	二(一對)	仝上
(三七)	玉人頭	一	傳世
(三八)	料小人	二 (共一盒)	仝上
(三九)	料人頭	一 (共一盒)	仝上
(四〇)	玉鏡	一	仝上
(四一)	鏤空花龍頭玉帶鈎	一	河南省洛陽金村出土
(四二)	滿花玉劍把	一	仝上
(四三)	金鱔骨鍊帶雷紋勒 計玉勒二蜜蠟珠二	一	仝上
(四四)	玉盤龍佩	一	仝上
(四五)	尖首帶花紋玉	一	仝上
(四六)	陰紋花玉蟬	一	仝上
(四七)	鏤龍鳳花紋玉雙連環	一	仝上
(四八)	八字玉璜	一	安徽省壽州出土
(四九)	雷文鏤空玉龍佩連 原有銅圈二	一	仝上
(五〇)	雷文花出脊梭式勒	一	仝上
(五一)	鏤粗細花玉璜	二(一對)	安徽省老虎山出土
(五二)	鐵心十三節玉龍鈎 失三節	一	仝上
(五三)	鏤空細花葉形玉刀柄	一	仝上
(五四)	鏤空龍文花圓片玉	一	仝上
(五五)	玉絞絲雙頭龍	一	仝上
(五六)	陰文雷文花瓶式玉片	一	仝上
(五七)	白玉粗細花紋四節刀把連刀柄鑲件 五小件合爲一付	一	仝上
(五八)	玉仝形立人	一	仝上
(五九)	素玉管	一	仝上
(六〇)	鎏金鑲骨細花小鐘形 此件出土時套在上件之中	一	仝上
(六一)	細花玉蟬	一	仝上

31. Turtle of Jade.
32. Wild Goose of Jade. Two pieces.
33. Bird of Jade, with two Small Birds on its wings.
34. Semicircular Piece of Dragon-Carved Jade, for hanging on the girdle.
35. Square Piece of Jade with Honeycoul design.
36. Phœnixes of Jade with Honeycoul design. Two pieces.
37. A Man's Head of Jade.
38. A Small Man of Jade. Two pieces.
39. Head of a Man of Jade.
40. Jade Mirror.
41. Jade Belt-Hook with open-work carving of a Dragon's Head.
42. Jade Sword Handle with Flower designs.
43. Jade Bridle, shaped like the bones of an Eel, with thunder pattern.
44. Jade Pendant with dragon-pattern design.
45. A Pointed Piece of Jade with carvings.
46. Jade Cicada, with designs carved on it.
47. Two Connected Rings, with open-work carvings of a Dragon and Phœnix.
48. Semicircular Piece of Jade with eight letters carved on it.
49. Jade Pendant with thunder pattern and open-work carving of a Dragon and two Brass Rings.
50. Jade Bridle with thunder pattern and projecting hanges.
51. Semicircular Piece of Jade with open-work carvings. Two pieces.
52. Jade Dragon-Shaped Hook, composed of thirteen pieces, with iron inside.
53. Leaf-Shaped Knife Handle with fine open-work carvings.
54. Round Piece of Jade with dragon-pattern open-work designs.
55. Doubled-Headed Dragon of Jade.
56. Piece of Jade, shaped like a Flower Vase, with thunder pattern.
57. Knife Handle of White Jade with carvings.
58. Jade in the shape of a Man standing.
59. Plain Jade Pipe.
60. Bone shaped like a Small Bell inlaid with gold.
61. Jade Cicada with five designs carved on it.

景　泰　藍

CLOISONNÉ

參加倫敦中國藝術國際展覽會
景泰藍照片目錄

CLOISONNÉ

一

景泰款景泰琺瑯三羊瓶　一件(院)

底有「大明景泰年造」六字楷款。有傷。口徑貳拾貳·肆公分。高叁拾玖·伍公分。底徑拾玖·壹公分。最大腹圍柒拾伍·柒公分。

1. Ching-t'ai Enamel Vase, with a Design of Three Sheep.

二

景泰款景泰藍花觚　一件（院）

底有「大明景泰年製」六字楷款。缺戟一件。有傷。口徑貳拾·壹公分。高叁拾柒·捌公分。底徑拾壹·叁公分。

2. Cloisonné Flower Vase, with Ching-t'ai Stamp.

One corner missing.

三

景泰款景泰藍海棠式雙耳花瓶一件(院)

底有「大明景泰年製」六字楷款。口徑拾貳·伍公分。橫拾肆·肆公分。高貳拾柒·玖公分。底徑拾壹·肆公分。橫拾叁·捌公分。

3. Cloisonné Flower Vase, with Two Ears.

Design of crab-apple blossoms. Ching-t'ai stamp.

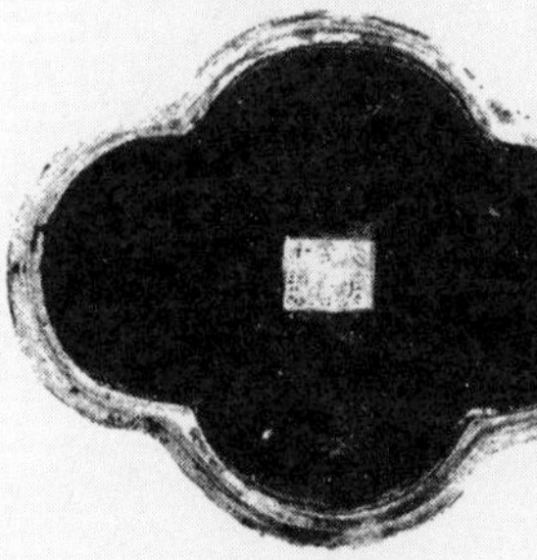

四

景泰款景泰琺瑯雙耳盂 ··件(院)

底有「景泰年製」四字楷款。口縱拾肆·貳公分。橫拾陸·叁公分。高拾肆公分。底縱玖·貳公分。橫拾·柒公分。最大腹圍叁拾捌·玖公分。

4. Ching-t'ai Enamel Bowl with Two Ears.

五

景泰款景泰藍三足盤　一件(院)

底有「大明景泰年製」六字楷款。口徑叁拾壹·叁公分。高拾貳公分。底徑貳拾肆公分。

5.　Cloisonné Plate with Three Legs.

With Ching-t'ai stamp.

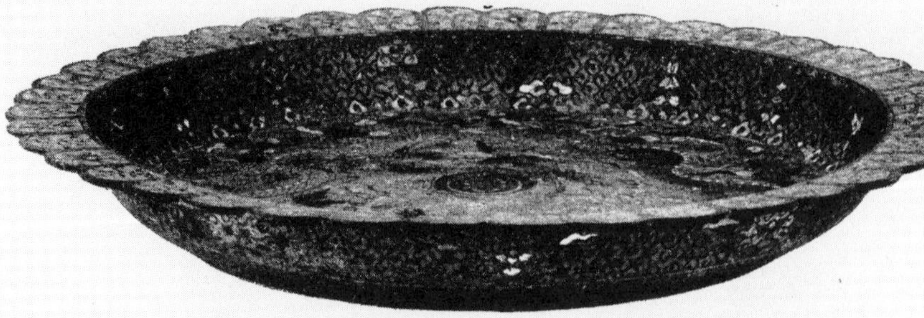

六

萬曆款景泰藍大盤　一件(院)

底有「大明萬曆年造」六字楷款。有傷。口徑肆拾叁公分。高陸捌公分。底徑叁拾壹公分。

6. Big Cloisonné Plate.

With Wan-li stamp.

七

乾隆款景泰藍犧尊　一件（院）

帶蓋。蓋上有「乾隆年製」四字楷款。通耳高貳拾·伍公分。最長貳拾捌·肆公分。最寬拾·貳公分。

7. Ch'ien-lung Cloisonné Goblet.

With cover.

八

乾隆款景泰藍雙連環瓶　　··件(院)

一環底有「大清乾隆年製」六字楷款。有微傷。一環口徑陸·伍公分。一環口徑伍·捌公分。最高貳拾柒公分。一環底徑捌·肆公分。一環底徑陸·陸公分。

8. Ch'ien-lung Cloisonné Vase.

With two connected rings.

(77)

九

康熙款銅胎畫琺瑯五彩牡丹黃地觀音瓶　一件(院)

底有「康熙御製」四字楷款。有傷。口徑玖公分。高叁拾肆·肆公分。底徑拾·叁公分。最大腹圍伍拾肆公分。

9. Vase, with Peony Flowers of Five Colors, and a Figure of Kwan-yin, on a Yellow Ground.

Enamel on a copper matrix. With K'ang-hsi stamp.

一〇

乾隆款金胎西洋琺瑯觀音瓶　一件(院)

底有「乾隆年製」四字楷款。口內有傷。口徑肆·叁公分。高貳拾·玖公分。底徑伍·壹公分。最大腹圍叁拾·玖公分。重市秤拾玖兩捌錢。

10. Ch'ien-lung Vase, with Figure of Kwan-yin on Western Enamel.

Gold matrix. Damaged inside the mouth.

一一

乾隆款金胎掐絲琺瑯蓋罐　一件(院)

底有「乾隆年製」四字楷款。蓋帶珊瑚頂。口徑叁·陸公分。通蓋頂高玖·壹公分。底徑叁·捌公分。重市秤捌兩正。

11. Ch'ien-lung Pot, with Cover.

Enamel on gold matrix. Coral top on cover.

(79)

一二

乾隆款金胎珐瑯盃盤壺　三件（院）

底均有「乾隆年製」四字楷款。壺蓋有珊瑚頂。盤壺均有傷。盃口徑肆·陸公分。通耳高肆公分。底徑貳公分。重市秤叁兩正。盤直徑拾叁·玖公分。最高貳·叁公分。底徑玖·伍公分。重市秤拾壹兩正。壺口徑貳·柒公分。通蓋頂高拾捌·捌公分。底縱叁·貳公分。橫叁·玖公分。重市秤拾陸兩陸錢。

12. Ch'ien-lung Pot, with Plate and Cup.

Coral top on cover. Three pieces.

(80)

一三

乾隆款金胎琺瑯盌　二件(院)

底均有「乾隆年製」四字楷款。一件口徑拾壹·陸公分。高伍公分。底徑陸·貳公分。重市秤捌兩貳錢。一件口徑拾壹·柒公分。高伍·壹公分。底徑陸公分。重市秤柒兩陸錢。

13. Enamel Bowls.

Enamel on gold matrix. Two pieces.

剔　　紅

RED LACQUER

参加倫敦中國藝術國際展覽會
剔紅照片目錄
RED LACQUER

一

明宣德款雕漆秋葵花大盤　一件(院)

底有「大明宣德年製」六字楷款。帶木座。有傷。口徑叁拾貳·壹公分。高肆·伍公分。底徑貳拾伍公分。

1. Big Plate, Carved with Malva Flowers.

Hsuan-tê, Ming Dynasty.

二

明嘉靖款雕漆龍鳳小盤　一件(院)

底有「大明嘉靖壬午年製」八字楷款。有裂紋。口徑貳拾陸公分。高貳·捌公分。底徑拾柒公分。

2. Small Plate, Carved with Dragons and Phœnixes.

Chia-ching, Ming Dynasty.

(85)

三

明雕漆繡墩　二件(院)

底破。有裂傷。足脫落不全。高肆拾肆·伍公分。面寬叁拾·伍公分。

3. Two Stools with Carvings.

Ming Dynasty.

四

明嘉靖款春字雕漆圓盒　一件（院）

底有「大明嘉靖年製」六字楷款。直徑叁拾伍·伍公分。通高拾叁·貳公分。

4. Ch'un Tze Round Box, with Carvings.

Chia-ching, Ming Dynasty.

(87)

摺　扇

FANS

參加倫敦中國藝術國際展覽會摺扇照片目錄

FANS OF THE MING DYNASTY

一

明范暹畫鷺鷥摺扇　一柄（院）

棕骨。計拾伍根。上端有「葦齋范暹」題款。背面素地有傷縱拾捌·肆公分。最寬伍拾貳·玖公分。骨長叁拾叁·貳公分。

1. Fan Hsien: "Herons."

二

明商喜畫濯足圖摺扇　一柄（院）

棕骨。計拾柒根。下端有「商喜」題款。背面素地。有傷。縱拾陸·柒公分。最寬伍拾·玖公分。骨長叁拾壹·伍公分。

2. Shang Hsi: "A Man Washing His Feet."

（91）

三

明唐寅畫玩月圖摺扇　·柄(院)

牙骨。計拾叁根。上端有「唐寅」題款背面素地有傷縱拾伍·伍公分。最寬肆拾伍·伍公分。骨長貳拾捌·肆公分。

3. T'ang Yin: "Enjoying the Moon."

四

明仇英畫漁笛圖摺扇　·柄(院)

竹骨貳根。棕骨計拾壹根。上端有「仇英」題款。背面素地。有傷。縱貳拾·叁公分。最寬伍拾陸·伍公分。骨長叁拾陸公分。

4. Ch'ou Ying: "Fishing and Music."

五

明仇英畫春郊摺扇　一柄(院)

竹骨貳根。棕骨計拾肆根。上端有「仇英」題款。背面素地。有傷。縱貳拾壹·壹公分。最寬陸拾·柒公分。骨長叁拾捌·伍公分。

5. Ch'ou Ying: "A Country Suburb in Spring."

六

明周臣畫掃葉烹茶摺扇　·柄(院)

棕骨。計拾陸根。下端有「周丞」題款。背面素地。縱拾柒·捌公分。最寬伍拾叁·叁公分。骨長叁拾壹柒公分。

6. Chou Ch'en: "Picking Leaves and Making Tea."

七

明文徵明畫古木寒鴉摺扇　一柄（院）

竹骨。計拾叁根。上端有「文徵明」題款。背面素地。有微傷。縱拾捌·叁公分。最寬伍拾陸公分。骨長叁拾叁·肆公分。

7. Wen Cheng-ming: "Old Trees and Winter Ducks."

八

明文徵明畫梅竹摺扇　一柄（院）

竹骨。計拾伍根。上端有「徵明」題款。背面素地。縱拾玖·壹公分。最寬伍拾叁·柒公分。骨長叁拾貳·叁公分。

8. Wen Cheng-ming: "Plum Blossoms and Bamboos."

九

明文伯仁畫采芝圖摺扇　一柄（院）

牙骨貳根。木骨計拾肆根。上端有「文伯仁」題款。背面素地。有傷。縱拾柒公分。最寬肆拾玖·叁公分。骨長貳拾玖·壹公分。

9. Wen Pe-jen: "Gathering Fungi."

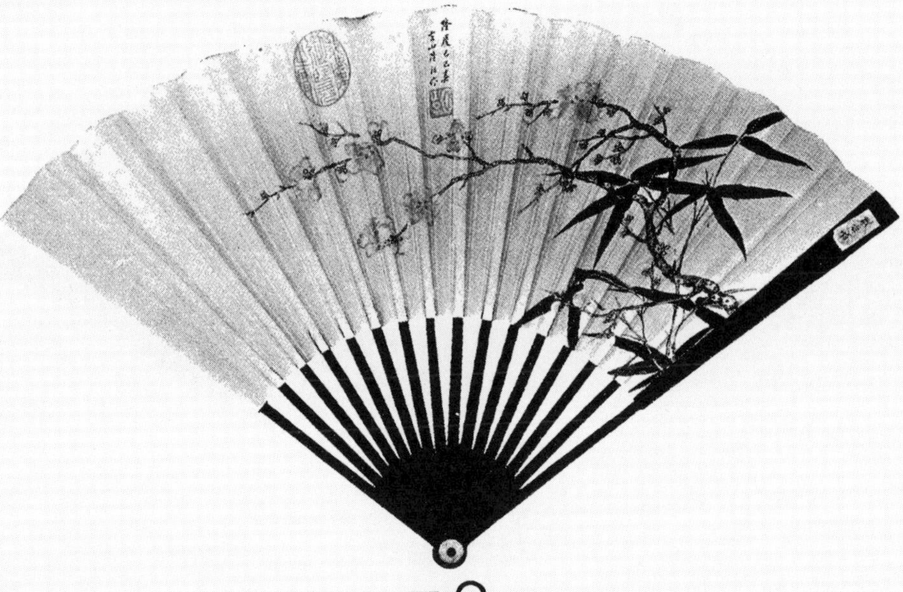

一〇

明陸治畫梅竹摺扇　一柄（院）

木骨。計拾陸根。上端有「陸治」題款。背面素地。有傷。縱拾柒公分。最寬伍拾·伍公分。骨長叁拾·叁公分。

10. Lu Chih: "Plum Blossoms and Bamboos."

一一

明董其昌畫雪山圖摺扇　一柄(院)

棕骨。計拾陸根。上端有「其昌」題款。背面素地。縱拾柒公分。最寬伍拾壹·肆公分。骨長叁拾壹·肆公分。

11. Tung Ch'i-ch'ang: "Mountains in Snow."

一二

明陳裸秋林茆舍摺扇　一柄(院)

竹骨。計拾陸根。下端有「陳裸」題款。背面素地。有傷。縱拾捌·柒公分。最寬伍拾伍·壹公分。骨長叁拾貳·玖公分。

12. Ch'en K'o: "A Thatched Hermitage in an Autumn Grove."

一三

明邵彌畫竹深荷淨摺扇　一柄（院）

竹骨。計拾陸根。上端有「邵彌」題款。背面素地。縱拾柒·陸公分。最寬伍拾壹·伍公分。骨長叁拾壹·柒公分。

13. Shao Mi: "The Profundity of Bamboos and the Quiet of Lotus Flowers."

一四

明趙文淑畫鶯粟圖摺扇　一柄（院）

棕骨。計拾陸根。上端有「趙文淑」題款。背面素地。有微傷。縱拾柒·捌公分。最寬伍拾貳·壹公分。骨長叁拾貳·伍公分。

14. Chao Wen-su: "Poppy Flowers."

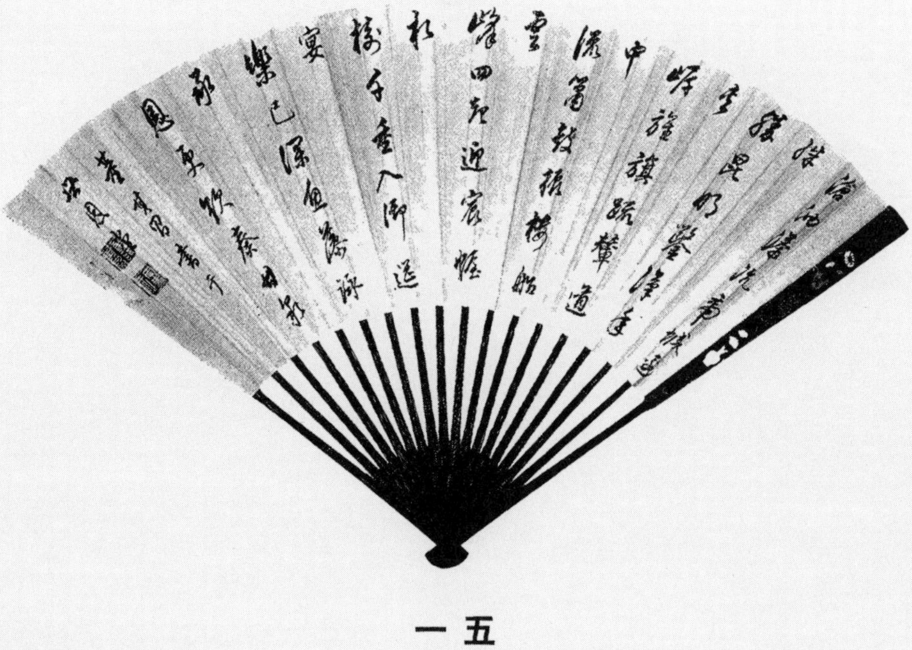

一五

明仇英畫抱琴圖董其昌書七言律摺扇　一柄(院)

棕骨。計拾捌根。上端有「仇英」題款。背面有「董其昌」題識。縱拾玖·肆公分。最寬伍拾陸公分。骨長叁拾伍·玖公分。

15. "Carrying the Lute," painted by Chou Ying, and a "Poem" transcribed by Tung Ch'i-ch'ang.

一六

明文徵明畫雲山圖並自書五言律摺扇　一柄（院）

牙骨貳根。木骨計拾根。兩面。上端有「徵明」題款·有傷·縱貳拾壹·貳公分·最寬伍拾柒·伍公分·骨長叁拾叁·玖公分。

16. Wen Cheng-ming: "Clouds and Mountains," with a "Poem" transcribed by himself.

一七

明談志伊畫秋花董其昌書五言絕句摺扇　一柄(院)

竹骨。計拾捌根。上端有「志伊」題款。背面有「董其昌」題款。有微傷。縱拾捌公分。最寬伍拾貳公分。骨長叁拾貳·肆公分。

17. "Autumn Flowers," painted by T'an Chih-i, and a "Poem" transcribed by Tung Ch'i-ch'ang.

一八

明趙左畫松林小坐董其昌書七言絕句摺扇　一柄（院）

竹骨。計拾捌根。下端有「趙左」題款。上端有「玄宰」題識。背面素地。有傷。縱拾陸·玖公分。最寬伍拾壹·伍公分。骨長叁拾壹·壹公分。

18. "Sitting in a Grove of Pines," painted by Chao Tso, and a "Poem" transcribed by Tung Ch'i-ch'ang.

一九

明 李士達畫飲中八仙 韓道亨書八仙歌 摺扇 一柄（院）

棕骨。計貳拾伍根。上端有「李士達」題款。背面下端有「韓道亨」題款。有微傷。縱拾陸·玖公分。最寬伍拾·伍公分。骨長叁拾·陸公分。

19. "Eight Arhats Drinking," painted by Li Shih-ta, and a "Song of Eight Arhats" transcribed by Han Tao-heng.

二〇

明 馬守貞畫花蝶圖 王穉登書五言絕句 摺扇 一柄（院）

竹骨。計拾陸根。上端有「馬守貞」題款及「王穉登」題識。背面素地。縱拾柒·捌公分。最寬伍拾壹·貳公分。骨長叁拾貳公分。

20. "Butterflies," painted by Ma So-chen, and a "Poem" transcribed by Wang Shih-teng.

傢　具　文　具

FURNITURE AND WRITING ACCESSORIES

參加倫敦中國藝術國際展覽會
傢具及文具照片目錄
FURNITURE AND WRITING ACCESSORIES

一

紫檀鑲景泰藍雲蝠寶座　一件（院）

紫檀木製。背刻雲蝠。附描金木脚踏及黃綾綉墊各一件。最高玖拾陸·叁公分。最長捌拾陸·伍公分。最寬壹百壹拾公分。綉墊縱柒拾肆·伍公分。橫捌拾玖·伍公分。厚拾貳公分。

1. A Throne of Teak Wood.

With cloisonné decorations, and carvings of "Cloud Scrolls and Bats," and a lacquer footstool, painted with golden-flower design.

（ 105 ）

二

紫檀鑲景泰藍仙山樓閣屏　一付（院）

紫檀木製。座叁塊合成一形、均嵌有景泰藍鑲件、屏身下節叁塊、上節叁塊帶葫蘆形頂叁個。屏身兩旁配件貳塊、原係鍍金今已退色、屏刻仙山樓閣圖、屏座中間壹塊高肆拾肆·陸公分。縱貳拾伍·肆公分。橫最長壹百貳拾貳·伍公分、兩旁兩塊均高肆拾肆·陸公分。縱貳拾伍·肆公分、橫最長捌拾叁·伍公分、屏身下節內壹塊連足高壹百玖拾玖·陸公分。寬壹百壹拾捌·伍公分、厚伍·玖公分、又兩塊均連足高壹百捌拾叁·伍公分、寬伍拾肆·陸公分。厚伍·玖公分。上節內壹塊連頂高柒拾玖·柒公分。寬壹百壹拾捌·伍公分、厚伍·陸公分、又兩塊均連頂高壹百零捌·陸公分。最寬柒拾肆·肆公分、厚伍·陸公分。配件貳塊均最高伍拾玖·捌公分。最寬貳拾壹·伍公分。厚伍·壹公分、

2. A Wind Screen of Teak Wood.

With cloisonné decorations and carvings of Mountains and Terraces. (A complete set.)

(106)

三

紅木畫案　一張（院）

原名「劉墉桌」。紅木製。四邊沿刻有「劉墉」「翁方綱」題識。屜面有「板橋」「錢維城」「南沙老人」「湯貽汾」「金農」「李育」「鄒一桂」等刻花。缺抽屜面一個。縱捌拾玖·伍公分。橫貳百壹拾玖·貳公分。高捌拾柒·貳公分。屜面均縱玖·伍公分。橫肆拾捌·肆公分。

3. A Teak Writing Desk.

Inscribed with the writings of Liu Yung, Weng Fang-k'ang, etc. With front piece of one of the drawers missing.

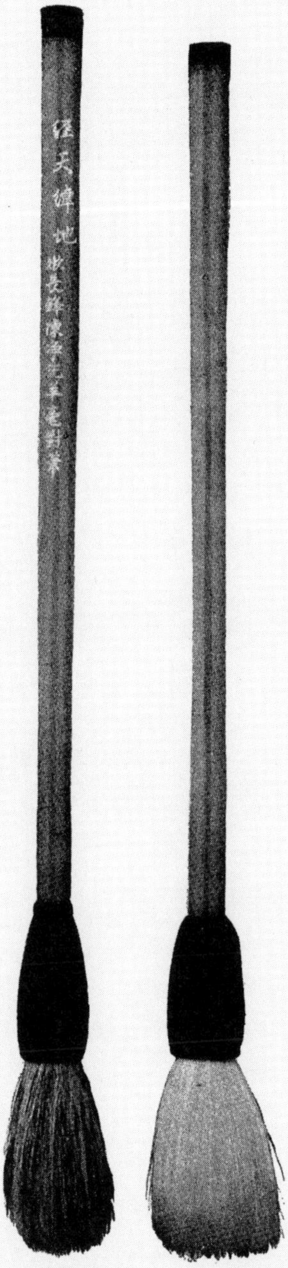

四

骨管小斗筆　二支(院)

內一支筆桿上刻有「經天緯地丙辰春月賀蓮青精製」等字。通筆尖約長貳拾陸公分。又一支筆桿上刻有「篆隸之筆丙辰秋月戴月軒精選」等字。通筆尖約長貳拾伍公分。

4. Writing Brushes.

Each with a brush-holder of bone. Two pieces.

五

白玉雕松筆筒　一件(院)

刻有「乾隆御題」。口沿有微傷。口徑捌·陸公分。高拾貳·柒公分。底徑拾壹·伍公分。中圍叁拾伍·叁公分。重市秤伍拾捌兩正。

5. Writing-Brush Holder of White Jade.

Carved with pine trees.

六

乾隆款魚形御墨　一件(院)

邊有「大清乾隆年製」六字。上有「御墨」二篆字。最寬貳·玖公分。最長柒·玖公分。最厚零·捌公分。重市秤捌錢正。

6. Fish-Shape Ink Tablet.

With the inscription "Made in Ch'ien-lung's Reign."

七

白玉墨床　一件(院)

帶木座。背後刻詩。寬伍·陸公分。長拾貳·捌公分。最厚零·柒公分。重市秤叁兩肆錢。

7. Ink Stand of White Jade.

八

白玉八卦印色盒　　·件(院)

原名「小玉八卦圓盒」有緒。口有微傷,口徑陸·柒公分。底徑肆·玖公分,通蓋高叁·貳公分。重市秤肆兩肆錢。

8. Seal Vermilion Box of White Jade.

With "Pa Kua" design.

九

白玉圖章　　三件(院)

帶木盒。盒面刻有「乾隆宸翰」「尋沿書屋」「圖書必有源」等字樣。之一獸紐。刻有「圖書必有源」五白文篆字。縱橫均叁·捌公分。通紐高陸·叁公分。之二獸紐。刻有「乾隆宸翰」四朱文篆字。縱橫均叁·捌公分。通紐高陸·叁公分。之三獸紐。刻有「尋沿書屋」四朱文篆字。縱叁·玖公分。橫貳·陸公分。通紐高陸·肆公分。三件共重市秤拾陸兩正。

9. Seal of White Jade.

Carved with the characters "Ch'ien-lung Chen Han."

Seal of White Jade.

Carved with the characters "Hsun Yen Shu Wu."

Seal of White Jade.

Carved with the characters "Tu Shu Pi Yu Yuan."

The above three pieces are contained in a wooden box.

(111)

一〇

宋澄泥石渠硯　一件(院)

帶木座及木蓋。蓋上有玉圭一塊(玉圭脫下)及「乾隆御題」。座上刻有「太上皇帝」四篆字。底有「乾隆御題」。縱拾肆·柒公分。橫玖·貳公分。厚叁·捌公分。

10. A Shih Chu Ink Stone of the Sung Dynasty.

Made of *ch'eng* clay. With a wooden box, the top of which has a piece of jade inserted into it.

一一

白玉五子筆架　一件（院）

帶雕花座。最高肆·捌公分。最長拾貳·捌公分。重市秤肆兩正。

11. A Writing-Brush Support of White Jade.

Carved with the figures of five children. With a wooden stand.

一二

白玉瓜形水盛　一件（院）

水盛帶玉水匙。口縱叁·伍公分。橫肆·捌公分。高肆·肆公分。水匙長捌公分。最寬壹·貳公分。連水匙共重市秤陸兩正。

12. A Melon-Shape Water Container of White Jade.

With a small jade spoon.

一三

明代雕漆圓盒　一件（院）

原名「明永樂年製雕光漆小盒」。無款。通蓋高肆·捌公分。口徑捌·柒公分。

13. A Small Round Box of Carved Lacquer of the Ming Dynasty.

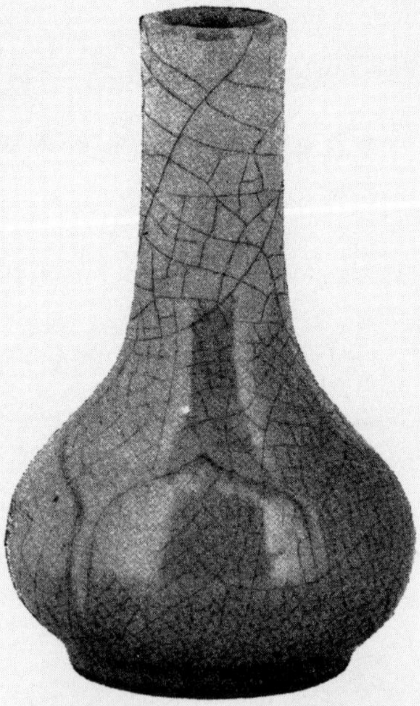

一四

宋哥窯月白蓮瓣瓶　一件(院)

原名「宋哥窯錐把瓶」。帶木座。口徑叁公分。高拾肆·陸公分。腹圍貳拾捌·叁公分。底徑陸·壹公分。

14. A Sung Ko Yao Vase.

Moon white in color, with lotus-flower design. With a wooden stand.

一五

白玉管筆　一支(院)

附玉筆帽。原名「玉筆」。筆長拾陸·叁公分。筆帽長捌·玖公分。共重市秤陸兩正。

15. A Writing Brush.

With a brush holder of white jade.

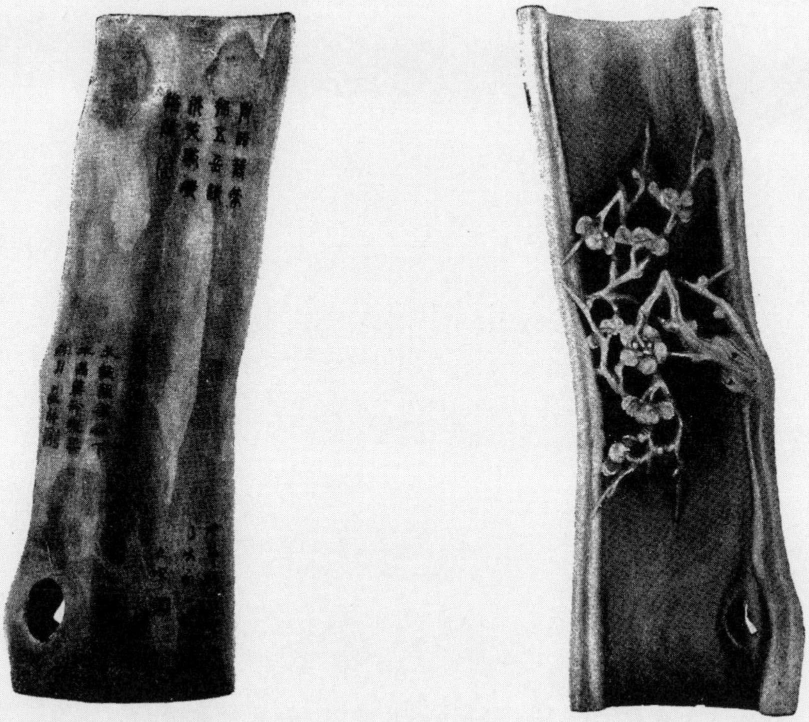

一六

黃楊木雕梅花臂擱　一件(院)

原名「黃楊木雕梅花文字臂擱」。上刻有「片月」「象軒」「之宰」等款。最高叁·肆公分。最長貳拾壹·柒公分。最寬陸·捌公分。

16. A Writing Arm-Rest of Huangyang Wood.

Carved with plum blossoms.

(115)

考 古 選 例

ARCHÆOLOGICAL EXHIBITS

國立中央研究院歷史語言研究所
考古組
送致
倫敦中國藝術國際展覽會
展覽品百件
簡目

展覽品百件中選自殷墟出土者九十七件;濬縣辛村出土者二件;其餘一件,由安陽古董市購買,並列於此,以資比較。共分十二大類:

(一) 卜用甲骨 . . . . 五件

(二) 甲骨文字 . . . . 十六件

(三) 鹿頭刻辭 . . . . 一件

(四) 石刀 . . . . 十件

(五) 石斧 . . . . 六件

(六) 骨笄 . . . . 十件

(七) 各種骨器 . . . . 七件

(八) 矢簇 . . . . 二十件

(九) 戈,矛,斧 . . . . 六件

(十) 銅器殘片 . . . . 八件

(十一) 銅笵 . . . . 六件

(十二) 骨刻,牙刻,與石刻 . . . . 五件

CATALOGUE

OF

THE ARCHÆOLOGICAL EXHIBITS

FOR

THE INTERNATIONAL EXHIBITION OF CHINESE ART IN LONDON

Contributed By

The Archæological Section

Institute of History and Philology

Academia Sinica

PRELIMINARY NOTES

The exhibits to be catalogued in the following pages have been chosen almost exclusively, from the artifacts recovered from Yinhsü, the site where the remains of the ancient capital of the Yin-Shang Dynasty are located. They are selected with a view to show some of the main characteristics of the culture of this period (*circa* 1400–1200 B.C.), the earliest of reliable Chinese history. Their value is therefore chiefly archæological. As no concensus of opinions has been reached regarding the exact chronology of this period, the date given in this connection must be considered as provisional only.

The Institute of History and Philology of Academia Sinica began to excavate this site in the fall of 1928. The work has been continued till the present with very little interruption and is still kept going on. For details concerning this work, see *Preliminary Reports of Excavations at Anyang*, published by the Institute.

The field work at Yinhsü, located in Anyang Hsien, Northern Honan, has been generously aided, financially and in many other respects, by a number of friendly institutes from time

殷墟出土卜用之甲骨及文字

一　卜用甲骨

龜卜之術，起源綦古，至殷商時代而大盛，事無巨細，必卜以決之，故殷墟出土之卜用龜甲極多。其卜法先將龜之背腹甲，剖分爲二，更將甲之表皮剔去，內外刮治平滑，更於內面施以鑽鑿，用時以火灼之，外面坼而成兆，以定吉凶。腹甲用全，背甲則於正中縱剖之，分左右爲二半。關於殷商龜卜之法，可參閱董作賓氏商代龜卜之推測一文（載安陽發掘報告第一期五九——一三〇葉）。

卜用龜甲，亦用牛肩胛骨，骨左右並用。以刀鋸剖刮，使之光滑平正。卜法同於龜甲，先施鑽鑿而後灼以求兆。有但施鑽或鑿者。殷墟出土亦極多。

AS 0.001　龜腹甲，尾部殘闕。外面有卜兆，內面有鑽鑿及灼痕各二十五。

AS 0.002　龜背甲，左半，尾部殘闕。外面有卜兆二十，內面有鑽鑿及灼痕二十八。

AS 0.003　牛胛骨，下半殘。正面有卜兆五，反面有鑽鑿灼痕八，一鑿而未灼。

AS 0.004　牛胛骨，下半殘。反面有鑿灼痕八，正面有卜兆六。

AS 0.005　牛胛骨，上、下、右皆殘，餘左邊。反面有鑽灼痕八，正面可見之卜兆三。

（121）

to time. Particular mention must be made of the Freer Gallery of Art, Smothsonian Institution, which contributed all the field expenses for the two seasons in 1929, and the China Foundation for the Promotion of Education and Culture, which, since 1931, has made annual grant to the Institute to carry on field work in archæology.

The present selection consists of one hundred articles (Cat. No. AS 0.001–AS 0.100); they are arranged consecutively in seventeen cases (AS-I–AS-XVII) and are to be divided into twelve groups. Each group, while made up from one to a number of objects, constitutes an organic whole, which aims at illustrating a characteristic point of the culture of this period.

GROUP A. Oracle Bones. AS-I: AS 0.001–0.005.

GROUP B. Inscribed Oracle Bones. AS-II–AS-V: AS 0.006–0.021.

GROUP C. Inscribed Frontal of a Deer's Skull. AS-VI: AS 0.022.

GROUP D. Stone Knives. AS-VII: AS 0.023–0.032.

GROUP E. Stone Axes. AS-VIII: AS 0.033–0.038.

GROUP F. Hairpins. AS-IX: AS 0.039–0.048.

GROUP G. Various Bone Works. AS-X: AS 0.49–0.055.

GROUP H. Arrowheads. AS-XI: AS 0.056–0.075.

GROUP I. Halberts, Spearheads, and Socketed Celt. AS-XII, AS-XIII: AS 0.076–0.081.

GROUP J. Fragments of Larger Bronze Works. AS-XIV: AS 0.082–0.089.

GROUP K. Moulds for Bronze Casting. AS-XV: AS 0.090–0.095.

GROUP L. Ivory, Bone, and Stone Carvings. AS-XVI, AS-XVII: AS 0.096–0.100.

GROUP A. ORACLE BONES

(AS-I: AS 0.001–0.005)

The use of tortoise shells and scapula for divination must have originated very early in Eastern Asia. In the time of the Yin-Shang Dynasty, the usage was apparently already deep rooted both among the populace and the ruling class. As is still evident from the records of these bones, the daily life of the king was minutely regulated by this practice. Whatever he was about to do, important or unimportant, inquiry must be first made on these bones. The oracle bones recovered from Yinhsü are extraordinarily abundant. Some idea of the technique with which the oracle bones were prepared before used for divination may be gathered

二　甲骨文字

殷墟出土甲骨文字,以記貞卜之事者爲多。此類卜辭,皆於每次後,記所卜事於兆旁。其事項約爲十二類:(一)祭;(二)告;(三)𩫖;(四)行、止;(五)田、漁;(六)征伐;(七)年;(八)風、雨;(九)霽;(十)瘳;(十一)旬與夕;(十二)雜卜。

卜辭自清光緒二十五年(公元一八九九)發現,三十年來,屢經土人挖掘,出土者達數萬版,已著錄之書十九種,凡一萬六千餘版。菁華幾盡於此。中央研究院殷墟發掘工作,始於民國十七年(公元一九二八),迄今工作九次,所得甲骨文字六千餘版,不過全量十之一二,然由科學發掘之結果,因地層、坑位、及其他各種標準,得斷代研究法,分卜辭爲五期:(一)武丁及其以前;(二)祖庚、祖甲;(三)廩辛、康丁;(四)武乙、文丁;(五)帝乙、帝辛;詳見董作賓氏甲骨文斷代研究例(集刊外編上三二三——四二四葉)。執此法以研究所有甲骨文字,使殷代寶貴之史料,劃然有時代之可分。以下就每期文字、甲骨各舉一例,附列說明,以見一斑。

AS 0.006　龜腹甲,左肩。外內皆有卜辭,大字,塗朱。內辭有帚好,爲武丁后。甲面刮治光澤,文字書法雄偉,可見此期工藝書法之精良。

AS 0.007　牛胛骨,上段。正、反面皆有文字,記征伐。史官永書,筆力秀勁,骨臼有記事刻辭,史官岳書。永岳皆武丁時人。

AS 0.009 AS 0.010 AS 0.011

AS 0.008

AS 0.012

AS 0.013

AS 0.015

AS 0.014

AS 0.020

AS 0.016 AS 0.017 AS 0.018 AS 0.019

(123)

by a study of these remnants. In the case of the tortoise shells, the first thing to be done was to separate the plastron from the carapace. Then the dermal part was skinned off, the ridges chipped away and smoothed, and sharp corners softened down so that the shell might become as platelike as possible. The next step was to drill a number of troughlike or circular cavities (AS 0.003, AS 0.004). When divination was to take place, a sort of brand, something perhaps like the burning joss-stick of later time, was applied to one side of one of the cavities. When it was sufficiently heated, the thin layer at the bottom of the cavity and the part that was particularly scorched naturally began to crack. This usually took place with a little explosion. Laboratory experiment has shown that the sound of the explosive created in such a manner is not unlike the phonetic value usually given to the character 卜 (p'o), a beautiful example of onomatope. It may be added that the arrangements of the different strokes possible for this same character are strangely resembling to the several varieties of the crack lines found on the oracle bones. The officers in charge of divination were evidently able to find out whether it was auspicious or not from the different arrangements of the crack lines, to do that particular thing for which the query was made. If it were a king's case, both the query and the answer were taken down and inscribed on these bones. Both carapace and plastron of the tortoise shell were used for the purpose; the latter, however, much more frequently, and used in entirety; while the former has usually been found in halves.

Although tortoise shells were better known as materials for divination, their use as a matter of fact was evolved from scapulimancy, existing in protohistorical China even earlier. In the remains of Yinhsü, more scapulæ have been found than tortoise shells. The preliminary preparation and the details of the divinatory procedure were the same for both materials.

AS 0.001 Scorched Plastron. 12.2×9.8 cm. 60.90 g.*

Almost complete, xiphiplastron missing. Note the crack lines on the external surface, and the twenty-five small cavities, each with a scorched mark, on the internal surface.

AS 0.002 Scorched Carapace. 11.1×11.7 cm. 50.20 g.

Left part, posterior missing. Twenty crack signs; twenty-eight scorched cavities.

*NOTE: The measurements given in each case are: maximum length, maximum width, and total weight.

AS 0.008 龜腹甲,左邊一部。內面記事文字。帚井武丁后。正面亦有卜辭。
AS 0.009 龜背甲,右半,中部。內面有卜辭,字形、書體、皆可知爲第一期物。
AS 0.010 牛胛骨,骨臼殘。有記事文。小臺,武丁史官。

以上第一期

AS 0.011 龜腹甲,右下邊緣。卜辭記祀祖丁。貞人大、祖甲時史。
AS 0.012 牛胛骨,中部。卜辭記祭祀。貞人行、祖甲時史。此期作風、字體、謹飭,行款嚴整,爲其特點。

以上第二期

AS 0.013 龜腹甲,右邊。文字記卜旬。有貞人口、逢,皆廪辛康丁時史。
AS 0.014 牛胛骨,中下一部。正、反皆有文字,記卜夕。彭、㚫皆廪辛康丁時人。此版書法幼稚,行款錯雜,爲第三期文風頹靡之代表作品。

以上第三期

AS 0.015 龜腹甲,左下邊。辭卜行止。由字形及出土地可證爲武乙文丁時物。
AS 0.016 牛胛骨,上半。卜祭祀。由出土地證之,父丁卽康丁,爲武乙時卜辭。此期不記貞人。書法勁峭,爲其特點。

以上第四期

AS 0.017 龜腹甲,右下邊。卜辭三,皆記田獵事。由書體、字形、出土地、定爲帝乙帝辛時物。此期文字行款工整,結構精嚴,書法纖麗,一望可辨。
AS 0.018 牛胛骨,右邊緣。記卜旬。字形、書體第五期。
AS 0.019 龜背甲,右半,右邊緣。記祭祀。由文法、字形、書體、皆可證爲第五期物。背甲之用,常見於第一期及第五期。

以上第五期

骨版書寫之文字

AS 0.020 牛胛骨,右邊。反面例書,殘辭『伐祖乙十人』等字,隱約可見。殷墟出土書寫之卜辭共三版,此其一也。此版可爲(一)殷人已用毛筆;(二)卜辭先書後契之證。

AS 0.003 Scorched Scapula. 7.7 × 7.6 cm. 37.80 g.

Fragment only. Five crack signs; eight cavities, one of which not yet scorched.

AS 0.004 Scorched Scapula. 12.6 × 6.4 cm. 66.65 g.

Fragment only. Eight scorched cavities; six crack signs. Shape of cavities, troughlike.

AS 0.005 Scorched Scapula. 14.6 × 4.3 cm. 53.00 g.

Fragment only. Eight scorched cavities, all circular shaped. Three crack signs.

Group B. Inscribed Oracle Bones

(AS-II--AS-V: AS 0.006–0.021)

Inscribed oracle bones form one of the most valuable groups of the finds from Yinhsü. The records were inscribed on the bones right besides the various crack lines evidently at the completion of every divinatory procedure. The events included in such queries and recorded in these inscriptions may be divided into a number of categories. The more important of these queries are about: offering sacrifice, festivity, traveling, hunting and fishing, military expedition, crops, weather forecasting, recuperation, decadary divination which occurred regularly on every tenth day in order to find out the fortune of the next ten days.

These records first became known to the general public in 1899. For thirty years native diggers had kept on digging the inscribed oracle bones and considered it a regular source of income. A recent estimate has been made of the number of the fragments of these bones that had been dug out in this way, the total is said to reach several tens of thousands. Of these, about 16,000 fragments have been already reproduced in rubbings or photographs and appeared in print. Many books have been written on these records; of these, nineteen have already been published.

The collection of the inscribed bones made by the Institute of History and Philology from the various excavations amount to a little over 6,000, less than 20% of what have already been known to the public. But the archæological value of this small collection is immeasurably greater. Owing to the field knowledge in the possession of the excavators, it has been possible to make a comparative study of these records and arrange them on a chronological basis, which may be divided into five different periods:

較完整之龜腹甲

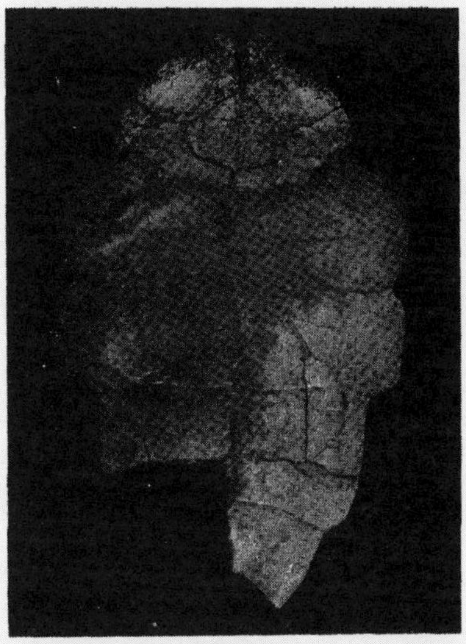

AS 0.021

AS 0.021 龜腹甲全形,殘左尾部下半。有卜辭八段,記方國雜卜。內面鑽鑿痕二十八,計全龜當爲三十。未灼者九。外面卜兆十九,不記卜辭者十一。此版可見全龜文字左右行之例。

三　鹿頭刻辭

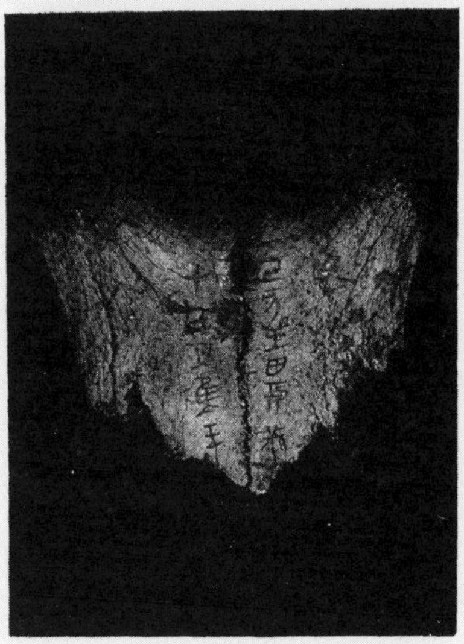

AS 0.022

1. Period of Wu-ting and earlier.
2. Period of Tsu-keng and Tsu-chia.
3. Period of Lin-hsin and K'ang-ting.
4. Period of Wu-i and Wen-ting.
5. Period of Ti-i and Ti-hsin.

For details on this particular problem, see Tung Tso-ping's "Criteria that May Be Used for a More Exact Dating of the Oracle Bone Records," *Studies Presented to T'sai Yuan-pei on His Attaining of 65th Birthday*, pp. 323-424.

AS 0.006 Inscribed Plastron. 7.4×3.3 cm. 22.00 g.

Fragment only. Well polished. Inscriptions on both sides. Large characters, filled with red pigments. Name of Wu-ting's queen occurs in the record. Style of writing bold and masterly, indicating a highly cultured period.

AS 0.007 Inscribed Scapula. 11.9×6.8 cm. 78.80 g.

Fragment only. Inscriptions on the glenoid cavity as well as the two sides; all recorded by chroniclers of Wu-ting's time. Their names occur in the records.

AS 0.008 Inscribed Plastron. 5.9×3.0 cm. 5.70 g.

Fragment only. Inscriptions on both sides. Names of Wu-ting's queens occur in the records.

AS 0.009 Inscribed Carapace. 9.0×5.7 cm. 26.50 g.

Fragment only. Style of writing characteristic of this period.

AS 0.010 Inscribed Glenoid Cavity. 3.4×3.5 cm. 6.90 g.

Fragment only. Name of chronicler of Wu-ting's period occurs in the record.

(The above five specimens may be assigned to Wu-ting's period.)

AS 0.011 Inscribed Plastron. 6.1×3.6 cm. 8.30 g.

Fragment only. Recording offering to Tsu-ting, recorded by chronicler of Tsu-chia's time.

AS 0.012 Inscribed Scapula. 6.4×2.5 cm. 9.20 g.

Fragment only. Recording sacrificial offering, recorded by chronicler of Tsu-chia's time. Inscription careful, formal almost stylized; characteristic of this period.

(The above two specimens may be assigned to the second period.)

AS 0.022 鹿頭骨，僅殘餘額面部及角礎。文字亦缺，記征伐、田獵事。由字形、書體可證爲第五期物。書法婉麗，有類鼎彝款識。文例下行而左，與其他獸頭刻辭二具同。可證殷人普通文例如此，卜辭之有左右行，爲迎合卜兆之一種特殊體式。

四　石刀

殷墟日用器之以石製者，刀類最多，出土之完全無缺者，在百數以上，殘破者數倍此數。石料多爲板岩或砂板岩。今就其形製不同者選十種（AS 0.023–AS 0.032），前七種較普通，後三種極少，或爲石器時代之遺留。

AS 0.023　AS 0.024　AS 0.025　AS 0.026　AS 0.027

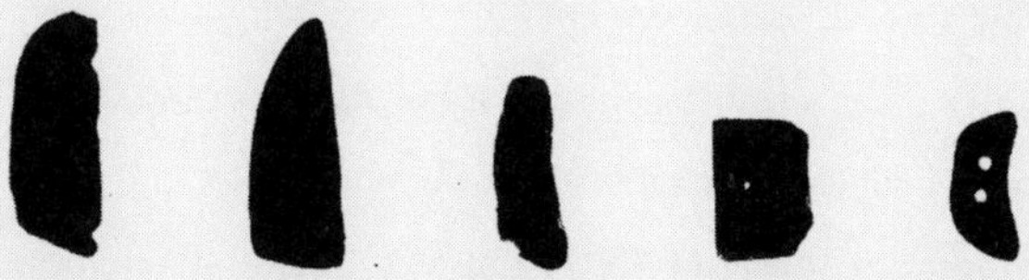

AS 0.028　AS 0.029　AS 0.030　AS 0.031　AS 0.032

AS 0.023 刀，砂板岩，21.7 cm.×7 cm.，269 g.

AS 0.024 刀，砂板岩，17.6 cm.×7.2 cm.，199 g.

AS 0.025 刀，砂板岩，17.6 cm.×7.2 cm.，231 g.

AS 0.026 刀，砂板岩，15.1 cm.×6.5 cm.，169.5 g.

AS 0.027 刀，板岩，14.3 cm.×6.6 cm.，118.5 g.

AS 0.028 刀，砂板岩，14.5 cm.×5.2 cm.，106 g.

AS 0.029 刀，板岩，14.7 cm.×5.3 cm.，124 g.

AS 0.030 刀，板岩，11.5 cm.×3.9 cm.，66.4 g.

AS 0.031 刀，閃長岩，8.3 cm.×5.3 cm.，90.5 g.

AS 0.032 刀，石灰岩，8.9 cm.×3.8 cm.，45.5 g.

（ 129 ）

AS 0.013 Inscribed Plastron. 6.3 × 3.5 cm. 8.60 g.

Fragment only. Recording decadary divination, recorded by chroniclers of Lin-hsin and K'ang-ting's time.

AS 0.014 Inscribed Scapula. 7.0 × 6.4 cm. 16.50 g.

Fragment only. Inscriptions on both sides. Recording evening divination recorded by chroniclers of Lin-hsin and K'ang-ting's time. Inscriptions carelessly and irregularly executed; no longer observing the old form. A period of decadence.

(The above two may be assigned to the third period.)

AS 0.015 Inscribed Plastron. 4.7 × 3.1 cm. 4.00 g.

Fragment only. Recording a journey. Both the location of this find and style of the inscription indicating it to be a relic of Wu-i or Wen-ting's period.

AS 0.016 Inscribed Scapula. 13.4 × 5.7 cm. 47.70 g.

Recording sacrificial offering. Location of this find indicating it to be a relic of Wu-i's time. As a rule chronicler's name does not occur in the records of this period. Inscription executed in a forcible manner.

(The above two may be assigned to the fourth period.)

AS 0.017 Inscribed Plastron. 5.2 × 3.2 cm. 7.70 g.

Fragment only. Three different records, all about hunting. From the style of writing, type of character, and the location of the find, it may be inferred that the relic belongs to the time of Ti-i and Ti-hsin. Inscriptions of this period are marked with precision and good workmanship, structurally accurate; the elegant and flowing style is very impressive.

AS 0.018 Inscribed Scapula. 5.2 × 3.2 cm. 7.70 g.

Fragment only. Recording decadary divination.

AS 0.019 Inscribed Carapace. 3.2 × 3.6 cm. 4.70 g.

Fragment only. Recording sacrificial offering. Carapace was frequently used both in the first and the fifth period.

(The above three may be assigned to the fifth period.)

AS 0.020 Scapula with Written Characters. 9.4 × 4.4 cm. 18.50 g.

Fragment only. Five characters written in some kind of ink still visible. One

五　石斧

殷墟石斧,大約可分帶穿與不帶穿兩類;每類又可依其形制分若干種。此中常用者似只一種,其餘或早期之遺留,或卽禮器,於祭祀舞蹈時用之。下六種,惟第一種所見較多,餘皆孤品。

AS 0.033 AS 0.034 AS 0.035 AS 0.036 AS 0.037 AS 0.038

AS 0.033 斧,閃長岩, 10.7 cm.×4.3 cm., 304 g.
AS 0.034 斧,閃長岩, 8.8 cm.×6.2 cm., 171 g.
AS 0.035 斧,石灰岩, 9.8 cm.×4.5 cm., 157.5 g.
AS 0.036 斧,石灰岩, 13.8 cm.×6.5 cm., 299 g.
AS 0.037 斧,磁土, 13.1 cm.×6.3 cm., 226 g.
AS 0.038 斧,象牙化石, 18.2 cm.×3.9 cm., 208 g.

六　骨笄

繫傳謂笄端刻雞形,想必有所本,殷墟所出骨笄多有刻雞形者,且其形變化極多;下列六種,代表較普通之笄形,皆骨製。

AS 0.039 AS 0.040 AS 0.041 AS 0.042 AS 0.043 AS 0.044 AS 0.045 AS 0.046 AS 0.047 AS 0.048

(131)

of the three pieces recovered from Yinhsü that show written characters. These three pieces show: (1) that some kind of brush must have been used during this period for writing purpose; (2) that inscription was most probably preceded by writing.

AS 0.021 Inscribed Plastron. 28.8 × 17.0 cm. 183.00 g.

Almost complete, missing only the right half of xiphiplastron. Eight different parts of divinatory records of miscellaneous character. Twenty-eight drilled cavities on the internal side; if complete, the number of such cavities would be thirty. Nine of the cavities were never scorched. Nineteen crack signs on the external surface; eleven of these bear no record. This example illustrates clearly the rule of symmetrical arrangements of the inscribed characters on an oracle bones of the plastron group.

Group C. Ancient Inscription on Frontal Bone of a Deer's Skull

(AS-VI: AS 0.022)

AS 0.022 Ancient Inscription on Frontal Bone of a Deer's Skull. 90.0 × 12.4 cm. 171.70 g.

Only the root of the horn and parts of the frontal left. Inscriptions also incomplete; recording military expedition and hunting, to be read downward and leftwise, an arrangement that is exactly the same as the two other inscribed skulls recovered from Yinhsü. It shows that this was probably the regular arrangement of an ordinary record. The symmetrical arrangement found on plastron records was probably dictated by the peculiar shape of the material and is to be considered as an exception rather than a rule. Style of the writing and type of the character conform quite closely to those of the fifth period.

Group D. Stone Knives

(AS-VIII: AS 0.023–0.032)

Stones were still extensively used in this period for making certain types of tools. Of these the knives have survived more abundantly in the remains of Yinhsü than most others. Slate

AS 0.039 11.9 cm.×1.1 cm., 6.15 g.

AS 0.040 12.5 cm., 3.50 g.

AS 0.041 11.6 cm.×.7 cm., 2.7 g.

AS 0.042 9 cm.×1.6 cm., 5.35 g.

AS 0.043 11.3 cm.×1.8 cm., 6.2 g.

AS 0.044 13.6 cm.×2.4 cm., 5.75 g.

AS 0.045 16.2 cm.×2.5 cm., 9.4 g.

AS 0.046 19.3 cm.×2.4 cm., 11.2 g.

AS 0.047 9.9 cm.×2.2 cm., 7.5 g.

AS 0.048 9.6 cm.×2.2 cm., 4 g.

七 骨器

殷墟骨製之器較他種保存者多,下列七種,爲示其用途之一般。

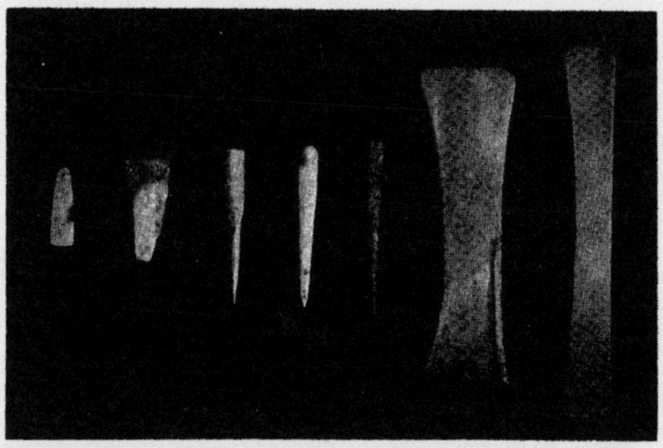

AS 0.049 AS 0.050 AS 0.051 AS 0.052 AS 0.053 AS 0.054 AS 0.055

AS 0.049 骨刀, 5.3 cm.×1.6 cm., 1.75 g., 一端帶穿,一端具刃,極薄,切刮用。

AS 0.050 骨楔, 6.9 cm.×2.9 cm., 25.9 g., 一端極厚,一端有刃,劈小物用。

AS 0.051 骨錐, 10.4 cm.×1.3 cm., 7 g., 一端尖銳,一端略刮治。

AS 0.052 骨釘, 10.6 cm., 10 g., 一端粗尖,中部隆起;似釘類。

AS 0.053 骨錐, 11.7 cm.×1.1 cm., 6.5 g., 一端尖銳,一端磨扁。

AS 0.054 骨柶, 20.8 cm.×5.9 cm., 60.2 g., 一端方頭,緣邊隆起,爲把握部份。一端具刃,爲剔性之用。

AS 0.055 骨柶, 24.8 cm.×3.3 cm., 49.9 g., 一端方頭帶穿,一端曲屈如爵之流,用之於酒漿者。

was usually chosen for shaping this particular tool; occasionally it was made of diorite or lime. More than one hundred complete specimens have been recovered from this site, and about ten times as many of the broken ones. Since the shapes vary a great deal, their functions must have differed accordingly.

AS 0.023 Knife. 21.3×7.0 cm. 269.00 g.

Sandy slate. Edge slightly convex. Back polished. Type common, but size unusual.

AS 0.024 Knife. 17.6×7.0 cm. 199.00 g.

Sandy slate. Edge straight. Back polished. A common type and a common size.

AS 0.025 Knife. 17.6×7.2 cm. 231.00 g.

Sandy slate. Edge slightly convex, polished but not sharpened. Curved back. Trianguloid shape with soft corners. A common type.

AS 0.026 Knife. 15.1×6.5 cm. 169.50 g.

Sandy slate. Edge slightly convex, polished but blunt. Back polished.

AS 0.027 Knife. 14.3×6.6 cm. 118.50 g.

Slate. Incomplete. Anterior part of a longer blade. Edge and back polished in the same manner.

AS 0.028 Knife. 14.5×5.2 cm. 106.00 g.

Sandy slate. Edge straight, sharpened and slightly worn off. Back polished; shape very unusual.

AS 0.029 Knife. 11.7×5.3 cm. 124.00 g.

Slate. Beautifully polished; sharp edge.

AS 0.030 Knife. 11.5×3.9 cm. 66.40 g.

Slate. Well-polished. Blade curved edgewise. Rare.

AS 0.031 Knife. 8.3×5.3 cm. 90.50 g.

Diorite. Beautifully polished. Rectangular shape. Back thickened, edge sharpened and worn off. Body of blade curved, uncommon. One perforation in the center. Rare.

八　矢簇

殷墟所出箭頭,有銅製與骨製兩種;骨製之形制變化甚多,可分爲四種:(一)圓錐式;(二)扁平式;(三)雙稜式;(四)叁稜式。第三式最爲普通。銅簇形制只有一種,屬第三式,惟大小不同而已。下列二十件,骨銅各十,略示變化之一般。

AS 0.056　AS 0.057　AS 0.058　AS 0.059　AS 0.060　AS 0.061　AS 0.062　AS 0.063　AS 0.064　AS 0.065

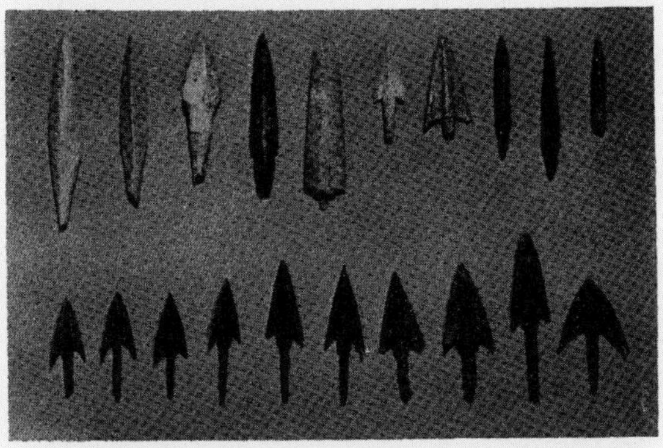

AS 0.066　AS 0.067　AS 0.068　AS 0.069　AS 0.070　AS 0.071　AS 0.073　AS 0.074　AS 0.072　AS 0.075

骨簇

AS 0.056	9.9 cm.×1.1 cm., 12.45 g., 雙稜式,單脊,骨簇中之最普通者。
AS 0.057	8.8 cm.×1.4 cm., 9.4 g., 雙稜式,銳脊。
AS 0.058	9.6 cm.×2 cm., 9.5 g., 殘,雙稜式,雙脊,極少。
AS 0.059	8.1 cm.×1.4 cm., 6.85 g., 雙稜式,下有托。
AS 0.060	9 cm.×2 cm., 11.55 g., 殘,雙稜式,下有托。
AS 0.061	5.55 cm.×1.6 cm., 2.05 g., 雙稜式,凹底,底兩尖,銳。
AS 0.062	5.2 cm.×2.4 cm., 4 g., 殘,雙稜式,凹底,底兩尖,銳。
AS 0.063	4.8 cm.×9 cm., 1.85 g., 叁稜式。
AS 0.064	7.2 cm.×9 cm., 4.5 g., 叁稜式,有托。
AS 0.065	6.2 cm.×8 cm., 4 g., 叁稜式,有托。

(135)

AS 0.032 Knife. 8.9×3.8 cm. 45.50 g.

Limestone. Beautifully polished. Semilunar rectangular shape, two perforations. Typical in æneolithic period. Very rare.

Group E. Stone Axes

(AS-VIII: AS 0.033–0.038)

Stone celts from Yinhsü are divisible into two classes: the unperforated and the perforated. Each class consists of a number of different types. Apparently only one of these types was used for ordinary purpose; the others are either rare, and therefore survivals of an earlier period, or belong to what the antiquarians of the older school have called ceremonial implements used by dancers during their professional performance celebrating religious festivals, sacrificial offering or any other state function. Most of these have a convex edge, polished but never sharpened, and showing no sign of having ever done any practical work.

AS 0.033 Ax. 10.7×4.3 cm. 304.00 g.

Diorite. Edge much worn off. Butt end oval shaped. Cross-section at the mid-point almost rectangular. Maximum thickness, 3.4 cm. A very common type of æneolithic period, but rather rare from Yinhsü.

AS 0.034 Ax. 8.8×6.2 cm. 171.00 g.

Diorite. Edge straight, sharpened, but never used. Body bladelike, thin, smooth and beautifully polished. Maximum thickness, 1.4 cm. only. Very rare.

AS 0.035 Ax. 9.8×4.5 cm. 157.50 g.

Limestone. Edge slightly convex. Rare.

AS 0.036 Ax. 13.8×6.5 cm. 299.00 g.

Limestone. Convex edge, spreading out laterally. Five indentations intervening six nipples on each of the lateral side. Perforation near the butt end. A familiar jade form, usually known as ch'i or dance ax. Rare.

AS 0.037 Ax. 13.1×6.3 cm. 226.00 g.

Kaolin. Unique for its material and shape. Convex and blunt edge, well polished. Hour-glass perforation, near the butt end. Maximum thickness, 2 cm. Lateral sides almost straight and the blade makes an elegantly curved sweep. Very rare.

銅鏃

AS 0.066　5.2 cm.×1.7 cm., 6.2 g.

AS 0.067　4.8 cm.×1.75 cm., 5 g.

AS 0.068　5.45 cm.×1.8 cm., 4.9 g.

AS 0.069　6.15 cm.×1.75 cm., 8.5 g.

AS 0.070　7 cm.×2 cm., 9.9 g.

AS 0.071　6.7 cm.×2.1 cm., 10.2 g.

AS 0.072　8.4 cm.×2.1 cm., 16.6 g.

AS 0.073　6.5 cm.×2.2 cm., 9.9 g.

AS 0.074　6.7 cm.×2.5 cm., 13.2 g.

AS 0.075　5.7 cm.×3.5 cm., 8.5 g.

九　戈，矛，斧

殷商期之武器，戈、矛最盛；一横擊，一直刺。此期之戈尚無胡，矛形極似西歐青銅時代第三期之矛。空頭銅斧亦在此期出現。下列六種，三種出自殷墟，二種出自濬縣新村，西周早期物；其一爲在安陽購買，周中期物。並置於此以示戈形之變化。

AS 0.076　AS 0.077　AS 0.078　AS 0.079　AS 0.080　AS 0.081

AS 0.076　戈殷墟，2.27 cm.×6.4 cm., 290.7 g.，戈之初期，無胡。

AS 0.077　戈濬縣，22.9 cm.×8.6 cm., 236.5 g.，胡甚短有穿一。

AS 0.078　戈安陽購，24.9 cm.×10.6 cm., 239 g.，胡較長。

AS 0.079　矛殷墟，25.2 cm.×6.9 cm., 343 g.，武器，直刺用。

AS 0.080　矛濬縣，26.1 cm.×6.7 cm., 153 g.，禮器，殉葬用。

AS 0.081　空頭銅斧殷墟，8.9 cm., 4.1 cm., 16.14 g.

AS 0.038 Ax. 18.2×3.9 cm. 208.00 g.

Fossilized ivory. Very unique material. Type also rare evolved probably from the shouldered celt. One side ivory white, marked with yellow spots; the other side, just the reverse; fine veins run longitudinally. Maximum length of blade, 16.7 cm. Beautifully polished with elegant curve near the edge. Maximum thickness, 1.4 cm. Haft seems to be rather disproportionately developed; it measures 1.5×3.2 cm. with a maximum thickness of 1.1 cm. The perforation, unlike most of the others, was drilled from one side only, slightly off the center. Most remarkable specimen.

Group F. Hairpins

(AS-IX: AS 0.039–0.048)

In one of the earlier dictionaries, under the heading of the character, "chi" (笄), or hairpin, the fact is mentioned that in earlier time the top of the hairpin was carved into the shape of a cock. The reference seems to be well grounded, though no authority was cited for this statement. The finds from Yinhsü amply testify its reliability. A number of these pins found from Yinhsü possess a very realistic cock-headed top, others however retain only some resemblance. There are also other types of hairpins.

AS 0.039 Hairpin. 11.9×1.1 cm. 6.15 g.

Top plain, but thickened a little.

AS 0.040 Hairpin. 12.5×0.4 cm. 3.50 g.

Plain top with incised marks. Probably also used as needle.

AS 0.041 Hairpin. 11.6×0.7 cm. 2.70 g.

Two knobs on the top.

AS 0.042 Hairpin. 9.0×1.6 cm. 5.35 g.

Two knobs on the top.

AS 0.043 Hairpin. 11.3×1.8 cm. 6.20 g.

Incomplete. Top enlarged into a small blade, thick in the middle, gradually thinning out into a sharp edge, with grooved lines on both sides.

一〇　銅器殘片

殷之亡,周人將其重器一掠而空;故殷墟遺址中無重要禮器,但下列殘片,已足證其存在。

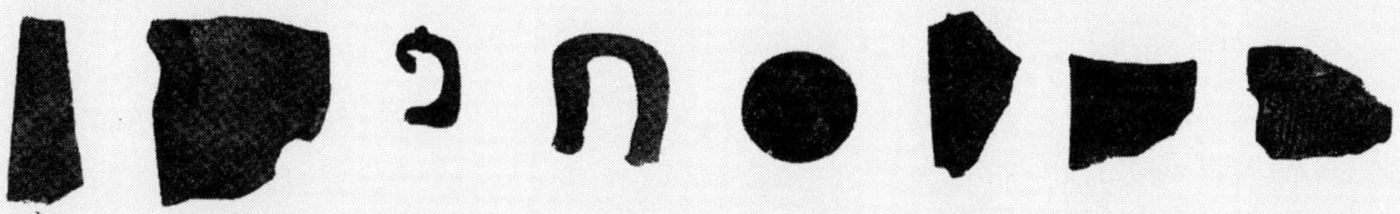

AS 0.082　AS 0.083　AS 0.084　AS 0.085　AS 0.086　AS 0.087　AS 0.088　AS 0.089

AS 0.082　刀柄殘片, 60 cm.×2.5 cm., 15.2 g.

AS 0.083　殘蓋片,中紐已失, 5.8 cm.×5.6 cm., 53 g.

AS 0.084　耳?, 3.2 cm.×1.9 cm., 5 g.

AS 0.085　鼎耳?, 4.2 cm.×3.3 cm., 36.3 g.

AS 0.086　觚或斝柱, 4.1 cm.×3.7 cm., 52.2 g.

AS 0.087　爵殘片, 5.3 cm.×3 cm., 15.2 g.

AS 0.088　殘片,細刻紋之一例, 3.9 cm.×3.8 cm., 24.9 g.

AS 0.089　殘片,深刻紋之一例, 4.5 cm.×3.7 cm., 24.6 g.

一一　銅范

銅范爲殷墟之一大發現,可證殷人青銅器皆自鼓鑄,並可證所鑄青銅器種類之夥。

AS 0.090　AS 0.091　AS 0.092　AS 0.093　AS 0.094　AS 0.095

(139)

AS 0.044 Hairpin. 13.6×2.4 cm. 5.75 g.

A fully developed cock-headed hairpin.

AS 0.045 Hairpin. 16.2×2.5 cm. 9.40 g.

Cock-headed with an exaggerated development of the crown.

AS 0.046 Hairpin. 19.3×2.4 cm. 11.20 g.

Still cock-headed top, but conventionalized.

AS 0.047 Hairpin. 9.9×2.2 cm. 7.50 g.

Another example of conventionalized cock-headed top.

AS 0.048 Hairpin. 9.6×2.2 cm. 4.00 g.

A further development from AS 0.047.

Group G. Various Bone Works

(AS-X: AS 0.049–0.055)

One of the most flourishing industries in the ancient capital of the Yin-Shang Dynasty was undoubtedly concerned with bone works. This material was utilized in a great variety of ways; works of bone have survived more abundantly than any other make. Ox bones constituted the bulk of this supply, supplemented by skeletal materials of many other animals—tiger, deer, whale, elephant, etc. The following shows only a few examples:

AS 0.049 Chisel. 5.3×3.6 cm. 1.75 g.

Narrow at the upper edge, with an eye for passing string. Lower edge sharpened, lateral sides smooth.

AS 0.050 Wedge. 6.9×2.9 cm. 25.90 g.

Sharpened edge, narrowed down from lateral side. Very thick butt end.

AS 0.051 Awl. 10.4×1.3 cm. 7.00 g.

Point broken off, evidently very sharp. Upper part retaining original shape of the material for a more convenient grasping.

AS 0.052 Nail. 10.6×1.2 cm. 10.00 g.

A type of nail that was used widely in later period.

AS 0.053 Awl. 11.7×1.1 cm. 6.50 g.

A commoner type than AS 0.051.

AS 0.090　?, 8.5 cm.×6.4 cm.×3.2 cm., 137.5 g.

AS 0.091　頂 盔, 6.8 cm.×6.6 cm.×4.2 cm., 116.6 g.

AS 0.092　?, 8.5 cm.×5.5 cm.×3.5 cm., 116.6 g.

AS 0.093　箭 頭, 4.4 cm.×4.8 cm.×3.7 cm., 62.6 g.

AS 0.094　?, 4.1 cm.×2.3 cm.×3.1 cm., 24.8 g.

AS 0.095　觚, 6.4 cm.×5.5 cm.×.4 cm., 37.95 g.

一二　骨刻,牙刻,與石刻

殷墟遺物最足以表示殷人藝術觀念者爲:銅范、骨刻、牙刻、與石刻。銅范已見上項,今再選骨刻、牙刻、與石刻共五種,以示其雕刻及鑲嵌之術。

AS 0.096

AS 0.097

AS 0.098

AS 0.099

AS 0.096　7.8 cm.×2.6 cm., 14.3 g., 牙鑴,解紐錐,兩面饕餮,帶穿。

AS 0.097　6.6 cm.×2.2 cm., 20.3 g., 牙製柱形裝飾,鑲松綠石,人字文套箭頭形。

AS 0.098　4.2 cm.×2.6 cm., 7.5 g., 骨製半面饕餮。

AS 0.099　3.4 cm.×1.0 cm., 2.8 g., 牙製,魚形。

(141)

AS 0.054 "Shih" (柶). 20.8×5.9 cm. 60.20 g.

A type of bone implements found relatively abundant. Shapes vary a great deal; but always curve in towards middle. Used in connection with dinner service, as a mixer, a cutter and a means to convey food from one vessel to another. The butt end is thickened on one lateral margin in order to stand the stress of grasping; the cutting edge is sharpened.

AS 0.055 "Shih" (柶). 20.8×5.9 cm. 60.20 g.

Another type. A small perforation at the butt end; the other end shaped like a shoe-horn used mostly in liquid. Curved towards middle very gracefully.

Group H. Arrowheads

(AS-XI: AS 0.056–0.075)

Arrowheads recovered from Yinhsü are mainly made of two different materials: bone and bronze. Some stone arrowheads have also been found. but they are so rare that they can be considered only as exceptions. A curious point to note is that while the shapes of the bone arrowheads vary a great deal, those cast from bronze conform essentially to only one type.

AS 0.056 Arrowhead. 9.9×1.7 cm. 12.50 g.

Bone. Double-edged. Mid-ridge on one side.

AS 0.057 Arrowhead. 8.8×1.4 cm. 9.40 g.

Bone. Double-edged. Sharp mid-ridge on one side.

AS 0.058 Arrowhead. 7.6×2.0 cm. 9.50 g.

Bone. Double-edged. Mid-ridges on both sides.

AS 0.059 Arrowhead. 8.1×1.4 cm. 6.85 g.

Bone. Double-edged. With a base, stem marked off. No mid-ridge.

AS 0.060 Arrowhead. 9.0×2.0 cm. 11.55 g.

Bone. Double-edged. More pronounced base. Stem broken.

AS 0.061 Arrowhead. 5.55×1.6 cm. 2.05 g.

Bone. Double-edged. Barbed base. No mid-ridge.

AS 0.062 Arrowhead. 5.2×2.4 cm. 4.00 g.

Bone. Double-edged. Barbed based. Extradeveloped mid-ridge. Stem broken off.

AS 0.100

AS 0.100 7.7 cm.×8.4 cm., 346 g., 大理石,殘琮,上刻饕餮。

加送品

下列選品十一件,照像一張,墓誌一張,由英選委之特別要求,加送展覽。

一二(續前) 石刻與白陶

AS 0.101

AS 0.063	Arrowhead.	4.8 × 0.9 cm.	1.85 g.
	Bone. Triple-edged. No base.		
AS 0.064	Arrowhead.	7.2 × 0.9 cm.	4.50 g.
	Bone. Triple-edged. Base slightly developed.		
AS 0.065	Arrowhead.	6.2 × 0.8 cm.	4.00 g.
	Bone. Triple-edged. Base developed.		

All the bronze arrowheads are: double-edged, with barbed base, pronounced mid-ridges on both sides.

AS 0.066	Bronze Arrowhead.	5.20 × 1.70 cm.	6.2 g.
AS 0.067	Bronze Arrowhead.	4.80 × 1.75 cm.	6.2 g.
AS 0.068	Bronze Arrowhead.	5.45 × 1.80 cm.	4.9 g.
AS 0.069	Bronze Arrowhead.	6.15 × 1.75 cm.	8.5 g.
AS 0.070	Bronze Arrowhead.	7.00 × 2.00 cm.	9.9 g.
AS 0.071	Bronze Arrowhead.	6.70 × 2.10 cm.	10.2 g.
AS 0.072	Bronze Arrowhead.	8.40 × 2.10 cm.	16.6 g.
AS 0.073	Bronze Arrowhead.	6.50 × 2.20 cm.	9.9 g.
AS 0.074	Bronze Arrowhead.	6.70 × 2.50 cm.	13.2 g.
AS 0.075	Bronze Arrowhead.	5.70 × 3.50 cm.	8.5 g.

Group I. Halberts, Spearheads, and Socketed Celt

(AS-XII, AS-XIII: AS 0.076–0.081)

Bronze objects found from Yinhsü may be divided into four classes: tools, weapons, ceremonial vessels, decorative pieces. Of these four weapons come first in quantity, if arrowheads are to be included. All the other three classes have survived in very fragmentary condition. Even among the weapons very few complete pieces have been found. The three specimens shown under this group are some of the best in the collection. Of the other three, two are selected from the Chünhsien collection; both of them are tomb furniture of the Western Chou period, and the remaining one was purchased from a curio shop in Anyang. These are shown here together with the Yinhsü specimens to illustrate certain features of the typological development of the two weapons.

AS 0.101 石刻人像下部,抱膝坐形,背面有槽。有紅土與石灰痕記;似爲附屬與建築之雕飾,殷墟出土。

最大寬度(穿過中心)	26.45 cm.
前後穿過中心之最大厚度	12.50 cm.
前寬(手以上)	22.00 cm.
後寬	20.20 cm.
兩肘最外相距之寬度	26.00 cm.
前左角高	22.50 cm.
前右角高	17.60 cm.
後左角高	18.40 cm.
後右角高	15.70 cm.
重	154,000 g.

AS 0.102

AS 0.102 刻紋白陶邊緣,獸耳作饕餮形,殷虛出土。

緣寬	7.7 cm.	正寬	13.6 cm.
高	9.9 cm.	左右對角	15.2 cm.
重	180 g.		

(145)

AS 0.076 Ko or Halbert. 22.7×6.4 cm. 290.70 g.

Yinhsü bronze. "Nei" well developed. Blade shows no curvature near the "nei"; hu hardly developed. Typical form of ko of the Yin-Shang Dynasty.

AS 0.077 Ko or Halbert. 22.7×8.6 cm. 236.50 g.

From Chünhsien collection. Early Chou. First development of hu, with one perforation.

AS 0.078 Ko or Halbert. 24.9×10.6 cm. 239.00 g.

Purchased in Anyang. Probably Middle Chou. Hu gradually lengthened, still with one perforation.

AS 0.079 Socketed Spearhead. 25.2×6.9 cm. 343.00 g.

Yinhsü bronze. Beautifully preserved. Blade strong with mid-ridges on both sides. Edge very sharp. Socket well developed, and thickened at the base. Two loops near the base for fastening.

AS 0.080 Spearhead. 26.1×6.7 cm. 153.00 g.

From Chünhsien collection. A curious contrast with the above specimen. Although the size is practically the same as the above, the weight is less than half. Manufactured specially for tomb consumption. The twenty perforations on the blade were probably an economical device rather than for any other purpose. The development of a barbed base is an interesting feature. Only one loop on the mid-ridge of the blade near at the base.

AS 0.081 Socketed Celt. 8.9×4.1 cm. 161.00 g.

Yinhsü bronze. Several specimens have been found from this site. As it shows no resemblance to any of the stone celts, its origin has aroused much interesting speculation.

Group J. Fragments of Larger Bronze Works

(AS-XIV: AS 0.082–0.089)

After the invading army of the Chou had finally captured the capital of the Yin, bronzes were undoubtedly one of the most important loots which the conquerors took away. The whole city must have been sacked quite thoroughly, and it is for this reason that no bronze

一三　黑陶精品

山東城子崖之石器時代黑陶文化，爲最近考古界之一大發現。其時代在殷商以前，爲殷商一部文化之所自出。下列黑陶四片，爲黑陶中之精品。看『中國考古報告集之一：城子崖』，中央研究院歷史語言研究所出版。

AS 0.103　　AS 0.104　　AS 0.105　　AS 0.106

AS 0.103　黑陶片，城子崖出土。

緣寬	2.30 cm.	正寬	3.20 cm.
高	4.85 cm.	左右對角	5.08 cm.
重	3.6 g.		

AS 0.104　黑陶片，城子崖出土。

緣寬	3.05 cm.	正寬	3.70 cm.
高	3.40 cm.	左右對角	4.80 cm.
重	2.96 g.		

AS 0.105　黑陶片，城子崖出土。

緣寬	5.25 cm.	正寬	5.4 cm.
高	3.20 cm.	左右對角	5.97 cm.
重	4.25 g.		

AS 0.106　黑陶片，城子崖出土。

緣寬	8.30 cm.	正寬	9.00 cm.
高	1.90 cm.	左右對角	9.10 cm.
重	9.05 g.		

of respectable size has ever been recovered from Yinhsü in all the diggings that have been carried out in the last six years. But their existence could not be disputed; it is proved by the many fragments that have been found; and still more substantially, by the moulds.

AS 0.082 Fragment of a Knife. 6.0 × 2.5 cm. 15.20 g.

AS 0.083 Part of a Lid. 5.8 × 5.6 cm. 53.00 g.

AS 0.084 Ear of a Vessel. 3.2 × 1.9 cm. 5.00 g.

AS 0.085 Ear of a Vessel. 4.2 × 3.3 cm. 36.30 g.

AS 0.086 Fragment of Ku, Chia. 4.1 × 3.7 cm. 52.20 g.

AS 0.087 Fragment of Chueh. 5.3 × 3.0 cm. 15.20 g.

AS 0.088 Fragment of a Vessel. 3.9 × 3.8 cm. 24.90 g.

AS 0.089 Fragment of a Vessel. 4.5 × 3.7 cm. 24.60 g.

The last three show the fine workmanship of bronze casting and are interesting examples of the decorative art of this period.

Group K. Moulds for Bronze Casting

(AS-XV: AS 0.090–0.095)

One of the most important discoveries from the Yinhsü excavations would always be the moulds used for bronzes casting. These finds conclusively prove that the people of this period not only used bronzes, but actually manufactured these articles. Quite a number of such fragments have been discovered; most of them were evidently used for casting large works.

AS 0.090 Bronze Mould. 8.5 × 6.4 × 3.2 cm. 137.50 g.

AS 0.091 Bronze Mould. 6.8 × 6.6 × 4.2 cm. 116.60 g.

AS 0.092 Bronze Mould. 8.5 × 5.5 × 3.5 cm. 116.60 g.

AS 0.093 Bronze Mould. 4.4 × 4.8 × 3.1 cm. 62.60 g.

Very distinct impressions of arrow-heads. Cf. Bronze arrow-heads.

AS 0.094 Bronze Mould. 4.1 × 2.3 × 3.1 cm. 24.80 g.

AS 0.095 Bronze Mould. 6.4 × 5.5 × 0.4 cm. 37.95 g.

For the lower part of ku.

一四

隋處士卜仁墓葬中隨葬器:處士卒於仁壽三年三月十六日,卽公元六〇三年五月二日,安陽小屯村出土。

AS 0.107

AS 0.107 高座盤,上部敷釉。

上盤徑	28.00 cm.	座徑	14.7–15.0 cm.
柱徑	8.8–9 cm.	高	12.4–13.7 cm.
重	2,650 g.		

AS 0.108　　AS 0.109

(149)

GROUP L. IVORY, BONE, AND STONE CARVINGS

(AS-XVI, AS-XVII: AS 0.096–0.100)

Among the art-objects of Yinhsü, bone, stone, and ivory carvings are undoubtedly of the most important. This group includes specimens of the decorative art current in the Yin-Shang period.

AS 0.096 Ivory Carving. 7.8 × 2.6 cm. 143.00 g.

Ivory carving. A tool used for untying knots. Double-faced t'ao t'ieh, with a perforation to pass string.

AS 0.097 Ivory Carving. 6.6 × 2.2 cm. 20.30 g.

Fragment only. Tube-shaped, inlaid with turquois. Zigzags, filled with arrow-head design.

AS 0.098 Bone Carving. 4.2 × 2.6 cm. 7.50 g.

Half a t'ao t'ieh, in relief. Originally attached to some other work.

AS 0.099 Ivory Carving. 3.4 × 1.0 cm. 2.80 g.

Fish.

AS 0.100 Stone Carving. 7.7 × 8.4 cm. 346.00 g.

Chung. A jade type. Another form of t'ao t'ieh in carving.

ADDENDA

At the request of Professor Paul Pelliott representing the British Committee, the following additional exhibits consisting of eleven articles and two photographs have been selected from the archæological collection of Academia Sinica.

GROUP L.

(Continued)

STONE CARVING AND WHITE POTTERY

AS 0.101 Lower half of a human figure in a squatting posture, carved of limestone, covered with incised ornament. Vertical trough on the back part, retaining traces of lime

AS 0.108　四耳罐，上部敷釉，帶蓋。

口徑	6.65 cm.	腹徑	15.1–15.3 cm.
底至口高	18.4 cm.	底至蓋頂高	20.1 cm.
重(連蓋)	1,300 g.		

AS 0.109　四耳罐，上部敷釉，帶蓋。

口徑	6.7 cm.	腹徑	14.8–15.1 cm.
底至口高	17.8 cm.	底至蓋頂高	19.7 cm.
重(連蓋)	1,200 g.		

AS 0.110　　　　AS 0.111

AS 0.110　杯，上部敷釉。

口徑	8.8 cm.	高	6.8 cm.
重	154.6 g.		

AS 0.111　杯，上部敷釉。

口徑	8.6–8.8 cm.	高	6.7 cm.
重	156.6 g.		

(151)

and red pigments, probably an architectural ornament. Found in several fragments, from Yinhsü.

Maximum width at mid-point	26.45 cm.
Maximum thickness at mid-point	12.50 cm.
Maximum frontal width (above hand)	22.00 cm.
Maximum width of back	20.20 cm.
Frontal height at left corner	22.50 cm.
Frontal height at right corner	17.60 cm.
Total weight	15,400 g.

AS 0.102 Incised white pottery shard; rim piece with a loop handle moulded in the form of a t'ao t'ieh, from Yinhsü. 13.6×99 cm.

GROUP M. BLACK POTTERY SHARDS

The following four specimens of black pottery shards are selected from the remains of Ch'êngtzŭyai, Shantung, the type site of the neolithic black pottery culture excavated by the Archæological Section of the Institute of History and Philology, Academia Sinica. For details see: ARCHÆOLOGIA SINICA, No. 1, Ch'êngtzŭyai, published by the Institute of History and Philology.

AS 0.103	Rim Piece of Black Pottery from Ch'êngtzŭyai.	3.2×4.85 cm.	3.60 g.
AS 0.104	Rim Piece of Black Pottery from Ch'êngtzŭyai.	3.7×4.80 cm.	2.96 g.
AS 0.105	Rim Piece of Black Pottery from Ch'êngtzŭyai.	5.4×3.20 cm.	4.25 g.
AS 0.106	Rim Piece of Black Pottery from Ch'êngtzŭyai.	9.0×1.90 cm.	9.05 g.

GROUP N. SUI POTTERIES

The following articles are all from the tomb furniture of Pu Jen (卜仁), who died on the 16th day of the 3rd month in the third year of Jen Shou (仁壽) of the Sui Dynasty (see AS-0.113), corresponding to the 2nd of May, 603 A. D. The tomb was found in Anyang, Honan and excavated in 1929.

AS 0.112

AS 0.112　卜仁墓葬全影。

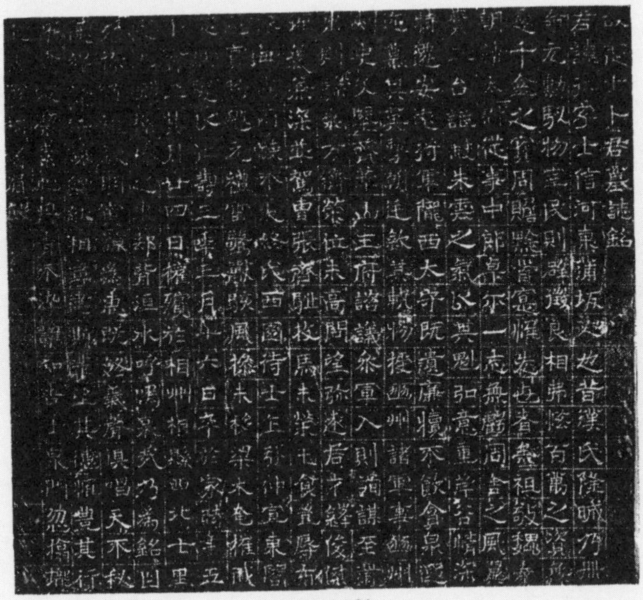

AS 0.113

AS 0.113　卜仁墓誌拓片。

（153）

AS 0.107 Plate with a tall pedestal. Greater part glazed.

Diameter of the Plate	28.00 cm.
Height	13.70 cm.
Weight	2,650 g.

AS 0.108 Jar with four loop handles and lid. Greater part glazed.

Height	18.40 cm.
Diameter of Rim	6.65 cm.
Maximum Diameter	15.30 cm.
Weight	1,300 g.

AS 0.109 Jar with four loop handles and lid. Greater part glazed.

Height	17.80 cm.
Rim Diameter	6.70 cm.
Maximum Diameter	15.10 cm.
Weight	1,200 g.

AS 0.110 Cup. Upper part glazed.

Height	6.80 cm.
Rim Diameter	8.80 cm.
Weight	154.60 g.

AS 0.111 Cup. Upper part glazed.

Height	6.70 cm.
Rim	8.80 cm.
Weight	156.60 g.

AS 0.112 Photograph showing the burial of Pu Jen before the removal of the tomb furniture.

AS 0.113 Photographic copy of the ribbing of the biographical record of Pu Jen inscribed on the stone tablet found in the above tomb.

珍 本 古 書

ANCIENT BOOKS

參加倫敦中國藝術國際展覽會 珍本古書照片目錄

（北平圖書館藏）

ANCIENT BOOKS FROM THE NATIONAL LIBRARY AT PEIPING

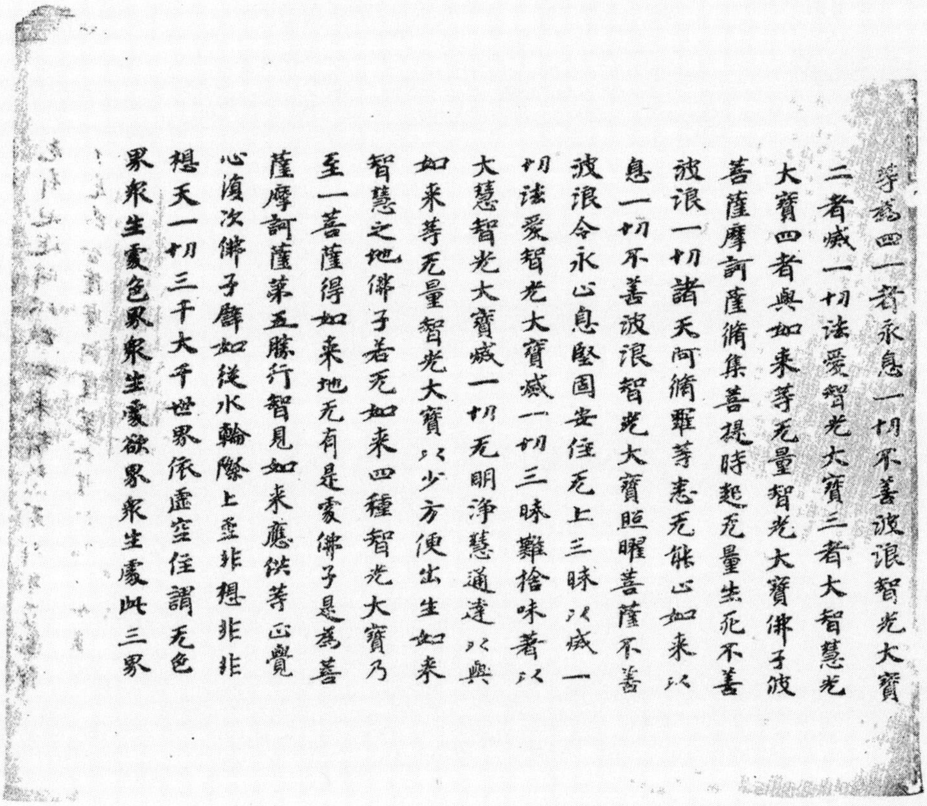
等為四一者永息一切不善波浪智光大寶
二者滅一切法愛智光大寶三者大智慧光
大寶四者與如来等无量智光大寶佛子彼
菩薩摩訶薩脩集菩提時起无量生死不善
波浪一切諸天阿脩羅等悉无能沮如来以
息一切不善波浪智光大寶照曜菩薩不善
波浪令永止息堅固安住无上三昧以滅一
切法愛智光大寶滅一切三昧難捨味著以
大慧智光大寶滅一切无明淨慧通達以與
如来等无量智光大寶以少方便出生如来
智慧之地佛子若无如来四種智光大寶乃
至一菩薩得如来地无有是處佛子是爲菩
薩摩訶薩第五勝行智見如来應供等正覺
心演次佛子譬如從水輪際上至非想非非
想天一切三千大千世界依虛空住謂无色
界衆生處色界衆生處欲界衆生處此三界

一

大方廣佛華嚴經

六朝寫本東晉佛駄陀羅譯敦煌莫高窟藏古寫本卷子之一。

1. **"The Buddhavatamsaka Mahavaipulya Sutra" (Circa 6th Century).**

A Chinese manuscript from T'un-huang.

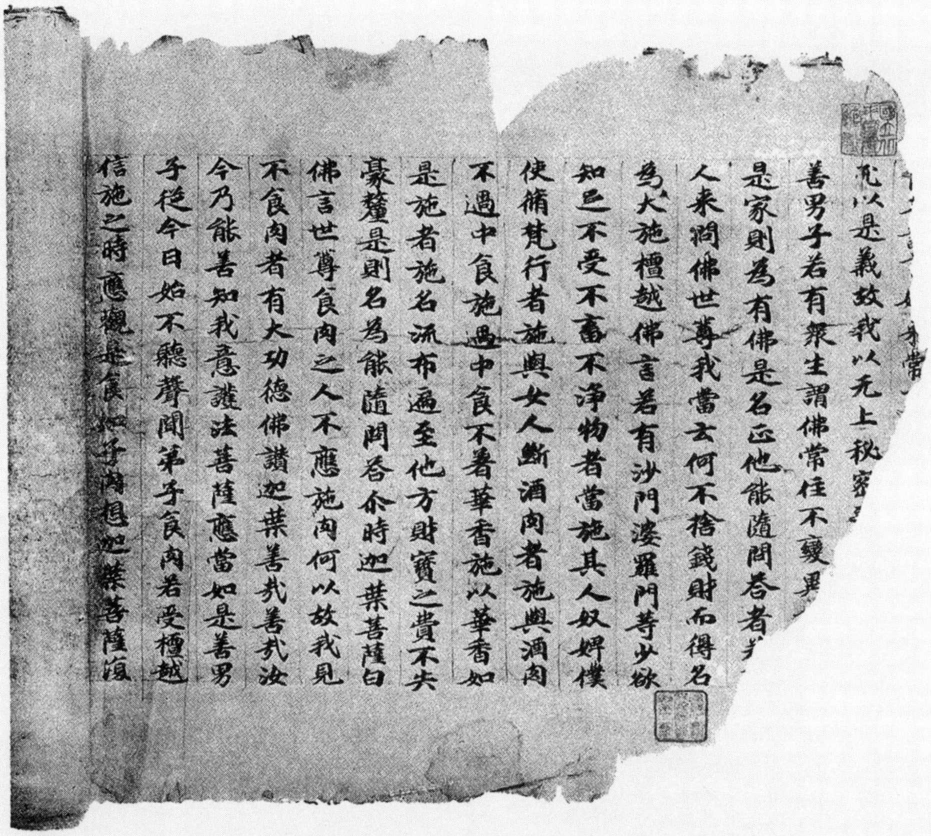

以是義故我以无上秘密
善男子若有衆生謂佛常住不變異
是家則為有佛是名正他能隨問答者
人來問佛世尊我當云何不捨錢財而得名
為大施檀越佛言若有沙門婆羅門等少欲
知足不受不畜不淨物者當施其人奴婢僕
使脩梵行者施與女人斷酒肉者施與酒肉
不過中食施過中食不著華香施以華香如
是施者施名流布遍至他方財寶之費不失
毫釐是則名為能隨問答尒時迦葉菩薩白
佛言世尊食肉之人不應施肉何以故我見
不食肉者有大功德佛讚迦葉善哉善哉汝
今乃能善知我意護法菩薩應當如是善男
子從今日始不聽聲聞弟子食肉若受檀越
信施之時應觀是食如子肉想迦葉菩薩復

二

大般涅盤經

六朝寫本。涼曇無讖譯。敦煌莫高窟藏古寫本卷子之一。

2. "The Mahaprajnaparamita Sutra" (Circa 6th Century).

A Chinese manuscript from T'un-huang.

(158)

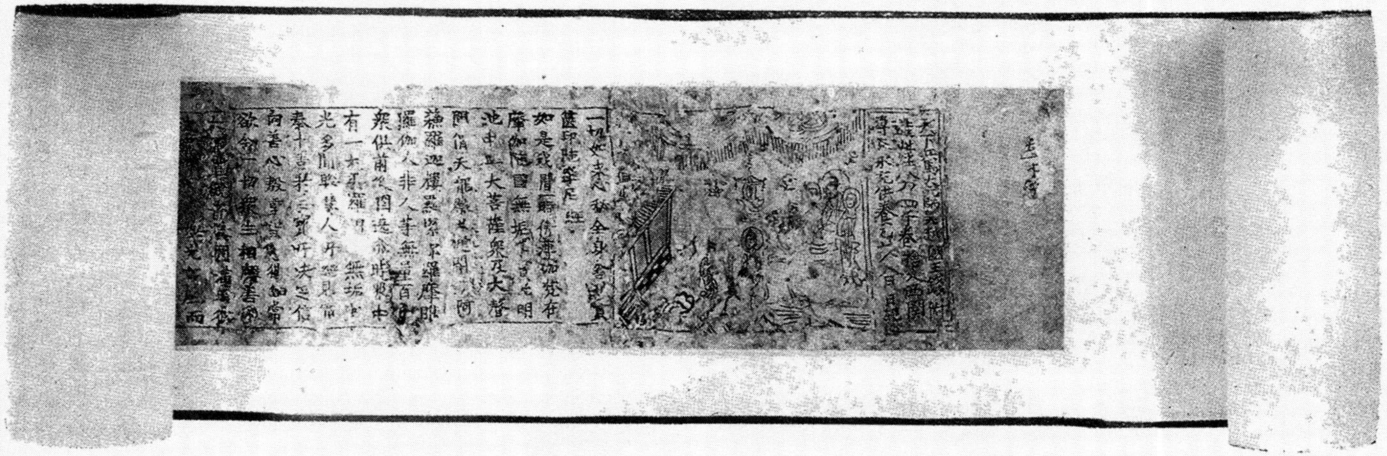

三

陀羅尼經

五代刻本。此卷出杭州雷峯塔。前有康有爲氏手跋。五代吳越國王錢俶時所雕。西歷九世紀中葉產物也。

3. "Dharani" (9th Century).

An early Chinese block print. This scroll came from the Laifeng Pagoda of Hangchow.

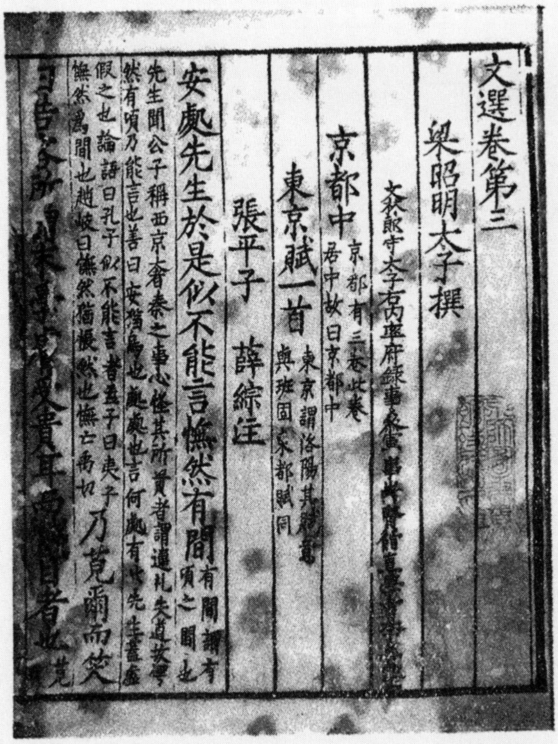
文選卷第三
梁昭明太子撰
文林郎守太子右內率府錄事參軍事[illegible]
京都中 京都有三卷此卷居中故曰京都中
東京賦一首 東京謂洛陽其[illegible]與班固東都賦同
張平子 薛綜注
安處先生於是似不能言憮然有間 有間謂有頃之間也
先生聞公子稱西京奢泰之事心怪其所貴者謂遵礼失道[illegible]
然有頃乃能言也善曰安猶焉也處處也言何處有此先生蓋虛
假之也論語曰孔子似不能言者孟子曰夷子
憮然爲間也趙岐曰憮然猶悵然也憮亡禹切 乃莞爾而笑
[illegible]者也 莞

四

文選

北宋刊本。梁蕭統輯。唐李善注。此本確爲仁宗天聖監本(西一〇二三至一〇三二)。緣卷中通字缺筆。通爲宋眞宗劉后父名。其避諱在仁宗初年。此爲本書舊槧傳世之最早者。

4. Hsiao T'ung (Prince of the Liang Dynasty): "Wên Hsuan" (Circa 1025 A. D.).

With notes by Li Shan. An official Northern Sung (960–1126 A. D.) edition of the well-known anthology. It is the earliest printed edition of this work, and a fine example of China's ancient printing.

(160)

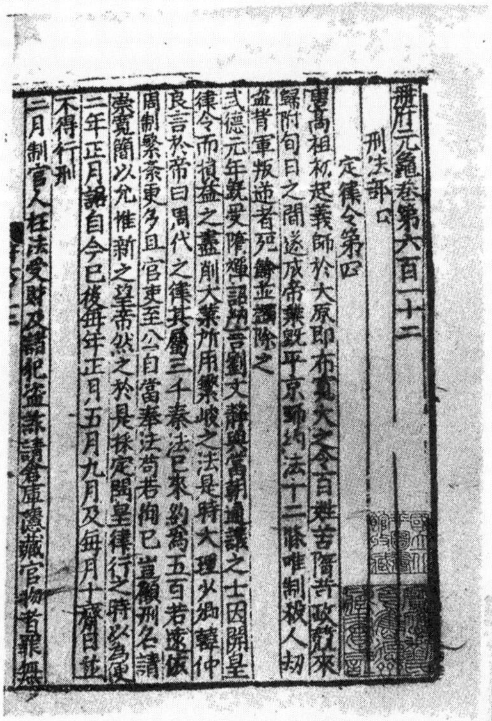
冊府元龜卷第六百一十二

刑法部四

定律令第四

五

冊府元龜

北宋刊本。宋王欽若等撰。輯錄六經子史。以部目類次。此北宋中葉眉山刊本。卷中朗敞驚殷等字俱減筆文字。遠勝通行本。內閣大庫書。

5. Wang Ch'in-jo, & etc.: "T'se Fu Yuan Kui" (Circa 1050 A. D.).

A Northern Sung (960–1126 A. D.) edition of this encyclopedic compilation. This particular volume is from an incomplete set formerly preserved in the Ch'ing Cabinet Library.

六

國朝二百家名賢文粹

南宋刊本。宋王稱輯。此編體例略如聖宋文海。而淵博則過之。刊於慶元丁巳（西一一九七）。亦蜀刊也。四庫全書失收。

6. Wang Ch'eng: "Kuo Ch'ao Er Pai Chia Ming Hsien Wên Ts'ui" (1197 A. D.).

A Southern Sung Dynasty (1127–1279 A. D.) edition, the blocks being cut and printed in Szechwan which was one of the important centers of printing in the Southern Sung Dynasty.

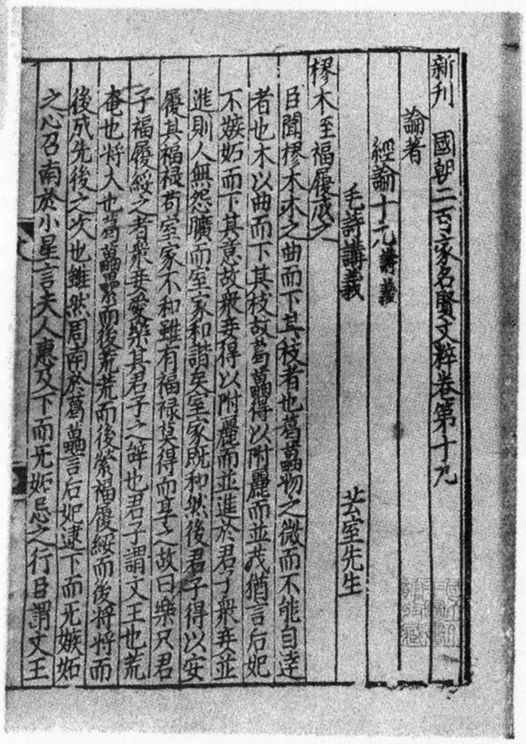
新刊國朝二百家名賢文粹卷第十九

論著

經論十九

毛詩講義

芸室先生

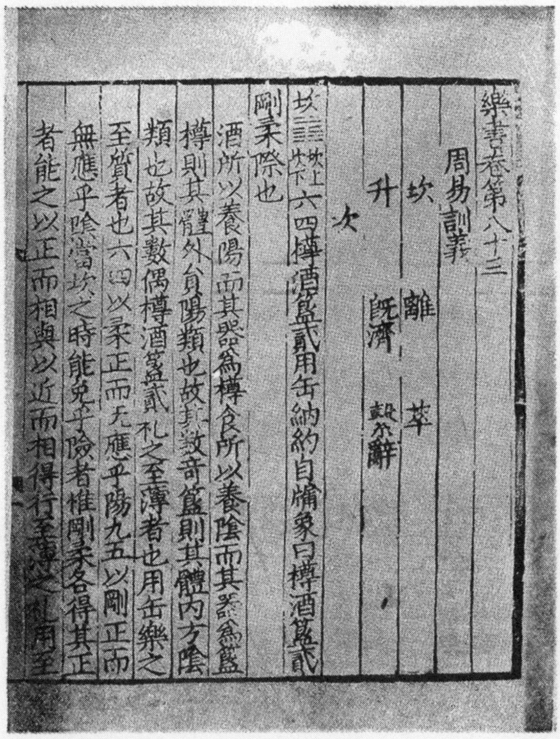

七

樂書

南宋刻本。宋陳暘撰。此書乃徽宗建中靖國間(西一一〇一)暘官祕書省正字時所進。論律呂本義樂器樂章及五禮之用樂者至詳。考古樂者所不廢也。

7. Ch'en Yang: "Yo Shu" (12th or Early 13th Century).

The work was completed in 1101 A. D., but not printed until much later, when the capital of the Sung Dynasty had been removed to Hangchow, and is thus known as a Southern Sung edition.

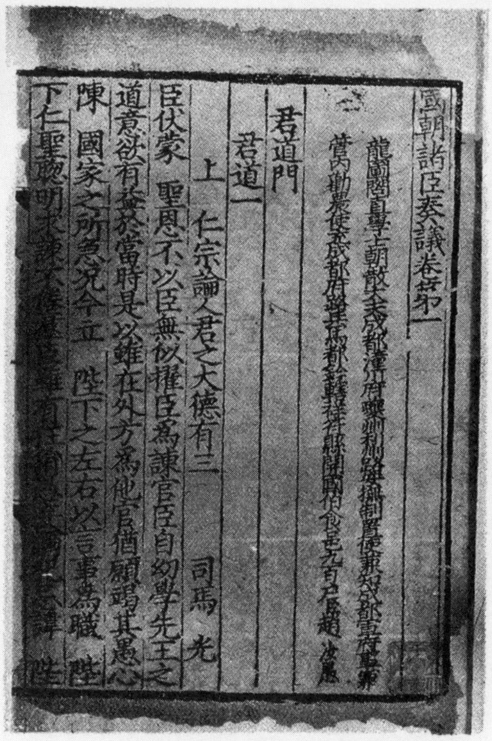

八

國朝諸臣奏議

南宋刻本。宋趙汝愚輯。全書分君道帝系天道百官儒學禮樂賞刑財賦兵制方域邊防總議十二門。輯錄北宋一代名臣奏議。自建隆迄靖康。此本乃淳祐間(西一二四一至一二五二)福建提舉史季溫所刊。其板明時入南監後印本也。

8. Chao Ju-yu: "Kuo Ch'ao Chu Ch'en Tsou I" (Circa 1245 A. D.).

The blocks of this book were cut in Fukien about 1245 A. D. The present copy was printed from the original blocks in Nanking during the Ming Dynasty (1368-1644 A. D.).

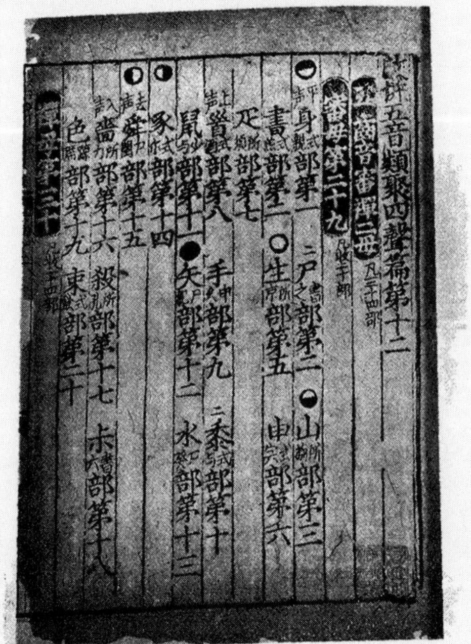

改併五音類聚四聲篇第十二

凡三十四部

審母第二十九　凡收十部

身部第一　尸部第二　山部第三

書部第四　生部第五　申部第六

疋部第七

晉部第八　手部第九　黍部第十

鼠部第十一　矢部第十二　水部第十三

豕部第十四

舜部第十五

嗇部第十六　殺部第十七　赤部第十八

色部第十九　束部第二十

禪母第三十

九

改併五音類聚四聲篇

金刻本。金韓道昭撰。以三十六字母各分四聲排比諸字之先後所收之字。大抵以廣韻集韻爲本。此金末平陽書肆刻本世所謂平水本也

9. Han Tao-chao: "Kai Pin Wu Yin Lei Chu Szu Sheng Pien" (Circa 1220 A. D.).

This is an edition printed about 1220 A. D. at P'ingyang in North China, which was then under the rule of the Chin Tartars. It is known in Chinese as the "Ping Shui Edition" from the name of the locality.

(163)

列傳第七　通志九十四

戰國　孟嘗君　平原君　虞卿

樂毅　廉頗　藺相如

趙奢　李牧

春申君　屈原　信陵君

秦

呂不韋　李斯　蒙恬

戰國

一〇

通志

元刻本宋鄭樵撰司馬氏史記後以紀傳體作通史者此書是也全書綱羅賅博。菁華全在二十略此本乃清內府天祿琳瑯舊藏元至治二年(西一三二二)福州路刊本尚是元印本也。

10. Cheng Ch'iao: "Tung Chih" (1322 A. D.).

A Yuan Dynasty (1279–1368 A. D.) edition. It was cut in Fukien in 1322 A. D. The present copy formerly belonged to Emperor Chien-lung's imperial library Tien Lu Ling Lang (see seal on first page).

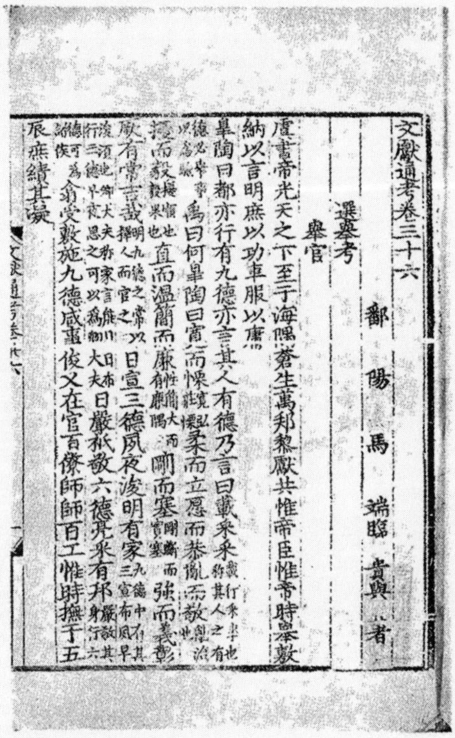

文獻通考卷三十六
鄱陽馬端臨貴與著
選舉考
舉官
虞書帝光天之下至于海隅蒼生萬邦黎獻共惟帝臣惟帝時舉敷
納以言明庶以功車服以庸
皋陶曰都亦行有九德亦言其人有德乃言曰載采采
禹曰何皋陶曰寬而栗柔而立愿而恭亂而敬
擾而毅直而溫簡而廉剛而塞彊而義彰
厥有常吉哉日宣三德夙夜浚明有家
翕受敷施九德咸事俊乂在官百僚師師百工惟時撫于五
辰庶績其凝

一一

文獻通考

元刻本。元馬端臨撰。此書蓋仿杜佑通典而作。上起遼古。下迄趙宋。以田賦錢幣等十九門叙歷代史事原委。此元至正初(西一三四一)重修泰定刻本。元時版置西湖書院。入明移南監。此入南監後印本也

11. Ma Tuan-lin: "Wên Hsien T'ung K'ao" (1341 A. D.).

A Yuan Dynasty (1277–1367 A. D.) edition. The blocks were actually first carved in 1324, but they were repaired in 1341. The present edition was printed in Nanking during the Ming Dynasty (1368–1644 A. D.).

一二

通鑑總類

元刻本。宋沈樞撰。此編取司馬氏資治通鑑爲藍本。仿冊府元龜之例。分爲三十七門。每門各以事標題。此元至正癸卯(西一三六三)蘇州郡庠刻本。明時移至南監後印本也。

12. Shen Shu: "T'ung Chien Tsung Lei" (1363 A. D.).

A Yuan Dynasty (1279–1368 A. D.) edition. The blocks were cut in Soochow in 1363 A. D., but the present copy was printed from the original blocks in Nanking during the Ming Dynasty.

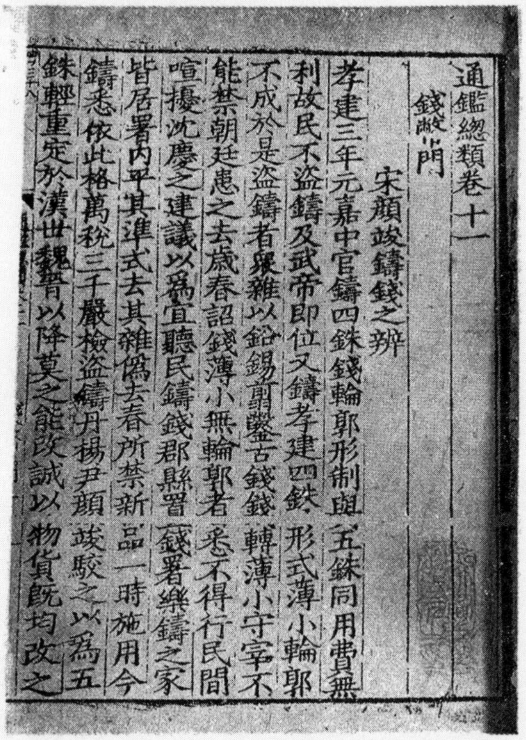

通鑑總類卷十一
錢幣門
宋顏竣鑄錢之辨
孝建三年元嘉中官鑄四銖錢輪郭形制與五銖同用費無
利故民不盜鑄及武帝即位又鑄孝建四銖形式薄小輪郭
不成於是盜鑄者衆雜以鉛錫翦鑿古錢錢轉薄小守宰不
能禁朝廷患之去歲春詔錢薄小無輪郭者悉不得行民間
喧擾沈慶之建議以爲宜聽民鑄錢郡縣置錢署樂鑄之家
皆居署內平其準式去其雜僞去春所禁新品一時施用今
鑄悉依此格萬稅三千嚴檢盜鑄丹楊尹顏竣駁之以爲五
銖輕重定於漢世魏晉以降莫之能改誠以物貨既均改之

(165)

一三

歷代十八史略

元刻本。元曾先之撰。記事自邃古迄宋季。治亂興亡之跡。略得其概而已。此至正二年(西一三四二)四明郡庠刻本。入明版入南監。內閣大庫書

13. Tseng Hsien-chih: "Li Tai Shih Pa Shih Lioh" (1342 A. D.).

A Yuan Dynasty (1279–1368 A. D.) edition. The blocks were cut in 1342 A. D. in Eastern Chekiang, but were moved to Nanking during the Ming Dynasty. The present copy formerly belonged to the Cabinet Library of the Ch'ing Dynasty.

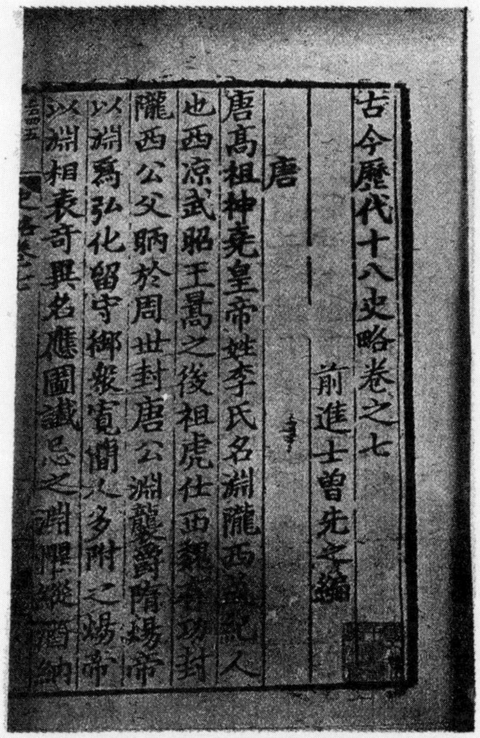

古今歷代十八史略卷之七
前進士曾先之編
唐
唐高祖神堯皇帝姓李氏名淵隴西成紀人
也西涼武昭王暠之後祖虎仕西魏有功封
隴西公父昞於周世封唐公淵襲爵隋煬帝
以淵爲弘化留守御衆寬簡人多附之煬帝
以淵相表奇異名應圖讖忌之淵懼縱酒納

一四

宣和博古圖

元刻本。宋王黼撰。此元至大間(西一三〇八至一三一一)刊本初印精美。世所罕見。內閣大庫書。

14. Wang Fu: "Hsuan Ho Po Ku Tu" (Circa 1310).

A Yuan Dynasty (1279–1368 A. D.) edition. Rare. A Ch'ing Dynasty (1644–1912 A. D.) black and block print

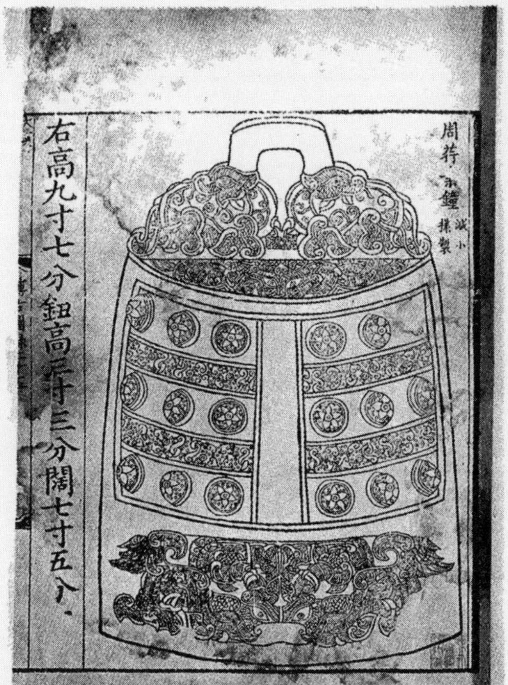

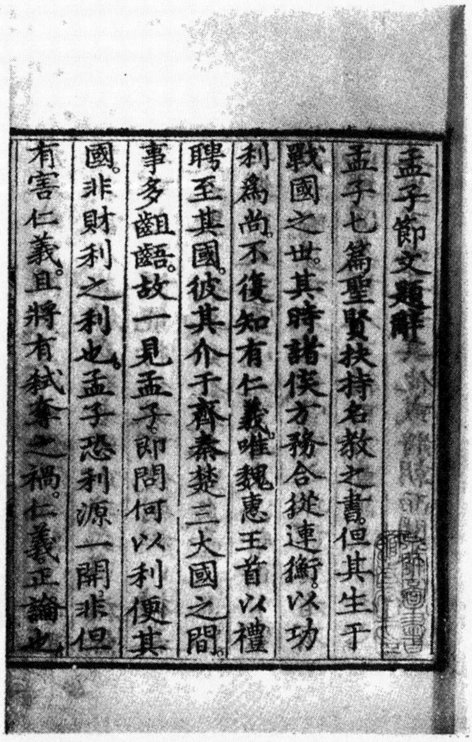

孟子節文題辭
孟子七篇聖賢扶持名教之書但其生于
戰國之世其時諸侯方務合從連衡以功
利為尚不復知有仁義唯魏惠王首以禮
聘至其國彼其介于齊秦楚三大國之間
事多齟齬故一見孟子即問何以利便其
國非財利之利也孟子恐利源一開非但
有害仁義且將有弑奪之禍仁義正論也

一五

孟子節文

明洪武官刻本。明劉三吾輯。書作于洪武二十七年(西一三九四)。以孟子涵義叢雜,故大加刪節而爲此書。內閣大庫書。

15. Liu San-wu: "Meng-tze Chieh Wên" (Circa 1394 A. D.).

A Ming Dynasty (1368–1644 A. D.) edition, printed by the government. The present copy formerly belonged to the Cabinet Library of the Ch'ing Dynasty.

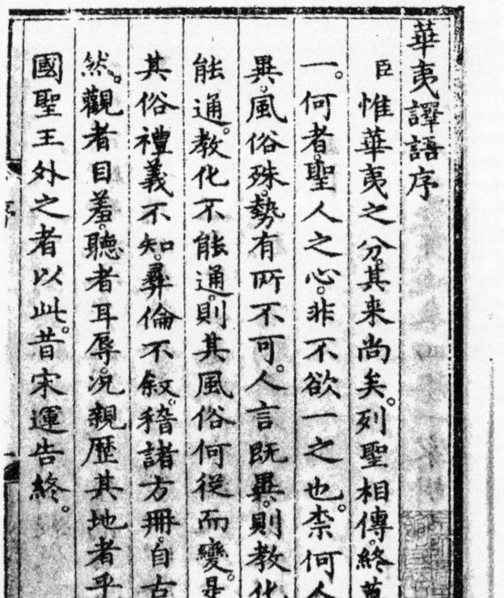

華夷譯語序
臣惟華夷之分其來尚矣列聖相傳終莫能
一何者聖人之心非不欲一之也柰何人言
異風俗殊勢有所不可人言既異則教化不
能通教化不能通則其風俗何從而變是以
其俗禮義不知彝倫不叙稽諸方冊自古為
然觀者目羞聽者耳辱况親歷其地者乎中
國聖王外之者以此昔宋運告終

一六

華夷譯語

明洪武官本。明火源潔撰。此書爲明初漢人習蒙古語者而設,故以漢文擬蒙古音分類編輯。四庫全書存目據永樂大典輯入,此尙是洪武原刊。可寶也。

16. Huo Yuan-chieh: "Hua I Yih Yu" (1389 A. D.).

A Ming Dynasty (1368–1644 A. D.) official edition. This is a Chinese Mongolian dictionary, and is quite rare.

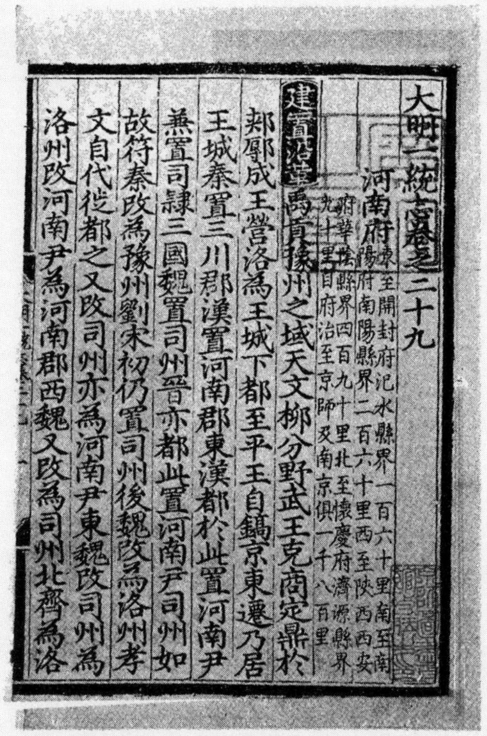

大明一統志卷之二十九

河南府東至開封府汜水縣界一百六十里南至南陽府南陽縣界二百六十里西至陝西西安府華陰縣界四百九十里北至懷慶府濟源縣界九十里自府治至京師又南京俱一千八百里

建置沿革禹貢豫州之域天文柳分野武王克商定鼎於郟鄏成王營洛為王城下都至平王自鎬京東遷乃居王城秦置三川郡漢置河南郡東漢都於此置河南尹兼置司隸三國魏置司州晉亦都此置河南尹司州如故苻秦改為豫州劉宋初仍置司州後魏改為洛州孝文自代徙都之又改司州亦為河南尹東魏改司州為洛州改河南尹為河南郡西魏又改為司州北齊為洛

一七

大明一統志

明天順官刻本明李賢等撰修據景泰修寰宇通志改編仿大元一統志例仍以一統志名書。黃綾包背裝尙是明代舊式也。

17. Li Hsien, & etc.: "Ta Ming I T'ung Chih" (Mid 14th Century).

A Ming Dynasty (1368–1644 A. D.) official edition. The present copy is in the original silk binding.

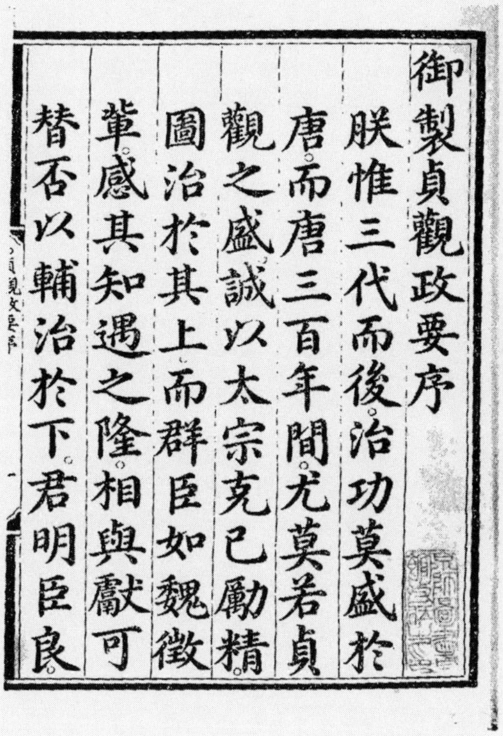

御製貞觀政要序

朕惟三代而後治功莫盛於唐而唐三百年間尤莫若貞觀之盛誠以太宗克己勵精圖治於其上而群臣如魏徵輩感其知遇之隆相與獻可替否以輔治於下君明臣良

一八

貞觀政要

明成化官刻本。唐吳兢撰。于唐太宗實錄外。采其與羣臣問答之語用備鑑戒。總四十篇。此成化元年(西一四六五)內府校刊本。有「廣運之寶」一印。初印精湛。經廠本之上駟也。

18. Wu Ching: "Chen Kuan Cheng Yao" (1465 A. D.).

A Ming Dynasty (1368–1644 A. D.) edition. This is an official publication, known in Chinese as "Ching Chang P'en."

(168)

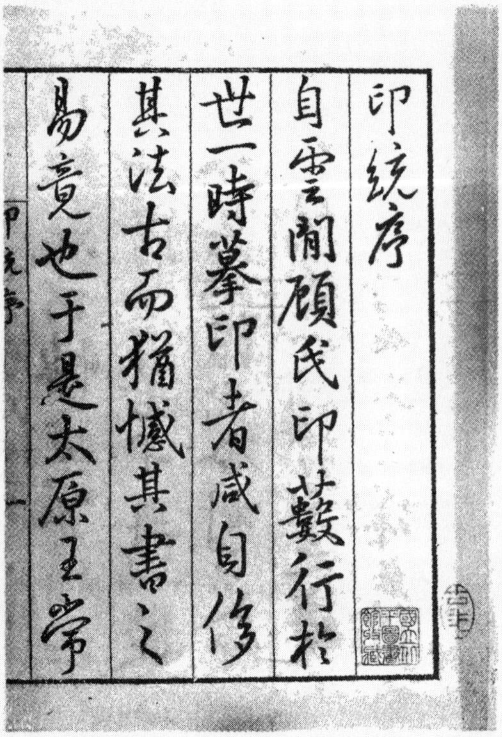

印統序

自雲間顧氏印藪行於

世一時摹印者咸自修

其法古而猶憾其書之

易竟也于是太原王常

一九

秦漢印統

明萬厯刻本。明羅王常撰。輯錄秦漢二代公私古鈐印而附著其說於下方。絕少贗品。不失爲謹嚴之作也此硃印本尤爲罕見可貴。

19. Lo Wang-ch'ang: "Ch'in Han Yin T'ung" (Circa 1608 A. D.).

A Ming Dynasty (1368–1644 A. D.) edition. This is a book of reproduction of ancient seals. Excepting the prefaces, the present copy was printed in vermilion.

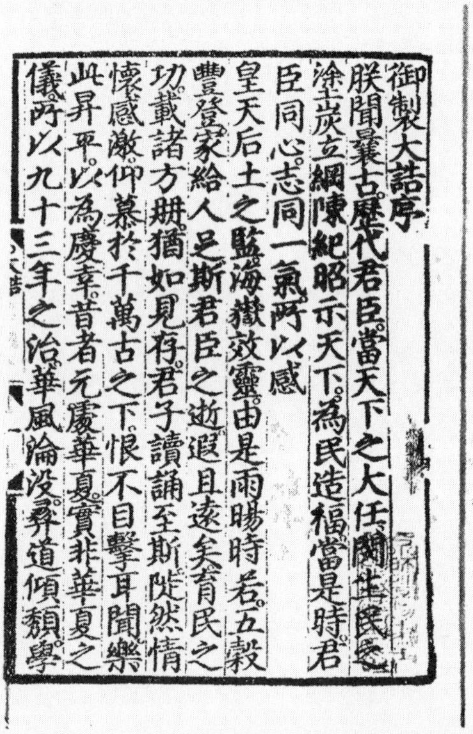

御製大誥序

朕聞曩古歷代君臣。當天下之大任。閔生民之

塗炭。立綱陳紀。昭示天下。爲民造福。當是時。君

臣同心。志同一氣。所以感

皇天后土之監。海嶽效靈。由是雨暘時若。五穀

豐登。家給人足。斯君臣之遊遐且遠矣。育民之

功。載諸方册。猶如見存。君子讀誦至斯。陡然情

懷感激。仰慕於千萬古之下。恨不目擊耳聞樂

此昇平。以爲慶幸。昔者元處華夏。實非華夏之

儀。所以九十三年之治。華風淪没。彝道傾頹。學

二〇

御製大誥

明洪武官刻本。洪武十八年(西一三八五)采輯官民過犯七十四條輯爲此編爲研究明代刑法史者唯一資料書絕罕見四庫全書失收

20. T'ai Tsu (Emperor of the Ming Dynasty, 1368-1398 A. D.): "Yu Chih Ta Kao" (1385 A. D.).

A Ming Dynasty (1368–1644 A. D.) edition. An official publication, indispensable for the study of Chinese law.

(169)

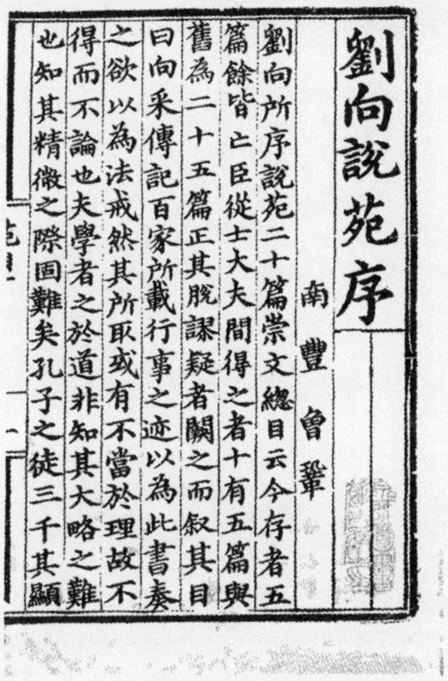

劉向說苑序

南豐曾鞏

劉向所序說苑二十篇崇文總目云今存者五篇餘皆亡臣從士大夫間得之者十有五篇與舊為二十五篇正其脫謬疑者闕之而叙其目曰向采傳記百家所載行事之迹以為此書奏之欲以為法戒然其所取或有不當於理故不得而不論也夫學者之於道非知其大略之難也知其精微之際固難矣孔子之徒三千其顯

二一

劉向說苑

明初官刻本漢劉向撰爲篇二十自君道迄反質向校書中祕時所輯此本字大悅目遠勝他本故前人誤以爲元刊也。

21. Liu Hsiang: "Liu Hsiang Shuo Yuan" (Late 14th Century).

A large character Ming Dynasty (1368–1644 A. D.) edition. This was printed under official auspices during the early years of the Ming Dynasty.

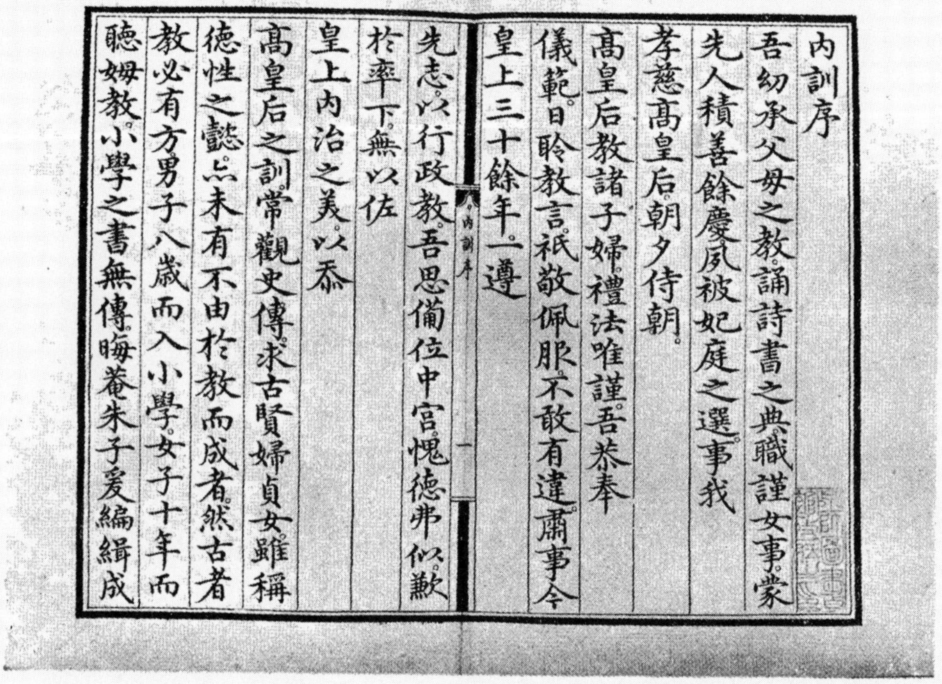

內訓序

吾幼承父母之教誦詩書之典職謹女事蒙

先人積善餘慶夙被妃庭之選事我

孝慈高皇后朝夕侍朝

高皇后教諸子婦禮法惟謹吾恭奉

儀範日聆教言祇敬佩服不敢有違肅事今

皇上三十餘年一遵

內訓序 一

先志以行政教吾思備位中宮愧德弗似歎

扵率下無以佐

皇上內治之美以忝

高皇后之訓常觀史傳求古賢婦貞女雖稱

德性之懿亦未有不由扵教而成者然古者

教必有方男子八歲而入小學女子十年而

聽姆教小學之書無傳晦菴朱子爰編緝成

二二

大明仁孝皇后內訓

明永樂官刻本。明仁孝皇后敕撰。爲篇二十。曹大家女戒之流亞。藍綾蝶裝。內閣大庫書。

22. "Ta Ming Jen Hsiao Huang Hou Nei Hsun" (Early 15th Century).

A Ming Dynasty (1368–1644 A. D.) edition. This was an official publication issued during the Yung-lo period (1399–1424 A. D.).

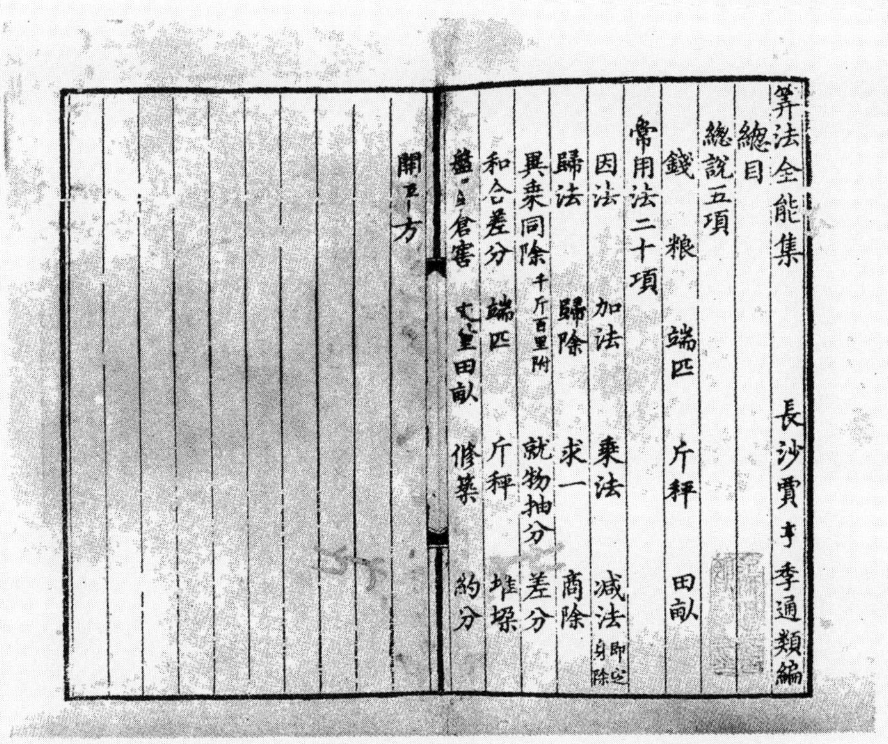

二三

算法全能集

明初刻本。元賈亨撰。首總說。次序常用法二十項。自因法加法乘法減法下迄開平方。各舉數例以明之。不啻算入門課本也。蝶裝書絕罕見。

23. Chia Heng: "Suan Fa Ch'uan Neng Chi" (Circa 1370 A. D.).

This work on mathematics was printed in the early years of the Ming Dynasty (1368–1643 A. D.). Attention is drawn to the "butterfly binding," in which the printed pages are folded facing each other. Early printed books in China were all bound in this way.

(172)

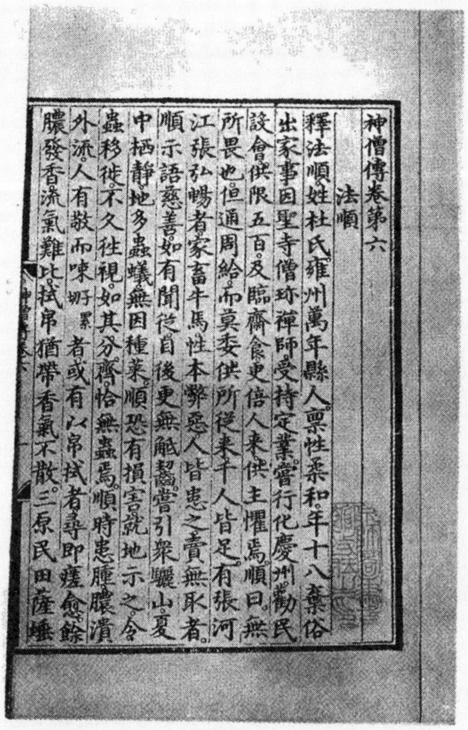
神僧傳卷第六
法順
釋法順姓杜氏雍州萬年縣人。稟性柔和。年十八棄俗
出家。事因聖寺僧珍禪師受持定業。嘗行化慶州。勸民
設會供限五百。及臨齋食更倍人來。供主懼焉。順曰。無
所畏也。但通周給。而莫委供所從來。千人皆足。有張河
江張弘暢者家畜牛馬性本弊惡人皆患之。賣無取者。
順示語慈善。如有聞從。自後更無觝齧。嘗引衆驪山夏
中栖靜。地多蟲蟻無因種菜。順恐有損。害就地示之。令
蟲移徙。不久往視。如其分齊。恰無蟲焉。順時患腫膿潰
外流。人有敬而嗽[illegible]者或有以帛拭者。尋即瘥愈。餘
膿發香流氣難比。拭帛猶帶香氣不散。三原民田薩蟠

二四

神僧傳

明永樂官刻本。明成祖敕撰。此書作於永樂十五年(西一四一七)。上自摩騰。下迄胆巴。體例蓋仿高僧傳。四庫著錄本不題作者姓氏。此本完整無缺。尚是明裝舊式可寶也。

24. "Shen Seng Chuan" (1417 A. D.).

A Ming Dynasty (1368–1644 A. D.) edition. This was an official publication and is bound in the original silk binding.

大明仁孝皇后勸善書卷之十三
嘉言
生長富貴。當念惜福。○崇善以廣德。則業泰而身安。○須惜福乃可延
年。○為善者未嘗無報也。不以其實。則以其名。不在其身。則在其子孫
若人為佛故建立諸形像。刻雕成衆相。皆已成佛道。○彩畫作佛像百
福莊嚴相。自作若使人。皆已成佛道。○若當有人。作佛形像。功德無量。天
上人中受諸快樂。○若作佛形像者。世世生處。身體完好。後死得生第七
梵天。○造佛形像。相好具足。令人見之。心生歡喜。能滅恒河沙劫生死之
罪。○敬像如敬佛。則法身應矣。
繪畫尊像。日夜虔成。尊重供養。當獲三十種上妙功德。○凡厥繫心皆
先造像。一念發心。得福無量。○聖相年久。風雨侵損。以時修復。得福無量。
○所造功德。第一造像。第二寫經。安置道場。傾心供養。當獲福報。○諸善
已備。得生有道之國。
感應

二五

勸善書

明永樂官刊小本。明仁孝皇后敕撰。書成於永樂三年(西一四〇五)。輯錄歷代釋典故事。四庫全書存目著錄本從永樂大典輯出。此永樂原刊小字本。尚有大字本。世均罕見。

25. "Ch'uan Shan Shu" (1405 A. D.).

A Ming Dynasty (1368–1644 A. D.) edition. This was an official publication.

(173)

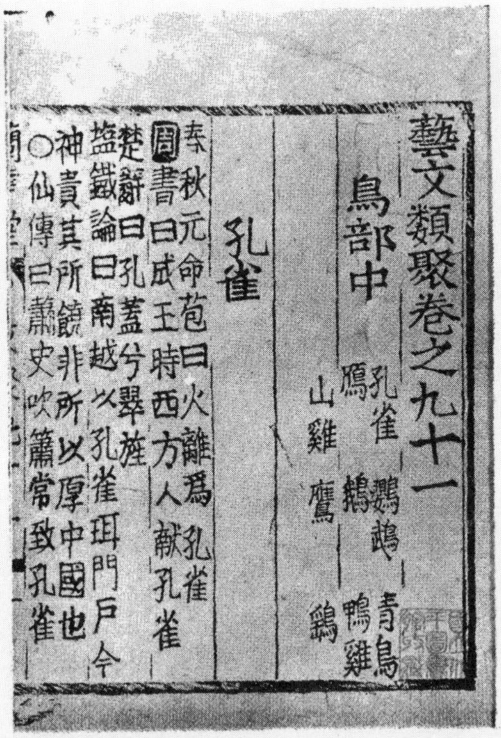

二六

藝文類聚

明正德活字印本。唐歐陽詢撰。此錫山華堅以銅活排印。首册目後有「乙亥冬錫山蘭雪堂華堅元剛活字銅版印行」二行可證。乙亥爲正德十年(西一五一五)。

26. Ou-Yang Hsun: "I Wên Lei Chu" (1515 A. D.).

Ming (1368–1644 A.D.) edition. This is a copper movable type edition printed in 1515 A. D. by the famous printer Hua Chien of Wusih. The Hua family is noted for movable type printing in the Ming Dynasty.

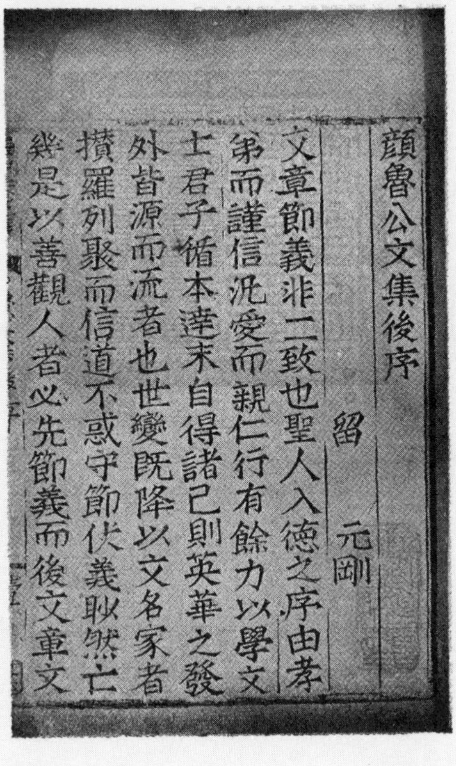

二七

顏魯公集

明嘉靖活字印本。唐顏眞卿撰。此嘉靖中(西一五二二至一五六六)無錫安國以銅活字版排印。版心有「錫山安氏館」五字可證。安氏以活字印書名於時。此外有初學記鶴山大全集。世俱罕見。

27. Yen Cheng-ch'ing: "Yen Lu Kung Chi" (Circa 1550 A. D.).

Ming (1368–1644 A. D.) edition. This is a copper movable type edition of "The Works of Yen Cheng-ch'ing," printed by An Kuo of Wusih.

二八

太平御覧

明隆慶活字印本。宋李昉等撰。此本從宋本出隆慶中(西一五六七至一五七二)。閩游廷桂以銅活字排印。世絕罕見。

28. Li Fang, & etc.: "T'ai Ping Yu Lan" (Circa 1570 A. D.).

A Ming Dynasty (1368–1644 A. D.) edition. This is a very rare Fukien edition printed from copper movable type.

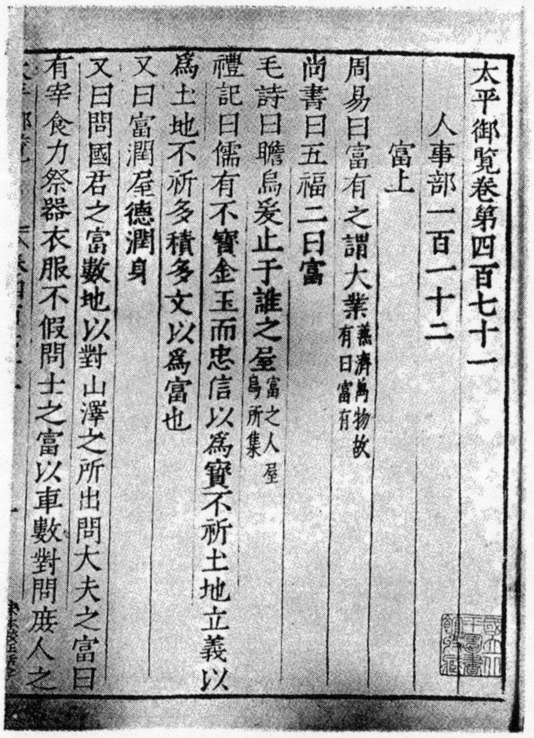

太平御覧卷第四百七十一
人事部一百一十二
富上
周易曰富有之謂大業義濟爲物故有日富有
尚書曰五福二曰富
毛詩曰瞻烏爰止于誰之屋富之人屋烏所集
禮記曰儒有不寶金玉而忠信以爲寶不祈土地立義以
爲土地不祈多積多文以爲富也
又曰富潤屋德潤身
又曰問國君之富數地以對山澤之所出問大夫之富曰
有宰食力祭器衣服不假問士之富以車數對問庶人之

二九

御世仁風

明萬曆刻本。明金忠撰。此書爲目凡五十有一。用備宸覽。帝鑑圖說之流也。葉各一圖。工整無比。

29. Chin Chung: "Yu Shih Jen Feng" (Circa 1600 A. D.).

An illustrated Ming Dynasty (1368–1644 A. D.) edition. The illustrations and text are on alternate pages.

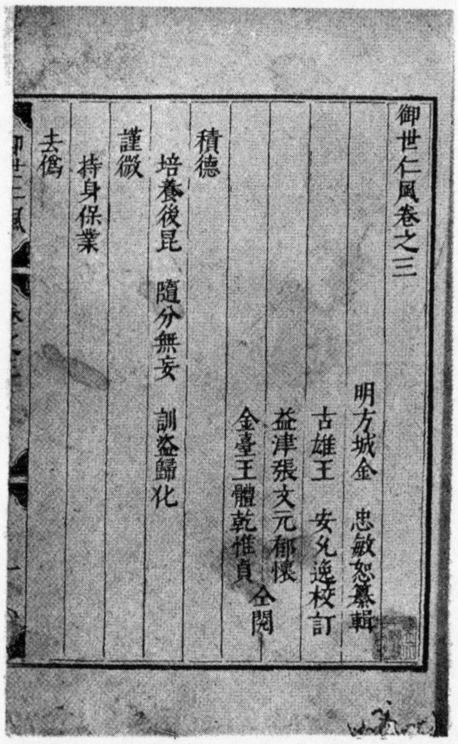

御世仁風卷之三
明方城金　忠敏恕纂輯
古雄王　安允逸校訂
益津張文元郁懷
金臺王體乾惟貞　仝閱
積德
培養後昆　隨分無妄　訓盜歸化
謹微
持身保業
去僞

(175)

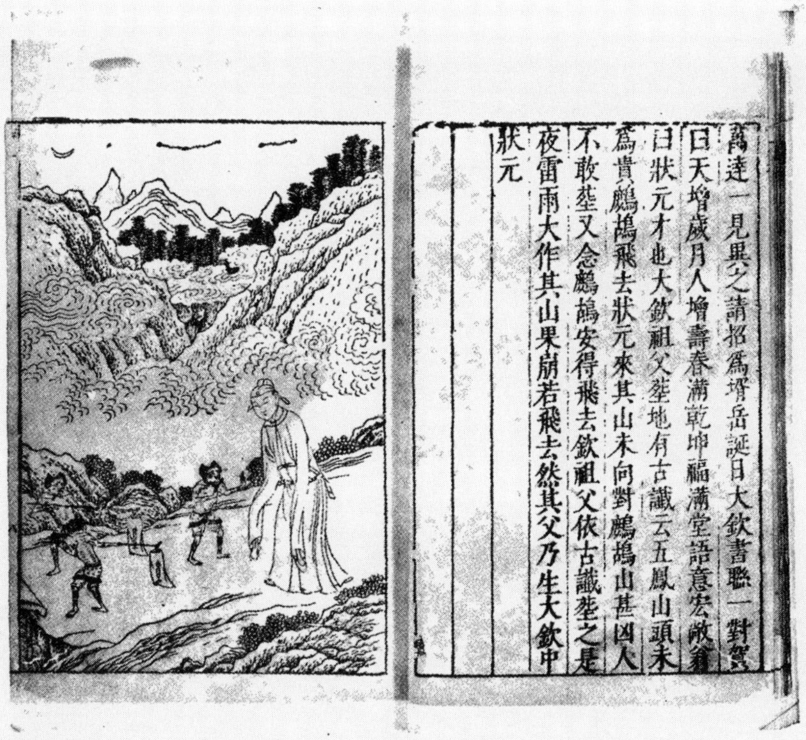

萬達一見異之請招爲壻岳誕日大欽書聯一對賀曰天增歲月人增壽春滿乾坤福滿堂語意宏敞翁曰狀元才也大欽祖父塟地有古讖云五鳳山頭未爲貴鷓鴣飛去狀元來其山未向對鷓鴣山甚凶人不敢塟又念鷓鴣安得飛去欽祖父依古讖塟之是夜雷雨大作其山果崩若飛去然其父乃生大欽中狀元

三〇

狀元圖考

明萬曆刻本。明顧鼎臣撰。錄有明一代狀元故事。刻圖出名工黃應瑞黃伯符手。明代徽郡書肆之代表作也。

30. Ku Ting-ch'en: "Chuang Yuan Tu K'ao" (Circa 1600 A. D.).

An illustrated Ming Dynasty (1368–1644 A. D.) edition. The illustrations were carved by famous artisans Huang Ying-jui and Huang Po-fu. This book is representative of the fine books published by booksellers in Huichow.

(176)

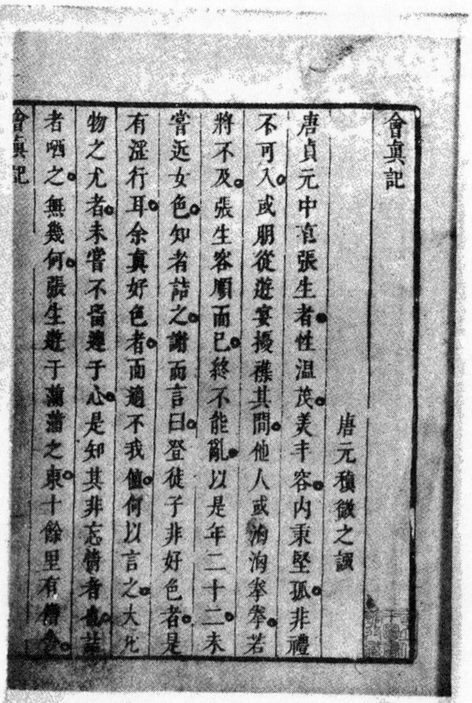

會眞記

唐元稹微之譔

唐貞元中有張生者。性温茂。美丰容。内秉堅孤。非禮
不可入。或朋從遊宴。擾雜其間。他人或洶洶拳拳。若
將不及。張生容順而已。終不能亂。以是年二十二。未
嘗近女色。知者詰之。謝而言曰。登徒子非好色者。是
有淫行耳。余眞好色者。而適不我值。何以言之。大凡
物之尤者。未嘗不留連于心。是知其非忘情者也。詰
者哂之。無幾何。張生遊于蒲。蒲之東十餘里有僧舍。

會眞記

三一

西廂記

明刻本。前四本元王實甫撰。後一本關漢卿撰。譜會眞記故事。此李卓吾批點本。頗罕見可貴。

31. Wang Shih-fu and Kuan Han-ch'ing: "Hsi Hsiang Chi" (1368–1644 A. D.).

An illustrated Ming edition of the drama "The Western Chamber."

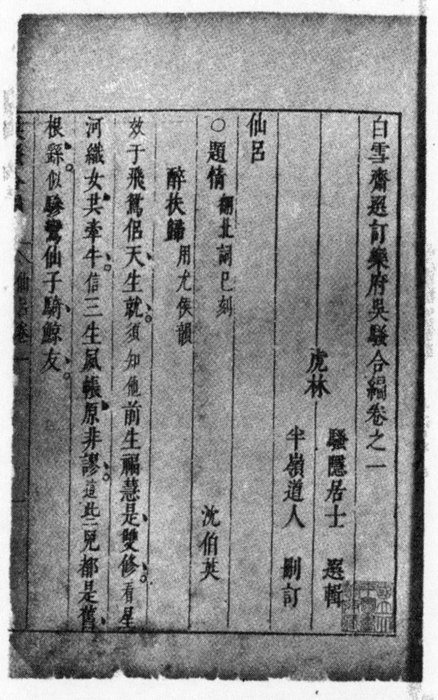

白雪齋選訂樂府吳騷合編卷之一

武林 騷隱居士 選輯

半嶺道人 刪訂

仙呂

○題情 翻北詞已刻

醉扶歸 用尤侯韻 沈伯英

效于飛鴛侶天生就。須知他前生福慧是雙修。看星
河織女共牽牛。信三生夙緣原非謬。道此兒都是舊
根蹤。似驂鸞仙子騎鯨友。

三二

吳騷合編

明崇禎刻本。明張楚叔輯。此錄明人所撰散曲。依宮調類次附圖。工緻絕倫。明末浙杭雕本中之代表作也。

32. Chang Ch'u-hsu: "Wu Sao Ho Pien" (Circa 1640 A. D.).

An illustrated Ming Dynasty (1368–1644 A. D.) edition. This book is representative of fine printing done at Hangchow at the end of the Ming Dynasty.

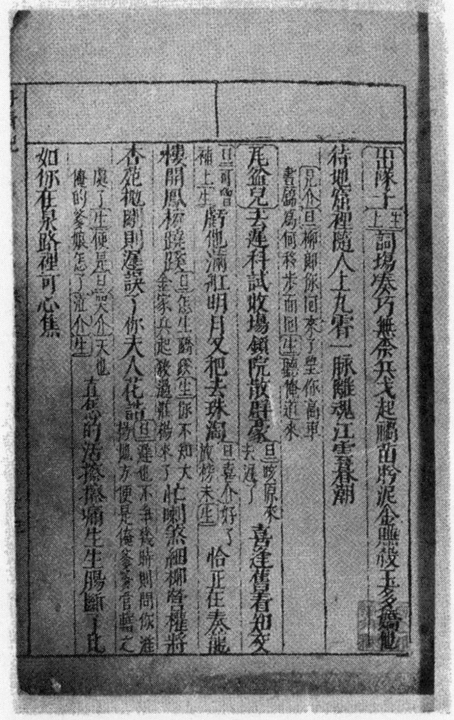

三三

丹青記

明萬曆刻本。明湯顯祖撰。此卽還魂記傳奇。譜杜麗娘柳夢梅故事。其中驚夢拾畫叫畫諸齣。現今中國舞臺尚有演之者。

33. T'ang Hsien-tsu: "Tan Ch'ing Chi" (Circa 1600 A. D.).

An illustrated Ming Dynasty (1368–1644 A. D.) edition of a musical drama.

三四

雙紅記

明萬曆刻本。題禹航更生氏撰。譜唐人小說紅線盜盒故事。此金陵書肆文林閣唐氏刻本。亦罕見之祕笈也

34. Yu Hang Keng-sheng: "Shuang Hung Chi" (Circa 1600 A. D.).

An illustrated Ming Dynasty (1368–1644 A. D.) edition. This was printed in Nanking.

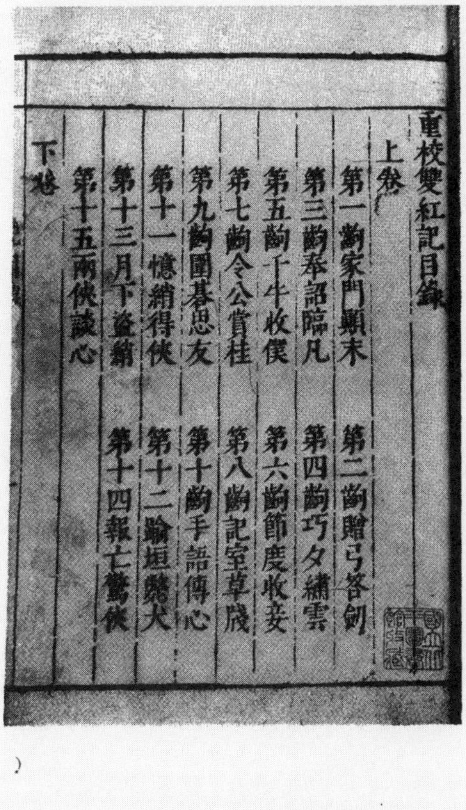
重校雙紅記目錄
上卷
第一齣家門顛末　第二齣贈弓客劍
第三齣奉詔臨凡　第四齣巧夕繡雲
第五齣千牛收僕　第六齣節度收妾
第七齣令公賞桂　第八齣記室草箴
第九齣圍碁忠友　第十齣手語傳心
第十一憶綃得俠　第十二驗垣獒犬
第十三月下盜綃　第十四報亡驚俠
第十五兩俠談心
下卷

三五

萬壽盛典

清康熙刻本。清馬齊等撰修。記康熙五十二年聖祖六旬壽辰故事。其中圖二卷繪臣庶迎鑾呼祝之儀。尤爲工緻。

35. Ma Chi, & etc.: "Wan Shou Sheng Tien" (Early 18th Century).

An illustrated Ch'ing Dynasty (1644–1912 A. D.) edition. The illustrations depict the celebration of the sixtieth birthday of Emperor Kang-hsi (1713 A. D.).

三六

皇清職貢圖

清乾隆刻本。清乾隆十六年敕撰。職貢圖之名昉於梁元帝。觀此可知當時聲教之盛。

36. "Huang Ch'ing Chih Kung Tu" (1751 A. D.).

An illustrated Ch'ing Dynasty (1644–1912 A. D.) edition.

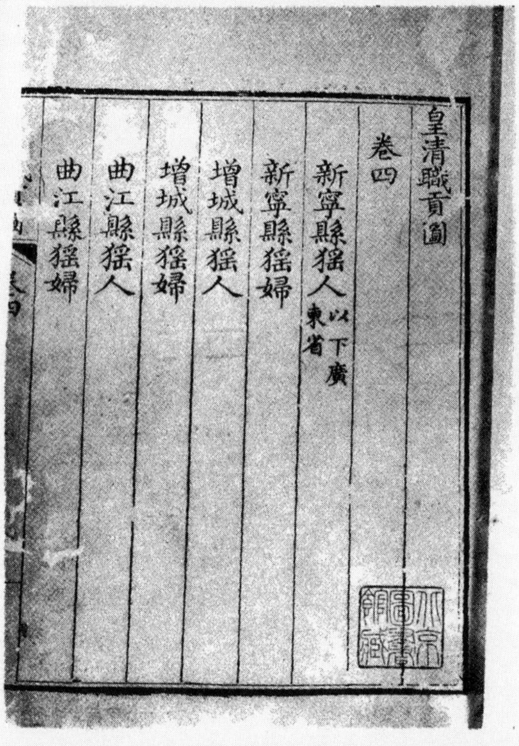
皇清職貢圖
卷四
新寧縣猺人 以下廣東省
新寧縣猺婦
增城縣猺人
增城縣猺婦
曲江縣猺人
曲江縣猺婦

三七

楚辭述註

清順治刻本。明來欽之撰。中載陳洪綬所繪雲中君湘君湘夫人大司命等十二圖。俱精絕。不在葉子格下也。

37. Lai Chin-chih: "Ch'u Tz'u Shu Chu" (Circa 1650 A. D.).

An illustrated Ch'ing Dynasty (1644–1912 A. D.) edition. This book contains twelve illustrations carved from drawings by Ch'en Hung-shou.

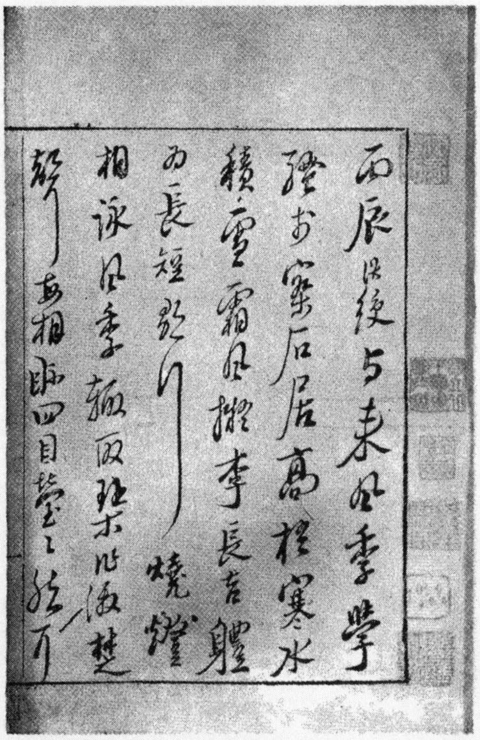

三八

天問圖

清初刻本。清蕭雲從繪。以楚辭天問本由壁畫而作。故爲此圖以記之。

38. Hsiao Yung-ts'ung (Illustrator): "Tien Wên Tu" (Mid 17th Century).

An early Ch'ing Dynasty (1644–1912 A. D.) edition prized for the illustrations.

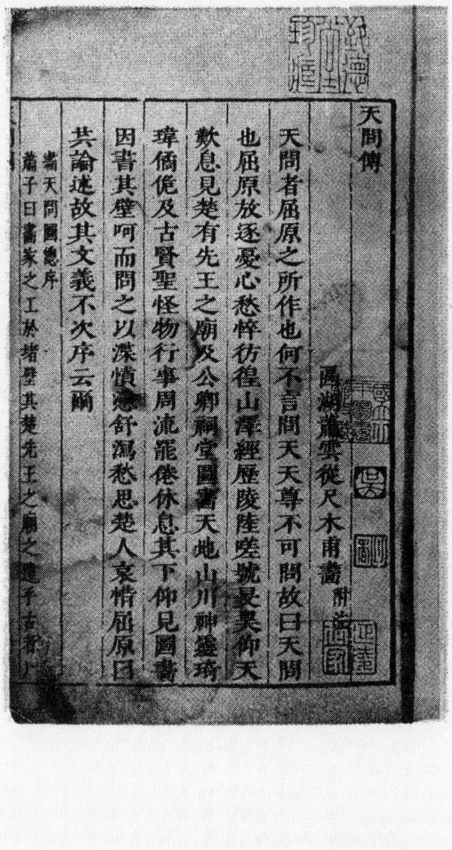

天問傳

天問者屈原之所作也何不言問天天尊不可問故曰天問也屈原放逐憂心愁悴彷徨山澤經歷陵陸嗟號旻昊仰天歎息見楚有先王之廟及公卿祠堂圖畫天地山川神靈琦瑋僪佹及古賢聖怪物行事周流罷倦休息其下仰見圖畫因書其壁呵而問之以渫憤懣舒瀉愁思楚人哀惜屈原因共論述故其文義不次序云爾

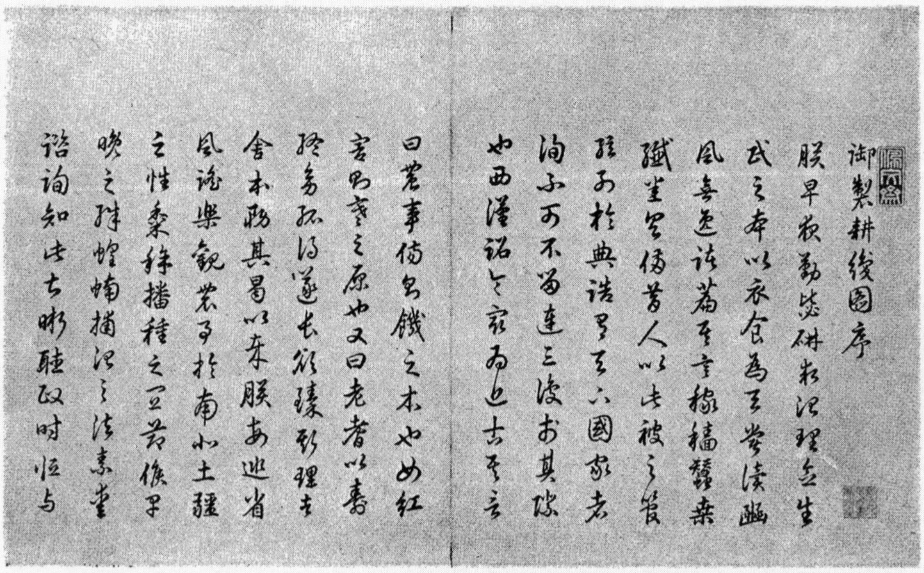

三九

耕織圖

清康熙刻本。此圖刊於康熙三十五年(西一六九七)。可稱清代雕板畫中之聖品。

39. "Keng Chih Tu" (1697 A. D.).

A Ch'ing Dynasty (1644–1912 A. D.) edition. An album illustrating methods of tilling and weaving as adopted in China. The colors were added by hand.

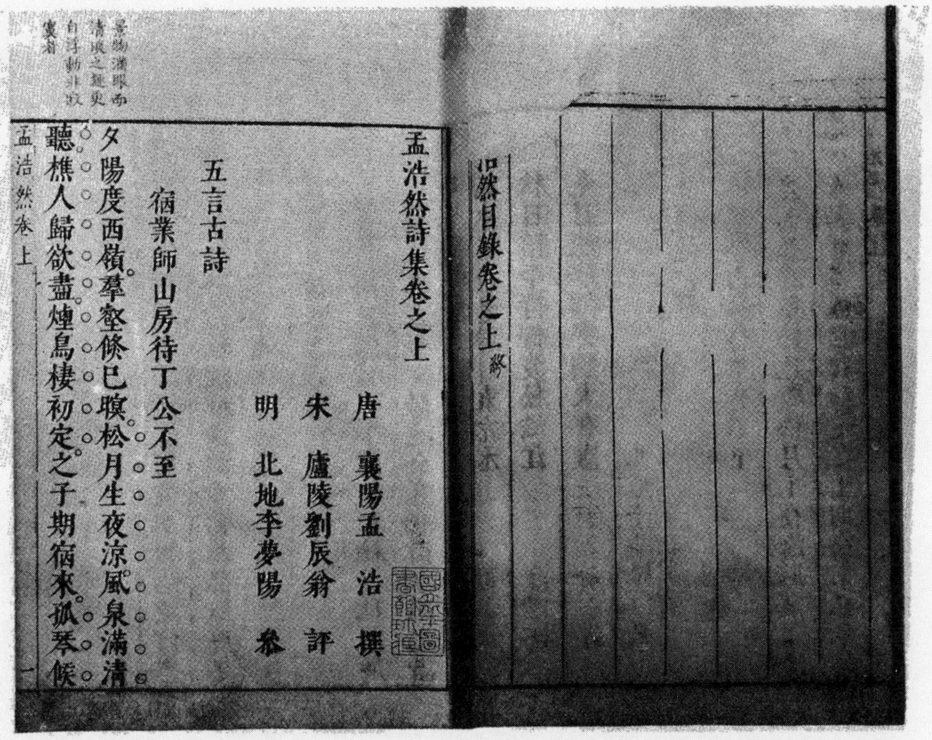
浩然目錄卷之上 終

孟浩然詩集卷之上
唐 襄陽孟 浩 撰
宋 廬陵劉辰翁 評
明 北地李夢陽 參
五言古詩
宿業師山房待丁公不至
夕陽度西嶺。羣壑倏已暝。松月生夜涼。風泉滿清聽。樵人歸欲盡。煙鳥棲初定。之子期宿來。孤琴候
孟浩然卷上 一

四〇

孟浩然詩集

明刻朱墨印本。唐孟浩然撰。宋劉辰翁評。此亦淩刻本與王摩詰集爲一時一地所刊。

40. Meng Hao-jan: "Meng Hao-jan Shih Chi" (Circa 1630 A. D.).

A Ming Dynasty (1368–1644 A. D.) edition printed in black and red.

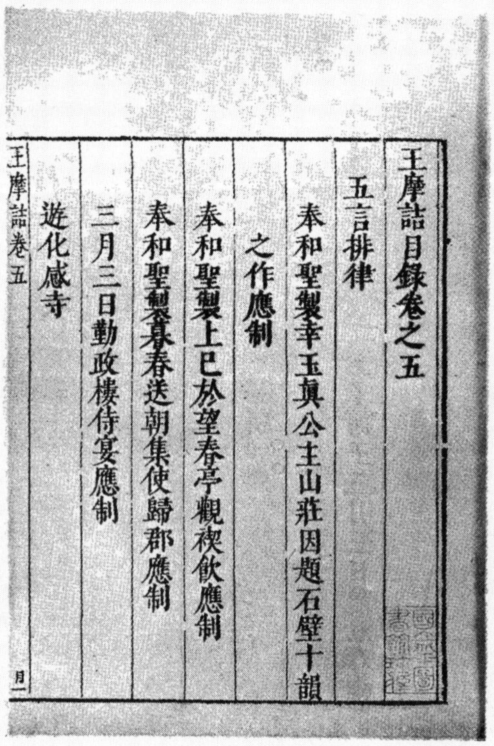
王摩詰目錄卷之五
五言排律
奉和聖製幸玉眞公主山莊因題石壁十韻之作應制
奉和聖製上巳於望春亭觀禊飲應制
奉和聖製暮春送朝集使歸郡應制
三月三日勤政樓侍宴應制
遊化感寺
王摩詰卷五 目一

四一

王摩詰詩集

明刻朱墨印本。唐王維撰。宋劉辰翁評。此明啓禎間吳興凌氏刊本。凌氏刻書多以朱墨二色套印。此其一也。

41. Wang Wei: "Wang Mo-chi Shih Chi" (Circa 1630 A. D.).

A Ming Dynasty (1368–1644 A. D.) edition, printed in black and red.

四二

十竹齋畫譜

明崇禎刻五色套印本。此崇禎中(西一六二八至一六四四)海陽胡正言所輯刻。原版初印。世間無兩。

42. "Shih Chu Chai Hua P'u" (Circa 1635 A. D.).

A Ming Dynasty (1368–1644 A. D.) edition. An example of five-color block printing.

(184)

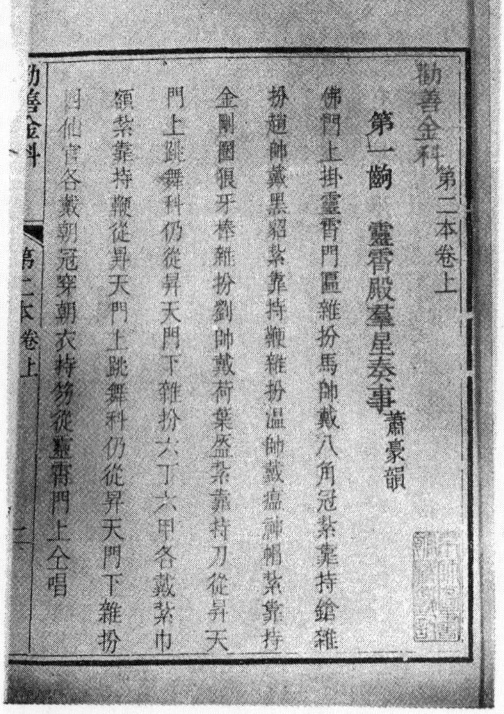
勸善金科 第二本卷上
第一齣 靈霄殿羣星奏事 蕭豪韻
佛門上掛靈霄門匾雜扮馬帥戴八角冠紮靠持鎗雜
扮趙帥戴黑貂紮靠持鞭雜扮温帥戴瘟神帽紮靠持
金剛圈很牙棒雜扮劉帥戴荷葉盔紮靠持刀從昇天
門上跳舞科仍從昇天門下雜扮六丁六甲各戴紮巾
額紮靠持鞭從昇天門上跳舞科仍從昇天門下雜扮
四仙官各戴朝冠穿朝衣持笏從靈霄門上仝唱
勸善金科 第二本卷上

四三

勸善金科

清康熙刻五色套印本。清聖祖勅撰。譜目蓮救母本事。明人鄭之珍有目蓮救母戲文。殆即此書所本。

43. Emperor K'ang-hsi (1662–1722 A. D.): "Ch'uan Shan Chin K'o" (Circa 1700 A. D.).

A Ch'ing Dynasty (1644–1912 A. D.) edition. An example of block printing in five colors.

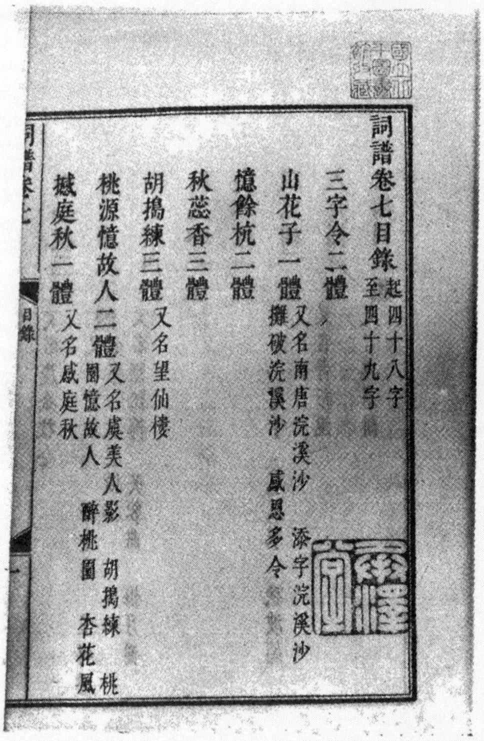
詞譜卷七目錄 起四十八字 至四十九字
三字令二體
山花子一體 又名南唐浣溪沙 攤破浣溪沙 感恩多令 添字浣溪沙
憶餘杭二體
秋蕊香三體
胡搗練三體 又名望仙樓
桃源憶故人二體 又名虞美人影 醉桃園 胡搗練 杏花風 桃
撼庭秋二體 又名感庭秋
詞譜卷七 目錄

四四

欽定詞譜

清康熙朱墨套印本。清聖祖勅撰。此編成於康熙五十四年(西一七一五)。共收八百二十六調。二千三百六十體。自唐迄元之遺編無不採入。體例與萬樹詞律略同。旁註平仄。以朱色套印。繕刻俱精。

44. Emperor K'ang-hsi (1662–1772 A. D.): "Ch'ing Ting Tz'u P'u" (1715 A. D.).

A Ch'ing Dynasty (1644–1912 A. D.) black and red block print.

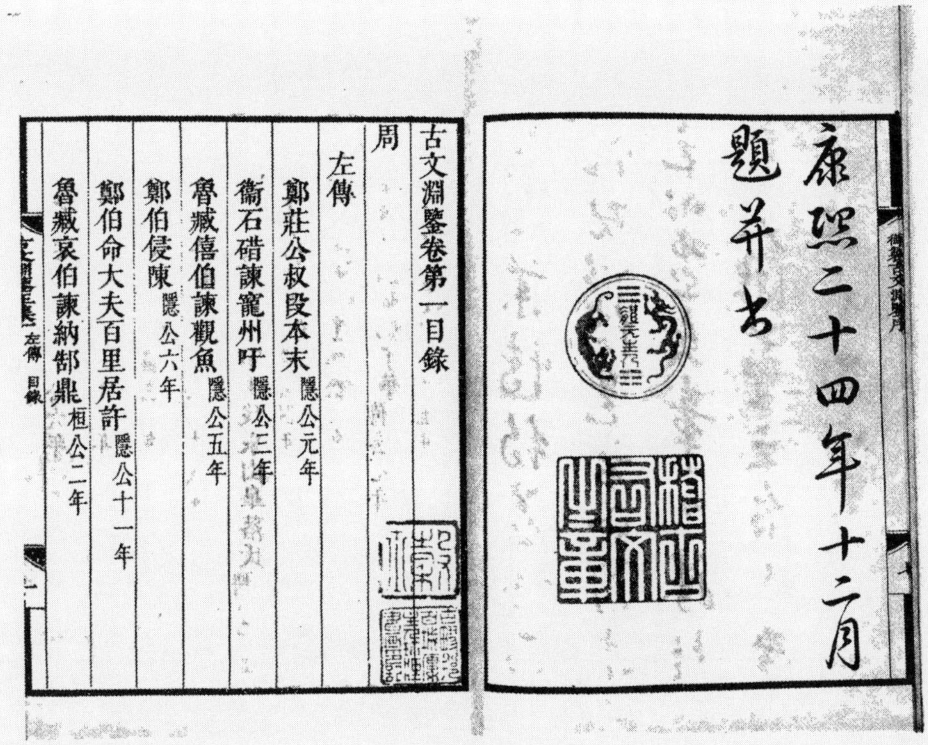

康熙二十四年十二月
題并書

古文淵鑒卷第一目錄
周
左傳
鄭莊公叔段本末 隱公元年
衛石碏諫寵州吁 隱公三年
魯臧僖伯諫觀魚 隱公五年
鄭伯侵陳 隱公六年
鄭伯命大夫百里居許 隱公十一年
魯臧哀伯諫納郜鼎 桓公二年

四五

古文淵鑒

清康熙刻五色套印本清聖祖敕撰此編成於康熙二十四年(西一六八五)用眞德秀文章正宗例錄宋以前人文。略加箋釋評點五色套印繕刻精絕。

45. Emperor K'ang-hsi (1662–1722 A. D.): "Ku Wên Yuan Chien" (1685 A. D.).

A Ch'ing Dynasty (1644–1912 A. D.) edition. An example of block printing in five colors.

(186)

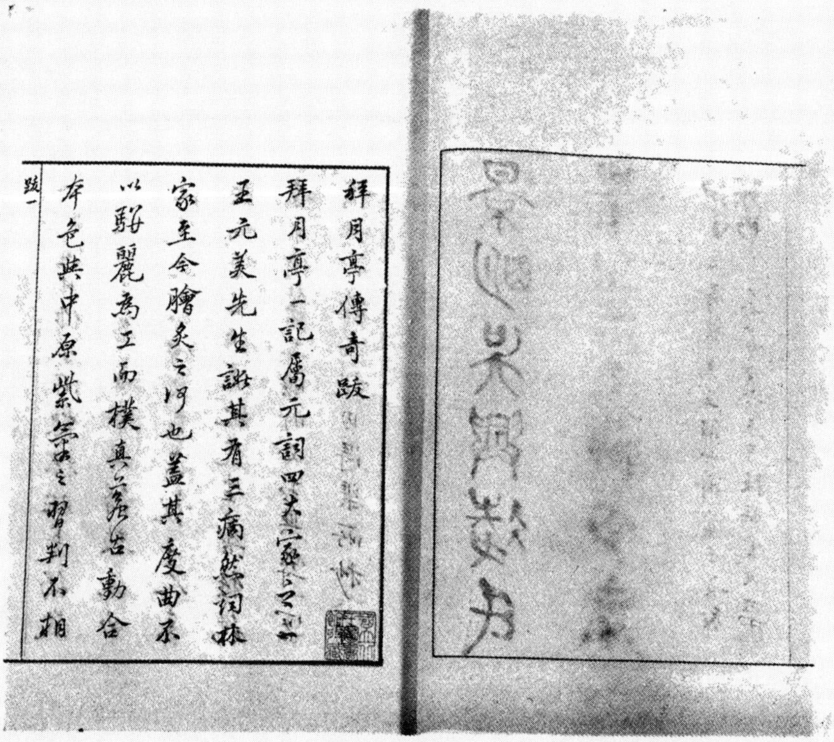

拜月亭傳奇跋

拜月亭一記屬元詞四大家之一王元美先生譏其有三病然詞林家至今膾炙之何也蓋其度曲不以駢麗爲工而樸真之意古勁合本色與中原紫箋之習判不相

跋一

四六

拜月亭傳奇

精鈔本。元惠施撰。此元明之際四大傳奇之一。從凌刻朱墨印本轉摹。附圖尤爲工緻。不在原本下也。

46. Hui Shih: "Pai Yueh T'ing Ch'uan Ch'i."

This is a manuscript facsimile of a Ming edition of a musical drama.

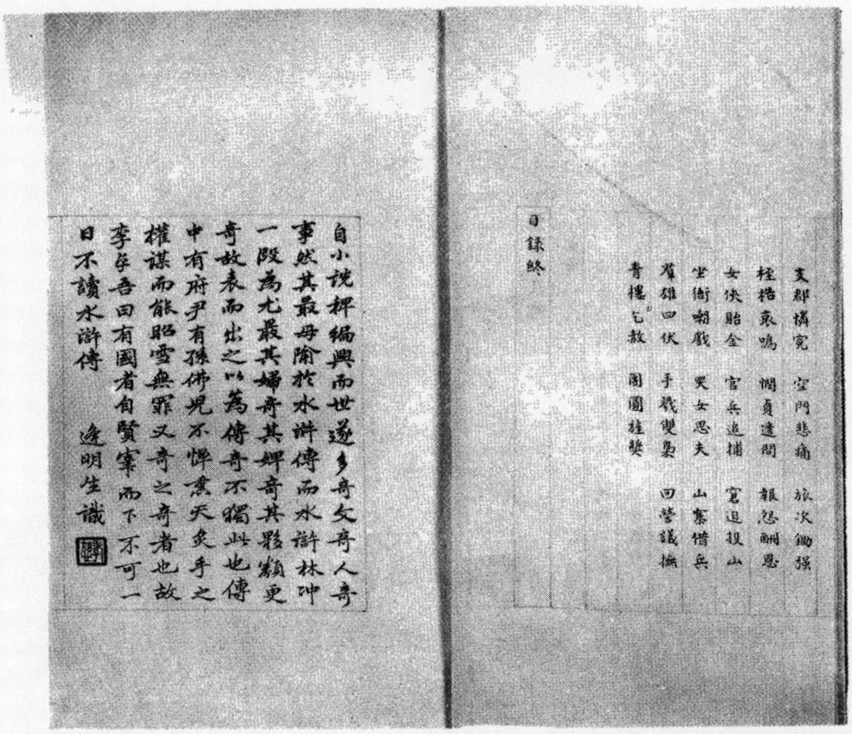

支郡構冤 空門悲痛 旅次鋤强
桎梏哀鳴 閫貞遣問 報怨酬恩
女俠貽金 官兵追捕 冤迫投山
坐衙嘲戲 哭女思夫 山寨借兵
羣雄四伏 手戮雙梟 回營議撫
青樓乞赦 團圓旌獎
目錄終

自小說稗編興而世遂多奇文奇人奇
事然其最毋險於水滸傳而水滸林冲
一段為尤最其婦奇其婢奇其影顯更
奇故表而出之以為傳奇不獨此也傳
中有府尹有孫佛兒不惮熏天炙手之
權謀而能昭雪無罪又奇之奇者也故
李卓吾曰有國者自賢宰而下不可一
日不讀水滸傳
逸明生識

四七

靈寶刀傳奇

精鈔本明陳與郊撰。此譜水滸傳林冲故事。世尚有演之者。此從萬曆丁巳(西一六一七)陳氏家刻本轉摹。紙墨工緻。不在毛鈔下也。

47. Chen Yu-chiao: "Ling Pao Tao Ch'uan Ch'i."

This is a manuscript facsimile of the 1617 A. D. edition of this musical drama.

四八

西夏文金光明最勝王經

西夏刻本近年甯夏某地出土。

48. "The Suvarnaprabhasothamaraja Sutra" (Circa 12th Century).

A Hsi Hsia (Tangut) block print, discovered in Ninghsia in 1930.

四九

西夏文經律異相

元刻本。此元成宗時(西一二九五至一三〇七)刊。河西字大藏經之一。近年甯夏某地出土。

49. "Ching Lu I Hsiang" (Circa 1300 A. D.).

A Hsi Hsia (Tangut) block print, discovered in Ninghsia in 1930.

(190)

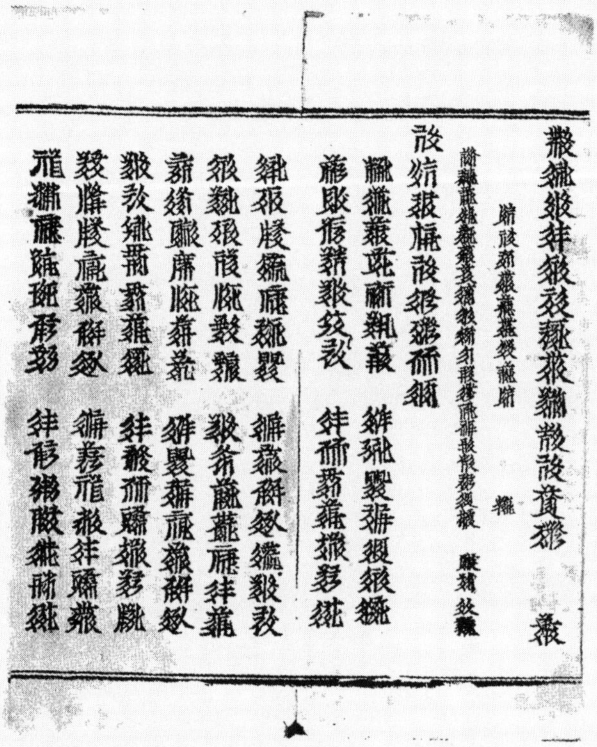

五〇

西夏文大方廣佛華嚴經

元刻本。此元成宗時(西一二九五至一三〇七)刊。河西字大藏經之一。近年甯夏某地出土。

50. "The Buddhavatamsaka Mahavaipulya Sutra" (Circa 1300 A. D.).

A Hsi Hsia (Tangut) block print, discovered in Ninghsia in 1930.

(191)

(72422D)

参加倫敦中國藝術國際展覽會
出品圖說

第四册 其他類

Illustrated Catalogue of Chinese Government Exhibits for the International Exhibition of Chinese Art in London

Volume IV Miscellaneous

編輯者 倫敦中國藝術國際展覽會籌備委員會

發行人 上海河南路 王雲五

印刷所 上海河南路 商務印書館

發行所 上海及各埠 商務印書館

定價國幣伍元 外埠酌加運費匯費

中華民國二十五年四月初版

（本書校對者吳麟璋）

(72422D)

参加倫敦中國藝術國際展覽會
出品圖說

第四册　其他類

Illustrated Catalogue of Chinese Government Exhibits for the International Exhibition of Chinese Art in London

Volume IV Miscellaneous

編輯者	倫敦中國藝術國際展覽會籌備委員會
發行人	上海河南路 王雲五
印刷所	上海河南路 商務印書館
發行所	上海及各埠 商務印書館

定價國幣伍元　外埠酌加運費匯費

中華民國二十五年四月初版

（本書校對者吳麟璋）